"If you are looking for a few bullet po
But if you are looking for a serious survey drawn from the Catholic Catechism and other
primary sources, along with an evangelical assessment of each point, Professor Allison's
labors will pay rich dividends."

Michael Horton, J. Gresham Machen Professor of Systematic Theology
and Apologetics, Westminster Seminary California; author, *Calvin on
the Christian Life*

"This book is good news to those who have long desired a reliable theological guide in
dealing with Roman Catholicism. Based on a painstaking analysis of the 1992 *Catechism
of the Catholic Church*, it covers the all-embracing trajectory of Roman Catholic theology and practice. Instead of juxtaposing ephemeral impressions and disconnected data,
Allison provides a theological framework that accounts for the complexity of the Roman
Catholic system and its dynamic unity. This book is to be commended for its biblical
depth, theological acuteness, historical alertness, and systemic awareness. My hope is
that this landmark book will reorient evangelical theology away from its attraction for a
shallow ecumenicity with Rome toward a serious dialogue based on the Word of God."

Leonardo De Chirico, Lecturer of Historical Theology, Istituto di Formazione
Evangelica e Documentazione, Padova (Italy); pastor, Breccia di Roma, Rome;
author, *Evangelical Theological Perspectives on Post-Vatican II Roman* and
A Christian Pocket Guide to the Papacy

"Writing with an irenic and thoughtful tone, Allison engages with Rome via the Church's
official Catechism and helps the reader understand what Protestants and Roman Catholics share in common and where they differ. This book is neither spinelessly ecumenical
nor harshly polemical, but a fair and principled engagement with the beliefs of Rome."

Carl R. Trueman, Professor of Church History, Westminster Theological
Seminary; author, *The Creedal Imperative* and *Luther on the Christian Life*

"A very useful evangelical assessment of Roman Catholicism. Unlike so many such
books, it does not concentrate merely on points of difference, but considers the whole
sweep of Roman Catholic teaching, as set out in the *Catechism of the Catholic Church*.
It affirms points of agreement as well as noting points of disagreement. It acknowledges
that evangelicalism is not monochromatic and points to areas where some evangelicals
would agree with Rome while others would not. This is a thorough guide that is warmly
to be commended."

Anthony N. S. Lane, Professor of Historical Theology, London School of
Theology; author, *Exploring Christian Doctrine*

Roman Catholic Theology and Practice

ROMAN CATHOLIC

THEOLOGY AND PRACTICE

An Evangelical Assessment

GREGG R. ALLISON

CROSSWAY

WHEATON, ILLINOIS

Trade paperback ISBN: 978-1-4335-0116-6
ePub ISBN: 978-1-4335-4541-2
PDF ISBN: 978-1-4335-4539-9
Mobipocket ISBN: 978-1-4335-4540-5

Library of Congress Cataloging-in-Publication Data
Allison, Gregg R.
  Roman Catholic theology and practice : an evangelical
assessment / Gregg R. Allison.
     pages cm
  Includes bibliographical references and index.
  ISBN 978-1-4335-0116-6 (tp)
    1. Catholic Church—Doctrines. 2. Catholic Church—
Customs and practices. 3. Evangelicalism. 4. Catholic
Church—Relations—Evangelicalism. 5. Evangelicalism—
Relations—Catholic Church. I. Title.
BX1753.A395   2014
282—dc23   2013047243

Crossway is a publishing ministry of Good News Publishers.

SH		24	23	22	21	20	19	18	17	16	15	14
15	14	13	12	11	10	9	8	7	6	5	4	3	2	1

Roman Catholic Theology and Practice is dedicated to several men who have exerted a deep and abiding influence on my life: Roy Allison, who was God's great gift to be my dear father, who unconditionally loved, counseled, guided, and provided for me; Steve Kovic, who discipled me during my university years and sacrificed his own dream for the sake of my further development; Wayne Grudem, whom God used to form me into a theologian who is unreservedly committed to the truthfulness and clarity of Scripture; Gerry Breshears, who shepherded me as my teaching career was beginning and knew just how to encourage and challenge me; John Feinberg, whose teaching, mentoring, and supervising have made me a better scholar and writer; and Bruce Ware, whose friendship and appropriately timed phone calls were God's instruments to direct me to the two faculty positions in which I have served. I love you men and am thankful to God for placing you in my life!

Contents

I

Catholic Theology according to the
Catechism of the Catholic Church

Part I: The Profession of Faith

II

Catholic Theology according to the
Catechism of the Catholic Church

Part 2: The Celebration of the Christian Mystery

III

Catholic Theology according to the
Catechism of the Catholic Church

Part 3: Life in Christ

Preface

Intrigue and Critique

The Catholic Church is everywhere one turns. In terms of its sheer size, the Church claims well over a billion adherents, so the Catholic faithful are present in most parts of the world. Wherever they are found, they are leaders in government, educational institutions, health care, social programs, law, business endeavors, the arts, and much more. The head of the Church, the pope, wields enormous influence on the international stage, not only in terms of spiritual matters but also in the realms of politics, ethics, education, culture building, and the like. Recent scandals—child abuse by priests, the Vatican banking fiasco—have propelled the Church into the limelight with widespread notoriety. Whether for good or for bad, the Catholic Church is in the center of public attention.

This Catholic Church finds itself celebrating the anniversaries of two monumental events in its recent past: Vatican Council II, the twenty-first general council of the Church, was convened from 1962 to 1965. This *aggiornamento*, or updating, launched the Church on the path of modernization, the process of which continues as the Church celebrates the fiftieth anniversary of Vatican II. One of the most significant results of this journey so far was the 1994 publication of the *Catechism of the Catholic Church*, a faithful and systematic presentation of the theology, liturgy, and practice of the Church. (For American Catholics, this *Catechism* replaced the *Baltimore Catechism* of 1885.) In 2014 the Church marks and celebrates the twentieth anniversary of the *Catechism*'s release.

Given the widespread profile of the Catholic Church and the conjunction of these two anniversaries, together with my own long-term familiarity with the Church, I offer this book. *Roman Catholic Theology and Practice: An Evangelical Assessment* seeks to accomplish two things: first, to note with fascination and appreciation the commonalities between Catholic and evangelical theology—which I shall describe as the *intrigue* component; and second, to examine the differences between the two, demonstrating how Catholic theology and practice at these points of divergence do not conform properly to Scripture—I'll call it the *critique* component. Though I offer this book primarily for evangelicals who want to become familiar with and assess Catholic theology and practice, I nourish a hope that some Catholics will also read it to learn what evangelicals think about Catholic theology and how they assess it. *Roman Catholic Theology and Practice* does not aim to be an anti-Catholic diatribe, though the critique that is offered is both sustained and pointed. It does not pretend to be an assessment of all things Catholic; indeed, it is quite circumscribed in its scope, focusing on Catholic doctrine and practice as unfolded in the *Catechism of the Catholic Church*. As such, it does not delve into how the Catholic faith is actually lived out by the faithful, nor does it engage the many faces of the Catholic Church in terms of its national, ethnic, theological, and liturgical varieties. Moreover, I do not claim to speak for all evangelicals or to represent the many versions of evangelical theology; given the expansive nature of evangelicalism, no one person and no one particular theological swath can accomplish that task. As for evangelical responses to this book, I anticipate that some will resonate thoroughly with its assessment, some will complain that it is too intrigued with and appreciative of Catholic theology, and some will object that it has overly criticized Catholicism. In any case, I hope to stimulate my readers' reflection on and assessment of Catholic theology and practice by holding up the Catholic faith to Scripture and evangelical theology.

All authors owe a debt of gratitude to many other people for their personal counsel, guidance, inspiration, suggestions, editorial help, corrections, and the like; *Roman Catholic Theology and Practice* is no exception.

Specific contributions from Catholics came from Father James Keleher, my professor for "The Documents of Vatican II" course at St. Mary of the Lake Seminary; Don Pio Iorg, with whom I worked in Lugano, Switzerland; Father Slider Steurnol, who contributed to my Catholic theology classes at Western Seminary; and various priests, monks, and deacons who have contributed to my Catholic theology classes at Southern Seminary. Many thanks go to the original members of Alfa-Omega for giving Nora and me such an incredible opportunity to work with their nascent movement: Don Carlo Stanzial, Mario and Giulia, Ruggiero and Theresa, Lilli, Andrea,

Luigi and Anna, Antonio, Margherita, Ninetta, Maria, Sandro and Velia, Sandro and Ornella, Annamaria, Stefano and Emilia, Roberto, la famiglia Poppi di Sorbara, and others who have faded from memory.

Specific contributions from evangelicals came from Dr. Harold O. J. Brown, my professor for "Roman Catholic Theology" at Trinity Evangelical Divinity School; Drs. Kenneth Kantzer and John D. Woodbridge, who shaped so much of my evangelical consciousness vis-à-vis other varieties of Christendom; and Dr. John Nyquist (and Peggy), who was a model of evangelical-Catholic dialogue.

Cru staff members who particularly shaped Nora and me while we were working in a Catholic context were Dennis Becker, campus director of Cru at Notre Dame; Kalevi Lethinen, European director of Cru; his close associates Piryo Salminen and Markuu Happonen; Paul Cowen, national director of Cru in France; Jose Monels, national director of Cru in Spain; and Gioele Baldari, Elfi Thaon de Revel, LeeAnn Weibel, and Donald Malcomb. More recently, sixteen Cru staff participated in my Institute of Biblical Studies elective course "Ministering to Catholics" in July 2013 and permitted me to use them as "guinea pigs" for the rough, rough draft of this book. Their discussion during class, and their insightful written comments on the draft, prompted numerous changes and have made the final product a much better book. Accordingly, I thank Mike Bost, Dawn Dishman, Jessica and Nate Gilbert, Dan Hardaway, Linda Harrah, Bret and Elizabeth Hern, Andi Mitchell, Marci Scholten, James and Sarah Ward, David Westmoreland, Brian and Erin White, and my graduate assistant, Ben McGuire. The students in my most recent "Contemporary Roman Catholic Theology" course at Southern Seminary also deserve thanks for their attentive reading and discussion of a draft of this book. A special thanks goes to our good friend Ann Casas for her suggested improvements.

Colleagues and friends who have encouraged me in both ministry and the writing of this book are Frank Beckwith, with whom I've had the privilege of interacting in both print and oral presentation; Rob Plummer, editor of *Journeys of Faith*, who provided a written platform for Frank and me to exchange views; Chris Castaldo, author of *Holy Ground: Following Jesus as a Former Catholic*, who knows how to do just that in a winsome, direct way; and Leonardo De Chirico, whose PhD dissertation, published as *Evangelical Theological Perspectives on Post-Vatican II*

Roman Catholicism, was crucial to my understanding Catholicism as a theological system.

Most of all, many thanks go to my family for their support of my life and ministry: Lauren, Troy, Caleb, Ali, and Zoe Schneringer; Hanell, Mike, Anni, Hudson, and Vaughan Schuetz; Luke Allison; and my wife, Nora. She sensed the same call of God, shared the dream of ministering to and with Catholics, labored so incredibly hard with me at Notre Dame and in Italy, left family and friends to move to a new country to learn a new language so as to start and develop a new ministry, discipled scores of women, and always encourages me to follow God's leading, whether that has been serving on Cru staff, pursuing advanced degrees in theology, teaching at two different seminaries, pastoring, writing books, or being her husband and the father of our children.

Abbreviations

Allison, *HT*   Gregg R. Allison, *Historical Theology: An Introduction to Christian Doctrine* (Grand Rapids, MI: Zondervan, 2011).

Allison, *SS*   Gregg R. Allison, *Sojourners and Strangers: The Doctrine of the Church* (Wheaton, IL: Crossway, 2012).

ANF   *Ante-Nicene Fathers*, ed. Alexander Roberts, James Donaldson, Philip Schaff, and Henry Wace, 10 vols. (Peabody, MA: Hendrickson, 1994).

Calvin, *Institutes* John Calvin, *Institutes of the Christian Religion*, ed. John T. McNeill, trans. Ford Lewis Battles (Philadelphia: Westminster, 1960). (See also the listings below for LCC 20 and LCC 21; references for the *Institutes* are provided in those sources as well.)

CCC   *Catechism of the Catholic Church* (New York: Doubleday, 1995).

De Chirico   Leonardo De Chirico, *Evangelical Theological Perspectives on Post-Vatican II Roman Catholicism*. Religions and Discourse, vol. 19 (Bern: Peter Lang, 2003).

Grudem, *ST*   Wayne Grudem, *Systematic Theology: An Introduction to Biblical Doctrine* (Grand Rapids, MI: Zondervan, 1994, 2000).

Heppe   Heinrich Heppe, *Reformed Dogmatics*, ed. Ernst Bizer, trans. G. T. Thomson (London: Allen & Unwin, 1950).

Kreeft   Peter Kreeft, *Catholic Christianity* (San Francisco: Ignatius, 2001).

LCC 20   John Calvin, *Institutes of the Christian Religion*, ed. John T. McNeill, trans. Ford Lewis Battles (Philadelphia: Westminster, 1960), in John Baillie, John T. McNeill, and Henry P. Van Dusen, gen. eds., Library of Christian Classics, 26 vols. (Philadelphia: Westminster, 1960), vol. 20.

LCC 21   John Calvin, *Institutes of the Christian Religion*, ed. John T. McNeill, trans. Ford Lewis Battles (Philadelphia: Westminster, 1960), in John Baillie, John T. McNeill, and Henry P. Van Dusen, gen. eds., Library of Christian Classics, 26 vols. (Philadelphia: Westminster, 1960), vol. 21.

LW   Martin Luther, *Luther's Works*, ed., Jaroslav Pelikan, Hilton C. Oswald, and Helmut T. Lehmann, 55 vols. (St. Louis: Concordia, 1955–1986).

NPNF[1]	*Nicene and Post-Nicene Fathers*, ed. Alexander Roberts, James Donaldson, Philip Schaff, and Henry Wace, 1st ser., 14 vols. (Peabody, MA: Hendrickson, 1994).
NPNF[2]	*Nicene and Post-Nicene Fathers*, ed. Alexander Roberts, James Donaldson, Philip Schaff, and Henry Wace, 2nd ser., 14 vols. (Peabody, MA: Hendrickson, 1994).
Schaff	Philip Schaff, *Creeds of Christendom*, 3 vols. (New York: Harper, 1877–1905).
Schmid	Heinrich Schmid, *The Doctrinal Theology of the Evangelical Lutheran Church*, trans. Charles A. Hay and Henry E. Jacobs (Minneapolis: Augsburg, 1899).
VC II-1	Austin Flannery, gen. ed., *Vatican Council II: Volume 1, The Conciliar and Post-Conciliar Documents*, new rev. ed. (Northport, NY: Costello; and Dublin: Dominican, 1998).
VC II-2	Austin Flannery, gen. ed., *Vatican Council II: Volume 2, More Post-Conciliar Documents*, new rev. ed. (Northport, NY: Costello; and Dublin: Dominican, 1998).

Introduction

Comically speaking, the genesis of this book occurred when I, as a five-year-old, was told by a similarly young (pre-Vatican Council II) Catholic neighbor girl that I was headed straight to hell because I wasn't Catholic. Greatly upset and fearing for my eternal destiny, I asked my parents if we could go to church, and they promptly responded by taking me to the local United Methodist church. Though that choice did nothing to change the neighbor girl's assessment of and warning about my future condemnation, it at least started me down the Protestant pathway. After nurturing me on the works of Martin Luther, Huldrych Zwingli, John Calvin, John Wesley, and many others, this road has brought me to the place where I am today: an evangelical systematic theologian of the Reformed Baptist variety.

Seriously, however, the origin of this book began in May 1976, when my fiancée (now wife, Nora) and I were visiting a businessman in Chesterton, Indiana, near South Bend. We had received permission from Campus Crusade for Christ (now Cru) to begin raising support for our future campus ministry with that parachurch organization. During our conversation, in which Nora and I presented our upcoming work, the businessman jokingly exclaimed, "Wouldn't it be interesting if the two of you were assigned to be Cru staff at the University of Notre Dame." After a hearty laugh—"Sure, a Protestant missionary movement on the campus of the premier Catholic university in the United States!"—we concluded our presentation and said our thanks and good-byes. Getting into our car to return home, Nora (from the passenger side) and I (from the driver's side) looked at each other and, together, with a strong, divinely given conviction, said, "God is calling us to the University of Notre Dame."

After our wedding, honeymoon, and the commencement of our preparation as Cru staff, we received a Placement Request Form as part of our training. One of the questions on this form had to do with where we hoped to be placed. We promptly wrote in our assignment preference: "the University of Notre Dame." Soon after receiving our response, Cru leaders responsible for staff placement called us in for a little chat. They were quite intrigued that we wanted to go to Notre Dame (ND), as the Cru ministry was just beginning on that campus, and they were looking to assign more staff to join the small initial team. Nora and I, however, failed to meet their three qualifications: we did not come from a Catholic background, we were not veteran staff (who usually are responsible for starting new campus ministries), and we did not have children (so as to be in a similar season of life as the Cru staff couple already working at ND). Strike one. Strike two. Strike three. The Allisons were not going to be Cru staff at Notre Dame.

A bit later, to the same question on the second Placement Request Form, we wrote, "the University of Notre Dame." Somewhat perturbed, our placement leaders called us in for another conversation, wondering what about the initial "No, you are not going to be assigned to Notre Dame" we didn't understand. They tried to comfort us with the possibility that we would end up at Notre Dame after we had been on Cru staff for a number of years, but they assured us ND was not in our immediate future. Of course, we assured them that we were willing to go anywhere they assigned us. But deep down inside lingered the firm conviction that God was calling us to Notre Dame.

Accordingly, when the third Placement Request Form was distributed a week or so later, our reply to the now infamous question was "the University of Notre Dame." The placement leaders' flustered and emphatic response to what seemed like an intractable stance on our part was, "Perhaps God is calling you to Villanova or some other Catholic university, but you are not going to the University of Notre Dame!"

Another strike three for the second out.

Shortly thereafter, and along with all the new Cru staff, Nora and I received our Placement Envelope. Written on the form inside was our future assignment. Bound by a promise that we would not discuss the enclosed content with anyone else for a period of silence (twenty-four hours, which was to be used solely for the purpose of praying about our assignment), we found an isolated spot outside under a palm tree and nervously yet excitedly ripped open the envelope:

Your mission, should you choose to accept it, is . . . the University of
Notre Dame.

After the day-long period of silence—which for us was filled with great
thanksgiving verging on giddiness—the Cru placement leaders confirmed
with us that our crystal clear call to be on staff at ND outweighed any
and all obstacles to our being assigned there. Upon completion of our
staff training, Nora and I raised our support, packed our belongings, and
moved to South Bend, Indiana, to begin our ministry at the University of
Notre Dame.

So began a two-year stint (1976–1978) as part of a Protestant missionary movement on the campus of the most well known and highly regarded
Catholic university in America. At the beginning of our second year, more
than two hundred and fifty students expressed a desire to be in one of our
weekly Bible studies; we ended up being able to accommodate one hundred
and fifty of them. Communicating the gospel with clarity, teaching how
to read and study the Word of God, discipling new believers, developing
leaders in ministry—these core Cru ministries were contextualized for a
Catholic university. Indeed, with more than 80 percent of Notre Dame students being Catholic, we learned a great deal about Catholic theology and
practice and developed a deep burden for ministering to and with Catholics.

Out of this burgeoning interest in Catholic ministry, Nora and I signed
up for a Cru summer project in Rome (1978), where the majority of our
first few weeks was spent sharing the gospel with students at the University
of Rome. Though we didn't know much Italian, we quickly learned one
phrase that was part and parcel of most of our conversations with Italian young people: "Non credo in Dio" (I don't believe in God). Because
this widely entrenched atheism had not been our experience working with
Catholics at Notre Dame, we desperately asked the Italian national director
of Cru if he knew any evangelical Catholics. "Do you mean Catholics who
have become evangelicals?" he replied. "No," we clarified, "do you know
any Catholics who are Catholics but who believe as we evangelicals believe
about the gospel, justification by grace through faith alone, and so forth?"
His response caught us by surprise: "Yes. Would you like to meet some?"
The next day, as we walked into a meeting of dozens of Catholics who
believed as evangelicals believe, we participated in the launch of a Catholic

lay evangelization movement called "Alfa-Omega: perché Cristo sia tutto in tutti" ("Alpha-Omega: that Christ may be all in all"). This encounter was the beginning of the fulfillment of a vision implanted several years earlier. Indeed, we committed to return to Italy to work with this movement.

After our return to the United States following the summer project, we raised support for our new assignment, completed three months of international staff training, and, moving to Firenze, studied Italian for six months before settling down in Rome. For the next three years (1979–1982), Nora and I were Cru staff embedded in Alfa-Omega. I served as the movement's first training center director, helping prepare Catholic laypeople in how to share the gospel, lead Bible studies, disciple new believers, prepare leaders, organize evangelistic meetings, train Bible study leaders, and the like. We also led weekly Reading Groups of the Gospel that, meeting during the week, would focus on the text of the Gospel reading for the upcoming Sunday mass while teaching a very simple inductive Bible study method consisting of the reading of the text, observation, interpretation, application, and prayer. Our goal was to expose Catholics to the person and work of Jesus Christ as presented in the Gospels so that they could embrace the good news of salvation. Following Alfa-Omega evangelistic campaigns in parishes in Sorbara and Nonantola (near Modena, in the province of Emilia-Romagna, in northern Italy), Nora and I would remain behind for several weeks to help train Bible study leaders to work with the hundreds of residents who signed up to be in weekly Reading Groups of the Gospel.

Along with our ministry within Alfa-Omega came numerous opportunities to work with priests, meet one of the bishops of the Province of Rome, attend a "private" audience with Pope John Paul II (along with 9,998 other invitees), sneak the *Jesus* film into what was then called Yugoslavia, speak before hundreds of Catholic clergy (bishops, priests, monks, nuns, and seminary professors) on the topic "The Importance of the Bible in Ministry," train other Cru staff for similar ministries with Catholics, and much more.[1]

In addition to this robust experience ministering to and with Catholics, when working on the MDiv degree at Trinity Evangelical Divinity School

---

[1] The claim by Dave Armstrong that I was "an undercover saboteur trying to find fault with Catholicism" during my ministry with Alfa-Omega is completely unfounded and false. I firmly deny the accusation (see http://art-of -attack.blogspot.com/2011/08/brief-refutation-of-gregg-r-allisons.html).

(1982–1985), I took a class, "The Documents of Vatican II" (S212; Fall 1983), at the nearby St. Mary of the Lake Seminary. Though this course was the extent of my formal training in Catholic theology and practice in a Catholic higher education context, I took a seminar on Roman Catholic Theology (DST 845A; Winter 1991) during my PhD studies at Trinity, regularly taught the Catholic theology elective course at Western Seminary (1994–2003), continue to regularly teach it at The Southern Baptist Theological Seminary, where I am Professor of Christian Theology (2003–present), and attempt to keep up with developments in Catholic theology through reading and writing. My writings that interact with Catholic theology and practice are, "The Bible in Christianity: Roman Catholicism," in the *ESV Study Bible* (Wheaton, IL: Crossway, 2008), 2613–2615; "The Theology of the Eucharist according to the Catholic Church," in *The Lord's Supper: Remembering and Proclaiming Christ until He Comes*, ed. Thomas R. Schreiner and Matthew R. Crawford (Nashville: B & H Academic, 2010), 151–192; and "A Response to Catholicism," in *Journeys of Faith*, ed. Robert Plummer (Grand Rapids, MI: Zondervan, 2012), 115–128.

This introductory background sketch serves to highlight two points: First, though I do not have a Catholic background, I am an evangelical theologian whose experience with Catholic theology and practice is more extensive and personal than that of most evangelicals. Hopefully, this familiarity puts me in a position to be a trustworthy guide for evangelicals who desire to know about Catholicism. Second, my experience helps to explain the purposes of this book, which are twofold. One purpose is to highlight the commonalities between Catholic and evangelical theology, agreements or similarities that prompt *intrigue*. These shared doctrines and practices—e.g., the Trinity; the full deity and full humanity of Jesus Christ; worship and prayer—need to be recognized and appreciated, and they lead to thanksgiving for a limited yet real unity between Catholicism and evangelicalism. The other purpose is to underscore the divergences between Catholic and evangelical theology—disagreements or dissimilarities that require *critique*. These doctrinal and practical disparities—e.g., apostolic succession, transubstantiation, the immaculate conception of Mary, praying for the dead in purgatory—are serious points of division that must be faced honestly and sorrowfully, yet with a humble conviction that avoids minimizing the substantive distance between Catholicism and evangelicalism.

Such a book is intended for two primary and two secondary audiences. As for its primary audience, the first group consists of evangelicals who desire to become familiar with Catholic theology and assess it in terms of both Scripture and evangelical theology. The second group is evangelicals who wish to know better their own evangelical theology as compared with and contrasted to Catholic theology. As for the book's secondary audience, the first group consists of Catholics who want to learn what evangelicals think about Catholic theology and how they assess it. The second group is Catholics who want to learn evangelical theology as it is compared with and contrasted to Catholic theology, perhaps because they are moving toward embracing the evangelical faith.

It should be underscored that this book is not intended as a rabid anti-Catholic diatribe. Though it will strongly critique certain Catholic doctrines and practices, this criticism must be placed in the context of *intrigue*—the book's appreciation of and thanksgiving for the many commonalities between Catholic and evangelical theology. Furthermore, it must be emphasized that this book is not intended as an ambiguous presentation emphasizing the similarities and minimizing the divergences between the two theological positions in an attempt to promote some type of "lowest common denominator" ecumenism. Though it will underscore with gratitude the many agreements between Catholic and evangelical theology, such approbation must be placed in the context of *critique*—the book's negative evaluation of certain Catholic doctrines and practices against which evangelical theology does and must take a strong stand.

To accomplish this task, I have designed *Roman Catholic Theology and Practice* to be a walk through the *Catechism of the Catholic Church*. Beginning in chapter 3 of this book, for each section of the *Catechism*, I first describe in summary form and without comment the Catholic theology or practice addressed in that section; then I offer an assessment of that Catholic theology or practice from the perspective of both Scripture and evangelical theology. In chapter 2, I explain my interpretive approach to Scripture and outline the evangelical theological perspective that I use throughout the book. In that chapter I also address my understanding of and approach to Catholic theology as a system that is characterized by two axioms: the interdependence between nature and grace, and the Catholic Church as the ongoing incarnation of Jesus Christ. I then briefly set forth how these two tenets manifest themselves in concrete Catholic doctrines and practices. I conclude this chapter with an assessment of the two axioms.

Following closely the structure of the *Catechism of the Catholic Church,* chapters 3 through 6 will cover its first part, entitled, "The Profession of Faith," because it describes Catholic theology as it is professed in the Apostles' Creed (with a few additions from the Nicene Creed). Chapters 7 through 11 treat the second part of the *Catechism,* "The Celebration of the Christian Mystery," which explains the Catholic Church's sacramental economy and seven sacraments. Chapters 12 and 13 discuss the third part of the *Catechism,* on "Life in Christ," which presents salvation, law, grace, justification, merit, and the like. Conclusions and applications will be drawn in chapter 14. The chapter divisions in this book are somewhat random and do not follow the divisions (noted according to their Part, Section, Chapter, Article, and Paragraph numbers) within the *Catechism* itself; rather, my chapter divisions are used to divide the large amount of Catholic theology and practice into manageable portions for readers.

For ease in following the flow of the *Catechism,* two structural notes may be helpful: From broadest to narrowest divisions, the *Catechism* moves from Part to Section to Chapter to Article, with some Articles being further divided into specific topics with Paragraph headings. For example, Part 1, "The Profession of Faith," is subdivided into two sections: Section One, treating "I Believe"—"We Believe"; and Section Two, covering The Creeds. This Section Two is further subdivided into twelve Articles, one of which is Article 3 on the doctrine of the person of Jesus Christ, entitled, "He Was Conceived by the Power of the Holy Spirit, and Was Born of the Virgin Mary." This Article 3 is further subdivided into three Paragraphs treating "The Son of God Became Man" (Paragraph 1), "Conceived by the Power of the Holy Spirit and Born of the Virgin Mary" (Paragraph 2), and "The Mysteries of Christ's Life" (Paragraph 3).

The second structural note is that every paragraph in the *Catechism* is consecutively numbered for easy reference. Here I use the word "paragraph" in a different sense than how it was just used as part of the overall structure of the *Catechism*—specifically, a Paragraph as a subheading under an Article. In contrast, "paragraph" is now used in a grammatical sense to refer to a series of sentences marked off by indentation and each of which expresses a self-contained idea or theme. Used in this grammatical sense, each paragraph of the *Catechism* is numbered, and throughout my book I will refer to these paragraph numbers (e.g., *CCC* 813) as I describe and assess each main idea or theme of Catholic theology and practice. It should be noted that paragraph numbers are different from page numbers. These paragraph numbers are the same for all versions and languages of the *Catechism*, while page numbers vary.

Three versions of the Bible are used in this book. Because citations of Scripture found in the *Catechism* are taken from the Revised Standard Version and the New Revised Standard Version, whenever the *Catechism* is quoted and a biblical citation is embedded in that quotation, it will come from either the RSV or the NRSV.[2] All other citations of Scripture will come from the English Standard Version.

---

[2] Because the *Catechism* makes no attempt to distinguish which version is being quoted, I will not indicate the version.

2

Scripture, Evangelical Theology, and Catholic Theology

My assessment of Roman Catholic theology and practice will be on the basis of both Scripture and evangelical theology, so this chapter will begin with a brief explanation of Scripture and its interpretation and will then concentrate on a presentation of evangelical doctrine. Additionally, it will propose for the purpose of understanding and assessment an approach that considers Catholic theology as a coherent, all-encompassing system with two major features: the nature-grace interdependence, that is, a strong continuity between nature and grace; and the Christ-Church interconnection, that is, an ecclesiology (a doctrine of the church) that views the Catholic Church as the ongoing incarnation of Jesus Christ. These axioms will also be assessed.

Scripture and Its Interpretation

According to evangelical theology, Scripture consists of sixty-six books—thirty-nine in the Old Testament and twenty-seven in the New Testament—and is interpreted according to a *grammatical–(redemptive) historical–typological method*.[1] This hermeneutic, or interpretive approach, focuses on the *grammar* of biblical passages, noting the meaning and function of words, the relation of words and phrases in sentences, the genre in which the text is written, the development of arguments, the flow of narratives, the imagery of poems and figurative expressions, allusions to ear-

---

[1] The Bible of the Roman Catholic Church contains more books than does its Protestant/evangelical counterpart. For further discussion of evangelical hermeneutics, see Grant R. Osborne, *The Hermeneutical Spiral: A Comprehensive Introduction to Biblical Interpretation*, rev. and expanded ed. (Downers Grove, IL: IVP Academic, 2006); William W. Klein, Craig L. Blomberg, and Robert L. Hubbard, Jr., *Introduction to Biblical Interpretation* (Dallas: Word, 1993); Robert L. Plummer, *40 Questions about Interpreting the Bible* (Grand Rapids, MI: Kregel Academic & Professional 2010).

lier passages, and the like.[2] This hermeneutic also focuses on the *historical* context in which the biblical passages were written, seeking to understand the socio-politico-economic-cultural background of texts, their authors and audiences, and the purposes for which the texts were written, all with the aim of interpreting them in that context and with those purposes.[3] Specific attention to the *redemptive-historical* context of the biblical passages is important for understanding their place in the progressive revelation of God, their connection to earlier passages, their anticipation of later passages, their connection to the biblical covenants, and the point they seek to drive home about Jesus Christ.[4] This interpretive approach focuses additionally on *typology*, or intentional relationships between an earlier person/place/institution/thing (the type) and a later person/place/institution/thing (the antitype), a structure that emphasizes the unity of Scripture and its promise-fulfillment or anticipation-consummation theme.[5] Evangelical interpretation does not follow the Roman Catholic "four-sense" approach to understanding Scripture, which seeks to discern four meanings—literal, allegorical, tropological, and anagogical—in most if not all biblical passages.[6] This view of Scripture and its interpretation stands as the base of the first element by which Catholic theology and practice will be assessed. The second element will be evangelical theology, to which we will now turn our attention.

An Evangelical Vision of Life with God and Human Flourishing

As for evangelical theology, one must understand first of all that evangelicalism is not a church or a denomination but a massive broad-tent move-

---

[2] For example, the story of the conversion of the Ethiopian eunuch (Acts 8:26–40) features *characterization* (vv. 26–28), or the introduction of the main characters (the eunuch, Philip, an angel of the Lord/the Holy Spirit) and the narrative setting (on the road to Gaza, a desert place); *rising action* (vv. 29–33), including the Spirit's direction of Philip, the eunuch's reading of Isaiah, inquiries about understanding and interpretation, and a citation from Scripture; *climax* (vv. 34–35), a dramatic crescendo reached in Philip's communication of the gospel; *falling action* (vv. 36, 38), focused on the legitimacy of baptism followed by the actual baptism of the eunuch (with v. 37 being a later and unnecessary addition for the purpose of clarification); and *resolution* (vv. 39–40), or the tying up of the various strands (the eunuch, Philip, and the Holy Spirit) so as to bring the story to a conclusion. Following this narrative flow is crucial for the proper interpretation of this passage.
[3] For example, understanding the background of mystery religions in Colossae is important for interpreting Paul's warnings about "the elemental spirits of the world" in his letter to the Colossians (Col. 2:8, 20).
[4] For example, biblical texts about the construction of and worship in Solomon's temple should be interpreted in light of earlier passages (antecedent revelation) about the construction of and worship at altars by the patriarchs and the construction of and worship in the tabernacle by the wandering people of Israel, and it should be understood as anticipating later passages (subsequent revelation) about the temple's destruction, the postexilic rebuilding of the temple, Jesus's insistence on worship in spirit and truth (John 4:24), the church as the temple of the Holy Spirit (1 Cor. 3:10–17), and God as the temple in the new heaven and new earth (Rev. 21:22).
[5] For example, Moses's action of lifting up the serpent in the wilderness (Num. 21:9) is the type, and Jesus's being lifted up on the cross is the antitype (John 3:14–15).
[6] These senses will be explained and assessed in a later discussion.

ment that encompasses thousands of churches and ministries from many different theological persuasions: Reformed, Lutheran, and Arminian; covenantal and dispensational; Pentecostal/charismatic and non-Pentecostal/non-charismatic; proponents of infant baptism and supporters of believer's baptism; complementarians and egalitarians; and much more. Given this amazing theological spectrum, it is not possible to define and present one evangelical theology; evangelical theologies—plural—are the reality. However, so as to avoid confusion in my evaluation of Catholic theology and practice, I will set forth and focus on a typical expression of evangelical theology—the one outlined below—while noting, where appropriate, important divergences within evangelical theology. To ward off an anticipated criticism by Catholics, this theological diversity is not a "problem" just for evangelicalism. Catholic theology itself "suffers" from the same reality as it embraces Augustinianism and semi-Augustinianism; progressive, liberation theology and conservative, Opus Dei theology; male-only priesthood proponents and supporters of women priests; inerrancy and non-inerrancy; inclusivism and exclusivism; and the like. The "problem" of theological diversity is not inherent in evangelicalism, nor is it confined therein, for it is encountered within Catholicism, despite claims to the contrary.

Accordingly, I proceed with a typical expression of evangelical theology, which I'll call "a vision of life with God and human flourishing."

God eternally exists as three persons—the Father, the Son, and the Holy Spirit—each of whom is fully God, yet there is only one God. Eternally existing, the Father, the Son, and the Holy Spirit are characterized by dynamic, loving relationships (John 17:24–26), mutual glory giving (John 17:4–5), and purposing (e.g., 1 Pet. 1:20–21), part of which included the decision to bring into existence our visible, tangible universe. This plan was actualized as the triune God created the world and everything in it *ex nihilo*, or "out of nothing" (Gen. 1:1; Heb. 11:3). Light and darkness, the dry land and the seas, the sun, moon, and stars, trees and plants, the fish, birds, land animals—everything was formed (Gen. 1:2–25), seemingly in preparation for a final, special, climactic creature; indeed, this being would be more like God than any other created being. God created human beings in his image and according to his likeness (Gen. 1:26–31), which means we both *reflect* God and *represent* him in the world in which we live. As for the reflective element, we human beings display God in whose image we are created, mirroring his love, justice, truth-telling, faithfulness, mercy, power, wisdom, and the like—always imperfectly, partially, and intermixed with sin because of our fallen reality. The representational aspect consists of two functions (Gen. 1:28): *procreation* ("be fruitful and multiply and fill the earth"), which means that most of us are or will be married and have children; and *vocation* ("subdue [the earth] and have dominion") or civilization building, which means that we work in such professions as education, politics, business, health care, construction and manufacturing, the arts, and so forth (e.g., Gen. 4:17–22).[7] We contribute to human flourishing by using our God-given human abilities. Through reflecting God (displaying glimmers of his character) and representing him (establishing a family and building civilization) we engage in the ultimate of purposes: glorifying God.

As divine image-bearers, we are hardwired with an innate sense of God (Acts 17:22–34), witness his eternal power and divine nature through what we observe in the created order (Rom. 1:18–25), experience further testimony of his goodness as he providentially cares and provides for us (Acts 14:8–18), and possess an intuitive sense of right and wrong through our conscience (Rom. 2:12–16). Through these modes of general revelation, we know that God exists, we know something about his attributes, and we know some basic moral principles that render us accountable before him. Because of this universal revelation of God, we should worship and honor him as God, give him thanks and depend on him for our very existence, and obey the moral sense in our heart.

Tragically, all image-bearers of God have fallen into sin and live in a world that is not the way it is supposed to be. Personally, we fall short of the glory of God (Rom. 3:23); that is, we do not worship and honor God as we should, we do not give him thanks and depend on him as we should, and we (often, not always) do not obey our moral sense of right and avoid doing what our moral sense indicates is wrong, as we should. All of this is evidence of our alienation from God. Still, our fallenness does not end here: We are also alienated from other human beings, consumed with ourselves rather than concerned about others, in competition with them, experiencing relational brokenness. Furthermore, we are alienated from ourselves,

---

[7] The divine command in Gen. 1:28 is traditionally referred to as the "cultural mandate," and the beginning of its fulfillment is narrated in Gen. 4:2, 17–22 in terms of shepherding, farming, building a city, tending livestock, engaging in artistic expression, and fashioning metal tools.

being darkened in our understanding, chasing after things that will never satisfy, even being self-deceived.

Indeed, we may not even be aware of our present condition of sinfulness: Our conscience may be calloused; we may judge ourselves morally upright by comparing ourselves to others who are worse than us; we may even engage in doing good works (this element does not necessarily mean that we are religious, but often being religious and being part of a faith community that emphasizes doing good contributes to this element), leading us to conclude that we have gained God's favor. Deep down inside, however, we know we are not fine: we have a disturbing sense of our own hypocrisy, and though we may hope that God will look favorably on us and our good works, we suspect—rightly—that a perfectly holy and just God does not grade on the curve, and that even the most momentous of human achievements, let alone the meager efforts of most human beings, cannot avail before a perfect God. So, we are not in a good state, nor are we merely in a neutral position; rather, we are in dire straits. We come into this world weighed down with original sin, and we manifest that reality throughout life: guilty before God, pervasively corrupt in nature (our mind, emotions, will, body, motivations, purposing—everything is marred), and incapable of rectifying our guilt and reorienting our sinful nature from self-centeredness to God-centeredness, from the life of self to life with God.[8]

In this tragic world of fallen human beings, God intervened to rescue his image-bearers. At the heart of this redemption is Jesus Christ, the eternal Son of God who, through a miracle wrought by the Holy Spirit, was conceived by the Virgin Mary and became incarnate (Matt. 1:18–25; Luke 1:26–38), taking on human nature (Phil. 2:5–7). As the God-man, Jesus lived a perfect life under the law of God (Gal. 4:4), performed miracles to demonstrate his deity,[9] walked in the power of the Holy Spirit (Luke 4:16–21; Acts 10:38; e.g., Luke 4:1), announced and inaugurated the kingdom of God (Mark 1:14–15), taught the masses (e.g., Matthew 5–7), discipled a handful

---

[8] Evangelical theology encompasses several varieties of views of sin. One example is the view that Adam's sin is imputed to all human beings so that all are guilty of his sin, as opposed by the view that only a sinful nature from Adam is inherited by human beings. A second example addresses the extent and intensiveness of original sin on human nature, with one view embracing total depravity and total inability, as opposed by another view embracing partial depravity and partial inability.

[9] For example, the Fourth Gospel narrates seven signs or miracles that Jesus performed to demonstrate his divine nature (John 2:1–11; 4:46–54; 5:1–18; 6:1–15; 6:16–21; 9:1–41; 11:1–45); as John explains toward the end of his Gospel, he could have recounted many other miraculous signs (John 20:30), but "these are written so that you may believe that Jesus is the Christ, the Son of God, and that by believing you may have life in his name" (John 20:31).

of men (Matt. 10:1–4), faced temptations and trials as every other real and fully human being does yet he never once sinned (Heb. 2:14–18; 4:14–16), flourished in his relationship with God (e.g., Matt. 11:25–27), enjoyed intimate personal relationships with people of all kinds (e.g., Mark 2:15–17), and rendered visible the invisible God (Col. 1:15; John 14:8–9; Heb. 1:3). Shortly before his death, Jesus was betrayed by a close friend, abandoned by his disciples, charged with and convicted of blasphemy though innocent, beaten, and finally crucified on a cross; his body was laid in a garden tomb, where it reposed for three days (e.g., Matt. 26:47–27:66).

On the third day, this once-crucified-and-buried Jesus rose from the dead through the power of God. For forty days he appeared to his disciples, after which he ascended back into heaven (Acts 1:2–3, 9–11) and sat down at the right hand of the Father, from which position he exercises all power and authority as the cosmic head of all created things (Eph. 1:19–21), directs the church or the body of which he is head (Eph. 1:22), intercedes for his followers (Heb. 7:25; Rom. 8:34), and prepares an eternal future for them (John 14:2–3). And he is poised to return again to earth, this time not as a suffering servant in shame and humiliation but as the triumphant King of kings and Lord of lords with power, might, and glory (Revelation 19).

This work of redemption, and how it becomes actualized in the lives of sinful people, is communicated through another means of divine revelation: special revelation, especially Scripture. This written Word of God is characterized by the following attributes: It is *inspired*, or breathed out by God (2 Tim. 3:16; 2 Pet. 1:19–21); that is, the Holy Spirit superintended the writers of the Bible in such a way that, preserving their personalities, writing styles, theological emphases, and grammatical abilities, they wrote exactly what God wanted them to write. Because this Word is God-breathed, it is wholly *true* (inerrant) in all it affirms (John 17:17), whether it addresses the person and work of Jesus Christ, the existence and nature of angels, the creation of the universe, the history of the Jewish people, the eternal destiny of both the righteous and the wicked, and so forth. Because it is God-breathed, Scripture is *authoritative*; that is, it is to be believed and obeyed (Rom. 6:17), just as God himself is to be believed and obeyed. It is *effective*, igniting faith (Rom. 10:17), exposing sin (Heb. 4:12–13), exhibiting the proper path on which to walk, saving hardened sinners, transforming and remaking ruined lives, always accomplishing the purpose for which God gives it (Isa. 55:10–11). Scripture is *sufficient*, containing everything people need to know in order to be saved and to live in a way that fully pleases God (Ps. 19:7–11; 2 Tim. 3:16–17). It is *necessary*, that is, needed for fallen human beings to understand the way of salvation, to know God's will, and to acquire wisdom for godly living (Matt. 4:4; 1 Pet. 2:1–3). Indeed, without Scripture, the church would not exist or be able to exist. Scripture is *clear*, written in such a way that ordinary human beings who possess the normal acquired ability to understand written/oral communication can read Scripture with understanding or, if they are unable to read, can hear Scripture read and comprehend it (Deut. 29:29). Finally, Scripture consists of sixty-six books—thirty-nine in the Old Testament and twenty-seven in the New Testament. These books compose the biblical *canon*, or proper list of writings that God wanted included in his inspired (God-breathed), truthful (inerrant), authoritative, effective (powerful), sufficient, necessary, and clear Word.

From this divine revelation of Scripture, fallen human beings come to know about and understand the gospel, which is the work of salvation that God accomplished in Christ and its actualization in human lives. As for the accomplishment of salvation, the focal point of the gospel is the death and resurrection of Jesus Christ (1 Cor. 15:1–4). By means of his atoning sacrifice, Jesus Christ paid the penalty for sin as a substitute for sinners; that is, Christ died in our place, for us (Eph. 5:2). His death overcomes four desperate consequences of human sin: as an *expiation*, it removes the liability to suffer death and eternal punishment due to guilt before God (Heb. 10:5–18); as a *propitiation*, it assuages the furious wrath of a righteously angry God (Rom. 3:23–26); as *reconciliation*, it removes the enmity between God and human beings by means of the mediation of Christ, restoring friendship between formerly opposing parties (2 Cor. 5:17–21); and as *redemption*, it frees sinful human beings enslaved under sin from such bondage through the payment of a purchase price or ransom, the blood of Christ (1 Pet. 1:18–21). Through this atonement as expiation/propitiation/reconciliation/redemption, Christ accomplished salvation for sinful human beings. The satisfactory nature of this sacrifice was confirmed when the Father raised his Son from the dead, for the resurrection signified that Christ had accomplished everything necessary for salvation (Rom. 1:4; 4:24–25). Additionally, through his death and resurrection, Jesus defeated Satan (Heb. 2:14–18) and triumphed over all created things (Eph. 1:19–21; Col. 2:15), a cosmic victory that will be fully manifested at the end of this age, when he comes again in conquering power and glory.

As for the actualization of this divine plan of salvation, the focal point of the gospel is on God's gracious work that is apart from any and all human effort and merit. This multifaceted application consists of the following mighty acts of God:

Election, or the sovereign, gracious, and eternal choosing of some people to be rescued from their sins and experience salvation, not conditional on anything they are or do but because of the good pleasure of God to save some of his image-bearers out of the hellish nightmare into which all have fallen. This divine decision is inscrutable and mysterious, personal and not random or fickle, gracious and unconditional, not dependent on human personality, religious inclinations, works, or any other such matters (Eph. 1:4; 2 Tim. 1:9).[10] Though an eternal and hidden choice, election becomes actualized through a series of mighty acts of God that take place in space and time, and from this application the divine choice can be known (1 Thess. 1:4–5).

Conviction of sin is the mighty work of the Holy Spirit (John 16:8–11) convincing unbelievers of their sin (specifically, their unbelief in Jesus), self-righteousness (their futile attempts to please God and merit salvation through engaging in good works, attending church, and the like apart from divine grace), and faulty judgment (assessing people by mere appearance and worldly standards). Through this convicting work of the Spirit, unbelievers stand exposed and guilty before God, sensing their need for salvation.

Effective calling is the mighty act by which God draws to himself his people, a summons that will certainly result in their embrace of salvation (Rom. 8:29–30). This calling is noncoercive yet sure, and it comes through the communication of the gospel message (2 Thess. 2:13–14).

Regeneration is the mighty work by which the Holy Spirit causes people dead in sin to be born again (John 3:1–8; Titus 3:5). Where once there was nothing but unresponsiveness to the things of God, new spiritual life exists;

---

[10] This view of election reflects Reformed theology. A different view, as embraced by Arminian theology, considers election to be based on God's foreknowledge of people's response of repentance and faith to the gospel for salvation, and their continuation in that salvation to the end of their life. Foreknowing such realities, God elects these people to belong to him forever. This view of election is held by many varieties of evangelical theology.

people are new creatures (2 Cor. 5:17), changed in their very being so as to be children of God (John 1:12).[11]

Justification is the mighty act by which God declares sinful people to be not guilty but righteous instead, being forgiven of their sins and having the righteousness of Christ accredited to them. Justification is grounded on the grace of God as accomplished by the atoning death of Christ, by which God justly announces that the penalty for sin has been paid and thus sinful people are not guilty (Rom. 3:25). Because of the divine demand for perfect righteousness, the perfect righteousness of Jesus Christ, achieved through his obedience in life and in death, is credited to sinful people. This declarative act is not based on any inherent goodness or any personally achieved righteousness of fallen human beings (Rom. 3:19–22), and it does not make them actually righteous; rather, the righteousness of Jesus Christ is imputed to their account. This gracious, mighty act of God is appropriated by faith (Gal. 2:15–16), and sinful people are justified completely, such that they will never face the condemnation of God (Rom. 8:1).

Adoption is the mighty work by which God brings sinful people into his family and embraces them as his children (Eph. 1:5).

Union with Christ is the multifaceted mighty act that includes believers being in Christ (Rom. 6:1–11), or identified with his death, resurrection, and ascension; Christ being in his followers (Gal. 2:20); and all believers being one in Christ (John 17:21–23).

All of these mighty acts of God—conviction of sin, effective calling, regeneration, justification, adoption, and union with Christ—are actualized at the beginning of God's gracious work of salvation. The human response to this multifaceted action is *conversion*, which entails hearing and understanding the gospel message, repentance from sin (turning from it, renouncing it, and purposing not to live anymore in sin; Luke 24:46–47; Acts 17:30), and faith (believing that Christ died for one's sins, trusting in his work for salvation, and forsaking all human effort and relying on Christ and Christ alone; Eph. 2:8–9; Rom. 10:9). Repentance and faith are not a human work, nor are they a merely human response. As *evangelical* virtues, they are tied to the *evangel*, or gospel, and are thus prompted by grace (Acts 18:27) and urged by the messengers of the gospel (1 Cor. 3:5; 2 Cor. 5:17–21). But they

---

[11] The relationship between effective calling, regeneration, and conversion (to be discussed shortly) is a disputed matter among the varieties of evangelical theology.

are the proper and necessary human response to the gospel. Indeed, without genuine repentance and faith, there can be no salvation.

Yet, salvation is much more than an individual matter, for the mighty works of God that rescue fallen human beings also lead redeemed people into the church. The particular mighty act involved is the *baptism with the Spirit*: Jesus baptizes (John 1:33) new believers with the Holy Spirit (Luke 3:15–17), thus incorporating them into his body, the church (1 Cor. 12:13). Christians are joined with both the universal church and a local church.[12]

The universal church is the fellowship of both the deceased believers who are presently in heaven and the living believers from all over the world. This universal church (at least its living members) is manifested (by Christ, its head, and the Spirit) and manifests itself (through Christians associating themselves with one another) in local churches. These communities are led by qualified and publicly recognized pastors or elders who have the responsibilities of teaching sound doctrine (1 Tim. 3:2; 5:17; Titus 1:9), governing (1 Tim. 3:4–5), praying (especially for the sick; James 5:13–18), and shepherding (protecting their flock and leading through exemplary lifestyles; 1 Pet. 5:2–3). These assemblies are also served by deacons (1 Tim. 3:8–13), qualified and publicly recognized members who serve Jesus Christ in the many church ministries. Local churches regularly gather to worship God, proclaim his Word through the reading and preaching of Scripture, celebrate the ordinances of baptism and the Lord's Supper, engage non-Christians with the gospel, exercise spiritual gifts, disciple their members, care for people through prayer and giving, exercise church discipline, and stand both for and against the world by helping the poor and marginalized through holistic ministries. Local churches also are strongly connected and cooperate with one another for high-impact ministries in their cities.

Two other mighty works of God accompany these acts and continue throughout the rest of life. *Sanctification* is the cooperative work of God and Christians (Phil. 2:12–13) by which ongoing transformation into ever-increasing Christlikeness takes place, particularly through the working of the Holy Spirit (2 Cor. 3:18; Gal. 5:16–23). Unlike the other divine works, which are *monergistic* (due to "one" [Gk. *mono*] who "works" [Gk. *ergon*], that is, God alone), sanctification is a *synergistic* ("working [Gk. *ergon*] together [Gk. *sun*]") process, with God working in ways that are proper to

---

[12] The following presentation is adapted from Allison, *SS*, 29–32.

his divine agency (e.g., convicting of sin, empowering by the Spirit, willing and working to accomplish his good pleasure) and Christians working in ways that are proper to their human agency (e.g., reading Scripture, praying, mortifying sin, yielding to the Spirit).

Perseverance is the mighty act by which God powerfully protects Christians through their ongoing exercise of faith so as to bring them securely into possession of the fullness of their salvation when Christ returns (1 Pet. 1:5). Because the preserving power of God is foundational for this process; because saving faith, by definition, perseveres fully throughout life (1 John 2:18–19); and because Scripture is replete with affirmations and promises of the resolute will of God to save completely all those in whom he has initiated his redemptive work (e.g., Rom. 8:28–35; Phil. 1:6), Christians enjoy the privilege of the assurance of their salvation.[13]

As Christians journey through life, they await several more mighty acts of God on both a personal and a cosmic level. Personally, as they age, suffer, become sick, and draw inexorably toward death, they anticipate with joy, and without becoming overwrought by fear, their homecoming. *Homecoming* is the mighty act of God at the end of life by which Christians slough off their body and go to be with the Lord. They pass immediately from this earthly life into the presence of God, though as disembodied beings (2 Cor. 5:1–10). Accordingly, they wait eagerly for the next mighty act of God, their *glorification*, which is the completion of their salvation when Christ returns (Phil. 3:20–21). Glorification features the resurrection of the body; disembodied Christians receive their glorified body—imperishable, glorious, powerful, and completely dominated by the Holy Spirit (1 Cor. 15:42–44).

Cosmically, the consummation of this present age will begin with *the return of Jesus Christ*. Descending from heaven, accompanied by his faithful people, the King of kings and Lord of lords will crush his enemies and manifest himself as the triumphant, sovereign Ruler (Revelation 19). Depending on their eschatology (view of the future), Christians believe either that the sovereign Ruler will exercise his reign for a thousand years—*the millennium* (Rev. 20:1–6)—on earth before inaugurating the new heaven and new earth, or that immediately after his triumphant return he will establish the

---

[13] Other varieties of evangelical theology believe that salvation can be lost; thus, they would qualify this discussion of the assurance of salvation.

new heaven and new earth. Accompanying these cosmic events are other future mighty acts of God: the *final judgment* (Acts 17:30–31), in which God will evaluate the works of all people (2 Cor. 5:10) and express either his remunerative justice through rewarding good deeds, or his retributive justice through the condemnation of evil deeds, leading to the *eternal punishment* of the wicked (Matt. 25:46). The ultimate mighty work of God will be the removal of this present heaven and earth and all it contains (2 Pet. 3:10) and the establishment of *a new heaven and new earth* (Revelation 21–22) in which there will be no more sin, no more suffering and disease, no more death, but in which redeemed human beings, fully renewed in the image of God, will dwell forever as worshipers of the Lord.

Catholic Theology as a Coherent, All-Encompassing System

It will be on the basis of Scripture and evangelical theology as outlined immediately above that this assessment of Catholic theology and practice will be carried out. Such an assessment will not be the first time evangelical theology has evaluated Catholicism, but this approach will be unique, for two reasons. First, the structure it will follow is a walk through Catholic systematic theology as articulated in the *Catechism of the Catholic Church*. As far as I know, evangelical theology has never undertaken an assessment of Catholic theology and practice in this manner. Second, most evangelical assessments of Catholic theology and practice have focused nearly exclusively on comparing agreements and differences between the two positions in an isolated, disconnected way—an atomistic approach resulting in Catholic doctrines such as transubstantiation, purgatory, the immaculate conception of Mary, and apostolic succession being described and critiqued as separate, unrelated beliefs. While such an approach has warrant and indeed is necessary, it is incomplete because it fails to understand the systemic nature of Catholic belief. Accordingly, this assessment will be different in that it will treat Catholic theology as a coherent, all-encompassing system and will evaluate it with this starting point. Thus, the remainder of this chapter will argue for viewing Catholic theology as a coherent, all-encompassing system; next it will detail the two axioms on which this Catholic doctrinal system is built (the nature-grace interdependence and the Christ-Church interconnection), assessing each of these two major tenets in turn. The bulk of the book (chs. 3–13) will walk through the *Catechism* offering agreements and expressing differences on a topic-by-topic basis while tying the evangelical disagreements to the evangelical critique of the Catholic doctrinal system grounded on its two axioms.

This systemic approach, necessary because Catholic theology is a coherent, all-encompassing system, owes much to the original and insightful conviction of Leonard De Chirico. His modified doctoral dissertation, entitled *Evangelical Theological Perspectives on Post-Vatican II Roman Catholicism*, evaluates several evangelical theologians and evangelical-Catholic dialogues and underscores that their appraisals of Catholicism suffer from an exclusively or nearly exclusively atomistic approach to Catholicism[14]—an evaluation of individual doctrines and practices viewed as discrete issues. He considers the advantages of a systemic approach to be the following: (1) It permits an evangelical assessment of Catholic theology that views the latter as a "stable yet dynamic pattern which enables the system to hold together different elements which other theological orientations [such as evangelical theology] consider to be incompatible";[15] and (2) it prepares an evangelical appraisal to "address it *as* Roman Catholicism, i.e. a religion enjoying or claiming to enjoy Catholic breadth and vision as well as institutional and historical particularity."[16]

When viewed from a systemic point of view, the assumption is that Catholic theology is "a complex unity, it really has a central core and its vast phenomenology [concrete manifestations] expressed by it can be legitimately thought of in terms of this core element."[17] De Chirico convincingly demonstrates that Catholicism as a system is unified but not uniform; indeed, as he underscores, within the systemic unity of Catholic theology an amazing degree of diversity exists and flourishes. Because of its unity and diversity, Catholicism is a dynamic system that is able to assimilate new ideas, increase in complexity, hold in tension disparate elements, and significantly develop without altering its basic unified identity. Moreover,

---

[14] Leonardo De Chirico, *Evangelical Theological Perspectives on Post-Vatican II Roman Catholicism*, Religions and Discourse, vol. 19 [hereafter De Chirico] (Bern: Peter Lang, 2003). Evangelical theologians with whom De Chirico interacts are G. C. Berkouwer, Cornelius Van Til, David Wells, Donald Bloesch, Herbert Carson, and John Stott. The evangelical-Catholic dialogues with which he interacts are the World Evangelical Fellowship and Evangelicals and Catholics Together. By atomism, he refers to "an epistemological framework which favours the analysis of components, parts, elements of a given reality, without appreciating sufficiently their inherent relationships and organic bond. In short, atomism is an analysis which falls short of synthesis, it emphasizes particulars while not adequately accounting for universals, it stresses the importance of particular aspects and underestimates the relevance of structures" (ibid., 204).

[15] Ibid., 18.

[16] Ibid., 24.

[17] Ibid., 186.

Catholicism is global, or all-encompassing, in nature: it is driven by its project of furthering its catholicity or universality, seeking to address, influence, and incorporate the whole of reality. Putting together these two elements of unity and universality, De Chirico explains, "In the Roman Catholic understanding, catholicity is a nuanced term and has to do simultaneously with unity and totality which the Church already enjoys and is called to increase. The basic premise is that the whole of reality, which is already one in essence, though this protological [divinely purposed] unity is marred by sin, should be brought into a Catholic unity."[18] At this point, the firm conviction that "since catholic unity can be achieved, it must be achieved and eventually will be achieved through the work of the system," takes over and becomes the goal of the system, with the key to this unity—the Catholic Church—at its center.[19]

Another key element of this Catholic system is its epistemology, or method of knowing. Catholic theology is characterized by the integration of divergent elements: it takes an "and-and" approach, rather than an "either-or" approach.[20] This principle of integration makes it difficult for evangelical theology to grasp the Catholic system, because evangelicalism is built on the five *solas* ("onlys") of Protestantism: *sola Scriptura* (only Scripture), not Scripture *and* Tradition, as it is in Catholicism; *sola gratia* (only grace), not grace *and* human cooperation, as it is in Catholic theology; *solus Christus* (only Christ), not Christ *and* the Church, as it is in the Catholic system; *sola fide* (only faith), not faith *and* good works/love that merits eternal life; and *soli Deo gloria* (glory only to God), not glory to God *and* special honor, for example, to Mary. At the same time, this openness to integration is not an undisciplined or anarchic approach, because the Catholic system filters and controls what is allowed into the system and assimilates new and disparate elements to its traditional foundations. But any proper evangelical assessment of Catholicism as a coherent, all-encompassing system must be aware of and consider carefully this integrative epistemological element.

Furthermore, the catholicity of the Catholic system "is never a merely abstract or ideal concept but, on the contrary, is always intertwined with visible, material, immanent, organised, social, juridical, and historical

---

[18] Ibid., 197.
[19] Ibid.
[20] Ibid., 199.

structures."[21] Indeed, such concrete catholicity is manifested in, and only in, the Catholic Church, which is a visible, material, concrete reality. The ground for this idea is "the incarnational principle"—"grace must be embodied in a tangible way"—which is the normative pattern for the way God manifests his grace in this world.[22] The prototype of this principle is the incarnation of the Son of God as the God-man Jesus Christ: God manifests his grace in an embodied, tangible way, in this case by means of the Son taking on human nature. But this principle is also operative in Catholic theology's concept of the Catholic Church as the embodiment—the tangible, visible, material, social, concrete manifestation—of the grace of God.

These last two examples—Catholic theology's principle of integration, bringing together Scripture *plus* Tradition, grace *plus* human effort, faith *plus* good works, and the like; and Catholic theology's principle of incarnation, manifesting itself in the perspective on the Catholic Church as means of grace—underscore this notion: Catholic theology is a coherent, all-encompassing system.[23] Accordingly, to engage in a proper assessment of Catholic theology, evangelical theology must approach it as a system and apply the appraisal not only to specific, crucial topics—transubstantiation, purgatory, Mary—as single, discrete issues, but to the system as a whole as well. As De Chirico pleads, "What is needed, instead [of an exclusively atomistic approach to assessing Catholic theology], is the appropriation of a distinctively systemic view to use in looking at every single issue, be it considered foundational or peripheral but always expressing the system as a whole. . . . Every part of the system is in some way causally connected to and operatively dependent on the theology of the system to the extent that the attempt to grasp the centre opens the way to an understanding of the whole."[24] Accordingly, the goal of this evangelical assessment is to take this systemic approach to Catholic theology and, dealing with "the framework while attempting to do justice to the particulars," offer a more robust appraisal of Catholicism.[25]

But more can and needs to be said about the core elements of Catholic

---

[21] Ibid., 201.
[22] Ibid.
[23] Another line of evidence that Catholicism is a system is the fact that it was countered by a movement that eventually became an opposing, coherent, and all-encompassing system—Protestantism—with its own axioms (the formal principle of *sola Scriptura*; the material principle of justification by grace through faith alone), its own marks of the true church (preaching, the sacraments), its own confessions of faith, and the like.
[24] De Chirico, 213, 218.
[25] Cf. ibid., 218.

theology as a coherent, all-encompassing system. De Chirico identifies two
axioms of the Catholic system: the nature-grace continuum (what I will call
the nature-grace interdependence) and the Catholic Church as the ongoing incarnation of the ascended Christ (what I will call the Christ-Church
interconnection).[26] Each of these two pillars will be discussed and assessed
in turn.

The Nature-Grace Interdependence

De Chirico defines the two key concepts of nature and grace: "In Christian vocabulary, nature has been considered the equivalent of the created
world as a whole which is both the result of God's creating activity and the
recipient of His saving purposes. As far as the latter is concerned, God's
dealings with the world (i.e. nature) have been accounted for theologically
in terms of 'grace'. Grace is what God does in relation to the world, both
providentially and redemptively."[27] In other words, nature, as the product
of the creative activity of God, is the entirety of the created order and includes inorganic reality (the seas, mountains), the plant world, the animal
kingdom, angels and demons, human beings, water, oil, bread and wine,
and the like. Grace, in an all-encompassing sense, is the providential activity
of God to sustain created nature in existence and to direct it to its divinely
designed end, and his redemptive activity to rescue this created order from
its fallenness due to sin.

Without flattening the diverse models of the relationship of nature to
grace as developed by different Catholic theologians and movements within
the Catholic theological system,[28] an overarching characterization of this
relationship is possible: Nature and grace are interdependent because they
exist in a continuum or continuity. The two were divinely designed to operate in reliance upon each other such that nature is to be a channel of grace,
and grace is to elevate or perfect nature.[29] To give a simple illustration, water

---

[26] The first of these, which treats the relationship between nature and grace, is the "theological scope" or "theological horizon" of the Catholic system. The second element, which focuses on the self-understanding of the Church,
is the "key theological reference point determining its [the system's] orientation and expressions" (ibid., 219).
[27] Ibid.
[28] De Chirico summarizes these divergent typologies presented as three polarities: the dualistic tendencies of the
rigid variety of the tradition of Thomas Aquinas, and the holistic tendencies of Henri de Lubac's *Surnaturel*; the
essentialist perspective of the patristic tradition, and the personalist/existentialist perspectives of twentieth-cen-
tury theologians; and the Augustinian tradition and the Thomistic tradition (the tradition that follows Thomas
Aquinas) (ibid., 222–229).
[29] As Aquinas affirmed, "grace does not destroy nature but perfects it" (Thomas Aquinas, *Summa Theologica*
pt. 1, q. 1, art. 8).

(in the realm of nature) is capable of receiving and becoming a conduit of grace when, consecrated by the Catholic Church, it is used for the sacrament of Baptism, which confers grace upon its recipients. Indeed, George Weigel affirms "that it is through the ordinary materials of life—the materials of the seven sacraments, such as bread, wine, oil, and water—that the extraordinary grace of God enters history, nourishes the friends of Jesus, and empowers them in their missionary discipleship."[30]

Continuing with his description of nature and grace, De Chirico explains, "there is a constitutive and irreversible link between them which sin, whatever its consequences, has not and cannot sever."[31] That is, at the fall of Adam and Eve, one of the consequences of that tragic event was a disturbance in this original nature-grace interdependence. Importantly, however, though marred by sin, tainted nature still possesses a capacity to receive, transmit, and cooperate with grace. The Catholic theological system thus has two poles, nature and grace, and it fits sin, which it takes seriously, in the sphere of nature, thereby relativizing the negative effects of sin on nature:

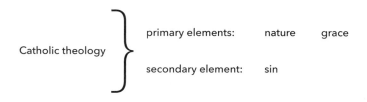

Catholic theology

primary elements: nature   grace

secondary element: sin

Nature and grace are the two constitutive elements of the Catholic system, with sin as a serious yet not devastating secondary element. Nature, while wounded by sin, retains a capacity for grace, and grace elevates or perfects nature.[32] The two continue to operate interdependently.

---

[30] George Weigel, *Evangelical Catholicism: Deep Reform in the 21st-Century Church* (New York: Basic, 2013), 44. Elsewhere, Weigel affirms that "the Church's sacramental system takes the stuff of the world and of human relationships with utmost seriousness, seeing in them the vehicles of divine grace" (ibid., 47; cf. 63–64).

[31] De Chirico, 236.

[32] Addressing Catholic theology's notion that, even before the fall, Adam and Eve's reason exercised a governing function over their passions and bodily desires, evangelical theology already senses that something is amiss: human nature, though not sinful as originally created, was nonetheless flawed or at least not in a state of integrity. Sin, therefore, is a *disturbance within nature*, not *a radical breach with nature*; nature already exhibited or was primed for a nature-sin continuum. Accordingly, the table is partially set for Catholic theology's submission of sin as a secondary element under the primary element of nature. Catholic theology's view of the original state of human beings before the fall will be discussed and assessed later.

By way of contrast, evangelical theology has three poles: creation, fall/ sin, and redemption/grace:[33]

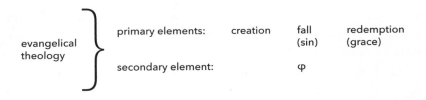

| evangelical theology | primary elements: | creation | fall (sin) | redemption (grace) |
| | secondary element: | | φ | |

In this system, sin is taken more seriously, and its corrupting impact on the creation is not mitigated by its being part of nature: "[N]ature is no longer considered as mere nature, not even an intrinsically graced nature, but always as a dramatically disrupted nature which needs to be restored by grace. In this view, nature is thought of as having experienced a radical breach at the fall and, in its post-fall outlook, which is the only historically real context in which creation finds itself, it cannot be anything but fallen nature."[34] Indeed, evangelical theology has three constitutive elements, with the fall or sin a primary, rather than secondary, element of its system. Because of the devastatingly deep impact of sin on creation, the notion of nature as possessing some capacity for grace is nonsensical in the evangelical system. A sin-riddled, totally marred creation "exists in a state of separation from God, incapable of restoring the relationship in its own strength, nor is it even willing to do so."[35]

In summary, "[t]he difference between the two systems revolves around differing understandings of nature and sin, and sin's impact on nature."[36] For Catholic theology, nature and grace are interdependent; for evangelical theology, nature and grace are at odds because of the devastating impact of sin on nature.[37]

---

[33] Some evangelical approaches would add a fourth element: consummation. The symbol φ stands for the null case; that is, evangelical theology does not have secondary elements. In particular, it does not consider sin to be a secondary element, but a primary element instead.

[34] De Chirico, 236.

[35] Ibid., 237.

[36] Ibid., 236. De Chirico rightly qualifies this discussion of the grave impact of sin on creation/nature by noting that evangelical theology also embraces two other doctrines that impinge on this topic: First, common grace is extended by God to preserve creation and encourage the building of civilization in spite of the extensive corruption introduced by the fall and continued by sin. Second, whereas the fall has "altered the 'direction' of creation," it has not destroyed its "structure." For example, while sin has devastatingly corrupted human nature, fallen human beings are still created in the image of God (ibid., 238–239).

[37] This does not mean that evangelical theology leads to gnosticism, which, according to Weigel, is a specter of the contemporary "spirit of the age." Evangelical theology embraces the goodness of the original creation, human

In one sense, these two divergent views reflect in part the different models of the nature-grace relationship as developed by Augustine and Thomas Aquinas: "[W]hereas the Augustinian tradition has stressed the concept of *natura vitiata* [spoiled or fallen nature], therefore underlining the pervasive and corrupting reality of sin and the utter primacy of grace, the Thomistic tradition has instead insisted on the inner resources of nature's *capacitas dei* [capacity for God], giving a more positive account of its intrinsic disposition towards the elevating operations of grace."[38] On this issue, evangelical theology follows the Augustinian tradition, with its pessimistic view of nature because of the devastating impact of sin on it, while Catholic theology follows the Thomistic tradition, with its relatively optimistic perspective on nature and its openness to and capacity for grace.

Up to this point, our focus has been on the constitutive element of nature, with a discussion of sin subsumed under this element, so attention must now turn to the second constitutive element of the Catholic theological system: grace. "An overall positive posture towards nature, coupled with a mild concept of sin, leads to a corresponding vision of grace."[39] This Catholic notion of grace "begins in nature . . . in the sense that in nature it finds a receptive attitude and potential resources which it can make use of in its operation. Nature always participates in grace whereas grace always presupposes the *ad intra* [from the inside; inherent] ability of nature to be stirred by it and co-operate with it. . . . The continuity between nature and grace allows the . . . mutual involvement between the forces of nature and those of grace. According to the Roman Catholic system, the methodology of grace always involves the participation of nature and the active collaboration of the latter [nature] in the outworking of the former [grace]."[40]

According to evangelical theology, grace has nothing to work with in nature because creation has been devastatingly tainted by sin; indeed, "grace cannot but operate *ad extra* [from the outside; extrinsically] with regard to nature because nature is so entrenched in sin to the point of not even being fully aware of its reprobate state, and only an external, unilateral operation

---

embodiment (because it is the divine design for human beings), the incarnation of the Son as the God-man, the resurrection (both of Christ and, in the future, of all his followers), and the new heaven and new earth. But evangelical theology maintains that the depravity due to sin is more extensive and intensive than its Catholic counterpart believes, and this depravity means that nature is not and cannot be a channel of grace; rather, nature must be re-created by grace.
[38] De Chirico, 228.
[39] Ibid., 240.
[40] Ibid.

of divine grace can redeem what is completely lost. Nothing that pertains to sinful nature is deemed to be capable of contributing to grace."[41] To summarize, the Catholic theological system is constructed on a continuum between nature and grace, whereas evangelical theology insists on a sin-produced divide or chasm between nature and grace.

A proper evangelical assessment of Catholicism will treat Catholic theology as a coherent, all-encompassing system with one of its two key tenets being the nature-grace continuum that underscores the less-than-devastating impact of sin on nature, which, as a consequence, retains some capacity to receive, transmit, and cooperate with grace. Specific theological doctrines and practices in which the outworking of this understanding of the nature-grace continuum can be seen are:

- *Epistemology* (the way of knowing): Catholicism expresses openness to all truth, whether that comes, for example, from Scripture *and* Tradition, or from Christianity *and* noble religious elements of non-Christian religions. Also, it elevates human reason (the realm of nature) as the essential element of the image of God, while also emphasizing the ability of human reason apart from grace to understand general revelation and theistic proofs so as to become convinced of the existence of God.
- *Biblical interpretation:* The words of Scripture—or, more specifically, the things to which the words of Scripture point (the realm of nature)—contain hidden meanings and are capable of communicating those deeper meanings as divine truths (the realm of grace).
- *Doctrine of humanity:* The Catholic system is characterized by a "moderate optimism regarding man's ability [the realm of nature] to be stirred by grace and to cooperate with its elevating process."[42] "Moreover, considering his ontological receptivity for grace, man is viewed as an intrinsically religious being in whom grace 'is experienced as a part of man's own self.'"[43] One manifestation of this characteristic is Adam and Eve's reason (in their original created state) exercising a controlling influence over their feelings/passions and bodily desires.
- *Doctrine of sin:* Catholic theology believes that, with the introduction of sin, this original structure of human nature was disrupted, with the lower aspects of Adam and Eve's nature usurping the role of reason. Yet

---

[41] Ibid., 241.
[42] Ibid., 242.
[43] Ibid., 84. Here De Chirico reflects David Wells's assessment of Catholic theology; the citation is from David Wells, *The Search for Salvation* (Leicester, England: Inter-Varsity Press, 1978), 144.

the Catholic system does not believe that sin's impact was so devastating that human nature lost its capacity for grace.

- *Doctrine of salvation*: Catholic theology views the process by which God rescues fallen human beings as being synergistic, that is, a cooperative venture between divine grace and human effort (the realm of nature), aided by grace, to work so as to merit eternal life. Moreover, it considers the operation of salvation to be an infusion of divine grace into people, by which their very nature is transformed. This point dovetails with Catholic theology's understanding of the goal of salvation as deification, or the process by which human nature, through grace, becomes more and more like God. If this process is interrupted through engaging in mortal sin, it can be restarted through the sacrament of Penance by which grace is conveyed again for the perfection of human nature. Finally, if this process is not completed in this earthly lifetime, that is, if grace has not fully elevated human nature to perfection before death, existence after death in purgatory promises to finish the purification procedure.

- *Sacramental theology*: Catholicism maintains that created elements in nature—for example, water, oil, bread and wine—are capable of transmitting divine grace as the sacraments of Baptism, Confirmation, and the Eucharist are administered. Moreover, these elements (the realm of nature), when consecrated (the realm of grace), are effective in conveying grace *ex opere operato*, that is, just by their administration as sacraments. Also, it views the Eucharist as conferring incorruptibility on the body and thus serving as a foretaste of the resurrection. Finally, Catholic theology understands the bread and the wine (the realm of nature) to be offerings to God by the Church (the realm of grace).

- *Ecclesiology:* For the Catholic system, grace must be concretely expressed in nature, and the highest tangible expression of grace (after Jesus Christ himself) is the Catholic Church. This aspect is especially seen in the Church's association of the forgiveness of sins with its priesthood. Indeed, by the sacrament of Holy Orders, men (the realm of nature) are consecrated so as to be able to administer the sacraments (the realm of grace).

- *Hierarchy:* The Catholic Church is characterized by hierarchy, specifically between the laity (on the low end) and the clergy (on the high end), with a hierarchical structure also existing among the clergy between deacons (on the lowest end), priests (in the middle), and bishops (on the highest end). A hierarchy is also generally in evidence between the faithful (on the lowest end), the religious (the middle), and the saints (the highest end).

- *Moral theology*: Catholic theology believes that the four cardinal human virtues (the realm of nature)—prudence, temperance, fortitude, justice—are understood, appreciated, and practiced by human beings apart from grace, which functions not to create but to purify and elevate these virtues. It also emphasizes that natural law—a law derived from the realm of human nature and known by human beings through reason, enabling them to know right from wrong—still functions, despite human sinfulness, in a somewhat intact manner to guide human choices.
- *Doctrine of Mary*: "Mariology expresses . . . the quintessential characteristics of the Roman Catholic nature-grace motif."[44] Mary, as a fully human being, is in the realm of nature; however, due to her immaculate conception, her human nature is not fallen, and, through her cooperation with grace, it remained unfallen throughout her life. Accordingly, in Mary's nature, grace found complete openness and full capacity for cooperation, leading to the incarnation of the Son of God and her meritorious sufferings at the foot of the cross.

Evangelical Assessment

Each of the above doctrines and practices will be assessed in due time in the remainder of this book, but an appraisal of the first pillar on which they are built—the nature-grace interdependence—will be undertaken now.

Evangelical theology disagrees strongly with its counterpart concerning the interdependence between nature and grace. One objection is that the Catholic system's concept of nature owes more to philosophical traditions—the Neoplatonism at the heart of Augustine's theology; the Aristotelian philosophy to which Thomas Aquinas's theology was wedded—than to Scripture. Because Catholic theology defines "nature" philosophically, rather than shaping this concept according to Scripture, evangelical theology considers its notion of nature to be fundamentally flawed. "The Evangelical systemic approach underlines the fact that building a whole system on a nature defined in this way is a structural fault of the Roman Catholic system, which is evident in every expression of the system itself and characterises its whole outlook."[45]

Indeed, rarely does evangelical theology address the topic of "nature":

---

[44] De Chirico, 243.
[45] Ibid., 234.

"It has gradually departed from using the language of nature and the theology it implied, preferring instead to develop its understanding of the created world in terms of creation," employing terminology like "created/creation order" and "creation ordinance."[46] Such reluctance to discuss the topic and the change in terminology for the issue is already a second objection to the Catholic understanding of the nature-grace relationship. Indeed, Eugene TeSelle believes that this relationship is "perhaps the only theological topic in which Catholic and Protestant thought have gone their own ways, passing like ships in the night, with no sense of common problems and standards of judgement."[47]

Assessing the Catholic system's nature-grace interdependence according to Scripture, evangelical theology offers a third objection: The continuity between nature and grace does not find biblical support. For example, the pristine state of the original creation, designed and executed to be a hospitable place in which human beings would enjoy a face-to-face relationship with God and flourish as vice-regents with him, was shattered when the original couple rebelled. This fall had ruinous consequences on Adam and Eve themselves, as they became guilty before God, enslaved to sin, broken relationally, and bound to death. But the biblical narrative also underscores the expansive, dreadful consequences of the disobedience of Adam and Eve on their relationship to the creation, as expressed in the divine damnation:

> cursed is the ground because of you;
> > in pain you shall eat of it all the days of your life;
> thorns and thistles it shall bring forth for you;
> > and you shall eat the plants of the field.
> By the sweat of your face
> > you shall eat bread,
> till you return to the ground,
> > for out of it you were taken;
> for you are dust,
> > and to dust you shall return." (Gen. 3:17–19)

Subjected to futility by God as a punishment for human sin (Rom. 8:20–22), the realm of nature becomes a cursed place. Emphatically, the one refuge

---

[46] Ibid., 232.

[47] Ibid., 233; citation is from Eugene TeSelle, "Nature and Grace in the Forum of Ecumenical Discussion," *Journal of Ecumenical Studies* (Summer 1971): 540.

in which Adam and Eve might have found rescue from ruin—the garden of Eden—becomes closed and shuttered to them as "[God] drove out the man, and at the east of the garden of Eden he placed the cherubim and a flaming sword that turned every way to guard the way to the tree of life" (Gen. 3:24). To use our terminology, if the garden of Eden represents the nature-grace interdependence, post-fall human beings are violently and decisively cut off from it, living instead in exile, the wilderness, a wasteland of their own undoing.

Furthermore, Scripture continues to emphasize the discontinuity, rather than the continuity, between the realm of nature and the realm of grace in John's portrayal of the creation's reception of its Creator, the Word of God, who is the life and the light of the world: "The true light, which gives light to everyone, was coming into the world. He was in the world, and the world was made through him, yet the world did not know him. He came to his own, and his own people did not receive him. But to all who did receive him, who believed in his name, he gave the right to become children of God, who were born, not of blood nor of the will of the flesh nor of the will of man, but of God" (John 1:9–13). The Word of God incarnate as Jesus Christ, the one through whom came "grace and truth" (v. 17), was rejected by the world that he created, more specifically, by his own people, the Jews. Again, to use our terminology, the realm of nature possesses no inherent capacity for God; even more, the realm of graced nature, the privileged people of God, possesses no intrinsic capacity for God. The only hope of rescue from this devastatingly grim nightmare is the new birth, being born of God, which has absolutely no connection to or continuity with family relationship, heritage (even Jewish), or human volition. Only by an external act of God—the Creator-Word coming into his inhospitable creation and to his unwelcoming people—and by a radical work of re-creation, can sinful human beings experience the grace of God.

The quintessential example of this radical work of salvation, rather than nature being primed for grace and then elevated by it, is Abraham (Rom. 4:17–22). This unbeliever from Ur, called by the one true God out of idolatrous paganism, believed the divine promise while he was still not circumcised and before works of the law were even possible. Accordingly, grace rescued Abraham *out of* nature; it did not remake him *from within* nature.[48] Moreover, the gracious promise of a son by which Abraham would become "the father of many nations" (v. 17) found no counterpart in either his or his wife's nature—"he did not weaken in faith when he considered his own body, which was as good as dead (since he was about a hundred years old), or when he considered the barrenness of Sarah's womb" (v. 19). On the contrary, grace operated apart from nature, and Abraham believed in the God "who gives life to the dead and calls into existence the things that do not exist" (v. 17). To use our terminology, nature is dead and nonexistent in relation to grace; but God's grace raises the dead and creates a new creation.

This emphasis on re-creation through grace, rather than grace finding a capacity in its counterpart of nature to be made over, is underscored in Scripture's final chapters, the vision of the new heaven and new earth to come (Revelation 21–22). Certainly, the consummation of this present age involves a renewal of the entire universe (Ps. 102:25–27; Rom. 8:21; 1 Cor. 7:31), but rather than understanding this renovation project in a continuity sense—grace reworking nature—it should be seen, in accordance with other biblical passages, as a renewal through destruction of the current reality: "the heavens and earth that now exist are stored up for fire, being kept until the day of judgment and destruction of the ungodly. . . . But the day of the Lord will come like a thief, and then the heavens will pass away with a roar, and the heavenly bodies will be burned up and dissolved, and the earth and the works that are done on it will be exposed" (2 Pet. 3:7, 10). The replacement for this radically burned, old reality is "a new heaven and a new earth, for the first heaven and the first earth had passed away, and the sea was no more" (Rev. 21:1). Furthermore, redeemed humanity's new place will not be renewed space made out of earthly nature, but "the holy city, new Jerusalem, coming down out of heaven" (vv. 2, 10).

In summary, for theological and biblical reasons, evangelical theology dissents from the Catholic theological system's axiom of the nature-grace continuum. Because this tenet is foundational for the entire system, it will manifest itself and undermine specific doctrines and practices, as the bulk of this book will demonstrate and critique. But this axiom is only the first of two supports for the Catholic system, and it is to the second element that this assessment now turns.

---

[48] Indeed, a constant theme of Scripture is the necessity of gracious salvation *out of* the idolatrous worship of nature (e.g., Acts 14:8–18; 17:22–31; Rom. 1:18–25).

The Christ-Church Interconnection

Continuing to follow De Chirico's presentation of the Catholic system as consisting of two pillars, the second element is the Catholic Church's understanding of itself as the continuation of the incarnation of Jesus Christ. This axiom is connected to the first in the following way: "Between the orders of nature and grace, a mediating subject is needed to represent nature to grace and grace to nature, so that nature will progressively and more fully be graced and grace will eventually achieve its final goal of elevating nature. That mediation is the theological *raison d'être* [reason for the existence] of the Roman Catholic Church and the chief role of the Church within the wider Roman Catholic system."[49] The mediatorial function of the Catholic Church is made possible by the interdependence of nature and grace: Nature, being open to grace, is capable of receiving the grace mediated to it by the Church, and grace needs nature because of the necessity for grace to be embodied, tangible, concrete—which is what the Catholic Church is. This mediation also depends on the principle or law of incarnation "as the pattern through which grace meets nature and nature receives grace."[50] The first and primary manifestation of this principle was the incarnation of the Son of God: as the incarnate God-man, Jesus Christ mediated grace to nature. But this specific event of the incarnation is not the only manifestation of this incarnational principle; this "basic pattern surpasses the particularity of the historical event of the mission of Jesus Christ and shapes the whole of salvation history . . . characterizing the on-going service of the Church. The Roman Catholic Church stands in continuity with the Incarnation and is the new enactment of the law of incarnation, being the post-ascension mediating agent which embodies the aspirations of nature and to which the mission of grace to nature is entrusted."[51] As the incarnate God-man Jesus Christ mediated grace to nature—the first and primary manifestation of the principle of incarnation—so the embodied, concrete Catholic Church mediates grace to nature in an analogous manifestation of the incarnational principle.

Specifically, Catholic theology "establishes a strong link between the incarnation of Christ and the Church as the prolongation of the Incarna-

---

[49] De Chirico, 247.
[50] Ibid., 249.
[51] Ibid.

tion whereby the latter [the Catholic Church] acts as *altera persona Christi* [another (or a second) person of Christ], standing therefore between God and the world."[52] Moreover, this mediatorial institution is characterized by hierarchy; just as there is the higher realm of grace and the lower realm of nature, so within the Catholic Church there is the higher realm of the clergy, who have the specific authority and responsibility to mediate grace, and the lower realm of the laity, who are to be open to and receive grace. At the head of this hierarchically structured, grace-mediating Church stands the pope.

This vision of the Catholic Church as the mediatorial agent between the grace of God and the world of nature is supported by several key considerations: the Christological analogy, the concept of the Church as the mystical body of "the whole Christ," and the notion of the Church as sacrament. The Christological analogy has already been treated when the incarnational principle was addressed above: As the Son of God became incarnate and thus mediated divine grace to nature, so the Catholic Church as the ongoing incarnation of the Son of God mediates divine grace to nature. Specifically, "the Church is seen as the same person as the Son of God who continues and renews the unique event of the Incarnation, being in herself the *locus* where the continuation of the Incarnation takes place and where the mission underlying the Incarnation is made present in an on-going way."[53] Reasoning from the traditional doctrine that Jesus Christ is both fully God and fully human, the result is that "in an analogous way the Church is made up of divine and human elements which are combined in the theandric [God-man] institution of the Church itself. The Church is deemed to be co-essentially divine and human, the two aspects being intertwined and inseparable in such a way that the human aspect carries the divine and the divine aspect is embodied in human forms."[54]

At first glance, this affirmation seems to be fraught with difficulties and dangers, and Catholic theology takes pains to clarify the analogy between Christ and his Church, underscoring both continuities and discontinuities between the two: "While the Son of God owns divine nature in a proper, ontological, and substantial way, the Church derives her divine elements by participating in the life of Christ which makes him present within the

---

[52] Ibid., 250.
[53] Ibid., 253.
[54] Ibid.

Church and through it."[55] Accordingly, Christ is not totally identified as the Church; rather, the Church is a prolongation of the incarnation of the Son of God, mediating the grace of God to the world as the incarnate Christ mediated the divine grace to the world.

A second support for this mediatorial role for the Catholic Church is the concept of the Church as the mystical body of Christ. Quite evidently, this understanding is rooted in the Pauline metaphor of the church as the body, of which Christ is the head. The apostle explains that this reality was God the Father's work to exalt his Son: "He [the Father] put all things under his [Christ's] feet and gave him as head over all things to the church, which is his body, the fullness of him who fills all in all" (Eph. 1:22–23; cf. 5:23; Col. 1:18, 24). Furthermore, Paul employs the sacrificial nature, love and respect, and intimacy of the relationship between husband and wife to illuminate the nature of the unity between Christ and the church, concluding, "This mystery is profound, and I am saying that it refers to Christ and the church" (Eph. 5:32). Accordingly, the Church is the mystical body of Christ. "The core of the metaphor refers to the indissoluble, organic bond between head (i.e. Christ) and members (i.e. the Church) within the unity of a single body so that what can be ascribed to the head can also be ascribed in some measure to its members."[56] The implication of the Church as this mystical body of Christ is key: "The Church is therefore organically related to, and pervasively inhabited by Christ and also subordinated to him in that both the Church and Christ are differently located, yet inseparable parts of the same body. While the members are dependent on the head in the sense that they receive from it direction and serve its cause, they are also so inextricably united to it as to form a single body so that the head cannot operate apart from its members and cannot be separated from them."[57]

Definitive support for this concept of the mystical body comes from Augustine's proposal of the *totus Christus* (the whole Christ); as he explained, "the whole Christ consists of Head and body. The Head is he who is the savior of his body, he who has already ascended into heaven; but the body is the Church, toiling on earth."[58] In other words, the whole Christ refers

---

[55] Ibid., 259.
[56] Ibid., 261.
[57] Ibid.
[58] Augustine, *Expositions of the Psalms*, in *The Works of Saint Augustine: A Translation for the 21st Century*, ed. John E. Rotelle, trans. Maria Boulding, 6 vols. (New York: New City, 2000–2004), 4:149.

to Christ as head, in the totality of his divine and human natures, together with his body, the church. For Augustine, the Pauline passages cited above cannot be understood merely metaphorically or symbolically; on the contrary, when Paul calls the church "the body of Christ," he is describing the church in terms of its actual reality.

The reason for this interpretation is the profound unity between the two through the incarnation; though ascended into heaven, Christ is still intimately united to his Church. Support for this unity was found in Matthew 25:31–46 and Acts 9:4–5. As for the latter passage, Augustine explained,

> Were it not for the body's linkage with its Head through the bond of charity, so close a link that Head and body speak as one, [Christ] could not have rebuked a certain persecutor from heaven with the question, *Saul, Saul, why are you persecuting me?* (Acts 9:4). Already enthroned in heaven, Christ was not being touched by any human assailant, so how could Saul, by raging against the Christians on earth, inflict injury on him in any way? He does not say, "Why are you persecuting my saints?" or "my servant," but *Why are you persecuting me?* This is tantamount to asking, "Why attack my limbs?" The Head was crying out on behalf of the members, and the Head was transfiguring the members into himself.[59]

Christ's impassioned cry when his church was suffering underscores the intimate unity between the two. Accordingly, Augustine formulated this idea: "Christ is not simply in the head and not in the body, but Christ whole is in the head and body."[60] Taking a realistic view of this concept, Augustine projected it onto his doctrine of Christ, proposing that there are three ways to understand Christ—his divine nature, his human nature, and his ecclesial nature—with the latter meaning "in some manner or other as the whole Christ in the fullness of the Church, that is as head and body, according to the completeness of a certain perfect man (Eph. 4:13), the man in whom we are each of us members."[61] Augustine's *totus Christus* lies at the heart of Catholic theology's concept of the mystical body of Christ, mediating the divine presence and grace.

---

[59] Ibid.
[60] Augustine, *Tractates on the Gospel of John* 28.1 (NPNF[1] 7:179).
[61] Augustine, Sermon 341, in *The Works of Saint Augustine: A Translation for the 21st Century*, Part 3: Sermons, vol. 10, *Sermons 341–400*, ed. John E. Rotelle, trans. Edmund Hill (Hyde Park, NY: New City, 1995), 19.

As a final support for the mediatorial agency of the Catholic Church, Catholic theology turns to the notion of the Church as sacrament, a category that is "paramount in dealing with the profoundly mysterious, yet vitally important relationship between Christ and the Church" as the ongoing incarnation of Christ.[62] According to Vatican Council II, "the Church, in Christ, is in the nature of sacrament" in that it is "a sign and instrument . . . of communion with God and the unity among all men."[63] Importantly, the Church as sacrament envisions itself both as representing the union with God and the unity of the human race and as working to actualize the reality that it symbolizes. "In other words, there is an intertwined relationship between her nature as sign and her role as instrument, in such a way that in being what she is, the Church performs her role efficaciously, and in doing what she does, the Church enacts her nature properly."[64]

In summary, the second pillar of the Catholic theological system, in addition to the nature-grace interdependence, is the Catholic Church's self-understanding as the prolongation of the incarnation of Jesus Christ—the Christ-Church interconnection. As such, the Church functions as the mediator between nature and grace. Additionally, because the nature-grace continuum is characterized by a hierarchical structure, so also the Catholic Church as the mediating agent is characterized by a hierarchical structure. Several lines of justification for this self-understanding are offered. One support is the Christological analogy: As the Son of God became incarnate and thus mediated grace to nature, so the Catholic Church as the ongoing incarnation of the Son of God mediates grace to nature. A second warrant is the concept of the Church as the mystical body of Christ. When combined with Augustine's proposal of the *totus Christus*, it means that the whole Christ, in the totality of his divine and human natures, together with his body, the Church, is currently present as and in the Catholic Church. A third support is the notion of the Church as sacrament, a sign and instrument of the union with God and the unity of the human race.

A proper evangelical assessment of Catholicism will treat Catholic theology as a coherent, all-encompassing system with one of its two key tenets being the Catholic Church's self-understanding as the prolongation of the

---

[62] De Chirico, 267.
[63] Vatican Council II, *Lumen Gentium* 1 (VC II-1, 350).
[64] De Chirico, 273.

incarnation of the ascended Jesus Christ; as such, the Church functions as the mediator between the realm of nature and the realm of grace (thus, the two key axioms are closely related). Specific theological doctrines and practices in which the outworking of this understanding can be seen are:

- *Scripture*: The Catholic Church claims to be the determiner of the canon of Scripture.
- *Faith*: The Church is the first to believe and indeed grants faith to human beings.
- *Christology*: Catholic doctrine certainly affirms the traditional view that, forty days after his resurrection, the God-man Jesus Christ ascended into heaven. However, it emphasizes a strong continuity between the incarnate Son of God who has ascended and now is seated at the right hand of God the Father in heaven and the extension of that incarnate Son in the life of the Catholic Church. Indeed, it maintains that the whole Christ, in the totality of his divine and human natures, is present in his body, the Church, and thus is here on earth.
- *Ecclesiology*: The Catholic system always associates Christ and the Church; the bond between the two is so essential and unbreakable that to think of Christ in isolation from the Church is impossible. Moreover, because the incarnate Christ mediated grace to nature, the Church as the continuing incarnation of the ascended Christ mediates grace to nature and thus is necessary for salvation. Additionally, the Church identifies itself as the universal Church that professes a common faith, engages in worshiping God with a common liturgy, is nourished by means of common sacraments, and is taught, governed, and sanctified by a common hierarchy through apostolic succession.
- *The only true church*: Because the Catholic Church is the prolongation of the incarnation of Jesus Christ, his mystical body, and a sacrament of union with God and the unity of the whole human race, it understands itself as the only true church, meaning that evangelical gatherings are only ecclesial communities, not actual churches. Moreover, for the Catholic system, the universal church is identified with the visible Catholic Church on earth. The Church is both Mother and Teacher.
- *Pneumatology (the doctrine of the Holy Spirit)*: Catholic theology clearly underscores the important role of the Holy Spirit in the world and the Church, but it fails to explain how the ascended Christ, who is wholly present here and now, relates to the Spirit, who as *another*

Helper/Comforter was sent to take the place of the absent (that is, the ascended) Christ.

- *Sacramental theology*: For Catholicism, when the sacraments are administered in the Church, Christ himself is the one who baptizes, Christ himself celebrates the Eucharist, Christ himself ordains, and so forth. Furthermore, these sacraments, as mediating divine grace, are necessary for salvation.
- *Priesthood*: For Catholic theology, the bishop/priest, in virtue of his consecration received through the sacrament of Holy Orders, acts in the person of Christ the head (*in persona Christi Capitis*) when he engages in the service of the Church; accordingly, it is Christ "who through the Church baptizes, teaches, rules, looses, binds, offers, sacrifices."[65]
- *Offices of Christ*: The Catholic theological system underscores that Christ delegates the exercise of his threefold office—kingly, prophetic, and priestly—to the Church. Because Christ is the king, the Church exercises his rulership through its authoritative leaders. Because Christ is the prophet, the Church exercises his teaching ministry through its *Magisterium*, or teaching office. Because Christ is the priest, the Church exercises his priestly ministry through its priesthood.
- *Hierarchy*: The Catholic Church as the mediatorial institution is characterized by hierarchy, which can been seen in the higher realm of its clergy—among which there is also a hierarchical order, from its highest officers, the bishops, and their assistants, the priests, to the lowest offices, the deacons—and the lower realm of the laity. At the head of this hierarchically structured Church stands the pope, who is the Vicar—the concrete, tangible, visible representative—of Christ himself.
- *Doctrine of Mary*: In relation to the Catholic Church's vision of its general mediatorial role in salvation, it elevates Mary to a particular mediatorial role in the distribution of grace, naming her as Mediatrix alongside her son, the Mediator.
- *The communion of saints and indulgences*: Catholicism embraces the interchange of spiritual goods (for example, prayers, sufferings, and merits) because of the communion of all the faithful in heaven, on earth, and in purgatory. Specifically this exchange means that indulgences may be obtained not only for oneself but also for those whose souls are in purgatory.

[65] Pope Pius XII, *The Mystical Body of Christ* (June 29, 1943), 54. Accessible at http://www.vatican.va/holy_father/pius_xii/encyclicals/documents/hf_p-xii_enc_29061943_mystici-corporis-christi_en.html.

- *Ecumenism*: Catholic theology's notion that the Church is a sacrament—and especially that, as such, the Church is an instrument of unity among the entire human race—results in ecumenism being a very important project for the Church in its mission to the world.
- *Transubstantiation*: Though presented and supported in a different way, Catholicism's understanding of the sacrament of the Eucharist (that during the mass, the bread is transubstantiated, or changed, into the body of Christ, and the wine is changed into the blood of Christ) is at home in the Catholic theological system grounded on the Church's understanding of itself as the prolongation of the incarnation of the ascended Jesus Christ. For a similar reason, the Church encourages the faithful to engage in ongoing worship of Christ, who is present in the unconsumed consecrated wafers stored in the tabernacle.[66]

Evangelical Assessment

Each of the above doctrines and practices will be assessed in due time in the remainder of this book, but an appraisal of the second pillar on which they are built, the Christ-Church interconnection, will be undertaken now.

Evangelical theology disagrees strongly with its counterpart's self-understanding as the ongoing incarnation of the ascended Christ. Such a construction posits far more of a continuity between the incarnation of the Son of God as Jesus Christ and the Church as the prolongation of this incarnation than is warranted. The incarnation of the second person of the Trinity was a unique event: There was no prefiguration of it in the Old Testament,[67] nor is a principle or law of incarnation articulated in the New Testament. Accordingly, there can be no continuation of the incarnation, nor any derivative, secondary instance of it, with respect to the church (or any other reality, for that matter).

Furthermore, evangelical theology finds much that is wrong with the *totus Christus*. The concept is based on a misunderstanding of Paul's body imagery, interpreting a metaphor in realistic terms. Indeed, the apostle em-

---

[66] The Eucharistic tabernacle is a consecrated, beautifully decorated, and secure furnishing placed in a prominent location in a Catholic Church and used to store the Eucharist outside of the mass. Because the consecrated host is the body of Christ, the faithful are encouraged to engage in adoration as they are near the tabernacle in which the sacrament is reserved. The Eucharist in the tabernacle may also be used to bring the sacrament to the sick as viaticum. "Viaticum" refers to preparations for a journey (Lat. *via*); this aspect of the sacrament of the Eucharist will be discussed in detail later.

[67] Theophanies were not prefigurations of the incarnation, because they consisted of temporary manifestations of God in human form but none of them was a hypostatic union between the divine nature and a human nature, as was the incarnation of Jesus Christ.

ploys analogical language when speaking of the head with its body: "For
the husband is the head of the wife *even as* Christ is the head of the church,
his body, and is himself its Savior" (Eph. 5:23). To apply the *totus Christus*
concept in interpreting this analogy results in the near identification of the
two marriage partners, with the primacy of the existence of the husband
and the contingency of the existence of the wife being reinforced; this is
neither a Pauline nor a biblical idea. Similarly, Jesus's affirmation (Matt.
25:31–46) that as people concretely and kindly treat (or overlook and do
not help) the least of his disciples, they do it to him, underscores that their
treatment or mistreatment of Christ's followers is a measure or reflection
of their attitude toward Jesus and their alignment with his kingdom. And
Jesus's warning to Paul (Acts 9:4–5) that, by his persecution of Christians,
Paul was persecuting Christ, certainly underscores the union of Christ with
his disciples, who share in his sufferings (Phil. 1:29). To be fair, "this somewhat ontological interpretation" of these passages by the Catholic system
is possible,[68] thus providing reinforcement for the Catholic Church's self-
understanding as the extension of the incarnation. However, it is countered
by the evangelical system's relational interpretation: These passages underscore that the church, which is "in Christ," stands in intimate *relationship*
to Christ but is not a prolongation of his ascended being—the *ontological*
interpretation. But there is another, more severe critique of the Catholic
Church's self-understanding, a criticism that renders the ontological interpretation of these passages quite implausible.

Often overlooked in this discussion is the fact of the ascension and its
implications for Christ: Presently, he is *not here* on earth but is ruling from
heaven from his position of authority at the right hand of the Father. It
was to heaven that Jesus ascended (Acts 1:11); it was to this exalted status
that the Father raised him (Eph. 1:20–21); it was from there that Christ
sent the Holy Spirit to take his place as another Helper (John 15:26; Acts
2:33); and it is from heaven that Jesus will return (Matt. 26:64; Acts 1:11;
1 Thess. 4:16). "The Roman Catholic system looks at the ascension within
the continuity of the pattern established with the Incarnation, even though
it recognises the newness of the post-ascension period of the same law. . . .
The Evangelical system tends to view the ascension in more abrupt, radical
ways in that it conceives it as the coming to an end of the earthly ministry

---

[68] De Chirico, 278.

of Jesus Christ which cannot be extended or prolonged in any form because of its uniqueness with the economy of salvation and its once and for all soteriological significance."[69]

This position of discontinuity is not to deny that the fullness of Christ fills his body (Eph. 1:23), but it must be understood with respect to his divine omnipresence and spiritual presence: Because he is fully divine, the Son of God is present everywhere with the entirety of his divine being at the same time, and that divine presence is manifested in specific ways in specific times, for example, to bring blessing when the church exercises discipline (Matt. 18:15–20), engages missionally (vv. 18–20), and celebrates the Lord's Supper (1 Cor. 10:14–22). Accordingly, to affirm *totus Christus* as the whole Christ—the divine-human God-man enthroned as king in heaven—being present in both the head and the body, is wrong. Indeed, it results in several grave errors (noted above, and to be discussed later), including the Catholic view of the presence of Christ in the Eucharist (transubstantiation); the substitution of "the church in the place of its absent Lord,"[70] especially noticeable in the Church's hierarchy standing in the place of Christ; and the identity of the universal church with the visible Catholic Church on earth.[71]

Moreover, evangelical theology objects to the essential mediatorial role ascribed to the Catholic Church as the prolongation of the incarnation of the ascended Christ. At this point, the first axiom of the Catholic theological system, the nature-grace interdependence, joins with the second axiom to exert a strong influence. While emphasizing the uniqueness of the mediation of Jesus Christ for salvation—an operation of grace clearly in line with Scripture (e.g., 1 Tim. 2:4–6)—Catholic theology incorporates the axiom of the interdependence of nature and grace, with the result that it "allows, indeed demands, the contribution of nature in the operation of grace. According to the Roman Catholic nature-grace pattern, the uniqueness of the mediation of Jesus Christ needs to be qualified in terms of requiring the participation of nature in the working out of the mediation. . . . The Church, therefore, as the body of Christ and the sacrament of the intimate union with God and humanity, shares the mediatory office of Jesus Christ whose Incarnation she extends."[72]

---

[69] Ibid., 276.
[70] Michael S. Horton, *People and Place: A Covenant Ecclesiology* (Louisville: Westminster John Knox, 2008), 5.
[71] For further discussion, see ibid., 155–189.
[72] De Chirico, 281.

It is important to underscore that, for Catholicism, such ecclesial co-operation and mediatorial assistance "neither take away from nor add anything to the dignity and efficacy of Christ the one Mediator."[73] While an evangelical assessment of the Catholic system must acknowledge the system's claim to hold in tension what seem to be mutually contradictory tenets of mediation—Christ's unique mediation is carried out through the Church's shared mediation—evangelical theology is at great pains to understand this conjunction. Its criticism focuses on the two axioms that support this Catholic concept of the mediatorial function of the Church: the nature-grace continuum is wrong, and the Church's self-understanding as the extension of the incarnation is wrong. And, in this case, two wrongs put together do not make a right. Accordingly, evangelical theology lives by the Protestant *solus Christus*—only Christ, not Christ *plus* the Church.

Evangelical theology makes a similar critique of its counterpart's theology of Mary, who is a particular expression of the more general expression of the Church's mediation in the operation of grace for salvation. Once again, the two axioms of the Catholic system undergird its elevation of Mary to Mediatrix. Nature possesses a capacity for grace, so when Mary's human nature was preserved from sin through her immaculate conception (a work of grace), and when she did not sin through her obedience of faith prompted by grace, then Mary became the graced mediator of grace, which must be embodied in (human) nature. Moreover, as the Church is the mediator between nature and grace, and Mary stands in relationship to the Church as its Mother, then she is its quintessential member who mediates grace to nature. But, objects evangelical theology, Mariology is grounded on the two wrongheaded axioms of the nature-grace continuum and the Church's understanding of itself as the extension of the incarnation of Jesus Christ. Accordingly, Christ and Christ only is the Mediator between God and man, grace and nature.

Conclusion

This chapter has accomplished four important matters: First, it has outlined the interpretive approach to Scripture, called a grammatical–(redemptive) historical–typological method, that will be the method of understanding

---

[73] Ibid., citing Vatican Council II, *Lumen Gentium* 62.

Scripture used in this evangelical assessment. Second, it has described a typical expression of evangelical theology—called a vision of life with God and human flourishing—that will be the general theological framework employed in this evangelical assessment. Third, it has argued for an approach to understanding and assessing Catholic theology that considers it to be a coherent, all-encompassing system based on two foundational tenets. And fourth, it has assessed these two axioms—the nature-grace interdependence and the Christ-Church interconnection—with a general critique.

The rest of this book will be an assessment of Catholic theology and practice within this broad Catholic system on the basis of both Scripture and evangelical theology.

I

Catholic Theology according to the
Catechism of the Catholic Church

Part I: The Profession of Faith

3

The Profession of Faith
(Part I, Section I, Chapters I–3)

The Human Capacity for God; the Doctrine
of Revelation; the Doctrine of Faith

Introduction: The Nature and Shape of the *Catechism*

Vatican Council II (1962–1965) developed and promoted doctrinal statements and ministerial principles to guide the Catholic Church into the
future, and the process of communicating and implementing the massive
changes called forth by the Council has been, is, and will be an ongoing
task. One of the chief means by which the Church effects this renewal is
through a reference text setting forth its doctrinal beliefs concerning both
faith and morals, entitled the *Catechism of the Catholic Church*. Though
catechism is not a concept with which many evangelicals are familiar, the
word refers simply to a teaching tool that can be used for the process of
catechizing, or instructing, people in the faith and its practice.

Work on the *Catechism* began in 1986 when Pope John Paul II established
a commission of cardinals and bishops for its preparation and writing. The
commission's chairman was Cardinal Joseph Ratzinger, who would later
become Pope Benedict XVI. Following nine drafts, the input of numerous
biblical and theological scholars, and many consultations, the *Catechism*
received approbation from the whole Episcopate (the office of the bishops)
of the Catholic Church, including Pope John Paul II,[1] and stands today as
a faithful and systematic presentation of the teaching of the Church according to its threefold structure of authority, that is, written Scripture, the

---

[1] The pope gave his approval on June 25, 1992, and promulgated the *Catechism* on October 11 of that same year
in his apostolic constitution *Fidei Depositum*, accessible at: http://www.vatican.va/holy_father/john_paul_ii
/apost_constitutions/documents/hf_jp-ii_apc_19921011_fidei-depositum_en.html.

Tradition of the Church (including its liturgy), and the Magisterium, or its teaching office. The *Catechism* was first published in English in 1994.[2]

Though the structure of the *Catechism* will seem unfamiliar to most evangelicals, its organization is quite traditional and consists of four parts. The first part, *The Profession of Faith*, or the *Creed*, treats initially the topic of humanity's capacity for God and the doctrines of revelation (God's disclosure or communication of himself to his human creatures) and faith (the human response to divine revelation), followed by other doctrines structured generally in accordance with the Apostles' Creed (written in the third to fourth century) and the Nicene-Constantinopolitan Creed (written in 381). The second part, *The Celebration of the Christian Mystery*, presents the *liturgy*, or the Church's celebration of divine salvation made present through its actions, particularly the *seven sacraments* of Baptism, Confirmation, the Eucharist, Penance, Anointing of the Sick, Holy Orders, and Matrimony. The third part, *Life in Christ*, develops the idea of *beatitude* or blessing as God's ultimate design for his image-bearers, a purpose that is to be realized through grace and law, particularly obedience to the Ten Commandments and Christ's teachings in the Sermon on the Mount. The fourth part, *Christian Prayer*, rehearses the seven petitions of the Lord's Prayer.[3] Though this structure results in some overlap (e.g., the doctrine of sin is treated in both parts 1 and 3), the *Catechism* is quite readable and easy to follow. A couple of final points for its readers: Scripture quotations, which are often and helpfully written out, are taken from the Revised Standard Version and the New Revised Standard Version.[4] Paragraphs with small print present historical or apologetic matters and, being supplemental materials, are not essential to read. Quotations in small print are taken from patristic, liturgical, and other sources and serve a catechetical, or teaching, purpose. Each unit concludes with a summary ("IN BRIEF"), which may be consulted both before and after reading the unit so that readers are sure to grasp the essential matters.[5]

---

[2] Following its translation from the original 1992 French version into the official Latin text in 1997, the *Catechism* underwent some revisions in its translations, including its English text, in 1997.

[3] This book will not discuss or assess the fourth part of the *Catechism*.

[4] When I quote sections of the *Catechism* that include biblical citations, those citations will be from either the Revised Standard Version or the New Revised Standard Version, but will not be marked as such.

[5] All citations of the *Catechism* will be abbreviated CCC and will indicate the paragraph number, not the page number, of the reference. Paragraph numbers are the same for all editions of the *Catechism*, while page numbers vary. For more explanation, see again my comments in the next-to-last paragraph of the "Introduction" to this book (ch. 1).

The Human Capacity for God (Sec. I, Ch. I)

The first section of Part 1 of the *Catechism*, The Profession of Faith, asks and answers the question of what it means to believe. Clearly, the *nature of faith* needs to be grasped before one can make a *profession of faith*. According to the *Catechism*, faith is a human response to God and his revelation of himself to his human creatures, whom he has created in his image and has called to know and love him. From the outset, then, human beings are designed to search for God; in a sense, they are hardwired to desire God through a divinely implanted longing. As religious beings, therefore, all people worship. God is the proper object of this veneration, but through human forgetfulness and even rejection, something or someone else becomes a substitute for the one, true, living God. Still, God continues to search out true worshipers amid the tragedy of human waywardness.

Specifically, God provides certain ways by which human beings can come to know him. Often called *proofs of God's existence*, they take their start from two points: (1) *Cosmological* and *teleological arguments* have the world (*cosmos*) and its evident design or purpose (*telos*) as their starting points. As people contemplate the universe and all it contains, its dependence on something or someone else for its existence rather than nonexistence, its design and order, and so forth, they rightly conclude that God exists. (2) *Aesthetic* and *moral arguments* take the human person as their point of departure. As people contemplate humanity's universal moral sense (the way things *ought* to be—e.g., fair trade laws); the human appreciation for goodness, truth, and beauty; and the human longing for perfection and happiness, they rightly conclude that God exists. Great Catholic scholars like Thomas Aquinas developed these arguments formally,[6] but they are not far removed from what Scripture affirms: All people everywhere see evidence of God and his personal characteristics in the creation that exists (Rom. 1:18–25) and know something of his moral laws through the human conscience (2:13–16). Also, through these ways human beings become disposed toward faith and grasp that faith is compatible with human reason. Indeed, the *Catechism* underscores that God "can be known with certainty from the created world by the natural light

---

[6] Interestingly, the *Catechism* does not present the ontological argument, one of the classical and time-honored proofs for God's existence, in its discussion of these proofs.

of human reason" because he created human beings as his image-bearers with this capacity to know him.[7]

Such knowledge of the existence of a personal God, however, is not sufficient for an intimate relationship with him. The cause of this insufficiency is the disturbing effects of sin on human reason, which, while providing certainty of the knowledge of God, becomes hindered by the senses, the imagination, and disoriented desires. Consequently, an intimate relationship with God requires divine revelation and grace to embrace that revelation by faith.

After these brief opening comments, the human ability to speak about God is clearly front and center. But why, especially in our postmodern context featuring great doubt about linguistic abilities in general and the possibility of religious language in particular, can such an assumption be made? Employing the *analogy of being (analogia entis)*, the *Catechism* maintains that, because there is a resemblance between finite human beings (creatures; the image-bearers) and the infinite God (Creator; the source who is imaged), human language about God is possible. Though human language cannot speak of God comprehensively and perfectly (that would be *univocal* language), it can do more than speak of God approximately and errantly (that would be *equivocal* language); indeed, human language can speak of God correspondingly and truly (using *analogical* language). Importantly, human language must be modified for any adequate speech about God. For example, when Christians address God as "our Father," they must purify their use of that term to remove all imperfect and sinful notions—for instance, an alcoholic and womanizing earthly father who abuses his children—and import into its use the highest qualities of a loving, protecting, providing earthly father, as the Church indicates such perfections.

Evangelical Assessment

Evangelical theology concurs with the *Catechism*'s notion of faith as a human response to God and his revelation of himself to his image-bearers, whom God has created to search for him. As the apostle Paul explained to the crowd gathered on Mars Hill,

---

[7] CCC 36; citation is from Vatican Council I, *Dei Filius* 2; further reference is made to Vatican Council II, *Dei Verbum* 12.

Men of Athens, I perceive that in every way you are very religious. For as I passed along and observed the objects of your worship, I found also an altar with this inscription, "To the unknown god." What therefore you worship as unknown, this I proclaim to you. The God who made the world and everything in it, being Lord of heaven and earth, does not live in temples made by man, nor is he served by human hands, as though he needed anything, since he himself gives to all mankind life and breath and everything. And he made from one man every nation of mankind to live on all the face of the earth, having determined allotted periods and the boundaries of their dwelling place, that they should seek God, and perhaps feel their way toward him and find him. Yet he is actually not far from each one of us, for "In him we live and move and have our being"; as even some of your own poets have said, "For we are indeed his offspring." (Acts 17:22–28)

This innate sense of God with which all human beings have been created is one of four modes of general revelation, or God's communication of himself to all peoples at all times and in all places. The four modes are the created order, or nature (Rom. 1:18–25); the human conscience (Rom. 2:13–16); God's providential care for what he has created (Acts 14:8–18); and the innate sense of deity (Acts 17:22–28). From this general revelation human beings know of God's existence, something of his divine characteristics, and broad principles of his moral law. The *intended*, or correct, response—how human beings *should* respond—is proper worship of the one, true, living God; thanksgiving to and dependence on him; and obedience to his moral law. Tragically, the *actual* response is far from the intended one; indeed, because of human sinfulness, worship is misdirected so that idolatry reigns, ingratitude and self-reliance dominate, and while some obedience is offered, disobedience to the moral law is commonplace. The outcome of all this tragic situation is not good: Paul speaks of human beings as having "no excuse" because of their suppression of the knowledge of God that is accorded to them through general revelation in creation (Rom. 1:20–23), and the apostle calls for all people to repent of their idolatrous response to the sense of deity embedded in their hearts (Acts 17:30–31). Furthermore, this dreary picture of the improper response to general revelation is found throughout Scripture and seems to be the constant and only reply given by sinful human beings, who then are certainly not in a good situation, nor even a neutral situation, before God; rather, everyone is in dire straits before him. Still, God is always at work to rescue his wayward creatures, but general revelation is not enough for such salvation to take place. Accordingly, evangelical theology would disagree with the *Catechism*'s rather hopeful attitude toward general revelation; how can it dispose nonbelievers to faith when they so steadily and completely reject general revelation? At the heart of this optimistic attitude is the nature-grace interdependence, one of the axioms of the Catholic theological system: while sin has seriously influenced nature, it has not so corrupted it that a positive human response to general revelation in nature is precluded. Evangelical theology strongly dissents from this position. Still, evangelical theology affirms the benefit of such a universal divine communication: despite deeply entrenched human rejection of him and his revelation, God does not give up on—indeed, he communicates himself to—all people at all times and in all places!

Concerning the proofs of God's existence, evangelical theology demonstrates various attitudes. Some versions affirm that certain of the proofs are sound arguments that can convince nontheists that God exists. Other varieties reject the proofs, denying that there are any rationally compelling arguments for God's existence. Still other evangelical approaches affirm presuppositionalism, the view that people must assume the existence of God and thus such proofs are wrongheaded. In all cases, however, evangelical theology would agree with the *Catechism* that the mere knowledge of the existence of God is insufficient for a personal relationship with him. This is so for two reasons: The first reason, not apparently affirmed by the *Catechism*, is that general revelation was not designed to foster a personal relationship with God; special revelation serves that role. The second reason, noted by the *Catechism* and in the above explanation, is that human sinfulness distorts the human perception of general revelation, rendering it incapable of establishing and cultivating an intimate fellowship with God. Accordingly, the *Catechism*'s view that God "can be known with certainty from the created world by the natural light of human reason"[8] (Vatican Council II adds "that those things, which in

---

[8] CCC 36; citation is from Vatican Council I, *Dei Filius* 2; further reference is made to Vatican Council II, *Dei Verbum* 12.

themselves are not beyond the grasp of human reason, can, in the present condition of the human race, be known by all men with ease, with firm certainty, and without the contamination of error"[9]) is problematic on three accounts: First, even granting some kind of sure knowledge of God through general revelation, the God who is assuredly known is a distortion of the one, true, living God. Second, too much confidence is shown in the "natural light of human reason" to perceive rightly the evidence for God's existence. The deceitfulness and destructiveness of sin, expressed in part by the *Catechism*, certainly extends to human rationality and corrupts its ability to gain sure knowledge of God through the created order, the human conscience, his providential care, the innate sense of deity, the proofs of his existence, or other means. Sinful human perception of God is most assuredly contaminated with error. Third, at the heart of these first two criticisms is evangelical theology's rejection of the Catholic system's axiom of a nature-grace continuum that is not thoroughly devastated by sin.

Finally, evangelical theology affirms the human ability to speak about God. Some varieties would embrace the analogy of being as the proper foundation for such an affirmation; other versions would reason differently yet come to the same conclusion. Examples of other grounds for the human ability to speak about God include: (1) God himself created human speech; this divine gift enables communication between God and his image-bearers. (2) When God became incarnate, the God-man Jesus Christ went around teaching about God and his ways in common human language, using metaphors (e.g., "For as the lightning comes from the east and shines as far as the west, so will be the coming of the Son of Man"; Matt. 24:27), figures of speech (e.g., "I am the vine, you are the branches"; John 15:5), and illustrations from common human endeavors (e.g., "A sower went out to sow"; Matt. 13:3). (3) When God willed to communicate himself and his ways through a written revelation, he employed common human languages—Hebrew, (some) Aramaic, and Greek—for his inspired Word. Whatever may be the justification for the affirmation, evangelical theology concurs with the *Catechism* that human language is sufficient, though not comprehensive, to speak about God. Such adequate, analogical language must, however, be refined so as to remove all imperfect and sinful notions, and it must

---

[9] Vatican Council II, *Dei Verbum* 6 (*VC II-1*, 752–753); citation is from Vatican Council I, *Dei Filius* 2.

be heightened in accordance with Scripture so as to attain an appropriate sense of excellence with respect to God.[10]

The Doctrine of Revelation: God Comes to Meet Human Beings (Sec. I, Ch. 2)

The Revelation of God (Art. 1)

Because knowledge of the existence of God through reason is not sufficient for a personal relationship with him, God provides another order of knowledge for human beings: *divine revelation* (evangelical theology commonly refers to this as *special revelation*). This self-disclosure is a completely free divine decision—God did not have to reveal himself—and has human salvation as its divine purpose. Such revelation "is realized simultaneously 'by deeds and words which are intrinsically bound up with each other' and shed light on each other."[11] For example, God's liberation of the people of Israel from enslavement in Egypt, which included the plagues, the Passover, the crossing of the Red Sea, the wilderness wanderings, the conquest of the Promised Land, and the like, was a series of mighty acts that revealed God in his power, holiness, jealousy, wrath, covenant faithfulness, mercy, and compassion. These deeds were at first rehearsed orally by his people and eventually narrated in written form (the Pentateuch), and these words reveal God in his might, righteousness, anger, love, grace, and patience. Moreover, this divine revelation is progressive, with God communicating himself to human beings gradually, leading up to his ultimate revelation in Jesus Christ.

Such revelation commenced with the first human beings, to whom God revealed himself both before they sinned and after their fall, in the latter instance in ways directed toward salvation. It continued with Noah, Abraham and the patriarchs, and the chosen people of Israel; indeed, the covenantal structure of divine revelation is clearly in evidence. Moreover, through the prophets, God announced the expectation of a new covenant that would ultimately bring salvation to all the nations. The apex of this divine revelation in acts and words is Jesus Christ, God's final Word (Heb. 1:1–2): "In him [Christ] he [God] has said everything; there will be no other

---

[10] An example from the evangelical world of these two steps of exclusion and excellence is J. I. Packer's best seller, *Knowing God* (Downers Grove, IL: InterVarsity Press, 1973), ch. 8.

[11] CCC 53; citation is from Vatican Council II, *Dei Verbum* 2.

word than this one."[12] No further public revelation is to be expected until Christ returns again.

The Transmission of Divine Revelation (Art. 2)

As to the transmission of divine revelation, the *Catechism* affirms two means: Tradition and Scripture. This twofold pattern of communication is grounded in the two ways of preaching the gospel by the apostles, as commanded by Christ himself:

- *"orally* 'by the apostles who handed on, by the spoken word of their preaching, by the example they gave, by the institutions they established, what they themselves had received—whether from the lips of Christ, from his way of life and his works, or whether they had learned it at the prompting of the Holy Spirit';
- *in writing* 'by those apostles and other men associated with the apostles who, under the inspiration of the same Holy Spirit, committed the message of salvation to writing.'"[13]

Furthermore, to ensure the preservation of this divine revelation in the Church, "the apostles left bishops as their successors" and "gave them 'their own position of teaching authority.'"[14] Through this apostolic succession the Church's Tradition is maintained.

Specifically, the *Catechism* affirms that Tradition and Scripture "are bound closely together and communicate one with the other. For both of them, flowing out from the same divine well-spring, come together in some fashion to form one thing and move toward the same goal."[15] Still, they are two distinct modes of transmitting divine revelation. *"Sacred Scripture* is the speech of God as it is put down in writing under the breath of the Holy Spirit";[16] this mode corresponds to the Catholic Bible. "And [Holy] Tradition transmits in its entirety the Word of God which has been entrusted to the apostles by Christ the Lord and the Holy Spirit"[17] and which the apostles have entrusted to their successors, the bishops of the Church. Two

---

[12] CCC 65. This statement does not rule out "private" revelations (e.g., the appearances of Mary) that are acknowledged by the Church, but such revelations do not constitute part of the deposit of faith nor contribute to the definitive revelation of Jesus Christ (CCC 67).
[13] CCC 76; citation is from Vatican Council II, *Dei Verbum* 7.
[14] CCC 77; citation is from Vatican Council II, *Dei Verbum* 7.
[15] CCC 80; citation is from Vatican Council II, *Dei Verbum* 9.
[16] CCC 81.
[17] Ibid.

examples of Tradition are (1) the immaculate conception of Mary; that is, she was "preserved from all stain of original sin" from the moment of her conception;[18] and (2) her bodily assumption—she "was taken up body and soul into heavenly glory"[19]—at the end of her life. Importantly, the Church "does not derive her certainty about all revealed truths from the holy Scriptures alone. Both Scripture and Tradition must be accepted and honored with equal sentiments of devotion and reverence."[20]

Both Scripture and Tradition, together composing the sacred deposit of the faith,[21] must be interpreted, and the *Catechism* affirms that, "[t]he task of giving an authentic interpretation of the Word of God, whether in its written form or in the form of Tradition, has been entrusted to the living, teaching office of the Church alone."[22] This Magisterium consists of the pope together with the bishops of the Church. The exercise of its authority is especially evident when the Magisterium defines doctrines contained in or connected to divine revelation, because these doctrines are binding for Catholics to believe. The two Marian doctrines—beliefs about Mary—noted above are examples.

Accordingly, the Catholic Church possesses a tripartite structure of authority: written Scripture, Tradition, and the Magisterium. Just as the three poles of a three-legged stool provide support for whoever sits on it, these three elements provide divine revelation and its authoritative interpretation for the Church.

Sacred Scripture (Art. 3)

As for the first of these three elements, Scripture, the *Catechism* affirms its importance, divine inspiration, and truth; provides instruction for its interpretation; discusses its canon; and encourages its reading in the Church.

Regarding the importance of Scripture, the *Catechism* closely links Scripture and the body of Christ, the Eucharist, and claims equal veneration of both for its historical practice.[23] Scripture is inspired because it has God

---

[18] Pope Pius IX, *Ineffabilis Deus* (December 8, 1854). Accessible at http://www.papalencyclicals.net/Pius09/p9ineff.htm.

[19] Pope Pius XII, *Munificentissimus Deus* (November 1, 1950). Accessible at http://www.vatican.va/holy_father/pius_xii/apost_constitutions/documents/hf_p-xii_apc_19501101_munificentissimus-deus_en.html.

[20] CCC 82; citation is from Vatican Council II, *Dei Verbum* 9.

[21] It may be helpful to think of Jude's words about "the faith that was once for all delivered to the saints" (Jude 3).

[22] CCC 85; citation is from Vatican Council II, *Dei Verbum* 10.

[23] This reverence is portrayed liturgically as the mass consists of two movements: the Liturgy of the Word (which features readings from the Old Testament, the New Testament, and one of the Gospels) and the Liturgy of the Eucharist. Both movements are necessary.

for its author. Yet this divine superintendence of the writing of Scripture did not minimize, curtail, or destroy the human writing of Scripture, as the biblical authors employed fully their personalities and writing abilities. Because Scripture is inspired, it is also truth-telling: "Since therefore all that the inspired authors or sacred writers affirm should be regarded as affirmed by the Holy Spirit, we must acknowledge that the books of Scripture firmly, faithfully, and without error teach that truth which God, for the sake of our salvation, wished to see confided to the Sacred Scriptures."[24]

The same Holy Spirit who inspired Scripture must illumine its readers' minds to understand it as they carefully follow sound interpretive principles. These principles include attentiveness to the authors'/Author's intent of their words, their historical context, the genre(s) they used (e.g., narrative, prophecy, poetry), and the grammar and syntax. Three criteria for proper interpretation of inspired Scripture in harmony with the Holy Spirit are special attention "to the context and unity of the whole Scripture," reading it within "the living Tradition of the whole Church," and consideration of "the analogy of faith" (emphasizing the coherence of truths in all of divine revelation). Through the interpretive process, the fourfold meaning of Scripture must be sought. The two senses of Scripture, which become its fourfold meaning, are:

- the *literal sense*: the meaning of the words of Scripture that is discovered by the application of sound interpretive principles;
- the *spiritual sense*: the meaning not of the words of Scripture, but of the things—the realities, events, institutions—about which Scripture speaks; this sense is distinguishable as
    - the *allegorical sense*: the Christological meaning; e.g., the crossing of the Red Sea as a sign of baptism;
    - the *moral sense*: the behavioral meaning; e.g., how we should live justly;
    - the *anagogical sense*: the future meaning or eternal significance; e.g., the Church on earth points to the heavenly Jerusalem.[25]

Of course, all interpretations of Scripture must conform to the authoritative judgment of the Magisterium.

---

[24] CCC 107; citation is from Vatican Council II, *Dei Verbum* 11.
[25] CCC 116–117. The three spiritual senses are based on the literal sense. The moral sense is also called the *tropological sense*, which is derived from the Greek word τρόπος (*tropos*), signifying "manner" or "way"; hence, the way one should live in light of the passage of Scripture. The *anagogical sense* is derived from the Greek word ἀνάγω (*anagō*), signifying "going up" or "leading up"; hence, the future fulfillment of the passage.

The Catholic Church affirms the canon of Scripture, the list of writings that properly belong in the Bible according to its apostolic Tradition; thus, the Catholic Old Testament contains seven additional writings, and several additional sections of two books, when compared with the Protestant Old Testament. The seven additional writings are: Tobit, Judith, the Wisdom of Solomon, Ecclesiasticus[26] (also called the Wisdom of Sirach), Baruch, and 1 and 2 Maccabees. The additional sections are found in the books of Esther (six additional chapters) and Daniel (three additional chapters). These additional writings and sections compose the Apocrypha, from a word signifying "hidden." The New Testament canon of the Catholic Church is exactly the same as that of Protestant churches. The *Catechism* underscores the necessity of both the Old and New Testaments, the Old being the preparation for Christ and thus to be read in light of what Christ did to accomplish salvation, and the New being the ultimate truth of divine revelation and thus to be read as the fulfillment of the Old.

Given all that is affirmed of Scripture, it should come as no surprise that the *Catechism* encourages Bible reading. The Church is to foster the regular practice of Scripture reading and studying by ensuring ready access to it, encouraging the ministry of the Word in its preaching and catechesis, and exhorting Catholics with Jerome's words: "Ignorance of the Scriptures is ignorance of Christ."[27]

Evangelical Assessment

Divine Revelation

Evangelical theology concurs with certain elements of the *Catechism*'s doctrine of revelation, beginning with its affirmation of the insufficiency of general revelation to establish and develop a personal relationship with God, and the consequent need for divine revelation (special revelation, in evangelical parlance) for such a relationship. Further agreement exists with regard to the freedom of God to disclose or not to disclose himself and his ways to fallen human beings for the sake of their salvation. Special revelation is a gracious divine gift, which has a very important implication that evangelical theology will emphasize in due course: The church's position with respect to divine revelation must be that of recipient, not giver or de-

---

[26] The title of this apocryphal writing should not be confused with the title of the canonical writing Ecclesiastes.
[27] CCC 133; citation is from St. Jerome, *Commentary on Isaiah*, book 18, prologue.

terminer of it. Moreover, evangelical theology agrees in principle with the *Catechism*'s affirmation of divine deeds and divine words working in tandem to reveal God and his ways. The event of the crossing of the Red Sea, for example, was a revelation of the power and faithfulness of God; Moses's text narrating this event (Exodus 14) is also divine revelation. Certainly, this mighty act of God was accessible to all who crossed on dry land through the walls of water, as well as to others to whom the story was told and retold orally; later, the narrative was written down as a text. Importantly, however, the church knows and is benefited by this mighty deed only by means of the written text; any surviving oral narrative would undoubtedly contain many and serious distortions and would not carry any authority for the church today. Indeed, authority attaches only to the written account of the exodus as narrated by Moses in Exodus 14, because that is the narrative inspired by the Holy Spirit.

Additionally, agreement is found on the issue of the progressive nature of divine revelation: God did disclose himself to Adam and Eve before the fall into sin (e.g., Gen. 2:15–17) and, after their debacle, through direct speech (e.g., 3:8–13). This revelation continued through more direct divine speech (e.g., 12:1–3), dreams and visions (e.g., Abimelech's dream, 20:1–7; Joseph's dreams, 37:1–11), historical events (e.g., the flood; Genesis 6–9), and written Scripture (e.g., Deut. 31:9). This ongoing communication was also progressive. For example, God taught his people to worship him in the tabernacle (e.g., Exodus 40); later, he gave instructions to them for worshiping him in the temple (e.g., 2 Chronicles 5). This progressive revelation is also clearly seen in the movement of the covenants that God established with his human partners: the Adamic, Noahic, Abrahamic, Mosaic (or old), and Davidic covenants were all operative before the coming of Jesus Christ, and a new covenant was prophesied (e.g., Jer. 31:31–34; Ezek. 36:25–27) that would eventually become the structured relationship between God and the members of the church. This new covenant would focus on the apex of divine revelation in both deeds and speech: Jesus Christ. His miraculous works were the climax of the many preceding mighty acts of God, and his words were the summit of divine speech—the fulfillment of all that was commanded and prophesied (e.g., Matt. 5:17–19) and the foundation for all that would be demanded and practiced afterwards (e.g., 1 Cor. 11:23). As promised, Jesus Christ is

God's final Word (Heb. 1:1–2), so no new revelation is to be expected or accepted until his second coming.

The Transmission of Divine Revelation/Sola Scriptura

Concerning the transmission of divine revelation, Catholic and evangelical theology part company in a very pronounced way. While Catholic theology affirms a twofold pattern of communication of divine revelation (oral Tradition and written Scripture), evangelical theology holds to the foundational tenet (called the *formal principle*) of Protestantism: the ultimate source of divine revelation is the written Word of God only (*sola Scriptura*) and not Scripture plus Tradition.

Several important reasons exist for evangelical theology's rejection of Tradition as a distinct mode of divine revelation, no matter how much the *Catechism* may insist on the "same divine well-spring" for Tradition and Scripture, the close bond and mutual communication between the two, even their oneness in essence and aim.[28] One reason is that the idea of Tradition as a supplement to written Scripture is based on weak biblical support. Catholic theology appeals for support of its view of Tradition to the words of Jesus to his disciples: "I still have many things to say to you, but you cannot bear them now" (John 16:12). Calvin objected to the Catholic (mis)interpretation of this passage:

> But what effrontery is this? I confess that the disciples were as yet untutored and well-nigh unteachable when they heard this from the Lord. But when they committed their doctrine to writing, were they even then beset with such dullness that they afterward needed to supply with a living voice [Tradition] what they had omitted from their writings through the fault of ignorance? Now, if they had already been led into all truth by the Spirit of truth [John 16:13, the immediately following verse] when they put forth their writings, what hindered them from embracing and leaving in written form a perfect and distinct knowledge of gospel doctrine?[29]

Calvin's criticism exposes the Catholic misunderstanding of Jesus's lament to his disciples at the time he uttered it: because of their place in the

---

[28] CCC 80; citation is from Vatican Council II, *Dei Verbum* 9.
[29] Calvin, *Institutes* 4.8.14 (LCC 21:1163–1164).

progress of salvation history—before Jesus's death, burial, resurrection, ascension, exaltation, and sending of the Holy Spirit—the disciples could not grasp everything that Jesus desired to communicate to them. However, on the other side of those salvation-accomplishing and church-launching events, the disciples did indeed possess the Holy Spirit, who guided them into all the truth (John 16:13) and taught them all things and brought to their remembrance all that Jesus had said to them (John 14:26). In other words, the handicap that once prevented the disciples from receiving full revelation from Jesus—and the cause of his lament—had been removed. Nothing prevented them from writing this whole divine revelation in their Gospels, the narrative of the early church (Acts), letters (of Paul, James, Peter, John, and Jude), and apocalyptic writing (Revelation). The disciples had no need for any supplemental body of oral communication—Tradition—that they were hindered from including in their writings because of their (previous) ignorance.

A second reason for evangelical theology's rejection of Tradition is the lateness of the development of such a concept. In support of its inclusion of Tradition as part of divine revelation, Catholic theology appeals to the diffusion of the church's theology and practice through both spoken word and written letter during its earliest centuries of existence (2 Thess. 2:15; cf. Jude 3). Such dual communication was certainly the manner of transmitting the gospel and sound doctrine in the early church, but there is no hint of it consisting of two sets that contained differing revelatory content—one set serving as a supplement to the other. Eventually, the original truth that had been necessarily communicated orally was written down and became the New Testament. As Irenaeus, an early church leader and defender of the Christian faith, explained concerning the apostles and their written Scripture,

> We have learned from none others the plan of our salvation, than from those through whom the gospel has come down to us, which they did *at one time proclaim in public*, and, *at a later period*, by the will of God, *handed down to us in the Scriptures*, to be the ground and pillar of our faith. For it is unlawful to assert that they preached before they possessed perfect knowledge, as some do even venture to say, boasting themselves as improvers of the apostles. For, after our Lord rose from the dead, [the apostles] were invested with power from on high when the

Holy Spirit came down [upon them], were filled from all [his gifts], and had perfect knowledge: they departed to the ends of the earth, preaching the glad tidings of the good things [sent] from God to us.[30]

Irenaeus's comments bear striking similarity to Calvin's chastisement of Catholic theology's notion of Tradition based on John 16:12: The disciples' "perfect knowledge," obtained as a gift from the Holy Spirit and originally spread widely as oral communication, was eventually written down and became New Testament Scripture. But Irenaeus gives no hint that this oral communication and its written, scriptural form were different in terms of content, with the one supplementing the other.

But Irenaeus also embraced and promoted a bona fide notion of church tradition. When the early church denounced heresies by exposing their contradiction of Scripture, the promoters of false doctrine accused Scripture itself of being in error, lacking authority, and possessing ambiguity that could be clarified only by means of the heretics' tradition. Indeed, these heretics alleged that "the truth was not delivered by means of written documents, but *vivâ voce* [a living voice]."[31] The early church's countermove was to insist on a proper tradition that originated with the apostles and that was preserved by means of the succession of leaders in the apostolic churches. The heretics offered their rejoinder: The church's tradition was wrong because it came from church leaders, from the apostles, and ultimately from Christ himself, all of whom were inferior in knowledge and truth to the heretics themselves, who alone possessed the unadulterated hidden mystery. As Irenaeus summarized the problem with the heretics, "these men do now consent neither to Scripture nor to tradition."[32] Accordingly, for Irenaeus, church tradition is apostolic doctrine, which provides for the proper understanding of Scripture. Such doctrine is preserved in apostolic churches.[33] But he did not propose a church tradition that was "a living

---

[30] Irenaeus, *Against Heresies* 3.1.1 (ANF 1:414, emphasis added).

[31] Irenaeus, *Against Heresies* 3.2.1 (ANF 1:415).

[32] Irenaeus, *Against Heresies* 3.2.2 (ANF 1:415).

[33] As to the identity of these apostolic churches, Irenaeus explained, "Suppose there arises a dispute relative to some important question among us, should we not have recourse to the most ancient churches with which the apostles held constant intercourse [discussion], and learn from them what is certain and clear in regard to the present question? For how should it be if the apostles themselves had not left us writings? Would it not be necessary, [in that case,] to follow the course of the tradition which they handed down to those to whom they did commit the Churches?" (Irenaeus, *Against Heresies* 3.4.1 [ANF 1:417]). Apostolic churches were founded by the apostles (e.g., Corinth, Ephesus, Galatia, Philippi) or engaged by the apostles (e.g., Rome) and thus preserved apostolic doctrine, which should be consulted in disputes. This would be the case even if the apostles had not committed their doctrine to writing; but, of course, apostolic doctrine had been written down as Scripture.

voice" containing truth that was not also written in Scripture. If this had been his tactic, he would have been arguing as the heretics argued, with a standoff being the result.

This proper tradition—apostolic doctrine that was in accordance with Scripture and that provided the correct framework for interpreting Scripture—was written out by Irenaeus himself:

> The Church, though dispersed throughout the whole world, even to the ends of the earth, has received from the apostles and their disciples this faith: [She believes] in one God, the Father Almighty, Maker of heaven, and earth, and the sea, and all things that are in them; and in one Christ Jesus, the Son of God, who became incarnate for our salvation; and in the Holy Spirit, who proclaimed through the prophets the dispensations of God, and the advents, and the birth from a virgin, and the passion, and the resurrection from the dead, and the ascension into heaven in the flesh of the beloved Christ Jesus, our Lord, and his [future] manifestation from heaven in the glory of the Father "to gather all things in one" [Eph. 1:10] and to raise up anew all flesh of the whole human race, in order that to Christ Jesus, our Lord, and God, and Savior, and King, according to the will of the invisible Father, "every knee should bow, of things in heaven, and things in earth, and things under the earth, and that every tongue should confess" [Phil. 2:10–11] to him, and that he should execute just judgment towards all; that he may send "spiritual wickednesses" [Eph. 6:12] and the angels who transgressed and became apostates, together with the ungodly, and unrighteous, and wicked, and profane among men, into everlasting fire; but may, in the exercise of his grace, confer immortality on the righteous, and holy, and those who have kept his commandments, and have persevered in his love, some from the beginning [of their Christian course], and others from [the date of] their repentance, and may surround them with everlasting glory.[34]

Irenaeus's tradition, called the canon of truth,[35] was an outline or summary of essential biblical doctrines. These truths were not in addition to Scripture; indeed, they had to find their source and warrant in Scripture itself, as Irenaeus affirmed in his justification of the doctrines of the apostles:

---

[34] Irenaeus, *Against Heresies* 1.10.1 (*ANF* 1:330).
[35] Irenaeus, *Against Heresies* 1.9.4 (*ANF* 1:330). "Canon" refers to a standard or rule.

"But while I bring out by these proofs the truths of Scripture, and set forth briefly and compendiously things which are stated in various ways, do you also attend to them with patience, and not deem them prolix [verbose]; taking this into account, that proofs [of the things which are] contained in the Scriptures cannot be shown except from the Scriptures themselves."[36] Apostolic doctrine had to derive from and be warranted by Scripture and did not consist of a supplement to Scripture.

This early church notion of tradition continued in the first part of the medieval period, as evidenced by Thomas Aquinas's argument for the supremacy of Scripture over the writings of the early church fathers in the determination of correct theology: "Theology properly uses the authority of the canonical Scriptures as an incontrovertible proof, and the authority of the doctors of the church as one that may properly be used, yet merely as probable. For our faith rests upon the revelation made to the apostles and the prophets who wrote the canonical books, and not on the revelations (if any such there are) made to other doctors."[37] This idea of tradition, then, was certainly not what it eventually came to be in later medieval Catholicism, as exemplified in these novel claims about tradition—first articulated in the fourteenth century:[38]

- "the doctrine and tradition of the apostles . . . without [outside of] Scripture";[39]
- "the unwritten words of the apostles and their unwritten traditions that would all belong to the canon of Scripture had they been written";[40]
- "such is the dignity of the apostolic traditions which did not transmit in the Scriptures, that the same veneration and the same fervent faith is due to them as to the written ones";[41]
- "truths that have come from the apostles by word of mouth or in the writings of the faithful, even though they may not be found in the Sacred Scriptures and may not be concluded with certainty from the Scriptures alone";[42]

[36] Irenaeus, *Against Heresies* 3.12.9 (ANF 1:434).
[37] Thomas Aquinas, *Summa Theologica* pt. 1, q. 1, art. 8.
[38] For further discussion of the development of this novel idea of tradition, see Allison, *HT*, 82–87.
[39] Gerald of Bologna, *Commentary on the Sentences*, 457, cited in George Tavard, *Holy Writ or Holy Church* (London: Burns & Oates, 1959), 27.
[40] Thomas Netter Waldensis, *Doctrinale Antiquatum Fidei Catholicae Ecclesiae*, ch. 23, in Tavard, *Holy Writ or Holy Church*, 58.
[41] Ibid.
[42] William of Ockham, *Dialogue against Heretics* bk. 2, ch. 5, in Tavard, *Holy Writ or Holy Church*, 35.

- "there is an infinity of truly catholic doctrines that could not be evidently concluded even from the contents of Sacred Scripture."[43]

This later-developed notion of Tradition is very far removed from the idea of tradition in the early church and the early medieval church.

A third reason for evangelical theology's rejection of Catholic theology's notion of Tradition is that the Church's claim to be the maintainer and promoter of such divine revelation essentially amounts to a claim of being infallibly led by the Holy Spirit apart from Scripture. Again, as just discussed, such a claim was novel, without precedent before the fourteenth century, at a time when the Catholic Church was struggling to maintain not only its spiritual authority but its sociopolitical authority as well.

Calvin noted two key passages to which the Catholic Church appealed as the biblical basis for its claim to infallibility: "that the church was cleansed 'with the washing of water in the word of life, that it might be . . . without wrinkle or spot' [Eph. 5:26–27], and therefore is elsewhere called 'the pillar and ground of truth' [1 Tim. 3:15]." To the first biblical passage, Calvin countered that it "teaches what Christ does each day in the church rather than what he has already accomplished"; indeed, the need for Christ's daily cleansing of the church, so empirically and readily obvious to everyone, demonstrates that it has not yet attained full sanctification. Accordingly, it does not and cannot yet possess infallibility. As for the second verse, Calvin argued that it means something entirely different from the Church's understanding of it: The church is "the pillar and ground of truth" not because it—the church—is infallible, but because "God's truth is preserved in the church, that is, by the ministry of preaching." As the "faithful custodian" of the truth, the church is to sustain it against all perversion and challenges; indeed, "this safekeeping of the truth wholly depends on whether the Word of the Lord is faithfully kept and preserved in its purity."[44] So the *Word of God* is infallible, not the church that guards and supports it.

Calvin went a step further, criticizing the Catholic Church's insistence on its own infallibility through the Holy Spirit as severing the inseparable bond between the Word of God and the Spirit of God. Appealing to passages noted earlier in connection with the Catholic Church's case for Tradition, Calvin explained that Jesus's promises of the Holy Spirit to "guide you

---

[43] William of Waterford, *LXXII Quaestiones de Sacramento Altaris*, in Tavard, *Holy Writ or Holy Church*, 43.
[44] Calvin, *Institutes* 4.8.12 (LCC 21:1161).

into all the truth" (John 16:13) and to "bring to your remembrance all that I have said to you" (John 14:26) mean that "we are to expect nothing more from his Spirit than that he will illumine our minds to perceive the truth of his [Christ's] teaching." Accordingly, while the Catholic Church may claim Spirit-granted infallibility to promote doctrines outside of Scripture, Calvin insisted that, all the while, "the Spirit wills to be conjoined with God's Word by an indissoluble bond, and Christ professes this concerning him when he promises the Spirit to his church."[45]

A fourth reason for evangelical theology's rejection of Tradition is that the Scripture-plus-Tradition structure is inherently unstable; in practice, when the two are in conflict, Tradition trumps Scripture in terms of authority. Though the Catholic Church claims that the two are in perfect harmony with each other, history bears witness that this is not always the case, and when the two aspects do indeed conflict, one of the two becomes the ultimate authority. This clash of the two, resulting in the elevation of the authority of Tradition above that of Scripture, can be clearly seen in the Church's promotion of the doctrine of Mary's immaculate conception. Without question, Scripture affirms the sinfulness of all human beings and does not allow for any exceptions; every human person, as a descendant of Adam, is conceived in sin, has a sinful nature, and sins in word, deed, thought, intention, and so forth. According to Catholic Tradition, however, there is one individual who was conceived without sin, did not possess a sinful nature, and never sinned in word, deed, thought, intention, or in any other way. In this clear case, Scripture and Tradition are diametrically opposed to each other; equally clearly, the Church has sided with Tradition over against Scripture and affirmed the immaculate conception of Mary. As James Warwick Montgomery pointed out, any two-source authority structure is inherently unstable because when the two authorities conflict, one inevitably rises to be the ultimate authority and the other cedes authority to it. The former becomes the *de facto* authority, despite claims to the contrary.[46] Thus, the inherent instability of the Scripture-plus-Tradition structure is a reason for evangelical theology's rejection of Tradition as a mode of divine revelation.

---

[45] Calvin, *Institutes* 4.8.13 (LCC 21:1162–1163).
[46] John Warwick Montgomery, "The Theologian's Craft: A Discussion of Theory Formation and Theory Testing in Theology," *Journal of the American Scientific Association* 18 (September 1966): 65–77, 92–95.

Finally, the idea of Tradition as a supplement to Scripture for divine revelation contradicts both the sufficiency and necessity of Scripture, two Protestant doctrines that evangelical theology embraces. The sufficiency of Scripture means that everything people need to know in order to be saved and to live in a way that fully pleases God is contained in Scripture. Biblical warrant for this attribute of Scripture includes David's testimony that "the law of the LORD is perfect" (Ps. 19:7) and Paul's affirmation that because God-breathed Scripture is "profitable for teaching, for reproof, for correction, and for training in righteousness," Christians are "complete, equipped for every good work" (2 Tim. 3:16–17).[47] Scripture is sufficient for rescuing sinful people and preparing them to walk in a way that pleases God as they engage in good works. Accordingly, no formulation of church doctrine or practice that comes from outside of Scripture—purgatory, transubstantiation, indulgences, prayers for the dead, penance—can bind the conscience of Christians as additional beliefs or actions required for salvation and holy living. But this is the very thing that Catholic Tradition claims: "the Church does not derive her certainty about all revealed truths from the holy Scriptures alone. Both Scripture and Tradition must be accepted and honored with equal sentiments of devotion and reverence."[48] Such a claim denies the sufficiency of Scripture.

Similarly, the Catholic notion of Tradition contradicts the necessity of Scripture, the attribute underscoring that the church needs Scripture just as "the daily bread is necessary, which this life cannot do without."[49] Although the Catholic Church would agree that Scripture is necessary for the *well-being* of the Church, it maintains—because of the existence of its Tradition—that Scripture is not necessary for the *being* of the Church; that is, the Church could still exist if Scripture would cease to be, because it would still be guided by Tradition. Evangelical theology decries this position and insists on the necessity of Scripture.

For these reasons, evangelical theology champions *sola Scriptura*: Scripture, not Scripture plus Tradition, is the source of divine revelation. Particular care needs to be exercised when promoting and discussing this concept,

---

[47] In another of his letters, Paul enjoins, "Remind them [Christians] . . . to be ready for every good work" (Titus 3:1). Joining this apostolic exhortation with Paul's affirmation that all God-breathed Scripture profitably prepares Christians for every good work, evangelical theology wonders what Tradition could possibly equip Christians to do?

[48] CCC 82; citation is from Vatican Council II, *Dei Verbum* 9.

[49] Amandus Polanus a Polansdorf, *Syntagma Theologiae Christianae* (Hanover, 1624), 1.35, cited in Heppe, 32.

because misunderstanding abounds. *Sola Scriptura* as originally conceived meant Scripture enjoys *primary* authority. It is not the only authority—indeed, the principle is not a rejection of other authorities—but in all theological matters, Scripture is the ultimate authority.[50] To take one example, whereas Luther and his developing Lutheran movement rejected Catholic Church Tradition and insisted instead on the sufficiency of Scripture,[51] the Lutheran Church did not dispense with or neglect the accumulated wisdom of the church throughout its many centuries. While affirming the supreme authority of Scripture,[52] the Formula of Concord (1580) underscored the importance of certain church traditions (called "symbols"):

> Inasmuch as immediately after the times of the apostles—indeed, even while they were yet alive—false teachers and heretics arose, against whom in the early church symbols were composed, that is to say, brief and explicit confessions, which contained the unanimous consent of the catholic Christian faith, and the confession of the orthodox and true church (such as the *Apostles'*, the *Nicene*, and the *Athanasian Creeds*). We publicly profess that we embrace them, and reject all heresies and all dogmas that have ever been brought into the church of God contrary to their decision.[53]

Accordingly, *sola Scriptura*, when rightly defined and championed, is not a rejection of church traditions like the early creeds that are summaries of sound doctrine, synopses that reflect and are grounded on a proper understanding of Scripture. "*Sola scriptura* [is] not *nuda scriptura*"[54]—Scripture and absolutely nothing else—and it should not be presented and argued as such today.[55]

---

[50] As the relevant section of the Westminster Confession of Faith states, "The Supreme Judge, by which all controversies of religion are to be determined, and all decrees of councils, opinions of ancient writers, doctrines of men, and private spirits, are to be examined, and in whose sentence we are to rest, can be no other but the Holy Spirit speaking in the Scripture" (Westminster Confession of Faith, "On the Holy Scripture," 10).

[51] As formulated in the Augsburg Confession, the sufficiency of Scripture means that "it is against the Scripture to ordain or require the observation of any traditions, to the end that we may merit remission of sins and satisfaction for sins by them" (Augsburg Confession, "Of Ecclesiastical Power," art. 7 [Schaff, 3:64]). As noted earlier, the idea of Tradition against which Luther contended was itself a recent development in the Church.

[52] *Formula of Concord*, Epitome 1, "Of the Compendious Rule and Norm" (Schaff, 3:93–94).

[53] Ibid. (Schaff, 3:94–95).

[54] Timothy George, *Theology of the Reformers* (Nashville: Broadman, 1988), 81, cf. 315. Cf. Alister McGrath, *Reformation Thought*, 2nd ed. (Oxford, UK; and Cambridge, MA: Blackwell, 1993), 144–147. Cf. Chris Castaldo, "A Journey to Evangelicalism," in Robert L. Plummer, ed., *Journeys of Faith: Evangelicalism, Eastern Orthodoxy, Catholicism, and Anglicanism* (Grand Rapids, MI: Zondervan, 2012), 156–158.

[55] Indeed, see Gregg R. Allison, "The *Corpus Theologicum* of the Church and Presumptive Authority," in Derek Tidball, Brian Harris, and Jason S. Sexton, eds., *Revisioning, Renewing, and Rediscovering the Triune Center: Essays in Honor of Stanley J. Grenz* (Eugene, OR: Wipf & Stock, 2014), ch. 16. A clear definition of *sola Scriptura* that is in harmony with the principle as articulated by the Protestant Reformers goes a long way in

Several key objections to the evangelical principle of *sola Scriptura* have been voiced by Catholic leaders and apologists and deserve a brief reply. For example, Peter Kreeft, rejecting the principle, avers that, "No Christian before Luther ever taught it, for the first sixteen Christian centuries."[56] Evangelical theology wonders what should be made of affirmations such as these from the early church fathers:

- Athanasius (4th cent.): "The sacred and inspired Scriptures are sufficient to declare the truth";[57]
- Cyril of Jerusalem (4th cent.): "For concerning the divine and holy mysteries of the faith, not even a casual statement must be delivered without the Holy Scriptures. . . . For this salvation which we believe depends . . . on demonstration of the Holy Scriptures";[58]
- Vincent of Lérins (died c. 450): "The canon of Scripture is complete, and sufficient of itself for everything, and more than sufficient."[59]

These examples affirming the sufficiency of Scripture could be multiplied. Given that the evangelical doctrine of the sufficiency of Scripture and its principle of *sola Scriptura* dovetail, evangelical theology wonders why Kreeft asserts that the idea is late in coming.

Kreeft again objects: "The first generation of Christians did not even *have* the New Testament."[60] But listen to the apostle Paul's affirmation of the sufficiency of the Old Testament, which the early church did indeed *have* as its *sola Scriptura*: "you have been acquainted with the sacred writings, which are able to make you wise for salvation through faith in Christ Jesus. All Scripture is breathed out by God and profitable for teaching, for reproof, for correction, and for training in righteousness, that the man of God may be complete, equipped for every good work" (2 Tim. 3:15–17). Before the

---

answering, for example, Frank Beckwith's rejoinder to my "Response to Catholicism," in Plummer, *Journeys of Faith*, 115–128. Frank seems to understand my appeal to *sola Scriptura* as precluding any and all appeals to extrabiblical resources—e.g., the early church creeds and its lists of canonical writings for both the Old and New Testaments—but his understanding of this Protestant principle is off target and, thus, so is the implication he draws from it (Francis J. Beckwith, "Catholicism Rejoinder," in ibid., 129–134).

[56] Kreeft, 20.

[57] Athanasius, *Against the Heathen* 1 (NPNF[2] 4:4). Elsewhere he offered, "Holy Scripture is of all things most sufficient for us" (*To the Bishops of Egypt* 4 [NPNF[2] 4:225]), and, "Divine Scripture is sufficient above all things" (*Councils of Ariminum and Seleucia*, pt. 1, 6 [NPNF[2] 4:453]).

[58] Cyril of Jerusalem, *Catechetical Lectures* 4.1 (NPNF[2] 7.23).

[59] Vincent of Lérins, *Commonitory* 2.5 (NPNF[2] 11:132). For further discussion of Vincent of Lerins and his role in formulating the notion of tradition, see Thomas G. Guarino, *Vincent of Lérins and the Development of Christian Doctrine*, Foundations of Theological Exegesis and Christian Spirituality (Grand Rapids, MI: Baker Academic, 2013).

[60] Kreeft, 20.

New Testament came into existence, the early church possessed the "sacred writings"/"Scripture"—the Hebrew Bible, *sola Scriptura* for the Jews, what Christians now call the Old Testament—which one of its founders considered to be sufficient with regard to providing wisdom leading to salvation by faith in Christ and equipping Christians for *every* good work—not just a few, or some, or many, or most good works—that God would give them to do. So before it had the additional writings that now compose its New Testament, the early church had the sufficient Word of God in its Old Testament. This attitude clearly reflected the viewpoint of its founder, Jesus Christ, who constantly appealed to, quoted, argued from, obeyed, came to fulfill, and trusted in the Bible of his people. So if Jesus Christ and the early church expressed such confidence in and reliance upon the completely sufficient written Word of God—the Old Testament—should we not expect that when additional written Scripture expanded that Word, the church should continue to express such confidence in and reliance upon the completely sufficient written Word of God—the Old Testament plus the New Testament?

A final objection: "Scripture never teaches *sola scriptura*. Thus *sola scriptura* is self-contradictory. If we are to believe only Scripture, we should not believe *sola scriptura*."[61] Evangelical theology wonders what Kreeft means when he says that Scripture does or does not *teach* something? Does Scripture, for example, *teach* the doctrine of the Trinity, clearly articulating in so many words that God eternally exists as Father, Son, and Holy Spirit, each of whom is fully God, yet there is only one God? Clearly, Scripture does not *teach* the doctrine of the Trinity in this fashion. If this is Kreeft's point, then evangelical theology gladly concurs that "Scripture never teaches *sola scriptura*." But certainly Kreeft will agree that even the Catholic Church believes certain doctrines—for example the doctrine of the Trinity—that Scripture does not *teach* in some manner similar to the one just described. But if it is legitimate for Catholic theology to embrace the doctrine of the Trinity because such a belief is an adequate summary of scriptural affirmations about the nature of the Godhead, or because such a belief is a logical entailment of other beliefs, then at least in principle it could be legitimate for evangelical theology to embrace *sola Scriptura* because such a belief is an adequate summary of scriptural affirmations about the nature of Scrip-

---

[61] Ibid.

ture and its benefits, or because such a belief is a logical entailment of other beliefs. Accordingly, the argument that "Scripture never teaches *sola Scriptura* and thus belief in *sola Scriptura*" is self-contradictory fails, because both Catholic and evangelical theology hold to beliefs that Scripture does not teach but that are summaries or entailments of Scripture and/or other beliefs.[62]

Scripture and Its Interpretation

More agreement between Catholic theology and evangelical theology is found in the *Catechism*'s discussion of the importance, divine inspiration, and truthfulness of Scripture. Though the two positions would ground the importance of Scripture differently—Catholic theology closely links Scripture with the Eucharist,[63] whereas evangelical theology would appeal to its inspiration, authority, sufficiency, necessity, clarity, power, and truthfulness—both insist on its vital role in the church.[64] Moreover, the *Catechism*'s presentation of the inspiration of Scripture resonates with an evangelical understanding of this doctrine. Especially to be highlighted is the *Catechism*'s fine balance, reflective of 2 Peter 1:21, in emphasizing both the human authorship of Scripture ("men [the biblical authors] spoke from God") and its divine authorship ("as they were carried along by the Holy Spirit"). Using the metaphor of confluence, the coming together of two bodies of water to form one common stream, evangelical theology

---

[62] Interestingly, Kreeft introduces the doctrine of infallibility into his objections to *sola Scriptura*: "If Scripture is infallible, as traditional Protestants believe, then the Church must be infallible too, for a fallible cause cannot produce an infallible effect, and the Church produced the Bible. The Church (apostles and saints) wrote the New Testament, and the Church (subsequent bishops) defined its canon" (ibid.). Employing this logic, we should also conclude that the nation of Israel was infallible because it produced the Old Testament. No one, not even the Catholic Church, has ever expressed or defended such an absurd idea. So if no claim is made for the infallibility of the nation of Israel based on the idea that an infallible cause is necessary to produce an infallible effect (the Old Testament), then why does Kreeft argue in this manner for the infallibility of the Catholic Church so as to produce an infallible effect (the New Testament)? What evangelical theology claims is not infallibility for the nation of Israel but the inspiration of the Holy Spirit as the prophets, sages, psalmists, and narrators were writing Jewish Scripture, even as it claims not infallibility for the church but the inspiration of the Holy Spirit as the writers of the Gospels, the narrator of Acts, the authors of the letters, and the seer of the apocalypse were writing Christian Scripture. For further discussion, see Chris Castaldo, "Journey to Evangelicalism" (155–156).
[63] For evangelical churches that stand self-consciously in the heritage of the Protestant "marks of the church"—true preaching of the Word of God and rightful administration of baptism and the Lord's Supper—this close connection between Scripture and the latter ordinance is greatly appreciated, even if the Protestant understanding of the Eucharist/Lord's Supper/Communion is very different from the Catholic doctrine of transubstantiation.
[64] The *Catechism*'s claim of equal veneration of Scripture and the Eucharist for its historical position—"the Church has always venerated the Scriptures as she venerates the Lord's Body" (CCC 103)—is disconcertingly exaggerated if put to the test of actual Church practice. For example, it was not without historical and empirical reason that the Reformers scorched the Catholic Church of their day for diminishing the Word of God and elevating the Eucharistic portion of the mass. That a balance between the Liturgy of the Word and the Liturgy of the Eucharist in the Catholic mass was championed by Vatican Council II is an encouraging development, but it remains precisely that—a development overcoming centuries of imbalance between the two elements.

commonly embraces a "confluence" model of inspiration: the Holy Spirit *came together* with the biblical authors in the writing of Scripture to produce the God-breathed and human-written Word of God. "Concursive" (*con* = with; *cursive* = writing) inspiration is another model used by evangelical theology: the Holy Spirit was *writing with* the biblical authors so as to produce Scripture. Accordingly, the biblical authors were fully engaged as they wrote Scripture, employing their personalities, grammatical abilities, writing styles, theological emphases, and the like, and the Holy Spirit was fully engaged, superintending the entire process. Furthermore, evangelical theology agrees with Catholic theology's move from its affirmation of the inspiration of Scripture to its truthfulness: because Scripture is God-breathed—that is, because the biblical authors were superintended by the Holy Spirit as they wrote Scripture—whatever they affirm, the Holy Spirit affirmed; thus, the biblical writings teach truth for salvation "firmly, faithfully, and without error."[65]

On biblical interpretation, both similarities and differences are found between Catholic and evangelical theology. One of the major distinctions is the ground for their approach to the interpretation of Scripture. Evangelical theology, following the theological legacy inherited from Protestantism, affirms the clarity of Scripture; from this doctrine flows its conviction that Scripture is understandable for Christians, who are also responsible for and capable of the task of interpreting it.[66] The clarity of Scripture means that it was written in such a way that ordinary human beings, possessing the normal acquired ability to understand written and/or oral communication, can read Scripture with understanding or, if they are unable to read, can

---

[65] CCC 107; citation is from Vatican Council II, *Dei Verbum* 11. *Dei Verbum*'s language—"we must acknowledge that the books of Scripture firmly, faithfully, and without error teach that truth which God, *for the sake of our salvation*, wished to see confided to the Sacred Scriptures" (emphasis added)—has generated significant controversy and ongoing debate. On the one side are non-inerrantists, who interpret the phrase as allowing for the portions of Scripture that do not treat salvific matters to contain error. They also point to the historical development of this section of *Dei Verbum*, particularly Cardinal Franz König's intervention at the Vatican Council (October 2, 1964) to insist that the existence of errors in Scripture (saying, e.g., that Mark 2:26 conflicts with 1 Sam. 21:1ff., or that Matt. 27:9 wrongly cites an unknown passage in Jeremiah rather than Zech. 11:12) means that the Council could not affirm the inerrancy of all Scripture. On the other side are the inerrantists, who, taking the whole sentence into account, insist that its first explanatory phrase—"since therefore all that the inspired authors or sacred writers affirm should be regarded as affirmed by the Holy Spirit"—precludes an errantist reading of the document. They further point to the footnotes to section 11 of *Dei Verbum*, where reference is made to Augustine, Thomas Aquinas, the Council of Trent, Leo XIII's encyclical *Providentissimus Deus*, and Pius XII's encyclical *Divino Afflante Spiritus*, as confirming their interpretation, because these authors, council, and encyclicals upheld the inerrancy of all Scripture. For a discussion of this debate, see Cardinal Alois Grillmeier, "The Divine Inspiration and the Interpretation of Sacred Scripture," in *Commentary on the Documents of Vatican II*, vol. 3, ed. Herbert Vorgrimler (New York: Crossroad, 1989),199–246.

[66] The following discussion is from Gregg R. Allison, *The Protestant Doctrine of the Perspicuity of Scripture: An Evangelical Reformulation* (PhD diss., Trinity Evangelical Divinity School, 1995).

hear Scripture read and comprehend it. Men and women, young and old, urbanites and desert nomads, seminary-trained and uneducated can read and understand the Bible.

How can evangelicals affirm such clarity? Scripture itself is characterized by the presumption of continued intelligibility; that is, it assumes that when the Word of God is read/heard, even in contexts far removed from the original settings in which it was written, people will comprehend it. For example, Moses affirmed that the Word of God that he was writing for the people of Israel was fully accessible to them:

> For this commandment that I command you today is not too hard for you, neither is it far off. It is not in heaven, that you should say, "Who will ascend to heaven for us and bring it to us, that we may hear it and do it?" Neither is it beyond the sea, that you should say, "Who will go over the sea for us and bring it to us, that we may hear it and do it?" But the word is very near you. It is in your mouth and in your heart, so that you can do it. (Deut. 30:11–14)

For Christians today, this exhortation means that Scripture need not be some obscure book far removed from them. Indeed, every time they sit on the side of the bed with their children and recite a Bible story, when they comfort their suffering friends with Scripture that they have memorized, when they hear a biblical passage read on their iPod as they are on their daily run, or when they discuss a biblically based sermon during their community group meeting, the intelligible Word of God is present—not "far off" but "very near."

Such a posture accounts for the subsequent instructions by Moses concerning his writing:

> Then Moses wrote this law and gave it to the priests, the sons of Levi, who carried the ark of the covenant of the LORD, and to all the elders of Israel. And Moses commanded them, "At the end of every seven years, at the set time in the year of release, at the Feast of Booths, when all Israel comes to appear before the LORD your God at the place that he will choose, you shall read this law before all Israel in their hearing. Assemble the people, men, women, and little ones, and the sojourner within your towns, that they may hear and learn to fear the LORD your God, and be careful to do all the words of this law, and that their children,

who have not known it, may hear and learn to fear the LORD your God, as long as you live in the land that you are going over the Jordan to possess." (Deut. 31:9–13)

Moses underscores the clarity of Scripture even in contexts far removed from the original setting of its writing. Though he, because of sinful rebellion, would not cross over to the Promised Land with his people (Num. 20:10–13), he commands the regular reading of Scripture in what would surely be new social/economic/political/religious/cultural contexts on the other side of the Jordan River. And his expectation was that the people of Israel—men, women, children, and the sojourners attached to Israel—would be able to grasp the Word of God read to them, wherever God would move them. From a forward-looking perspective, the Old Testament is characterized by the presumption of continued intelligibility.

A similar expectation characterizes the New Testament writings. Abraham, the founder of the people of Israel and the Jewish faith, stands as the quintessential example of God's gracious justification of people by faith apart from works—an example not only for the Jews but also for the Greek-speaking, Roman empire–ruled Gentile Christians in Rome (Rom. 4:22–25) and Galatia (Gal. 3:7–29). Indeed, Paul rehearses four episodes of Jewish sin and divine judgment—idolatry (Exodus 32), sexual immorality (Num. 25:6–9), testing the Lord (Num. 21:4–9), and grumbling (Numbers 14)—with the anticipation that the Gentile Corinthians would be warned by these examples and not commit the same heinous crimes (1 Cor. 10:6–13). As the apostle summarizes, "For whatever was written in former days was written for our instruction, that through endurance and through the encouragement of the Scriptures we might have hope" (Rom. 15:4). From a backward-looking perspective, Scripture is characterized by the presumption of continued intelligibility.

Add to this evidence the biblical exhortations to the church—all its members, not just its leaders—to pay attention to and be nourished by the Word of God (1 Pet. 2:1–3; 2 Pet. 1:19–21) and to read it publicly (1 Tim. 4:13), together with examples of its being understood (e.g., Nehemiah 8; Acts 17:10–12), and a strong biblical case in support of Scripture's clarity can be marshaled. At the heart of it is this principle from Moses: "The secret things belong to the LORD our God, but the things that are revealed belong to us and to our children forever, that we may do all the words of this law" (Deut. 29:29). Much about God remains obscure or mysterious to us, but what God has sovereignly willed to reveal to his people is sufficiently clear. Though Scripture does not exhaust the category of "revealed things," it is most certainly included in it, which means that Scripture is accessible and intelligible for the people of God—the clarity of Scripture.[67]

This doctrine is one of the reasons why the Reformers engaged in the translation of Scripture into the languages of the common people, why Protestants distribute millions of copies of Scripture, and why evangelicals encourage and engage in personal Bible reading and home Bible studies. While a heartening development following Vatican Council II is the Catholic Church's encouragement of Bible reading and study by Catholics, it pales in comparison with the prevalence of Bible study within evangelical churches, and an important reason for this is the doctrine of the clarity of Scripture as affirmed by evangelical theology.

The Canon of Scripture

On the canon of Scripture, the list of the God-breathed, authoritative writings that belong in Scripture, both similarities and differences are once again found. Two important agreements between Catholicism and evangelical theology are the canon of the New Testament—there are twenty-seven writings (and no serious dispute to these has ever been mounted[68])—and the acknowledgment that the church's recognition of which writings should be included in both the Old Testament and New Testament was the result of a

---

[67] Notice should be made that at no time in my discussion of this doctrine do I use the words "obvious" or "easy" in connection with the understanding of Scripture. This misconception is frequently foisted on the doctrine, as evidenced again by Frank Beckwith's rejoinder to me in my "Response to Catholicism," in Plummer, *Journeys of Faith*, 131. According to Peter's comments on the writings of the apostle Paul, "there are some things in them that are hard to understand, which the ignorant and unstable twist to their own destruction, as they do the other Scriptures" (2 Pet. 3:16). While thanking Peter for his honesty, we should also observe that his comment is quite circumscribed. He does not say that *all things*, or even *many things*, in Paul's writings bear this trait; "*some things* in them" is what he writes. We should also observe that Peter does not lament that these several matters are *impossible* to grasp; "*hard* to understand" is what he writes. So Peter's frank admission that the apostle Paul's writings include some things that are difficult to understand can in no way be taken to mean that all Scripture is obscure or that laypeople should be prohibited from reading and studying the Bible. So the clarity of Scripture does not and cannot be misconstrued to mean that Scripture is easy to understand, and, in fact, my discussion of it does not take that tack. Beyond this point, if Beckwith represents the Catholic position as standing against the clarity of Scripture, then this mode of divine revelation is obscure for the Catholic Church as well, including all the passages (e.g., Matt. 16:13–20) to which it appeals in support of its doctrines of justification, tradition, transubstantiation, purgatory, Mary, and the like—including its doctrine of papal infallibility for the interpretation of divine revelation. Apparent victories may end up being Pyrrhic for those who achieve them.

[68] Martin Luther's well-known wrestling with four New Testament books—Hebrews, James, Jude, and Revelation—and his consignment of them to the end of his German translation of the Bible following the twenty-three "true and certain chief books of the New Testament"—was clearly an anomaly and not a serious challenge to the New Testament canon (Martin Luther, *Prefaces to the New Testament* [*LW* 35:394–399]). For further discussion, see Allison, *HT*, 53–54n66.

relatively lengthy historical process that featured agreements and disagreements and was guided by the Holy Spirit.

One of the major differences between the Catholic Church and Protestant churches is the canon of the Old Testament. The Protestant Old Testament is composed of thirty-nine writings, while the Catholic Old Testament is more extensive. It includes the Apocrypha or apocryphal writing, seven additional books—Tobit, Judith, the Wisdom of Solomon, Ecclesiasticus (the Wisdom of Sirach), Baruch, and 1 and 2 Maccabees—and additional sections to the Protestant books of Esther and Daniel.

This important difference arose in the early church due to the presence of two different versions of the collection of books that were written before the coming of Jesus Christ. On the one hand, the Hebrew Bible consisted of twenty-two (or twenty-four, according to a different numbering system) writings, distributed in three divisions: the Law, the Prophets, and the Writings:

- the Law: Genesis, Exodus, Leviticus, Numbers, Deuteronomy;
- the Prophets: Joshua, Judges–Ruth (one book), Samuel (one book), Kings (one book), Jeremiah–Lamentations (one book), Ezekiel, Isaiah, the Twelve Minor Prophets (one book), Job, Daniel, Ezra–Nehemiah (one book), Chronicles (one book), Esther;
- the Writings: Psalms, Proverbs, Ecclesiastes, Song of Songs.[69]

On the other hand, the Greek translation of the Hebrew Bible—called the Septuagint, and abbreviated LXX—contained additional writings that had never been part of Jewish Scripture. As a Palestinian Jew well versed in Hebrew, Jesus used the Hebrew Bible (e.g., the scroll of Isaiah that he read from in the synagogue [Luke 4:16–20] was in Hebrew), and this collection did not include the extra books that were found in the LXX. But the early church, expanding into the Greek-speaking Gentile world, used the Septuagint with its additional writings.

This situation raises the question, What was the Old Testament canon that was acknowledged in the early church? Was it a canon reflective of the lengthier Septuagint, or did it correspond to the shorter Hebrew Bible?

---

[69] Josephus, *Against Apion* 1.37. Later Jewish reckonings typically listed twenty-four books. Following is the Talmud's canon: the Law (Genesis, Exodus, Leviticus, Numbers, Deuteronomy); the Prophets (Joshua, Judges, Samuel, Kings, Jeremiah, Ezekiel, Isaiah, the Twelve Minor Prophets); the Writings (Ruth, Psalms, Job, Proverbs, Ecclesiastes, Song of Songs, Lamentations, Daniel, Esther, Ezra-Nehemiah, and Chronicles) (*Baba Bathra* 14b-15a).

Evidence can be marshaled in favor of both positions. In favor of the first view is the fact that the New Testament authors and early church leaders cited readily from the Septuagint in their many writings. Such evidence is understood to support the idea of an early church endorsement of a more extensive canon of the Old Testament, including the apocryphal writings. In support of the second position are several actual early church lists of canonical Old Testament Scripture that correspond to the canon of the Hebrew Bible and that explicitly deny that the apocryphal writings belong in the canon. For example, Melito of Sardis composed the first extant list of "the books of the old covenant" (AD 170) and it included all the books of the Hebrew Bible with the exception of Esther but did not contain any of the apocryphal writings. The canon of Origen (died 254) corresponded to the Hebrew canon, with the exception that he included the Letter of Jeremiah.[70] Athanasius, whose *Thirty-ninth Easter Letter* (AD 367) contains a list of both New Testament and Old Testament books, continued this tradition of mirroring the canon of the Hebrew Bible (though he included the Letter of Jeremiah and Baruch in his Old Testament list). Additionally, Athanasius rejected "the Wisdom of Solomon, the Wisdom of Sirach [Ecclesiasticus], and Esther, and Judith, and Tobit," though he pointed out that these books, while "not indeed included in the canon," had been "appointed by the Fathers [the early church leaders] to be read by those who newly join us, and who wish for instruction in the word of godliness."[71] Cyril of Jerusalem listed twenty-two books in the Old Testament, corresponding to the writings of Hebrew Scripture, and warned, "have nothing to do with the apocryphal writings. Study earnestly these only which we read openly in the church. Far wiser and more pious than you were the apostles, and the bishops of old time, the presidents of the church who handed down these books. Being therefore a child of the church, do not transgress its statutes."[72]

In AD 382, the bishop of Rome commissioned Jerome to produce a new Latin translation of the Bible. For his work on the Old Testament, Jerome commenced with the Hebrew Bible rather than the Septuagint. In his preface to his translations of the books of Samuel and Kings, Jerome composed

[70] This additional writing was eventually added to the end of Baruch (another apocryphal writing) and included in the Roman Catholic canon.
[71] He also listed two additional noncanonical New Testament writings: the *Didache*, or *Teaching of the Twelve*, and the *Shepherd of Hermas* (Athanasius, *Thirty-Ninth Easter Letter* [367] 7 [NPNF² 4:552]).
[72] Cyril of Jerusalem, *Catechetical Lectures* 4.35 (NPNF² 7:27). The text has been rendered clearer.

a list of canonical Scripture. The writings corresponded to those in the Hebrew Bible; these and these alone, he said, were Scripture. He added, "This preface to the Scriptures may serve as a 'helmeted' [general] introduction to all the books which we turn [translate] from Hebrew into Latin, so that we may be assured that what is not found in our list must be placed among the apocryphal writings."[73] These noncanonical Old Testament books, according to Jerome, were Wisdom (of Solomon), the Book of Jesus Ben Sirach (Ecclesiasticus), Judith, Tobit, and 1 and 2 Maccabees.[74] Elsewhere, Jerome dismissed Baruch, and though he translated the additional parts of Daniel from the LXX, he placed them in an appendix to that book. Moreover, commenting on the Wisdom of Solomon and Ecclesiasticus, he expressed the purpose for the Apocrypha: "As then the church reads Judith, Tobit, and the books of Maccabees, but does not admit them among the canonical Scriptures, so let it read these two volumes for the edification of the people, not to give authority to doctrines of the church."[75] Important to note is that Jerome continued the tradition that has been traced from Melito and that included such church leaders as Origen, Cyril of Alexandria, and Athanasius.[76]

The decisive intervention that propelled the church to include the apocryphal writings in its Old Testament canon was made by Augustine, who believed that "one and the same Spirit" had spoken through both the writers of the Hebrew Bible and the translators of the Septuagint. This must have been the case, he surmised, because the apostles cited both the Hebrew Bible and the Septuagint in their New Testament writings. Thus, Augustine adopted the apostolic perspective on this matter: "I also, according to my capacity, following the footsteps of the apostles, who themselves have quoted prophetic testimonies from both, that is, from the Hebrew Bible

---

[73] Jerome, *Preface to the Books of Samuel and Kings* (NPNF[2] 6:490).

[74] Ibid.

[75] Jerome, *Preface to the Books of Proverbs, Ecclesiastes, and the Song of Songs* (NPNF[2] 6:492).

[76] Certainly not unaware of these historical advocates of a shorter canon of the Old Testament, the Catholic Church does not side with their position. But why not? The *Catholic Encyclopedia* provides an example of such a dismissal: "Obviously, the inferior rank to which the [apocryphal writings] were relegated by authorities like Origen, Athanasius, and Jerome, was due to too rigid a conception of canonicity, one demanding that a book, to be entitled to this supreme dignity, must be received by all, must have the sanction of Jewish antiquity, and must moreover be adapted not only to edification, but also to the 'confirmation of the doctrine of the Church', to borrow Jerome's phrase" (*Catholic Encyclopedia*, "Canon of the Old Testament"; accessible at http://www.newadvent.org/cathen/03267a.htm). The question becomes, in a historical study such as the development of the canonical consciousness of the early church, on what grounds is it possible to judge these contributors to that consciousness as possessing "too rigid a conception of canonicity?" The *Encyclopedia*'s anachronistic approach and evaluation is evident and wrongheaded.

and the Septuagint, have thought that both should be used as authoritative, since both are one and divine."[77]

Corresponding in a series of letters with Jerome, Augustine urged his colleague to translate the Old Testament into Latin from the Septuagint rather than from the Hebrew; Jerome capitulated to his friend's request and included translations of the apocryphal writings in his Latin Vulgate. As this new Bible became widely known, its Old Testament, including the Apocrypha, became the Bible of the church. Shortly thereafter, this longer Old Testament canon was ratified by three regional councils: the Council of Hippo (393), the Third Council of Carthage (397), and the Fourth Council of Carthage (419). Thus, the Old Testament with the apocryphal writings (including Tobit, Judith, additions to Esther, 1 and 2 Maccabees, the Book of Wisdom, Ecclesiasticus, Baruch, and the additions to Daniel), together with the New Testament, would be canonical Scripture for the Church.

This view went without significant challenge until the Reformation of the sixteenth century. Spurred on by humanism—a significant cultural and educational movement in the fourteenth through sixteenth centuries that promoted eloquence in speech and writing and advocated a return to the classical sources of Western society—the Church rediscovered its foundational writings: the Hebrew Old Testament, the Greek New Testament, and the writings of the early church. The difference between the shorter Hebrew Bible and the longer Old Testament of the Latin Bible became an issue and raised the question, On which of these two versions should the Church's Old Testament be based? Additionally, Jerome's ancient distinction between canonical and apocryphal writings was revived, and his contention that the Apocrypha could be read for edification but not to authorize church doctrine raised another question: If the Church appealed to an apocryphal writing for justification of one of its beliefs or practices, should it dismiss those doctrines and discontinue those practices? As a specific example, if the basis for the Church's belief in purgatory and its practice of praying for the dead was the apocryphal writing 2 Maccabees (12:38–45), should the church continue affirming these matters?

The Protestant Reformers, beginning with Martin Luther, maintained that the church's Old Testament should be based on the shorter Hebrew Bible and should not include the apocryphal writings merely because they

---

[77] Augustine, *The City of God* 18:43–44 (*NPNF*[1] 2:386–387).

were included in the Septuagint. Key to their decision was the fact that Jewish Scripture, with its twenty-two (or twenty-four) books, had been the Word of God used by Jesus and the disciples.[78] Additionally, some of the apocryphal writings contained incorrect historical or chronological details, and many of them had not been considered sound by the early church. Appealing to Jerome's classical distinction, the Reformers insisted that the church could appeal to canonical Scripture alone as the foundation for its doctrines and practices. Because the Apocrypha was noncanonical, it could not be used as the basis for the church's beliefs. Accordingly, one of the major differences between the Catholic Church and the nascent Protestant churches was the canon of the Old Testament.

The Catholic Church reacted strongly to this Protestant challenge to its canonical Scriptures. At the Council of Trent (1546), the Church affirmed, "If anyone does not receive, as sacred and canonical, these books, with all their parts, as they have been read in the Catholic Church and as they are contained in the old Latin Vulgate edition, and knowingly and deliberately rejects the above mentioned traditions, let him be anathema [cursed]."[79] Thus, Protestants were threatened with Church condemnation for adopting a Bible without the apocryphal writings. This denunciation created another major difference with regard to the official version of canonical Scripture: based on the Council's decision, the Latin Vulgate is the Catholic Church's official Bible. While Protestant theology did not promote an official version, its practice has always been to appeal to the Hebrew Bible and the Greek New Testament.

Catholicism's ongoing opposition to this Protestant reformulation of the canon of Scripture (specifically, the Old Testament) often focuses on the Catholic Church being the divinely appointed determiner of the canon. As Kreeft expresses it, "The Church (apostles and saints) wrote the New Testament, and the Church (subsequent bishops) defined its canon."[80] This focus is wrong on at least two accounts: First, it ignores the actual historical development of the recognition of the canon, specifically during the first

---

[78] Jesus, as a Palestinian Jew, was well versed in Hebrew and used the Hebrew Bible, as illustrated by his reading from the scroll of Isaiah in the synagogue of Nazareth (Luke 4:16–20). It is also the case that the New Testament writers quoted from the Septuagint, so they were clearly familiar with that translation of the Hebrew Bible. Importantly, however, no New Testament author quotes from the apocryphal writings.

[79] *Canons and Decrees of the Council of Trent*, 4th session (April 8, 1546), *Decree Concerning the Canonical Scriptures* (Schaff, 2:80). The text has been rendered clearer.

[80] Kreeft, 20.

five centuries of the church. It often overlooks the fact that Augustine broke with a well-developed tradition, embodied in his contemporary Jerome, that did not include the apocryphal writings in the canon of the Old Testament, and it fails to note that the councils that approved this lengthier Old Testament canon were regional councils—not ecumenical councils—that reflected the influence of Augustine.[81] The second and more problematic reason flows from the second axiom of the Catholic system, the Christ-Church interconnection, according to which Christ has delegated his authority to the Catholic Church to be, in this case, the determiner of the canon of Scripture. As this axiom has already been critiqued (ch. 2), only one comment is needed, and that is a reminder from John Webster: "Scripture is not the word of the church; the church is the church of the word. . . . The church exists in the space which is made by the Word."[82] Evangelical theology blisters at its counterpart's insistence on the priority of the Catholic Church over the Word of God. Such an insistence fails to account for the preexisting written Jewish Scripture, which prophesied of a fresh, new, unprecedented outpouring of the Holy Spirit,[83] the event that historically gave birth to the church.[84] That is, Scripture did indeed precede the church in time and brought the church into existence, not vice versa. Moreover, despite its many denials to the contrary, such an insistence elevates the Catholic Church above Scripture. It becomes the determiner of the Word of God rather than the thankful recipient of it. But if divine revelation is a free act of the gracious God, how can the Church position itself in any way other than being a grateful beneficiary of that divine, inscripturated grace?

The Authoritative Interpretation of Scripture

Another crucial difference separating Catholic and evangelical theology in this realm of Scripture concerns the authoritative interpretation of the Bible. The Catholic Church insists that the prerogative to determine the proper and authoritative interpretation of Scripture belongs solely to its

---

[81] It was not until the Council of Trent proclaimed the canon of the Old Testament as including the apocryphal writings that an ecumenical council of the Catholic Church officially determined that canon (*Canons and Decrees of the Council of Trent*, 4th session [April 8, 1546], *Decree Concerning the Canonical Scriptures* [Schaff, 2:80]).
[82] John Webster, *Holy Scripture: A Dogmatic Approach*, Current Issues in Theology (Cambridge: Cambridge University Press, 2003), 46; cf. Michael Horton, *People and Place: A Covenant Ecclesiology* (Louisville: Westminster John Knox, 2008), 72–98.
[83] E.g., Ezek. 36:25–27; Joel 2:28–32; continued by John the Baptist (Luke 3:15–17) and Jesus (Luke 24:44–49; Acts 1:4–5).
[84] Acts 2:1–4, explained as a fulfillment of Joel's prophecy (Acts 2:16–21).

Magisterium, or teaching office (consisting of the pope and bishops). This was a decision made in response to the growing Protestant movement by the Council of Trent (1546), which decreed "that no one relying on his own judgment shall, in matters of faith and morals pertaining to the edification of Christian doctrine, distorting the Holy Scriptures in accordance with his own conceptions, presume to interpret them contrary to that sense which holy mother Church, to whom it belongs to judge of their true sense and interpretation, has held and holds. . . ."[85] Thus, the Catholic Church claims that it possesses the sole right to interpret Scripture.

Evangelical churches do not have a Magisterium to decide the authentic and authoritative interpretation of Scripture. However, they urge all believers to engage in careful and responsible interpretation of the Bible by observing sound interpretive principles (including those highlighted in the *Catechism*) under the guidance of the Holy Spirit (as also affirmed by the *Catechism*) and with the help of divinely ordained and gifted elders (1 Tim. 3:2; 5:17; Titus 1:9) or pastor-teachers (Eph. 4:11). Unlike the Catholic interpretive approach that seeks to discern a fourfold sense of Scripture, evangelicals follow the Protestant heritage that focuses on the grammatical–(redemptive) historical meaning of Scripture, together with an eye toward typology, especially as that typology considers Old Testament people, events, institutions, and the like as foreshadowing a later fulfillment in the person and work of Jesus Christ.

The reasons for evangelical theology's approach to biblical interpretation are several. As discussed above, this approach to biblical interpretation is grounded in the doctrine of the clarity of Scripture. It also reflects a deep distrust of the fourfold meaning of Scripture. This Catholic approach is grounded on the nature-grace interdependence: the words of Scripture— or, to be more precise, the things to which those words point (the realm of nature)—contain hidden meanings that are capable of communicating grace. This nature-grace axiom has already been demonstrated to be faulty. Historically, Martin Luther, though trained in this interpretive approach, rejected it because the method, as practiced in the Catholic Church, so emphasized the spiritual sense—the allegorical, moral (tropological), and anagogical meanings—that the literal sense was overlooked or dismissed.

---

[85] *Canons and Decrees of the Council of Trent*, 4th session (April 8, 1546), *Decree Concerning the Canonical Scriptures* (Schaff, 2:82).

He championed the literal, or the "grammatical, historical meaning,"[86] which is "the highest, best, strongest, in short, the whole substance, nature and foundation of Holy Scripture."[87] Indeed, Luther insisted that biblical interpreters "should strive, so far as possible, to get one, simple, true, and grammatical meaning from the words of the text."[88] Similarly, John Calvin rejected the allegorical interpretation of Scripture, urging instead "that the true meaning of Scripture is the natural and obvious [not hidden] meaning,"[89] the sense that the biblical authors intended their readers to grasp. Thus, an interpreter's task is to discern the author's intent: "It is almost his only work to lay open the mind of the writer whom he undertakes to explain."[90] To instruct the growing number of Protestants, both Luther and Calvin advocated principles of biblical interpretation to guide them into a proper understanding of Scripture: familiarity with Paul's letter to the Romans,[91] a sound theological framework, a Christocentric focus, consideration of the context, the analogy of faith (interpretation of any particular passage in conformity with the entirety of Scripture), and being the right kind of interpreter in terms of godliness, humility, willingness to learn and obey, persistence, and the like. Additionally, both men underscored the necessity of the illumination of the Holy Spirit to understand Scripture rightly. Luther and Calvin also preached the Word of God and wrote commentaries for its proper interpretation, responsibilities that were incumbent upon them as pastors of their churches. Advocating the clarity of Scripture, and taking seriously their office of pastor-teachers in helping Christians to grasp the Word of God rightly, the Reformers broke from the centuries-old position of the Catholic Church regarding the fourfold sense of Scripture and the sole prerogative to interpret it as belonging to the Church's Magisterium.

But there is more to this evangelical rejection of the Magisterium. Historically, Protestants have disputed the Church's alleged biblical support for this authoritative teaching office that centers on its bishops with the pope

---

[86] Martin Luther, *Answers to the Hyperchristian, Hyperspiritual, Hyperlearned Book by Goat Emser in Leipzig* (*LW* 39:181).
[87] Ibid. (*LW* 39:178).
[88] Martin Luther, *Lectures on Genesis: Chapters 45–50* (*LW* 8:146).
[89] John Calvin, *Commentaries on Galatians and Ephesians*, trans. William Pringle (repr., Grand Rapids, MI: Baker, 2005), 136.
[90] John Calvin, *Institutes* 4.11.1 (LCC 21:1212).
[91] This emphasis was due to the fact that the letter to the Romans is a clear articulation of the gospel and the mighty work of justification by divine grace through faith in Jesus Christ.

at their head. As more will be said about this topic later, no comment will be made at this point.

In summary, Catholic and evangelical theology on the doctrine of Scripture contain both areas of agreement and areas of disagreement. As for agreement, both affirm the need for divine/special revelation (given the inadequacy of general revelation for salvation); the gracious, gifted, and progressive nature of such revelation; the working in tandem of divine deeds and divine words as composing divine revelation; the importance, divine inspiration, and truthfulness of Scripture; and some important principles for biblical interpretation. The two theologies clash, however, over several critical issues: (1) the transmission of divine revelation: Catholic theology insists on the two modes of written Scripture and Church Tradition, while evangelical theology champions *sola Scriptura* (Scripture alone); (2) the interpretation of Scripture: Catholic theology focuses on a fourfold meaning of Scripture and insists that the Magisterium of the Church possesses the sole prerogative to interpret it, while evangelical theology underscores the clarity of Scripture and follows a grammatical–(redemptive) historical–typological approach to discerning the one meaning of Scripture; and (3) the canon of the Old Testament: Catholic theology includes the apocryphal writings and additions in its canon, while evangelical theology holds that these additional writings are not inspired, authoritative, and wholly true.

The Doctrine of Faith: The Human Response to God (Sec. I, Ch. 3)

The proper and intended response to divine revelation is faith, and the *Catechism* next addresses the doctrine of faith. The *Catechism* highlights the instrumental role of faith: *by faith*, a person submits his intellect and will to God. Given this notion of submission, a further emphasis becomes the biblical expression "the obedience of faith" (Rom. 1:5; 16:26). Examples of those who submitted freely to the word that they heard are Abraham and the Virgin Mary. The definition of faith focuses on the idea of personal adherence to God that is also a "free assent to the whole truth that God has revealed."[92] The object of faith for a Christian is Jesus Christ, and Christian belief is prompted by the Holy Spirit. Specifically, faith is characterized as:

---

[92] *CCC* 150.

- a *grace/gift*: it is "a gift of God, a supernatural virtue infused by him";[93]
- a *human act*: "the human intellect and will cooperate with divine grace";[94]
- linked with *understanding*: faith is not counter to reason; it goes beyond reason to bring certainty, because it is grounded on the true word of God; faith seeks understanding as a Christian grows in knowledge of God and his revelation; and it is in accord with, not in conflict with, science;[95]
- *free*: it cannot be coerced;[96]
- *necessary*: faith in Christ is necessary for salvation;[97]
- can be *lost*: because faith is a free gift, human beings can lose it; to avoid this possibility, therefore, faith must be nourished on the word of God; it requires "working through charity" while grounded in the Church's faith;[98]
- a *beginning*: it gives a foretaste of seeing God face-to-face; thus, faith is the beginning of eternal life;[99]
- not in the propositions, but *in the realities* they express: because divine revelation is both propositional (including both orally transmitted Tradition and written Scripture) and personal (revealing God, with whom people may have an intimate relationship), that in which Christians ultimately believe is the reality of God made known through doctrines of the faith.[100]

But faith is more than an individual matter, a personal act, because no person can believe alone. Indeed, faith is received from others, specifically, from the Catholic Church: "It is the Church that believes first, and so bears, nourishes, and sustains my faith."[101] Nowhere is the ecclesial nature of faith more evident than in the sacrament of Baptism. To the infant who is being baptized, the Church grants faith. To the adult who is ready to be baptized, the priest poses this question: "What do you ask of God's Church?" The response: "Faith."[102] Accordingly, one of the rich metaphors for the Church

[93] CCC 153.
[94] CCC 155.
[95] CCC 156–159.
[96] CCC 160.
[97] CCC 161.
[98] CCC 162; the biblical citations are Gal. 5:6 and Rom. 15:13.
[99] CCC 163.
[100] CCC 170.
[101] CCC 168.
[102] Ibid. The interchange is part of the Roman Ritual, Rite of Baptism of Adults.

is that of mother: "We believe the Church as the mother of our new birth, and not *in* the Church as if she were the author of our salvation."[103] It is the Catholic Church that from the beginning to the end confesses this one faith inherited from the apostles.

Evangelical Assessment

This notion of faith bears some similarities with its evangelical counterpart, but it also evidences a number of differences. In terms of similarities, evangelical and Catholic theology alike affirm that faith is personal adherence, a disposition of trust, which is indeed a human act linked with understanding (especially grounded on the Word of God) that is free (noncoerced) and necessary for salvation. Moreover, the object of faith is God as he has revealed himself and his way of salvation through the gospel, which has been communicated to fallen human beings through propositional truth expressed by means of various genres (narrative, poetry, letter, prophecy, and the like) in Scripture (not Scripture and Tradition). This revelation does indeed serve to establish a personal relationship between the Revealing and Redeeming God and those who have faith in him.

In terms of differences, evangelical theology underscores the influence of both axioms of the Catholic system (the nature-grace interdependence and the Christ-Church interconnection) on its formulation of the doctrine of faith. Aligned with its first axiom, Catholic theology emphasizes that human nature—intellect and will—is capable of cooperating with divine grace such that faith is a human act, and is able to cease cooperating with that grace so that faith is lost. Moreover, Catholic theology highlights that divine grace received by faith is infused into human nature so as to elevate and perfect that nature. From its second axiom, Catholic theology highlights the fact that the Catholic Church, as the ongoing incarnation of Christ, mediates between nature and grace in such a way that the Church is the first to believe and indeed grants faith (the realm of grace) to human beings (the realm of nature). The evangelical critique of both of these axioms has already been expressed, which means that the points of the Catholic system's doctrine of faith that are grounded on these axioms are without foundation.

---

[103] CCC 169; citation is from Faustus of Riez, *On the Holy Spirit* 1, 2.

In terms of specific criticisms, evangelical theology agrees that faith is a gift of God in terms of it not being an ingrained disposition or natural response, but it denies the notion that faith is infused by God. In its discussion of this matter, the *Catechism* appeals to Peter's confession of the identity of Jesus as the Christ, the Son of the living God, and Jesus's subsequent comment that "this revelation did not come 'from flesh and blood,' but from 'my Father who is in heaven.'"[104] The *Catechism* apparently draws this implication from this passage: "Faith is a gift of God, a supernatural virtue infused by him."[105] Actually, however, Jesus does not address Peter's faith as a gift but underscores the origin of the divine revelation that Peter received; the revelation of Jesus's identity, not Peter's faith, was a divine gift. So it is hard to see what this passage has to do with faith itself as a gift. Furthermore, evangelical theology would insist that before faith can be expressed, the grace of God's mighty acts of conviction of sin, calling, justification, regeneration, adoption, and union with Christ make it possible that formerly callous and rebellious people who are now effectively summoned, declared not guilty but righteous instead, given a new spiritual nature that is receptive to God, brought into the family of God, and united with Christ, do indeed respond with faith to this gracious, divine work. Indeed, Paul expresses it this way: "For by grace you have been saved through faith. And this is not your own doing; it is the gift of God, not a result of works, so that no one may boast" (Eph. 2:8–9). What Paul affirms is that this entire reality—salvation by grace through faith—is a gift of God, not just faith. As will be discussed later, grace is not something that is infused into people—hence, neither is faith—but is instead God's goodness expressed to those who deserve only condemnation; this divine goodness summons and prompts a positive response to—faith in—the gospel, resulting in salvation.

A second major disagreement centers on whether saving faith can be lost. Catholic theology maintains that it can be lost. One stream of evangelical theology agrees; another stream—and I place myself here—maintains that genuine faith is permanent and cannot be abandoned. The *Catechism* offers the example of "certain persons [who] have made shipwreck of their faith" (1 Tim. 1:18–19) in support of the possibility of the

---

[104] CCC 153; citation is from Matt. 16:17.
[105] Ibid.

loss of faith.[106] But the example of Hymenaeus, one of the persons named as ruined with respect to faith (v. 20), seems unconvincing, for he turns out to be a false teacher, "saying that the resurrection has already happened"; indeed, Hymenaeus's heretical doctrine was "upsetting the faith of some" (2 Tim. 2:17–18). In his apostolic comment on this situation, Paul explains, "But God's firm foundation stands, bearing this seal: 'The Lord knows those who are his,' and, 'Let everyone who names the name of the Lord depart from iniquity'" (v. 19). That is, Paul erects a contrast between those who genuinely belong to Christ (e.g., those whose faith was upset by false teaching) and those who are Christians in name only but who engage in iniquity (e.g., Hymenaeus, who engaged in false teaching). Accordingly, Hymenaeus is not a bona fide example of a Christian who lost his faith.

Other alleged examples of Christians who lost their faith could be marshaled in defense of this position: Ananias and Sapphira (Acts 5:1–11); the followers of Jesus who prophesied, cast out demons, and performed miracles in the name of Jesus (Matt. 7:21–23); the believers described in the Letter to the Hebrews as "those who have once been enlightened, who have tasted the heavenly gift, and have shared in the Holy Spirit, and have tasted the goodness of the word of God and the powers of the age to come, and then have fallen away" (Heb. 6:4–6); and others.

But do these passages actually affirm that the people described therein lost their salvation? In the case of Ananias and Sapphira, Luke gives insufficient details to determine if they were genuine believers or not. From one perspective, they were believers who committed a heinous sin that threatened to disrupt the sacrificial giving leading to the remarkable unity of the early church (described in Acts 2:42–47; 4:32–37); accordingly, God removed them through a severe intervention to prevent their example from spreading like cancer in the community.[107] From another perspective, the couple had associated themselves with the church in Jerusalem and sought to imitate the generosity exhibited by that community; however, their egregious act of deceit revealed that they were not true Christ-followers.

In the next example, though the followers of Jesus engaged in mighty

---

[106] CCC 162.

[107] A possible parallel is the divine discipline meted out on the Corinthian church for its abuse of the Lord's Supper, with some of its members being sick and even dying prematurely (1 Cor. 11:17–34).

signs and wonders in his name, Jesus explains that on the day of judgment, he himself "will declare to them, 'I never knew you; depart from me, you workers of lawlessness'" (Matt. 7:23). They were not people who had genuine faith.

As for the people noted in the Letter to the Hebrews, on the surface the description of them may seem to indicate that they were real Christians, but the writer's comment to his readers (Heb. 6:9–10) steers us away from that conclusion: "Though we speak in this way, yet in your case, beloved, we feel sure of better things. . . ." But what things could possibly be better than being enlightened, tasting the heavenly gift, sharing in the Spirit, tasting the goodness of God's word and the power of the age to come? The writer continues: ". . . we feel sure of better things—things that belong to salvation. For God is not unjust so as to overlook your work and the love that you have shown for his name in serving the saints, as you still do." In other words, the writer first describes people who have participated in the church with great blessing, received answers to prayer, experienced the movement of the Holy Spirit at work in the community, and the like, but because they are not genuine Christians, they fall away—not from saving faith (which they never had) but from the religious persuasion that once attracted them to the church. In the case of his readers, however, the writer is convinced that their faith is true, resulting in salvation, as evidenced by the persistent fruit that their lives put forth.

A helpful passage for understanding this phenomenon is 1 John 2:19: "They went out from us, but they were not of us; for if they had been of us, they would have continued with us. But they went out, that it might become plain that they all are not of us." The apostle's point can be diagrammed and personalized with respect to members of the church in two ways, one positive, one negative. Positively:

- If people are "of us"—that is, if they have saving faith—then they will continue with us; that is, they will remain faithfully in the community of the church until the end.
- You have saving faith.
- Therefore, you continue faithfully with us in the church.

Negatively:

- If people go out from us, they were not "of us"—that is, then they did not have saving faith.

- You do not have saving faith.
- Therefore, you will go out from us—you will depart from the community of the church.

Specifically, saving faith by definition perseveres; a constitutive element of genuine faith is perseverance.[108] Those who do not have genuine faith will eventually fall away. Because their faith was not saving faith, however, but a spurious faith, their desertion is not from salvation but from the religious persuasion they once held. Oppositely, those who have saving faith in the gospel of Jesus Christ will indeed remain Christians to the end. Of course, such perseverance is not solely up to them and their best efforts to remain faithful; indeed, "by God's power [they] are being guarded through faith for a salvation ready to be revealed in the last time" (1 Pet. 1:5). The protective power of God, operating through these believers' daily and consistent faith, preserves them for their future, awaiting salvation.

Because salvation cannot be lost once genuinely obtained, saving faith cannot be lost. This is the consistent teaching of Scripture. Christ himself pledged not to lose any of his followers (John 10:27–29; 6:37–40), and his ongoing intercession for them results in their ultimate salvation (Heb. 7:25). The Holy Spirit has sealed genuine believers, his mark serves as the guarantee of God's preserving work in their lives (2 Cor. 1:22; 3:18; Eph. 1:13–14; 4:30), and his inner testimony bears witness that they are truly children of God (Rom. 8:16). To those who have the Son of God, his Word promises eternal life, giving them the assurance that such is their possession (1 John 5:11–13); indeed, there is nothing at all that can ever separate Christians from the love of God in Jesus Christ (Rom. 8:31–39). Moreover, the persevering faithfulness of genuine believers is consistent with and grounded in the faithfulness of God (1 Cor. 1:9; Phil. 1:6), who has chosen them (Rom. 8:32; Eph. 1:4), justified them (Rom. 3:21–31; 8:1), regenerated them (John 3:1–8), adopted them (Rom. 8:14–15; Gal. 4:5–6), and united them with Christ (Rom. 6:1–11), who also has baptized them with the Holy Spirit into his body (1 Cor. 12:13).

A final key contrast is between the Catholic view that faith comes from others, especially the Catholic Church, and the evangelical view that faith is a personal responsibility that, while aided and nourished by the church,

---

[108] For further discussion, see Gregg R. Allison, "Eternal Security," in A. Scott Moreau, ed., *Evangelical Dictionary of World Missions*, Baker Reference Library (Grand Rapids, MI: Baker, 2000), 318–319.

does not come from it. As already noted, the Catholic view is dependent on its underlying assumptions regarding the Christ-Church interconnection. Moreover, a weakness of the *Catechism*'s discussion of this point is its lack of biblical support. Its claim that the Church is the mother of Christians because they "receive the life of faith through the Church"—specifically, through the Church's administration of Baptism[109]—is certainly an important part of the Church's Tradition: In the middle of the third century, Cyprian, bishop of Carthage (North Africa), claimed, "He can no longer have God for his Father, who has not the church for his mother."[110] While Scripture uses a vivid feminine image for the church—it is the bride of Christ (2 Cor. 11:1–4; Eph. 5:25–33; Rev. 19:7; 21:2, 9; 22:17)—it does not employ the metaphor of mother.

At the same time, evangelical theology doesn't necessarily shy away from the church-as-mother image, as long as it is understood in a certain way.[111] For example, John Calvin favorably quoted Cyprian's dictum as he advocated for the necessity of the church, "into whose bosom God is pleased to gather his sons, not only that they may be nourished by her help and ministry as long as they are infants and children, but also that they may be guided by her motherly care until they mature and at last reach the goal of faith."[112] He insisted that believers know the church as their mother, "For there is no other way to enter into life unless this mother conceive us in her womb, give us birth, nourish us at her breast. . . . Our weakness does not allow us to be dismissed from her school until we have been pupils all our lives. Furthermore, away from her bosom one cannot hope for any forgiveness of sins or any salvation. . . . [I]t is always disastrous to leave the church."[113]

Clearly, Calvin was not promoting the Catholic Church's concept of itself as the mother of all believers; indeed, it is arguable that his discussion was offered as a corrective to the Catholic idea with its focus on Mary. For Calvin, the focus of the church-as-mother metaphor is the ministry of the Word of God as preached by the church's pastors and their administration of the sacraments, all of which is empowered and rendered effective

---

[109] CCC 168–169.
[110] Cyprian, *Treatise* "On the Unity of the Church," 1.6 (*ANF* 5:423).
[111] Martin Luther, *Large Catechism*, part 2, the Creed, art. 3.
[112] Calvin, *Institutes* 4.1.1 (LCC 21:1012).
[113] Ibid., 4.1.4 (LCC 21:1016).

by the Holy Spirit. But the authority of these pastors is not a magisterial authority, as it is for the Catholic Church, but a ministerial authority. It is the ministerial nature of the pastoral office that Paul highlighted to the Corinthian church: "What then is Apollos? What is Paul? Servants *through whom you believed*, as the Lord assigned to each" (1 Cor. 3:5, emphasis added)—not *from whom* you received faith. This same ministerial authority is emphasized for Apollos in another context: "he greatly *helped those who through grace had believed*" (Acts 18:27, emphasis added)—not *from whom* they had received grace so as to have faith. The church as the mother of Christians, when understood as serving as the Spirit-anointed minister of the grace of God through the preaching of the gospel and the celebration of the sacraments, is proper within an evangelical theological framework.

In summary, the doctrine of faith finds some overlap between Catholic and evangelical theology: faith is personal adherence, a disposition of trust; it is linked with understanding, free (noncoerced), necessary for salvation, and directed toward God as its object and the one to whom believers are joined in a personal relationship. But there are key differences as well: faith as infused (Catholic) versus faith as a non-infused virtue linked to God's gracious acts of conviction of sin, calling, justification, regeneration, adoption, and union with Christ (evangelical); the possibility of faith being lost; and faith's relationship to the church.

4

The Profession of Faith
(Part I, Section 2, Chapter I,
Article I–Chapter 3, Article 8)

The Doctrines of God, Angels, Humanity, and Sin; the Doctrines of the Person of Jesus Christ, the Incarnation, and the
Immaculate Conception of Mary; the Doctrine of the Work of
Jesus Christ; the Doctrines of Christ's Resurrection, Ascension,
and Second Coming; the Doctrine of the Holy Spirit

Having treated the doctrines of revelation and faith, the *Catechism* turns
next to twelve doctrines that flow from the Church's creeds, specifically, the
Apostles' Creed as supplemented by the Nicene-Constantinopolitan Creed
(abbreviated as the Nicene Creed).

The Doctrines of God, Angels, Humanity, and Sin: "I believe in God the Father almighty, creator of heaven and earth" (Sec. 2, Ch. I, Art. I)

There is one and only one God, whose name is "I am who I am" and who is
truth and love. This one and only living God is triune, eternally existing as
Father, Son, and Holy Spirit. Each of the three persons is eternally and fully
God and distinguishable by his eternal relationship to the other two (known
as the *ontological* Trinity: "It is the Father God who generates, the Son who
is begotten, and the Holy Spirit who proceeds")[1] and by his personal work
that is nonetheless the common work of all three (known as the *economic*

---

[1] CCC 254; citation is from the Fourth Lateran Council (1215). Where the three traditions of Christendom
(Roman Catholic, Protestant, and Eastern Orthodox) disagree is on the eternal procession of the Holy Spirit,
which will be discussed later.

Trinity).[2] Furthermore, God is almighty, and he created the universe and everything in it *ex nihilo* (out of nothing);[3] the *Catechism* explicitly denounces pantheism, dualism (Manichaeism), deism, and materialism, and avoids any explicit discussion of evolution.[4] In addition to creating all that exists, God upholds and sustains creation in existence and carries out his eternal purpose through his work of providence. The problem of evil must be considered in the context of the entire Christian faith—creation, fall, redemption, and consummation—and the free will defense seems to be the preferred approach to the problem.

The Apostles' Creed's confession that God is "Creator of heaven and earth" (Nicene Creed: "all that is, seen and unseen") leads to a brief discussion of the angels, which are spiritual, noncorporeal beings belonging to Christ, and which assist him in his mission of salvation. Some attention is given to the role of angels in the Church's liturgy—specifically, their assistance is invoked in the adoration of God—and to protection by guardian angels.

As for the creation of the visible universe, God created human beings as creatures who bear his image, which means that humanity alone is "able to know and love his creator," is "the only creature on earth that God has willed for its own sake," and is called to share in the very life of God

---

[2] For example, the triune God created the entire universe and everything it contains; this was the inseparable operation of the three persons. Yet the Father spoke the universe and its elements into existence (e.g., Gen. 1:3), the Son was the divine agent through whom it was created (John 1:3; Col. 1:15–16), and the Holy Spirit prepared and protected the original created world (Gen. 1:2) in anticipation of the divine fashioning of it into an inhabitable world for human beings.

[3] On the divine creation in relationship to modern theories of evolution, the *Catechism* points to "many scientific studies which have splendidly enriched our knowledge of the age and dimensions of the cosmos, the development of life-forms and the appearance of man. These discoveries invite us to even greater admiration for the greatness of the Creator, prompting us to give him thanks for all his works and for the understanding and wisdom he gives to scholars and researchers" (CCC 283). As for the biblical account of creation, the *Catechism* offers, "Scripture presents the work of the Creator symbolically as a succession of six days of divine 'work,' concluded by the 'rest' of the seventh day. On the subject of creation, the sacred text teaches the truths revealed by God for our salvation, permitting us to 'recognize the inner nature, the value, and the ordering of the whole of creation to the praise of God'" (CCC 337); citation is from Vatican Council II, *Lumen Gentium* 36.2. Pope John Paul II broached the issue of science and creation in his October 22, 1996, address before the Pontifical Academy of Sciences, explaining that, "some new findings lead us toward the recognition of evolution as more than an hypothesis." (The text is that of the English edition of *L'Osservatore Romano* and follows the other language editions of the pope's original message in French. It is not the text of the original English translation of the message in French.) The text of the papal address is accessible at http://www.ewtn.com/library/papaldoc/jp961022.htm.

[4] *Pantheism* is the view that everything is God, making him identical with, and thus dependent on, the creation. *Dualism*, or *Manichaeism*, is the position that two equal and eternal powers—for example, God and evil—exist and are locked in combat. Manichaeism was a dualistic movement that flourished in the early church and that captivated Augustine before he became a Christian. *Deism* is the perspective that God created the initial universe with its physical matter and physical laws and set it on its course, but he does not and cannot intervene (for example, through miraculous activity). A common metaphor for this position is that of a watchmaker who assembles the timing instrument with all of its mechanisms, then winds it up and lets it go, never to tinker with it again. *Materialism* is the philosophy that everything that exists can ultimately be explained by material realities and material processes; immaterial things like God and the human soul do not exist.

himself.[5] Given this dignity of personhood, the human being is "capable of self-knowledge, of self-possession and of freely giving himself and entering into communion with other persons."[6] Because all humans are image-bearers created by the one God, the unity of the human race encourages solidarity and love among all people everywhere.

Specifically, being created in the image of God means that a person is a complex being consisting of both a material aspect and an immaterial aspect. The latter element, or soul, "refers to the innermost aspect of man, that which is of greatest value to him, that by which he is most especially in God's image."[7] Still, this emphasis is not intended to denigrate or minimize the physical aspect of human beings, for the "human body shares in the dignity of 'the image of God': it is a human body precisely because it is animated by a spiritual soul."[8] This immaterial element and the material element are so intimately and intricately united that "one has to consider the soul to be the 'form' of the body," such that, in a human being, they "are not two natures united, but rather their union forms a single nature."[9] Theologically, then, Catholic anthropology holds to (1) *dichotomy* rather than *trichotomy*, that is, the human constitution consists of two aspects (body and soul) and not three (body, soul, and spirit);[10] (2) *creationism* rather than *traducianism*, that is, the soul is created immediately (i.e., out of nothing) by God and is not transmitted from parents to their children; and (3) the *immortality of the soul*, that is, "it does not perish when it separates from the body at death."[11]

The created genderedness of human beings as designed by God means that men and women are "equal as persons" who are alike made in the divine image, as well as different from each other for the purpose of being "'helpmate' to the other."[12] Together, then, men and women as stewards of God engage in the vocation of ruling over the created world.

Adam and Eve, the first human creatures created by God, "were

---

[5] CCC 356; citations are from Vatican Council II, *Gaudium et Spes* 12.3; 24.3.
[6] CCC 357.
[7] CCC 363.
[8] CCC 364.
[9] CCC 365.
[10] The *Catechism* does note that at times the soul and spirit are distinguished (e.g., 1 Thess. 5:23), concluding, "this distinction does not introduce a duality into the soul" but merely provides two ways of considering the one immaterial aspect of human beings (CCC 367).
[11] CCC 366.
[12] CCC 372. The *Catechism* interprets the account of Gen. 2:18–25 first in a generic way, as applying to all human beings as men and women, then in a specific way, as applying to a husband and wife in marriage.

constituted in an original 'state of holiness and justice.'"[13] Original holiness means that they shared in the life of God, with no fear of suffering or death. Original justice means that (1) individually, Adam and Eve each experienced an inner harmony within him/herself; (2) relationally, the two together experienced harmony between themselves; and (3) environmentally, they experienced harmony with their surrounding created world. Specifically, with regard to the first point, the spiritual faculties of Adam's soul (likewise for Eve) controlled his body and its passions so that "he was free from the triple concupiscence that subjugates him to the pleasures of the senses [lust], covetousness for earthly goods [greed], and self-assertion [pride], contrary to the dictates of reason."[14] Placed in the garden of Eden, Adam and Eve collaborated together with each other and with God in developing the created order.

Into this harmonious state another reality was introduced sometime at the origin of humanity. While some would explain this interruption "as merely a developmental flaw, a psychological weakness, a mistake, or the necessary consequence of an inadequate social structure, etc.," divine revelation presents it as the fall, "a primal event, a deed that took place at the beginning of the history of man."[15] Even before this debacle, the fall of a portion of the angels, who were originally created good, had taken place; they abused their free choice to rebel, rejected God and his reign, and thus committed an unforgivable sin. Satan and his minions, the demons, while wreaking havoc among the human race, are nonetheless providentially hemmed in by God and permitted to accomplish only what God wills. It was this Satan or the devil who engaged in "the mendacious seduction that led man to disobey God."[16]

In the midst of this satanic temptation, Adam and Eve wrestled with the divine prohibition regarding the tree of the knowledge of good and evil, which "symbolically evokes the insurmountable limits that man, being a creature, must freely recognize and respect with trust."[17] They did not follow God: "Man, tempted by the devil, let his trust in his Creator die in his heart and, abusing his freedom, disobeyed God's command. This is

---

[13] CCC 375; citation is from the *Canons and Decrees of the Council of Trent*, 5th session (June 17, 1546), *Decree Concerning Original Sin* 1 (Schaff, 2:88).
[14] CCC 377. For further discussion, see Kreeft, 62.
[15] CCC 387, 390 (emphasis removed).
[16] CCC 394.
[17] CCC 396.

what man's first sin consisted of. . . . In that sin man *preferred* himself to God and by that very act scorned him. He chose himself over and against God, against the requirements of his creaturely status and therefore against his own good."[18] The devastating consequences of this rebellious decision included the following: First, *the loss of original holiness*: Adam and Eve immediately fear God, and death—the penalty threatened for disobedience to the divine prohibition—enters into the human race. Second, *the loss of original justice*: the spiritual faculties of their souls no longer exercise dominion over their bodies with their passions; their interpersonal harmony is ruined and their relationship is now characterized by tensions, lust, and domination; and their harmony with the created order is broken, with work taking on a painful, arduous character.

But the consequences of the fall are not contained, affecting only Adam and Eve; rather, sin will spread universally to all human beings, as all people are implicated in Adam's sin. Original sin, or the "death of the soul,"[19] is transmitted from Adam to all human beings, and it is the sin with which all are born. The *Catechism* explains this transference mostly in terms of *realism* ("the whole human race is in Adam 'as one body of one man'");[20] that is, all human beings were present in Adam and thus actually sinned when he sinned. But its explanation has an element of *representation* as well: "Adam had received original holiness and justice not for himself alone, but for all human nature."[21] The transmission of original sin occurs by propagation; fallen human nature, devoid of original holiness and original justice, is transmitted to the entirety of the human race. Specifically, this is not personal sin; original sin is a state that is contracted, not an act of sin that is committed. Moreover, original sin does not result in total depravity and total inability: human nature "is wounded in the natural powers proper to it; subject to ignorance, suffering, and the dominion of death; and inclined to sin—an inclination to evil that is called 'concupiscence.'"[22] The Catholic Church's solution to the problem of original sin is the sacrament

---

[18] CCC 397–398.

[19] CCC 403; citation is from the *Canons and Decrees of the Council of Trent*, 5th session (June 17, 1546), *Decree Concerning Original Sin* 2 (Schaff, 2:85).

[20] CCC 404; citation is from Thomas Aquinas, *On Evil* 4, 1.

[21] CCC 404.

[22] CCC 405. The *Catechism* explicitly denounces Pelagianism, the view that the sin of Adam in no way affects the human race after him. It also explicitly denies the Reformers' doctrine of total depravity, the view "that original sin has radically perverted man and destroyed his freedom," and their doctrine of total inability, the view that identifies original sin with concupiscence, the tendency to evil that is "insurmountable" (CCC 406).

of Baptism, in particular infant Baptism, which forgives original sin and wipes away its corruption through regeneration, or the provision of a new spiritual nature.

Evangelical Assessment

The doctrine of God as affirmed by the *Catechism* is thoroughly biblical, consistent with the historical belief of the church throughout its existence, and held by all Catholics, Protestants, and Orthodox alike. The only difference appears with the ontological Trinity, specifically the eternal procession of the Holy Spirit. The *Catechism*, representing the Western Church tradition—Catholic and Protestant/evangelical—affirms "the Holy Spirit proceeds from the Father and the Son" and explains why the addition of the *filioque* clause ("and the Son") was proper.[23] The Orthodox tradition confesses the procession of the Holy Spirit from the Father and denies the *filioque*.[24]

Strong biblical support for this double procession can be marshaled and includes the following: The Holy Spirit is described (Rom. 8:9) as both the Spirit of God (i.e., the Father) and the Spirit of Christ (i.e., the Son); both the Father and the Son send the Holy Spirit on the day of Pentecost (John 14:16, 26; 15:26; 16:7), implying that he proceeds from both of them; and Christ breathed the Spirit on his disciples, implying that, together with the Father, the Son gives the Holy Spirit (Acts 2:33). Furthermore, the Orthodox objection (that the West's theology creates a situation in which there are two principles or sources of Holy Spirit) has been answered well by theologians such as Augustine. He explained that through one action of the Father and the Son together, the Spirit proceeds.[25] Catholic and evangelical theology of the procession of the Spirit are in full accord.

Between Catholic and evangelical theologies of creation, intramural disagreements exist over theistic evolution, old age creationism, young earth creationism, and other views. With regard to the doctrine of providence and its corollary, the problem of evil, Catholicism proposes the free will

---

[23] The Nicene Creed, as originally written, affirmed "the Holy Spirit proceeds from the Father." At the Third Council of Toledo (Spain) in 589, the *filioque* clause was added to the Creed, yielding the affirmation "the Holy Spirit proceeds from the Father *and the Son*."

[24] CCC 243–248.

[25] Specifically, in generating or begetting the Son, the Father established that the Spirit would proceed from both of them: "He [the Father] so begat him [the Son] as that the common Gift [the Holy Spirit] should proceed from him also, and the Holy Spirit should be the Spirit of both" (Augustine, *On the Trinity* 15.17/29 [NPNF[1] 3:216]).

defense,[26] a view that is also embraced by some proponents of evangelical theology.

The Catholic theology of angels finds accord with evangelical angelology, with these two exceptions. First, the Church's liturgical emphasis on joining with the angels in adoring God, entailing the invocation of their assistance, has no biblical basis and seems to be contradicted by Scripture. Certainly, angels worship God. Additionally, the church—including Christians who have died and are now with the Lord in heaven as members of the heavenly church, and Christians who by faith walk with him as members of the church on earth—joins with the angelic host in adoring God (Heb. 12:18–24). But as for the perspective that these God-adoring angels assist the church's worship, Scripture emphasizes that "angels long to look" into matters of salvation (which only human beings can experience; 1 Pet. 1:12) and that angels learn about "the manifold wisdom of God" through the church (Eph. 3:10), but the notion that they assist the church in its worship finds no scriptural support.

Second, the *Catechism*'s affirmation that "beside each believer stands an angel as protector and shepherd leading him to life"[27] needs to be cautiously affirmed, if at all. According to the book of Daniel (10:13, 20; 12:1), it appears that particular angels have been assigned to particular earthly nations, and Jesus suggests (Matt. 18:10) that specific angels protect children. The most compelling support for this view is in Acts (12:15), which presents the humorous story of Peter's release from prison and appearance at the door of the house in which the church was gathered to pray for his release. When told that the apostle was standing outside seeking entrance, the shocked disciples replied, "It is his angel!" However, to draw the conclusion from these passages that each person has a specific guardian angel assigned to him or her is speculative. Moreover, the view seems to overlook the biblical emphasis that God provides a host of angels to defend and help his people (e.g., 2 Kings 6:17; Luke 16:22). Accordingly, Calvin may be more on

---

[26] A common version of the free will defense is that, in creating the universe, God had to choose between creating a world in which no sin and evil would exist, and creating a world in which human beings would possess free will. In this latter case, sin and evil would indeed exist, because for the will of human beings to be absolutely free, it must be free to rebel against God in an abuse of its freedom, thereby introducing sin and evil into the world. If God had chosen the first option, the resultant world would have been a good creation. But in choosing the second option, God did something at least as good, if not even better, than the first option. In creating human beings with free will, a free will that would and did indeed rebel against him and thus introduce sin and evil into a good creation, God did nothing wrong; he is justified in his choice.
[27] CCC 336.

target: "We ought to hold as a fact that the care of each one of us is not the task of one angel only, but all with one consent watch over our salvation."[28]

Concerning the doctrine of humanity, Catholic and evangelical theology share broad strokes of agreement interspersed with some areas of disagreement. Agreement is found in the following affirmations: First, human beings alone are created in the divine image, which is the source of their dignity, the reason for their unique ability to enjoy a personal relationship with God, and the ground of the solidarity of the human race. Second, humans are complex beings, consisting of both material (the body) and (at least one) immaterial aspects. With respect to this latter element, most evangelicals hold to *dichotomy* (two constitutive aspects of human nature—the body and the soul, which is also called the spirit), in agreement with Catholic theology. However, some evangelicals hold to *trichotomy* (three constitutive aspects: one material element [the body] and two immaterial elements [the soul and the spirit]).[29] Both dichotomy and trichotomy stand over against *monism*, the view that human nature is simple, composed of a material aspect only.[30] Such a position is outside the pale of orthodox Christian belief, as it contradicts the biblical presentation of the intermediate state (2 Cor. 5:1–9)[31] and flies in the face of the historic position of Christianity. Furthermore, evangelical theology is divided over the issue of the origin of the immaterial element of human nature. Some hold to *creationism*, believing that God creates the soul out of nothing and joins it to material reality at conception;[32] this position is in agreement with Catholic theology.[33] Other evangelicals hold to *traducianism*, the view that the soul is passed on from parents to their children.[34] Still others are undecided on this issue or think

---

[28] Calvin, *Institutes* 1.14.7 (LCC 20:167).

[29] Augustine's fluctuating views regarding dichotomy and trichotomy can be followed in his *On Faith and the Creed* 10.23 (NPNF[1] 3:331); cf. *On the Soul and Its Origin* 4.3 (NPNF[1] 5:355).

[30] Only very rarely has anyone championed monism in terms of the one element being immaterial. George Berkeley's philosophy featured this notion of monism, as did German idealism.

[31] If human nature is monistic, consisting only of a material aspect, then upon the death of the body, a person cannot continue to exist as an immaterial being in the presence of Christ, in the intermediate state.

[32] Reformed evangelical theology traces its view to Leonard Riissen, *Francisci Turretini Compendium Theologiae* (Amsterdam, 1659), 7.52.2, in Heppe, 227–228; Amandus Polan, *Syntagma Theologiae Christianae* (Hanover, 1624–1625), 5.23, in Heppe, 229; Gisbert Voetius, *Selectarum Disputationum Theologicarum* (Utrecht, 1648–1669), 1.798, in Heppe, 229–230.

[33] Augustine pleaded ignorance as to the origin of the soul (Augustine, *On the Soul and Its Origin* 4.6[5] [NPNF[1] 5:356]; later retracted in Augustine, *Retractions* bk. 2, ch. 56 (NPNF[1] 5:310). Ultimately, he did not find the biblical case for either view convincing and held that God did not reveal truth about this matter (Augustine, *On the Soul and Its Origin* 1.17, 21–29 [NPNF[1] 5:324–328]); ibid., 4.5 (NPNF[1] 5:355–356).

[34] Evangelical Lutheran theology traces its view to Martin Luther, *Table Talk Recorded by John Mathesius* (LW 54:401); John Quenstedt, *Theologia Didactico-Polemica* 1.519 (Schmid, 166–167); Leonard Hutter, *Compendium Locorum Theologicorum* 319 (Schmid, 249). Though a Reformed theologian, William G. T. Shedd vigorously defended traducianism in his *Dogmatic Theology*, ed. Alan W. Gomes (Philipsburg, PA: P & R, 2003), 429–493.

a more holistic explanation—for example, William Hasker's emergent dualism or emergent personalism—is likely better.[35] Third, Catholic and evangelical theology agree that human existence does not end at death but continues for eternity.[36]

Fourth, Catholic and evangelical theology are in agreement that the fact that both men and women are made in the image of God means they are equal with respect to human personhood and they together exercise stewardship of the created order. The historical and contemporary disparagement of one or the other of the genders finds no support from Scripture and is contradicted by creation in the divine image. Indeed, the church should be a leader in encouraging men and women to honor, love, and respect one another as divine image-bearers. At the same time, both Catholic and evangelical theology affirm the divinely designed differences between men and women, but many evangelicals would not agree that the purpose for this created difference was so that the two may be "helpmate" to each other.[37] That men and women complement one another in fulfilling the cultural mandate—"Be fruitful and multiply and fill the earth and subdue it, and have dominion" (Gen. 1:28)—is certainly true: The divine purpose is that most men and most women will be married and have children, and that both men and women will contribute to the building of civilization. But the biblical narrative of the creation of the first woman (2:18–25) for the purpose of being "a helper fit for" the first man (v. 18) refers to God's plan to fashion Eve to be the wife of Adam; the idea of reciprocity—i.e., the two are helpmates for each other—is not present in the story. Indeed, this narrative becomes the basis for later biblical instruction concerning the loving headship of the husband and the submission of the wife (1 Cor. 11:2–16; cf. Eph. 5:22–33). Certainly, the interdependence of men and women is affirmed by Scripture; for example, Eve was taken from Adam, and ever since that event, every man who has ever lived has been born of a woman (1 Cor. 11:11–12). But the mutuality and interdependence that typifies the

---

[35] William Hasker, *The Emergent Self* (Ithaca and London: Cornell University Press, 1999); cf. John Cooper, *Body, Soul, and Life Everlasting: Biblical Anthropology and the Monism-Dualism Debate* (Grand Rapids, MI: Eerdmans; and Leicester, England: Apollos, 1989, 2000).

[36] There is some debate over the phrase "the immortality of the soul," used to describe the Catholic position, because the expression seems to reflect Greek philosophy more than biblical teaching. But the substance of the belief is held by both Catholic and evangelical theology.

[37] On this point, evangelicals are divided between complementarians and egalitarians. The first position is well represented by the Council on Biblical Manhood and Womanhood, and the second view is well represented by Christians for Biblical Equality. A similar division is present within the Catholic Church.

relationship between men and women in certain areas of life does not apply wholesale to the relationship between husbands and wives.

The first major area of disagreement in the doctrine of humanity concerns the Catholic concept of the original state of Adam and Eve. Evangelical theology shares the Catholic view that the first man and the first woman were created in a state of integrity, with (1) individual inner harmony, with no sin nature to produce a tendency toward evil; (2) relational harmony between themselves, with no embarrassment and shame to provoke a separation between the two; and (3) external harmony with the created order, with no disturbance in the environment to resist their exercise of dominion. But the point of disagreement comes with the Catholic notion that the soul of Adam (likewise for Eve)—specifically, his rationality—governed his passions and body. The first objection to be raised is the apparent identification of the image of God with reason or intellect, thus elevating one aspect of human nature above other aspects. Though Catholic theology can point to historical precedent for this view—for example, Irenaeus and Thomas Aquinas emphasized the intellect in their theologies of the image of God[38]—the biblical narratives of human creation in the divine image do not support it; indeed, they contain no hint that some potential inner struggle was headed off by reason controlling the passions and the body. On the contrary, Scripture presents the divine creation of human beings in a holistic fashion—"So God created man in his own image, in the image of God he created him; male and female he created them" (Gen. 1:27)— followed by an emphasis on how these holistically created human beings are to function: as stewards engaging in procreation and vocation so as to establish and build a thriving human civilization on earth (v. 28).[39] Moreover, the Catholic emphasis on the human soul—reason, intellect—as the seat of the image of God seems to betray more of an attachment to Platonic/ Gnostic philosophy than to Scripture.

The second major disagreement introduces the next topic and thus needs only a brief mention here: Catholic theology believes that the fall of Adam and Eve entailed a disruption of the soul's control over the passions

---

[38] Irenaeus, *Against Heresies* 4.4.3 (*ANF* 1:466); Thomas Aquinas, *Summa Theologica* pt. 1, q. 93.

[39] Indeed, biblical scholarship for the last century or so, through its study of ancient Near Eastern creation literature, has helpfully turned the discussion of the image of God away from substantive matters (the image consists of human rationality, morality, free will, or other attributes) to functional matters: human beings as divine image-bearers are designed for a working purpose—rulership.

and the body. Thus, a great reversal was introduced when sin entered the human race, with sinful human beings experiencing a loss of integrity and now being dominated by their lower elements. As will be explained later, evangelical theology holds that this Catholic belief shortchanges the fall's impact on all aspects of human nature, reason and intellect included.

Turning to the doctrine of sin, widespread agreement between Catholic and evangelical theology can be verified. More than an interruption and certainly not a myth, the fall was an event in space and time that devastated everything in existence as God had designed it. It was preceded by a fall in the angelic realm, which introduced an evil spiritual being, Satan, who would seek to murder—that is, rob of God-given life (John 8:44)—the first human beings through its lying seduction. Creating an atmosphere of trickery, Satan in the guise of a serpent tempted Eve to doubt God's word, question God's goodness, and disobey God's authority (Gen. 3:1–7). Adam, while not deceived by the machinations of the Evil One, sinned with his eyes wide open (1 Tim. 2:14). Disobedience. Unfaithfulness. Mistrust. Rebellion. Transgression. Trespass. Abuse of human freedom. Disregard for divinely imposed human limitation. Usurpation of the place of the Creator by his creatures. All of these expressions capture some aspect of the catastrophic event of the fall into sin, about which there is broad agreement between Catholic and evangelical theology.

Further agreements include the following: Adam and Eve immediately experienced fear of God, and the threat of death became a reality. Having a double sense, this death was at first a spiritual reality: Adam and Eve died in terms of being separated from God, cut off from the open, face-to-face relationship they had enjoyed with him up to the point of their fall. Later, they would die physically, returning to the dust of the ground from which they had been taken (Gen. 2:7; 3:19). Moreover, the former interpersonal harmony between the two was wrecked; henceforth, their relationship would be characterized by competition, lust, rebellion and harsh domination (3:16), and shame (2:25; 3:7). Further breakdown of a former harmony occurred with the creation in which Adam and Eve lived, as the fruitfulness of the original pristine world would be tempered, consigning them to hard labor for the rest of their lives (3:17–19). Finally, these devastating consequences of the fall reverberated far beyond their impact on the first human beings, spreading beyond and from them to ravage all human beings.

Before treating this doctrine of original sin, one important point, already mentioned above, must be addressed. This disagreement concerns the fall of Adam and Eve as resulting in a disruption of the soul's control over the passions and the body. This view elevates the human immaterial element—specifically, human reason or intellect—over the emotional and physical elements. As discussed earlier, this understanding of the image of God in human beings is overly reductionistic, fraught with difficulties, and should be abandoned. Moreover, the Catholic position minimizes the devastating effect of sin on human reason or intellect. This view is consistent with the first axiom of the Catholic theological system—the nature-grace interdependence—which fits sin under the realm of nature, thereby blunting sin's impact on nature or, in this case, on human nature governed by reason. An evangelical theology that takes a holistic view of the image of God—human beings in their entirety are created in the divine image—does not permit a dominating role for human reason or intellect ruling over passions and body. Such a view must posit an original instability within human beings as created, rather than seeing Adam and Eve as existing in an original state of integrity. Consequently, their fall into sin does not result in a loss of control by their higher nature so that their lower nature becomes dominant, but produces instead a state of corruption, the extensiveness and intensiveness of which is total and which is passed down as original sin to every human being since then. Finally, the evangelical critique of the nature-grace interdependence, with its tempered effect of sin on human nature, has already been offered (ch. 2).

It is with this doctrine of original sin that other important differences between Catholic and evangelical theology arise. While both agree that original sin is the state or condition into which all human beings are born as a result of the originating sin of Adam (Rom. 5:12–21; 1 Cor. 15:21–22), evangelical theology has several points of disagreement with Catholic theology's understanding of it. First, evangelicals differ among themselves as to how original sin is transmitted. Some evangelicals—e.g., from a Lutheran perspective—agree with Catholic theology's *realism* that original sin is passed down from parents to their children. Other evangelicals—e.g., from a Reformed perspective—embrace the view of *representation*; that is, because Adam was constituted by God as the head of the human race, when he sinned, he sinned as the representative of all humanity. As Adam went, so went all human beings, with the result that they all inherit original sin. Still other evangelicals *combine realism and representation*. They affirm that all human beings were seminally present in Adam when he sinned (realism); thus, original sin is transmitted from parents to their children. Because realism struggles to explain why only the first sin of Adam, and not all of his sins, is transmitted to the human race, this combined view also maintains that Adam was the head of the entire human race (representation). When he sinned and broke the covenant with God, his one sin affected all human beings, whom he represented; accordingly, they all inherit original sin from their representative head.[40]

Second, whereas Catholic theology affirms that human nature is weakened by original sin, it does not embrace total depravity and total inability, as do some versions of evangelical theology. *Total depravity* is the view that original sin impacts every aspect of human nature. It does not mean that human beings are as evil as they could possibly be, or that they lack a will or moral aptitude; rather, it has to do with the extensiveness of original sin. Total depravity means that every element of human nature—intellect/reason, feelings/sentiments, will/volition, body, motivations, purposing—is infected by sin. No element—e.g., reason, intellect, will—escapes the corrupting influence of original sin. *Total inability* is the position that original sin renders human beings incapable of doing anything to earn or merit divine favor; the intensity of the corrupting influence of original sin is such that it is insurmountable. Specifically, the freedom that sinful human beings possess is never exercised to do good, at least good with respect to pleasing God; human free will is enslaved by sin, so human beings sin as a matter of course.

Accordingly, evangelical theology joins Catholic theology in denouncing Pelagianism, which denied that Adam's sin affects human beings at all. But some varieties of evangelical theology depart from Catholic theology's denial of total depravity and total inability. They disagree with the Catholic view that, in some sense, human reason/will is sufficiently free so that, when moved by the grace of God, it is capable of cooperating with it. And they disagree with the Catholic notion that original sin does not include concupiscence, the

---

[40] For a succinct discussion of these positions, see John Murray, *The Imputation of Adam's Sin* (Grand Rapids, MI: Eerdmans, 1959); Henri Blocher, *Original Sin: Illuminating the Riddle*, New Studies in Biblical Theology (Grand Rapids, MI: Eerdmans, 1999).

proclivity to evil that is insurmountable. According to the Council of Trent, "This concupiscence, which the apostle sometimes calls sin, the holy Synod declares that the Catholic Church has never understood it to be called sin, as being truly and properly sin in those born again, but because it is of sin, and inclines to sin."[41] These versions of evangelical theology dissent from this position, insisting that fallen human nature, which produces the tendency to sin (concupiscence), is an aspect of original sin and thus incurs the wrath of God (Eph. 2:1–3). In summary, these varieties of evangelical theology maintain that, because of the pervasiveness of original sin (it infects every element of human nature and does not leave any aspect unaffected), and because of its perversity (original sin renders human beings incapable of doing anything that will fundamentally please God), all human beings are in dire straits before God and deserving of judgment, condemnation, and wrath.

The solution to this grave problem of original sin is, for Catholic theology, Baptism, especially infant Baptism. Through this sacrament, original sin is removed and the infant is regenerated, bringing salvation out of this hellish nightmare. Because a full treatment of that sacrament comes later in the *Catechism*, the evangelical assessment of Baptism will be postponed.

The Doctrine of the Person of Jesus Christ: ". . . and in Jesus Christ, his only Son, our Lord" (Sec. 2, Ch. 2, Art. 2)

The gospel, or good news, centers on the gracious act of God the Father in sending his Son for the purpose of rescuing divine image-bearers who have fallen into sin. As the gospel is focused on the Son of God, the Lord Jesus Christ, so is the *Catechism*. In its opening treatment of this doctrine, it notes that the name "Jesus" means "God saves"; the word "Christ" is the Greek translation of the Hebrew "Messiah," meaning "anointed one"; the title "Son of God" refers to the unique and eternal relationship of the second person of the Trinity to God the Father; and the title "Lord" indicates divine sovereignty.

Evangelical Assessment

This doctrine of the person of Christ is embraced fully by evangelical theology; indeed, this traditional theology serves as the historical foundation for the development of evangelical christology.

---

[41] *Canons and Decrees of the Council of Trent*, 5th session (June 17, 1546), *Decree Concerning Original Sin 5* (Schaff, 2:88). The references to "the apostle" are to Paul's affirmations in Rom. 6:12 and 7:8.

The Doctrine of the Incarnation and the Doctrine of the Immaculate Conception: "he was conceived by the power of the Holy Spirit, and was born of the Virgin Mary" (Sec. 2, Ch. 2, Art. 3)

The second person of the Trinity, the preexistent Word of God, the eternal Son of God became incarnate (literally, "in flesh") about two thousand years ago as Jesus of Nazareth. This incarnation had four purposes: to accomplish salvation for fallen human beings (1 John 4:10, 14; 3:5); to demonstrate the love of God (Rom. 5:8; 1 John 4:9); to be a model of holiness for redeemed people (Matt. 11:29; John 14:6; 15:12); and to make Christians partakers of the divine nature (2 Pet. 1:4). The biblical warrant for the doctrine of the incarnation includes Philippians 2:5–8 and Hebrews 10:5–7; belief in the incarnation is "the distinctive sign of Christian faith," according to 1 John 4:2.

This belief entails commitment to the full deity and full humanity of the God-man. The *Catechism* explicitly denounces the following historical heresies:

- *gnostic docetism:* the denial of the true humanity of the incarnate Son;
- *Arianism:* the denial of the true deity of the Son of God; countered by the Council of Nicea (325) and, later, the First Council of Constantinople (381), which insisted that the Son is *homoousios*—of the same substance or nature as the Father;
- *Nestorianism:* the belief that the divine person of God's Son joined to the human person of Jesus of Nazareth; opposed (431) by the Council of Ephesus's confession that two natures united in one person;
- *monophysitism/Eutychianism:* the view that the divine nature so absorbed the human nature that the latter did not continue in the incarnation, or, alternatively, that the two natures fused to form a hybrid entity, a type of "d ^{h} i ^{u} v ^{m} i ^{a} n ^{n} e" nature; contradicted (451) by the Council of Chalcedon's affirmation that each nature retained its specific properties and did not undergo change or fusion with the other nature;
- *Apollinarianism:* a truncation of the humanity of Christ, with the Logos, or divine Word, replacing the immaterial aspect of the God-man such that the only element of human nature that he took on was his body; refuted by the statement of the Council of Ephesus (also, later, the Council of Chalcedon) that the Son assumed a rational (i.e., human) soul.

The Church's christology is also informed by the Second Council of Constantinople (553), which maintained that the person who was crucified was one and the same with the second person of the Trinity; the Third Council of Constantinople (681), which denounced *monothelitism*, the view that Christ had only one will; and the Second Council of Nicea (787), which permitted the representation of Christ's body in holy images. Accordingly, the Church affirms that, in the incarnation, the eternal Son of God assumed, or took on, a complete human nature consisting of both a material aspect (a body) and an immaterial aspect (a soul, with intellect and will). It confesses that the God-man consists of two natures—a fully divine nature and a fully human nature—in one person, Jesus Christ.

Associated with the incarnation is an important aspect of Catholic theology, part of its doctrine of Mary. Jesus Christ "was conceived by the power of the Holy Spirit," meaning that the Spirit was "sent to sanctify the womb of the Virgin Mary and divinely fecundate [i.e., render fertile] it, causing her to conceive the eternal Son of the Father in a humanity drawn from her own."[42] Biblical support for this powerful work of the Holy Spirit is Luke 1:34–35 (cf. Matt. 1:18–25). This was the divine side of the incarnation.

As for the human side of the incarnation, the *Catechism* affirms several important points in its doctrine of Mary, beginning with her predestination: Mary was eternally ordained to become the mother of Jesus. Indeed, "from all eternity God chose for the mother of his Son . . . 'a virgin betrothed to a man whose name was Joseph, of the house of David; and the virgin's name was Mary' [Luke 1:26–27]."[43] Importantly, God "willed that the Incarnation should be preceded by assent on the part of the predestined mother, so that just as a woman [Eve] had a share in the coming of death, so also should a woman [Mary] contribute to the coming of life."[44]

This participation on Mary's part was prepared for by her immaculate conception. This doctrine, which was proclaimed by Pope Pius IX in his encyclical *Ineffabilis Deus* (December 8, 1854), stated, "The most Blessed Virgin Mary was, from the first moment of her conception, by a singular grace and privilege of almighty God and by virtue of the merits of Jesus Christ, Savior of the human race, preserved immune from all stain of original sin."[45] Additionally, Mary was "redeemed, in a more exalted fashion, by

---

[42] CCC 485.
[43] CCC 488.
[44] Ibid.; citation is from Vatican Council II, *Lumen Gentium* 56; cf. 61.
[45] CCC 491. The encyclical is accessible at: http://www.papalencyclicals.net/Pius09/p9ineff.htm.

reason of the merits of her Son"[46] and was blessed by God more than any other human being. Moreover, by this same divine grace, "Mary remained free of every personal sin her whole life long."[47] By this singular reality, Mary was well prepared to become the mother of the Savior, and the words of the angel Gabriel at the annunciation echo rightly: he salutes her as "full of grace." Mary's response, a free assent to the angelic announcement, was the obedience of faith: "Behold, I am the handmaid of the Lord; let it be [done] to me according to your word" (Luke 1:28–38). "Espousing the divine will for salvation wholeheartedly, without a single sin to restrain her, she gave herself entirely to the person and to the work of her Son."[48] The contrast between Mary's obedience of faith and Eve's response when tempted is a stark one, as underscored by several early church fathers: "The knot of Eve's disobedience was untied by Mary's obedience: what the virgin Eve bound through her disbelief, Mary loosed by her faith. . . . Death through Eve, life through Mary."[49]

From her immaculate conception and obedience of faith in joining herself to the divine plan of salvation flows Mary's divine motherhood: She is *theotokos*, literally, "the one who bears [the one who is] God,"[50] or, for short, "the Mother of God."[51] Accordingly, the Son of God was conceived in her womb by the Holy Spirit, not by means of sexual intercourse with Joseph (or any other man, for that matter); hers was a virginal conception. Moreover, Mary remained a virgin during childbirth; her physical integrity was not compromised by the birth process.[52] Furthermore, she remained a virgin throughout her entire life; Mary is called "*Aeiparthenos*, the 'Ever-virgin.'"[53] This means that Mary, even after the birth of Jesus, never engaged in sexual intercourse with Joseph (or any other man). Apparent biblical references to the brothers and sisters of Jesus (Mark 3:31–35; 6:3; 1 Cor. 9:5; Gal. 1:19; Matt. 13:55; 28:1) are to his close relations, not his actual nuclear family members. Such perpetual virginal integrity is "the sign of

---

[46] CCC 492; citation is from Vatican Council II, *Lumen Gentium* 53, 56.

[47] CCC 493.

[48] CCC 494.

[49] Ibid.; citations are from Irenaeus, *Against Heresies* 3.22.4 (*ANF* 1455); Epiphanius, *Heresies* 78.

[50] Jaroslav Pelikan, *Mary through the Centuries* (Cambridge: Yale University Press, 1998), 55.

[51] As first affirmed by the Council of Ephesus (431), the word is a combination of two Greek words, θεός (*theos*), God; and τόκος (*tokos*), childbirth.

[52] According to Ludwig Ott, "Mary gave birth in miraculous fashion without opening of the womb and injury to her hymen, and consequently without pain" (Ludwig Ott, *Fundamentals of Catholic Dogma*, ed. James Canon Bastible, trans. Patrick Lynch [Rockford, IL: Tan, 1960], 205). Aquinas attempted to provide reasons why Mary's intact condition was fitting for the birth of Jesus (Thomas Aquinas, *Summa Theologica* pt. 3, q. 28, art. 2).

[53] CCC 499; citation is from Vatican Council II, *Lumen Gentium* 52.

her faith 'unadulterated by any doubt'"[54] and manifests Mary's sinlessness throughout her life. She is also "the symbol and the most perfect realization of the Church,"[55] which itself becomes a mother by giving its members the new birth through preaching and Baptism, while retaining itself as a virgin, faithful and obedient to its spouse, Jesus Christ.

Conceived by the Holy Spirit and born of the Virgin Mary, the Son of God became incarnate, being born in a normal way and experiencing the development of a real and fully human being. The *Catechism* traces his early life and three-year ministry under the heading "the mysteries of Christ's life."[56] These include revelation (he reveals God the Father), redemption (including his passive and active obedience in life and death), and recapitulation (he summed up human history while reversing the disobedience of Adam), accomplishing what he did as a substitution for human beings whom he came to save and as a model for his disciples to follow. Union with him makes people participants in his mysteries. The specific events in his life are detailed in the *Catechism*: the promise of Christ's coming in the Old Testament; the preparation for his coming through John the Baptist; Jesus's birth; his infancy and hidden early life (on which light is shown only in the episode of Jesus remaining behind in the temple at the age of twelve); his baptism to initiate his public ministry, followed immediately by his temptations in the wilderness; his announcement of the kingdom of God through proclamation, messianic signs (miracles and exorcisms), and the commissioning of twelve disciples, to whom (with Peter at their head) Jesus gave the keys of the kingdom; his transfiguration; and his ascent to and entrance into Jerusalem.

Evangelical Assessment

The doctrine of the incarnation of Jesus Christ, the *Catechism*'s denunciation of the historical Christological heresies, and its emphasis on both the full deity and the full humanity of Jesus Christ resonate fully with evangelical theology; indeed, such traditional formulations and censures provide the historical framework for the evangelical doctrine of the incarnation. Moreover, the *Catechism*'s affirmation that Jesus Christ "was conceived

---

[54] CCC 506 (emphasis removed); citation is from Vatican Council II, *Lumen Gentium* 63; cf. 1 Cor. 7:34–35.
[55] CCC 507.
[56] CCC 512–560.

by the power of the Holy Spirit," meaning that the Spirit miraculously overshadowed Mary so as to render this young virgin pregnant with the Son of God (who, at the moment of this conception, assumed a full human nature), is embraced by evangelicals as well. This divine side of the incarnation is unmistakably supported by Scripture (Matt. 1:18–25; Luke 1:34–35).

A deep division between Catholic and evangelical theology comes over the next point, about the human side of the incarnation. Almost all of the *Catechism*'s teachings about Mary are challenged and rejected by evangelicals. Still, three commonalities about her are shared. The first is acknowledgment of and gratitude for the unique role Mary played in the incarnation of the Son of God. Specifically, the recognition of her as *theotokos* (literally, "bearer of God"[57]), in terms of the historical sense that the one whom Mary bore was fully God,[58] unites Catholics and evangelicals.[59] A second agreement is Mary's stellar example of faith and obedience, as demonstrated in her response to the annunciation (Luke 1:26–38) and her personal suffering tied to the life and death of her son (Luke 2:35; John 19:25–27). The third commonality is calling her "blessed" (Luke 1:48) because of the mighty work that God did on her behalf and, through her, on behalf of all human beings in fulfillment of his promise of salvation (Luke 1:46–55).

On all other Marian doctrines, Catholic theology and evangelical theology part company. Four disagreements separate the two positions. First, the *Catechism*'s emphasis on Mary's predestination, which it then ties to her "free cooperation" and an alleged divine design for a woman to parallel Eve and undo her disobedience, is both exaggerated and not grounded properly. That God predestines individuals for salvation (e.g., Eph. 1:4, 11) and for specific service (e.g., Jer. 1:5; Gal. 1:15–16) is clearly biblical, so in one sense there is nothing remarkable about Mary's predestination to become the mother of Jesus Christ. Accordingly, Catholic theology's elevation of Mary (describing her as "the exalted Daughter of Sion," adding that "after a long period of waiting the times are fulfilled in her . . . and the new plan of salvation is established"[60]) is exaggerated. Indeed, Scripture itself ties

---

[57] As noted earlier, Jaroslav Pelikan renders the translation as "the one who gives birth to the one who is God" (Pelikan, *Mary Through the Centuries*, 55).
[58] This sense was at the heart of the affirmation at the Council of Ephesus (431), which battled against the heretical christology of Nestorius.
[59] However, evangelical theology denies *theotokos* as a statement about some kind of exalted status for Mary, which is a common misconception of its historical meaning.
[60] CCC 489; citation is from Vatican Council II, *Lumen Gentium* 55.

the fulfillment of the lengthy time of waiting not to Mary but to Jesus: "But *when the fullness of time had come*, God sent forth *his Son*, born of woman, born under the law, to redeem those who were under the law, so that we might receive adoption as sons" (Gal. 4:4–5, emphasis added).[61] This correction is not to deny the uniqueness of Mary's predestination to her particular role; after all, as Vatican Council II affirms, she is "already prophetically foreshadowed in the promise of victory over the serpent which was given to our first parents after their fall into sin (cf. Gen. 3:15). Likewise she is the virgin who shall conceive and bear a son, whose name shall be called Emmanuel (cf. Is. 7:14; Mic. 5:2–3; Mt. 1:22–23)."[62] The one and only Son of the Father became incarnate as the one and only God-man, and only one woman—Mary—was chosen to be the one through whom he would be conceived. But Catholic theology seems to initiate the exalted status of Mary with its emphasis on her predestination.

Accompanying this focus on Mary's predestination is the assertion that "to prepare a body for him [the Son], he [God the Father] wanted the free cooperation of a creature."[63] Echoes of the nature-grace interdependence are readily heard in this statement. According to the Catholic system, nature is capable of receiving grace; indeed, nature must cooperate with grace for grace to become activated. This nature-grace interdependence has already been critiqued. A specific criticism of its manifestation in the doctrine of Mary will now be offered: According to the Catholic theology of freedom, human beings possess libertarian free will, or "power to contrary," meaning that in their decisions and actions, they are able by the grace of God either to assent to his design or, refusing to cooperate with divine grace, to disobey his purpose. Applying this to Mary's response to the angel's announcement that she would become the mother of the Son of God, Mary as an ordinary human being could have either assented or refused the divine will. Because this latter option could not possibly be actualized, Mary had to be uniquely prepared to render with certainty a positive response. This preparation will be treated in the second disagreement—the immaculate conception—below.

---

[61] The two phrases "born of woman" and "born under the law" are dependent clauses and should not be misconstrued as receiving the emphasis in the statement, as the *Catechism* seems to do. Interestingly, the *Catechism* begins its discussion with the citation "God sent forth his Son," which is the main clause of Gal. 4:4, but it quickly turns to a discussion of Mary's predestination.

[62] Vatican Council II, *Lumen Gentium* 55 (VC II-1, 415).

[63] CCC 488.

Additionally, her predestination is tied to an alleged divine plan for Mary to be a parallel to Eve and, by her obedience, to reverse the disobedience of Eve. No biblical support for this idea is forthcoming, but an early tradition, arising from Justin Martyr,[64] Irenaeus,[65] and Tertullian,[66] drew this parallelism:

first Adam   second Adam   ‖ ‖   first Eve   second Eve
(Adam)   (Jesus Christ)   (Eve)   (Mary)
disobedience   *obedience*   *disobedience*   *obedience*

Biblical support for the first parallel comes from Paul's discussion in Romans 5:12–21 (cf. 1 Cor. 15:45–49); through his obedience, Jesus the second Adam does indeed undo the disobedience of the first Adam. But no biblical parallel is found for the Mary-Eve relationship. Accordingly, evangelicals dismiss Catholic theology's presentation of Mary's predestination and consent that rendered her the divinely designed parallel to Eve.

As noted above, Mary's consent to God's predestination entailed her free cooperation with that divine plan. But for Mary to grant her approval, she needed to be prepared: "In fact, in order for Mary to be able to give the free assent of her faith to the announcement of her vocation, it was necessary that she be wholly borne by God's grace."[67] A key element in this gracious preparation for her consent was Mary's immaculate conception, which is the second disagreement between Catholic theology and evangelical theology.

To review, this is the doctrine: "The most Blessed Virgin Mary was, from the first moment of her conception, by a singular grace and privilege of almighty God and by virtue of the merits of Jesus Christ, Savior of the human race, preserved immune from all stain of original sin."[68] At the same time, Catholic theology maintains that Mary was "redeemed, in a

[64] Justin Martyr, *Dialogue with Trypho the Jew* 100 (ANF 1:249).
[65] Irenaeus, *Against Heresies* 3.22.4 (ANF 1:455); 5.19.1 (ANF 1:547).
[66] Tertullian, *On the Flesh of Christ* 17 (ANF 3:536).
[67] CCC 490.
[68] CCC 491. The relevant encyclical is accessible at: http://www.papalencyclicals.net/Pius09/p9ineff.htm.

more exalted fashion, by reason of the merits of her Son."[69] Such gracious work was extended throughout her entire life, that "Mary remained free of every personal sin."[70] Uniquely blessed, more than any other human being, by divine grace, she was made ready to become the mother of the Son of God. This preparedness is clearly seen when the angel Gabriel approaches and salutes her as "full of grace" (Luke 1:28). Mary's free—and graciously prepared—response was the obedience of faith: "Behold, I am the handmaid of the Lord; let it be [done] to me according to your word" (Luke 1:38). Conceived without a sin nature, born without original sin, and preserved free from all sin, she was enabled to give her wholehearted consent to the divine plan for her to become the mother of Jesus Christ.[71]

Evangelical objections to this Marian doctrine focus on the Catholic misinterpretation of its alleged biblical support.[72] Specifically, in Luke 1:26–38, the narrative of the annunciation centers on God and his powerful salvation, not on Mary. Beverly Gaventa describes the story:

> Luke identifies Mary with the leanest of descriptions, especially when considered against the role about to be handed to her. He introduces her by means of a report that Gabriel is sent by God to Nazareth in Galilee to "a virgin engaged to a man by the name of Joseph, from the house of David, and the name of the virgin is Mary" (Luke 1:26–27). By stunning contrast with his introduction of Elizabeth and Zechariah, Luke says not a word about Mary's righteousness, her faithfulness to the Law, or her family of origin (see 1:5–25). Nothing in the introduction of Mary qualifies her for this role apart from God's own favor dispensed to her. . . . As Joel Green has put it, Mary "is not introduced in any way that would recommend her to us as particularly noteworthy or deserving of honor. In light of the care with which other characters are introduced and portrayed as women and men of status in Luke 1–2, this is remarkable."[73]

---

[69] CCC 492; citation is from Vatican Council II, *Lumen Gentium* 53, 56. According to Pope John Paul II, this redemption has to do with "sharing in the salvific and sanctifying grace and in that love which has its beginning in the 'Beloved,' the Son of the Eternal Father" (Pope John Paul II, *Redemptoris Mater* [March 28, 1978], 10).
[70] CCC 493.
[71] CCC 494.
[72] In the following comments, I interact with *Redemptoris Mater*, which is a biblical theology of Mary (accessible at http://www.vatican.va/holy_father/john_paul_ii/encyclicals/documents/hf_jp-ii_enc_25031987_redemptoris -mater_en.html).
[73] Beverly Gaventa, "Nothing Will Be Impossible with God," in Carl E. Braaten and Robert W. Jenson, eds., *Mary: Mother of God* (Grand Rapids, MI: Eerdmans, 2004), 23–25. As Joel Green adds elsewhere, "Her insignificance seems to be her primary significance for the Lucan narrative" (Joel Green, "Blessed Is She Who Believed," in Beverly Roberts Gaventa and Cynthia L. Rigby, eds., *Blessed One: Protestant Perspectives on Mary* [Louisville: Westminster John Knox, 2002], 14).

These observations urge caution about finding an exaggerated role for Mary in this narrative.

Moreover, in his annunciation, the angel makes three affirmations: using lofty language and Old Testament terminology, he describes who Mary's son Jesus will be; the angel explains that the power of the Holy Spirit will bring about the incarnation; and he illustrates from Elizabeth's miraculous pregnancy that "nothing will be impossible with God" (Luke 1:37).[74] Accordingly, Mary's response to Gabriel's announcement—"Let it be done to me" (γένοιτό μοι; *genoito moi*)—is optative, not imperative, as Catholic theology takes it. Mary is not expressing her fiat[75] (i.e., her authoritative decree to Gabriel/God); rather, she expresses her wish to submit to God's will, which has been communicated to her by Gabriel's final words, "nothing will be impossible with God" (v. 37). This text is not about Mary and her unique preparation; it is about the power of God to effect the incarnation of his Son.

What is key is that Mary responds with faith to the angel's word about the identity of her Son Jesus, the powerful overshadowing of the Holy Spirit, and the impossibility of God finding this virginal conception impossible to do. Mary responds rightly to Gabriel's announcement, and for her response, evangelicals look to her as a stellar example of faith and obedience—but not because of her "entirely special and exceptional" place in the divine plan, not because of "the extraordinary greatness and beauty of her whole being," and not because of her "perfect cooperation with 'the grace of God that precedes and assists.'"[76] This is the notion of exceptional perfection, but it is absent from the biblical account; indeed, it completely misses the point of the passage. What is to transpire within Mary's womb is impossible for Mary as a human being. Add as she might her obedience of faith, cooperation, or whatever, none of this changes the impossible into possible; nothing that Mary is or does is "decisive on the human level" in contributing to this miracle.[77] Certainly, there is great blessing both to Mary and to all humanity because of her obedience, but she believed "that there would be a fulfillment of what was spoken to her

---

[74] Gabriel's final assertion is well supported by Old Testament illustrations and statements; e.g., Gen. 18:10–15; Job 42:2–3; Isa. 50:2; 59:1; Jer. 32:17; Zech. 8:6. It is echoed later in Luke's Gospel (18:24–27).
[75] Pope John Paul II, *Redemptoris Mater* 13.
[76] Ibid., 8, 9, 11, 13.
[77] Ibid., 13.

from the Lord" (Luke 1:45); that is, she believed that *God himself* would fulfill his promised word.

Furthermore, Gabriel's address to her—"Hail, full of grace, the Lord is with you" (Luke 1:28)[78]—is misunderstood by Catholic theology. "Full of grace" is certainly not her new and real name.[79] Nor does the adjective "full" signify that Mary is more blessed than any other human being ever was; this notion betrays a misunderstanding of grace as some type of substance or commodity that is infused into people and that is capable of increase or decrease (this topic will be discussed later). This misunderstanding further contributes to the mistaken notion of Mary's exceptional and perfect cooperation in the incarnation. As Nancy Duff explains,

> In contrast, for [evangelical] theology this emphasis on perfection contradicts the doctrine of incarnation summarized in Gabriel's proclamation that "the Lord is with you." That Mary was full of grace does not mean that she was created without sin in order to be *worthy* of giving birth to the Son of God, for God enters a world that is *un*worthy of the presence of God, a world that is sinful and broken. If Mary must be perfect in order to be worthy of carrying the Savior, the message is lost. . . . Mary's perfection . . . presents a field of holiness capable of receiving God rather than the sinful and unworthy world in which God chooses to be present.[80]

Again, the axiom of the nature-grace interdependence prompts the Catholic system to misunderstand Mary and her exceptional role (the realm of nature) as being capable of receiving divine grace.

Accordingly, evangelicals should embrace Mary and her example of faith and obedience without elevating her above the rest of humanity endued with the grace of God, placing her in a category all by herself and rendering her example as unattainable for all others. Duff offers this important correction:

> In spite of their rejection of Mary's perfection, [evangelicals] have, nevertheless, sometimes allowed Mary to be understood as the ideal woman. Mary's passive acceptance of Gabriel's pronouncement, her obedience, and the absence of resistance or rebellion . . . have at times

---

[78] Ibid., 8.
[79] Ibid.
[80] Nancy Duff, "Mary, Servant of the Lord," in Gaventa and Rigby, *Blessed One*, 64.

been held up as the ideal model for women of faith to follow. This notion of Mary as an ideal woman or even an ideal disciple, however, is
actually inconsistent with [evangelical] theology. God does not encounter Mary or any of us as ideals, nor does God transform us into ideals.
We are like Mary, real human beings of flesh and spirit, body and soul,
in need of the power of God as we seek to give glory to the One who
saves and sustains us in grace. Mary, like all of us, was called not into
perfection but into discipleship.[81]

Third, evangelical theology disagrees with Catholic theology's insistence on "Mary's real and perpetual virginity," again tracing this wrong
idea to a lack of biblical warrant or a misinterpretation of Scripture. That
Mary was a virgin when she conceived the Son of God in her womb is
categorically true; both the Gospel of Matthew (1:18, 25) and the Gospel
of Luke (1:27, 34) underscore that Mary had never engaged in sexual intercourse with Joseph (or any other man, for that matter) resulting in the
conception of Jesus.[82] Indeed, his conception in the womb of Mary, a virgin,
was a miracle. Matthew 1:25 further notes that she did not engage in intercourse during the time of her pregnancy. But the idea that, in giving birth,
Mary's virginity was preserved intact is not affirmed in Scripture; indeed,
it is contradicted by the very simple and straightforward account of the
event: "And she gave birth to her firstborn son and wrapped him in swad-
dling cloths and laid him in a manger, because there was no place for them
in the inn" (Luke 2:7). There is no hint of a miraculous, virginity-preserving
intervention at Jesus's birth. What is more, after this birth, Mary did engage in sexual intercourse with Joseph, as described in Matthew (1:24–25):
"He took his wife, but knew her not until she had given birth to a son."
The word "until" (ἕως; *heōs*), used as a conjunction, indicates an end point
to an ongoing state of things.[83] That is, while Joseph did not engage in
intercourse with Mary during the entire time of their engagement (which
corresponded to the nine months of her pregnancy), they did so engage
after the birth of Jesus. This fact is confirmed by references to Jesus being

---

[81] Ibid., 65.

[82] Affirmation or denial of the virgin birth was one of the major points of division between evangelical theology (affirmation) and liberal Protestant theology (denial) in the first part of the twentieth century.

[83] It is true that "until" can connote an ongoing state of things that continues past the specified time, which is indicated for its particular importance rather than as an end point. For example, if I exclaim, "I will be a Chicago Cubs fan *until* they win the World Series!" I am not indicating that as soon as the Cubs win the championship, I will cease to be a fan. But in its twenty-five occurrences in the Gospel of Matthew, this sense of "until" is not found, making it highly unlikely that it is Matthew's sense in 1:24–25.

Mary's "firstborn son" (Luke 2:7), and to his brothers and sisters (Matt. 12:46 [par. Mark 3:31; Luke 8:19]; 13:55–56; Acts 1:14). The *Catechism* misidentifies these brothers and sisters as "the sons of another Mary, a disciple of Christ, whom St. Matthew significantly calls 'the other Mary' . . . [making them] close relations of Jesus, according to an Old Testament expression."[84] Catholic theology's embrace of the perpetual virginity after the birth of Jesus is not supported by Scripture.[85]

A fourth and final evangelical objection to this Marian doctrine moves from interaction with Catholic biblical (mis)interpretations to the Church's elevation of its Tradition regarding Mary over Scripture. Because criticism of the Scripture-plus-Tradition formula has already been offered,[86] it will not be repeated. Rather, it will suffice here to contrast key biblical affirmations relevant to our discussion—all human beings are conceived with a sin nature, born with original sin, and engage in sin throughout their entire lifetime—with the Church's Tradition regarding Mary: she was conceived without a sin nature, born without original sin, and preserved free from all sin throughout her entire life.[87] Tradition flatly contradicts Scripture; thus, Catholic theology of Mary is based on unchastened Tradition. As the evangelical participants in Evangelicals and Catholics Together affirmed, "The doctrine of the Immaculate Conception is incongruent with Sacred Scripture because it exempts Mary from original sin and declares that she is thus saved by Jesus in a unique manner."[88]

In summary, while three commonalities—Mary as *theotokos*, a stellar example for Christians, and blessed—are shared between Catholic theol-

---

[84] CCC 500. For James and Joseph—called "brothers of Jesus" (Matt. 13:55)—being the sons of "the other Mary," the *Catechism* references Matt. 28:1; cf. Matt. 27:56; but neither of these verses gives any clue as to the other Mary being the mother of James and Joseph. For the Old Testament expression, the *Catechism* references Gen. 13:8; 14:16; 29:15; etc.

[85] Catholic theology does make appeals to Old Testament types that prefigured the virginity of Mary, including her perpetual virginity. One is the ark of the covenant and the temple, upon which the Holy Spirit descended with glory, which are allegedly types of the Spirit's descent upon the womb of Mary. A second, the divine command that the outer gate of the sanctuary of the temple should be shut (Ezek. 44:1–3), is an alleged type of Mary's perpetual virginity. A third is the description of the woman in Song of Solomon: "A garden locked is my sister, my bride, a spring locked, a fountain sealed" (4:12). These appeals do indeed find early church support but are clearly fanciful and exaggerated, and the lack of the New Testament's appeal to them in its presentations of the Virgin Mary steers evangelicals clear of such whimsical typology.

[86] Chapter 3.

[87] Sadly, the Catholic (mis)interpretation of three passages—John 2:1–11; Luke 11:27–28; Mark 3:20–35 (esp. vv. 20–21 and 31–35)—as presented in *Redemptoris Mater* obscures Jesus's distancing of himself from his mother that is underscored in those texts. Such (mis)understanding of Scripture perpetuates the (wrong) notion of the lifelong sinlessness of Mary.

[88] Evangelicals and Catholics Together, "Do Whatever He Tells You: The Blessed Virgin Mary in Christian Faith and Life" (November 2009), section entitled, "An Evangelical Word to Catholics," 3. Accessible at http://www .firstthings.com/article/2009/11/do-whatever-he-tells-you-the-blessed-virgin-mary-in-christian-faith-and-life.

ogy and evangelical theology of Mary, more disagreement than agreement exists. These mistaken claims about Mary—her predestination for cooperation in the divine plan to be a parallel to the first Eve, her preparation for such a role through her immaculate conception, her perpetual virginity—are due to either poor interpretation of Scripture or elevating an unchastened Tradition above Scripture.[89]

The remainder of the *Catechism*'s teachings about the life of Christ is very biblically grounded and traditionally presented, with little to which evangelicals will object. Of concern is its presentation of Jesus's circumcision as prefiguring "that 'circumcision of Christ' which is Baptism";[90] some speculative material about Jesus's early hidden life and its application for people today;[91] the emphasis on Baptism as assimilating Christians to Jesus;[92] and the elaboration on "the college of the Twelve" as establishing the papacy centered on Peter.[93] These objections will be treated in other sections dealing with the sacrament of Baptism and the Church's hierarchy.

The Doctrine of the Work of Jesus Christ: "Jesus Christ suffered under Pontius Pilate, was crucified, died, and was buried" (Sec. 2, Ch. 2, Art. 4)

The life of Jesus culminates in his cross and resurrection, and the *Catechism* devotes its next two sections to these two critical events at the heart of the gospel. The circumstances leading up to the cross include Jesus challenging the Jewish people of his day, particularly the religious leaders, with respect to three essential institutions: the law, the temple, and faith. Though Jesus did not abolish the law (of the old covenant), he did fulfill it (Matt. 5:17–19) and thus provided its authoritative interpretation in light of the grace of the new covenant that he would institute. Additionally, Jesus redeemed human beings, all of whom have transgressed the law, from its curse. While Jesus

---

[89] More discussion on the doctrine of Mary is forthcoming in chapter 5 under the topic of the doctrine of the church. For a collaborative book on the doctrine of Mary from Catholic and Anglican perspectives, see Tim Perry and Daniel Kendall, *The Blessed Virgin Mary* (Grand Rapids, MI: Eerdmans, 2013). Cf. Tim Perry, *Mary for Evangelicals: Toward an Understanding of the Mother of Our Lord* (Downers Grove, IL: IVP Academic, 2006).
[90] CCC 527.
[91] CCC 531–533.
[92] CCC 537.
[93] CCC 551–553. For example, the *Catechism* explains the power of the keys to bind and loose (Matt. 16:19): "The power to 'bind and loose' connotes the authority to absolve sins, to pronounce doctrinal judgments, and to make disciplinary decisions in the Church. Jesus entrusted this authority to the Church through the ministry of the apostles and in particular through the ministry of Peter, the only one to whom he specifically entrusted the keys of the kingdom" (CCC 553).

as an observant Jew participated in the temple and its celebrations, he also announced its destruction and denounced the shameful use to which it had been subjected. With his body as the new temple, Jesus transferred genuine worship from a place to an identity ("worship in spirit and truth"; John 4:21–24). Jesus also challenged the people's faith in God by riveting attention on himself as the one who forgives sins. By pardoning sins, Jesus showed himself to be the Savior God himself, yet he was judged by certain Jews as engaging in blasphemy. In summary, by his opposition to these three institutions of Israel, Jesus placed himself in opposition to the Jewish people and their leaders, putting into motion events that would culminate in his death.[94]

Jesus's crucifixion "was not the result of chance in an unfortunate coincidence of circumstances, but is part of the mystery of God's plan,"[95] which Scripture foretold (e.g., Isa. 53:7–8). For the sake of fallen human beings, God made Christ to be sin (2 Cor. 5:21), and Christ came "to give his life as a ransom for many" (Matt. 20:28), not in a limited sense of many, but in many who are all; indeed, the *Catechism* emphasizes unlimited atonement, or the position that Christ died to pay the penalty for the sins of all human beings.[96] Christ offered himself to the Father, to accomplish his will, and was "the Lamb of God, who takes away the sin of the world" (John 1:29). At his Last Supper, Jesus anticipated the free offering of his life, and in the garden of Gethsemane he wrestled with the choice between self-preservation (his human will) and crucifixion (the will of the Father), which he voluntarily and obediently embraced. His death was unique and definitive, "both the Paschal sacrifice that accomplishes the definitive redemption of men . . . and the sacrifice of the New Covenant, which restores man to communion with God by reconciling him to God."[97] Indeed, his death is an atonement for sins and a satisfaction for sins to God, with Christ accomplishing "the substitution of the suffering Servant, who 'makes himself an offering for sin,' when 'he bore the sin of many,' and who 'shall make many to be accounted righteous.'"[98] His sacrifice merited jus-

---

[94] The *Catechism* takes pains to underscore that "Jews are not collectively responsible for Jesus' death," thus reversing the long-standing tradition of placing the burden for his death on them (*CCC* 597). This trend of reversal began with Vatican Council II (e.g., *Nostra Aetate* 4) and has continued since then as post-conciliar popes have echoed it. For example, see Pope Benedict XVI, *Jesus of Nazareth: Holy Week: From the Entrance into Jerusalem to the Resurrection* (San Francisco: Ignatius, 2011).

[95] *CCC* 599.

[96] *CCC* 605.

[97] *CCC* 613 (emphases removed).

[98] *CCC* 615; citations are from Isa. 53:10–12.

tification for fallen human beings, all of whom participate in Christ's sacrifice "because in his incarnate divine person he has in some way united himself to every man"; thus, to everyone is offered "the possibility of being made partners, in a way known to God, in the paschal mystery."[99]

Having been crucified, Jesus experienced "the condition of death, the separation of his soul from his body, between the time he expired on the cross and the time he was raised from the dead."[100] His body was placed in a tomb, as his material aspect and immaterial aspect were disconnected for three days. At the same time, "the divine person of the Son of God necessarily continued to possess his human soul and body, separated from each other by death."[101]

Evangelical Assessment

Catholic and evangelical doctrines of the work of Christ are in agreement on almost every aspect of his death on the cross, the focus of this section in the *Catechism*. His suffering, due in particular to his challenges to the Jewish leaders and their sacred institutions and traditions; his crucifixion, not as an accident but willingly endured in fulfillment of the Father's will; his death as an atonement for human sin; and his burial are the key elements of Christ's work. Two points of disagreement on tangential matters—tangential here, in the sense that they are not the primary focus of the present doctrinal discussion, but which will appear later as important matters—are the *Catechism*'s embrace of unlimited atonement, and its vague notion of a universal participation in Christ's sacrifice. As for the first point, evangelical theology embraces three main positions on the extent of the atonement: *limited atonement*, the view that Christ died to atone for the sins of, and secure salvation for, the elect alone; *unlimited atonement*, the view, similar to the one espoused by Catholic theology, that Christ died to atone for the sins of all human beings (with the corollary that prevenient grace, a universal divine blessing, enables all human beings to respond properly to the gospel and meet the requirements of salvation); and the *multiple intentions* theory, the view that God had multiple intentions in the death of Christ, including the intention to secure the salvation of the elect, the

[99] CCC 618; citation is from Vatican Council II, *Gaudium et Spes* 22.
[100] CCC 624.
[101] CCC 626.

intention to provide atonement for the sins of all people, the intention to establish another basis for the eternal condemnation of the impenitent, and so on.[102] Accordingly, some evangelicals will agree with Catholic theology's position of unlimited atonement, while others will disagree.

As for the second point, about the ambiguous notion of universal participation in Christ's sacrifice, Vatican Council II, in its Pastoral Constitution *Gaudium et Spes*, provides a bit more detail. After rehearsing Christ's work and its many benefits, the Constitution concludes, "All this holds true not for Christians only but also for all men of good will in whose hearts grace is active invisibly. For since Christ died for all, and since all men are in fact called to one and the same destiny, which is divine, we must hold that the Holy Spirit offers to all the possibility of being made partners, in a way known to God, in the paschal mystery."[103] If, by this vague notion, Catholic theology means that a universal provision for the forgiveness of sins of all human beings has been made by the sacrifice of Christ, and that through the universal announcement concerning how this atoning work can be appropriated, the gospel is communicated to all human beings, thereby bringing the possibility of salvation to all, evangelicals holding to an unlimited atonement or to a multiple intentions theory of the atonement will agree (limited atonement proponents will not agree, because they deny the universal provision of atonement for all human beings). But if Catholic theology holds to some kind of universal salvation that is brought to Christians through the gospel and (secretly, mysteriously) is conveyed to non-Christians in some way—even (allegedly) involving the Holy Spirit—apart from the gospel, evangelicals of all stripes on the issue of the extent of the atonement will disagree strongly.[104]

The Doctrine of the Resurrection: "he descended into hell, on the third day he rose again" (Sec. 2, Ch. 2, Art. 5)

The doctrine of the resurrection presupposes a state or existence of Jesus Christ between his crucifixion and resurrection, and the Apostles' Creed, building off of 1 Peter 3:18–19, affirms that he descended into hell. Ac-

---

[102] For an overview of these positions, see Bruce Demarest, *The Cross and Salvation: The Doctrine of Salvation*, Foundations of Evangelical Theology (Wheaton, IL: Crossway, 1997, 2006), 189–193.

[103] Vatican Council II, *Gaudium et Spes* 22 (*VC II-1*, 924). For the idea of invisible grace, reference is made to Vatican Council II, *Lumen Gentium* 16. Biblical support for Christ's death for all people is listed as Rom. 8:32.

[104] More detailed discussion and assessment will come in chapter 5.

cording to the *Catechism*, in his human soul united to his divine person, the Savior descended into the realm of the dead, or hell, not "to deliver the damned, nor to destroy the hell of damnation, but to free the just who had gone before him"[105] through the proclamation of the gospel (4:6).

Death and this descent into hell did not get the last word, for on the third day Christ rose from the dead, "a real event, with manifestations that were historically verified" (e.g., 1 Cor. 15:3–4).[106] The first event in this Easter drama was the empty tomb. Though not a direct proof of resurrection—other explanations could be offered for it—it nonetheless awakened the hope of the resurrection in those who saw the grave clothes devoid of Jesus's body. The next events were Jesus's appearances—first to Mary Magdalene and other women, then to Peter, then to the Twelve, even to more than five hundred people at the same time—creating witnesses to his resurrection, who would constitute the foundation of the Christian community. The *Catechism* explicitly denounces deviant explanations for the resurrection—e.g., it was the product of mystical exaltation, or a myth stirred up by the apostles' faith—insisting "it is impossible not to acknowledge it as an historical fact."[107]

As for the nature of Christ's resurrected body, the *Catechism* affirms both continuity with his pre-resurrected body (for example, it still bears the marks of his crucifixion) and discontinuity: his resurrected body is not bound by space and time. Importantly, his resurrection "was not a return to earthly life, as was the case with the raisings from the dead that he had performed before Easter: Jairus' daughter, the young man of Naim, Lazarus."[108] Resurrected from the dead by Christ's power, these people returned to earthly living and would eventually die again. But Christ's resurrection involved passing "from the state of death to another life beyond time and space."[109] Indeed, his resurrection was a work of the triune God, as the Father raised up Jesus, thus revealing him as the Son of God (Rom. 1:3–4); the Son exercised the power he possessed to lay down his life and take it up again (John 10:17–18); and the Holy Spirit gave life to the Son's mortal body and raised him (Rom. 8:11).

[105] CCC 633.
[106] CCC 639.
[107] CCC 643–644.
[108] CCC 646. "Naim" (Luke 7:11, Douay-Rheims Bible) is spelled "Nain" in the Bible versions most familiar to Protestants.
[109] CCC 646.

The significance of Christ's resurrection is multifold: it confirms all Christ's works and teachings; it is the fulfillment of Old Testament prophecies and Jesus's own promises; it authenticates Jesus Christ as the divine Son of God; it accomplishes the justification of sinful human beings; and it is the guarantee of the future resurrection of Christians.

Evangelical Assessment

Catholic theology and evangelical theology agree fully on the doctrine of the resurrection, including its reality in space and time, the rejection of naturalistic explanations for it, the nature of the resurrected body of Christ, its Trinitarian dimension, and its multifold significance. As to Christ's descent into hell between his death and resurrection, some evangelicals agree while others disagree. Agreement comes from evangelicals who accept the descriptive clause—"he descended into hell" (*descendit ad inferna*)—in the Apostles' Creed, in most cases finding warrant for it in 1 Peter 3:18–19 (appeal is also made to Acts 2:27; Rom. 10:6–7; Eph. 4:8–9; and 1 Pet. 4:6). Evangelicals who disagree with the affirmation note problems with the historical development of the expression, specifically that (1) the earliest versions of the Apostles' Creed did not include it; (2) it does not find clear attestation until the end of the fourth century in Rufinus's commentary on the Creed of Aquileia;[110] (3) at the same time, it is not found in the Old Roman Creed of Rufinus, who understood the expression to refer to Christ's burial ("descended into the grave"); and (4) its next clear attestation is not found until the middle of the seventh century in the *Sacramentarium Gallicanum* (c. 650). Accordingly, whatever claim it may lay to the title "Apostles'," the Creed does not have firm apostolic lineage, and the phrase "descended into hell" is a later addition to it. Moreover, these evangelicals point to the lack of clear biblical warrant for the affirmation. For example, 1 Peter 3:18–19 is quite problematic, as it does not teach that Christ went into hell "to free the just who had gone before him."[111] On the contrary, Peter's point has nothing to do with the righteous, as he singles out "the spirits in prison . . . [who] formerly did not obey, when God's patience waited in the days of Noah, while the ark was being prepared" (1 Pet. 3:19–20). Though it is beyond

---

[110] Rufinus, *A Commentary on the Apostles' Creed* (NPNF² 3:541–563).
[111] CCC 633.

the scope of this discussion to demonstrate the meaning of this biblical text,[112] Augustine's proposal may offer good direction: "The preexistent Christ proclaimed salvation through Noah to the people who lived before the flood."[113]

The Doctrine of the Ascension: "he ascended into heaven and is seated at the right hand of the Father" (Sec. 2, Ch. 2, Art. 6)

For forty days after his resurrection, Jesus appeared to his disciples numerous times. His "final apparition ends with the irreversible entry of his humanity into divine glory," which is "the historical and transcendent event of the Ascension."[114] As the Son of God descended from heaven, so he ascended back to heaven (John 3:13; Eph. 4:8–10). Seated bodily at the right hand of the Father (Acts 2:33; Eph. 1:20; Heb. 1:3; 1 Pet. 3:22), he has been exalted and now shares "in God's power and authority" as the incarnate Son whose "flesh was glorified."[115] As such, he is the High Priest of the new and eternal covenant, who intercedes for his followers and who reigns over the messianic kingdom.

Evangelical Assessment

There is full accord between Catholic and evangelical theology on most aspects of the doctrine of the ascension, including Christ's post-resurrection appearances preceding it, its reality in space and time, and its significance for the exalted Christ and his intercessory ministry in glory. However, the Catholic system's axiom of the Christ-Church interconnection—the idea that the Catholic Church is the prolongation of the incarnation of the ascended, whole Christ (*totus Christus*)—is a serious misunderstanding of the ascension; it has already been assessed and found to be in error. More will be said about this misunderstanding later on.

---

[112] For further discussion, see Wayne Grudem, *The First Epistle of Peter*, Tyndale New Testament Commentaries (Grand Rapids, MI: Eerdmans, 1999), 157–162, 203–239; idem, "He Did Not Descend into Hell: A Plea for Following Scripture instead of the Apostles' Creed," *Journal of the Evangelical Theological Society* 34/1 (March 1991): 103–113.

[113] Augustine, *Letter* 164 (*NPNF*[1] 1:515–521). Confirmation of the work of the preexistent Christ "in the Spirit" making proclamation is found in 1 Pet. 1:11. That Noah was a preacher of righteousness while he was building the ark is affirmed in 2 Pet. 2:5. Accordingly, Noah's preaching to those in his time was a case of the preincarnate Christ preaching "in the Spirit" to those people who, because of their disobedience in not heeding the Noah/Christ message, died in the flood. Though their bodies perished in this way, their spirits (i.e., their immaterial being) were imprisoned and continue to be in prison, that is, in hell, awaiting the last judgment.

[114] CCC 659–660.

[115] CCC 668, 663.

The Doctrine of the Second Coming and Divine Judgment: "from thence he will come again to judge the living and the dead" (Sec. 2, Ch. 2, Art. 7)

This current reign of Jesus Christ is both inaugurated and still to come. As the cosmic Lord over all created things, he is the head of his body, the church (Eph. 1:22–23); accordingly, he "dwells on earth in his Church," already exercising authority over it through redemption, though such sanctifying work is "real but imperfect."[116] Additionally, his reign is under attack by the defeated evil powers. His complete supremacy, therefore, is still to come, when the king returns to earth, definitively destroys all that is set against him, and establishes the new heavens and new earth.

The second coming of Christ has been imminent ever since his ascension, though the timing of this event is unknown and unknowable by human beings. It is tied to the recognition of Messiah "by 'all Israel,' for 'a hardening has come upon part of Israel' in their 'unbelief' toward Jesus."[117] Eventually, "the 'full inclusion' of the Jews in the Messiah's salvation, in the wake of 'the full number of the Gentiles,'"[118] will mean the completion of the people of God as "the fullness of Christ" (Eph. 4:13). Before Jesus returns again, the church must suffer one last trial during which "the mystery of iniquity" (2 Thess. 2:7), the machinations of the Antichrist, will be unveiled "in the form of a religious deception offering men an apparent solution to their problems at the price of apostasy from the truth."[119]

Accompanying the return of Jesus Christ is the last judgment. On that last day, culpable unbelief will be exposed, and "acceptance or refusal of grace and divine love" will be disclosed by attitudes toward one's neighbor (Matt. 25:40).[120] Christ himself possesses authority delegated to him by the Father to pass definitive judgment (John 5:22, 27). At the same time, the *Catechism* introduces the idea of a self-judgment and self-condemnation through the rejection of love.[121]

---

[116] CCC 669–670; citation in this latter paragraph is from Vatican Council II, *Lumen Gentium* 48.

[117] CCC 674; citations are from Rom. 11:20–26 and Matt. 23:39.

[118] CCC 674; citations are from Rom. 11:12, 25; cf. Luke 21:24.

[119] CCC 675–676. Biblical support for this belief is 2 Thess. 2:4–12; 1 Thess. 5:2–3; 2 John 7; 1 John 2:18, 22. The *Catechism* denounces "millenarianism"—specifically of the secular variety—that claims to be able to usher in this messianic hope through historical movements, including "a historic triumph of the Church through a progressive ascendancy" (CCC 677).

[120] CCC 678.

[121] CCC 679.

Evangelical Assessment

Much agreement is found between Catholic and evangelical theology on the second coming of Christ and his last judgment. Specific items of accord are the inaugurated nature of Christ's rule (evangelicals term this the "already–not yet" reality of his reign), which progresses toward its full realization at his return; the imminency and unknown (and unknowable) timing of the second coming; the great tribulation, featuring an assault by the Antichrist that precedes that event; the last judgment before Christ as Judge, to be faced by all human beings who have ever existed; and the future hope of the new heavens and new earth.

Points of disagreement are, first, the nature of Christ's dwelling on earth with his Church. As the axiom of the Christ-Church interconnection has already been subjected to critique, it will suffice to offer a specific criticism here of its implication: evangelical theology wonders how, in light of Catholic theology, it can be said in any meaningful way that Christ, who ascended to heaven and is thus not here (physically) on earth, will return (physically) to earth at his second coming. If the ascended Christ, in his whole being—the head, including both his divine and human natures, and the body—continues to be incarnated in the Catholic Church, it does not seem that he is absent from this world in any significant sense, nor does it seem possible that the return of one who has never left is of any significant importance.

A second point of disagreement concerns the last judgment. While the *Catechism* affirms that Christ will "pass definitive judgment" (a right that he "acquired" by his death) at this climactic event, it tempers this affirmation with a contrasting one: "Yet the Son did not come to judge, but to save," appealing to biblical passages such as John 3:17 and 5:26. The *Catechism* seems to deal with this tension by focusing on self-judgment and self-condemnation: "By rejecting grace in this life, one already judges oneself, receives according to one's works, and can even condemn oneself for all eternity by rejecting the Spirit of love."[122] Evangelicals are concerned that other biblical passages may have been overlooked or misunderstood in this discussion: "Whoever believes in him [Christ] is not condemned, but whoever does not believe is condemned already, because he has not

---

[122] Ibid. Biblical support marshaled is John 3:18; 12:48; Matt. 12:32; 1 Cor. 3:12–15; Heb. 6:4–6; 10:26–31.

believed in the name of the only Son of God. . . . Whoever believes in the Son has eternal life; whoever does not obey the Son shall not see life, but the wrath of God remains on him" (John 3:18, 36).[123] Certainly, the primary purpose of Christ's atoning sacrifice was to accomplish redemption for fallen human beings; no one disputes the salvific mission of the Son. But the appropriation of this divine provision is the responsibility of all who hear the gospel ("And this is his commandment, that we believe in the name of his Son Jesus Christ and love one another, just as he has commanded us"; 1 John 3:23), and this charge is obeyed by some, leading to eternal life, and disobeyed by others, leading to eternal death. And this latter condemnation, while certainly the result of a personal decision, is far more than self-judgment; indeed, it is divine condemnation, as the wrath of God already abides on the one who does not obey the commandment.

A third point will find disagreement among certain varieties of evangelical theology. The *Catechism* ties the second coming of Jesus to the wholesale recognition of him as the Messiah by the Jewish people, with appeal to Paul (Rom. 11:20–26) and Jesus (Matt. 23:39). One branch of evangelical theology—Reformed theology—disagrees, generally speaking, with this eschatological viewpoint, though some within it do hold out this hope for Israel. Evangelicals of the dispensational persuasion will certainly concur with the *Catechism*, but they will disagree with a fourth point, namely, that the church will suffer through the great tribulation, spurred on by the Antichrist, which will precede Christ's return. Their view maintains that the church, which is promised exemption from divine wrath, will be removed from the earth—the technical term is the "rapture"—just prior to the onset of the period of tribulation, during which the fierce anger of God will be poured out in punishment on unbelievers on the earth.

[123] The *Catechism* does cite the first verse (John 3:18) in its discussion, but the key affirmation in the verse—"whoever does not believe is condemned already"—refers not to self-condemnation but to divine condemnation (taking the passive "is not condemned" as a divine passive, i.e., God condemns), as verse 36 confirms. Additional appeal is made to John 12:48 (better, vv. 47–48), which emphasizes what has already been noted: The mission of the Son was to bring salvation and not judgment. But this point cannot be misconstrued to mean that Jesus does not judge those who reject him and his provision of salvation. Indeed, the passage indicates that judgment in the case of unbelievers, though not directly meted out by Christ, is carried out by Christ's word: "the word that I have spoken will judge him on the last day" (v. 48). To understand this passage as indicating self-condemnation misses its meaning. Furthermore, Matt. 12:32 addresses a particular rejection of the Holy Spirit's work attesting to Christ—he refers to it as "blasphemy against the Spirit" (v. 31) and explains that it is an unforgivable sin—and cannot be generalized to include all types of rejection of divine grace. And it does not support the notion that such a sin brings self-condemnation; again, the passive expression "will not be forgiven" is a divine passive, understood properly to mean that God will not forgive this heinous sin. Finally, how 1 Cor. 3:12–15 and the Hebrews passages (6:4–6; 10:26–31) support the *Catechism*'s argument is not evident.

The Doctrine of the Holy Spirit: "I believe in the Holy Spirit" (Sec. 2, Ch. 3, Art. 8)

The doctrine of the Holy Spirit treats both the divine personhood and the many works or ministries of the Holy Spirit. Before commencing with these matters of belief, however, the *Catechism* demonstrates that Christians who profess the faith already know and experience the power of the Holy Spirit in their lives. For example, the ability to state "Jesus is Lord" comes by the Holy Spirit (1 Cor. 12:3); "to be in touch with Christ, we must first have been touched by the Holy Spirit."[124] It is he who grants the grace of regeneration, or the new birth, awakening faith in people, and it is he who will complete their salvation. Indeed, "[t]o believe in the Holy Spirit is to profess that the Holy Spirit is one of the persons of the Holy Trinity, consubstantial [of the same divine nature] with the Father and the Son," with whom "he is worshipped and glorified."[125] Furthermore, the church knows the Holy Spirit in the Scripture that he inspired, in its Tradition, and in its Magisterium that he assists; in the sacramental liturgy; in prayer, in which the Spirit intercedes; and more.[126]

Concerning the doctrine of the Holy Spirit, the *Catechism* affirms that he is of the same divine nature as the Father and the Son, both inseparable from them in the unity of the Trinity and a person distinct from them. The joint mission of the Son and the Spirit means that, "[w]hen the Father sends his Word, he always sends his Breath";[127] this collaborative work is seen especially "in the children adopted by the Father in the Body of his Son" through "the mission of the Spirit of adoption."[128] His proper name is "Holy Spirit," and his titles are "Paraclete"—"literally, 'he who is called to one's side,' *ad-vocatus*" or consoler[129] (John 14:16, 26; 15:26; 16:7); "the Spirit of truth" (John 16:13); "the Spirit of the promise" (Gal. 3:14; Eph. 1:13); "the Spirit of adoption" (Rom. 8:15; Gal. 4:6); "the Spirit of the Lord" (2 Cor. 3:17); "the Spirit of God" (Rom. 8:9); and "the Spirit of glory" (1 Pet. 4:14). Symbols of the Spirit include water, anointing, fire, cloud and light, the seal, the hand, the finger, and the dove.[130]

---

[124] CCC 683.
[125] CCC 685; citation is from the Nicene Creed.
[126] CCC 688.
[127] CCC 689.
[128] CCC 690.
[129] CCC 692.
[130] CCC 694–701.

Before the incarnation, the Holy Spirit was active in various ways (e.g., creation), but of great importance is the development of two prophetic lines in the Old Testament, "one leading to the expectation of the Messiah, the other pointing to the announcement of a new Spirit."[131] Prophetic passages like Isaiah 11:1–2, Ezekiel 36:25–28, and Joel 2:28–32 pointed to a fresh, unprecedented outpouring of the Spirit. At the beginning of his messianic ministry, Jesus of Nazareth noted, "The Spirit of the Lord is upon me, because the Lord has anointed me" (Luke 4:18–19, citing Isa. 61:1–2), and Peter announced the inauguration of the fulfillment of prophecies about the Spirit in his Pentecost sermon (Acts 2:17–21, citing Joel 2:28–32).

Prior to the incarnation, the Holy Spirit was powerfully at work in John the Baptist, a man who was "filled with the Holy Spirit, even from his mother's womb" (Luke 1:15, 41). The Spirit also prepared Mary for the incarnation: "She was, by sheer grace, conceived without sin as the most humble of creatures, the most capable of welcoming the inexpressible gift of the Almighty"; accordingly, "the Father found the dwelling place where his Son and his Spirit could dwell among men."[132] It was by the Holy Spirit that Mary as ever-virgin conceived and gave birth to the Son of God, rendering him visible to the world. Indeed, as Mary made known the Son to the poor and humble (the shepherds, magi, Simeon and Anna, the couple at the wedding of Cana, and the twelve disciples), through her the Spirit began to introduce human beings "into communion with Christ."[133] Finally, as "the mother of the 'whole Christ,'" Mary was present in the upper room with the twelve disciples as the Holy Spirit was about to inaugurate his new work (Acts 1:14).[134]

The incarnation is thus a miracle wrought by the Holy Spirit; even more, "Christ's whole work is in fact a joint mission of the Son and the Holy Spirit."[135] Christ made allusions to the Spirit and his fresh, unprecedented future work in his conversations with Nicodemus (John 3:5–8), the Samaritan woman (4:10, 14, 23–24), and the participants at the feast of Tabernacles (7:37–39).[136] More openly, Jesus spoke to his twelve disciples about the Spirit's role in prayer (Luke 11:13) and in bearing witness (Matt.

---

[131] CCC 711.
[132] CCC 722, 721 (emphasis removed).
[133] CCC 725 (emphasis removed).
[134] CCC 726.
[135] CCC 727.
[136] CCC 728.

10:19–20). But Jesus reserved his promise of the coming of the Holy Spirit to his last hour, as he explained that he (i.e., the Son) would pray for the Father to send the Spirit; the Father would send the Spirit in his (i.e., Jesus's) name; he (i.e., the Son) would send the Spirit from the Father; and the Spirit proceeds from the Father. This promised and sent Spirit would be with Christ's disciples forever, teach them everything, recall to mind what Christ said, bear witness to Christ, lead his disciples into all truth, glorify Christ, and convict the world of sin, righteousness, and judgment (John 14:16–17, 26; 15:26; 16:7–15; 17:26).[137]

Jesus's promise was fulfilled on the day of Pentecost as he poured out the Holy Spirit in a fresh, unprecedented way. At last, the triune God is fully revealed and gives a new gift: The first gift is love (Rom. 5:5), the effect of which is the forgiveness of sins, or restoration of that which was once lost through sin. Other gifts include the Spirit as "pledge" or "firstfruits" of a future inheritance (1 John 4:11–12; Rom. 8:23; 2 Cor. 1:21–22); love as the source of the new life in Christ through the power of the Spirit (Acts 1:8; 1 Corinthians 13); and the fruit of the Spirit (Gal. 5:22–23), as Christians "live/walk by the Spirit" (Gal. 5:25).[138]

"The mission of Christ and the Holy Spirit is brought to completion in the Church, which is the Body of Christ and the Temple of the Holy Spirit."[139] The role of the Spirit is specifically to prepare people with divine grace so as to draw them to Christ; manifest the risen Lord to them through opening their minds to the gospel of his death and resurrection; make present the mystery of Christ, especially in the Eucharist; and bring them into communion with God. Accordingly, the mission of the Church is the sacrament of the mission of Christ and the Holy Spirit: it announces, bears witness to, makes present, and extends the mystery of the communion of the triune God. Christ's gift of the Spirit is particularly tied to the Church's sacraments.[140]

Evangelical Assessment

For the most part, evangelical theology's doctrine of the Holy Spirit accords with, because it is largely dependent on, Catholic theology's development

[137] CCC 729.
[138] CCC 732–736.
[139] CCC 737.
[140] CCC 738–739.

of it from Scripture. The Spirit is divine, equal in essence and attributes to the Father and the Son, and he is a person distinct yet inseparable from those two in the unity of the Trinity; this belief is affirmed in Scripture and was defended by the early church against heretical ideas. The Spirit's works in creation, incarnation (prophecies of the coming of Messiah; the miraculous conception of the Son of God in the womb of the Virgin Mary; the anointing of Jesus for his messianic ministry), salvation (including conviction of sin, drawing to Christ, illuminating the gospel, regeneration, igniting faith, adoption, and intercession), and consummation (the resurrection of the body) are well attested in Scripture. Moreover, the Spirit foretold his own upcoming new covenant ministry (a fresh, unprecedented, future outpouring of the Spirit on all people), a prophetic word that was continued and heightened by both John the Baptist and Jesus himself. Indeed, Jesus promised to send the Holy Spirit[141] to be with the disciples forever, teach and lead them into the truth, bring to their memory all that he had said and done, bear witness to Christ, and glorify him. These prophecies and promises began their fulfillment on the day of Pentecost, when the Holy Spirit was poured out in his new covenant ministry and gave birth to the church. Now, indwelling all Christians, the Spirit gives love, fosters sanctification, develops Christlikeness, empowers for service, prompts faithfulness and obedience as Christians are filled with/walk in the Spirit, and much more.

Despite this widespread agreement, several important differences exist with regard to the doctrine of the Holy Spirit. First, evangelical theology is suspicious of Catholic theology's neglect of the Holy Spirit as "another Paraclete" (helper/counselor/consoler; John 14:16). Though the *Catechism* does note that Jesus is "the first consoler" (referencing 1 John 2:1 in support),[142] it does not trace out the important biblical point that the Holy Spirit is "another" or "the second" consoler. Biblically speaking, Jesus makes much of his forthcoming sending of the Spirit in this capacity because it means that the Spirit, as another Paraclete, will take the place of Jesus, who is going away: "Nevertheless, I tell you the truth: it is to your advantage that I go away, for if I do not go away, the Helper will not come to you. But if I go, I will send him to you" (John 16:7). Evangelical theology

---

[141] As discussed earlier under the doctrine of the Trinity, Jesus's promises to send the Spirit, and to send him from the Father, who would in turn send the Spirit in Jesus's name, are the basis for the Catholic and Protestant belief of the double procession of the Spirit: he proceeds from both the Father and the Son.
[142] CCC 692.

questions whether the reason for this neglect is the Catholic system's axiom of the Christ-Church interconnection, that is, the whole Christ is fully present in the Catholic Church. This axiom seems to contradict Jesus's point that he is leaving this world so that *he (Jesus) is not here*—which will be an advantage for the church—but he is sending another Paraclete to take his place in this world so that *the Holy Spirit is here*. Certainly, Catholic theology underscores the present operation of the Holy Spirit in the world and in the church, but it fails to explain how the Spirit's presence relates to Christ's presence, especially in light of Jesus's own affirmations that he is leaving and the Spirit is taking his place. Evangelical theology offers this simple idea: Jesus Christ, who left this world and ascended into heaven, is present in the world and with his church through the person and work of the Holy Spirit, whom he sent to be the Paraclete in his place.

Whereas both theological perspectives agree concerning the Spirit's work of inspiring Scripture, evangelical theology parts company when Catholic theology also associates the Spirit's work with both the Church's Tradition and its Magisterium. As presented earlier in the *Catechism*,[143] this work of the Spirit means that (1) Tradition is one mode of authoritative divine revelation (along with Scripture); (2) the Magisterium exercises ultimate authority in the interpretation of Scripture and Tradition; and (3) this teaching office makes infallible pronouncements of official Catholic dogma when the pope speaks *ex cathedra*. As explained earlier, evangelical theology rejects this overreaching authority, fueled by Catholic theology's claim of the work of the Holy Spirit in and through both Tradition and the Magisterium. Furthermore, evangelical theology disagrees with Catholic theology's claim that the Spirit was operative in Mary, in some exalted sense, to introduce human beings to life with Christ. Additionally, while agreeing that God gives the gift of the Spirit as a down payment or guarantee of the future inheritance of genuine Christ-followers, evangelical theology questions why Catholic theology does not include as part of this divine gift the assurance of salvation, as the apostle Paul underscored: "The Spirit himself bears witness with our spirit that we are children of God" (Rom. 8:16). Tragically, Catholic theology denies that the faithful can possess such confidence because it maintains that salvation can be forfeited and is indeed lost when mortal sin is committed. But this position does not accord with

---

[143] See the discussion in chapter 3.

Scripture, which assures genuine believers that the Holy Spirit both seals them for the day of redemption—an objective work—and provides certainty that they belong to God in Christ forever—a subjective confidence.

One area that is not developed in the *Catechism* is the Church's renewed emphasis on the person and work of the Holy Spirit as seen particularly in the Catholic charismatic movement. Rooted in the Pentecostal revival that began in the early part of the twentieth century, the charismatic movement was fueled by Pentecostal theology's core belief called baptism by/with the Spirit.[144] Charismatics see this "second blessing" as a potent work of the Spirit subsequent to conversion that renews Christians and equips them with evangelistic zeal, supernatural love for God and others, devotion to Christ and his church, power for service, and even miraculous ministries of healing, prophecy, speaking in tongues, and the like. This Spirit-baptism theology, while penetrating many denominations and theologies such as Lutherans, Methodists, Presbyterians, Baptists, and Anglicans, also had an immense impact on the Catholic Church; indeed, millions of the faithful have been influenced by the Catholic Charismatic movement. Numerous evangelicals are thankful for this charismatic renewal of the Catholic Church, sensing that in many instances the encounter with the Holy Spirit has brought a deeply rooted experience of salvation evidenced by prayer and praise, joyfulness, and devotion to Christ and his gospel.

---

[144] See Gregg R. Allison, "Baptism of and Filling with the Holy Spirit," *Southern Baptist Journal of Theology* (Winter 2012): 4–20.

5

The Profession of Faith
(Part I, Section 2, Chapter 3, Article 9)

The Doctrine of the Church

The Doctrine of the Church: "I believe in the holy catholic church" (Sec. 2, Ch. 3, Art. 9, Para. 1–3)

Following its discussion of the doctrines of Christ and the Holy Spirit, and in light of and in dependence on those doctrines, the *Catechism* next addresses the doctrine of the church. Indeed, to believe that the Church is one, holy, catholic, and apostolic "is inseparable from belief in God, the Father, the Son, and the Holy Spirit."[1] Furthermore, Christians profess "the church" but do not believe *in* the Church, "so as not to confuse God with his works."[2] In this first part of the chapter, the first three paragraphs of the *Catechism*'s doctrine of the Church will be discussed and then evaluated. In the latter half of the chapter, the second three paragraphs of the *Catechism*'s ecclesiology will be presented and then evaluated.

The word "church" is taken from the Latin *ecclesia*, from the Greek ἐκκαλεῖν (*ekkalein*), signifying "to call out of"; thus, it refers to an assembly and, in this case, an assembly for religious purposes. In the Greek Old Testament, "church" referred to the gathering of the people of Israel before God, especially on Mount Sinai for the reception of the law. The first Christian community, calling itself "church," readily identified itself as heir to that assembly, yet now consisting of people from the entire world who are "called together" by God. In its Christian context, three meanings of "church" are identified and are inseparable: the liturgical assembly

[1] CCC 750.
[2] Ibid.

(Christians actually gathered together for worship), the local community (a local church composed of its members), and the whole universal community of believers. The universal church manifests itself in local churches and "is made real as a liturgical, above all a Eucharistic, assembly."[3] Symbols of the Church abound. They center on the image of the body of Christ and include a sheepfold/flock (e.g., John 10:1–10), a cultivated field or vineyard (1 Cor. 3:9; Rom. 11:13–26), the building of God (e.g., 1 Cor. 3:9, 11; 1 Pet. 2:7), a family (1 Tim. 3:15), the temple (1 Cor. 3:16–17; Rev. 21:3; 1 Pet. 2:5), "Jerusalem which is above" (Rev. 21:1–2), and "our mother."[4]

The *Catechism* makes numerous affirmations about this Church: It is established in and by the triune God; specifically, it was predetermined by God the Father in accordance with his eternal plan. The Church began as a gathering together of God's people the moment that sin wrecked their communion with God; more precisely, its remote preparation began with the calling of Abraham and the election of Israel to be the covenant people (who tragically broke their covenant with God). The Church was instituted by Christ, who ushered in the kingdom of God, the Church as Christ's inaugurated reign on earth; hierarchically, it is structured around Christ's "choice of the Twelve with Peter as their head."[5] "The Church is born primarily of Christ's total self-giving for our salvation, anticipated in the institution of the Eucharist and fulfilled on the cross."[6] It is revealed by the Holy Spirit and constituted as missional—sent to make disciples of all the nations—by Christ and the Spirit. Ultimately, the Church will one day be perfected in glory when Christ returns.

Mysteriously, the Church is both visible and spiritual, both human and divine: visible and human in its hierarchy and earthly society; spiritual and divine in being the mystical body of Christ and the spiritual community given heavenly riches. Such characteristics pertain not only to local churches but to the universal church as well. Moreover, the Church is the universal sacrament of salvation: "The Church, in Christ, is like a sacrament—a sign and instrument, that is, of communion with God and of unity among all men."[7] Christ uses the sacrament of the Church as his instrument of uni-

---

[3] CCC 752.
[4] CCC 753–757. Nowhere in Scripture is the church called "our mother," and the *Catechism* (757) notes various passages in support of the biblical description of the church "as the spotless spouse of the spotless lamb."
[5] CCC 765; reference is made to Mark 3:14–15.
[6] CCC 766.
[7] CCC 775. The Greek word μυστήριον (*mystērion*), used about a dozen times in the New Testament, was translated into Latin by two words: *mysterium* and *sacramentum*. This latter term was defined by Augustine as "the visible sign of an invisible grace," which is the hidden reality of salvation referred to by the former term.

versal salvation, uniting all human beings with God and, as a consequence, all human beings with one another.

The *Catechism* presents three key descriptors of the Church: First, the Church is the people of God, who are a priestly, prophetic, and royal people. Second, the Church is the body of Christ, united with him who is the head as one body with a great diversity of many members. Indeed, "Christ and his Church thus together make up the 'whole Christ' (*Christus totus*)."[8] Additionally, the Church is the bride of Christ. Third, the Church is the temple of the Holy Spirit, fostering Baptism, the sacraments, grace, the virtues, and special graces or gifts for service, called "charisms," for the building up of the Church.[9]

Following the more detailed profession of faith in the Nicene Creed, the *Catechism* discusses the identity of the Church in terms of its four historical or classical attributes: oneness, holiness, catholicity, and apostolicity. The Church is *one* because of (1) its source, who is the triune God, three persons in perfect unity; (2) its founder, the incarnate Son who reconciled all people to God by his sacrificial death and thereby unites all people into his one body; and (3) its "soul," who is the Holy Spirit dwelling in all believers and thereby joining them together. For these reasons, "[u]nity is the essence of the Church."[10] But this unity is not uniformity or sameness, because the one Church is also characterized by a great diversity, due to the variety of God's gifts, the diversity of the people from all over the world who receive them, and the variety of local churches that retain their own traditions. Specifically, the bonds that unite the Church are "profession of one faith received from the Apostles; common celebration of divine worship, especially of the sacraments; [and] apostolic succession through the sacrament of Holy Orders."[11] The Creed, the liturgy, and apostolic succession belong to "[t]he sole Church of Christ which our Savior . . . entrusted to Peter's pastoral care, commissioning him and the other apostles to extend and rule it. . . . This Church . . . subsists in (*subsistit in*) the Catholic Church, which is governed by the successor of Peter and by the bishops in communion with

---

Specifically, the seven sacraments of the Church are the signs and means by which the Holy Spirit communicates the grace of Christ throughout his body, the Church. "The Church, then, both contains and communicates the invisible grace she signifies. It is in this analogical sense, that the Church is called a 'sacrament'" (*CCC* 774).

[8] *CCC* 795.

[9] *CCC* 799–801 provides a short discussion of these charisms, which are commonly known to evangelicals as spiritual gifts.

[10] *CCC* 813.

[11] *CCC* 815.

him."[12] Because only the Catholic Church possesses these three elements of unity, through it alone, as "the universal help toward salvation, . . . the fullness of the means of salvation can be obtained."[13]

The *Catechism* laments the many "wounds to unity" that have wreaked havoc with the unity of the one Church, confessing that people on both sides of the divisions were in sin and thus to blame. Such historical division does not mean that members of current churches estranged from the Catholic Church are culpable of the sin of separation; rather, they are accepted as brothers: "All who have been justified by faith in Baptism are incorporated into Christ; they therefore have a right to be called Christians, and with good reason are accepted as brothers in the Lord by the children of the Catholic Church."[14] Beyond this, "'many elements of sanctification and of truth' are found outside the visible confines of the Catholic Church":[15] Scripture; grace; faith, hope, and love; the gifts of the Spirit; and visible elements.[16] Indeed, "from the fullness of grace and truth that Christ has entrusted to the Catholic Church," these other churches and ecclesial communities derive their power to be means of salvation, while also being called to "Catholic unity."[17] Because of the great importance of the Church's attribute of oneness, the *Catechism* underscores Christ's gift of, and the Spirit's call to, a recovery of unity, and lists elements (e.g., renewal, conversion of heart, praying together, ecumenical dialogue) to bring about such desired restoration.[18]

The second attribute of the Church is holiness. The Church is *holy* because it is "endowed already with a sanctity that is real though imperfect."[19] At the heart of this confession is Christ's parable of the wheat and the tares, applied to all the members of the Church: "In everyone, the weeds of sin will still be mixed with the good wheat of the Gospel until the end of time."[20] Composed of sinners who continue to sin and are in constant need of repentance and renewal, the Church possesses holiness only in part. At the same time, some of its members, moved by "the power of the Spirit of

---

[12] CCC 816; citation is from Vatican Council II, *Lumen Gentium* 8.2.
[13] CCC 816; citation is from Vatican Council II, *Unitatis redintegratio* 3.5.
[14] CCC 818; citation is from Vatican Council II, *Unitatis redintegratio* 3.1.
[15] CCC 819; citation is from Vatican Council II, *Lumen Gentium* 8.2.
[16] CCC 819; citation is from Vatican Council II, *Unitatis redintegratio* 3.2; cf. *Lumen Gentium* 15.
[17] CCC 819.
[18] CCC 820–821.
[19] CCC 825; citation is from Vatican Council II, *Lumen Gentium* 48.3.
[20] CCC 827; reference is to Matt. 13:24–30.

holiness," have "practiced heroic virtue and lived in fidelity to God's grace" and are thus recognized by the Church (the technical term is "canonized") as saints. The Church proposes them "as models and intercessors" and looks to them as its agents of renewal.[21] The highest example of all is Mary, to whom the faithful turn their eyes because "in the most Blessed Virgin the Church has already reached that perfection whereby she [the Church] exists without spot or wrinkle."[22]

The Church's third attribute is catholicity, from the word "catholic," which means "universal." The Church is *catholic* because of (1) the presence of Christ in it, and (2) the universal commission given to it by Christ. With regard to the first reason, Ignatius offered, "Where there is Christ Jesus, there is the Catholic Church."[23] As the *totus Christus*, the whole Christ as the head united to the fullness of his body, the Church possesses the fullness of the means of salvation, specifically, the Creed, the liturgy with its sacraments, and apostolic succession. With regard to the second reason, Christ commissioned his disciples with the following order: "Go therefore and make disciples of all nations, baptizing them in the name of the Father and of the Son and of the Holy Spirit" (Matt. 28:19). This Great Commission is universal in scope. This catholicity pertains not only to the Church in general. Each particular church (or diocese)—"a community of the Christian faithful in communion of faith and sacraments with their bishop ordained in apostolic succession"—is fully catholic through its communion with the Church of Rome.[24]

The *Catechism* raises an important question: "Who belongs to the Catholic Church?" To envision its response, think of concentric circles with the Catholic faithful in the center, others who believe in Christ—Orthodox Christians, Protestant Christians, evangelical Christians—in the circles farther out, and all the rest of humanity, "called by God's grace to salvation," in the more remote circles.[25]

Starting with the innermost circle of Catholics, the *Catechism* affirms,

Fully incorporated into the society of the Church as those who, possessing the Spirit of Christ, accept all the means of salvation given to

---

[21] CCC 828.
[22] CCC 829; citation is from Vatican Council II, *Lumen Gentium* 65.
[23] CCC 830; citation is from Ignatius, *Letter to the Smyrneans* 8 (shorter version; *ANF* 1:90).
[24] CCC 833–834.
[25] CCC 836; citation is from Vatican Council II, *Lumen Gentium* 13.

the Church together with her entire organization, and who—by the bonds constituted by the profession of faith, the sacraments, ecclesiastical government, and communion—are joined in the visible structure of the Church of Christ, who rules her through the Supreme Pontiff [i.e., the pope] and the bishops. Even though incorporated into the Church, one who does not however persevere in charity is not saved. He remains indeed in the bosom of the Church, but "in body" not "in heart."[26]

Thus, the Catholic faithful occupy the innermost circle.

In the circles farther out are found "the baptized who are honored by the name of Christian, but do not profess the Catholic faith in its entirety or have not preserved unity or communion under the successor of Peter [i.e., the pope]."[27] These believers who have been properly baptized—i.e., in the name of the triune God in water—"are put in a certain, although imperfect, communion with the Catholic Church."[28] While Protestants and evangelicals belong in this category, the description pertains especially to members of the Orthodox Churches.

Moving into circles extending even farther out are found Jews, Muslims, and adherents of other non-Christian religions, people "who have not yet received the Gospel" yet "are related to the People of God in various ways."[29] Concerning the Jews, the Church has in common with them faith in God's revelation in the old covenant, the law, the patriarchs, and the Christ (cf. Rom. 9:4–5); indeed, both the Jews and the Church expect "the coming (or the return) of the Messiah," even though the Jewish "waiting is accompanied by the drama of not knowing or of misunderstanding Christ Jesus."[30] With regard to Muslims, the *Catechism* affirms that "[t]he plan of salvation also includes those who acknowledge the Creator, in the first place amongst whom are the Muslims; these profess to hold the faith of Abraham, and together with us [i.e., the Catholic Church] they adore the one, merciful God, mankind's judge on the last day."[31] As for adherents of non-Christian religions—for example, Hindus, Buddhists, Sikhs, Baha'is,

---

[26] CCC 837; citation is from Vatican Council II, *Lumen Gentium* 14.
[27] CCC 838; citation is from Vatican Council II, *Lumen Gentium* 15.
[28] CCC 838; citation is from Vatican Council II, *Unitatis redintegratio* 3.
[29] CCC 839; citation is from Vatican Council II, *Lumen Gentium* 16.
[30] CCC 840.
[31] CCC 841; citation is from Vatican Council II, *Lumen Gentium* 16; cf. *Nosta Aetate* 3. The *Catechism* also refers to Pope Paul VI's *Evangelii nuntiandi* 53. Accessible at http://www.vatican.va/holy_father/paul_vi/apost _exhortations/documents/hf_p-vi_exh_19751208_evangelii-nuntiandi_en.html.

Zoroastrians, Shintoists, animists[32]—"the Catholic Church recognizes in other religions that search, among shadows and images, for the God who is unknown yet near since he gives life and breath and all things and wants all men to be saved. Thus, the Church considers all goodness and truth found in these religions as 'a preparation for the Gospel and given by him who enlightens all men that they may at length have life.'"[33] At the same time, the *Catechism* acknowledges and decries the satanically induced deception that leads to idolatry and despair in the religious behavior of these non-Christians. Indeed, Vatican Council II cautioned, "But very often, deceived by the Evil One, men have become vain in their reasonings, have exchanged the truth of God for a lie and served the world rather than the Creator (cf. Rom. 1:21 and 25). Or else, living and dying in this world without God, they are exposed to ultimate despair."[34] Thus, though Catholicism embraces a pathway to salvation for adherents of non-Christian religions, it also acknowledges that the journey they must travel is wrought with grave difficulties.

Because these other churches, ecclesial communities, and non-Christian religions are to a lesser or greater degree removed from the fullness of salvation that exists at the center of the circle, "the Father willed to call the whole of humanity together into his Son's Church. The Church is the place where humanity must rediscover its unity and salvation. The Church is 'the world reconciled.'"[35] The *Catechism* raises another important question: How is the traditional affirmation "outside the Church there is no salvation"[36] to be understood today? "Re-formulated positively, it means that all salvation comes from Christ the Head through the Church which is his Body"; indeed, the Church is "necessary for salvation" because Christ "himself explicitly asserted the necessity of faith and Baptism, and thereby affirmed at the same time the necessity of the Church."[37] The *Catechism* further explains, "Hence they could not be saved who, knowing that the Catholic Church was founded as necessary by God through Christ, would refuse either to enter it or to

---

[32] Though the *Catechism* does not provide a list of the non-Christian religions envisioned in its discussion, I list these as the religions represented at the first World Day of Prayer for Peace on October 27, 1986, in Assisi (repeated January 24, 2002).
[33] CCC 843; citation is from Vatican Council II, *Lumen Gentium* 16; cf. *Nosta Aetate* 2.
[34] *Lumen Gentium* 16 (*VC II-1*, 368).
[35] CCC 845; citation is from Augustine, *Sermon* 96.7, 9.
[36] The first to make this statement was Cyprian in his *Epistle* 73.21 (*Letter* 72.21 in *ANF* 5:384); he developed the idea further in his *Treatise* 1: *On the Unity of the Church* 1.6 (*ANF* 5:423).
[37] CCC 846; citation is from Vatican Council II, *Lumen Gentium* 14, with biblical support given as Mark 16:16 and John 3:5.

remain in it."[38] The *Catechism* then offers a caveat: "This affirmation is not aimed at those who, through no fault of their own, do not know Christ and his Church."[39] Indeed, sincere God-seekers who, "moved by grace, try in their actions to do his will as they know it through the dictates of their conscience—those too may achieve eternal salvation."[40] What God accomplishes mysteriously in these cases does not and must not detract from the Church's obligation to reach out to all people with the gospel.

Accordingly, its catholicity demands that the Church be missional. To it has been given the Great Commission (Matt. 28:19–20), a missionary mandate that has the love of the triune God for its origin and the establishment of loving communion between God and all human beings for its purpose. Moved by the love of Christ (2 Cor. 5:14), motivated by the knowledge that God desires everyone to be saved (1 Tim. 2:4), and being led by the Spirit, the Church engages in missionary endeavors to bring the truth of salvation to those who already desire the truth.[41]

The fourth attribute of the Church is apostolicity. The Church is *apostolic*, or founded on the apostles, in three ways: (1) its underpinning was and is "the foundation of the apostles" (Eph. 2:20; cf. Rev. 21:14), who were duly appointed by Christ; (2) it keeps and passes on the "good deposit" (2 Tim. 1:13–14) or sound teaching/words that it has learned from the apostles; and (3) it "continues to be taught, sanctified, and guided by the apostles until Christ's return, through their successors in pastoral office: the college of bishops, 'assisted by priests, in union with the successor of Peter, the Church's supreme pastor.'"[42] According to Scripture, Jesus Christ chose twelve disciples and named them apostles, or emissaries (ambassadors, missionaries), in whom he continues his mission: "As the Father has sent me, even so I am sending you" (John 20:21). "The apostles' ministry is the continuation of his mission; Jesus said to the Twelve: 'he who receives you receives me'" (Matt. 10:40; cf. Luke 10:16).[43] The office of apostleship has an aspect that *cannot* be transmitted

---

[38] Ibid.
[39] CCC 847.
[40] Ibid.; citation is from Vatican Council II, *Lumen Gentium* 16.
[41] In these endeavors, the *Catechism* urges "a respectful dialogue" between the Church and those who do not yet accept the gospel and notes that believers can gain from such interaction a greater appreciation for "those elements of truth and grace which are found among peoples, and which are, as it were, a secret presence of God." Indeed, the gospel functions in such a way "to consolidate, complete, and raise up the truth and the goodness that God has distributed among men and nations, and to purify them from error and evil 'for the glory of God, the confusion of the demon, and the happiness of man'" (CCC 856); citations are from Vatican Council II, *Ad gentes* 9.
[42] CCC 857; citation is from Vatican Council II, *Ad gentes* 5.
[43] CCC 858.

and an aspect that *can* be transmitted. The first and nontransferable aspect is being eyewitnesses of Christ's resurrection and thus the foundation stones of the Church; only the original apostles exercised this aspect of the apostolic office. The second and permanent aspect, based on Christ's promise to be with his disciples always, is the appointment of successors to the apostles, i.e., apostolic succession. These successors are the bishops of the Church; the apostles "consigned, by will and testament, as it were, to their immediate collaborators the duty of completing and consolidating the work they had begun. . . . They accordingly designated such men and then made the ruling that likewise on their death other proven men should take over their ministry."[44] This episcopal office of shepherding or pastoring the Church is a permanent one, carries with it divine approbation, and demands obedience to it.

In addition to apostolic succession through the office of bishop, the whole Church is apostolic in that all its members participate in the apostolate, or mission to the world. They carry out this apostolate in various ways, with some engaging in it as ordained ministers (priests, bishops, cardinals) and others serving in it as laypeople.

In summary, the Church is one, holy, catholic, and apostolic. These attributes are its fundamental identity markers, and the fullness and splendor of the Church's unity, holiness, universality, and apostolicity will be ultimately revealed when Christ returns in his glory.

Evangelical Assessment

Though the *Catechism* continues its lengthy discussion of the doctrine of the church, an assessment of what it has affirmed thus far (para. 1–3) is appropriate. As will become evident, one of the doctrines that most separates Catholic theology and evangelical theology is this doctrine of the church. Before presenting the many areas of disagreement, however, several areas of accord need to be underscored.

General Assessment

For the most part, Catholic and evangelical theology agree that the basic notion of the church is that of an assembly.[45] Both identify two types of

---

[44] CCC 861; citation is from Vatican Council II, *Lumen Gentium* 20. Biblical support listed is Acts 20:28, and early church attestation is Clement of Rome, *Letter to the Corinthians* 42, 44 (*ANF* 1:16, 17).

[45] To make a minor adjustment to the *Catechism*'s discussion of the word "church," it should be noted that the Latin *ecclesia* is from the Greek ἐκκλησία (*ekklēsia*), which is regularly used to refer to an assembly. While this

this assembly: the gathering of Christians to worship God together, and the members of a local church. As will be noted, they disagree about the third type of assembly, the universal church. Further accord consists in seeking to understand the nature of the church in terms of the biblical images (e.g., building, family) used to present it. Moreover, evangelical theology embraces the Trinitarian nature of the church, its missional identity, and its eschatological orientation. Even the three descriptors of the church—the people of God, the body of Christ, the temple of the Holy Spirit—and Catholic theology's understanding of them resonate to some extent with evangelical theology.[46]

As to the origin of the church, two theological positions are quite common: The *continuity* position holds that the church began with Adam and Eve, after the fall into sin necessitated salvation to rescue fallen human beings. Accordingly, there is one people of God—the church—composed of all the faithful beginning with Adam and Eve, including the patriarchs, extending to the people of Israel under the old covenant, and encompassing Christians under the new covenant. That is, there is continuity between the faithful Jewish people before Jesus Christ and the faithful Christian people after him: together they compose the one people of God. This continuity position is embraced by Catholic theology as well as by many types of evangelical theology, including Reformed and Lutheran theology.

The *discontinuity* position holds that the church began at Pentecost; as I have defined it elsewhere, "The church is the people of God who have been saved through repentance and faith in Jesus Christ and have been incorporated into his body through baptism with the Holy Spirit."[47] The church is characterized by certain realities: faith, specifically in the death, burial, and resurrection of Jesus Christ; incorporation into his body through baptism with the Spirit; the permanent indwelling of the Spirit in his new covenant ministry; spiritual gifts distributed by the Spirit; Jews and Gentiles joined together in one new entity; and baptism and the Lord's Supper as signs of the new covenant. Because these realities were not applicable to the people of Israel before the coming of Christ, the church did not and could not exist

latter word is derived from the Greek ἐκκαλεῖν (*ekkalein*), caution is urged not to commit the root word fallacy and make too much of the fact that ἐκκαλεῖν signifies "to call out."
[46] Differences would include evangelical theology's rejection of the *totus Christus* and its redefinition of the sacraments as given and empowered by the Word of God and the Holy Spirit, rather than by the Church.
[47] Allison, *SS*, 29.

before then. Accordingly, because there is discontinuity between the people of Israel before the coming of Christ and Christians of the new covenant, the church did not exist prior to Christ but began on the day of Pentecost.[48] Catholic theology does not hold this discontinuity position, but it is embraced by many types of evangelical theology, often under the umbrella term "dispensationalism."

One of the major points of disagreement on the doctrine of the church is the idea of the universal church. Catholic theology identifies this as one of the three types of assembly (along with a worship gathering and the local church); evangelical theology concurs, but with a very different understanding of the universal church. For Catholic theology, the universal church is the Catholic Church as a concrete, actual reality in addition to being a spiritual and mystical reality. As visible and human, the universal or Catholic church professes a common faith, engages in worshiping God with a common liturgy, is nourished by means of common sacraments, and is taught, governed, and sanctified by a common hierarchy through apostolic succession. Evangelical theology conceives of the universal church as the fellowship of all the faithful, incorporating both the deceased believers who are presently in heaven and the living believers from all over the world. The former aspect of this universal church is gathered together as the "heavenly" church (Heb. 12:23). Though "the latter aspect does not assemble, does not possess a structure or organization, does not have human leaders, and does not have a specific space-time address,"[49] such intangibles do not render it any less real, as the universal church is manifested in local churches. Accordingly, a wide divide exists between Catholic theology's notion of the universal church and evangelical theology's idea. One implication of this divergence is that evangelical theology dissents from the Catholic Church's claim to be the universal sacrament of salvation. Certainly, local churches are divinely designed to be the instruments of salvation as their pastors and members proclaim the gospel, disciple, worship, baptize, celebrate the Lord's Supper, pray, educate, fellowship, provide care, exercise spiritual gifts, and the like. But such instrumentality pertains to local churches and does not stretch to include a universal church as a concrete, actual assembly—the Catholic Church.

At the heart of evangelical theology's disagreement is the Catholic

---

[48] For further discussion, see ibid., 61–89.
[49] Ibid., 31.

system's two axioms. The nature-grace interdependence requires that divine grace be concretely manifested in nature. Accordingly, the church as the body of Jesus Christ cannot be some invisible, spiritual, intangible entity; on the contrary, it must be a visible, material, concrete reality—the Catholic Church. The Christ-Church interconnection means that the Catholic Church is the extension of the incarnation of the ascended Christ. To be specific, the Catholic Church concretely mediates divine grace to (human) nature so as to be the universal and only means of salvation. As both of these axioms at the core of the Catholic theological system have already received critique (ch. 2), this assessment turns to specific criticisms of Catholic ecclesiology, particularly its presentation of the four historical or classical attributes of the church.

Importantly, the Protestant Reformers criticized and broke from the Catholic Church as the "one, holy, catholic, and apostolic" church, not because these historic attributes were unbiblical and hence untrue of the church, but because the Church of the sixteenth century claimed them as its characteristics but belied their truthfulness and reality by the decrepit state into which it had fallen. Accordingly, while holding that the church is one, holy, catholic, and apostolic, the Reformers had to distinguish true churches—those started by Martin Luther, Huldrych Zwingli, John Calvin, and others—from the false Catholic Church. This situation led to their formulation of the marks of a true church, which were two in number. As the Augsburg Confession (Lutheran theology) affirmed, "The church is the congregation of the saints in which the gospel is rightly taught and the sacraments [baptism and the Lord's Supper] rightly administered."[50] Calvin (Reformed theology) concurred: "Wherever we see the Word of God purely preached and heard, and the sacraments administered according to Christ's institution, there, it is not to be doubted, a church of God exists."[51] Some later Protestant churches added a third mark: church discipline.[52]

Oneness/Unity

Consequently, while Catholic theology underscores three concrete bonds— the Creed, the liturgy,[53] and apostolic succession—of the *oneness* of the

---

[50] Augsburg Confession 7 (Schaff, 3:11–12).
[51] Calvin, *Institutes* 4.1.8 (LCC 21:1022).
[52] Thirty-Nine Articles (Anglican), 19 (Schaff, 3:486); Belgic Confession (Reformed), 29 (Schaff, 3:383); Scottish Confession of Faith (Reformed), 18 (Schaff, 3:461–462).
[53] Every worship service celebrated by the Catholic Church worldwide follows the same liturgy, with the same prayers, readings of Scripture, Eucharist, etc.

Church, evangelical theology emphasizes that "unto the true unity of the church, it is sufficient to agree concerning the doctrine of the gospel and the administration of the sacraments."[54] Moreover, evangelical theology understands unity in three ways: Positionally, unity is a reality of the church; that is, it is already united because it has been given the gift of oneness by the Holy Spirit (Eph. 4:3). Purposively, the church aims to "attain to the unity of the faith and of the knowledge of the Son of God, to mature manhood, to the measure of the stature of the fullness of Christ" (v. 13). This attainment of unity as a goal entails a process. Instrumentally, unity among its members fosters growth in unity; for this reason, the church works hard to maintain the unity with which it has been endowed (v. 3). "Thus, affirming the unity of the church means affirming that the church, which is endowed with oneness, pursues the end of perfect unity by working diligently to maintain its unity."[55]

As for the three concrete bonds of unity affirmed by Catholic theology, because only the Catholic Church possesses them, it is only through the Church, as "the universal help toward salvation, . . . [that] the fullness of the means of salvation can be obtained."[56] Clearly, evangelical theology dissents from this position, together with its corollary that "[t]he sole Church of Christ . . . subsists in (*subsistit in*) the Catholic Church, which is governed by the successor of Peter and by the bishops in communion with him."[57] While Catholic theology does not refrain from calling evangelicals "Christians" and even appreciates their commitment to Scripture, divine grace, and the like, it does deny that their assemblies are churches; they are, instead, "ecclesial communities."[58] Furthermore, Catholic theology insists that the salvation offered to people through evangelical ecclesial communities actually flows from the "fullness of grace and truth that Christ has entrusted to the Catholic Church."[59] What is more, if unity is ever to be recovered among evangelical ecclesial communities and other churches, those evangelical assemblies must join the Catholic Church.

In addition to the critique of the two axioms upon which Catholic

[54] Augsburg Confession 7 (Schaff, 3:11–12).
[55] Allison, *SS*, 168.
[56] CCC 816; citation is from Vatican Council II, *Unitatis redintegratio* 3.5.
[57] CCC 816; citation is from Vatican Council II, *Lumen Gentium* 8.2.
[58] This point was underscored and clarified in the *motu proprio* of Pope Benedict XVI, "Responses to Some Questions Regarding Certain Aspects of the Doctrine of the Church" (July 10, 2007), accessible at http://www.vatican.va/roman_curia/congregations/cfaith/documents/rc_con_cfaith_doc_20070629_responsa-quaestiones_en.html.
[59] CCC 819.

ecclesiology is grounded, several specific criticisms are in order. Certainly, evangelical theology appreciates the clarity of Catholic theology on this point. Following Vatican Council II, a great degree of ambiguity on the connection of evangelical churches to the Catholic Church clouded that relationship and hence was unhelpful. Additionally, evangelical theology embraces all the common doctrine it shares with Catholic theology, as noted in this book, and rejoices with Catholics who, through repentance from sin and faith alone in the saving work of Jesus Christ as announced in the gospel, have embraced salvation. However, it notes that because of Catholic theology's stance, the journey of some evangelicals toward the Catholic Church—and the accompanying encouragement from Catholics to do so—in response to a longing for the unity of all churches and the overcoming of historic and current divisions between them, is not satisfied by this move. Catholicism's position that evangelical ecclesial communities are not even churches does nothing to overcome the problem of disunity. Moreover, the utopian vision of other churches and ecclesial communities finally becoming united by being joined to the Catholic Church will not be actualized, nor should it even be pursued. Such a dream would entail evangelical theology and churches agreeing with the axioms of the nature-grace interdependence and the Christ-Church interconnection, yielding to the doctrines that separate it from Catholic theology (as noted in this book), and abandoning the Protestant principles of *sola Scriptura* and justification by grace alone through faith alone. Such moves are not permissible.

Holiness

Concerning the attribute of *holiness*, evangelical and Catholic theology agree that the purity with which the church has been endowed is a real though imperfect gift. Evangelical theology affirms three ways in which the church is holy. Positionally, the church is already holy, or set apart from sin and the world for God's special use (1 Cor. 1:1–2). Purposively, the church aims at perfect purity in response to the biblical vision of its future as "holy and without blemish" (Eph. 5:27). Instrumentally, the church fosters greater and greater purity by pursuing the holiness of its members (2 Cor. 6:14–7:1).

The major point of disagreement on this attribute of the church is over the extent of holiness that is possible during this earthly pilgrimage. Catholic theology maintains that some of the faithful have "practiced heroic virtue and lived in fidelity to God's grace" and thus are to be canonized as saints.[60] With reference to the axiom of the nature-grace interdependence, this view of holiness is based on grace completely elevating (human) nature so as to render it perfect. This axiom fails, as explained in the earlier critique of the Catholic system. But a few specific criticisms may also be offered now. A chief critique is that this position of achieving complete holiness—even fostered and empowered by divine grace, as Catholic theology strongly insists—is contradicted by Scripture. Even when the Bible presents its "heroes" as righteous and blameless, fearing God and walking with him—e.g., Noah (Gen. 6:9), Job (Job 1:1, 8), Zechariah and Elizabeth (Luke 1:6)—Scripture also takes note of their failures. Beyond these examples, the apostle John warns Christians, "If we say we have no sin, we deceive ourselves, and the truth is not in us. If we confess our sins, he is faithful and just to forgive us our sins and to cleanse us from all unrighteousness. If we say we have not sinned, we make him a liar, and his word is not in us" (1 John 1:8–10). Given the standard of righteousness enjoined by Jesus—"You therefore must be perfect, as your heavenly Father is perfect" (Matt. 5:48)—it is little wonder that he also charged his disciples with daily confession of sin (Matt. 6:12). The actualization of complete obedience and faithfulness to God and his will has not been granted to Christians during their earthly lives; hence, Catholic theology is wrong to claim that some of the faithful have achieved this unattainable holiness.[61]

Besides the problem that this position runs into with Scripture, it is wrong for other reasons. For one thing, it represents what evangelical theology calls "overrealized eschatology." This expression refers to realities that are reserved for the future, after Jesus Christ returns, being prematurely brought into and actualized in the present. For example, some people insist that because human beings, in the future age, will not be married, they should forgo marriage now, in this present age. A future reality is prematurely brought into and realized in the present. For evangelical theology, Catholic theology's doctrine of sainthood suffers from such overrealized eschatology: a reality that is promised as a future blessing is prematurely

---

[60] CCC 828.

[61] This discussion also links with Catholic theology's notion of salvation as a synergistic effort between divine grace and human cooperation, with the expectation that salvation comes to those who do what is within their reach to do (*facere quod in se est*)—not, as evangelicals assert, that salvation is granted to those who are counted as perfectly righteous (not by their own righteousness, but because Jesus Christ imputes perfect righteousness to their account). Critique of this notion comes later in the book.

brought into and actualized in the present age. A second problem questions the actual help that fully sanctified human beings provide for people who are struggling with sin and suffering. It is one thing for Christians, when they are tempted and tried, to turn to their sympathetic High Priest, who has been tempted and has suffered in every way that they have been, yet without sin. For in his case, Jesus the God-man not only empathizes with them but he also gives grace, mercy, and help in their time of need (Heb. 2:14–18; 4:16–18). But holy human beings as models do not actually encourage those who are weak and struggling; rather, perfect people function as burdens of law for sinners: What is wrong with these abject failures, that they cannot be like the saints? Moreover, these saints cannot offer grace and mercy to them, only an unattainably high standard that functions as a law that brings greater condemnation as it is not reached. A third problem, one that has been addressed and will be again later on, is the doctrine of Mary's sinlessness.

Catholicity

As understood by Catholic theology, the attribute of *catholicity*, or universality, both accords and clashes with evangelical theology's understanding of it. Both agree that the Great Commission (Matt. 28:18–20) is a foundation for the church's universality: As the giver of this mandate, Jesus Christ will not permit his church to be parochial in its interests; rather, it must take the gospel into every corner of the globe and make disciples of all people. Accordingly, its catholicity requires the church to be missional. Other foundational elements of this attribute on which the two theologies agree are the love of Christ moving the church to engage in its ministry of reconciliation (2 Cor. 5:14–21); the biblical affirmation that God does not wish that anyone should perish apart from Christ, but desires for all people to be saved (2 Pet. 3:9; 1 Tim. 2:4); and the empowerment of the Holy Spirit for the church's worldwide missional endeavors (Acts 1:8). Some camps within evangelical theology—for example, Reformed theology—would add another foundational element to those already presented: proclamation of the gospel for those chosen by God. As the apostle Paul explained, "I endure everything for the sake of the elect, that they also may obtain the salvation that is in Christ Jesus with eternal glory (2 Tim. 2:10). Accordingly, the missional church moves into the whole world to reach people who have been divinely chosen to embrace the good news. Indeed, from this perspective, the church does not seek to announce the truth of salvation to people who already desire the truth (as Catholic theology holds), but proclaims the gospel as the truth, empowered by the Spirit, that awakens a longing for the truth and ignites faith in those whom God has chosen and called (Rom. 10:17; cf. 8:29–30; 2 Thess. 2:13–14).

Despite these points of agreement, Catholic and evangelical theology are largely at odds with one another on this attribute of the church's catholicity. The major source of this disagreement is the Catholic system's axiom of the Christ-Church interconnection. If the Church is the prolongation of the incarnation of Jesus Christ such that the whole Christ subsists in the Catholic Church, and if the whole Christ is present everywhere, then logically the Catholic Church is universal as well. Moreover, it alone possesses "the fullness of the means of salvation."[62] This axiom has already been critiqued.

As for specific criticisms, evangelical theology is deeply concerned by Catholic theology's answer to the important question, "Who belongs to the Catholic Church?" Not surprisingly, the first part of the answer affirms that the Catholic faithful are situated at the heart of the Church, in the innermost circle of concentric circles; to them belongs the fullness of salvation. Moving from this center circle to those just outside of it, we find Christians of the Orthodox churches as well as those in Protestant/evangelical communities. Though properly baptized, all of these in one way or another do not enjoy the fullness of salvation, which is found only by those in full unity or communion with the Catholic Church. Given Catholic theology's axiom of the Christ-Church interconnection, evangelical theology can understand this diminished stature that the Church accords to other parts of Christendom, even while disagreeing with it. But what is most disturbing is the rest of the discussion.

Farther out from these inner circles, members of non-Christian religions who have not heard the gospel—specifically, Jews and Muslims—are situated. What distinguishes this circle from those still farther removed from the center is that their knowledge of God is based on biblical revelation: in the case of the Jews, the Old Testament, including the promise of the Messiah; for Muslims, the faith of Abraham and knowledge of God the Creator and merciful Judge. Jews and Muslims can be saved. Still farther removed

---

[62] CCC 830; citation is from *Unitatis redintegratio* 3; *Ad gentes divinitus* 6.

from the center circle are adherents of other non-Christian religions—e.g., Hindus and Buddhists—who "search, among shadows and images," for the unknown God who has created them and desires that they be saved.[63] Other non-Christians who, through divine grace, believe in God, are situated in the penultimate concentric circle. For them also eternal salvation is possible, if they "seek God with a sincere heart, and, moved by grace, try in their actions to do his will as they know it through the dictates of their conscience."[64] Still farther removed are those located in the outermost concentric circle. These people live without an explicit knowledge of God, yet salvation is available to those who, through divine grace, strive to lead a good life.[65] This salvation is designed for them because God desires that all people become saved, it is operative in them because of the grace of God,[66] and it joins them to the Catholic Church in virtue of the fact that it is "the universal sacrament of salvation."[67] Just how the Church can exercise an instrumental role in the salvation of non-Christians who have neither knowledge of Christ nor acquaintance with his Church is not spelled out.[68] Moreover, the Church considers "[w]hatever good or truth is found amongst them [non-Christians] . . . to be a preparation for the Gospel" given by God as light to them.[69] Consequently, when the Church engages in evangelization of these non-Christians, the effect of its missional endeavor "is that whatever good is found sown in the minds and hearts of men or in the rites and customs of people, these not only are preserved from destruction, but are purified, raised up, and perfected for the glory of God, the confusion of the devil, and the happiness of man."[70] Thus, Catholic theology finds an important role for non-Christian religions in preparing their adherents for salvation.

---

[63] CCC 843.

[64] CCC 847; citation is from Vatican Council II, *Lumen Gentium* 16.

[65] For a summary of the historical development of inclusivism in the Catholic Church, see Francis A. Sullivan, "Vatican II on the Salvation of Other Religions," in *After Vatican II: Trajectories and Hermeneutics*, ed. James L. Heft (Grand Rapids, MI: Eerdmans, 2012), 68–95.

[66] In the case of non-Christians who have some knowledge of God, his grace prompts their seeking him and undergirds their attempts to do his will through obeying their conscience; for non-Christians who do not have knowledge of God, his grace prompts their striving to live a good life.

[67] Vatican Council II, *Lumen Gentium* 48 (*VC II-1*, 407).

[68] One conjecture is offered by Sullivan, who links the Church's instrumental role in the salvation of non-Christians with the Church's offering of Christ in the sacrament of the Eucharist, which is universally effective as a sacrifice: "The fact that only the church can offer this sacrifice justifies describing the church as efficacious sign of the salvation of non-Christians even when it cannot play a more directly instrumental role by preaching the gospel to them" (Sullivan, "Vatican II on the Salvation of Other Religions," 76).

[69] Vatican Council II, *Lumen Gentium* 16 (*VC II-1*, 368); cf. CCC 843.

[70] Vatican Council II, *Lumen Gentium* 17 (*VC II-1*, 368–369).

Evangelical theology decries this notion of the Church's universality as embracing inclusivism, the view that though (1) salvation has been accomplished objectively by the death and resurrection of Jesus Christ, (2) explicit knowledge of the gospel of Christ and faith in him are not necessary for people to embrace salvation subjectively.[71] Evangelical theology objects to inclusivism because its second tenet has no biblical support; indeed, Scripture contradicts the idea that faith in Christ through the gospel is not needed for salvation (e.g., Rom. 10:13–17). Moreover, the church historically has never believed this; specifically, the Catholic Church did not begin to entertain the idea that non-Christians can be saved apart from becoming Christians until the following pronouncement from Pope Pius IX in 1863:

> Here, too, our beloved sons and venerable brothers, it is again necessary to mention and censure a very grave error entrapping some Catholics who believe that it is possible to arrive at eternal salvation although living in error and alienated from the true faith and Catholic unity. Such belief is certainly opposed to Catholic teaching. There are, of course, those who are struggling with invincible ignorance about our most holy religion. Sincerely observing the natural law and its precepts inscribed by God on all hearts and ready to obey God, they live honest lives and are able to attain eternal life by the efficacious virtue of divine light and grace. Because God knows, searches and clearly understands the minds, hearts, thoughts, and nature of all, his supreme kindness and clemency do not permit anyone at all who is not guilty of deliberate sin to suffer eternal punishments.[72]

Even then, Vatican Council I (1870) did not include the idea, which did not appear again until Pope Pius XII's 1943 encyclical *The Mystical Body of Christ*.[73] After a lengthy development, Vatican Council II's *Lumen Gentium*

---

[71] Though various permutations of inclusivism may be found today, the one just described corresponds with the inclusivism promoted by Catholic theology, as evidenced in a document from the Pontifical Council for Interreligious Dialogue: "[A]ll men and women who are saved share, though differently, in the same mystery of salvation in Jesus Christ through his Spirit. Christians know this through their faith, while others remain unaware that Jesus Christ is the source of their salvation. . . . Concretely, it will be in the sincere practice of what is good in their own religious traditions and by following the dictates of their conscience that the members of other religions respond positively to God's invitation and receive salvation in Jesus Christ, even while they do not recognize or acknowledge him as their savior" (Pontifical Council for Interreligious Dialogue, "Dialogue and Proclamation," 29. Accessible at http://www.vatican.va/roman_curia/pontifical_councils/interelg/documents/rc_pc_interelg_doc _19051991_dialogue-and-proclamatio_en.html).

[72] Pope Pius IX, *Quanto conficiamur moerore* (August 10, 1863), paragraph 7. Accessible at http://www.papal encyclicals.net/Pius09/p9quanto.htm).

[73] Pope Pius XII, *Mystici Corporis Christi* (June 29, 1943). Accessible at http://www.vatican.va/holy_father/pius _xii/encyclicals/documents/hf_p-xii_enc_29061943_mystici-corporis-christi_en.html.

articulated inclusivism as just described, while forging new ground in its affirmation of the goodness of non-Christian religions. Several other conciliar
documents—*Nostra aetate*, *Ad gentes*, and *Gaudium et Spes*—echo similar
ideas.[74] But the point stands: inclusivism as Catholic theology of the salvation of non-Christians is a novel belief and hence a betrayal of the Catholic
Church's lengthy tradition.

Evangelical theology objects to inclusivism on many other grounds as
well. Inclusivism has an inadequate view of human sinfulness and its impact on the human response to the general revelation of God. According to
Scripture, (1) the response of non-Christians to the witness of God in the
created order is idolatry that leaves them without excuse before him (Rom.
1:18–25); (2) their adherence to the dictates of their conscience is at best
partial and leaves them in no better a state than Jews who have the law and
disobey it (Rom. 2:13–16); (3) their reaction to God's providential care is
superstition and idolatry (Acts 14:8–18); and (4) the stirring in their hearts
to search for God (of whom they have an innate sense) results in ignorant
worship that is culpable before the divine Judge, who demands that they
repent (Acts 17:22–31). That is, the biblical portrait of the status of non-
Christians is not a pretty one; rather, it presents them as being in dire straits
before God. This dismal situation is even underscored by Vatican Council
II, whose *Lumen Gentium* (16), as quoted earlier, concludes its presentation of inclusivism with strong words of caution about the facility of non-
Christians traveling a path to salvation apart from the Catholic Church's
missional assistance.[75]

Furthermore, Catholic inclusivism assumes that worship, prayer, spirituality, good deeds, and other "religious" or "positive" activities in which
non-Christians engage are evidences of divine grace rather than the perverted responses of intractably sinful hearts. Evangelical theology would
agree that any "good" that human beings do is the result of being created in the image of God and being recipients of "common" grace (or, for
other proponents of evangelical theology, prevenient grace). But it would
not agree that such grace is in any way salvific, that is, effecting salvation,

---

[74] Sullivan notes these conciliar contributions to the topic and points to several post-conciliar documents—Pope Paul VI's *Evangelii Nuntiandi*; Pope John Paul II's *Redemptor Hominis, Dominum et Vivificantem; Redemptoris Missio, Ecclesia in Asia*—that continued its development in Catholic theology (Sullivan, "Vatican II on the Salvation of Other Religions," 77–88).
[75] This very important fact is well discussed and defended in Ralph Martin, *Will Many Be Saved? What Vatican II Actually Teaches and Its Implications for the New Evangelization* (Grand Rapids, MI: Eerdmans, 2012).

apart from a response of faith to the gospel of Jesus Christ. And evangelical theology would dissent from the idea that any "good" activity achieves divine favor. Additionally, later Catholic theological development of this inclusivism attaches such positive activities to the work of the Spirit who, like the wind, "blows where it wishes" (John 3:8).[76] This idea is contradicted by Jesus himself, who associates the wind-like activity of the Holy Spirit with regeneration (John 3:1–8)[77] and promises to the apostles the gift of the Spirit, "whom the world cannot receive, because it neither sees him nor knows him" (John 14:17). If the gift of the Holy Spirit is promised to Christians but denied to outsiders, how can these versions of Catholic inclusivism claim a role for the Spirit in the religions and activities of non-Christians? Catholic inclusivism also assumes a divine activity to prompt faith apart from knowledge of the gospel, though Catholic theology considers such work to be a mystery and thus, one would assume, not revealed by God. As Vatican Council II's *Ad gentes* offered, ". . . *although in ways known to himself* God can lead those who, through no fault of their own, are ignorant of the Gospel to that faith without which it is impossible to please him."[78] If such ways are "known to God," the implication seems to be that they are not known to people; hence, if such divine activity is not a matter of divine revelation, how can Catholic theology affirm anything about it? Accordingly, inclusivism seems to be speculation at best.

As a final objection to Catholic inclusivism, evangelical theology draws attention to its view of the possibility of salvation for Jews and Muslims. Importantly, though the *Catechism* draws specific attention to the fact that the Jewish waiting for the Messiah "is accompanied by the drama of not knowing or misunderstanding Christ Jesus,"[79] it makes no mention of the major tenets of Islam that deny the Trinity (Sura 4:171) and denounce the idea that God has a Son (e.g., Sura 4:171; 6:101; 9:30). But in the case of both Judaism and Islam, their lack of acknowledgment, or outright denial, of the Trinity and of the deity of Jesus Christ places them outside the pale of salvation, as explained by Jesus himself:

---

[76] As Sullivan notes, this emphasis on the unregulated blowing of the Holy Spirit—that is, his work outside of the Catholic Church—was a favorite theme of Pope John Paul II (e.g., *Dominum et Vivificantem*) (Sullivan, "Vatican II on the Salvation of Other Religions," 82).

[77] If this activity of the Spirit is associated with regeneration, and if the Catholic Church insists that such regeneration is effected by Baptism, then how can people experience this wind-like activity, or regeneration, of the Spirit apart from the sacrament? Further discussion of this issue comes later in the book.

[78] Vatican Council II, *Ad gentes* 7 (*VC II-1*, 821, emphasis added).

[79] CCC 840.

So Jesus said to them, "Truly, truly, I say to you, the Son can do nothing of his own accord, but only what he sees the Father doing. For whatever the Father does, that the Son does likewise. For the Father loves the Son and shows him all that he himself is doing. And greater works than these will he show him, so that you may marvel. For as the Father raises the dead and gives them life, so also the Son gives life to whom he will. The Father judges no one, but has given all judgment to the Son, that all may honor the Son, just as they honor the Father. Whoever does not honor the Son does not honor the Father who sent him. Truly, truly, I say to you, whoever hears my word and believes him who sent me has eternal life. He does not come into judgment, but has passed from death to life. (John 5:19–24)

The work of the Father and the Son (the work of the Spirit, though not discussed here, could be added) accomplished eternal salvation, and God cannot be honored apart from honoring the Son. Moreover, eternal life is appropriated by faith in the gospel of Christ. Given the major tenets of their religions, the adherents of Judaism and Islam are excluded from eternal salvation. This position of exclusivism is embraced by evangelical theology, in contradistinction to the inclusivism maintained by Catholic theology.

In summary, the attribute of the catholicity of the church engenders a deep divide between Catholic and evangelical theology.

Apostolicity

As for the attribute of *apostolicity*, agreement between the two positions centers on the emphasis accorded to the foundational role of the apostles in the church (Eph. 2:20) and on the New Testament as the writing of the apostles. Differences abound from this point on. Evangelical theology dissents especially from Catholic theology's doctrine of apostolic succession. Certainly, Jesus chose the twelve disciples to engage in ministry (Matthew 10), and after his death and resurrection, he appointed them to fulfill the Great Commission (Matt. 28:18–20). Specifically, the mission with which the Father had commissioned the Son became the mission with which the Son commissioned the church: "As the Father has sent me, even so I am sending you" (John 20:21). This mission was evangelistic in nature, proclaiming the gospel of the forgiveness of sins through Jesus Christ (Luke

24:44–48; John 20:23), and it involved making disciples throughout the world (Matt. 28:18–20). The beginning of the fulfillment of the missionality of the church is narrated in Acts. What is striking is the apostles' concentration on announcing the good news; calling people to repent of their sins and trust in Jesus Christ by faith; promising the forgiveness of sins and the gift of his Spirit to those who so call upon the Lord; and baptizing these disciples and incorporating them into the church, where apostolic teaching, the Lord's Supper, worship, prayer, fellowship, sacrificial generosity, signs and wonders, and multiplication took place (e.g., Acts 2:38–47). This narrative does not present the development of a self-perpetuating hierarchy, nor does it offer the template for a line of succession from the apostles. Indeed, many non-apostolic characters figure in the story: Stephen, the first Christian martyr (Acts 7); Philip, the evangelist to the Samaritans and the Ethiopian eunuch (Acts 8); "men of Cyprus and Cyrene" who evangelize the Greeks (Acts 11:19–22) and launch the first Gentile church, led by Barnabas, in Antioch (vv. 22–26); and others. Certainly, the apostles selected leaders in the churches they had planted (e.g., 14:23), but such appointments did not transfer some type of apostolic authority to their recipients.

The episcopalian form of church government, which led eventually to the Catholic Church's hierarchical structure with the papacy at its head, awaited historical development and is not without its problems. Its three-tiered pattern of leadership—episcopate (or office of bishop); eldership/priesthood/pastorate; and diaconate—contradicts the two-tiered pattern of leadership as set forth in Scripture: The New Testament presents one office of teaching and oversight that is exercised by leaders who are called elders, bishops, overseers, or pastors (these terms are used interchangeably in the New Testament),[80] and a second office of ministry or service that is exercised by deacons and deaconesses. Another problem is that the historical development of this three-tiered ministry was a pragmatic solution to contextual factors, specifically the rise of heresy and the splintering of churches through division. The *monoepiscopalian* form of government elevated one bishop (Gk. *mono* = one; *episcopos* = bishop) around whom the entire church would congregate in hopes that he would stave off division and maintain the unity of the church. Though biblical support for this polity is offered—e.g., James's role at the council of Jerusalem is similar to the func-

---

[80] For support for this claim, see Allison, *SS*, 211–212.

tion of a bishop; Paul's appointment of apostolic legates (Timothy, Titus), who in turn appointed others, approaches the authority of a bishop—such support is only a seed awaiting the full flowering of the concept later in the early church. This point introduces a further problem: Episcopalianism leading to the papacy departs from the sufficiency of Scripture because it is dependent on developments in the following centuries for its justification. Even here, the development of this structure is only part of the story, as some type of congregational form of church government was present at the same time in the early church.[81]

Part of this development focused on Jesus's promise to Peter, who confessed the identity of his friend as "the Christ, the Son of the living God" (Matt. 16:16): "And I tell you, you are Peter, and on this rock I will build my church, and the gates of hell shall not prevail against it. I will give you the keys of the kingdom of heaven, and whatever you bind on earth shall be bound in heaven, and whatever you loose on earth shall be loosed in heaven" (vv. 18–19). Several points need to be made: Whereas some evangelical theologians interpret "this rock" as a reference to Peter, and others as a reference to his confession, a more plausible understanding is that the rock is *Peter in virtue of his confession*. Thus, Jesus promises that he is about "to institute a new assembly of his people gathered under him—'my church,' he calls it—involving the Twelve and built on Peter and his authoritative word—the confession of faith in the identity of Jesus of Nazareth."[82] The promised "keys of the kingdom" will be the crux of Christ's building of his church. Again, how we see the apostles in the book of Acts employing these gifts is crucial for our understanding of Jesus's promise. "These keys have to do with the gospel and people's response to it: those who repent of sin and embrace Jesus Christ by faith are 'loosed' from their sin, death and condemnation, domination by the world, and enslavement to the evil one. In contrast, those who refuse to heed the good news are 'bound' in that

---

[81] See, for example, Clement of Rome, *Letter to the Corinthians* 44 (ANF 1:16); *Didache* 15 (ANF 7:381).

[82] Allison, *SS*, 94. This interpretation should not be taken to be minimizing Peter's salvation-historical privilege among the apostles; after all, Peter is the first to announce the gospel to the Jews (Acts 2:14–41), confirms (along with John) the inclusion of the Samaritans in the church (Acts 8:14–25), and is the apostle who is instrumental in the conversion of the first Gentiles (Acts 10, 11). However, Matt. 16:13–20 must be set in the context of the entire Gospel of Matthew: "the disciples [all of them] were called to be fishers of men (4:19), to be salt (5:13) and light (5:14–16), to preach the good news of the kingdom (10:6–42), and, after the Resurrection, to disciple the nations and teach them all that Jesus commanded (28:18–20)" (D. A. Carson, "Matthew," in Frank E. Gaebelein, ed., *Expositor's Bible Commentary*, 12 vols. [Grand Rapids, MI: Zondervan, 1984], 8:370–372). To Christ's disciples (all of them, with the special role of Peter) is given the responsibility of the exercise of the keys and, later in the Gospel, it is given to the entire church (Matt. 18:15–20; confirmed by 1 Cor. 5:1–13; 2 Cor. 13:10; Titus 2:15; 3:10–11).

persistent hellish nightmare."[83] Accordingly, this passage is not support for the episcopalian hierarchy of the Catholic Church with the pope at its head and dependent on apostolic succession for its authority.[84]

At the heart of evangelical theology's rejection of apostolic succession is the doctrine's basis in the Christ-Church interconnection, with its implication that somehow Christ transferred his ministerial authority and activity to the apostles, who in turn transferred it to their successors, the bishops, who continue it in the Catholic Church as the ongoing incarnation of Christ. To its credit, the *Catechism* affirms that one aspect of apostleship cannot be and has not been transmitted: being eyewitnesses of the resurrection and as such being the foundation of the church. Where the *Catechism* goes wrong is in its insistence that another aspect of the apostolic office can be and has been transferred: the appointment of successors to the apostles; thus, apostolic succession. John Webster well represents evangelical theology's specific critique of this notion:

> First, the ministerial acts of Jesus Christ in the Spirit, by which he gathers, protects, and preserves the church, are, properly speaking, incommunicable [non-transferrable] and non-representable. That is to say, if by 'communication' or 'representation' we mean the assumption of Christ's proper work by agents other than himself, we may not make use of such concepts in a Christologically and pneumatologically structured theology of ministry. The dogmatic premises of an evangelical ecclesiology—that, as the risen and ascended Lord, Jesus Christ is present and active—do not permit any such transference of agency. Christ distributes his own benefits through his Spirit, that is, by his own hand; they are not to be thought of as some treasure turned over to the church for it to dispense.[85]

Evangelical theology dissents from Catholic theology's notion that Christ has transferred his authority and activity through the successors of the apostles through the line of apostolic succession.

Positively, evangelical theology understands apostolicity to refer to the

[83] Allison, ibid.
[84] For the historical development of the use of Matthew 16 in support of the papacy, see Michael A. G. Haykin, "The Development and Consolidation of the Papacy"; and Gregg R. Allison, "The Papacy from Leo I to Vatican II," in Thomas Schreiner and Benjamin Merkle, eds., *Shepherding God's Flock* (Grand Rapids, MI: Kregel, 2014).
[85] John Webster, *Word and Church: Essays in Christian Dogmatics* (Edinburgh and New York: T & T Clark, 2001), 199–200.

church's focus on preaching, hearing, believing, and obeying the teachings of the apostles, written down in the canonical New Testament writings. Promised the guidance of the Holy Spirit for this very task, the apostles' memories were aided by the Spirit as they wrote, rendering them and their writings bona fide witnesses of Jesus Christ (John 14:26). Importantly, the apostle Peter himself underscores the manner in which he sought to ensure that the teachings that he had received from Christ would be transmitted to the church after his death ("departure"): "Therefore I intend always to remind you of these qualities, though you know them and are established in the truth that you have. I think it right, as long as I am in this body, to stir you up by way of reminder, since I know that the putting off of my body will be soon, as our Lord Jesus Christ made clear to me. And I will make every effort so that after my departure you may be able at any time to recall these things" (2 Pet. 1:12–15). Following this point, Peter explains that as an eyewitness of Jesus Christ's glory on the Mount of Transfiguration, he heard the very voice of God the Father commending his Son (vv. 16–18).[86] Amazingly, however, Peter professes that "we have the prophetic word more fully confirmed" and discourses on the written Word of God, the product of the biblical authors being moved by the Holy Spirit (vv. 19–21). If he, as the chief apostle, considered Scripture to be the sure, divine instruction for the church in the post-apostolic era, it is hard to see how apostolic succession could add to this already-certain foundation. Accordingly, evangelical theology embraces apostolicity as the logocentricity, or Word-centeredness, of the church that is focused on the writings of the apostles.

This point concludes the evangelical assessment of the first section of the *Catechism*'s doctrine of the church. The presentation of the second part, followed by another section of assessment, follows next.

The Doctrine of the Church: "I believe in the holy catholic church" (Sec. 2, Ch. 3, Art. 9, Para. 4–6)

The *Catechism* now turns to a specific discussion of the people of the Church: "the faithful," as they are commonly called, composed of the hierarchy, the laity, and the monks and nuns who are dedicated to the consecrated life. As explained earlier, the faithful share in Christ's threefold

---

[86] Matt. 17:1–9 and parallels relate the event of the transfiguration.

office—priestly, prophetic, and royal—in various ways as they engage missionally with the world.

The Church is hierarchical because Christ designed it this way. Preaching the gospel, speaking to the community, bestowing grace—these are not self-initiated activities that one does to oneself; rather, these ministries of grace presuppose "ministers of grace, authorized and empowered by Christ. From him, they receive the mission and faculty ('the sacred power') to act *in persona Christi Capitis* ['in the person of Christ the Head']."[87] This ministry is conferred by the sacrament of Holy Orders. As ecclesial ministry, it is characterized by (1) *service* on the part of ministers who freely become slaves of Christ to be slaves of others; (2) *collegiality*, or a harmonious collaboration among bishops within the episcopal college in communion with its head, the bishop of Rome, and among priests "within the *presbyterium* of the diocese, under the direction of their bishop"; and (3) *personal responsibility* to respond to one's call and to exercise one's ministry.[88]

The episcopal college and its head, the pope, finds its origin in Christ's institution of the Twelve: "[H]e constituted [them] in the form of a college or permanent assembly, at the head of which he placed Peter, chosen from among them."[89] The parallelism is this: As Peter and the other eleven apostles constituted a single apostolic college, so the pope, Peter's successor, and the bishops, the apostles' successors, form the one episcopal college. Biblical support for this structure is found in Matthew 16:18–19 (cf. John 21:15–17), interpreted in the following way: "The Lord made Simon alone, whom he named Peter, the 'rock' of his Church. He gave him the keys of his Church and instituted him shepherd of the whole flock. 'The office of binding and loosing which was given to Peter was also assigned to the college of apostles united to its head.'"[90] Accordingly, the papacy and the ecclesial college is not just an administrative convenience or pragmatic arrangement; it "belongs to the Church's very foundation" in an essential manner.[91] To be underscored is the fact that the pope—also called the "Roman Pontiff"—is the bishop of Rome and the successor of Peter; as the Vicar (i.e., visible representative) of Christ and the pastor of the entire Catholic Church, he

[87] CCC 875.
[88] CCC 876–878.
[89] CCC 880; citation is from Vatican Council II, *Lumen Gentium* 19.
[90] CCC 881; citation is from Vatican Council II, *Lumen Gentium* 22.2.
[91] CCC 881.

possesses "full, supreme, and universal power over the whole Church, a power which he can always exercise unhindered."[92]

As united with the pope, the college of bishops, meeting in an ecumenical council, has "supreme and full authority over the universal Church; but this power cannot be exercised without the agreement of the Roman Pontiff."[93] Each bishop has both local and universal responsibilities: Locally, he is the center of unity for his own particular church or diocese, exercising his ministry over the faithful assigned to him, assisted by priests and deacons. Universally, as a member of the episcopal college, he is concerned for all the churches. Regional gatherings of bishops are called synods or provincial councils; national gatherings are called episcopal conferences (e.g., the U. S. Conference of Catholic Bishops).

The bishops of the Church engage in three specific ministries: teaching, sanctifying, and ruling. The teaching office focuses on preaching the gospel; and to preserve the apostolic faith in the Church, this office is characterized by infallibility. At the most general level, the membership of the Church "unfailingly adheres to this faith" as it is guided by the Magisterium.[94] But it is the Magisterium that particularly enjoys this "charism [i.e., gift] of infallibility in matters of faith and morals,"[95] the exercise of which takes on several forms: With respect to the pope, according to the doctrine of papal infallibility promulgated by Vatican Council I,[96] "[t]he Roman Pontiff, head of the college of bishops, enjoys this infallibility in virtue of his office, when, as supreme pastor and teacher of all the faithful—who confirms his brethren in the faith—he proclaims by a definitive act a doctrine pertaining to faith or morals."[97] With respect to the episcopal college, "[t]he infallibility promised to the Church is also present in the body of bishops when, together with Peter's successor, they exercise the supreme Magisterium,"[98] especially when gathered in an ecumenical council. All infallible definitions promulgated by the Magisterium are binding on all Catholics (they "must be adhered to with the obedience of faith"),[99] and "[t]his infallibility ex-

---

[92] CCC 882; citation is from Vatican Council II, *Lumen Gentium* 22.
[93] CCC 883; citation is from Vatican Council II, *Lumen Gentium* 22.
[94] CCC 889; citation is from Vatican Council II, *Lumen Gentium* 12; cf. *Dei Verbum* 10.
[95] CCC 890.
[96] Vatican Council I (1870), *First Dogmatic Constitution on the Church of Christ*, session 4. Accessible at http://www.papalencyclicals.net/Councils/ecum20.htm#papal infallibility defined.
[97] CCC 891; citation is from Vatican Council II, *Lumen Gentium* 25; cf. Vatican Council I.
[98] CCC 891.
[99] Ibid.; citation is from Vatican Council II, *Lumen Gentium* 25.2.

tends as far as the deposit of divine Revelation itself."[100] On a lesser level, when the bishops in communion with the pope, "without arriving at an infallible definition and without pronouncing in a 'definitive manner,' . . . propose in the exercise of the ordinary Magisterium a teaching that leads to better understanding of Revelation in matters of faith and morals," divine assistance is also provided. In such a case, the faithful, though not owing the obedience of faith, "are to adhere to it with religious assent," which is an extension of the obedience of faith.[101]

The sanctifying office centers on the administrations of the sacraments, especially the celebration of the Eucharist. Other activities encompassed by this office include prayer, work, the ministry of the word, and an exemplary lifestyle.

The governing office applies to the particular churches assigned to the bishops and is carried out "by their [the bishops'] counsels, exhortations, and example . . . in the spirit of service which is that of their Master."[102] As noted before, the authority of the bishops must be exercised in tandem with the pope and is ultimately controlled by him. At the same time, episcopal authority is personal, ordinary, and immediate because it is exercised in the name of Christ, the Good Shepherd, who is the model for the bishop's pastoral office.

The second segment of the faithful consists of the laity of the Church; as those who have been incorporated into Christ through Baptism, they engage in his threefold ministry in carrying out the mission of the Church. The laity differ from the hierarchy because they have not been ordained through the sacrament of Holy Orders, and they differ from monks and nuns of the religious life because they have not taken the three evangelical counsels or vows of chastity, poverty, and obedience.[103] Their vocation engages them in temporal matters—education, business, government, science, the arts, farming, construction—which they seek to guide according to the will of God and for the glory of Christ, with the salvation of all people as their duty.

Laypeople participate in Christ's priestly office through their Spirit-led sacrifices of work, prayer, family and married life, leisure, and the like.

---

[100] CCC 891.
[101] CCC 892; citation is from Vatican Council II, *Lumen Gentium* 25.
[102] CCC 894; citation is from Vatican Council II, *Lumen Gentium* 27; cf. Luke 22:26–27.
[103] The adjective "evangelical" in this expression means "related to the gospel" (in Greek, *euaggelion*).

188 The Profession of Faith

Their participation in Christ's prophetic office is as witnesses and teachers: they engage in evangelization through their proclamation of Christ and the testimony of their life, and they help with catechesis, or the communication of the faith. Lay participation in Christ's kingly office takes on two forms: Personally, laypeople govern themselves, exercising royal power so that their soul/reason rules over their body/passions, thereby prohibiting themselves from being imprisoned by sin and evil. Publicly, laypeople "remedy the institutions and conditions of the world when the latter are an inducement to sin, that these may be conformed to the norms of justice, favoring rather than hindering the practice of virtue."[104] Additionally, they collaborate with the members of the hierarchy for the growth of the Church, serving on parish councils, diocesan synods, finance committees, and so forth.[105]

The third sector of the faithful consists of the men and women who dedicate themselves to the consecrated life through the profession of the three evangelical counsels. In one sense, Christ calls all his faithful to these counsels so they may be perfected in charity. For those men and women who are called to the consecrated life, this call entails "the obligation of practicing chastity in celibacy for the sake of the Kingdom, poverty and obedience."[106] The results of living in this religious state include a "more intimate" consecration to God, a following of Christ "more nearly,"[107] and the growth of the Church. Two types of the religious life exist in the Church: one lives in solitude; the other lives in community. The first type, the eremitic life, entails a devotion "to the praise of God and salvation of the world though a stricter separation from the world, the silence of solitude and assiduous prayer and penance";[108] the Carthusian and Camaldolese orders are examples. The religious life in community is represented by such orders as the Franciscans and the Dominicans, whose members live life in common and collaborate with diocesan bishops in their pastoral work. Consecrated virgins are women who have been dedicated to a life in the state of virginity by a solemn rite—the *Consecratio Virginum*—which renders them "betrothed mystically to Christ" for service to the Church.[109] Some religious serve in

---

[104] CCC 909; citation is from Vatican Council II, *Lumen Gentium* 36.3.
[105] CCC 910.
[106] CCC 915.
[107] CCC 916.
[108] CCC 920; citation is from the Code of Canon Law 603.1. The Code of Canon Law is a centuries-old system of laws and legal principles governing the Roman Catholic Church. It was last revised in 1983.
[109] CCC 923; citation is from the Code of Canon Law 604.1. This solemn rite of consecration is a sacramental, not a sacrament. Sacramentals "are sacred signs which bear a resemblance to the sacraments" and which dis-

secular institutions, seeking the sanctification of the world from within it. Still others of the faithful, without taking (all of) the religious vows, serve in societies of apostolic life. What all these religious have in common is a special consecration to God that is manifested in a life that is fully dedicated to him and engagement in missional endeavors.

As it nears the completion of its discussion of the doctrine of the church, the *Catechism* returns to the Apostles' Creed and its confession of belief in "the holy catholic Church," which is followed immediately by the confession of faith in "the communion of saints." Accordingly, "[t]he communion of saints is the Church."[110] This belief is based on the idea that "the riches of Christ are communicated to all the members, through the sacraments," so that all the goods that the Church has received "necessarily become a common fund."[111] This communion in spiritual goods includes communion in the faith, the sacraments, charisms (gifts), possessions (in every sense of that word), and charity. The sharing of such goods is not confined to the Church that is seen, because the Church actually exists in three states: the *earthly church*, consisting of sojourners living in this world; the *purgatorial church*, consisting of the souls who are being purified in purgatory; and the *heavenly church*, consisting of perfected Christians in glory. The communion of the saints means that the fellowship of the members of these "churches" is uninterrupted so that an exchange of spiritual goods takes place. Such exchange is seen in intercession: the faithful in the heavenly church unceasingly pray for the faithful in the earthly and purgatorial churches. Regarding this latter intercession, prayers for the dead are offered "that they may be loosed from their sins"[112] and thus be transferred to the heavenly church. The exchange is further seen in the experience of closer communion with Christ through communion with the saints in heaven.

Having treated the Virgin Mary's role in the doctrines of Christ and the Holy Spirit, the *Catechism* turns to a discussion of Mary's place in the doctrine of the Church. Accordingly, Mary must be considered as both the mother of Christ and the mother of the Church.

---

pose the faithful "to receive the chief effects of the sacraments" (CCC 1667; citation from Vatican Council II, *Sacrosanctum concilium* 60).

[110] CCC 946.

[111] CCC 947; citations are from Thomas Aquinas, *On the Apostles' Creed*, 10, and *Roman Catechism* 1.10, 24. The *Roman Catechism*, or the *Catechism of the Council of Trent*, was published in 1566. Accessible at http://www.cin.org/users/james/ebooks/master/trent/tindex.htm.

[112] CCC 958; citation is from Vatican Council II, *Lumen Gentium* 50, with its basis in the apocryphal writing 2 Macc. 12:45.

Mary was in union with her Son throughout his entire life, from his virginal conception up to his death, but especially during his suffering on the cross: "There she stood, in keeping with the divine plan, enduring with her only begotten Son the intensity of his suffering, joining herself with his sacrifice in her mother's heart, and lovingly consenting to the immolation [sacrificial offering] of this victim, born of her: to be given, by the same Christ Jesus dying on the cross, as a mother to his disciple [John], with these words: 'Woman, behold your son.'"[113] Furthermore, after the ascension, "Mary 'aided the beginnings of the Church by her prayers.' . . . imploring the gift of the Spirit, who had already overshadowed her in the Annunciation."[114] Lastly, Mary was united to her Son in her assumption into heaven. This dogma of the Bodily Assumption of Mary, promulgated by Pope Pius XII, means that "the Immaculate Virgin, preserved free from all stain of original sin, when the course of her earthly life was finished, was taken up body and soul into heavenly glory, and exalted by the Lord as Queen over all things, so that she might be the more fully conformed to her Son, the Lord of lords and conqueror of sin and death."[115] Accordingly, Mary has participated in a singular way in the resurrection of her Son, such that she is the only believer in heaven who is embodied. Furthermore, her assumption is "an anticipation of the resurrection of other Christians."[116]

"Mary's role in the Church is inseparable from her union with Christ and flows directly from it."[117] Specifically, "the Virgin Mary is the Church's model of faith and charity. Thus she is a 'preeminent and . . . wholly unique member of the Church'; indeed, she is the 'exemplary realization' (*typus*) of the Church."[118] In light of her obedience, faith, hope, and love, through which she cooperated in Christ's work of salvation, Mary is the mother of the Church in the order of grace. Her saving office did not cease with her bodily assumption but continues unhindered through her intercession. "Therefore the Blessed Virgin is invoked in the Church under the titles of Advocate, Helper, Benefactress, and Mediatrix."[119] The *Catechism* explic-

---

[113] CCC 964; citation is from Vatican Council II, *Lumen Gentium* 58; the biblical citation is from John 19:26–27.
[114] CCC 965; citations are from Vatican Council II, *Lumen Gentium* 69, 59; the biblical allusion is to Acts 1:14.
[115] CCC 966; citation is from Vatican Council II, *Lumen Gentium* 59; for the proclamation of the dogma, see Pius XII, *Munificentissimus Deus* (November 1, 1950); accessible at http://www.vatican.va/holy_father/pius_xii /apost_constitutions/documents/hf_p-xii_apc_19501101_munificentissimus-deus_en.html.
[116] CCC 966.
[117] CCC 964.
[118] CCC 967; citations are from Vatican Council II, *Lumen Gentium* 53; 63.
[119] CCC 969; citation is from Vatican Council II, *Lumen Gentium* 62.

itly denies that Mary's maternal role in the Church detracts from or minimizes the unique mediatorial role of Christ.[120]

Because of Mary's unique person and work, acknowledged very early
on in the Church through its title for her as *theotokos*, or "Mother of
God," the Church is devoted in a special way to her. Such special devotion is not *latria* (Gk. *latreia*, worship), for *worship* or *adoration* belongs
to God alone; nor is it mere *dulia* (Gk. *doulia*, service), for *veneration* is
given to all the saints; but it is *hyperdulia*, or *super-veneration*, which is
reserved for her.

The *Catechism* concludes its doctrine of the Church by looking to Mary
as the eschatological icon, the future image, of the Church: "In her we contemplate what the Church already is in her mystery on her own 'pilgrimage
of faith,' and what she will be in the homeland at the end of her journey."[121]

Evangelical Assessment

The first part (para. 1–3) of the *Catechism*'s lengthy discussion of the doctrine of the church has already been assessed; the second part (para. 4–6)
will now be assessed. As has been noted and will become even more evident,
this doctrine significantly separates Catholic theology and evangelical theology. As before, the areas of agreement will be presented before discussing
the many areas of disagreement.

Catholic Clergy/Hierarchy

At the conclusion of the first part of the evangelical assessment, it was
pointed out that Jesus Christ did not transfer his authority and activity
through his apostles to their successors through the line of apostolic succession. Evangelical theology's challenge to Catholic theology's notion of
apostolicity does not mean, however, that Christ eliminated human ministry, which is ordained by himself, in the church. As John Webster explains,
"For although the acts of Christ are incommunicable, non-representable,
Christ himself freely chooses to represent himself through human ministry. . . . He is not delivered into the hands of his servants, who remain
entirely at his disposal. But in his lordly freedom, he elects that alongside
his triumphant self-manifestation there should also be human service in

---
[120] CCC 970.
[121] CCC 972.

the church."[122] Accordingly, evangelical theology embraces human ministry focused on the Word of God and empowered by the Spirit of God, but in a significantly different way than Catholic theology does.

Still, there is some agreement between the two positions. The hierarchical nature of the church is one such point, with this qualification: Whereas the Catholic Church is structured according to an episcopalian hierarchical system, evangelical churches, reflective of the broad spectrum of evangelical theology, are organized according to several different forms of government. Some evangelical churches are episcopalian, thus sharing some similarities with the Catholic Church's polity, with authority residing in the bishop (Gk. *episcopos*). Other evangelical churches hold to a presbyterian form of government, with elders (Gk. *presbuteroi*) as representatives of the church, teaching and leading their own local congregations as a session or consistory, as well as governing in a series of authoritative graded bodies—presbytery or classis, synod, general assembly—above the local church level. Still other evangelical churches are congregational, with the members of the congregation exercising authority in their sphere of responsibility, the pastor or elder council exercising authority in his/its sphere of responsibility, and no person or organization having jurisdiction above the local church level. Consequently, evangelical churches, even those whose polity is episcopalian, are governed in significantly different ways than is the Catholic Church.

Evangelical theology rejects the Catholic episcopalian structure with the pope at its head for several reasons. The most important reason is a lack of biblical support, as evangelical theology does not believe that Jesus's promise to build his church on Peter and his confession, and Christ's gift of the keys to Peter and the apostles (Matt. 16:18–19), can bear the weight placed on it by the Catholic (mis)interpretation.[123] Moreover, whereas the pope, Peter's successor, and the bishops, the apostles' successors, constitute a single episcopal college leading the Catholic Church today, Catholic theology searches in vain for a parallel structure during the ministry of Jesus and afterwards during the apostolic age, with Peter and the apostles composing one apostolic college leading the church in their day. On the contrary, Jesus engaged his disciples in proclamation of the gospel, healing, and exorcis-

---

[122] Webster, *Word and Church*, 200.
[123] See again the section on "Apostolicity," earlier in this chapter.

ing demons in an itinerant ministry (Matthew 10). He did not organize them into a presiding hierarchy; indeed, the only ruling authority Jesus promised to them was reserved for the age to come: "You [Jesus's disciples] are those who have stayed with me in my trials, and I assign to you, as my Father assigned to me, a kingdom, that you may eat and drink at my table in my kingdom and sit on thrones judging the twelve tribes of Israel" (Luke 22:28–30). This promised kingdom in which the apostles would rule would not correspond to the earthly church, as evidenced by Jesus's preceding promise, at his institution of the Lord's Supper, that he would not celebrate this feast "until the kingdom of God comes" (Luke 22:18)—that is, at his return in glory. To take some creative liberties, the apostolic college that Jesus instituted is a future ruling body in the kingdom of God to come. Furthermore, only by a stretch of the imagination can the council of Jerusalem (Acts 15) be appealed to as an exhibit of this college with Peter at its head.[124] Finally, the actual institution of the Catholic episcopal college and the papacy has a history of lengthy debate and intense struggle in the early church (e.g., the pitched debate between Stephen, the bishop of Rome, and Cyprian, the bishop of Carthage [North Africa] over the proper interpretation of Matthew 16:18–19),[125] a development that was fueled as much by political, economic, and social factors as religious ones.[126]

At the apex of the Church's episcopal college is the pope, and here evangelical theology joins all other non-Catholic Christian theologies (e.g., that of the Orthodox churches) in rejecting the Catholic notion of the papacy. To maintain that the current pope, through an unbroken line of apostolic succession, is the heir of Peter requires turning a blind eye to the actual history of the popes, many of whom were nothing more than worldly princes ruling over vast amounts of land and wielding political, economic, and military might.[127] Moreover, the "Babylonian Captivity of the Church," a

---

[124] For further discussion, see Allison, SS, 261, 298–301.

[125] Cyprian, Treatise 1.4, "On the Unity of the Church" (ANF 5:422); Letter 51.21 (ANF 5:332); Letter 71.3 (ANF 5:379); Letter 70.3 (ANF 5:377).

[126] See Haykin, "Development and Consolidation of the Papacy"; and Allison, "Papacy from Leo I to Vatican II," in Schreiner and Merkle, Shepherding God's Flock.

[127] The claim that the pope possesses "full, supreme, and universal power over the whole Church, a power which he can always exercise unhindered" (CCC 882), must be juxtaposed with papal claims, broached in the early church and on the ascendency particularly in the medieval period, not only to rule over the church but to extend that power so as to rule over the entire world. E.g., Gelasius, To the Emperor Anastasius, in Eric G. Jay, ed., The Church: Its Changing Image through Twenty Centuries, vol. 1: The First Seventeen Centuries (London: SPCK, 1977), 98. Such claims were grounded on transparently ridiculous interpretations of biblical passages (e.g., Pope Innocent III, "The Moon and the Sun," based on Gen. 1:16–18; Pope Boniface VIII's "Two Swords," based on Luke 22:38) and were indefensible. See Allison, HT, 599.

seventy-year period in which the papacy was hijacked to Avignon, France, and the popes were little more than puppets of the French government, and the Great Schism, an epoch in which two and even three men staked claims to be the pope, underscore the turbulent, even anti-Christian, nature of this office. If the pope is the Vicar of Christ, his visible representative on earth, then the Catholic Church must reckon squarely with the fact that for vast periods of its history, the Vicar has been absent or a non-representative.

More foundationally yet, the entire hierarchical structure of the Catholic Church, together with the notion of the vicarage of Christ being tied to the papacy, is based on the two faulty axioms at the heart of the Catholic system. The nature-grace interdependence supports the hierarchical structure of the Catholic Church because of the hierarchy that exists from nature (at the low end) to grace (at the high end). This nature-grace hierarchy must be mirrored in the Catholic Church and is indeed manifested in the ordering from laity (at the low end) to clergy (at the high end). This nature-grace continuum also demands that grace be manifested concretely in nature. To this requirement, the Christ-Church interconnection corresponds: The Catholic Church, as the prolongation of the incarnation of Jesus Christ, performs the necessary mediation between nature and grace. Moreover, this axiom functions as the ground for the idea that the pope is the Vicar—the concrete, tangible, visible representative—of Christ himself. The critique of these two axioms has already been offered.

Still, a specific evangelical criticism remains to be offered. Jesus Christ, seated at the right hand of the Father, is ruling his body, the church, from heaven, and the vicar that he promised and did indeed send to represent him on earth is the other Paraclete, the Holy Spirit, who operates as such in the church. As John Calvin offered,

> He [Christ] uses the ministry of men to declare openly his will to us by mouth, as a sort of delegated work, not by transferring to them his right and honour, but only that through their mouths he may do his own work—just as a workman uses a tool to do his work. . . . [T]hrough the ministers to whom he has entrusted this office and has conferred the grace to carry it out he dispenses and distributes his gifts to the church; and he shows himself as though present by manifesting the power of his Spirit in this his institution, that it be not vain or idle.[128]

---

[128] Calvin, *Institutes* 4.3.1, 2 (LCC 21:1053, 1055).

The association of the pope as the Vicar of Christ with the doctrine of papal infallibility is another major disagreement between Catholic and evangelical theology of the church. Support for this doctrine is found in both Scripture and Tradition. The biblical grounds include Jesus's promise to Peter, as head of the church, that "the gates of hell shall not prevail against it" (Matt. 16:18), as well as his promise to the disciples that the Holy Spirit would guide them into all truth (John 16:13). Evangelical theology questions this alleged biblical basis. For one thing, there is a vast difference between Christ's promising the protection of the church against comprehensive defeat and his promising the perfection of its knowledge; the former, which is surely the nature of the pledge that Jesus made, does not necessarily entail the latter. As for the promise of Spirit-led guidance of the disciples, the exhibition of its fulfillment is rightly seen in the doctrine of the inerrancy of Scripture. The Holy Spirit superintended the biblical authors so that what they wrote—the Gospels, Acts, the letters, Revelation—was exactly what God wanted them to write: the truthful Word of God.

This perspective was certainly the one that the early church's leaders held, as they honored the truthfulness of authoritative Scripture.[129] And this view is better able to account for the fact that, despite the Church's claim that the bishop of Rome has always championed orthodoxy and refuted heresy, the Roman bishop played only a minor role in some of the early ecumenical councils (e.g., the Council of Nicea [325]),[130] and some contradictory examples sully this impeccable reputation (e.g., Vigilius [537–555] and Honorius I [625–638]).[131] Certainly, all of Christendom is indebted to such bishops of Rome as Leo I and his articulation of the orthodox doctrine of Christ[132] that paved the way for the Chalcedonian Creed.[133] But the regular championing of orthodoxy by the bishop of Rome and the claim of

---

[129] For examples, see Allison, *HT*, chs. 4 and 5.

[130] Accordingly, the claim of Gelasius, bishop of Rome from 492–496, that ecumenical councils of the church—and there had been four such councils (Nicea, Constantinople I, Ephesus, and Chalcedon) up to that point—derived their authority from the bishop of Rome, was historically inaccurate (though it did much to advance the development of the papacy in Rome).

[131] Vigilius capitulated to the enticements of the Empress Theodora by compromising on the Chalcedonian Creed; his compromised position was addressed by the Second Council of Constantinople (553). Honorius affirmed monothelitism, the view that in the incarnation, the God-man possessed only one will. The Third Council of Constantinople (680–681) condemned Honorius as a heretic. Pope Leo II (682–683) also condemned Honorius, creating the embarrassing situation in which one pope denounced another. Sadly, Pope Gregory VII (1073–1085), claiming in his *Memorandum* (*Dictatus Papae*; 1075) that the pope had never erred and would not err, overlooked the case of Honorius.

[132] Leo I, "The Tome of Leo," in Henry Bettenson and Chris Maunder, eds., *Documents of the Christian Church*, 3rd and new edition (Oxford and New York: Oxford University Press, 1999), 54–55.

[133] "The Definition of Chalcedon," in Bettenson, *Documents of the Christian Church*, 56.

papal infallibility are two very different matters; moreover, the former can be empirically verified, while the latter can be empirically refuted.

Another criticism of the doctrine of papal infallibility can be offered. Though certainly the case can be made that, prior to its promulgation by Vatican Council I, the Catholic Church affirmed infallibility, concern is raised that it was not until the middle of the nineteenth century when it was officially proclaimed. Many factors other than religious ones converged to influence this decision: The Church was under intense political and social attack for being on the wrong side of Italian nationalistic fervor, especially when Pope Pius IX (1846–1878) alienated the Italian people by refusing to participate in a war against Austrian forces to liberate the papal states for inclusion in the Italian confederation. Additionally, the Church was still reeling from the debacle of the Constitutional Church during the Napoleonic empire in France earlier in that century, and the ugly specter of modern ideologies—pantheism, naturalism, rationalism, indifferentism and latitudinarianism (types of soteriological pluralism), socialism, communism, liberalism, and the like—led to the Church taking a strong defensive posture.[134] Moreover, recent concordats—papal political agreements with the sovereign rulers of other nations—had given away more and more of the temporal holdings of the papacy. Accordingly, the day after Vatican Council I had proclaimed papal teaching infallible, the Franco-Prussian war broke out, and within two months, the papacy was stripped of its vast lands and left with the Vatican, the Basilica of St. John Lateran (in Rome), and Castel Gandolfo (the pope's summer residence, outside of Rome). In other words, the onslaught of many nonreligious factors fostered the promulgation of the doctrine of papal infallibility, which was in turn a defensive reaction to them.

One final criticism from evangelical theology: papal infallibility results in dogmatic proclamations—for example, the Bodily Assumption of Mary—that are binding on the conscience of the faithful (they "must be adhered to with the obedience of faith").[135] Even if, for the sake of argu-

---

[134] All of these movements and ideologies were condemned by Pope Pius IX, *Quanta Cura* (December 8, 1864), with the Syllabus of Errors. Accessible at http://www.archive.org/stream/QuantaCuraTheSyllabusOfErrors_247/pius_ix_pope_quanta_cura_and_the_syllabus_of_errors_djvu.txt.

[135] CCC 891. Additionally (from CCC 891–892), what is the concrete difference, other than semantic, between an infallible papal pronouncement to which is owed "the obedience of faith," and a sub-infallible Magisterial teaching to which is owed "religious assent," which "is nonetheless an extension of the obedience of the faith" (CCC 892)?

ment, these dogmas do not contradict Scripture, they go beyond it, thus contradicting its sufficiency.

Catholic Laity

Turning to Catholic theology's presentation on the laity of the Church, evangelical theology applauds several of its affirmations. One such matter is the elevated position accorded to laypeople, an encouraging development set in motion by Vatican Council II. Lay participation in the mission of the Church finds wide agreement with evangelical theology, which has several varieties that call the laity to carry out the threefold office—priestly, prophetic, and kingly/royal—of Christ. Consequently, all Christians are called to preach the gospel to, and pray for, one another, exercising the priesthood of all believers. Additionally, they are summoned as ambassadors of Christ to evangelize nonbelievers by engagement in the ministry of reconciliation (2 Cor. 5:14–21). Though evangelical theology would not see participation in the royal office of Christ as involving the exercise of self-mastery— critique has already been made of Catholic theology's notion that human reason/intellect must rule over the body with its passions—it certainly affirms that this kingly function involves vocational responsibilities for all Christians, who also, in the case of personal and systemic evils, are called to stand against injustice and champion the cause of the marginalized, the poor, orphans and widows, and others. Finally, like its Catholic counterpart, evangelical theology encourages lay collaboration with the clergy for the advancement of churches.

Catholic Religious

In terms of Catholic theology's approach to the life of consecration for those in religious orders, evangelical theology agrees in part and disagrees in part. First, agreement consists over the fact that Christ calls all his faithful to live lives that are conscientiously and completely devoted to him. To be discarded from both discussion and reality is any type of division between Christians as to their holiness or spirituality. Whether that distinction (and the following examples are found within evangelicalism) is between Spirit-baptized Christians and ordinary Christians (encountered in Pentecostal/charismatic theology), spiritual Christians and carnal Christians (evidenced in Keswick theology), disciples and believers (found in the

Grace Evangelical Society), or some other permutation, a biblical view of holiness repudiates it.[136]

Accordingly, evangelical theology takes issue with Catholic theology's threefold division of the faithful into saints, religious, and ordinary Christians. The necessity of such a hierarchical structure, being grounded on the axiom of the nature-grace interdependence, has already been critiqued; so has the overrealized eschatology of Catholic theology's doctrine of sainthood. Accordingly, attention here will be focused on its view of the religious state and the evangelical counsels of chastity, poverty, and obedience. Evangelical theology's chief objection is to the notion that this state leads to living in "more intimate" consecration to God and following Christ "more nearly."[137] Beginning with Martin Luther, and especially his 1520 *Treatise on Good Works*, evangelical theology has refused to elevate "religious" activity above other types of human work in terms of what is more pleasing to God and what contributes more effectively to personal sanctification. Because the divine call to, and enablement for, the pursuit of holiness (e.g., 2 Pet. 1:3–4) intersects with all believers no matter what their vocation may be, those in religious professions—for example, priests and religious for Catholic theology, pastors/elders and missionaries for evangelical theology—are not in a more favorable state before God nor in a more advantageous position to please him.

Taking the evangelical counsels one by one, evangelical theology affirms that *celibacy* is a choice that a believer may make, with this stipulation: that Christian must have the gift of celibacy from God (1 Cor. 7:7). Indications that one possesses this gift include contentment not to be married and the God-given ability to control one's sexual desires in God-honoring ways (vv. 8–9, 36–38). Additionally, evangelical theology affirms that temporary celibacy is conceded, though not commanded, for married couples, with these stipulations: it is mutually agreed upon, temporary, and for a spiritual purpose, and it terminates in renewed sexual intercourse (vv. 5–6). Furthermore, evangelical theology acknowledges that the celibate Christian is spared "worldly troubles" (v. 28) and marital and family anxieties, being instead anxious only about "the things of the Lord" (vv. 32–35). Accordingly, celibacy and the life of singleness is a wonderful gift to the church.

---

[136] For further discussion, see Grudem, *ST*, 775–776.
[137] *CCC* 916.

However, evangelical theology objects when celibacy becomes a requirement for a type of service to the church. Though it is conceptually possible that the gift of celibacy corresponds to the group of unmarried men and women in the consecrated state (we could add the group of priests ordained by Holy Orders as well), the reality of sexual immorality, in terms of both heterosexual and homosexual sin, among those who have taken the vow of celibacy is evidence against it. Indeed, evangelical theology wonders if a misunderstanding of celibacy is not a contributor to failure in this area. After all, when Paul indicates that one who "refrains from marriage will do even better" (v. 38), he is addressing those who are engaged to be married yet abstain from getting married "in view of the present distress" (v. 26; probably a reference to intense persecution of the church) and because they are able to master their sexual desires (vv. 36–38). This instruction is not a manifesto on celibacy for everyone at all times.

As for the evangelical counsel of *poverty*, evangelical theology underscores both the compassion of Jesus for the poor and disenfranchised of society (e.g., Mark 14:7; Luke 4:18) and the church's mission to care for the poor (e.g., Acts 4:32–35; Gal. 2:10; 1 Tim. 5:3–16; James 1:27; 2:15–16).[138] What it dissents from is the notion that poverty enhances one's sanctification. Biblical spiritual disciplines are many: prayer, reading and meditating on Scripture, fasting, accountability, solitude, and the like. Even giving is a discipline enjoined upon all Christians (2 Corinthians 8–9). And even though examples of extensive giving are presented in Scripture (e.g., Zaccheus promised to give half of his wealth to the poor; Luke 19:1–10), they focus on a specific person (e.g., the refusal of the rich young ruler to give away his money exposed his idolatry; Luke 18:18–30) or on specific acts of generosity (e.g., Christians with financial and physical means in the Jerusalem church gave sacrificially, Acts 2:44–45; 4:32–35; Barnabas sold a field, Acts 4:36–37). But giving is never presented in Scripture as an obligation to divest oneself of all one's assets; for example, even Ananias and Sapphira sinned, not by keeping back a portion of the proceeds from the sale of their land, but by making it seem as if they were giving away the entire amount (Acts 5:1–11). Giving is a discipline, but poverty is not. Moreover, the apostle

---

[138] An example of an evangelical affirmation of help for the poor and marginalized is The Gospel Coalition's "Theological Vision for Ministry," V. 5; accessible at http://thegospelcoalition.org/about/foundation-documents/vision/.

Paul encourages those who are rich "to do good, to be rich in good works, to be generous and ready to share" while they are enjoying the riches that God richly gives to them (1 Tim. 6:17–19). Importantly also, Paul addresses the financial status of presbyters in the church: "Let the elders who rule well be considered worthy of double honor [respect and remuneration], especially those who labor in preaching and teaching. For the Scripture says, 'You shall not muzzle an ox when it treads out the grain,' and, 'The laborer deserves his wages'" (5:17–18). Poverty is not prescribed for servants in the church.

The evangelical counsel of *obedience* finds support from evangelical theology in that submission to God, conformity to all the commandments—and avoidance of all the prohibitions—of Scripture, and compliance with all good and licit directives of those in authority (government officials, parents, employers, church leaders) are proper for Christians. But if obedience is the normal course of the Christian life, how can it be more so for those living the consecrated life, unless it entails submission to rules and regulations that go beyond what Scripture and legitimately constituted authorities legitimately prescribe? In this latter case, the issue is not with obedience but with the unbiblical supplements and the illegitimate authorities or the illegitimate prescriptions of legitimate authorities.

Thus, evangelical theology has deep concerns about the evangelical counsels of chastity, poverty, and obedience that are enjoined on men and women seeking to live the consecrated life.

A final issue with points of both agreement and disagreement: Evangelical theology concurs with living life in community with others, which is one type of the religious life in the Catholic Church. It dissents from the other type, the eremitic life, that demands solitude through separation from the world. A key reason for this disagreement is that this structured withdrawal contradicts the very thing for which Jesus prayed to the Father concerning his disciples:

> I have given them your word, and the world has hated them because they are not of the world, just as I am not of the world. I do not ask that you take them out of the world, but that you keep them from the evil one. They are not of the world, just as I am not of the world. Sanctify them in the truth; your word is truth. As you sent me into the world, so I have sent them into the world. And for their sake I consecrate myself, that they also may be sanctified in truth. (John 17:14–19)

Withdrawal from the world, which through its carnal philosophies and ungodly systems stands against the church and seeks to pollute and derail it, is no more an option for Christians than it was for Jesus himself: As Jesus was in the world though not of it, the church is to be in the world though not of it. Indeed, as the Father sent the Son into the world to accomplish salvation, so the Son sends the church into the world to announce how that accomplished salvation is to be appropriated (cf. John 20:21). And Jesus's consecration of himself for the sake of the church, together with his provision of the Word of God, is sufficient for the church to be in the world and not of the world, engaging in its missional endeavors and remaining faithful and obedient to God.

The Communion of Saints

Catholic and evangelical theology also agree in part and disagree in part concerning the communion of saints. Agreement consists in the affirmation that the church exists in two states, as the *earthly church*, consisting of all Christians living in this world, and the *heavenly church*, consisting of perfected Christians in glory. Disagreement exists over the third state of the church, the *purgatorial church*. As noted earlier and as will be further discussed later, Catholic theology's doctrine of purgatory depends on the mistaken axiom of the nature-grace interdependence, lacks biblical warrant, and contradicts the doctrine of justification. Furthermore, the notion that the communion of saints entails the exchange of spiritual goods between the various states of the church lacks scriptural support. Accordingly, to believe that the members of the heavenly church engage in constant intercession for the members of the earthly church (and those of the purgatorial church as well) is speculative at best. What is biblically affirmed, and thus of the greatest and surest comfort for Christians living today, is that both the Holy Spirit and Jesus Christ intercede for them (Rom. 8:26–27, 34).[139] The sufficiency of Scripture reminds Christians that

---

[139] As the evangelical participants in Evangelicals and Catholics Together affirmed, "Whether Mary and other departed believers with the Lord in glory can hear and answer words addressed to them from this life, the Bible does not say. Evangelicals believe that through the finished work of Christ on the cross, and by the power of the Spirit who intercedes for us, we may come directly and 'boldly to the throne of grace' (Heb. 4:16). Although the Church triumphant [the heavenly church] and the Church militant [the earthly church] join together in common worship by means of the one Spirit (Rev. 5:6–14), there is no mention of prayers to Mary or the saints in the witness of the New Testament and the first two hundred years of the Church" (Evangelicals and Catholics Together, "Do Whatever He Tells You: The Blessed Virgin Mary in Christian Faith and Life" [November 2009], section entitled "An Evangelical Word to Catholics," 4). Accessible at http://www.firstthings.com/article/2009/11/do-whatever-he-tells-you-the-blessed-virgin-mary-in-christian-faith-and-life.

what God has provided for them, the tandem intercession of the second and third persons of the Trinity, is the sufficient resource upon which they are to rely.

Mary as Mother of the Church

Once again, the *Catechism* returns to a discussion of the role of Mary, not in relation to Christ and the Holy Spirit, as it did earlier, but now in relation to the doctrine of the Church. Here, its emphasis is on Mary as the mother of the Church. Catholic theology closely associates the sufferings of Christ on the cross and Mary's sufferings as she endured the crucifixion of her son, joined herself with his sacrifice, and consented to his execution as a sacrificial victim. Evangelical theology objects to this portrayal of the role of Mary. Certainly, she must have been horrified by the spectacle of her son suffering execution by crucifixion, and she must have known unspeakable heartache because of her loss. However, beyond these expected human emotions that one imagines from the simple statement of the text of Scripture— "standing by the cross of Jesus were his mother and his mother's sister, Mary the wife of Clopas, and Mary Magdalene" (John 19:25)—anything else is mere speculation.

But there is more. The narrative continues: "When Jesus saw his mother and the disciple whom he loved standing nearby, he said to his mother, 'Woman, behold, your son!' Then he said to the disciple, 'Behold, your mother!' And from that hour the disciple took her to his own home" (John 19:26–27). Catholic theology misinterprets this passage and develops an exaggerated role for Mary—her motherhood of all humanity: "The Mother of Christ, who stands at the very center of this mystery . . . is given as mother to every single individual and all mankind. The man at the foot of the Cross is John. . . . But it is not he alone."[140] Specifically, John represents the offspring of Adam and the Church. To its credit, Catholic theology acknowledges that "we find here an expression of the Son's particular solicitude for his Mother, whom he is leaving in such great sorrow."[141] But Catholic theology goes on to say, "And yet the 'testament of Christ's Cross' says more."[142] Indeed, this interpretation finds more in the passage and

---

[140] Pope John Paul II, *Redemptoris Mater* 23.
[141] Ibid.
[142] Ibid.

tends "not so much to see Mary as coming under the care of the beloved disciple, as the reverse:"[143] John comes under her care. Through a symbolic turn, this interpretation then considers John as the model of all true disciples, thus paving the way for Mary to be the mother of humanity and mother of the Church. But what does the text actually say? The disciple took Mary into *his* home. As one of his final acts before dying, Jesus properly and lovingly displayed his concern for his mother as she witnessed the horrendous and tragic crucifixion of her son. The temporal clause ("and from that hour") once again underscores the death of Jesus Christ. Indeed, the following three verses recount his last few climactic moments of life: his words "I thirst"; the offering of sour wine to quench his thirst; and his last affirmation, "It is finished," as "he bowed his head and gave up his spirit" (John 19:28–30). The narrative is all about Jesus and his finished work on the cross. It does not indicate in any way a role for Mary as mother of all humanity and of the church.

Neither is her motherhood confirmed in Luke's notation that, after Jesus's ascension, the eleven apostles gathered in the upper room and were praying "together with the women and Mary the mother of Jesus, and his brothers" (Acts 1:12–14). Whereas Catholic theology makes much of her presence for the birth of the church and for a type of apostleship,[144] that is not in Luke's narrative. Instead, he emphasizes the abnormality of only eleven apostles—Judas's absence from the Twelve is striking, and serves as a lead into Luke's subsequent narrative (vv. 15–26)—and the continuing presence of key women in the ministry of Jesus and the disciples, as Luke had previously emphasized (e.g., Luke 8:1–3). Two new items are introduced in Acts 1:14: "Mary the mother of Jesus, and his brothers" also joined with the apostles in prayer. We learn from this statement that Mary his mother continues to be one of Jesus's followers. Though this outcome was left in doubt in the Gospel of Luke (Luke 8:19–21), happily we learn that Mary continues as a disciple. To her have been added her sons, the brothers of Jesus. Though they had not believed in him during his life (John 7:5), they have become Jesus's disciples following his death and resurrection. Luke will not allow us to imagine more of a role for Mary (nor for any of the

---

[143] D. A. Carson, *The Gospel according to John* (Leicester, England: Inter-Varsity Press; and Grand Rapids, MI: Eerdmans, 1991), 617.
[144] Pope John Paul II, *Redemptoris Mater* 24, 26.

other women and Jesus's brothers) than this. She is not apostle-like, nor is she aiding in the creation of the church.

Even more disturbing for evangelical theology is the dogma of the Bodily Assumption of Mary. The doctrine is based on her sinlessness: absent any original sin or actual sins, Mary did not undergo the corruption that is a consequence of sin, but her body was taken up into heaven. Evangelical theology's main objection is to Mary's sinlessness; with that ground removed, there is no reason to believe that her body was not sloughed off at death and subsequently decayed in the tomb in which it was buried. A second objection is that heaven is not a place of embodiment but of disembodiment, as the apostle Paul affirms (2 Cor. 5:1–9). In the intermediate state—the period between death and the return of Jesus Christ, which will be accompanied by the resurrection of the body—Christians as disembodied people enjoy the presence of the Lord, a type of existence that is appropriate to heaven. Only after Christ returns and establishes his kingdom can Christians be re-embodied with their glorified bodies (1 Cor. 15:42–44, 49); embodiment is the type of existence appropriate to this state. Thus, Catholic theology errs in its doctrine of the bodily assumption.

Accordingly, the Marian doctrines of the immaculate conception, sinlessness, perfect obedience of faith, cooperation in the salvific work of her son, assistance in the birth of the church, and motherhood of all humanity and of the church is grounded on poor interpretation of Scripture and unchastened Tradition that contradicts Scripture. Moreover, these Marian doctrines are the quintessential implications of the two axioms of the Catholic theological system, which have been found to be wanting. With deep perplexity and unmitigated concern, evangelical theology laments and rejects the Catholic Church's invocation of Mary "under the titles of Advocate, Helper, Benefactress, and Mediatrix."[145] Despite Catholic theology's denial that Mary's maternal role detracts from or minimizes the unique mediatorial role of Christ, evangelical theology insists otherwise. Through the Son of God's immaculate conception, sinlessness, perfect obedience of faith, passion, death, burial, resurrection, ascension, sending of the Holy Spirit to give birth to the church, baptism of Christians with the Spirit to incorporate them into his body, and union with them, Jesus Christ has accomplished salvation completely. Nothing more is or can be added to

[145] CCC 969.

that which he did to perfectly save fallen human beings, and God has not designed salvation, which he could have done through his Son alone, to include the work of his Son's mother. Yes, Mary is *theotokos* as the mother of *the one who is God*. No, Mary is not *theotokos* as the *Mother* of God and of the Church, which engages in *hyperdulia*—super-veneration—of her as Advocate, Helper, Benefactress, and Mediatrix. Her mediatorial role is wrong because there is no need for it, as the writer to the Hebrews affirms:

> Since then we have a great high priest who has passed through the heavens, Jesus, the Son of God, let us hold fast our confession. For we do not have a high priest who is unable to sympathize with our weaknesses, but one who in every respect has been tempted as we are, yet without sin. Let us then with confidence draw near to the throne of grace, that we may receive mercy and find grace to help in time of need. (Heb. 4:14–16)

With Jesus as the God-man who is the perfect advocate, helper, benefactor, and mediator, there is no need for Mary to exercise those roles as ascribed to her by Catholic theology.

6

The Profession of Faith
(Part I, Section 2, Chapter 3, Articles IO–I2)

The Doctrines of Salvation, Our Future
Resurrection, and Eternal Life

The Doctrine of Salvation: "I believe in the forgiveness of sins" (Sec. 2, Ch. 3, Art. IO)

Following the structure of the Creed—"I believe in the Holy Spirit, the holy catholic church, the communion of saints"—the *Catechism* notes that the Creed "associates faith in the forgiveness of sins not only with faith in the Holy Spirit, but also with faith in the Church and in the communion of saints."[1] The *Catechism* points to Christ's conferring of the Holy Spirit, along with "his own divine power to forgive sins," on the apostles as the biblical basis for this belief. On the day of his resurrection, Jesus said to his disciples, "Receive the Holy Spirit. If you forgive the sins of any, they are forgiven; if you retain the sins of any, they are retained" (John 20:22–23).[2] Moreover, Christ linked the forgiveness of sins to faith and Baptism; Jesus's Great Commission, as narrated in the Gospel of Mark, is the biblical basis for this association: "Go into all the world and preach the gospel to the whole creation. He who believes and is baptized will be saved" (Mark 16:15–16). As will be discussed more fully later, the cleansing of Baptism effects the full and complete effacement of original sin in the case of baptized infants, and the full and complete effacement of original sin and all personal acts of sin

---
[1] CCC 976.
[2] Ibid.

in the case of baptized youth and adults; accordingly, there is no longer "any penalty to suffer in order to expiate them."[3] Baptism is one of the uses of the keys of the kingdom granted by Christ to his Church (Matt. 16:13–20).

At the same time, "the grace of Baptism delivers no one from all the weakness of nature. On the contrary, we must still combat the movements of concupiscence that never cease leading us to evil."[4] To overcome this proclivity that lures toward sin and ends in actual sin, the faithful must have another remedy besides Baptism. Accordingly, another use that the Church makes of the keys of the kingdom is the sacrament of Penance, which is its power "to forgive all penitents their offenses."[5] Penance, traditionally described as "'a laborious kind of baptism' . . . is necessary for salvation for those who have fallen after Baptism."[6] By this sacrament, post-baptismal sins (later on, it will be specified that the sins that the sacrament targets are mortal, not venial, sins) are forgiven by the Church, and the penitents are restored to communion with God through the grace of justification.

Evangelical Assessment

Because this doctrine of the forgiveness of sins is so closely linked to Baptism and Penance, a full evaluation of it awaits the *Catechism*'s presentation of the sacraments. However, as noted earlier, Catholic theology's close association of forgiveness with the apostles—and, hence, their successors, the bishops of the Catholic Church—is problematic because it is grounded on the two axioms of the Catholic system: The nature-grace interdependence manifests itself in the need for grace to be conferred in a tangible manner; hence, it must be granted concretely, first by the apostles and, after their death, by the bishops of the Catholic Church. The Christ-Church interconnection expresses itself in the requirement of mediation between the two realms of nature and grace; thus, the Catholic Church must convey grace to nature. These two axioms have already been critiqued (ch. 2).

A specific criticism may also be offered at this point. Certainly, evangelical theology acknowledges Jesus's gift to, and commission of, his disciples:

---

[3] CCC 978; citation is from *Roman Catechism* 1.11, 3.
[4] Ibid.
[5] CCC 979; citation is from *Roman Catechism* 1.11, 4.
[6] CCC 980; citation is from *Canons and Decrees of the Council of Trent*, 14th session (November 25, 1551), *On the Most Holy Sacraments of Penance and Extreme Unction* 2 (Schaff, 2:143). The Council cites Gregory of Nazianzus, *Oration* 39.17 (NPNF[2] 7:358) and John of Damascus, *The Orthodox Faith* 4.9 (NPNF[2] 9:77–79, second set of page numbers).

"Receive the Holy Spirit. If you forgive the sins of any, they are forgiven; if you retain the sins of any, they are retained" (John 20:22–23). The question becomes, How does Scripture present the apostolic initiative to fulfill this missional task? Following the Gospel of John in canonical order, the book of Acts narrates the period of waiting and praying in anticipation of the coming of the Holy Spirit (Acts 1:12–14) and his descent on the day of Pentecost to initiate his new covenant ministry and to inaugurate the church (Acts 2). Jesus's disciples—not only the newly constituted Twelve (Acts 1:15–26), but about 120 in all (v. 15)—were baptized, or filled, with the Holy Spirit, thus receiving Christ's promised gift of the Spirit (vv. 4–5; 2:4). Empowered from on high with the needed divine resource (1:8), these disciples were launched on their gospel mission, which is narrated throughout the rest of Acts. The aspects of this missional endeavor were the announcement of the work of Jesus of Nazareth on behalf of fallen human beings; instruction to repent from sin and believe in Christ; the promise of forgiveness and the gift of the Spirit; baptism; and incorporation into the church (2:22–47). Engagement in the Great Commission was not restricted to the apostles; Stephen (Acts 7), Philip (Acts 8), and the men of Cyprus and Cyrene (Acts 11:19–26) are specifically mentioned as non-apostolic heralds of the gospel. Accordingly, the forgiveness of sins is not the prerogative of a special caste of men, nor does it attach to their ministries alone. Whatever institutional and hierarchical realities were introduced later in history to confine the remission of sins to the priests/bishops of the Catholic Church, they cannot alter what Scripture enjoins on all Christ-followers empowered by the Spirit of God. When a Christian mother shares the gospel of Jesus Christ and her lost son repents and believes, that mother's announcement—"Your sins are forgiven"—expresses the truth of sins already loosed in heaven because of Christ's sacrifice (Matt. 16:19, 21), and it provokes "joy before the angels of God" over another prodigal who has returned home and been found (Luke 15:10, 11–32).

The specific connection of this forgiveness of sin with the Catholic sacraments of Baptism and Penance will be explored and assessed later.

The Doctrine of Our Future Resurrection: "I believe in the resurrection of the body" (Sec. 2, Ch. 3, Art. II)

The work of salvation accomplished by Jesus Christ through his death and resurrection, and the working out of that salvation in the lives of fallen human beings, is not complete during this present age but awaits the *eschaton*, or the age to come, of which the bodily resurrection of Christians and their experience of everlasting life are essential elements.

The doctrine of the resurrection of the body, a belief held by the church from its very beginning, signifies that God's work of salvation applies not only to the soul (the immaterial aspect of human beings will live on after death) but to the body as well (the material aspect, sloughed off at death, will come to life again). Biblically, this doctrine is progressively revealed[7] but finds its clearest and fullest expression in Jesus's linking of "faith in the resurrection to his own person: 'I am the Resurrection and the life.' It is Jesus himself who on the last day will raise up those who have believed in him, who have eaten his body and drunk his blood."[8] From the beginning, belief in the resurrection has met stiff resistance: "On no point does the Christian faith encounter more opposition than on the resurrection of the body."[9]

In order to explain the resurrection, the *Catechism* first discusses death: "In death, the separation of the soul from the body, the human body decays and the soul goes to meet God, while waiting its reunion with its glorified body."[10] Accordingly, the existence of believers in heaven with Christ is a disembodied one (with the one exception of Mary, whose body was assumed into heaven at the end of her life). When Christ returns, all disembodied believers will be raised and given a new, glorious body; they will be re-embodied by the power of Christ and the Holy Spirit (1 Cor. 15:35–53; Phil. 3:21; Rom. 8:11).

While this hope lies in the future, a certain foretaste of the resurrection is given during this earthly life. Participation in the sacrament of Christ's body and blood means that "our bodies, which partake of the Eucharist, are no longer corruptible, but possess the hope of resurrection."[11] Participation in the sacrament of Baptism means that the faithful are already identified with Christ's resurrection; indeed, they "truly participate in the heavenly life of the risen Christ" in a hidden manner.[12] Implications of the hope of resurrection include respecting one's own body and the bodies of other people (1 Cor. 6:13–15, 19–20).

---

[7] CCC 992. The *Catechism* references Dan. 12:1–13 along with the apocryphal writing 2 Macc. 7:9, 14, 29.
[8] CCC 994; citation is from John 11:25. The affirmation about Christ's body and blood is from John 5:24–25; 6:40, 54.
[9] CCC 996; citation is from Augustine, *Expositions on the Psalms,* Psalm 88(89), 32 (NPNF[1] 8:437).
[10] CCC 997.
[11] CCC 1000; citation is from Irenaeus, *Against Heresies* 4.18.5 (ANF 1:486).
[12] CCC 1002–1003; the biblical basis for these affirmations is Col. 2:12; 3:1, 3; cf. Phil. 3:20.

Of course, rising with Christ is contingent on dying with Christ, and the *Catechism* returns to its discussion of death. In one sense, bodily death is natural—it is common to all people; but in another sense it is unnatural, in that it is the penalty for sin (Rom. 6:23; cf. Gen. 2:17). Death is (1) the end of earthly life; (2) a consequence of sin; and (3) transformed by Christ. Specifically, for Christians, death has a positive and new meaning: They gain the presence of Christ himself as they live with him (Phil. 1:21; 2 Tim. 2:11), and their dying with Christ, initiated in baptism, becomes complete. Death also marks the end of opportunities to avail oneself of divine grace for salvation; there is no chance to decide one's eternal destiny after death (Heb. 9:27). In preparation for death, the faithful pray, "From a sudden and unforeseen death, deliver us, O Lord"; they ask Mary to intercede for them "at the hour of our death"; and they entrust themselves to "St. Joseph, the patron of a happy death."[13]

Evangelical Assessment

With few exceptions, Catholic and evangelical theology agree on the doctrine of the resurrection. The ultimate hope of Christians is not to die and go to heaven as disembodied people; rather, the proper anticipation is the resurrection of the body. Only when believers are re-embodied with imperishable, glorious, strong, and spiritual (i.e., completely controlled and dominated by the Holy Spirit) bodies (1 Cor. 15:42–44, 49) will they experience the fullness of salvation. All who are united with Christ—an identification with his death, burial, and resurrection that is vividly portrayed in baptism—have this hope. Positionally, therefore, Christians are already raised with Christ, and the reality of their heavenly citizenship should motivate and guide their earthly citizenship (Phil. 3:20; Col. 2:12; 3:1–4). Finally, the resurrection will be the miraculous work of the Holy Spirit (Rom. 8:11) that reunites disembodied believers with their glorious new bodies.

The key point of disagreement centers on the source of the foretaste of the resurrection body during the earthly life of believers. Evangelical theology does not hold that the sacrament of the Eucharist confers incorruptibility on the body, the result of an inner transformation through the grace of God infused into believers, as Catholic theology maintains.[14] Echoes of

---

[13] CCC 1014; citations are from the Roman Missal, "Litany of the Saints," and the "Hail Mary."
[14] CCC 1000.

the nature-grace interdependence are heard: grace operates so as to elevate and eventually perfect (human) nature. Rather, evangelical theology points to Christ's resurrection as the harbinger of the resurrection of his followers (1 Cor. 6:13–14); this belief is also embraced by Catholic theology, but evangelical theology insists that Christ's resurrection is the *only* foretaste of resurrection. Baptism, by which Christians are identified with Christ's resurrection, concretely depicts this hope.

The doctrine of the resurrection is affirmed against the backdrop of a theology of death, and here again Catholic and evangelical theology share much in common. Death is the cessation of the functioning of the material aspect of human nature as well as the "unzipping" of this material element from the immaterial element; thus, the body dies and is sloughed off while the soul or spirit continues its existence, now temporarily separated from the body. Accordingly, death is the end of this earthly life, but not of all existence. Moreover, though natural in the sense of being common to everyone, death is unnatural, being the punishment for sin and not part and parcel of the original created order. Christians face death not with fear (Heb. 2:14–18) but with joy (2 Cor. 5:8; Phil. 1:21–23), not because death itself is good (on the contrary, it is an enemy to be defeated; 1 Cor. 15:26, 54–56) but because it is the gateway, or point of departure, from this earthly existence into life with Christ in heaven (2 Tim. 4:6; 2 Pet. 1:15).

Where the two positions part company on the theology of death is the Catholic encouragement of the faithful to enlist the aid of Mary's intercession at the time of death and to entrust themselves to St. Joseph as the patron of a happy death. Evangelical theology dismisses these aids of comfort and insists that the true source of comfort is a robust faith in the sustaining power of God, the Good Shepherd who walks with his people trudging through the valley of the shadow of death (Psalm 23), and in the assurance of salvation as promised in the gospel (e.g., Rom. 8:1). The solace offered by family, friends, and fellow believers—those alive on earth—is also a great source of help in facing death.

The Doctrine of Eternal Life: "I believe in life everlasting" (Sec. 2, Ch. 3, Art. 12)

Another essential element of the completion of salvation in the *eschaton*, or the age to come, is eternal life. This hope is sealed for the faithful through the administration of the sacrament of last rites, which includes "viaticum,"[15] an aspect of the sacrament of the Eucharist. By this means the Church prepares its dying faithful members.

As death ends human earthly life, it is followed by divine judgment: Each person "will be rewarded immediately after death in accordance with his works and faith."[16] One of two eternal destinies awaits the judicial verdict: "either entrance into the blessedness of heaven—through a purification or immediately—or immediate and everlasting damnation."[17]

As for the first possible eternal destiny, heaven is the reward for the faithful "who die in God's grace and friendship and are perfectly purified."[18] Specifically, they experience the beatific vision; that is, they "see the divine essence with an intuitive vision, and even face to face, without the mediation of any creature."[19] Moreover, "[h]eaven is the ultimate end and fulfillment of the deepest human longings, the state of supreme, definitive happiness" and "consists in the full and perfect possession of the fruits of the redemption accomplished by Christ."[20]

Heaven is the ultimate destiny not only for these faithful who are perfectly purified but also eventually for the faithful whose purification is not complete in their earthly lifetime: "All who die in God's grace and friendship, but still imperfectly purified, are indeed assured of their eternal salvation; but after death they undergo purification, so as to achieve the holiness necessary to enter the joy of heaven."[21] Purgatory is "this final purification of the elect, which is entirely different from the punishment of the damned."[22] Biblical support for purgatory includes passages about a cleansing fire (1 Cor. 3:15; 1 Pet. 1:7) and Jesus's stern warning that those who commit blasphemy against the Holy Spirit "will be pardoned neither in this age nor in the age to come" (Matt. 12:32), his threat implying that "certain offenses *can* be forgiven . . . in the age to come."[23] The *Catechism* also

---

[15] As previously noted, "viaticum" refers to preparations for a journey (Lat. *via*); this aspect of the sacrament of the Eucharist will be discussed in detail later.

[16] CCC 1021. Biblical support for this judgment includes the parable of Lazarus and the rich man (Luke 16:19–31), the words of the dying Christ to the good thief (Luke 23:39–43), and other New Testament passages (2 Cor. 5:8–10; Heb. 9:27; 12:23).

[17] CCC 1022.

[18] CCC 1023.

[19] Ibid.; citation is from Pope Benedict XII, *Benedictus Deus* (1336). Accessible at http://www.papalencyclicals .net/Ben12/B12bdeus.html. Cf. CCC 1028.

[20] CCC 1024, 1026.

[21] CCC 1030.

[22] CCC 1031.

[23] Ibid. (emphasis added); citation is from Gregory the Great, *Dialogue* 4.39. Accessible at http://www.tertullian .org/fathers/gregory_04_dialogues_book4.htm#C39.

appeals to the practice of praying for the dead, as found in the apocryphal writing 2 Maccabees: "Therefore [Judas Maccabeus] made atonement for the dead, that they [the Jewish soldiers slain in battle] might be delivered from their sin" (2 Macc. 12:46).[24] On the basis of such support, the Catholic Church formulated its doctrine of purgatory, particularly at the Councils of Florence and Trent. Accordingly, the Church encourages various practices done on behalf of the dead and in their honor: praying, offering Eucharistic sacrifices, almsgiving, purchasing or earning indulgences, and engaging in works of penance.

The other possible eternal destiny is hell, which is the "state of definitive self-exclusion from communion with God and the blessed," to which are consigned all who "die in mortal sin without repenting and accepting God's merciful love" by their own free choice.[25] Failure "to meet the serious needs of the poor and the little ones" who are one's brothers and sisters specifically manifests one's rejection of God.[26] Jesus himself spoke often of "Gehenna" and its "unquenchable fire" (e.g., Matt. 5:22, 29; 10:28; 13:42, 50; Mark 9:43–48). Accordingly, the Church affirms that "[i]mmediately after death the souls of those who die in a state of mortal sin descend into hell, where they suffer the punishments of hell, 'eternal fire.' The chief punishment of hell is eternal separation from God."[27] In light of the above, the *Catechism* urges two considerations: it is incumbent on every person to respond responsibly and freely to the call to conversion, and "God predestines no one to go to hell; for this, a willful turning away from God (a mortal sin) is necessary, and persistence in it until the end."[28]

In addition to the reward that comes to individuals immediately after their death, the last judgment will occur when Christ returns at his second coming, a time that has been determined by God but that cannot be known by human beings (Mark 13:32). All the dead, both the just and the unjust, will be resurrected, and Christ will separate them into two groups. The righteous will go into eternal life; the unrighteous will go into eternal punishment (Matt. 25:31–46). Going beyond the individual assessment undertaken at death, the "Last Judgment will reveal even to its furthest con-

---

[24] According to the *Catechism*, this passage is numbered as verse 46; in the RSV, it is verse 45.
[25] CCC 1033.
[26] Ibid.; the biblical allusion is to Matt. 25:31–46.
[27] CCC 1035.
[28] CCC 1037. The latter affirmation is reinforced by appeals to the Council of Orange II (529) and the Council of Trent (1547), as well as the biblical assertion of God's desire that all would come to repentance (2 Pet. 3:9).

sequences the good each person has done or failed to do during his earthly life."[29] As before, this threat of judgment should prompt a positive response to the divine call to conversion.

Following the last judgment, "[at] the end of time, the Kingdom of God will come in its fullness . . . [and] the righteous will reign for ever with Christ, glorified in body and soul."[30] Additionally, the whole universe, whose destiny is intricately tied to that of humanity, will be entirely renewed: according to the eternal plan of God, the final state will be "new heavens and a new earth" (2 Pet. 3:13), summed up under the single head, Jesus Christ (Eph. 1:10). This consummation has far-reaching consequences for both humanity in particular and the cosmos in general: "For *man*, this consummation will be the final realization of the unity of the human race, which God willed from creation and of which the pilgrim Church has been 'in the nature of sacrament.' Those who are united with Christ will form the community of the redeemed, 'the holy city' of God, 'the Bride, the wife of the Lamb.'"[31] There will be no more sin and self-ishness that destroy community, and the beatific vision will be the source of all joy and communion. Tied closely to this ultimate human destiny is the destiny of the *cosmos* (Rom. 8:19–23), which "is itself destined to be transformed, 'so that the world itself, restored to its original state, facing no further obstacles, should be at the service of the just,' sharing their glorification in the risen Jesus Christ."[32] This hope for the transformation of the universe should not detract from the Church's concern for the current earth. While earthly progress must be clearly distinguished from the expansion of the kingdom of God, the progression of both is welcomed; in particular, earthly progress "can contribute to the better ordering of human society."[33]

Evangelical Assessment

Continuing on with its discussion of eschatology, or the doctrine of last things, the *Catechism* addresses personal eschatology under the topic of judgment after death, and cosmic eschatology under the topics of the return

---

[29] CCC 1039.
[30] CCC 1042.
[31] CCC 1045; citation is from Vatican Council II, *Lumen Gentium* 1; the biblical references are Rev. 21:2, 9.
[32] CCC 1047; citation is from Irenaeus, *Against Heresies* 5.32.1 (*ANF* 1:561).
[33] CCC 1049; citation is from Vatican Council II, *Gaudium et Spes* 39.2.

of Christ, the last judgment, the millennium, and the new heaven and new earth. Each of these elements will be assessed.

In terms of personal eschatology, death ends human earthly life and is followed by divine judgment, with one of two eternal destinies awaiting each and every person. According to Catholic theology, one of these futures is *heaven*, the immediate eternal destiny of those who die in the grace and friendship of God and are perfectly purified. While evangelical theology agrees that heaven is one of two eternal destinies awaiting people, it disagrees with Catholic theology's ground for people entering into that state. According to the Catholic system based on the nature-grace interdependence, grace operates so as to elevate nature, and heaven is the reward for the faithful whose (human) nature has been perfected by grace. Because this axiom, which has already been critiqued, is wrong, it means that Catholic theology's notion of the ground for the faithful entering into heaven is wrong.

In terms of evangelical theology's specific criticism of this Catholic doctrine of heaven (and as will be discussed fully later on), salvation—and, hence, life with Christ in heaven after death—is based on God's declarative judgment and not on some (unattainable) purification in this life. The evangelical doctrine of justification, which is completely different from the Catholic idea of it, maintains that one of the mighty acts of God in saving fallen human beings is his declarative pronouncement that they are not guilty, but righteous instead, because God the Judge credits the perfect righteousness of Jesus Christ to their account, thus rendering them completely righteous before him. This justification is grounded on the grace of God alone—accomplished through the death, burial, and resurrection of Jesus Christ—and is appropriated by faith alone, that is, trust in the finished work of Christ without any mixture of good works, human effort, church involvement, participation in the sacraments, and/or anything else added to saving faith. Accordingly, all who are justified by grace through faith await the eternal destiny of heaven.

This evangelical critique of the Catholic system's axiom of the nature-grace interdependence, together with the evangelical doctrine of justification, further means that Catholic eschatology's notion of purgatory is wrong. According to Catholic theology, heaven is the ultimate destiny not only for the faithful who are perfectly purified but also, eventually, for those whose purification is not complete in their earthly lifetime. Upon the death of these faithful, their souls go immediately into *purgatory*, their temporary destiny and a state of suffering in which they "undergo purification, so as to achieve the holiness necessary to enter the joy of heaven."[34] While in this state, their souls may be helped by the prayers of the faithful in heaven as well as those on earth, the purchase of indulgences to lessen the time needed for purification, the dedication of masses said for them, and other means.

For Catholic theology, purgatory is necessary because it views salvation—and, hence, life with Christ in heaven after death—as based on "not only the remission of sins, but also the sanctification and renewal of the interior man."[35] If such renewal and elevation of human nature by God's grace does not reach perfection in this life, something more is required for salvation. Accordingly, what is needed is "a state of temporary punishment for those who, departing this life in the grace of God, are not entirely free from venial sins or have not yet fully paid the satisfaction due to their transgressions."[36] This Catholic doctrine is incorrect theologically because it is based on a misunderstanding of justification and a wrong view of the nature-grace interdependence.

Biblically, Catholic theology finds support for this doctrine in the apocryphal writing of 2 Maccabees:

> Then Judas [Maccabeus] assembled his army and went to the city of Adullam. As the seventh day was coming on, they purified themselves according to the custom, and they kept the sabbath there. On the next day, as by that time it had become necessary, Judas and his men went to take up the bodies of the fallen [Jewish soldiers] and to bring them back to lie with their kinsmen in the sepulchres of their fathers. Then under the tunic of every one of the dead they found sacred tokens of the idols of Jamnia, which the law forbids the Jews to wear. And it became clear to all that this was why these men had fallen. So they all blessed the ways of the Lord, the righteous Judge, who reveals the things that are hidden; and *they turned to prayer, beseeching that the sin which had been committed might be wholly blotted out.* And the noble Judas

---

[34] CCC 1030.
[35] CCC 1989. This is Catholic theology's definition of justification, which will be discussed later.
[36] Joseph Pohle, *Eschatology; or The Catholic Doctrine of the Last Things: A Dogmatic Treatise*, reprint of 1923 text (Ulan Press, 2012), 77.

exhorted the people to keep themselves free from sin, for they had seen with their own eyes what had happened because of the sin of those who had fallen. He also took up a collection, man by man, to the amount of two thousand drachmas of silver, and sent it to Jerusalem *to provide for a sin offering*. In doing this he acted very well and honorably, taking account of the resurrection. For if he were not expecting that those who had fallen would rise again, it would have been superfluous and foolish *to pray for the dead*. But if he was looking to the splendid reward that is laid up for those who fall asleep in godliness, it was a holy and pious thought. Therefore *he made atonement for the dead, that they might be delivered from their sin*. (2 Macc. 12:38–45, emphasis added)

This passage from 2 Maccabees narrates the aftermath of a battle (c. 180–160 BC) between Jewish conspirators, led by Judas Maccabeus, and a pagan army. The discovery of amulets on the bodies of the slain Jewish soldiers brought to light the reason why these particular men had died: they were idol worshipers, a grievous sin prohibited by Jewish law. Moreover, this discovery prompted action: prayer that the idolatry of these deceased men would be forgiven, and the collection of money to purchase a sin offering on their behalf. The hope expressed by this action was that the atonement offered for these dead soldiers would result in their deliverance from sin and their future resurrection. Catholic theology considers 2 Maccabees to be part of canonical Scripture and thus authoritative for its formulation of the doctrine of purgatory. Evangelical theology rejects the canonicity of 2 Maccabees and thus does not consider it to be Scripture; accordingly, this text does not provide biblical support for purgatory.

However, Catholic theology points to several New Testament passages for biblical warrant that evangelical theology should accept. In the first passage, the apostle Paul describes the judgment of certain people: "If anyone's work is burned up, he will suffer loss, though he himself will be saved, but only as through fire" (1 Cor. 3:15). Catholic theology finds here the idea of purgatorial fires burning away the dross of sin in preparation of the souls in purgatory for their ultimate salvation. But evangelical theology calls attention to the context of this passage (1 Cor. 3:10–14) and notes that Paul is describing, not the sufferings of people in purgatory, but the assessment of the works of people, primarily the leaders of the church, who build on its one foundation of Jesus Christ with either good works (gold, silver, precious stones) or bad works (wood, hay, straw). On the Day of Judgment (thus, this assessment is not executed immediately after death), each person's works will be evaluated by fire. The first scenario is promising: "If the work that anyone has built on the foundation survives, he will receive a reward" (v. 14). This Christian not only enjoys eternal salvation but is also rewarded for his good works for the sake of Christ. The second scenario is both reassuring and tragic: "If anyone's work is burned up, he will suffer loss, though he himself will be saved, but only as through fire" (v. 15). While this Christian, like his counterpart in the first scenario, enjoys eternal salvation, his poor labor for the cause of Christ results in a loss of (potential) rewards. This evaluation of the works of Christians for the purpose of giving—or not giving—rewards on the Day of Judgment cannot be understood to refer to a personal judgment immediately after death leading to banishment in purgatory for the purpose of purging away the dross of sin in preparation for ultimate salvation.

A second New Testament passage used in support of purgatory is Jesus's instructions about blasphemy against the Holy Spirit: "And whoever speaks a word against the Son of Man will be forgiven, but whoever speaks against the Holy Spirit will not be forgiven, either in this age or in the age to come" (Matt. 12:32). Catholic theology focuses on the implication of the last phrase, reasoning in this fashion: if there is one sin—blasphemy against the Holy Spirit—that cannot be forgiven either in this current age or in the one to come, then there may be other sins that, if not forgiven in this present age, *can* be forgiven in the age to come—that is, in purgatory. Evangelical theology objects to this implication as being far removed from Jesus's point, which is to emphasize the heinousness of one particular sin against the Holy Spirit: it is unpardonable both now and in eternity. The fact that forgiveness of such blasphemy is *impossible* even after death does not make forgiveness of other sins *possible* even after death, in purgatory.

Besides the lack of biblical support for this Catholic doctrine, the evangelical doctrine of justification renders purgatory useless. Christians have been declared not guilty but completely righteous because the perfect righteous of Jesus Christ has been imputed to them—credited to their account. As a result, they stand clothed in Christ's righteousness before God, and salvation—and, hence, entrance into heaven to enjoy eternal life with Christ after death—is granted to them. This standing before God is based on his declarative judgment, his justification, and not on some (unattainable) perfection in this life or in purgatory. For this reason, evangelical theology affirms and rejoices in the assurance of salvation, which is the privilege of all sinful human beings who embrace the grace of God in the work of Christ by faith alone. Evangelical theology therefore dissents from and laments Catholic theology's misunderstanding of justification and purgatory, with its corollary that the faithful cannot find comfort and strength in the assurance of salvation.

Having completed the assessment of one of the two eternal destinies of people after death—heaven—and the evaluation of the temporary destiny of purgatory, the second of the two eternal destinies awaits appraisal. According to Catholic theology, this other future is *hell*, the immediate eternal destiny of all who "die in mortal sin without repenting and accepting God's merciful love" by their own free choice.[37] The unrepentant wicked suffer eternal punishments in hell, the chief of which is eternal separation from the presence of God.

While evangelical theology agrees that hell is one of two eternal destinies awaiting people, it hesitates to affirm certain aspects of this Catholic doctrine. One point of hesitancy is the ground for consigning people to this destiny. Because evangelical theology does not accept Catholic theology's distinction between mortal and venial sins, it maintains that anyone who commits sin—mortal or venial, presumptuous or unintentional, sins of commission or sins of omission—is guilty before God and thus condemned to hell. Furthermore, rejecting the inclusivism of Catholic theology (discussed earlier), evangelical theology underscores that it is only through a conscious appropriation of the gospel of Jesus Christ that any sinful person escapes the deserved destiny of hell.

A second hesitation is voiced by many proponents of evangelical theology, but not all. This point has to do with the doctrine of predestination as it relates to this topic. *Predestination* has to do with the decree of God, in particular his decision from all eternity regarding the ultimate destiny of all persons. There is a theology that denies divine predestination: God does not make any decision about the eternal destiny of people, but each person makes the choice to follow Christ so as to be saved or not to follow him so as to be condemned. Another theology holds to divine *election*: that

---
[37] CCC 1033.

is, from eternity past, God has chosen some people, the elect, to be saved through repentance from sin and faith in Christ. Still another theology embraces "double" predestination, that is, both election (as defined above) and *reprobation*, the divine decision to pass over some persons, in sorrow deciding not to save them. Catholic theology seems to fall in the second group: Whereas it acknowledges some type of election of those who will be saved, it holds further that God does not predestine anyone to hell; that destiny is a matter of personal choice. People who persist in mortal sin and refuse to embrace the forgiveness provided for them exclude themselves from heaven; God does not consign them to the horrific future of hell. This view finds support from certain varieties of evangelical theology; specifically, it is the belief of evangelical Arminian theology. In contrast, evangelical Reformed theology takes the third position of double predestination, holding not only to election but also to reprobation. At the same time, this Reformed theology agrees with Catholic theology on the matter of personal choice: the eternal decision to pass over some people—reprobation—belongs to God, but this divine choice is completely compatible with the belief that those people willfully turn away from God and intractably persist in that state of unrepentance and unbelief, resulting in their condemnation in hell.

A final point of agreement on the doctrine of hell: As Catholic theology underscores the duty incumbent on every person to respond responsibly to the gospel, so does evangelical theology. Indeed, the threat of eternal conscious punishment awaiting the wicked in hell is a primary motivator for missional endeavors by the church.

This individual evaluation of each person at death for the purpose of conferring upon that person his or her eternal destiny in either heaven or hell anticipates one aspect of cosmic eschatology, and this evangelical assessment moves now to this topic. Because the "last times" refers to the entire period between the first and second comings of Jesus Christ, the next great event to which the church looks forward is his glorious return. Catholic theology rightly points out that, although this is a definite event established by God, he has not revealed its timing (Mark 13:32), so the church cannot know when Christ will come again. Accompanying that event will be the resurrection of both the righteous and the unrighteous and their appearance before Christ at the last judgment (Matt. 25:31–46), which the apostle Paul describes: "For we must all appear before the judgment seat

of Christ, so that each one may receive what is due for what he has done in
the body, whether good or evil" (2 Cor. 5:10). The eternal destinies already
meted out at the individual judgment at death will now be displayed publicly for the entire world to see. The divine righteousness will be vindicated
as God is demonstrated to be holy and true in all his ways and as his "justice
triumphs over all the injustices committed."[38] For the most part, Catholic
and evangelical theology agree on the return of Christ and the last judgment. Evangelical theology would make a stronger point that the evaluation
to be undergone at the last judgment centers upon one's appropriation, or
lack thereof, of the gospel, that life-changing decision from which flow all
good and bad works. It would add also that those who have not heard of
Jesus Christ will not be judged on the basis of their acceptance or rejection
of the gospel but on the grounds of their response to the light of general
revelation received from God.

For Catholic theology, the return of Jesus Christ and the last judgment
bring an end to this present age and initiate the *eschaton*, or age to come,
in which the kingdom of God is established in its fullness. Some proponents
of evangelical theology agree with this scenario, while others disagree. The
doctrine that treats this aspect of cosmic eschatology is called *millennialism* because it focuses on the place of Revelation 20:1–6—particularly the
recurring expression "the/a thousand years" (Lat., *mille* = thousand; *annus*
= year)—in relation to our present existence and the return of Christ. *Amillennialism*[39] holds that the thousand years is not a literal period of time but
corresponds to the age of the church between the first and second comings
of Christ; thus, there is no future thousand-year period. At the conclusion of the church age, or millennium, Christ will return and establish the
kingdom of God, or the new heavens and new earth. Augustine, in the fifth
century, developed amillennialism, and beginning from that point it became the church's standard millennial doctrine. It is the millennial view of
Catholic theology as well as of many types of evangelical theology (e.g., Reformed theology). *Postmillennialism*[40] holds that through the preaching of
the gospel and the Christianization of the world, the church age will gradu-

---

[38] CCC 1040.
[39] *Amillennialism* comes from the prefix *a* (the alpha-privative), expressing negation, and *millennium*, or a thousand years. Thus, amillennialism signifies "no thousand years" or, to be more precise, "no *future* thousand years."
[40] *Postmillennialism* derives from the prefix *post* (= after) and *millennium*, or a thousand years. Thus, postmillennialism signifies "after the thousand years."

ally give way to the millennium, a golden age (not necessarily a thousand years) of peace and prosperity, after which Christ will return. Though never finding widespread support, postmillennialism was championed by some notable people (e.g., Jonathan Edwards) and is still a minority view within evangelical theology. *Premillennialism*[41] holds that Jesus Christ will return before the millennium and will set up an authoritative reign on the earth for a literal thousand years. This millennial position was pervasive in the early church up to the time of Augustine; consequently, it is often referred to as *historical* or *classical premillennialism*. A version of it—called *pretribulational*[42] *premillennialism*—was introduced in the nineteenth century. It is differentiated from the classical position on the issue of the church's relationship to the tribulation, the seven-year period of intense suffering, satanic attack, human evil, and divine wrath described in Scripture (e.g., Dan. 12:7; Rev. 7:14). Whereas classical premillennialism maintains that the church will experience this tribulation period, pretribulational premillennialism believes that the church will be taken out of the world—the technical term for this event is the *rapture* of the church—before the tribulation begins. Both versions of premillennialism are found extensively within evangelical theology. Accordingly, some parts of evangelical theology concur with Catholic millennialism while others parts do not.

Despite the existence of many perspectives on the doctrine of the millennium, Catholic and evangelical theology are in complete agreement that the final stage in cosmic eschatology is the new heavens and new earth. After the return of Jesus Christ, the resurrection from the dead, and the last judgment (here, premillennialism would add the thousand-year reign of Christ on the earth), the eternal state will be initiated. All existence will be summed up in Christ (Eph. 1:10). The church—"the Bride, the wife of the Lamb" (Rev. 21:9)—will yield its place to the New Jerusalem as the splendid dwelling of God among human beings (vv. 2–4, 10–21), all of whom will have been completely conformed to the image of Christ and united forever (Rev. 21:5; Rom. 8:29). The entire universe will be remade or renewed (Rom. 8:18–23; 2 Pet. 3:10–13; Rev. 21:1) such that God's original design for it will be restored forever.

---

[41] *Premillennialism* stems from the prefix *pre* (= before) and *millennium*, or a thousand years. Thus, premillennialism signifies "before the thousand years."

[42] *Pretribulational* comes from the prefix *pre* (= before) and *tribulation*, or suffering. Thus, pretribulational signifies coming "before the (period of) suffering."

Conclusion

Part 1 of the *Catechism*, the Profession of Faith, comes to completion, having treated the doctrines of revelation and faith, and the twelve doctrines that flow from the Church's creeds, specifically, the Apostles' Creed as supplemented by the Nicene Creed. Working through this first part, section by section, and cognizant of the Catholic system's two axioms, an evangelical assessment of this Catholic theology in the light of Scripture and evangelical theology has been offered, resulting in areas of both intrigue and critique. Part 2 of the *Catechism*, the Celebration of the Christian Mystery, with its focus on the sacramental economy of the Catholic Church together with its seven sacraments, becomes the next topic of discussion.

II

Catholic Theology according to the
Catechism of the Catholic Church

Part 2: The Celebration of the Christian Mystery

7

The Celebration of the Christian Mystery (Part 2, Section I)

The Liturgy and the Sacramental Economy

Introduction: Why the Liturgy?

Following its presentation of the doctrines of the Church under the heading "The Profession of the Faith," the *Catechism* next turns to an expanded discussion of the liturgy of the Church, entitled "The Celebration of the Christian Mystery," with particular attention paid to two areas: the sacramental economy of the Church, and the theology and practice of its seven sacraments. The word "mystery" is used in two specific ways: First, "mystery" refers to the economy of salvation, the work God did in Christ to accomplish the redemption of fallen human beings. This salvific work was especially centered on Christ's Paschal[1] mystery, composed of his passion, death, burial, resurrection, and ascension. From this sacrificial act of Christ on the cross, "there came forth 'the wondrous sacrament of the whole Church.'"[2] Second, and as a consequence, "mystery" refers to the Church's proclamation of the gospel and its celebration of Christ's Paschal mystery—his work of salvation, the first sense of "mystery"—in its liturgy: "For it is in the liturgy, especially in the divine sacrifice of the Eucharist, that 'the work of our redemption is accomplished,' and it is through the liturgy especially that the faithful are enabled to express in their lives and manifest to others the mystery of Christ and the real nature of the true Church."[3]

---

[1] The word "Paschal" is from Hebrew and Greek words meaning "passing over," as in the Jewish Passover, transformed into the Christian Good Friday and Easter Sunday.
[2] CCC 1067; citation is from Vatican Council II, *Sacrosanctum concilium* 5.2.
[3] CCC 1068; citation is from Vatican Council II, *Sacrosanctum concilium* 2.

Indeed, liturgy is "the participation of the People of God in 'the work of God.' Through the liturgy Christ, our redeemer and high priest, continues the work of our redemption in, with, and through his Church."[4] Liturgy is not confined to the service of worship but refers also to the communication of the gospel and to works of charity; at the heart of all of these activities is the idea of service to God and others. Most importantly, the Catholic notion of the liturgy (Gk. λειτουργία, *leitourgia*, "ministry"; Heb. 8:6) is connected to *the* "minister" (Gk. λειτουργὸς, *leitourgos*; Heb. 8:2), Jesus Christ:

> The liturgy then is rightly seen as an exercise of the priestly office of Jesus Christ. It involves the presentation of man's sanctification under the guise of signs perceptible by the senses and its accomplishment in ways appropriate to each of these signs. In it full public worship is performed by the Mystical Body of Jesus Christ, that is, by the Head and his members. From this it follows that every liturgical celebration, because it is an action of Christ the priest and of his Body which is the Church, is a sacred action surpassing all others. No other action of the Church can equal its efficacy by the same title and to the same degree.[5]

Accordingly, the liturgy is characterized by dual agency: on the divine side, it is the work of Christ; on the human side, it is the work of the Church, rendering the Church present and revealing it "as the visible sign of the communion in Christ between God and men."[6] Furthermore, the liturgy is not the only work of the Church; "it must be preceded by evangelization, faith, and conversion."[7] For the faithful in the Church, the liturgy is "the privileged place" for their catechesis as it proceeds "from the visible to the invisible, from the sign to the thing signified, from the 'sacraments' to the 'mysteries.'"[8]

Evangelical Assessment

Not a familiar concept for many evangelicals, "liturgy" can simply refer to a rite, an ordered structure, of public worship. Most evangelical church services follow a designated rhythm, beginning with a call to worship, mov-

---

[4] CCC 1069. The expression "the work of God" alludes to Christ's statement in John 17:4.
[5] CCC 1070; citation is from Vatican Council II, *Sacrosanctum concilium* 7.2–3.
[6] CCC 1071.
[7] CCC 1072.
[8] CCC 1074–1075.

ing into singing hymns and/or songs of praise and thanksgiving, turning to corporate and/or individual prayers including confession of sin and the promise of forgiveness, followed by the reading and preaching of the Word of God, often including a celebration of the two ordinances or sacraments of baptism and the Lord's Supper, and concluding with more singing of praise to God and a benediction. Thus, evangelical churches, while not accustomed to calling such structure "the liturgy," do engage in worship services that are liturgical.

However, the Catholic notion of liturgy is much more exalted, because it is associated with mystery.

As for Catholic theology's idea of mystery, evangelical theology concurs that this centers on the church's proclamation of the gospel. Specifically, in the New Testament, "mystery" primarily refers to a truth known originally and only to God in ages past but which has now been disclosed, especially through the announcement of the good news of Jesus Christ, for human beings to embrace. Even then, not everyone is the recipient of this revelation (e.g., to the disciples only, and not to outsiders, was the secret [mystery] of the kingdom of God, voiced in parables, explained; Matt. 13:11). Specific mysteries revealed in Christ are God's ultimate goal to sum up all things in Christ (Eph. 1:10); the participation of the Gentiles in Christ and their inclusion together with the Jews in his body, the church (Eph. 3:6); and Christ in believers as their hope of glory (Col. 1:27; 2:3). In particular, church leaders as servants of Christ are stewards of these mysteries (1 Cor. 4:1), in the sense of "the mystery of the faith" (1 Tim. 3:9) or "the mystery of godliness," which is true belief, or sound doctrine, about Christ (1 Tim. 3:16–17).

Because Scripture presents mystery in these ways, evangelical theology does not accept the different and primary sense of it found in Catholic theology: the economy, or work, of salvation. Certainly, the passion, death, burial, resurrection, and ascension of Jesus Christ is the foundation for everything that the church is, believes, and does. But why does Catholic theology consider it to be a mystery? Furthermore, with the New Testament's emphasis on the *proclamation* of this mystery, evangelical theology asks why Catholic theology expands the idea to include the church's *celebration* of this mystery. The answer to evangelical theology's puzzlement is the Catholic system's two axioms. The nature-grace interdependence underscores the capacity of nature—water, oil, bread and wine—to convey the grace of God, which must be expressed in a tangible manner. The result is the ability of the sacraments—Baptism, Confirmation, the Eucharist—to be instruments of grace that operate concretely through these visible means. Moreover, the Christ-Church interconnection highlights that when the Catholic Church celebrates the liturgy, it is the mystical body of Jesus—the whole Christ, both head and body—as the continuation of the incarnation of Christ that performs the liturgy. Indeed, it is Christ himself, acting in and through the priest, who celebrates it. Thus, the Catholic Church as a sacrament is the revealer of hidden divine grace, which it discloses and mediates through its administration of its seven sacraments. In the Catholic liturgy, these two foundational tenets of the Catholic system combine and manifest themselves clearly. Because these axioms are rejected by evangelical theology—and rightly so, because they are faulty, as critiqued earlier—the Catholic liturgy is very difficult for evangelicals to understand.

That the salvation accomplished by Christ, revealed through the gospel, is and must be applied in a continuous fashion is certainly true, but evangelical theology objects to the Catholic notion of a fresh revelation of the word of Christ and an ongoing accomplishment of salvation through the liturgy of the Church. For Catholic theology, this reality is termed "the sacramental economy," the subject to which the *Catechism* next turns.

The Sacramental Economy (Sec. I)

The sacramental economy of the Church can be represented by the accompanying diagram. As Redeemer and High Priest, Jesus Christ accomplished the salvation of fallen human beings through his Paschal mystery—his passion, death, burial, resurrection, and ascension—that occurred in history and that gave birth to the sacrament of the Church. As Redeemer and High Priest, Jesus Christ continues accomplishing the salvation of fallen human beings through his Church, with particular reference to the apostles and their successors—consisting of the pope and the college of bishops—who teach, govern, and sanctify the Church through the gospel, works of charity, and above all else, the seven sacraments. Accordingly, the benefits of Christ's saving work, or Paschal mystery, are communicated or dispensed through the Church's liturgy to the world.

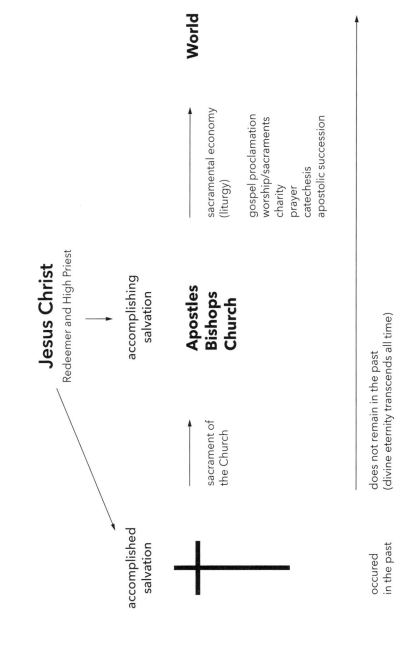

THE SACRAMENTAL ECONOMY

Jesus Christ
Redeemer and High Priest

accomplishing
salvation

accomplished
salvation

Apostles
Bishops
Church

sacrament of
the Church

World

sacramental economy
(liturgy)

gospel proclamation
worship/sacraments
charity
prayer
catechesis
apostolic succession

occured
in the past

does not remain in the past
(divine eternity transcends all time)

The Liturgy—Work of the Holy Trinity (Sec. I, Ch. I, Art. I)

The *Catechism* treats this sacramental dispensation, or "the Paschal mystery in the age of the Church," by focusing on the various agents and instruments at work in the liturgy. Specifically, this is the work of the triune God.

The work of God the Father, as the source of the liturgy, is to give a blessing. Additionally, he is acknowledged and adored as the goal of the liturgy, indeed, as "the end of all the blessings of creation and salvation."[9]

The work of God the Son is his activity "through the sacraments he instituted to communicate his grace"; by Christ's action and the power of the Holy Spirit, the sacraments "make present efficaciously the grace that they signify."[10] More specifically, the Son signifies and makes present his own work of salvation as a unique event to which a divine attribute is applied:

> His Paschal mystery is a real event that occurred in our history, but it is unique: all other historical events happen once, and then they pass away, swallowed up in the past. The Paschal mystery of Christ, by contrast, cannot remain only in the past, because by his death he destroyed death, and all that Christ is—all that he did and suffered for all men—participates in the divine eternity, and so transcends all times while being made present in them all. The event of the Cross and Resurrection *abides* and draws everything toward life.[11]

Jesus Christ died and rose from the dead only one time, about two thousand years ago; he accomplished the salvation of fallen human beings once and for all. However, his cross work and resurrection cannot remain confined to the past, locked in space and time like all other historical events. Rather, this Paschal mystery is *made present*, or *re-presented*, in all times (as we will see, this has particular reference to the celebration of the sacrament of the Eucharist) because that once-and-for-all event shares in the divine attribute of eternality, or atemporality (note, again, the bottom lines of diagram 7.1). God's existence is not a temporal one, having beginning and end and succession of moments, and he himself is not and cannot be limited in time; on the contrary, God exists outside of time and thus is present everywhere at all times. As Christ's work of salvation participates in this divine attribute, it too is not and cannot be limited in time but exists

---

[9] CCC 1082.
[10] CCC 1084.
[11] CCC 1085.

outside of time and thus is re-presented, or made present, in the Church's Eucharistic celebrations.

This re-presentation is associated with the Church: Christ, by the power of the Holy Spirit, accomplishes this work of re-presentation through his apostles and those to whom the apostles, through the power of the same Spirit, transferred this power by means of apostolic succession—the bishops of the Church. Thus, Christ is present in the Church's liturgy specifically in two ways: in the priest and in the Eucharist. Christ is present "in the person of his minister, 'the same now offering, through the ministry of priests, who formerly offered himself on the cross.'"[12] Christ is also present "especially in the Eucharistic species," that is, the two elements of bread and wine (mixed with water).[13] Crucial to this reality is the conviction that Christ "always associates the Church with himself in this great work in which God is perfectly glorified and men are sanctified."[14]

The work of God the Holy Spirit in the Church's liturgy is multifold. He is "teacher of the faith of the People of God and artisan of 'God's masterpieces,' the sacraments."[15] As the one who stirs up faith, the Spirit meets the Church's faithful in the response of faith, thus stimulating a synergistic cooperation and prompting a divine-human collaboration in the Church's liturgy. Additionally, the Holy Spirit "prepares the Church to encounter her Lord; he recalls and makes Christ manifest to the faith of the assembly[;] . . . he makes the mystery of Christ present here and now[; and he] . . . unites the Church to the life and mission of Christ."[16] The preparatory work of the Spirit is matched by the faithful's own preparation and the work of the Church's ministers to prepare its people to meet Christ. The grace of the Holy Spirit stimulates faith, conversion, and commitment to God's will, dispositions that are "the precondition" for receiving other graces made available through the liturgy.[17]

Specifically, the work of the Holy Spirit in the liturgy focuses on recalling the mystery of Christ. Because the liturgy "is the *memorial* of the mystery of salvation," the Spirit "is the Church's living memory."[18] This

---

[12] CCC 1088; citation is from Vatican Council II, *Sacrosanctum concilium* 7.
[13] Ibid.
[14] CCC 1089.
[15] CCC 1091.
[16] CCC 1092.
[17] CCC 1098.
[18] CCC 1099.

work has particular reference to the Word of God: "The Holy Spirit first recalls the meaning of the salvation event to the liturgical assembly [the faithful gathered to worship] by giving life to the Word of God, which is proclaimed so that it may be received and lived."[19] This role of Scripture has reference not only to the portions of it that are read during the liturgy and upon which the homily, or sermon, is based; rather, Scripture is at the heart of the songs, prayers, collects (short, structured prayers), and liturgical actions as well. Moreover, the Spirit illumines the Word of God, giving "a spiritual understanding" to its hearers/readers "according to the dispositions of their hearts."[20] Furthermore, the Word of God "elicits the *response of faith* as consent and commitment"; such nourishing of faith causes the Church to grow.[21] Specifically, in the Liturgy of the Word (the first part of the Church's liturgical celebration, with the Liturgy of the Eucharist being the second part), the Spirit "recalls" to the Church the work of Christ for its salvation. This recollection, or awakening of the Church's memory, is called the *anamnesis*; thus, "the celebration 'makes a remembrance' of the marvelous works of God in an anamnesis."[22]

As noted above, however, the liturgy does not entail a mere memory of the events of Christ's work of salvation "but actualizes them, makes them present. The Paschal mystery of Christ is celebrated, not repeated. It is the celebrations that are repeated, and in each celebration there is an outpouring of the Holy Spirit that makes the unique mystery present."[23] This work of the Spirit has particular reference to the liturgical element called the *epiclesis*: "The *Epiclesis* ('invocation upon') is the intercession in which the priest begs the Father to send the Holy Spirit, the Sanctifier, so that the offerings [the elements of the bread and the wine (mixed with water)] may become the body and blood of Christ and that the faithful, by receiving them, may themselves become a living offering to God."[24] These two elements, the *anamnesis* and the *epiclesis*, are the core of the liturgical celebration, especially of the sacrament of the Eucharist. With and through the Holy Spirit, the Church is intimately united with Christ and is formed as his body, with its members being rendered "a living sacrifice to God by

---

[19] CCC 1100.
[20] CCC 1101.
[21] CCC 1102.
[22] CCC 1103.
[23] CCC 1104.
[24] CCC 1105.

their spiritual transformation into the image of Christ," knit together in unity, and equipped for the Church's "mission through the witness and service of charity."[25]

Evangelical Assessment

Evangelical theology has almost nothing in common with Catholic theology's concept and practice of the sacramental economy, other than the same object of worship (the triune God), the same participants (the leaders of the liturgy and the congregation), and the same external rites or activities of worship (e.g., praying, the reading and preaching of the Word of God, singing, observing the Lord's Supper). Beyond these formal similarities, however, Catholic theology's sacramental economy and evangelical theology's doctrine of worship are far, far removed from each other.

Evangelical theology rejects the sacramental economy's central point of Jesus Christ's ongoing accomplishment of salvation, which is particularly associated with the Catholic Church, its hierarchy, and its sacraments. Certainly, Jesus Christ as High Priest died on the cross once, and only once. Indeed, evangelical theology urges its adherents not to misunderstand Catholic theology on this point: Catholic theology does not teach that Christ is re-sacrificed each and every time the sacrament of the Eucharist is celebrated. Today, at a Catholic mass, Jesus is not dying for the 2,503,693,176th time. He died once, and both evangelical and Catholic theology affirm this truth.

Where the two part company is over the notion of the *re-presentation* of that once-and-for-all sacrifice each and every time the sacrament of the Eucharist is administered. The Catholic notion that the cross work of Christ participates in the divine attribute of eternality (always in existence), or atemporality (without time limitations; note, once again, diagram 7.1), has no warrant whatsoever. Accordingly, the sacrifice of Christ two thousand years ago, like all other historical events, took place once then and does not transcend all times so as to be made present now (or, for that matter, anytime after it occurred). The idea of atemporality may be invoked in an attempt to explain how the body and blood of Christ are present in the Eucharist, but the whole matter is grounded on a misinterpretation of Christ's

---

[25] CCC 1109.

words as he spoke of the bread when he instituted the Lord's Supper: "This is my body" (Matt. 26:26). Just as it was not his physical body when the disciples and he ate it during Christ's Last Supper—how could it be, given that he was not yet crucified?—neither is it his physical body now when the faithful eat the wafer during the Eucharistic celebration. Moreover, the sacramental interpretation of Jesus's "Bread of Life" discourse in John 6, upon which Catholic theology is dependent for its concept of the sacramental economy in general and the sacrament of the Eucharist in particular, is not very plausible. These issues will be fully discussed later on.

Catholic theology's view of the re-presentation of Christ, as associated with the Church through its hierarchy, especially suffers from being grounded on the Christ-Church interconnection, an axiom that has already been critiqued (ch. 2). Christ is not now in the Church as both its Head and its Body. He is not here on earth with the fullness of his entire being; rather, in his human nature, the exalted Lord is seated at the right hand of the throne of God in heaven. Two implications flow from this truth, both of which contradict Catholic theology on this matter: Christ is not and cannot be present in the priest as the latter engages in the liturgy. And Christ is not and cannot be present in the bread and cup of the sacrament of the Eucharist. On this point, evangelical theology does not maintain that Christ is absent from his church, its worship, its celebration of the Lord's Supper, and the like. On the contrary, as the fully divine Son of God, he is omnipresent—present everywhere. Moreover, he manifests his spiritual presence in particular ways at particular times—for example, to empower the church's missional engagement (Matt. 28:18–20), to support the church's exercise of discipline (Matt. 18:15–20), and to bless a proper administration or judge an unworthy observation of the Lord's Supper (1 Cor. 10:14–22; 11:17–33). Accordingly, he is not absent from, but present with, his church as it engages in evangelism, worship, teaching, and the like. But this spiritual presence is mediated through the agency of the Holy Spirit, whom Christ sent as "another Helper" (John 14:16) to take his place on the earth during his absence from it between his ascension and return. Additionally, Christ's spiritual presence is mediated through the instrumentality of written Scripture, which he gave through the Spirit by the ministry of human authors to be his inspired, truthful, authoritative, sufficient, necessary, clear, and powerful Word. Moreover, it is mediated through the ordinances of the new covenant, baptism and the Lord's Supper, that Christ commanded his church to administer until he returns. But the presence that these elements mediate is not the fullness of the whole Christ, including his human nature with his body and blood, but his spiritual presence only.[26]

With specific regard to the agency of the Holy Spirit in the liturgy, evangelical theology agrees in part with its Catholic counterpart that the Spirit stirs up faith, mediates the presence of Christ in the church and the world, converts, teaches the faith to God's people, and illumines Scripture. It disagrees that the Spirit, as an artisan, confects the sacraments; renders Christ's sacrifice present here and now in the church, especially through its sacraments; stimulates certain dispositions that serve to predispose people for receiving divine grace through the liturgy; and functions as the church's living memory of the mystery of salvation. A liturgical action that is especially troubling is the *epiclesis*, the priest's invocation of God the Father to send the Holy Spirit to transubstantiate the bread and cup into the body and blood of Christ during the celebration of the Eucharist. Evangelical theology also hesitates to agree with Catholic theology's idea of a Spirit-stimulated synergy between God and his people in the liturgy. While evangelical theology affirms a dual dimensionality present as the church worships—in ways proper to his divine agency, God is active; and in ways proper to their human agency, clergy and laity are active—it ascribes a very different role to the clergy than Catholic theology does.

As for the instrumentality of Scripture in the liturgy, evangelical theology agrees with Catholic theology that the Word and the Spirit of God are tightly connected in this regard. Specifically, this means that the Spirit empowers the proclamation of the Word, illumines it so that it is grasped and put into practice, and nourishes a response of faith to it. Furthermore, this proclamation is not limited to the specific passages read and preached during the liturgy, but Scripture undergirds the songs, prayers, responses, and other liturgical actions. Evangelical theology voices caution, however, when Catholic theology speaks of the Spirit giving a spiritual understanding to readers/hearers of the Word of God, the hesitation being due to the possibility that

---

[26] Anyone who objects that this position separates the divine and human natures of Christ (the heresy of Nestorianism) must confront this issue: it is not possible to meaningfully affirm that Christ as the God-man ascended into heaven forty days after his resurrection, is currently seated at the right hand of the Father's throne in heaven, and will return to earth at his second coming without saying that this is true of his human nature alone and not of his divine nature (which is omnipresent). My position is firmly grounded on, and in accord with, this preceding statement, so it is not open to the charge of Nestorianism.

this spiritual understanding is code for some (mis)interpretation that goes beyond the grammatical–(redemptive) historical–typological sense of Scripture. Another concern is raised over the idea of the Spirit giving life to the Word of God, which describes itself as "living and active" (Heb. 4:12) in itself.

In summary, while there are some formal similarities between Catholic and evangelical theology, for the most part the Catholic concept of the Church's sacramental economy is very far removed from the evangelical notion of worship. This divergence becomes even more pronounced when it comes to the sacraments.

The Paschal Mystery in the Church's Sacraments (Sec. I, Ch. I, Art. 2)

As noted above, the seven sacraments are at the heart of the Catholic Church's sacramental economy, and the *Catechism* offers a general discussion of these sacraments before engaging in a more detailed exposition of them.[27] This general discussion focuses on the commonalities of the sacraments both from a doctrinal point of view and in terms of their celebration; the detailed exposition underscores their distinctive elements.

Following the classical definition given by Augustine, a sacrament is a tangible or visible sign of an intangible or invisible grace. Baptism, for example, involves immersing under water or sprinkling with water, so the action involving the water is a concrete sign. At the same time, the sign is not an empty sign, as the sacrament actually effects that which it symbolizes: baptismal grace cleanses from original sin (and all actual sins, in the case of adults) and causes regeneration. For the Catholic Church, there are seven such *sacraments of Christ*: "Baptism, Confirmation or Chrismation, Eucharist, Penance, Anointing of the Sick, Holy Orders, and Matrimony."[28] Differing from Protestant churches, which claim that Jesus Christ ordained only two ordinances or sacraments—baptism and the Lord's Supper—the Catholic Church professes that seven sacraments were "instituted by Jesus Christ."[29] Other terms used to describe these seven sacraments of Christ are "'powers that come forth' from the Body of Christ," "actions of the Holy Spirit" at work in the Church, and "the masterworks of God."[30]

---

[27] These detailed presentations will be discussed and assessed in chapters 8–11.
[28] CCC 1113.
[29] CCC 1114; citation is from *Canons and Decrees of the Council of Trent*, 7th session (March 3, 1547), *Decree on the Sacraments*, Canon 1 (Schaff, 2:119).
[30] CCC 1116; the biblical basis for the first descriptor is Luke 5:17; 6:19; 8:46, passages that describe the power that emanated from Jesus Christ during his earthly ministry.

These sacraments of Christ are also *sacraments of the Church* in a double sense: they are "by her" and "for her." They are "by her" in that the Church "is the sacrament of Christ's action at work in her through the mission of the Holy Spirit." They are "for her" in that "the sacraments make the Church" by presenting the mystery of communion with the triune, loving God through priestly actions.[31] This priesthood also has a double aspect to it: The "baptismal priesthood" is composed of all the faithful who have been baptized and confirmed, and thus prepared as priestly people to celebrate the liturgy. The "ministerial priesthood" is composed of all the ordained men who are "at the service of the baptismal priesthood" and who, when they administer the sacraments, guarantee "that it really is Christ who acts in the sacraments through the Holy Spirit for the Church." Thus, there is a "sacramental bond" beginning with Christ, proceeding through the apostles, and continuing with those who are ordained, which "ties the liturgical action" that the ministerial priesthood performs to "Christ, the source and foundation of the sacraments."[32]

Three sacraments are unique in terms of the indelible mark they bestow: "Baptism, Confirmation, and Holy Orders confer, in addition to grace, a sacramental *character* or 'seal' by which the Christian shares in Christ's priesthood and is made a member of the Church according to different states and functions."[33] Because of their indelible quality, these three sacraments can never be repeated.

The sacraments are also *sacraments of faith*. Taking its cue from the Great Commission (Matt. 28:19), the *Catechism* explains, "The mission to baptize, and so the sacramental mission, is implied in the mission to evangelize, because the sacrament is prepared for *by the word of God and by the faith* which is assent to this word."[34] Indeed, the ministry of the Word of God is necessary for the ministry of the sacraments because the latter finds its source in and draws its sustenance from the Word. Accordingly, they are sacraments *of faith* in a double sense: They presuppose faith, and "they also nourish, strengthen, and express it."[35] Moreover, "[t]he Church's

---

[31] CCC 1118; the second citation is from Augustine, *The City of God*, 22.17.
[32] CCC 1120.
[33] CCC 1121.
[34] CCC 1122 (emphasis added).
[35] CCC 1123; citation is from Vatican Council II, *Sacrosanctum concilium* 59.

faith precedes the faith of the believer who is invited to adhere to it,"[36] and as it celebrates the liturgy, the Church believes.

In addition to being sacraments of Christ, sacraments of the Church, and sacraments of faith, the sacraments are also *sacraments of salvation*; that is, "[c]elebrated worthily in faith, the sacraments confer the grace that they signify. They are *efficacious* because in them Christ himself is at work: it is he who baptizes, he who acts in his sacraments in order to communicate the grace that each sacrament signifies."[37] The expression for this reality is *ex opere operato*: the sacrament is effective, literally, "by the very fact of the action's being performed"; that is, "by virtue of the saving work of Christ, accomplished once for all."[38] The validity and effectiveness of the sacraments is not dependent on the one who administers them—e.g., the priest who baptizes or celebrates the Eucharist—nor is it dependent on the one who receives them—e.g., the infant who is baptized or the faithful who eats the wafer and drinks from the cup (the communicant). Their legitimacy and benefit is dependent only on the power of Christ and his Holy Spirit acting through the sacraments, "independently of the personal holiness of the minister. Nevertheless, the fruits of the sacraments also depend on the disposition of the one who receives them."[39] As the means by which sacramental grace is conferred by Christ and his Spirit through the Church, the sacraments are necessary for salvation. Finally, they prefigure the future glory, the eternal life, that is still to come to the Church when Christ returns.

In summary, this general discussion of the sacraments focused on their commonalities from a doctrinal point of view. The next general discussion treats the commonalities of the sacraments in terms of their celebration in and by the Church. Before embarking on the liturgical celebration of the sacraments, an assessment of Catholic theology's general idea of the sacraments is in order.

Evangelical Assessment

As heir of the Protestant Reformation, evangelical theology widely disagrees with the Catholic theology of the sacraments. Four major diver-

---

[36] CCC 1124.
[37] CCC 1127.
[38] CCC 1128.
[39] Ibid.

gences are the terminology for these rites, their proper number, sacraments as means of grace, and the ground of their validity or effectiveness.

Before addressing the issue of terminology, a bit of background needs to be provided on how the word "sacrament" came to be associated with the church's administration of these rites. As noted earlier, the New Testament uses the word μυστήριον (*mustērion* = mystery) to refer to a long-held divine secret that has now been revealed through the proclamation of the gospel, as well as the sound doctrine to which the church is beholden. Historically, the term was applied to the early church's celebrations of baptism and the Lord's Supper in the context of mystery religions, which featured secret ceremonies that channeled spiritual goods and power to their participants. The church's understanding of "mystery" in the context of mystery religions produced this result: Baptism and the Lord's Supper were considered to reveal a mystery of divine grace, conferring spiritual goods and power on their recipients. Furthermore, as the universal language of Greek yielded to the new common language of Latin, the Greek μυστήριον (*mustērion*) was translated into Latin by *sacramentum*. This word could refer either to a sacred object or rite, or to an oath of allegiance. Catholic theology's use of *sacramentum* depended to a large degree on Augustine, who defined "sacrament" as "an outward and visible sign of an inward and invisible grace"; moreover, it is a sacred sign divinely designated to indicate a divine reality, and that includes that reality within itself. Accordingly, baptism and the Lord's Supper, as sacred rites, were seen as both signs and means of divine grace.

When the Protestant Reformation broke with the Catholic Church, it set in motion ripple effects that eventually resulted in challenges to almost everything associated with Catholic theology and practice. One such challenge focused on the proper terminology for the rites of the liturgy. While one large segment of Protestant theology continued to use the word *sacrament* (though with a different understanding of its meaning), another large segment dismissed the term because of its Catholic association and opted for the word *ordinance*. This term was chosen because it signifies rites that were instituted, or ordained, by Christ himself and thus enjoined on the church to be observed.[40]

---

[40] Some Protestants avoided the latter term as well, so as to not associate baptism and the Lord's Supper with the Catholic Church's theology and practice of them.

This issue of the rites ordained by Christ introduces the second matter of the proper number of sacraments. Whereas Catholic theology acknowledges seven sacraments—Baptism, Confirmation, the Eucharist, Penance and Reconciliation, Anointing of the Sick, Holy Orders, and Matrimony—evangelical theology affirms only two: baptism and the Lord's Supper. The reason for this reduction in number from seven to two is that only baptism and the Lord's Supper were ordained by Christ and have accompanying tangible signs. As part of his Great Commission, Jesus ordered the church to "make disciples of all the nations, baptizing them in the name of the Father and of the Son and of the Holy Spirit" (Matt. 28:19). Baptism was ordained by Christ, and the accompanying sign is water; therefore, it is a rite to be observed by the church. Additionally, at his Last Supper with his disciples, Jesus instituted the Lord's Supper: "Now as they were eating, Jesus took bread, and after blessing it broke it and gave it to the disciples, and said, 'Take, eat; this is my body.' And he took a cup, and when he had given thanks he gave it to them, saying, 'Drink of it, all of you, for this is my blood of the covenant, which is poured out for many for the forgiveness of sins. I tell you I will not drink again of this fruit of the vine until that day when I drink it new with you in my Father's kingdom'" (Matt. 26:26–29). The Lord's Supper was ordained by Christ, and the accompanying signs are bread and the cup containing the fruit of the vine (i.e., wine or grape juice); therefore, it is a rite to be observed by the church.

Taking the other five Catholic sacraments one by one, they were dismissed by the Reformers for the following reasons: Confirmation is not found in Scripture and has no tangible sign associated with it. Penance and Reconciliation is based on a misunderstanding of Jesus's command, "Repent, for the kingdom of God is at hand" (Matt. 4:17). Jesus did not institute a sacramental action involving contrition, confession of sins to a priest, absolution, and rendering of satisfaction to make amends for harm done. Rather, he called for a change of mind and life, a break from sin and self together with a turn toward God. Anointing of the sick finds support in James 5:13–17 and has oil as its accompanying sign, but Jesus himself did not ordain the practice. Holy orders, the rite by which men are consecrated to the priesthood, has no biblical support. Marriage, while mandated by Scripture (Gen. 1:28; 2:24) and endorsed by Jesus (Matt. 19:1–9), is a creation ordinance, established by God at the beginning of the creation of the human race (Gen. 1:28). It is not a distinctively Christian rite, and Jesus himself did not institute it. Accordingly, because these five Catholic sacraments were not ordained by Christ and/or lack accompanying signs for their observance, evangelical theology does not consider them to be rites enjoined upon the church.

The next two issues—sacraments as means of grace, and the grounds of their validity or effectiveness—go hand in hand and will be addressed together. The Protestant Reformation broke not only from the number of Catholic sacraments but also from the Church's sacramental theology. Catholic theology holds that the sacraments are means of grace that actually convey the divine benefits of which they are signs. Moreover, the grace communicated through the sacraments is infused into their recipients, thereby transforming their very nature and rendering them capable of meriting eternal life. While one large segment of Protestant theology continued to embrace the sacraments as means of grace, another large segment moved to a view far removed from any notion of means of grace. Evangelical theology, therefore, encompasses these two positions.

As for the first position, Charles Hodge summarized the Reformed theology of the sacraments as "real means of grace, that is, means appointed and employed by Christ for conveying the benefits of his redemption to his people." Unlike Catholic sacramental theology, this Reformed perspective regards them as means, but not the exclusive means, of grace. And it does not consider these means as infusing grace for salvation. Rather, as the sacraments are administered, "a promise is made to those who rightly receive the sacraments that they shall thereby and therein be made partakers of the blessings of which the sacraments are the divinely appointed signs and seals."[41] For infants who are baptized, Reformed theology sees their baptism as a sign of their incorporation into the new covenant community, the church, and as a promise of future repentance and faith. As for the Lord's Supper, Reformed theology views the elements of bread and the cup as signs of God's favor through participation in the body and blood of Christ (who is spiritually present in the celebration of the Lord's Supper) and as means of spiritual nourishment that sustains and increases faith. Thus, the water of baptism, and the bread and cup of the Lord's Supper, are signs, but they are not empty signs, because they

---

[41] Charles Hodge, *Systematic Theology*, 3 vols. (Grand Rapids, MI: Eerdmans, 1946), 3:499.

244   The Celebration of the Christian Mystery

are means of grace conferring divine blessing and mercy upon those who participate in them.

If this Reformed theology of the sacraments sounds similar to Catholic sacramental theology, it is not. The great distance between the two resides in the ground of the validity or effectiveness of the sacraments. For Catholic theology, the sacraments are means of grace *ex opere operato* (literally, "by the work worked"), or simply by their administration. Their validity is completely attached to their sign, which is virtuous or powerful in and of itself. For example, when a priest baptizes an infant following the Catholic rite of the sacrament of Baptism, his action of administering water in proper Christian manner cancels the infant's original sin, causes her to be born again, and incorporates her into the Catholic Church. The effectiveness of the sacrament is not dependent in any way upon the state of the priest who administers the baptism (i.e., he may be a saintly man or entrenched in mortal sin), and it clearly bears no relationship to the infant's faith or disposition to be baptized. Reformed theology of the sacraments dissents from their validity being *ex opere operato*. Rather, it holds that their efficacy is dependent solely on God who promises to bless, the Spirit's work in those who receive the sacraments, and the Word of God upon which the institution of the sacraments is grounded. Accordingly, "There is, in every sacrament, a spiritual relation, or sacramental union, between the sign and the thing signified: whence it comes to pass, that the names and effects of the one are attributed to the other."[42] None of this should be understood to mean that the sacraments are salvific; that is neither the purpose nor the effect of either baptism or the Lord's Supper. Though not effective for salvation, however, they do confer God's blessing and mercy on their recipients.

The second evangelical position emphasizes that these rites function especially as concrete reminders of what God in Christ has done for Christians, and serve as testimonies of faith and obedience on the part of Christians who participate in them. This position is well represented by the article on the ordinances in the Baptist Faith and Message of the Southern Baptist Convention:

> Christian baptism is the immersion of a believer in water in the name of the Father, the Son, and the Holy Spirit. It is *an act of obedience*

---

[42] Westminster Confession of Faith, "On the Sacraments," 27.2.

symbolizing the believer's faith in a crucified, buried, and risen Saviour, the believer's death to sin, the burial of the old life, and the resurrection to walk in newness of life in Christ Jesus. It is *testimony to his faith* in the final resurrection of the dead. Being a church ordinance, it is prerequisite to the privileges of church membership and to the Lord's Supper.

The Lord's Supper is *a symbolic act of obedience* whereby members of the church, through partaking of the bread and the fruit of the vine, *memorialize* the death of the Redeemer and *anticipate* His second coming.[43]

According to this second view, these rites symbolize the faith and obedience of Christians who are baptized and who participate in the Lord's Supper. They do not confer divine grace and, for this reason, the question of their validity *ex opere operato* is a moot one. What is important is the disposition of those to whom these ordinances are administered: for those being baptized, faith in Christ's saving work on their behalf, and obedience to the command to be baptized; for those taking the Lord's Super, obedience to the command to remember what Christ accomplished on the cross, and faith in his return. Some who hold this position would also affirm that various benefits—sanctification, fellowship with Christ—accrue to those who participate in the ordinances. This position developed over against Catholic sacramental theology and even some Protestant views of the sacraments, with a strong suspicion of the means of grace as being mechanical, impersonal, and effective apart from faith and obedience.

Despite these divergences within evangelical theology, both positions are aligned against the notion that the sacraments/ordinances of baptism and the Lord's Supper are means of a grace that is effective *ex opere operato*, as Catholic theology of the sacraments maintains.

The Sacramental Celebration of the Paschal Mystery (Sec. I, Ch. 2)

Having concluded its discussion of—and in light of—the *doctrine* of the sacramental economy that centers on the Paschal mystery of Christ, the *Catechism* addresses the issue of how the Church is to *celebrate* this Paschal mystery, particularly in its administration of the seven sacraments. Important questions need to be addressed: Who celebrates the liturgy?

---

[43] Baptist Faith and Message, art. 7 "Baptism and the Lord's Supper" (emphasis added). This statement of faith represents the generally held convictions of the churches of the Southern Baptist Convention.

How is it celebrated? When is the liturgy celebrated? Where is it celebrated?

Celebrating the Church's Liturgy (Sec. I, Ch. 2, Art. I), and Liturgical Diversity and the Unity of the Mystery (Sec. I, Ch. 2, Art. 2)

As for *who* celebrates the liturgy, it is "an 'action' of the *whole Christ (Christus totus)*,"[44] meaning both the Head and his Body, the Church, which includes both its heavenly celebrants engaged in the eternal liturgy and the earthly celebrants of the sacramental liturgy. The former group (according to Rev. 4–5; 7:1–8; 14:1; cf. Isa. 6:2–3) includes "the heavenly powers, all creation (the four living beings), the servants of the Old and New Covenants (the twenty-four elders), the new People of God (the one hundred and forty-four thousand), especially the martyrs 'slain for the word of God,' and the all-holy Mother of God (the Woman), the Bride of the Lamb [Rev. 6:9–11; 21:9; cf. Revelation 12] and finally 'a great multitude which no one could number, from every nation, from all tribes, and peoples and tongues' [Rev. 7:9]."[45] The Church participates in this "eternal liturgy" when it celebrates its sacramental liturgy. In this latter case, the celebrating Church consists of the community of the baptized (the common or baptismal priesthood), its ordained ministers (the hierarchical or ministerial priesthood), and other particular (non-ordained) ministers such as "[s]ervers, readers, commentators, and members of the choir," all of whom "exercise a genuine liturgical function."[46]

How is the liturgy celebrated? There are various modes: signs and symbols, words and actions, singing and music, and holy images. "A sacramental celebration is woven from signs and symbols," which are part and parcel of human existence.[47] Being complex creatures, human beings are composed of both a material and an immaterial aspect—body and spirit/soul—and thus they express and perceive "spiritual realities through physical signs and symbols."[48] Just as they need such signs and symbols to communicate with other human beings, so human beings need signs and symbols to communicate with God in a personal relationship. Indeed, God reveals himself

---

[44] CCC 1136.
[45] CCC 1138.
[46] CCC 1143.
[47] CCC 1145.
[48] CCC 1146.

to his human creatures through a visible creation (Rom. 1:19); accordingly, tangible realities—e.g., "washing and anointing, breaking bread and sharing the cup"—that are perceptible by the senses "can become means of expressing the action of God who sanctifies men, and the action of men who offer worship to God."[49] Such signs and symbols receive their significance as they are attached to a covenant. For example, "circumcision, anointing and consecration of kings and priests, laying on of hands, sacrifices, and above all the Passover" were the signs and symbols marking the liturgical life of the old covenant and prefiguring the sacraments of the new covenant.[50]

Furthermore, a sacramental celebration takes the form of a dialogue, involving "actions and words," between God and his children.[51] Here, the Liturgy of the Word, the first part of the liturgical celebration, comes into focus. This liturgical movement includes signs accompanying the Word of God: "the book of the Word (a lectionary or a book of the Gospels), its veneration (procession, incense, candles), the place of its proclamation (lectern or ambo), its audible and intelligible reading, the minister's homily which extends its proclamation, and the responses of the assembly (acclamations, meditation psalms, litanies, and profession of faith)."[52] The Liturgy of the Eucharist, which follows the Liturgy of the Word, "makes present the 'wonders' of God which it [the Word] proclaims."[53] Moreover, a sacramental celebration involves singing and music, as enjoined on the Church by Scripture (Eph. 5:19).

Finally, a sacramental celebration includes holy images that represent Christ. The *Catechism* offers this cautionary note about a sacred image: "It cannot represent the invisible and incomprehensible God," but because the Son became incarnate, an image of the visible God-man is appropriate.[54] Importantly, "Christian iconography expresses in images the same Gospel message that Scripture communicates by words."[55] Appropriate subject matter for such icon making includes the incarnate Son, his cross, his mother Mary, the angels, and the saints; appropriate artistic media include

---

[49] CCC 1148.
[50] CCC 1150.
[51] CCC 1153.
[52] CCC 1154. The *lectionary* is a book containing the Scripture readings for the liturgical year. The *ambo* is the podium or lectern from which Scripture is read. *Litanies* are prayers that consist of petitions or invocations voiced by the minister or leader and the alternating responses of the congregation.
[53] CCC 1155.
[54] CCC 1159.
[55] CCC 1160. Indeed, the *Catechism* points out that a sacred image "confirms that the incarnation of the Word of God was real and not imaginary."

paintings, mosaics, and other suitable materials; the appropriate display of such icons and paintings includes church buildings, sacred vessels like the tabernacle (the receptacle in which are placed the remaining Eucharistic wafers), the priestly vestments, homes, and outdoor exhibits.[56]

Turning to the question of *when* the liturgy is celebrated, "certain days throughout the course of the year" should be reserved for such observances. These include: (1) once each week on Sunday, or the Lord's Day, in remembrance of Christ's resurrection; (2) once each year on Good Friday/ Easter, in remembrance of Christ's passion, death, and resurrection; and (3) special annual celebrations of the liturgical year.[57] This latter point stems from the Church's belief that "[t]he economy of salvation is at work within the framework of time."[58] Specifically, the Annunciation, Christmas, and Epiphany (Easter has already been discussed) are celebrated as formative events in Christ's Paschal mystery: the announcement of his miraculous conception to Mary, his birth, and his revelation to the wise men. As Mary is intimately linked with the mystery of her Son, certain annual days are also dedicated to her, such as the feast of the Immaculate Conception (December 8 of most years). Additionally, "the Church keeps the memorial of martyrs and other saints during the annual cycle" as celebrations of the Paschal mystery in the faithful "who have suffered and have been glorified with Christ."[59]

While noting the importance of these regular weekly and annual celebrations of the liturgy, the *Catechism* also explains that the Paschal mystery of Christ "permeates and transfigures the time of each day, through the celebration of the Liturgy of the Hours, 'the divine office.'"[60] These official daily prayers, designed to be recited throughout the day at specified times, are eight in number: Matins, Lauds, Prime, Terce, Sext, None, Vespers, and Compline. They extend the celebration of the Eucharist and serve to complement it.

Where is the liturgy celebrated? In accordance with Jesus's affirmation that genuine worship under the new covenant is worship "in Spirit and in truth" (John 4:24), the *Catechism* explains that worship is "not tied exclu-

---

[56] As established by the Council of Nicea II.
[57] CCC 1163.
[58] CCC 1168.
[59] CCC 1173.
[60] CCC 1174.

sively to any one place. . . . What matters above all is that, when the faithful assemble in the same place, they are the 'living stones,' gathered to be 'built into a spiritual house' . . . [composing] 'the temple of the living God.'"[61] When the faithful are free to gather together and "construct buildings for divine worship," these structures "signify and make visible the Church" in that place and consequently "ought to be in good taste and a worthy place for prayer and sacred ceremonial."[62] Specifically, a church building must contain the following physical elements for a proper liturgical celebration: At the center of the structure is the *altar*, upon which "the sacrifice of the Cross is made present under sacramental signs" through the liturgy of the Eucharist, in which the faithful participate.[63] As the receptacle of the remaining Eucharistic elements not consumed during the mass, the *tabernacle* is located in a place of honor that is accessible to the faithful for adoration of the Lord who is really present in the Eucharistic sacrament. In another secure location is the *sacred chrism (myron)*, the oil that is used for anointing catechumens and the sick "as the sacramental sign of the seal of the gift of the Holy Spirit."[64] The *chair (cathedra)* symbolizes the presiding and directing authority of the bishop/priest. Because of the dignity of the Word of God, the *lectern (ambo)* enjoys a central place for the proclamation of the Word and directing the faithful's attention to it during the Liturgy of the Word.[65] As the place for the celebration of the sacrament of Baptism and "for fostering the remembrance of the baptismal promises," the *baptistery* and the *holy water font* are located at the entrance of the building, symbolic of Baptism providing entrance into the life of the Church. The *confessional* is the place for penitents engaged in the sacrament of penance. The whole structure is designed to foster "the recollection and silent prayer that extend and internalize the great prayer of the Eucharist."[66] Because of its eschatological significance, the building has a *threshold* over which the faithful cross to enter the house of God, symbolizing "passing from the world wounded by sin to the world of the new Life to which all men are called."[67]

The *Catechism* concludes its discussion of the celebration of the liturgy

---

[61] CCC 1179; the biblical references are 1 Pet. 2:4–5 and 2 Cor. 6:16.
[62] CCC 1180–1181; citation is from *Presbyterorum ordinis* 5; cf. *Sacrasanctum concilium* 122–127.
[63] CCC 1182.
[64] CCC 1183.
[65] CCC 1184.
[66] CCC 1185.
[67] CCC 1186.

by noting that, whereas the Paschal mystery of Christ that is celebrated is one, "the forms of its celebration are diverse."[68] This reality flows from the ongoing fulfillment of the Church's mission to bring "Christ, the light and salvation of all peoples . . . to the particular people and culture to which that Church is sent and in which she is rooted."[69] The specific legally recognized rites current in the Church are the Latin (principally the Roman rite, but including some others), Byzantine, Alexandrian (Coptic), Syriac, Armenian, Maronite, and Chaldean rites. The *Catechism* underscores the importance of the contextualization of the Church, because "[i]t is with and through their own human culture, assumed and transfigured by Christ, that the multitude of God's children has access to the Father, in order to glorify him in the one Spirit."[70] The contextualization of the liturgy in general and of the sacraments in particular consists of two poles: an *immutable part* "that is divinely instituted and of which the Church is the guardian," and a *mutable part* that is adapted "to the cultures of recently evangelized people,"[71] while disavowing cultural elements that are incompatible with the Catholic faith. That such contextualization is not easy, and often fraught with difficulty, is acknowledged by the *Catechism*, which ends its discussion with a call to unity amid diversity.

Evangelical Assessment

Following the order of discussion in the *Catechism*, an evangelical assessment of the *doctrinal commonalities* of the sacraments has already been rendered.[72] At this juncture, the assessment will be of the commonalities of the sacraments in terms of the celebration in and by the Church. On this topic, Catholic and evangelical theology share some points of agreement and others of disagreement.

As for *who* celebrates the liturgy, Catholic and evangelical theology concur that the participants in worship are twofold: On the one hand, the heavenly multitudes are already engaged in uninterrupted adoration around the throne of God, as pictured in the scenes of worship in heaven (e.g., Revelation 4–5). This heavenly crowd is not limited to Christians

---

[68] *CCC* 1200.
[69] *CCC* 1202.
[70] *CCC* 1204.
[71] *CCC* 1205.
[72] See above, under the subheading "The Paschal Mystery in the Church's Sacraments (Sec. 1, Ch. 1, Art. 2)."

of the universal church who have died and are living in heaven as disembodied people awaiting the return of Christ and the resurrection of their bodies ("the assembly of the firstborn who are enrolled in heaven"; Heb. 12:23). This throng of worshipers includes "innumerable angels in festal gathering" and old covenant saints ("the spirits of the righteous made perfect"; vv. 22–23), not to mention the four living creatures with eyes and wings (Rev. 4:6–9) and the twenty-four elders (vv. 10–11). On the other hand, Christians on earth gather together regularly to worship God in local churches. In some sense, these local assemblies of worship join in with their heavenly analogue in adoring God; as it is in heaven, so it is on earth, even if the fullness of worship is not and cannot yet be experienced by the earthly analogue.

This agreement must be tempered by two points of disagreement. Because evangelical theology dissents from the axiom of the Christ-Church interconnection, it does not ground this heavenly-earthly worshiping assembly on the idea that evangelical churches are extensions of the incarnation of the ascended Christ. Furthermore, because it departs from Catholic theology's notion of the communion of saints—the interchange of spiritual goods between the church in heaven and the church on earth (Catholic theology would add the church in purgatory as well)—evangelical theology does not view this twofold gathering of worshipers in that manner.

How is the liturgy celebrated? In one sense, Catholic masses and evangelical worship services have many formal similarities, including praying, singing, reading Scripture, preaching, giving, celebrating the Eucharist/Lord's Supper, and the like. Behind these similarities, however, are two important differences.

One difference, which for many evangelicals is also easily detectable, is the meticulously structured or ritualistic nature of the Catholic mass. Being familiar with a less extensively ordered and often a more relaxed pattern of worship in their services, these evangelicals are immediately aware of what they commonly call the difference between "high church" liturgy and "low church" liturgy.[73] The former, exemplified by the Catholic mass, is thoroughly scripted, so that all the prayers, the congregational participation, the Liturgy of the Eucharist, and the like are prescribed—even word by word. The latter—exemplified by some evangelical services—is not as

---

[73] These terms are not being used in their historic sense to differentiate between types of Anglican churches.

systematized and may even incorporate spontaneous activities (e.g., prayers, congregational sharing, testimonies). Important to keep in mind is the fact that, except in the most intentionally unstructured evangelical churches, all worship services follow some type of pattern or order. Indeed, many evangelical churches (e.g., Presbyterian) follow a strict order of worship and could be characterized as "high church." Accordingly, though evangelical theology does not often speak of liturgy, evangelical worship services, like the Catholic mass, are liturgical.

A second key difference centers on the reason why the various liturgical elements are incorporated into the worship service. Driven by the biblical insistence that the church must worship God according to the way he finds acceptable, two different positions have developed historically on the issue of what constitutes acceptable worship. The *regulative principle* "teaches that with regard to worship whatever is commanded in Scripture is required, and whatever is not commanded is forbidden."[74] The *normative principle* permits the church to incorporate any elements into its worship unless Scripture prohibits them. Historically, one of the Protestant Reformation's criticisms of the Catholic Church was that its mass incorporated many unbiblical elements. Indeed, the Westminster Confession of Faith addressed the many Catholic accretions to the worship service: "The acceptable way of worshipping the true God is instituted by himself, and so limited by his own revealed will, that he may not be worshipped according to the imaginations and devices of men, or the suggestions of Satan, under any visible representation or any other way not prescribed in the holy Scripture."[75] At the heart of this Protestant rejection of these unbiblical elements was the doctrine of the sufficiency of Scripture (the substance of divine worship is to be ordered solely by the explicit or implicit instruction of the Word of God) and the principle of the freedom of conscience (the church may not impose any activity that is only of human invention, because to do so would bind the conscience of worshipers).[76]

Although evangelical churches do not necessarily adhere consciously to the regulative principle, the elements of their worship services are generally limited to scripturally warranted components: singing of praise and

---

[74] Frank L. Smith, "What Is Worship?" in Frank L. Smith and David C. Lachman, eds., *Worship in the Presence of God* (Greenville, SC: Greenville Seminary Press, 1992), 16–17.
[75] Westminster Confession of Faith, 21.1.
[76] For example, see the Westminster Confession of Faith, 20.

thanksgiving to God, praying, giving, preaching, baptism, the Lord's Supper, and the like. By contrast, the Catholic mass consists of those biblically justified elements as well as many other prescribed parts—for example, crossing oneself with holy water, genuflecting (kneeling down) at certain junctures of the mass, and repeating specific prayers before participating in the Eucharist.

At the heart of Catholic theology's incorporation of these additional elements is the Catholic system's axiom of the nature-grace interdependence, specifically that nature possesses a capacity for grace, and grace must be embodied in nature. Accordingly, physical elements can become channels of spiritual realities, which must be concretely conveyed through physical elements. As already noted, this view is part and parcel of its theology of the sacraments: they are visible and concrete signs of an invisible yet real grace. Evangelical theology's critique of this nature-grace interdependence, together with its criticism of Catholic theology's doctrine of the sacraments, has already been offered.

But Catholic theology extends this notion beyond the sacraments to include other matters. Evangelical theology concurs that God reveals himself through the visible creation (Rom. 1:19); thus, Catholic theology's idea that tangible realities "can become means of expressing the action of God" to his human creatures is correct, with certain qualifications.[77] Certainly, the rainbow in the sky, the circumcision of eight-day-old Jewish boys, the laying on of hands, the sacrifices of bull and goats, and other concrete actions receive a new significance—the promise to never destroy the world by a flood, membership in the old covenant community, consecration to God's service, mercy in the place of judgment—when attached to a covenant between God and his people. However, just how far this principle can be extended becomes the point of contention. Evangelical theology limits these concrete signs to what is prescribed in Scripture; thus, its emphasis on baptism and the Lord's Supper as the signs of the new covenant. It dissents from Catholic theology's adding other required elements to the liturgy. And, importantly, it diverges from Catholic theology's understanding of what these symbols convey and accomplish. For example, the Passover meal as celebrated by the Jews (Ex. 12:1–28) was not an infusion of divine grace to render them more holy in character. The chosen lamb was the spotless victim whose life was

---

[77] CCC 1148.

sacrificed for the people of Israel, and they were spared from the just and wrathful judgment of God by the imposition of blood on the doorposts and lintel of the Jewish houses. This action was a forensic, or legal, acquittal of the guilty people of Israel: God did not destroy but passed over them, even though they deserved the same fate as the Egyptians. Accordingly, evangelical theology does not dissent from the incorporation of signs in the worship service, but it restricts these elements to those called for by Scripture and interprets what the signs convey and accomplish differently from their Catholic understanding.

Finally, regarding the use of holy images, evangelical theology concurs with its Catholic counterpart that no image can be made of the invisible and incomprehensible God, and it cautiously agrees that an image representing Christ may confirm the reality of the incarnation. But it moves away from Catholic theology's embrace of icons as being capable of expressing "the same Gospel message that Scripture communicates by words."[78] In this case, the common aphorism "a picture is worth a thousand words" is not correct. The divinely breathed revelation is not pictorial in nature, but verbal, and nothing is equivalent to the written/spoken Word of God in terms of its truthfulness, authority, and clarity. Moreover, the sufficiency of this Word means that its account, for example, of the dying Jesus's instructions to his mother Mary and the apostle John (John 19:25–27) contains all that the church needs to know about this touching moment in which a son provides for his mother, as "from that hour the disciple took her to his own home" (v. 27). No painting or statue can fairly and adequately represent that inscripturated interchange, and to the degree that the icon exaggerates Mary's role as the newly constituted mother of all the faithful, it is not the same as the gospel but an obstacle to it. It is certainly true that written stories such as this one, and paintings and statues of it, require interpretation. But the biblical narrative has contextual clues and restraints that are missing in any icon, and to the degree that a painting or statue fosters an unchecked imagination, it leads not to a true understanding of what Jesus did but to mere speculation, perhaps even error. A further problem with icons from an evangelical perspective is that they are necessarily limited in their portrayal; thus, if one icon is not supplemented by other ones, a truncated message results. For example, the Catholic crucifix—Jesus hanging on the cross—

---

[78] CCC 1160.

may succeed in capturing one important aspect of the work of Christ on behalf of sinful human beings. At the same time, the crucifix is isolated in its portrayal of Christ's accomplishments, for it does not—indeed, cannot—communicate that he did not remain dead but rose on the third day. In this case, another difficulty arises because the crucifix is a helpful device to remember the re-presentation of Christ on the cross during the mass, an idea that evangelical theology soundly dismisses. Additionally, evangelical theology rejects icons of Mary and the saints.

Turning to the question of *when* the liturgy is celebrated, Catholic and evangelical theology agree that weekly worship on Sunday, the day of the resurrection, is proper. Though Scripture points minimally in this direction (e.g., 1 Cor. 16:2; illustrated in Acts 20:7), early church literature underscores this weekly pattern (e.g., Justin Martyr, *First Apology*)[79] and it became widely established in the church. Some segments of evangelical theology further agree with following the liturgical year to celebrate important events in the life and ministry of Christ and the church—for example, Christmas, Good Friday, Easter, and Pentecost. Other varieties of evangelical theology disagree with these particular observances because they reject the Catholic rationale for them ("[t]he economy of salvation is at work within the framework of time").[80] While this principle is certainly true in one sense—God is at work so as to save fallen human beings in their concrete realities—it is not true, they believe, in the sense of a cyclical repetition of these saving highlights that should dominate the church year. Furthermore, evangelical theology does not incorporate any celebrations in honor of Mary and the saints, for obvious reasons. Finally, though it does not follow Catholic theology's Liturgy of the Hours, evangelical theology embraces the concept and importance of daily prayer (and, it would add, reading and studying Scripture) while not prescribing particular times for it to be practiced.

Where is the liturgy celebrated? In accord with its Catholic counterpart, evangelical theology insists that the location of worship is not key, in light of Jesus's instruction that genuine worship is not confined to Mount Gerizim nor to the temple in Jerusalem (John 4:20–21), but is to be exercised "in spirit and truth" (John 4:24). Genuine worship requires genuine believers,

[79] Justin Martyr, *First Apology* 67 (*ANF* 1:186).
[80] *CCC* 1168.

those who, through the Holy Spirit, have been transposed from the realm of "flesh" into the realm of *"spirit"* (John 3:5–6)—the realm of God himself ("God is spirit"; 4:24)—and who have embraced the truth of Jesus, who is "the way, and *the truth*, and the life" (14:6). Gathered together to praise and honor the triune God according to the ways that he has fixed for his proper adoration, these genuine worshipers compose the "living stones" of the temple of the living God (1 Pet. 2:4–5; cf. 2 Cor. 6:16).

Additionally, Catholic and evangelical theology concur that when cultural and contextual factors permit the faithful to own a building for regular worship services, theological reflection on the nature, design, architecture, and furnishings of the building is in order. Whereas Catholic Church buildings have numerous specified elements—the altar, the tabernacle, the sacred chrism (*myron*, or oil), the chair (*cathedra*), the lectern (*ambo*), the baptistery, the holy water font, the confessional, and the threshold—only some evangelical churches are this elaborate, and none contain all of these items. On the one hand, many evangelical church buildings are intentionally simple, in reaction to the sumptuous ornamentation of a typical Catholic church building. At the heart of this rejection is an evangelical sentiment that such ostentatious display detracts from, rather than enhances, the worship of God, and that the vast amounts of money spent on such elaborate architecture and decoration could have been better spent on missional endeavors, ministries, staffing, assistance to the poor, and other priorities. On the other hand, some evangelical church buildings are quite substantive, but for diverse reasons. One tragic motivation is for honoring a particular pastor by constructing a notable physical legacy that will endure for decades to come; more disappointingly yet, some pastors themselves engage in elaborate building campaigns to enhance their reputation and ensure their memory. Positively, the more substantial nature of some evangelical church buildings reflects careful theological reflection and vision for significant impact to accommodate God-given growth. Because human beings are embodied creatures, the impact of their physical surroundings on their worship of God is significant, even if the idea is overlooked or even dismissed. Careful theological reflection—not veering toward the Catholic direction but substantive nonetheless—on church buildings is proper.[81]

The final topic to be addressed regarding the celebration of the liturgy

---

[81] For a brief discussion, see Allison, *SS*, 148–152.

concerns its contextualization. For both Catholic and evangelical theology, this need for adaptation arises as the church moves into new people groups with their particular cultures, worldviews, religious influences, and the like. Interestingly, the legally recognized rites of the Catholic Church—Latin (primarily Roman), Byzantine, Alexandrian (Coptic), Syriac, Armenian, Maronite, and Chaldean—are ancient liturgies, and evangelical theology wonders about the Church's contextualization efforts during the last half millennium, during which it established itself in lands in South and Central America, Asia, and other regions that are remarkably different from the lands represented by those ancient rites. Despite this question, evangelical theology concurs that contextualization is necessary, but the practice of adapting the church is far from easy. For Catholic theology, contextualization moves between two poles: one is immutable; the other is mutable. This latter pole is where cultural elements from the newly reached people (but never ones that are antithetical to Catholicism) may be incorporated into the Church's liturgy. In principle, evangelical theology would agree, and it has developed several models of contextualization that may be found in different churches throughout the world.[82]

---

[82] For example, see A. Scott Moreau, *Contextualization in World Missions: Mapping and Assessing Evangelical Models* (Grand Rapids, MI: Kregel, 2012).

8

The Celebration of the Christian Mystery (Part 2, Section 2, Chapter I, Articles I–2)

The Seven Sacraments; The Sacraments of Christian
Initiation: Baptism and Confirmation

The Seven Sacraments of the Church (Sec. 2)

Having treated the commonalities of the sacraments both from a doctrinal
perspective and in terms of how they are celebrated, the *Catechism* moves to
a detailed exposition underscoring the distinctive elements of the seven rites.
The discussion is categorized under three headings or types, with the specific
sacraments presented under their appropriate type: the three sacraments of
Christian initiation (Baptism, Confirmation, the Eucharist), the two sacraments of healing (Penance and Reconciliation, Anointing of the Sick), and
the two sacraments at the service of communion (Holy Orders, Matrimony).
In general, the discussion of each sacrament develops along the following
line: an introduction, the names of the sacrament, its biblical basis (both
Old and New Testaments), the mode of its celebration, and specific matters.

The Sacraments of Christian Initiation (Sec. 2, Ch. I)

The three sacraments of Christian initiation establish the foundation of
the Christian life for each person. "The faithful are born anew by Baptism,
strengthened by the sacrament of Confirmation, and receive in the Eucharist the food of eternal life," thereby receiving the divine life in increasing
measure and advancing "toward the perfection of charity."[1]

---

[1] CCC 1212; citation is from Paul VI, apostolic constitution, *Divinae consortium naturae* (August 15, 1971),
para. 1. The Latin text is accessible at http://www.vatican.va/holy_father/paul_vi/apost_constitutions/documents
/hf_p-vi_apc_19710815_divina-consortium_lt.html.

The Sacrament of Baptism (Sec. 2, Ch. I, Art. I)

For its introductory comments on the first sacrament, the *Catechism* affirms, "Holy Baptism is the basis of the whole Christian life, the gateway to life in the Spirit . . . , and the door which gives access to the other sacraments. Through Baptism we are freed from sin and reborn as sons of God; we become members of Christ, are incorporated into the Church and made sharers in her mission: 'Baptism is the sacrament of regeneration through water in the word.'"[2]

The name *Baptism* comes from the mode by which the sacrament is administered: the Greek βαπτίζειν (*baptizein*) "means 'to plunge' or 'immerse,'"[3] and the action of submerging a catechumen under the water powerfully portrays his identification with the death, burial, and resurrection of Christ, establishing him as "a new creature" (2 Cor. 5:17). Another name for this sacrament is *the washing of regeneration and renewal by the Holy Spirit*, taken from Titus 3:5 and applied to the sacrament, "for it signifies and actually brings about the birth of water and the Spirit without which no one 'can enter the kingdom of God' [John 3:5]."[4] The sacrament is also called *enlightenment*, because catechumens have received instruction in, and thereby have been enlightened in their understanding of, the Christian faith before participating in the rite. Moreover, they receive "in Baptism the Word, 'the true light that enlightens every man' [John 1:9],"[5] thereby becoming "enlightened" (Heb. 10:32), "children of light" (1 Thess. 5:5), and a "light" themselves (Eph. 5:8).[6]

The biblical basis for this sacrament begins with prefigurations of baptism in the Old Testament. At the creation, water was "the source of life and fruitfulness" as "'overshadowed' by the Spirit of God [Gen. 1:2]."[7] Noah's ark prefigured salvation by Baptism as "a few, that is, eight persons, were saved through water" (1 Pet. 3:20). The waters of the great flood are "a symbol of death and so can represent the mystery of the cross. By this symbolism Baptism signifies communion with Christ's death."[8] The most

---

[2] CCC 1213. The paragraph is based on affirmations from the Council of Florence (1314) and the *Roman Catechism* 2.2, 5.
[3] CCC 1214.
[4] CCC 1215.
[5] CCC 1216.
[6] Other names associated with this sacrament include gift, grace, anointing, clothing, bath, and seal, as affirmed by Gregory of Nazianzus, *Oration* 40.3–4 (*NPNF*[2] 7:360); CCC 1216.
[7] CCC 1218.
[8] CCC 1220.

pronounced prefiguration is the crossing of the Red Sea: The liberation of the people of Israel from enslavement in Egypt foreshadows the liberation accomplished by Baptism. A final harbinger is the crossing of the Jordan River: The people of Israel traversed the water so as to enter the Promised Land, presaging the water of Baptism leading to eternal life.

Baptism in the Gospels starts with Jesus of Nazareth being baptized by John the Baptist in the Jordan River (Matt. 3:13) and ends with the resurrected Christ commissioning his apostles to baptize disciples from all the nations (Matt. 28:19–20; cf. Mark 16:15–16). Jesus's baptism was "to fulfill all righteousness" (Matt. 3:15) and manifested his self-emptying (Phil. 2:7); furthermore, he spoke of his impending death as a "Baptism" with which he would have to be baptized (Mark 10:38; cf. Luke 12:50). Indeed, "[t]he blood and water that flowed from the pierced side of the crucified Jesus are types [foreshadowings] of Baptism and the Eucharist, the sacraments of new life. From then on, it is possible 'to be born of water and the Spirit' in order to enter the Kingdom of God."[9]

In the Church, from its very beginning, Baptism has been celebrated and administered. On the day of Pentecost, in response to the crowd's inquiry about the proper course of action to take in light of the gospel that he preached, Peter declares, "Repent and be baptized every one of you in the name of Jesus Christ for the forgiveness of your sins; and you shall receive the gift of the Holy Spirit" (Acts 2:38). Baptism is administered immediately to the Jewish audience (v. 41) and subsequently to the Samaritans (8:12–13), an Ethiopian eunuch (v. 38), and God-fearing Gentiles like Cornelius (10:48), Lydia (16:15), and the Philippian jailer together with his family (vv. 31–33). The apostle Paul underscores the identification with Christ's death, burial, and resurrection that is wrought by baptism (Rom. 6:3–4; cf. Col. 2:12); he affirms that the baptized have "put on Christ" (Gal. 3:27). "Through the Holy Spirit, Baptism is a bath that purifies, justifies, and sanctifies."[10] The baptismal water is closely associated the Word of God: "Baptism is a bath of water in which the 'imperishable seed' of the Word of God produces its life-giving effect. St. Augustine says of Baptism: 'The word is brought to the material element, and it becomes a sacrament.'"[11]

---

[9] CCC 1225; the biblical support referenced is John 19:34; 1 John 5:6–8; John 3:5.
[10] CCC 1227; the biblical support referenced is 1 Cor. 6:11; 12:13.
[11] CCC 1228; the biblical reference is 1 Pet. 1:23 (cf. Eph. 5:26); citation is from Augustine, *Homilies on the Gospel of John* 80.3 (NPNF[2] 7:344).

The *Catechism* presents the mode of the administration of this sacrament by first recounting its celebration historically and then rehearsing how baptism is administered today. The brief historical section notes the presence of certain essential elements in its celebration: "proclamation of the Word, acceptance of the Gospel entailing conversion, profession of faith, Baptism itself, the outpouring of the Holy Spirit, and admission to Eucharistic communion."[12] Though no biblical reference is provided, the *Catechism* clearly depends on the narrative of Acts 2:22–47: Peter preaches the gospel (vv. 22–36) that is accepted by the people through repentance (vv. 37–40) and faith (they are called "believers" in v. 44), and three thousand are baptized (v. 41), receive the Spirit (as promised in v. 38), and celebrate "the breaking of bread" in community (vv. 42, 46–47). This common pattern gave way to a great amount of variation in the coming centuries, with two key developments underscored by the *Catechism*: a lengthy period called the *catechumenate*, or the communication of and formation in the faith as a preparation for participation in baptism and the other sacraments of initiation,[13] and infant Baptism as the usual form of administering the sacrament, "a single act encapsulating the preparatory stages of Christian initiation in a very abridged way."[14] As for catechesis in relation to infants who have been baptized, the *Catechism* affirms, "By its very nature infant Baptism requires a post-baptismal catechumenate. Not only is there a need for instruction after Baptism, but also for the necessary flowering of baptismal grace in personal growth."[15] As for the baptism of adults, the *Catechism* refers to the rites for their catechumenate as found in the *Rite of Christian Initiation of Adults* (*RCIA*), rites that closely link the catechumenate with the three sacraments of initiation, which compose a single celebration of Baptism, Confirmation, and the Eucharist.[16]

As for the contemporary celebration of Baptism, several elements are involved. Before the Baptism itself, the rites are: the sign of the cross, marking the catechumens and signifying Christ's salvation on the cross; the proclamation of the Word of God, enlightening the catechumens and eliciting faith;[17] exor-

---

[12] CCC 1229.
[13] CCC 1230.
[14] CCC 1231.
[15] Ibid.
[16] CCC 1232.
[17] As will be more fully discussed shortly, the *Catechism* underscores that "Baptism is 'the sacrament of faith' in a particular way, since it is the sacramental entry into the life of faith" (CCC 1236).

cisms, because "Baptism signifies liberation from sin and from its instigator the devil," which include anointing with oil (alternatively, the laying on of hands) and the renunciation of Satan;[18] and the consecration of the water by a prayer of *epiclesis*, by which "[t]he Church asks God that through his Son the power of the Holy Spirit may be sent upon the water, so that those who will be baptized in it may be 'born of water and the Spirit.'"[19] In terms of the essential act itself, Baptism is expressed most vividly by triple immersion (plunging three times) in the consecrated water, though the practice of pouring the water three times over the head has been common from the early church age; also included is an anointing with sacred, consecrated oil (chrism), signifying the gift of the Holy Spirit and portraying Christians as "anointed ones" like Christ ("the anointed one"). The effect of the sacrament is to signify and actually bring about "death to sin and entry into the life of the Most Holy Trinity through configuration to the Paschal mystery of Christ."[20] Throughout the ceremony, the white robes portray that the catechumens have "put on Christ" (Gal. 3:27) and have risen with him, and the candle "signifies that Christ has enlightened" these new Christians.[21] In the case of adults, Baptism is followed by another sacrament: they participate in their First Holy Communion. Baptized children, by contrast, are "brought to the altar for the praying of the Our Father [the Lord's Prayer]."[22] A solemn blessing concludes the celebration.

Participation in this sacrament is open to "[e]very person not yet baptized and only such a person is able to be baptized."[23] In places "where the proclamation of the Gospel is still new," adults are baptized after a period of catechumenate in which "their conversion and faith" is brought to "maturity," and the three sacraments of initiation are administered together.[24] Infants are baptized because of original sin: "Born with a fallen human nature and tainted by original sin, children also have need of the new birth in Baptism to be freed from the power of darkness and brought into the realm of the freedom of the children of God, to which all men are called. The sheer gratuitousness of the grace of salvation is particularly manifest

---

[18] CCC 1237.
[19] CCC 1238.
[20] CCC 1239.
[21] CCC 1243.
[22] CCC 1244.
[23] CCC 1246; citation is from canon 864 of the Code of Canon Law.
[24] CCC 1247–1248. This period of formation prepares catechumens—who "are already joined to the Church" and "are quite frequently already living a life of faith, hope, and charity"—for Baptism, Confirmation, and the Eucharist (CCC 1249; citation is from Vatican Council II, *Lumen Gentium* 14.3).

in infant Baptism."[25] The *Catechism* appeals to historical precedent for the practice of infant Baptism, claiming it to be "an immemorial tradition of the Church" for which explicit testimony exists "from the second century on."[26] It finds "possible" biblical support in New Testament references to household baptisms (Acts 16:15, 33; 18:8; 1 Cor. 1:16), during which "infants may also have been baptized."[27]

The *Catechism* addresses next the issue of faith and Baptism. This matter does not pertain only to infant Baptism, for even in the case of adult Baptism, the faith that is expressed is not the catechumen's faith, but the faith of the Church: "Baptism is the sacrament of faith. But faith needs the community of believers. It is only within the faith of the Church that each of the faithful can believe. The faith required for Baptism is not a perfect and mature faith, but a beginning that is called to develop. The catechumen or the godparent is asked, 'What do you ask of God's Church?' The response is: 'Faith!'"[28] In other words, the faith of an adult who comes to be baptized is the gift of faith given to him by the Church, and in the case of an infant, who cannot personally believe, her faith is the faith of the Church as received vicariously by her parents and godparents. Moreover, the faith of both the baptized adult and the baptized infant "must grow after Baptism" as the new life in Christ, initiated in Baptism, must be nurtured.[29] Crucial help in this faith development comes from both parents and godparents, "who must be firm believers, able and ready to help the newly baptized—child or adult—on the road of Christian life."[30] Additionally, the entire community is responsible for providing help in the growth and protection of baptismal grace.

Ordinarily, the bishops, priests, or deacons of the Church administer Baptism. However, "[i]n case of necessity, any person, even someone not baptized, can baptize, if he has the required intention. The intention required is to will to do what the Church does when she baptizes, and to apply the Trinitarian baptismal formula. The Church finds the reason for this possibility in the universal saving will of God and the necessity of Baptism for salvation."[31] To give

---

[25] CCC 1250.
[26] CCC 1252.
[27] Ibid.
[28] CCC 1253.
[29] CCC 1254.
[30] CCC 1255.
[31] CCC 1256.

an example, during a pitched battle in war, a soldier repents of his sins and believes in Jesus Christ for salvation. Understanding the necessity of Baptism and calculating that he will not emerge alive from the skirmish, the soldier explains the basic contours of the sacrament of Baptism to his unbaptized colleague and requests that this fellow combatant pour water over his head three times in the name of the triune God. Such an emergency Baptism is valid.

This practice, as noted above, is predicated on the necessity of Baptism, belief in which is supported by Jesus's words, "Truly, truly, I say to you, unless one is born of water and the Spirit, he cannot enter the kingdom of God" (John 3:5). Furthermore, Jesus commanded his gospel-announcing apostles to make disciples everywhere and to baptize them (Matt. 28:19–20). Accordingly, "Baptism is necessary for salvation for those to whom the Gospel has been proclaimed and who have had the possibility of asking for this sacrament. The Church does not know of any means other than Baptism that assures entry into eternal beatitude."[32] This belief propels the Church into mission.

At the same time, the *Catechism* affirms, "God has bound salvation to the sacrament of Baptism, but he himself is not bound by his sacraments."[33] Four examples follow: martyrs, catechumens who prematurely die, the un-evangelized, and unbaptized infants. First, *martyrs* undergo a *"Baptism of blood"*: "[T]hose who suffer death for the sake of the faith without having received Baptism are baptized by their death for and with Christ."[34] In the second case, a *"desire for Baptism"* is valid: "For *catechumens* who die before their Baptism, their explicit desire to receive it, together with repentance for their sins, and charity, assures them the salvation that they were not able to receive through the sacrament."[35] For the third example, appeal is made to the unlimited atonement of Jesus Christ, the universal call to divine blessing, and the mystery of God, with this conclusion: "[W]e must hold that the Holy Spirit offers to all the possibility of being made partakers, in a way known to God, of the Paschal mystery."[36] Accordingly, in the case of the *unevangelized*, the *Catechism* affirms, "Every man who is ignorant of the Gospel of Christ and of his Church, but seeks the truth

---

[32] CCC 1257.
[33] CCC 1257 (emphasis removed).
[34] CCC 1258.
[35] CCC 1259.
[36] CCC 1260; citation is from Vatican Council II, *Gaudium et Spes* 22.5; cf. *Lumen Gentium* 16; *Ad gentes* 7. See the earlier discussion of this theology of inclusivism, on pages 175 and 180.

and does the will of God in accordance with his understanding of it, can be saved." But what of Baptism in such instances? "It may be supposed that such persons would have *desired Baptism explicitly* if they had known its necessity."[37] In the fourth case, regarding "children who have died without Baptism, the Church can only entrust them to the mercy of God."[38] Cheered on by God's desire for everyone to be saved (1 Tim. 2:4) and Jesus's own compassion toward children (Mark 10:14), the Church hopes for their salvation and is spurred on to greater efforts to baptize children.

The two principal effects of Baptism, as symbolized by the elements of the sacrament—immersion in water—are purification from sins and regeneration in the Holy Spirit.[39] As for the first effect, "*all sins* are forgiven, original sin and all personal sins, as well as all punishment for sin"; accordingly, entrance into the kingdom of God is completely unimpeded.[40] Still, "certain temporal consequences of sin remain," including suffering, illness, death, character weaknesses, and concupiscence, or the inclination toward evil with which the baptized must wrestle by resisting through divine grace.[41] The second effect of Baptism—regeneration, or the new birth—renders the newly baptized "a new creature" (2 Cor. 5:17) and a "partaker of the divine nature" (2 Pet. 1:4), as well as an adopted son of God, a member of and coheir of Christ, and a "temple of the Holy Spirit" (1 Cor. 6:19). "The Most Holy Trinity gives the baptized sanctifying grace, the grace of justification," with three results: enablement to believe in, hope in, and love God through the theological virtues; power to live through the prompting and gifts of Holy Spirit; and growth in goodness through the moral virtues.[42] Additional effects of Baptism are incorporation into the Church (Eph. 4:25); a sharing in the priestly, prophetic, and royal offices of Christ, as well as the common priesthood of all believers; responsibilities to and privileges in the Church; participation in the mission of the Church; and "the sacramental bond of unity" with all Christians, "including those who are not yet in full communion with the Catholic Church."[43]

In conclusion of its detailed presentation of Baptism, the *Catechism*

---

[37] CCC 1260.
[38] CCC 1261.
[39] CCC 1262.
[40] CCC 1263 (emphasis added).
[41] CCC 1264.
[42] CCC 1266.
[43] CCC 1271.

underscores the indelible quality of this sacrament: "Baptism seals the Christian with the indelible spiritual mark (*character*) of his belonging to Christ. No sin can erase this mark, even if sin prevents Baptism from bearing the fruits of salvation. Given once for all, Baptism cannot be repeated."[44] This rule of non-repetition is applicable to Protestants who convert to the Catholic faith.[45] As long as their baptism was carried out "by immersion, pouring or sprinkling, together with the trinitarian formula," it is "of itself valid."[46] Indeed, "if they freely wish to embrace the Catholic faith, they have no need to be absolved from excommunication."[47] By faithfully maintaining this "seal of eternal life" and obeying its demands until his death, a Christian "will be able to depart this life 'marked with the sign of faith,' with his baptismal faith, in expectation of the blessed vision of God—the consummation of faith—and in the hope of resurrection."[48]

Evangelical Assessment

Introductory Matters

Because baptism is such an important sacrament for Catholic theology, as evidenced by the extensive discussion of it in the preceding section, it warrants a significant assessment. In part, evangelical theology in its many stripes both agrees with this Catholic treatment of baptism and disagrees with it, making the task of assessment straightforward. But it is complicated in other parts because of the noticeable variety in the evangelical theology of baptism, making the job somewhat more challenging.

Agreement is found in what to call this rite. *Baptism* is a transliteration of the common Greek word βαπτίζειν (*baptizein*), meaning "to plunge" or "to immerse."[49] Moreover, both Catholic and evangelical theology consider baptism to be the initiatory rite of the Christian faith. With few exceptions, both insist that people be baptized at some beginning point, whether in the case of adults at the beginning of their consciously Christian profession of faith (for Protestant credobaptists) or, in the case of infants, soon after their birth (for Protestant paedobaptists). The initiatory nature of this rite is

---

[44] CCC 1272.
[45] "It is never lawful to repeat it if it has been validly celebrated, even by our separated fellow Christians" (*Per initiationis Christianae* [June 24, 1973], 4 [*VC II-2, 23*]).
[46] *Ad Totam Ecclesiam* (May 14, 1967), 13 (a) (*VC II-1, 488*).
[47] Ibid., 19 (*VC II-1, 490*).
[48] CCC 1274; citation is from the Roman Missal, Eucharistic Prayer 1 (Roman Canon), 97.
[49] CCC 1214.

supported by several considerations: the pattern of baptizing new believers soon after their conversion, as narrated in the book of Acts; the assumption of the New Testament that all Christ-followers had been baptized;[50] and the insistence of the early church that, before people could participate in the Lord's Supper/Eucharist, they had to be baptized.[51] Further agreement is found in Catholic theology's emphasis on this sacrament, supported by the fact that Jesus's ministry began with his baptism (Matt. 3:13–17 and par.) and ended with his commissioning his disciples to baptize disciples in all the nations (28:18–20). Additionally, Catholic theology's discussion of other elements associated with Christian baptism—for example, the communication of the gospel, reception of the message through repentance and faith, the gift of the Holy Spirit, and participating in the Lord's Supper/Eucharist—is echoed in evangelical theology's presentation of this ordinance, because the baptismal narratives in the book of Acts note the presence of these other elements (e.g., Acts 2:22–47).

These points of accord are greatly overshadowed by the many divergences between Catholic and evangelical theology of baptism. These disagreements commonly center on matters of biblical support for and/or interpretation of the sacrament, and the importance of its historical development for Catholic theology and practice of baptism.

Biblical Basis

One of the most important points of divergence is Catholic theology's appeal to John 3:5 as support for the necessity of baptism for salvation. In response to Nicodemus's misunderstanding of the statement that "unless one is born again he cannot see the kingdom of God" (v. 3), "Jesus answered, 'Truly, truly, I say to you, unless one is born of water and the Spirit, he cannot enter the kingdom of God'" (v. 5).[52] Catholic theology interprets the water as a reference to baptism, concluding from this ultimatum of Jesus that the sacrament is necessary for salvation.

Though various segments of evangelical theology interpret the water in

---

[50] The New Testament seems to lack a category for unbaptized Christians, presenting instead the picture that all who had believed in Christ had been baptized (e.g., Gal. 3:23–29). The only way for this picture to be an accurate portrait of the universality of baptism is that the rite was initiatory.

[51] For example, *Didache* 9.5 (*ANF* 7:380).

[52] Because Greek did not employ capital letters for the same purposes as English does, there is some question of whether the phrase should be translated "born of water and spirit," referring to the spiritual reality that is imparted by God, who is spirit (John 4:24), or "born of water and the Spirit," referring to the Holy Spirit. The point is not crucial, for the Spirit's work to effect this new spiritual reality is underscored in 3:8.

a similar way—though often minimizing the aspect of baptism's necessity that seems to be demanded by this understanding—a significant portion finds this Catholic interpretation to be off target.[53] The case against this interpretation is summarized in the following points:[54] First, it is an anachronistic understanding of the passage, reading the later-developed sacrament of Christian baptism into it. Accordingly, "John's words could have had no relevance to the historical Nicodemus. This part of the account, at least, becomes a narrative fiction designed to instruct the church on the importance of baptism."[55] Thus, the view that "water" in verse 5 refers to baptism would mean that Jesus then went on to scold Nicodemus (v. 10) for failing to grasp something that he certainly was in no position to grasp. Second, if the water refers to baptism, which then becomes necessary for salvation, "it is surprising that the rest of the discussion never mentions it again: the entire focus is on the work of the Spirit (v. 8), the work of the Son (vv. 14–15), the work of God himself (vv. 16–17), and the place of faith (vv. 15–16)."[56] Third, if the water is a reference to baptism, which is an ecclesially administered and controlled rite, the analogy between the wind that "blows where it wishes" and the sovereign movement of the Holy Spirit to bring about the new birth (v. 8) is hard to understand. Fourth and last, nowhere else in Jesus's presentation of the Holy Spirit in the Gospel of John is the Spirit linked with baptism, making the referent of water to baptism in John 3 highly doubtful.

If the water does not refer to baptism, then what is Jesus demanding for entrance into/seeing the kingdom of God? Again, several points are key to a proper interpretation of John 3:5. First, Jesus's insistence on being born again (v. 3) is parallel to his insistence on being born of water and the Spirit (v. 5); conceptually, they refer to the same experience, "and so only one birth is in view."[57] The second point is a grammatical one: one preposition, "of," governs the two nouns "water" and "the Spirit" ("born of *water and the Spirit*"). This point means that the two items are linked conceptually: "there is a water-spirit source . . . that stands as the origin of

---

[53] To discuss other common interpretations of the water—it refers to the amniotic fluid in the womb, or it is a metaphor for semen, meaning that one must be born physically and be born again spiritually—would take the discussion far afield. It seems that none of these other understandings is well supported by the biblical text.
[54] The following is adapted from D. A. Carson, *The Gospel according to John* (Leicester, England: Inter-Varsity Press; and Grand Rapids, MI: Eerdmans, 1991), 185–203.
[55] Ibid., 192.
[56] Ibid.
[57] Ibid., 194.

this regeneration."[58] Third, several Old Testament passages that strongly associate water with the work of the Spirit provide the background for Jesus's amazement at Nicodemus's ignorance of what Jesus was saying. As a teacher of Israel, Nicodemus should have been aware that his Hebrew Bible linked water and the Spirit, just as Jesus was doing in conversation with him. The Spirit of God, who anointed the prophets, judges, and kings of Israel, was promised as the bearer of an even greater anointing in the future (e.g., Joel 2:28–32). And water was often an image of cleansing from sin and renewal of the people of God. One passage that joins water as a figure of cleansing with the Spirit as the giver of renewal stands out in particular: "I will sprinkle *clean water* on you, and *you shall be clean* from all your uncleannesses, and from all your idols *I will cleanse you*. And I will give you a new heart, and *a new spirit* I will put within you. And I will remove the heart of stone from your flesh and give you a heart of flesh. And *I will put my Spirit within you*, and cause you to walk in my statutes and be careful to obey my rules" (Ezek. 36:25–27, emphasis added). Accordingly, Jesus instructs Nicodemus with truth from Scripture that the teacher of Israel should have known. Furthermore, Jesus urges this "man of the Pharisees" (John 3:1) who had come secretly to him and expressed curiosity in him (v. 2) to be "born again" or "born of water and the Spirit," that is, to undergo cleansing from his sin and renewal of his inner being through the miraculous and sovereign regenerative work of the Spirit God. As a man of flesh born of the flesh—i.e., as only a naturally born person—Nicodemus needed regeneration by the Spirit to become spirit—a Spirit-born, spiritual person (v. 6)—and thus a participant in the kingdom of the God, who exists in the realm of spirit (4:24).

This interpretation, which is plausible and avoids the difficulties associated with the "water as baptism" interpretation, is a ground for evangelical theology's rejection of Catholic theology's insistence, based on John 3:5, on the necessity of baptism for salvation.[59]

But other divergences between the two theologies are equally important and flow also from evangelical theology's questioning of the biblical basis for Catholic baptismal theology. Evangelical theology does not call this rite "enlightenment," because of the lack of any biblical basis for this name.

---

[58] Ibid.
[59] This non-necessity of baptism does not render it unimportant, however, as will be discussed.

Certainly, Scripture frequently employs the metaphor of light in association with Christ and his work. For example, the incarnate Word was "the true light, which gives light to [enlightens] everyone" (John 1:9), resulting in Christians being "enlightened" (Heb. 10:32) and "light" (Eph. 5:8; 1 Thess. 5:5). But none of these biblical passages to which Catholic theology appeals in support of calling baptism "enlightenment" has any association with the immersion of people in water. It seems that Catholic baptismal theology takes its lead from early church writers who referred to this rite as enlightenment,[60] with particular reference to catechumens being instructed in the faith, and thereby becoming enlightened, before being baptized. But this is unchastened Tradition.

Catholic theology's appeal to several Old Testament prefigurations of baptism is also met with suspicion by evangelical theology. The original dark and watery creation was "without form and void" (Gen. 1:2), not a latent source of light and fertility. The light and the created order that succeeded this original state of the world were spoken into existence from the outside, by God himself (vv. 3–31). Accordingly, this creational water was no prefiguration of Christian baptism. Neither was the crossing of the Jordan River, which Scripture never employs as imagery of baptism. Because the New Testament points to the great flood, and Noah's escape from divine judgment through water (1 Pet. 3:20), as symbolic of baptism, Catholic theology rightly finds a prefiguration of baptism in this event. Many holding to evangelical theology also agree that the crossing of the Red Sea is a type of baptism, with biblical support in 1 Corinthians 10:1–2.

Turning to New Testament support for baptism, points of agreement have already been noted. Strong disagreement comes when Catholic baptismal theology finds a foreshadowing of the sacraments of baptism and the Eucharist in the blood and water flowing out of the pierced body of the crucified Jesus (John 19:34). Evangelical theology detects no mystical meaning in the physiological reality that when Jesus's side was stabbed with the spear, the fluid that had accumulated between his lungs and ribs (fluid that would have separated into clearer liquid at the top and red liquid at the bottom) flowed out. Jesus was dead; this is John's point in recounting the escape of what looked like blood and water from Jesus's

---

[60] Justin Martyr, *First Apology* 61 (ANF 1:183); Augustine, *On the Forgiveness of Sin, and Baptism* 39[26] (*NPNF*[1] 5:30).

side, and it is no prefiguration of baptism (nor of the Eucharist, for that matter).

Further disagreement is found in Catholic theology's statement that "Baptism is a bath that purifies, justifies, and sanctifies," with appeal made to several biblical passages.[61] Taking Romans 6:3–4 and Galatians 3:27 together, evangelical theology certainly concurs that the apostle Paul presents baptism as powerfully portraying the identification of Christians with the death, burial, and resurrection of Christ (Rom. 6:3–4), such that those baptized are said to "have put on Christ" (Gal. 3:27). But the first of these affirmations is actually used by Paul to demonstrate the incongruity of both continuing in sin and being dead to it as people who now live in newness of life (Rom. 6:4). This is a positional truth that encourages reckoning oneself "dead to sin and alive to God in Christ Jesus" (Rom. 6:11), which is about neither purification nor justification, nor is it about sanctification as envisioned by Catholic theology. Thus, Catholic theology's association of Baptism with the mighty, divine acts of purification, justification, and sanctification, supported by these passages, is not warranted. The second affirmation, that the baptized "have put on Christ" (Gal. 3:27), is employed by Paul to support his contention that "in Christ Jesus you are all sons of God, through faith" (v. 26). Accordingly, Paul's point about baptism is not that it purifies, justifies, and sanctifies, but that it portrays adoption into the family of God, thereby rendering national, class, and gender differences moot, "for you are all one in Christ Jesus" (vv. 27–28). Unity and adoption into community are what Paul emphasizes in this passage, and the common baptism of all Christians symbolizes their adoption into the one family of God and their subsequent unity. Not to be overlooked in this passage as well is the apostle's constant emphasis on faith (vv. 22, 23, 24, 25, 26), whose connection to baptism will be treated later.

Taking the next two passages (1 Cor. 6:11 and 12:13) to which Catholic theology appeals for New Testament support for its baptismal theology, Paul's assuring words to the Corinthians—"And such were some of you. But you were washed, you were sanctified, you were justified in the name of the Lord Jesus and by the Spirit of our God" (1 Cor. 6:11)—stand in stark contrast to his sober warning that "the unrighteous will not inherit the kingdom of God" (vv. 9–10). Importantly, the apostle differentiates the

---

[61] CCC 1227.

three mighty divine acts—purification, sanctification, and justification—without indicating that any of them individually, or all three collectively, is/are dependent on baptism. At most, one could associate "washing" with baptism—Titus 3:5 does this—but to make baptism the ground of sanctification and justification as well is not warranted by this passage. Support for the sacrament is not forthcoming from the second passage either: "for in one Spirit we were all baptized into one body—Jews or Greeks, slaves or free—and all were made to drink of one Spirit" (1 Cor. 12:13). The point Paul makes is not about baptism with water, but about baptism with the Spirit. One of the mighty acts of God in saving his people is that Jesus Christ baptizes them with the Spirit and incorporates them into the body of Christ, the church. The exact relationship between this divine act involving Christ and the Spirit, and the ecclesial act of baptizing with water, is not spelled out in Scripture, but while certainly related to purification, justification, and sanctification, baptism with the Spirit is a distinct act. Accordingly, this passage does not support what Catholic theology claims it does.

As for Catholic theology's close link between Baptism and Scripture, the *Catechism* proposes that "Baptism is a bath of water in which the 'imperishable seed' of the Word of God produces its life-giving effect. St. Augustine says of Baptism: 'The word is brought to the material element, and it becomes a sacrament.'"[62] In support of this perspective, the *Catechism* references 1 Peter 1:23, which assures Christians, "you have been born again, not of perishable seed but of imperishable, through the living and abiding word of God." Evangelical theology calls attention to the context of Peter's affirmation about regeneration through the Word. He appeals to the prophet Isaiah [40:6, 8] to justify his point: "All flesh is like grass, and all its glory like the flower of grass. The grass withers, and the flower falls, but the word of the Lord remains forever." The apostle concludes, "And this word is the good news that was preached to you" (1 Pet. 1:23–25). At no point does Peter join the Word of God, which is the message of the gospel that is announced, to baptism. His emphasis is on the instrumentality of the preached word to effect regeneration, and any connection to baptism is read into Peter's presentation.

That leaves one other passage, together with the citation from Augustine,

---

[62] *CCC* 1228; the biblical reference is 1 Pet. 1:23 (cf. Eph. 5:26); citation is from Augustine, *Homilies on the Gospel of John* 80.3 (NPNF² 7:344).

to support the link between baptism and the Word of God. As Paul affirms, "Christ loved the church and gave himself up for her, that he might sanctify her, having cleansed her by the washing of water with the word, so that he might present the church to himself in splendor, without spot or wrinkle or any such thing, that she might be holy and without blemish" (Eph. 5:25–27). If "the washing of water" refers to baptism, and if "the word" refers to the Word of God, this verse is the only one that explicitly links baptism with the Word of God. This fact alone should prompt a good deal of caution in interpreting this verse in this way.

As Markus Barth argues, a metaphorical understanding may be in order. According to this approach, the phrase "having cleansed her by the washing of water with the word" figuratively, and thus succinctly, portrays all that Jesus Christ did to accomplish salvation for sinful human beings. Through his sacrificial, loving death on the cross, he gave himself up for the church in order to sanctify it, or set it apart, for God's purposes, which have a future orientation encompassing complete holiness on the day of Christ's return. These truths have already been thematized at the beginning of this letter (1:3–14): First, Paul highlights the work of Christ: "In him we have redemption through his blood, the forgiveness of our trespasses" (v. 7); other specific mighty acts by which fallen human beings are rescued and blessed are election, adoption, the revelation of God's eternal will, an inheritance, predestination, and the sealing with the Holy Spirit. Second, the apostle underscores that God purposed to effect this salvation: "in love he predestined us for adoption as sons through Jesus Christ, according to the purpose of his will, to the praise of his glorious grace" (vv. 5–6; cf. vv. 9, 12, 14). Third, Paul emphasizes the design of sanctification: "he [God] chose us in him [Christ] before the foundation of the world, that we should be holy and blameless before him" (v. 4). Importantly, the divine work and design are activated as people "heard the word of truth, the gospel of salvation, and believed in him [Christ]" (v. 13). As for "the washing with water," the expression may recall Ezekiel's prophecy that uses the idea of sprinkling with water as a metaphor for the cleansing or forgiveness of sins, which is associated with God giving a new heart/a heart of flesh, a new spirit, and the Holy Spirit to effect obedience to the covenant (Ezek. 36:25–27). Thus, Paul's point is "a praise of the new life given in common to all members of the church through the death of Christ and the Spirit of God" as announced through the word of the gospel.[63] Therefore, Ephesians 5:26 does not support the sacramental notion that the Word of God effects a change in ordinary water so as to render it capable of transmitting grace. Such an interpretation reflects Augustine's theology (the next point), but it is certainly an anachronistic understanding of Paul's intention when writing.

As for Augustine's view that the Word of God, when joined to the water, makes that water the sacrament of Baptism, the idea reflects the Catholic system's axiom of the nature-grace interdependence. Because nature—in this case, water—possesses a capacity for grace, and because grace must be conveyed concretely through nature, the water becomes a channel or means of grace: the sacrament of Baptism. As this axiom has already been critiqued and found wanting, nothing more will be said here.

Historical Development

Still other divergences on baptism flow from evangelical theology's questioning of the impact of this rite's historical development on Catholic theology's current understanding and practice of it. As the *Catechism* correctly notes, numerous elements were added to the administration of this rite, and these additions deeply influenced the baptismal theology of the early church. Given that these elements lack clear biblical support, evangelical theology must again confront the unchastened Tradition of Catholicism. Each element will be taken and explored one by one.

Though the clear biblical pattern was for those who heard the gospel, repented of their sins, and believed in Jesus Christ to be baptized immediately, this common practice gave way to a period of catechesis being inserted between hearing the message of salvation and baptism. Catechesis involved catechists teaching Scripture and the doctrines of the Christian faith, and the learners who participated in this instructional formation were called catechumens; they were being prepared for the rite of Christian initiation. A key reason for this development can be found in the legalization of Christianity as a religion in the Roman empire. As a large influx of new people streamed into the church—and not always for the right reasons—the genuineness and seriousness of their commitment had to be assessed, and what better way was there to accomplish this goal than making entrance

---

[63] Markus Barth, *Ephesians 4–6: A New Translation with Introduction and Commentary*, The Anchor Bible, vol. 34A (Garden City, NY: Doubleday, 1960), 699.

into the church a rather long and demanding process? Thus, their baptism was delayed, having to await their successful completion of the period of catechesis.

A wide swath of evangelical theology assesses this delay negatively. Though the pragmatic move to test the authenticity of one's Christian commitment is understandable and perhaps even commendable under certain circumstances, three questions deserve consideration: Why should pragmatic matters be allowed to break a clear biblical pattern of conversion followed quickly by baptism? Why didn't the early church better anticipate and prepare itself for the negative consequences of its growing relationship with the state? If the church's Lord emphasized that his kingdom is not of this world, why would his church identify itself with a worldly kingdom? The results bear out the wrongness of the state-church relationship: secular emperors becoming involved in sacred theological debates; the church that once was persecuted becoming the persecutor; the Crusades attempting to retake the Holy Land (or even Christendom's Constantinople) by force while warring against Islamic forces; the papacy reigning as one kingdom or monarchy among others, with the same political intrigue, financial misconduct, immorality, and military subterfuge as any earthly power; concordats with international despots such as Napoleon, Mussolini, and Hitler. These results were not due to the delay of baptism; that is not the point. Rather, the postponement of baptism in order to prepare candidates for the rite represents a capitulation to pragmatic matters, the breaking of a clear biblical pattern, confusion over making new disciples (with their baptism as part of that responsibility) and making mature church members by baptism, and a freighting of the baptismal water with a weightiness that it was never intended to have. This last point leads to a discussion of infant baptism.

The greatest change that was introduced to the rite of baptism in the early church was the baptism of infants. Although Scripture consistently presents the recipients of baptism as those who had already heard the gospel and appropriated it through repentance and faith, in the latter part of the second century the church began to view infants as the recipients of baptism, with this practice being firmly established by the fifth century. Important to remember is that this historical development had both supporters and detractors; sometimes this fact is overlooked. For example, the *Catechism* invokes second-century support for this practice but fails to mention that the extant account in which infant baptism is addressed at that time is Tertullian's *objection* to this novel practice, complaining that "innocent infancy" does not need to "rush to the forgiveness of sins." On the contrary, argued Tertullian, "Let them become Christians when they become able to know Christ" and then be baptized.[64] Similarly, when in the middle of the third century Origen claimed, "The church has received a tradition from the apostles to give baptism even to little children,"[65] he too objected to this practice, arguing that innocent people—that is, children who have not yet personally sinned—do not need forgiveness.

So how did infant baptism develop? Origen underscored the key point in its development: "No one is clean of filth, not even if his life on earth has only been for one day. . . . Because the filth of birth is removed by the sacrament of baptism, for that reason infants, too, are baptized."[66] In other words, the practice of infant baptism developed as a strong link between baptism and the removal of original sin was forged. Original sin—the doctrine that Adam has transmitted his guilt and corruption to all human beings, so that everyone is born into this world guilty before God and tainted with a corrupt, sinful nature—must be dealt with, or only judgment leading to condemnation is the result. Because baptism was considered to effect the forgiveness of sins, and because infants are born with Adamic guilt and corruption (original sin), they must be baptized in order to be saved. With this theology firmly in place by the beginning of the fifth century, infant baptism became the official practice of the church.

Evangelical theology objects strongly to the theology and practice of infant baptism. To be precise, even though some portions of evangelical theology practice infant baptism—thus, there is a family resemblance between those churches and the Catholic Church in terms of administering baptism to infants—the theology that warrants the evangelical practice is completely different from its Catholic counterpart. As just noted, Catholic baptismal theology centers on original sin and its forgiveness through the baptism of infants. Evangelical baptismal theology, with its several varieties, has a much different focus. For example, Reformed theology grounds its

---

[64] Tertullian, *On Baptism* 18 (ANF 3:678).
[65] Origen, *Commentary on Romans* 5.9.3, in Origen, *Commentary on the Epistle to the Romans*, trans. Thomas P. Scheck, 2 vols., in *The Fathers of the Church: A New Translation* (Washington, DC: Catholic University of America Press, 2001), 1:367.
[66] Origen, *Homilies on the Gospel of Luke* 14:5; cited in Jaroslav Pelikan, *The Christian Tradition: A History of the Development of Doctrine*, 5 vols. (Chicago and London: University of Chicago Press, 1971–1991), 1:291.

practice of infant baptism on covenantal membership: children of believing parents are to be baptized because, like their parents, they are part of the covenant community, the church, and therefore they are entitled to the sign of covenant membership, which is baptism. Historically, Huldrych Zwingli underscored the analogy between the old covenant practice of circumcision and the new covenant practice of infant baptism. Because circumcision was applied on the eighth day after an infant boy's birth, so baptism should be administered to infants, both boys and girls. John Calvin also emphasized this analogy, noting the benefits that accrue to both believers and their children. The parents are encouraged to see God's covenant of mercy extended to their offspring, while the children receive this benefit: "[B]eing engrafted into the body of the church, they are somewhat more commended to the other members. Then, when they have grown up, they are greatly spurred to an earnest zeal for worshipping God, by whom they were received as children through a solemn symbol of adoption before they were old enough to recognize him as Father."[67] To be noted is that Reformed theology does not appeal to the need to remove original sin and the necessity of baptismal regeneration as the ground for infant baptism. Indeed, Reformed baptismal theology distances itself from Catholic baptismal theology, disagreeing that baptism cleanses infants of their original sin and regenerates them.

While infant baptism is the practice of a significant portion of evangelicals, others baptize only those who can offer a credible profession of faith in Jesus Christ. Historically, this development began with the Anabaptists, whose baptismal theology was built on several arguments. First, a negative case was presented to disqualify the practice of baptizing infants: the Anabaptists found no explicit biblical warrant for it and noted that none of the New Testament accounts of baptism mention infants participating in this rite. Then, a positive case was made for the baptism of believers: in every case of baptism in the New Testament, faith preceded water baptism; accordingly, Anabaptist theology concluded that people must experience the saving intervention of God and have faith before they can properly be baptized. Adding to this was the fact that, in his Great Commission, Jesus himself commanded the baptism of those who had been made disciples (Matt. 28:18–20). Baptists developed a similar baptismal theology, disavowing the legitimacy of any type of infant baptism, whether that be the

---

[67] Calvin, *Institutes* 4.16.9 (LCC 21:1332).

Catholic rite grounded on the cleansing from original sin and regeneration, or Protestant paedobaptism grounded on the analogy between the old and new covenants and the incorporation of the infants of believing parents into the church. Instead, Baptists insisted on baptism following a credible profession of faith in Christ.

For evangelical proponents of believer's baptism, Catholic theology's appeal to historical precedent and Scripture to support the practice of infant baptism falls short. Taking the latter support first, the examples of baptism that pepper the pages of the New Testament champion believer's baptism, not infant baptism. On the day of Pentecost, in response to Peter's proclamation of the gospel and his command to "Repent and be baptized every one of you in the name of Jesus Christ for the forgiveness of your sins, and you will receive the gift of the Holy Spirit" (Acts 2:38), "those who received his word were baptized, and there were added that day about three thousand souls" (v. 41). Baptism was preceded by hearing and responding to the gospel by repentance from sin and faith in Jesus Christ (in v. 44, these people are referred to as "all who believed"). This same pattern is repeated in the book of Acts: among those who believe and are baptized are Samaritans (8:12); an Ethiopian eunuch (8:36, 38); Saul, a persecutor of the church (9:18; 22:16); Gentiles (10:47–48; 11:16–17); a businesswoman and her household (16:15); a jailer and his family (16:33); a large number of Corinthians (18:8); and a dozen disciples of John the Baptist (19:3–7). Extending beyond this early period, believer's baptism continued to be the practice, as evidenced by the *Didache* (mid-second century), which provides instructions for the rite, directions that would be inapplicable for infants.[68]

Despite this clear biblical pattern, Catholic theology points to the instances of household baptisms as "possible" support for infant baptism. The four passages will be considered one by one: The baptism of Lydia and her family (Acts 16:15) provides no information about the makeup of her household. The assumption that some who were baptized were infants is as unfounded as is the assumption that none were infants. What is clear is that this businesswoman heard the gospel and as a consequence was baptized. The Philippian jailer, after crying out to know how he could be saved, was

---

[68] The *Didache* prescribes that both the baptizer and the one to be baptized fast before the baptism, and it prohibits participation in the Lord's Supper by those who have not yet been baptized (*Didache* 7 [*ANF* 7:379]; 9:5 [*ANF* 7:380]).

commanded by Paul and Silas, "'Believe in the Lord Jesus, and you will be saved, you and your household.' And they spoke the word of the Lord to him and to all who were in his house. . . . [A]nd he was baptized at once, he and all his family" (Acts 16:25–33). In this case of a household baptism, sufficient information is known about the recipients: all of them first heard the gospel, then all of them were baptized. The case of the Corinthians is similar. As Paul was "occupied with the word, testifying to the Jews that the Christ was Jesus" (Acts 18:5), a great result took place: "Crispus, the ruler of the synagogue, believed in the Lord, together with his entire household. And many of the Corinthians hearing Paul believed and were baptized" (v. 8). Again, the common pattern is verified: Paul announced the gospel, and Crispus and his whole household, like many other Corinthians, believed and were baptized. The fourth passage is in Paul's first letter to the church of Corinth, in which he recalls, "I did baptize also the household of Stephanas" (1 Cor. 1:16). Though insufficient information is provided about the composition of this family, to entertain the possibility that it included infants who were thus baptized would be wrong, on the basis of more information that is given elsewhere. In his final instructions in this letter, the apostle notes "that the household of Stephanas were the first converts in Achaia, and that they have devoted themselves to the service of the saints" (1 Cor. 16:15). Clearly, Stephanas's household consisted of people who had embraced the gospel and engaged in fruitful ministry, thereby excluding infants.

Accordingly, the biblical pattern, continued as the common practice in the early church, is baptism following hearing and embracing the gospel by repentance and faith. Thus, evangelical proponents of believer's baptism have strong biblical support for their baptismal theology and practice, and rightly underscore the corollary of the weakness of the case for infant baptism.

While admitting that the biblical support for infant baptism is only "possible," Catholic baptismal theology appeals secondly to historical precedent to support its practice. As noted above, the evidence for this development, at least in its earliest phases, is mixed: Some in the church supported infant baptism, while others lamented it. However, by the beginning of the fifth century, the official practice had become the baptism of infants. How does evangelical theology assess this evolution?

As for evangelical credobaptists, this development both contradicts the clear pattern of believer's baptism as established by Scripture and is grounded on a misunderstanding of baptism as cleansing from original sin and regenerating its recipients. Accordingly, evangelical theology of this persuasion views the baptism of infants as an unwarranted, even tragic, accretion to the baptismal theology and practice of the early church, going back to its inception on the day of Pentecost. Similarly, evangelical paedobaptists dissent from this development because, even though their practice bears a family resemblance to Catholic infant baptism, they reject Catholic theology's grounds for it. Evangelical paedobaptism is not grounded on the need for cleansing from original sin and the necessity of baptismal regeneration; rather, it points to the analogy between the old covenant rite of circumcision and the new covenant rite of baptism and consequently applies this sign of covenant membership to the infants of believing parents. Thus, both evangelical credobaptism and evangelical paedobaptism dissent from this historical precedent and its use in support of Catholic paedobaptism.

Evangelical theology also laments the other accretions to the rite of baptism that occurred in the early church. For example, the celebration of this rite is preceded by an exorcism and a renunciation of Satan. Certainly, Scripture describes sinful human beings as "following the prince of the power of the air, the spirit that is now at work in the sons of disobedience" (Eph. 2:2) and as "children of the devil" (1 John 3:8, 10; cf. John 8:44) who are under "the power of Satan" (Acts 26:18). Catholic theology ties this satanic domination to both original sin and actual sins, as one of their consequences; the devil is the instigator of sin and thus rules those who are under its control. Release from sin and this devilish jurisdiction is one of the effects of regeneration. Because regeneration is effected by baptism, exorcism and renunciation of Satan became an element of the baptismal rite of the early church. Evangelical theology criticizes this accretion because of its lack of biblical support and laments the fact of another unchastened Tradition in Catholic theology and practice.[69]

Other examples of lamentable accretions to the administration of

---

[69] Indeed, in Scripture, exorcisms are carried out on demonically *possessed* people, not on those who were merely subject to demonic influence. Catholic theology promotes exorcism in association with baptism, not because it holds that catechumens are demonically possessed before they are baptized, but because it holds that they have fallen under the power of Satan due to their sins. Evangelical theology objects to extending the use of exorcism to these lesser cases.

baptism are the use of consecrated water and the act of anointing with oil those who have been baptized. As for the first of these, the consecration of the water is seen as necessary because those who are to be baptized in it must be "born of water and the Spirit" (John 3:5). As noted earlier, this theology is based on a misunderstanding of Jesus's affirmation, taking it to refer to baptismal regeneration and its necessity. The consecration of the water is also dependent on the Catholic system's axiom of the nature-grace interdependence. The natural element of water, possessing a capacity for grace, must be consecrated so that grace is conveyed concretely through it as the sacrament of Baptism. This nature-grace interdependence is tied closely to Catholic theology's notion of the sacraments being valid *ex opere operato*. Because divine grace is communicated by the act of Baptism itself, the power to effect the forgiveness of original sin (and, in the case of adults, their actual sins as well) and to bring about the new birth necessarily adheres in the water, to which God through his Son has sent the power of the Holy Spirit in the act of its consecration. Evangelical objections to the nature-grace axiom and the *ex opere operato* validity of the sacraments have already been offered. As for the anointing with oil of the recently baptized, signifying the gift of the Spirit and portraying these new Christians as "anointed ones" like Christ (literally, "the anointed one"), evangelical theology objects. God has given baptism to the church of the new covenant, and this covenantal sign is one visible, concrete element: water. Elaboration on this rite with other elements does not enhance the administration of baptism but detracts from its straightforward meanings.

Indeed, baptism powerfully portrays the various meanings or effects of baptism as presented in the New Testament: association with the triune God, who is eternally Father, Son, and Holy Spirit (Matt. 28:19); identification with the death, burial, and resurrection of Jesus Christ (Rom. 6:3–5; cf. Gal. 3:26–28); cleansing from sin (Acts 22:16; 2:38); escape from divine judgment (1 Pet. 3:20–21);[70] an act of obedience on the part of those who have repented and believed in Christ (Acts 2:38); and the sign of entrance and incorporation into the new covenant community, the church (vv. 42–47). Evangelical theology embraces, with greater or lesser degrees of emphasis,

---

[70] Importantly, Peter emphasizes that it is not the external rite of baptism itself that saves by some external act of cleansing. Rather, baptism associated with a transaction between God and those being baptized—an appeal on their part for or from a good conscience—is what rescues them from divine judgment.

depending on what variety it is, these meanings of baptism. Additional meanings or effects are rejected as being without biblical support or because their theological basis is wrong. For example, the infusion of grace resulting in an increase of the divine life leading toward perfection in love—held as an effect of Baptism by Catholic theology—depends on the nature-grace interdependence, particularly its emphasis that grace must elevate and eventually perfect nature. Accordingly, it misunderstands the working of divine grace, which is not infused into its recipients but imputed to them, a subject that will be addressed later in more detail.

Faith and Baptism

Because the *Catechism* next addresses the issue of faith and Baptism, this evangelical assessment turns to that topic. Both Catholic and evangelical theology associate faith with baptism, so there is agreement on this point. However, disagreement is found over the nature of the relationship between faith and baptism. Of particular importance is Catholic theology's emphasis on the faith of the Church as the foundation for personal faith; as the *Catechism* explains, "It is only with the faith of the Church that each of the faithful can believe."[71] In the case of the Baptism of an infant, then, her faith is the faith of the Church as received vicariously through her parents and godparents. In the case of the Baptism of an adult, his faith is the gift of faith given to him by the Church. Clearly, at the heart of this emphasis is the necessity of the Church and its sacrament of Baptism for salvation.

As much as evangelical theology wishes to underscore the importance of the church, it does not concur with Catholic theology's exaggerated ecclesial sense as evidenced in its grounding of personal faith on the faith of the Church. At the heart of this disagreement lies the Christ-Church interconnection, an axiom of the Catholic system: the Catholic Church is the extension of the incarnation of Christ; as such, the Church, and the Church alone, is the mediator between nature and grace, conveying salvation through its sacrament of Baptism and, what is more, the very faith involved in salvation. This overarching principle has received critique already (ch. 2).

But specific criticisms may also be offered. Another reason for disagree-

---

[71] CCC 1253.

ment is the lack of biblical support for this role of the church in faith. In every instance of baptism in the New Testament, the person being baptized had expressed faith in Christ individually. Certainly, it is true that other "players" were active in these dramas of salvation: Peter made the first proclamation of the gospel on the day of Pentecost, leading three thousand to faith followed by baptism (Acts 2:22–41), and he was in the midst of speaking about Christ when the first Gentiles became Christians and were baptized (10:34–48). Philip the evangelist announced Jesus Christ to the Samaritans (8:5–24) and to the Ethiopian eunuch (vv. 26–40). These examples could be multiplied. But biblically speaking, Peter, Philip, and the others are responsible servants, not representatives of a church that supplies faith to those who hear the gospel. Indeed, Paul rejected any exaggerated role for himself and Apollos as leaders of the church of Corinth: "What then is Apollos? What is Paul? *Servants through whom you believed, as the Lord assigned to each.* I planted, Apollos watered, but God gave the growth. So neither he who plants nor he who waters is anything, but only God who gives the growth" (1 Cor. 3:5–7, emphasis added; cf. 4:1–5). To be the servant of those coming to believe in Christ as Lord is a very different matter from being the repository of faith that is then given as the foundation for the faith of others. The first is the instrument for faith; the second, the ground of faith.

Additionally, the New Testament presentation of faith focuses on individual responsibility to believe in Christ for salvation. For example, taking a key passage for Catholic theology's baptismal regeneration, Jesus told Nicodemus, "unless one is *born again* he cannot see the kingdom of God" (John 3:3, emphasis added). This instruction recalls the vivid affirmation of John's Prologue about the Word of God: "He came to his own, and his own people did not receive him. But to all who did receive him, who believed in his name, he gave the right to become children of God, who were *born*, not of blood nor of the will of the flesh nor of the will of man, but *of God* (1:11–13, emphasis added). Being born again and being born of God mean the same thing, and as the latter, divinely engineered birth is intimately linked with receiving the Word of God and believing in his name, the former new birth must similarly be joined. To be noted here is the individual responsibility for reception/belief; this is far removed from the notion of faith found in Catholic baptismal theology in which the faith of the Church rather than the faith of the individual comes to the forefront.

Moreover, Catholic theology's idea that the Church is that which gives the gift of faith to the faithful conflicts with Scripture's emphasis that faith leading to salvation is the gift of God (Eph. 2:8–9), and that a genuine profession of faith is prompted by the Holy Spirit ("no one can say 'Jesus is Lord' except in the Holy Spirit"; 1 Cor. 12:3). Again, this rejoinder is not to deny the instrumental role of the church in proclaiming the gospel, urging repentance and faith, praying for the conversion of nonbelievers, and the like. Rather, it denies the foundational role of the Church for the faith of the faithful. According to the apostle Paul, "But what does it [the righteousness based on faith; Rom. 10:6] say? 'The word is near you, in your mouth and in your heart' (that is, the word of faith that we proclaim); because, if you confess with your mouth that Jesus is Lord and believe in your heart that God raised him from the dead, you will be saved. For with the heart one believes and is justified, and with the mouth one confesses and is saved" (vv. 8–10). Transposing the words of the *Catechism*, then, when the catechumen is asked, "What do you ask of God's Church?" the proper response is not "Faith!" but "the word of faith that [the Church proclaims]," because "faith comes from hearing, and hearing through the word of Christ" (v. 17). Positively, then, the church is the servant and instrument of faith through its proclamation of the Word of God, which ignites faith leading to salvation, all of which is the gift of God. Negatively, the faith of the church is not the foundation for, or dispenser of, faith.

Extraordinary Scenarios

With all that has been affirmed by Catholic theology concerning the necessity of Baptism for salvation and the foundational role of the Church for faith associated with Baptism, it comes as no surprise that the ordinary administrators of this rite are the leaders—the bishops, priests, and deacons—of the Church. This raises the important question about what to do in the case in which the Church, in the person of one of its leaders, is not present to baptize people, or the case in which people die before they are baptized. Does the necessity of Baptism for salvation, and the Church's role in its administration, spell doom for those who are not able to avail themselves of clergy-conferred Baptism?

Catholic baptismal theology addresses several extraordinary scenarios, and an evangelical assessment will follow each of them. One scenario focuses on the case in which Catholic clergy cannot administer this rite; Catholic theology allows for anyone to baptize, as long as the required intention is present. In this case, the emergency Baptism is valid. For the most part, evangelical theology, which does not deem baptism necessary in the way Catholic theology does, would not see the lack of baptism as a hindrance to salvation. The non-baptism of the thief on the cross may be appealed to as a parallel exceptional case. Another scenario focuses on four cases in which people die before they are baptized. The first extraordinary case is martyrs. Evangelical theology may make the same appeal as in the case of the thief on the cross, concluding that martyrs who die before they are able to be baptized are not hindered from salvation. It would not invent—indeed, it decries—a "Baptism of blood" to substitute for water baptism. The second case, of catechumens dying before they are baptized, raises a more fundamental objection: their baptism should not have been delayed, so the Church is at fault for prohibiting them from obediently being baptized according to the biblical pattern. Evangelical theology would not contrive—indeed, it would lament—a "desire for Baptism" to make up for the lack of water baptism.

Even more disturbing is the third case, the fate of the unevangelized who clearly have not been baptized. Appealing to the unlimited atonement of Christ, the universal call to divine blessing, and the mystery of God, Catholic theology concludes that "we must hold that the Holy Spirit offers to all the possibility of being made partakers, in a way known to God, of the Paschal mystery."[72] Evangelical theology has already assessed and condemned this Catholic inclusivism, insisting instead that (1) the atonement of Christ is the only objective basis for the salvation of sinful human beings (Catholic theology agrees with this first point) and (2) faith is the necessary subjective or personal appropriation of this atoning sacrifice, knowledge of which comes through the gospel and leads to salvation. Catholic theology disagrees with this second point, inventing some other possible way for the unevangelized to be saved—by seeking the truth through non-Christian religions, following the dictates of conscience, or in some other manner. In such instances, Catholic theology

---

[72] CCC 1260.

supposes "that such persons would have *desired Baptism explicitly* if they had known its necessity."[73]

Evangelical theology objects: This theory is completely speculative, not being grounded on any divine revelation, as even Catholic theology admits, and it stands against nearly eighteen hundred years of Catholic Tradition. Though it may posit the possibility of their salvation coming about "in a way known to God,"[74] and though it may imagine that "God has bound salvation to the sacrament of Baptism, but he himself is not bound by his sacraments,"[75] Catholic theology does not offer any support for these contentions.[76] Catholic inclusivism further ignores the explicit biblical emphasis joining together the atonement of Christ (point 1) and its announcement through the gospel and the response of faith (point 2), apart from which there can be no salvation. Lastly, it does not take into account the intractable sinfulness of all people, Christians as well as non-Christians, which evacuates the supposition that if the unevangelized had only known about the necessity of Baptism, they would have explicitly desired it.[77]

The fourth extraordinary case concerns unbaptized infants. Historically, "the [Church's] traditional teaching on this topic has concentrated on the theory of *limbo*, understood as a state which includes the souls of infants who die subject to original sin and without baptism, and who, therefore, neither merit the beatific vision, nor yet are subjected to any punishment, because they are not guilty of any personal sin."[78] However, Catholic theology notes that this theory finds no explicit teaching in divine revelation, and was never dogmatically defined by the Magisterium; hence, it is only a hypothesis. Accordingly, the current focus of Catholic theology is on entrusting unbaptized infants to the mercy of God. Whereas some varieties of evangelical theology go beyond this position—some affirm that all infants who die are saved, others that the infants of believers are saved,

---

[73] Ibid.
[74] Ibid.
[75] CCC 1257 (emphasis removed).
[76] Indeed, if Catholic theology is wrong on the first affirmation—that God has bound salvation to baptism—what confidence does that instill with respect to the second affirmation—that God is not bound by his sacraments?
[77] As noted earlier, though Catholic theology acknowledges the barriers that Satan, sin, and the world present for the unevangelized to gain eternal salvation (*Lumen Gentium* 16), it does not consider these obstacles to be so intractably obstinate that in some way they cannot be vanquished by some unbelievers.
[78] International Theological Commission, *The Hope of Salvation for Infants Who Die without Being Baptized* (January 19, 2007), opening paragraphs. Accessible at http://www.vatican.va/roman_curia/congregations/cfaith /cti_documents/rc_con_cfaith_doc_20070419_un-baptised-infants_en.html.

still others that infants who die are condemned to hell because of Adamic guilt through original sin—the careful handling of this matter by Catholic theology should caution against such definitive stances. For this reason, other varieties of evangelical theology are silent on the issue of the fate of infants who have died.[79]

The preceding discussion and evangelical assessment of extraordinary cases and their relationship to baptism is capable of misunderstanding, so to avoid any such confusion, a word needs to be said about this ordinance and its necessity for salvation. Many variations of evangelical theology make a distinction between baptism as the ground, or efficient cause, of salvation, and baptism as the means, or instrumental cause, of salvation. In the first sense, evangelical theology denies that baptism is the ground, or efficient cause, of salvation; on the contrary, the foundation of salvation—its accomplishment—is the redemptive work of God through the death, burial, and resurrection of Jesus Christ alone. Accordingly, baptism is not necessary for salvation in this first sense. In the second sense, many varieties of evangelical theology embrace baptism as one of the means, or instrumental causes, of salvation. Together with repentance from sin and faith in Jesus Christ (Acts 2:38–44), baptism is a divinely appointed means for the appropriation of salvation; baptism is necessary for salvation in this second sense. The fact that there may be and indeed are extraordinary cases in which Christians are not able to be baptized (e.g., martyrdom, premature death, the thief on the cross) does not mean that these people were not saved, but neither does it lessen the importance of baptism as an instrumental means to appropriate salvation. Many evangelical churches, obeying the Great Commission's insistence on the baptism of disciples (Matt. 28:18–20) and following clear biblical examples (Acts 2:38), teach and urge people to be baptized. Though not necessary for salvation (in the first sense), baptism is necessary as an act of obedience in appropriating salvation (in the second sense).[80]

One final issue: Catholic theology proposes Baptism for anyone not yet baptized, and does not permit the Baptism of people who have been

---

[79] Such studied agnosticism does not leave its proponents devoid of words to say to parents who have lost infants to death. The ultimate comfort of the survivors of such tragedies is God himself (2 Cor. 1:3–7), who is afflicted when his people are afflicted (Isa. 63:9) because he is well acquainted with such cases, and who is also great and powerful enough to bring hope out of such suffering.

[80] For further discussion, see Allison, SS, 357–360.

baptized already because of the indelible character of the sacrament. Given the permanent nature of the sacrament, Catholic theology denies that Protestants who have been baptized with Christian baptism, and who want to convert to Catholicism, can be rebaptized. Evangelical theology approaches this topic in different ways. As for the proper recipients of baptism, evangelical paedobaptists generally restrict baptism in some way—for example, to the infants of believing parents—while evangelical credobaptists limit it to those who can offer a credible profession of faith. In terms of rebaptism, many varieties of evangelical theology would require people who have been baptized in the Catholic Church to be baptized in order to become members of an evangelical church. This position is due either to the fact that (1) Catholic paedobaptism is wrongly considered to remove original sin and bring about regeneration (thus, it is invalid), or (2) any type of paedobaptism (Catholic, Orthodox, or Protestant) is not a true baptism. In the latter case, people are not rebaptized, but baptized, because their infant baptism is not considered to be a valid baptism.

In summary, Catholic and evangelical baptismal theology and practice, while possessing a few commonalities, are substantially different because of different interpretations of biblical passages narrating or presenting baptism, different assessments of the historical precedents for baptism, different understandings of the meanings and effects of baptism, and much more.

The Sacrament of Confirmation (Sec. 2, Ch. I, Art. 2)

The second sacrament of Christian initiation is Confirmation, known also in the Eastern Churches as "*Chrismation*, anointing with chrism, or *myron* which means 'chrism.'"[81] Following Baptism, "the reception of the sacrament of Confirmation is necessary for the completion of baptismal grace. For 'by the sacrament of Confirmation, [the baptized] are more perfectly bound to the Church and are enriched with a special strength of the Holy Spirit,'" leading to a greater missional obligation.[82] Indeed, this sacrament both ratifies and strengthens baptismal grace.

The biblical basis for this sacrament begins with Old Testament prophecies of the Holy Spirit's anointing of the Messiah for his work of salvation (e.g., Isa. 11:2; 61:1; fulfilled in Luke 4:16–22). Jesus of Nazareth, who was

---

[81] CCC 1289.
[82] CCC 1285; citation is from Vatican Council II, *Lumen Gentium* 11; cf. *Ordo confirmationis*, Introduction 2.

conceived by the Holy Spirit, was marked out as the Messiah at his baptism by the descending Spirit; indeed, Jesus lived his entire life and carried out his whole mission with dependence on the Holy Spirit, whom the Father gave him "without measure" (John 3:34). Furthermore, during his ministry, Jesus promised a fresh, new, unprecedented outpouring of the Spirit (e.g., Luke 12:12; John 3:5–8; 7:37–39; 16:7–15; Acts 1:4–5, 8), a promise that "he fulfilled first on Easter Sunday and then more strikingly at Pentecost" (John 20:22; Acts 2:1–4), when the fullness of the Spirit was poured out on "the whole messianic people."[83] "From that time on the apostles, in fulfillment of Christ's will, imparted to the newly baptized by the laying on of hands the gift of the Spirit that completes the grace of Baptism. . . . The imposition of hands is rightly recognized by the Catholic tradition as the origin of the sacrament of Confirmation, which in a certain way perpetuates the grace of Pentecost in the Church."[84]

The early church signified this gift of the Spirit through Confirmation by adding an anointing with perfumed oil (*chrism*) to the laying on of hands. This sign of anointing both signifies and impresses a spiritual mark, "the *seal* of the Holy Spirit. A seal is a symbol of a person, a sign of personal authority, or ownership of an object."[85] Christ himself marks his followers with the seal of the Holy Spirit, who is the guarantee of their belonging to Christ, enrollment in his service, and the promise of divine protection (e.g., 2 Cor. 1:21–22; cf. Eph. 1:13; 4:30; Rev. 7:2–3; 9:4).

This sacrament is celebrated with the following rites: Preceding the celebration of Confirmation, the oil has been consecrated by the bishop as part of the Chrism Mass of Holy Thursday. The celebration itself "begins with the renewal of baptismal promises and the profession of faith by the confirmands [those to be confirmed]."[86] In the case of those who were baptized as infants, years of time separate the administration of Baptism and Confirmation, but in the case of adults, there is no separation; they are baptized and "immediately receive Confirmation and participate in the Eucharist."[87] The bishop signifies the conferring of the Holy Spirit

---

[83] CCC 1287 (emphasis removed).
[84] CCC 1288; citation is from Pope Paul VI, *Divinae consortium naturae*, 2 (accessible at https://archive.org /stream/paulvisapostolic00cath/paulvisapostolic00cath_djvu.txt); biblical support listed is Acts 8:15–17; 19:5–6; Heb. 6:2.
[85] CCC 1295 (emphasis added).
[86] CCC 1298.
[87] Ibid.

by extending "his hands over the whole group of the confirmands" while pronouncing set words that include the invocation "Send your Holy Spirit upon them."[88] The essential rite follows: "[T]he sacrament of Confirmation is conferred through the anointing with chrism on the forehead, which is done by the laying on of hands, and through the words: '*Accipe signaculum doni Spiritus Sancti*' [Be sealed with the Gift of the Holy Spirit]."[89] The celebration ends with the sign of peace,[90] signifying and manifesting full communion with the bishop and the other faithful.

The sacrament's effect, clearly portrayed and actualized, "is the full outpouring of the Holy Spirit as once granted to the apostles on the day of Pentecost."[91] This outpouring results in "an increase and deepening of baptismal grace": a deepening of divine sonship, a firmer union with Christ, an increase in the Spirit's gifts, a strengthening of the bond with the Church,[92] and the power of the Spirit to be on mission "publicly and as it were officially."[93] Like the sacrament of Baptism, this sacrament confers an *indelible spiritual mark* and may not be repeated.

As for the recipients and ministers of the sacrament, Confirmation can and should be conferred on everyone who has been baptized; indeed, as the three sacraments of Christian initiation form a unity, all the baptized are obligated to participate in Confirmation. For those baptized as infants, the appropriate time is "about the age of discretion,"[94] which is between seven and sixteen years of age.[95] For adults, this sacrament accompanies Baptism and the Eucharist. Apart from Confirmation, "Baptism is certainly valid and efficacious, but Christian initiation remains incomplete."[96] Reception of the sacrament is preceded by preparation through catechesis and the sacrament of Penance, which restores the confirmands to a state of grace and renders them ready for the reception of the Holy Spirit. A Confirmation *sponsor*, preferably one of the baptismal godparents, provides spiritual help for the confirmands. The sacrament is

---

[88] CCC 1299. The prayer of invocation comes from the *Ordo confirmationis* 25.
[89] CCC 1300; citation is from Pope Paul VI, *Divinae consortium naturae*, 5 (accessible at https://archive.org/stream /paulvisapostolic00cath/paulvisapostolic00cath_djvu.txt).
[90] A handshake accompanied by the expression, "The peace of the Lord be with you always."
[91] CCC 1302.
[92] CCC 1303.
[93] CCC 1305; citation is from Thomas Aquinas, *Summa Theologica*, pt. 3, q. 72, art. 5, reply 2.
[94] CCC 1307; citation is from the Code of Canon Law 891.
[95] As set by the United States Conference of Catholic Bishops, November 15, 2000, in accord with canon 891 of the Code of Canon Law. Accessible at http://www.usccb.org/beliefs-and-teachings/what-we-believe/canon-law /complementary-norms/canon-891-age-for-confirmation.cfm.
[96] CCC 1306.

administered ordinarily by the bishop, although concession may be made for its celebration by priests in emergency situations (e.g., a confirmand is in danger of death).

Evangelical Assessment

Though many varieties of evangelical theology incorporate confirmation as part of their preparation of people for conversion to or growth in the Christian faith, none of them considers it to be a sacrament. As noted above, the reason for this rejection of confirmation as a sacrament is that Jesus did not ordain it as a rite to be administered by the church.

At the heart of the Catholic theology of Confirmation is the nature-grace interconnection. This axiom emphasizes the concrete conferring of grace through nature (in this case, oil), which possesses the capacity to convey grace, a capacity that is actualized through the Church's consecration of the oil. This grace, infused into the confirmands, further elevates their (human) nature beyond the effects of the grace conferred on it by their Baptism. Given this understanding, baptismal grace initiates the process, removing original sin and causing baptized persons (in most cases, infants) to have a new nature through regeneration by the Spirit. Baptismal grace also introduces them into the Church and launches them on mission for Christ. As these baptized infants reach the age of discretion, sometime between seven and sixteen years of age, an advanced infusion of grace is necessary, and this increase in grace is provided through the sacrament of Confirmation. Indeed, Catholic theology's descriptors of this sacrament underscore the augmentation that it confers on its recipients: It *increases/ deepens/perfects* baptismal grace, *binds* the baptized *more perfectly* to the Church, *enriches* them with a *special strength* through a *full outpouring* of the Holy Spirit, *intensifies* their missional obligation while *amplifying* the Spirit's gifts, *deepens* the roots of sonship, *unites more firmly* to Christ. The quantitative nature of grace, and its elevation of (human) nature through Confirmation, is evident.[97]

This nature-grace interdependence has already been critiqued; thus, the grounding for this sacrament is lacking. Another specific criticism focuses on the notion that grace is infused into the baptized and the confirmands,

---

[97] CCC 1285, 1294, 1302, 1303, 1316 (emphasis added).

thereby changing their nature for the journey toward perfection in love. Rather, grace is *imputed* to people, credited to their account, such that they stand perfect, clothed in the righteousness of Jesus Christ, before God. Accordingly, descriptors of a sacrament that augments a divine substance or power make no sense. If the faithful are united to Christ—identified with his death, burial, and resurrection (Rom. 6:3–5)—how can they be *more united* to him? If the faithful have been adopted as sons and daughters into the family of God, how can they be *more adopted*? If the faithful have been made members of the body of Christ, how can they become *more membered*? If the faithful have been baptized by Jesus with the gift of the Holy Spirit (John 1:33; 1 Cor. 12:13), how can they be *more gifted* with him? These questions are at the heart of evangelical theology's concern that grace viewed as a divine substance or power that is infused into the faithful so as to elevate their nature is a very problematic concept.

Evangelical theology encounters other problems with this Catholic sacrament, most important of which is its weak biblical basis.[98] Certainly, the anointing of the Messiah, Jesus of Nazareth, by the Holy Spirit is well attested by Scripture. So too is Christ's prophecy of the outpouring of the Spirit on Christ's disciples in a fresh, new, and unprecedented manner, a promise that was fulfilled on the day of Pentecost. But Scripture underscores that the gift of the Holy Spirit is received at conversion, conferred by Jesus himself. Evidence for this includes the following: John the Baptist explained that the Messiah would baptize people with the Holy Spirit (Luke 3:15–17); indeed, John identified Jesus as "he who baptizes with the Holy Spirit" (John 1:33). On the day of Pentecost, together with the Father, Christ poured out the Spirit on his followers (Acts 2:1–4, 33), and this same gift was received by the three thousand people who heard Peter's message (v. 38). The apostle Paul further explains that this baptism with the Spirit—which is true of all Christians, because it is an initial experience accompanying the other mighty acts of God in saving people—incorporates them into Christ's body, the church (1 Cor. 12:13). Accordingly, all Christians have been baptized with the Spirit as part of their conversion. The fact that successive and multiple fillings of the Spirit (e.g., Acts 4:8, 31; 13:9) take place and should be desired for empowerment for ministry

---

[98] For more on the following discussion, see Gregg R. Allison, "Baptism of and Filling with the Holy Spirit," *Southern Baptist Journal of Theology* (Winter 2012): 4–20.

should not detract from the reality that all Christ-followers have been endowed with the Spirit from the beginning of their Christian journey. And that Christians are commanded to be filled with the Spirit, guided and dominated by him as a way of life (Eph. 5:18), should not diminish the fact that the gift of the Holy Spirit has been conferred when they embraced the gospel of Jesus Christ.

Accordingly, evangelical theology wonders about the biblical basis for Catholic theology's affirmation that, following the outpouring of the Spirit on the day of Pentecost, "the apostles . . . imparted to the newly baptized by the laying on of hands the gift of the Spirit that completes the grace of Baptism."[99] This notion depends on the Christ-Church interconnection that places the Catholic Church in the role of mediator. A critique of this overarching axiom has already been offered (ch. 2). In terms of other criticisms, the idea that the apostles imparted the Holy Spirit through the laying on of hands is grounded on two unusual events narrated in Acts that somehow (and wrongly) become paradigmatic for the Catholic Church. The first instance followed the conversion of the Samaritans: "Now when the apostles at Jerusalem heard that Samaria had received the word of God, they sent to them Peter and John, who came down and prayed for them that they might receive the Holy Spirit, for he had not yet fallen on any of them, but they had only been baptized in the name of the Lord Jesus. Then *they laid their hands on them and they received the Holy Spirit*" (Acts 8:14–17, emphasis added). The theology[100] that has developed out of this passage is sadly the result of a poor interpretation. Verse 16 is key, because it explains (the first word is "for" or "because") the delay of the Samaritan's reception of the Holy Spirit. An explanation is needed only in cases in which something unusual has taken place. Accordingly, when Luke offers a reason for Peter and John's action of laying their hands on the Samaritan Christians, he underscores not some normal event but an abnormal occurrence. The apostles' conferring of the Holy Spirit through the laying on of hands on baptized Christians is highlighted as an uncommon, not a common, experience; thus, it cannot serve as paradigmatic for the church today.

---

[99] CCC 1288.
[100] In some circles this is called the *doctrine of subsequence*: the Holy Spirit baptizes Christians at some point *subsequent to* their conversion.

The second instance took place when Paul encountered some disciples of John the Baptist:

> And he said to them, "Did you receive the Holy Spirit when you believed?" And they said, "No, we have not even heard that there is a Holy Spirit." And he said, "Into what then were you baptized?" They said, "Into John's baptism." And Paul said, "John baptized with the baptism of repentance, telling the people to believe in the one who was to come after him, that is, Jesus." On hearing this, they were baptized in the name of the Lord Jesus. And when *Paul had laid his hands on them*, the Holy Spirit came on them, and they began speaking in tongues and prophesying. There were about twelve men in all. (Acts 19:2–7, emphasis added)

Key to a proper interpretation of this passage is Paul's opening question (v. 2), which arose from what the apostle must have detected to be a lack or shortcoming in these disciples of John the Baptist: "Did you receive the Holy Spirit when you believed?" Their negative reply underscored the fact that these men were not even Christians, so how could they have received the Spirit? Accordingly, Paul's inquiry represents the normal Christian experience: when one believes in Jesus Christ, one receives the Holy Spirit, a pattern that is confirmed in the preceding examples of conversion in the book of Acts. Thus, this episode is highlighted as an uncommon, not a common, event; it cannot serve as paradigmatic for the church today.

As for the apostles' laying on of hands for the reception of the Spirit (and, to be more precise, following baptism), though in both of the above passages this was the case, they are the only two accounts in which this model is found. This means that no definitive pattern can be established from the Acts narratives. Indeed, one story clearly belies the notion of an established pattern—the conversion of Cornelius, his family, and his friends:

> While Peter was still saying these things [the details of the gospel; Acts 10:34–43], the Holy Spirit fell on all who heard the word. And the believers from among the circumcised who had come with Peter were amazed, because the gift of the Holy Spirit was poured out even on the Gentiles. For they were hearing them speaking in tongues and extolling God. Then Peter declared, "Can anyone withhold water for baptizing these people, who have received the Holy Spirit just as we have?"

> And he commanded them to be baptized in the name of Jesus Christ.
> (Acts 10:44–48)

In this conversion story, the Holy Spirit falls upon the Gentiles as they are listening to Peter's announcement of the gospel, so no laying on of hands for the reception of the Spirit occurred here. And the coming of the Spirit upon these Gentiles preceded their baptism with water.

To summarize, the Acts accounts of the laying on of hands by the apostles for the purpose of conferring the gift of the Holy Spirit upon new believers after their baptism demonstrate no established pattern that would make these events in this order a formula for the normal Christian initiation process. Yet the Catholic sacrament of Confirmation appeals to Acts as support for the normal pattern of receiving the Holy Spirit through the laying on of hands by the Church at some time after Baptism.

The further development of this sacrament, in which an anointing with consecrated oil was added to the laying on of hands, has no biblical basis either. Certainly, Jesus baptizes Christians with the Holy Spirit, who is described in Scripture as the seal of their redemption (Eph. 1:13–14; 4:30), marking them out as belonging to God with the Spirit as the firstfruits (Rom. 8:23) or down payment (2 Cor. 1:22; 5:5), the guarantee that they will one day experience the fullness of salvation when Christ returns (1 Pet. 1:5). Furthermore, Scripture commonly employs "oil" to portray consecration to God and his service/mercy (e.g., Lev. 8:12; 1 Sam. 16:13; James 5:14). However, though in Scripture there are several tangible metaphors for the Holy Spirit—wind, water, fire, dove—his presence or ministry is never represented by oil.[101] Moreover, the varieties of evangelical theology that affirm the perseverance of genuine Christians in salvation find a disconnect between, on the one hand, Catholic theology's affirmation that this sacrament imparts an indelible mark on the faithful and, on the other hand, its denial that the faithful will necessarily persist in salvation all the way to its consummation. Crassly put, what good is an indelible mark—the sign of the Spirit who pledges the fullness of salvation—if the guarantee can be broken?

In summary, evangelical theology does not consider confirmation to

---

[101] The one biblical passage in which anointing with oil is found in conjunction with the Holy Spirit is 1 Sam. 16:12–13, but in this case the act of anointing is symbolic of David's kingship (in accordance with 1 Sam. 9:16, 10:1; 16:1, 3; cf. 1 Kings 1:39; 2 Kings 9:1, 3, 6), not the conferral of the Spirit.

be a sacrament. Even evangelical denominations that administer the rite of confirmation agree that it is not a sacrament, in the sense of conferring grace. Rather, confirmation is a public profession of the faith into which confirmands were introduced at their baptism. They acknowledge before the church the work of divine grace, which they now intentionally accept by faith.

9

The Celebration of the Christian Mystery
(Part 2, Section 2, Chapter I, Article 3)

The Eucharist

The Sacrament of the Eucharist (Sec. 2, Ch. I, Art. 3)

The third sacrament of Christian initiation, and the one that completes commencement in the faith, is the Eucharist. Superlatives abound in its description: The Eucharist is "the source and summit of the Christian life" toward which the other six sacraments, not to mention all of the Church's ministry and mission, are oriented.[1] The "whole spiritual good of the Church, namely Christ himself," is contained in the Eucharist,[2] which is also "the efficacious sign and sublime cause of that communion in the divine life and that unity of the People of God by which the Church is kept in being."[3] In this sacrament is reached the culmination of the divine work of salvation and the human work of worshiping the triune God, an earthly liturgy that is united with the heavenly liturgy by its celebration in anticipation of eternal life.

This sacrament is known by various names, reflective of its various aspects. It is called the *Eucharist* from the Greek words εὐχαριστειν (*eucharistein*; Luke 22:19; 1 Cor. 11:24) and εὐλογειν (*eulogein*; Matt. 26:26; Mark 14:22) used to narrate Jesus's giving of thanks to the Father during his Last Supper. The words also recall the Jewish blessings for the divine works of creation, salvation, and sanctification. It is called the *Lord's Supper* because

---

[1] CCC 1324; citation is from Vatican Council II, *Lumen Gentium* 11.
[2] CCC 1324; citation is from Vatican Council II, *Presbyterorum ordinis* 5; cf . *Eucharisticum mysterium* 6 (VC II-1, 106.
[3] CCC 1325; citation is from the Sacred Congregation of Rites, instruction on Eucharistic worship, *Eucharisticum mysterium* 6 (VC II-1, 106, with this rendering: "The Eucharist both perfectly signifies and wonderfully effects that sharing in God's life and unity of God's people by which the Church exists").

of its association with Jesus's Last Supper (1 Cor. 11:20) and because of its anticipation of the wedding feast of the Lamb in the New Jerusalem (Rev. 19:9). Another name is the *Breaking of Bread* because of Jesus's action with the loaves as he fed the five thousand (Matt. 14:19) and the four thousand (Matt. 15:36), his action with the unleavened bread during his Last Supper (Matt. 26:26; 1 Cor. 11:24), and his action during a resurrection appearance by which he made himself known to two disciples (Luke 24:30–31). The phrase was also used by the first Christians "to designate their Eucharistic assemblies" (Acts 2:42, 46; 20:7, 11).[4] The breaking of bread "signified that all who eat the one broken bread, Christ, enter into communion with him and form but one body in him" (1 Cor. 10:16–17).[5]

This sacrament is further called the *Eucharistic assembly* (*synaxis*) because it is celebrated during a gathering of the faithful. It is a *memorial* of Christ's death and resurrection. Furthermore, "because it makes present the one sacrifice of Christ the Savior and includes the Church's offering," it is called the *Holy Sacrifice*; other similar terms—"*holy sacrifice of the Mass, 'sacrifice of praise,' spiritual sacrifice, pure and holy sacrifice*"—emphasize that "it completes and surpasses all the sacrifices of the Old Covenant."[6] The names *Holy and Divine Liturgy* and *Sacred Mysteries* underscore its central and powerful role in the Church's worship; the *Most Blessed Sacrament*—the name used especially for the species preserved in the tabernacle—accentuates that it is the Sacrament of sacraments.[7] It is called *Holy Communion* because it unites the faithful to Christ, in whose body and blood they share so as to form one body (1 Cor. 10:16–17). Other names include *the holy things, the bread of angels, bread from heaven, medicine of immortality*,[8] and *viaticum*. Finally, the sacrament is referred to as *Holy Mass* (Lat., *Missa*) because the last element in the liturgy is the sending forth (*missio*) of the faithful.[9]

The *Catechism* explores the biblical forerunners of the Eucharist by focusing on the signs of the sacrament—the bread and wine: "At the heart of the Eucharistic celebration are the bread and wine that, by the words

---

[4] CCC 1329.
[5] Ibid.
[6] CCC 1330.
[7] Ibid.
[8] CCC 1331. The phrase "medicine of immortality" goes back to Ignatius in his *Letter to the Ephesians* 20 (*ANF* 1:57).
[9] CCC 1332.

of Christ and the invocation of the Holy Spirit, become Christ's Body and Blood."[10] At the Last Supper, as he instituted the Lord's Supper, Jesus himself took both bread and a cup of wine; these elements "become, in a way surpassing understanding, the Body and Blood of Christ; they continue also to signify the goodness of creation."[11] Because of this symbolism, during the Offertory—the liturgical moment in which the bread and the wine are presented to God before their consecration, accompanied by prayers and singing—thanks is given to God, who is the creator of the bread and wine, "fruit of the 'work of human hands,' but above all as 'fruit of the earth' and 'of the vine.'"[12] The Church's offering is prefigured in the Old Testament by the action of Melchizedek, who "brought out bread and wine" (Gen. 14:18). Other Old Testament prefigurations include the unleavened bread of the exodus, the manna in the wilderness, and the cup of blessing at the conclusion of the Jewish Passover.

As for New Testament prefigurations, Jesus's multiplication of the loaves of bread at the feeding of the five thousand (Matt. 14:19) and the four thousand (Matt. 15:36), and his miracle of turning the water into wine at the marriage in Cana (John 2:11), were harbingers of the Eucharistic elements. Jesus's "Bread of Life" discourse in John's Gospel (6:25–71) is considered to be "[t]he first announcement of the Eucharist," with this important explanation: Just as Jesus's announcement of the Eucharist divided the disciples, so also his announcement of his impending Passion scandalized them; accordingly, both "[t]he Eucharist and the Cross are stumbling blocks. It is the same mystery and it never ceases to be an occasion of division."[13] Moreover, "to receive in faith the gift of his Eucharist is to receive the Lord himself."[14]

As recounted in the Synoptic Gospels and in Paul's First Letter to the Corinthians, Jesus inaugurated the Eucharist during his Last Supper with his disciples, a Passover feast that they as Jews celebrated annually. Importantly, "he instituted the Eucharist as the memorial of his death and Resurrection, and commanded his disciples to celebrate it until his return; 'thereby he constituted them priests of the New Testament.'"[15] His

---

[10] CCC 1333.
[11] Ibid.
[12] Ibid.
[13] CCC 1336.
[14] Ibid.
[15] CCC 1337; citation is from the *Canons and Decrees of the Council of Trent*, 22nd session (September 17, 1562), *Decree concerning the Most Holy Sacrifice of the Mass* 1 (Schaff, 2:177).

command, "do this in memory of me," does not only have reference to remembering him and his work. "It is directed at the liturgical celebration . . . of the *memorial* of Christ, of his life, of his death, of his Resurrection, and of his intercession in the presence of the Father."[16] Accordingly, it is not just a *subjective* experience—the *memory* of Christ—but an *objective* celebration—the *memorial* of Christ, as observed by the Church from its very outset (Acts 2:42, 46). Historical accounts of the early church's celebration of the Eucharist begin with Justin Martyr's *First Apology* (c. 155), in which he outlines the basic contours of the Eucharistic celebration: readings from the Word of God, preaching, prayers, the sign of peace, the offering of thanksgiving to God for "bread and a cup of water and wine mixed together," a community acclamation of "Amen," and the distribution of "the 'eucharisted' bread, wine and water" by the deacons to all those present and those who are absent.[17]

* * *

Excursus: The Contemporary Celebration of the Sacrament of the Eucharist

Today, the sacrament of the Eucharist is structured with "two great parts that form a fundamental unity . . . 'one single act of worship'":[18] the Liturgy of the Word and the Liturgy of the Eucharist. Accordingly, "the Eucharistic table set for us is the table both of the Word of God and the Body of the Lord."[19] Both of these main parts, with their corresponding elements, are presented in detail in the following paragraphs.

Before the celebration begins, the faithful *all gather together* in the Eucharistic assembly. Jesus Christ himself is its head, high priest, and presider. *In the person of Christ the head (in persona Christi capitis)* presides the bishop or his delegated representative, a priest, who also presents the homily after the readings, receives the offerings of the bread and wine, and prays the Eucharistic Prayer. Others who gather and who play crucial roles are the readers, those who bring the offerings forward,

---

[16] CCC 1341 (emphasis added).
[17] CCC 1345; citations are from Justin Martyr, *First Apology* 65–67 (ANF 1:185).
[18] CCC 1346; citation is from Vatican Council II, *Sacrosanctum concilium* 56.
[19] CCC 1346.

those who serve Communion, and the faithful who participate by their "Amen."

The *Liturgy of the Word* features three *readings*: one from the Old Testament, one from the New Testament (other than the Gospels), and one from the Gospels. These readings are followed by a *homily*, which is an exhortation to accept and live out the Word of God, and *intercessions* for all people (in accordance with 1 Tim. 2:1–2).

The *Liturgy of the Eucharist*[20] begins with the *Offertory*, or the procession to the altar and the presentation of the bread and wine; these elements will later be consecrated for the Eucharistic sacrifice. Gifts to share with those in need, the *collection*, accompany this offering of bread and wine (1 Cor. 16:1; 2 Cor. 8:9). The "heart and summit of the celebration" is reached with the *anaphora*.[21] The *preface* features thanksgiving to God for his work of creation, redemption, and sanctification. "In the *epiclesis*, the Church asks the Father to send his Holy Spirit" to transform the bread and wine to become the body and blood of Christ.[22] Specifically, the priest requests, "Be pleased, O God, we pray, to bless, acknowledge, and approve this offering in every respect; make it spiritual and acceptable, so that it may become for us the Body and Blood of your most beloved Son, our Lord Jesus Christ."[23] Next comes the recitation of the *institution narrative*, the words of Jesus during his Last Supper as he instituted the Lord's Supper (Matt. 26:26–29; Mark 14:22–25; Luke 22:19–20). By the power of these words, the action of Christ, and the power of the Holy Spirit, Christ's body and blood are made "sacramentally present under the species of bread and wine."[24] As the priest recites, "On the day before he [Jesus] was to suffer," he elevates the bread slightly above the altar, then continues, "he took bread in his holy and venerable hands [the priest raises his eyes] and with eyes raised to heaven to you, O God, his almighty Father, giving you thanks he said the blessing, broke the bread, and gave it to the disciples, saying [the priest bows

---

[20] The following discussion is adapted from my chapter "The Theology of the Eucharist according to the Catholic Church," in Thomas R. Schreiner and Matthew R. Crawford, eds., *The Lord's Supper: Remembering and Proclaiming Christ until He Comes*, NAC Studies in Bible and Theology (Nashville: B & H Academic, 2010), 152–155.

[21] CCC 1352. *Anaphora* is, literally, "carrying up"; thus, this part of the celebration is an offering to God.

[22] CCC 1353. *Epiclesis* is, literally, "calling upon"; thus, this part of the celebration is an invocation to God.

[23] Roman Missal, Eucharistic Prayer 1 (Roman Canon) (International Commission on English in the Liturgy [hereafter ICEL], 88). This commission, composed of bishops from countries in which the mass (according to the Roman Rite) is celebrated in English, prepares English translations of Latin liturgical books and texts. For more discussion, see: http//www.icelweb.org/.

[24] CCC 1353.

slightly], 'Take this, all of you, and eat of it, for this is my body, which will be given up for you.'" Displaying the consecrated host (the wafer) to the faithful, the priest places it on the paten (the tray), and genuflects (bends one knee) in adoration.[25] As he next announces, "In a similar way, when supper was ended," the priest elevates the cup slightly above the altar and continues, "he took this precious chalice in his holy and venerable hands, and once more giving you thanks, he said the blessing and gave the chalice to his disciples, saying [the priest bows slightly], 'Take this, all of you, and drink from it, for this is the chalice of my blood, the blood of the new and eternal covenant, which will be poured out for you and for many for the forgiveness of sins. Do this in memory of me." Displaying the chalice to the faithful, the priest places it on the corporal (the linen cloth covering the altar), and genuflects (bends one knee) in adoration.[26] He then says, "The mystery of the faith."[27]

The *anaphora* just recounted is followed by the *anamnesis*[28] and offering, in which "the Church calls to mind the Passion, resurrection, and glorious return of Christ Jesus; she presents to the Father the offering of his Son which reconciles us with him."[29] The priest prays, "Therefore, O Lord, as we celebrate the memorial of the blessed Passion, the Resurrection from the dead, and the glorious Ascension into heaven of Christ, your Son, our Lord, we, your servants and your holy people, offer to your glorious majesty from the gifts that you have given us, this pure victim, this holy victim, this spotless victim, the holy Bread of eternal life and the Chalice of everlasting salvation."[30] The intercessions that come next underscore that "the Eucharist is celebrated in communion with the whole Church in heaven and on earth."[31] The priest leads the faithful in the recitation of the Lord's Prayer, after which they exchange the sign of peace. The priest then takes the host, breaks it, and places a small amount in the cup, saying, "May this mingling of the Body and Blood of our Lord Jesus Christ bring eternal life to us who receive it."[32] The congregation prays, "Lamb of God, you take away the sins

---

[25] Roman Missal, Eucharistic Prayer 1 (Roman Canon) (ICEL, 89).
[26] Ibid., 90.
[27] Ibid., 91.
[28] *Anamnesis* is, literally, "remembering"; thus, this part of the celebration is the remembrance of Christ's suffering, death, resurrection, and ascension.
[29] CCC 1354.
[30] Roman Missal, Eucharistic Prayer 1 (Roman Canon) (ICEL, 92).
[31] CCC 1354.
[32] Roman Missal, Eucharistic Prayer 1 (Roman Canon) (ICEL, 129).

of the world, have mercy on us. Lamb of God, you take away the sins of the world, have mercy on us. Lamb of God, you take away the sins of the world, grant us peace."[33] Genuflecting, the priest displays the host as he elevates it slightly above the paten (or above the chalice) and announces, "Behold, the Lamb of God, behold him who takes away the sins of the world. Blessed are those called to the supper of the Lamb." The priest and the faithful together pray, "Lord, I am not worthy that you should enter under my roof, but only say the word and my soul shall be healed."[34] As he faces the altar, the priest says, "May the Body of Christ keep me safe for eternal life," then he consumes the Body of Christ. Similarly, he takes the chalice and prays, "May the Blood of Christ keep me safe for eternal life," then he consumes the Blood of Christ.[35] He then offers the host to the faithful, saying, "the Body of Christ," before he gives it to them. Similarly, the chalice is offered, preceded by the saying, "the Blood of Christ."[36]

To conclude the Liturgy, the priest announces, "Go forth, the Mass is ended" (Lat., *Ite, missa est*). As noted earlier, the word *missa* is the reason that the Liturgy is called *the mass*, as it implies "mission" (Lat., *missio*). The faithful, nourished by the Word of God and the Body and Blood of Christ during the celebration of the mass, are sent off to embark on their mission in this world.

• • •

Several key themes course through the celebration of the Eucharist: memorial, sacrifice, offering, and presence. Indeed, this sacrament celebrates the "*memorial of his* [Christ's] *sacrifice*," with its participants *offering* to the Father his creational gifts of bread and wine that, "by the power of the Holy Spirit and by the words of Christ, have become the body and blood of Christ. Christ is thus really and mysteriously made *present*."[37] Within this trinitarian structure, the Eucharist must be considered as three realities: thanksgiving (to the Father), sacrifice (of the Son), and presence (by the word and the Spirit).[38]

---

[33] Ibid., 130. The reference to Jesus as the Lamb of God recalls John the Baptist's words (John 1:29; cf. v. 36).
[34] Ibid., 132. The profession of unworthiness echoes the centurion's humility before Jesus (Matt. 8:8).
[35] Ibid., 133.
[36] Ibid., 134.
[37] CCC 1357 (emphasis original).
[38] Much of the following discussion is adapted from my chapter (cited above), "Theology of the Eucharist according to the Catholic Church," 158–164.

As for the first reality, and in keeping with the sense of the Greek word, "[t]he Eucharist is a sacrifice of thanksgiving and praise to the Father . . . for all that he has accomplished through creation, redemption, and sanctification."[39]

In terms of the second reality, and in keeping with the sense of the word *anamnesis*, "[t]he Eucharist is the memorial of Christ's Passover, the making present and the sacramental offering of his unique sacrifice."[40] As noted earlier, this reality is not just the subjective "recollection of past events" or *memory of Christ*; rather, it is an objective *memorial of Christ* and his sacrifice, which "is made present: the sacrifice of Christ offered once for all on the cross remains ever present" by means of sharing in the atemporality or eternality of the divine nature.[41] Because the Eucharistic celebration is a memorial, Christ's death is not just to be remembered, but is re-presented in the liturgy. Accordingly, it is a memorial of his sacrifice; thus, the Eucharist itself is a sacrifice. This idea is confirmed by Jesus's words of institution, understood literally: "This is my body which is given for you" and "This cup which is poured out for you is the New Covenant in my blood."[42] Indeed, "[i]n the Eucharist Christ gives us the very body which he gave up for us on the cross, the very blood which he 'poured out for many for the forgiveness of sins.'"[43] Specifically, it is "a sacrifice because it *re-presents* (makes present) the sacrifice of the cross, because it is its memorial, and because it applies its fruit."[44] In this explanation, there is no note of the repetition of Christ's death on the cross over and over again. On the contrary,

> The sacrifice of Christ and the sacrifice of the Eucharist are *one single sacrifice*: "The victim is one and the same: the same now offers through the ministry of priests, who then offered himself on the cross; only the manner of offering is different." "In this divine sacrifice which is celebrated in the Mass, the same Christ who offered himself once in a bloody manner on the altar of the cross is contained and is offered in an unbloody manner."[45]

The once-and-for-all atoning sacrifice of Christ on the cross of Calvary nearly two thousand years ago is not time-bound to that moment but is

---

[39] CCC 1360.
[40] CCC 1362.
[41] CCC 1363, 1364.
[42] CCC 1365; citations are from Luke 22:19–20.
[43] CCC 1365; citation is from Matt. 26:28.
[44] CCC 1366.
[45] CCC 1367 (emphasis added); citations are from the *Canons and Decrees of the Council of Trent*, 22nd session (September 17, 1562), *Decree concerning the Most Holy Sacrifice of the Mass* 2 (Schaff, 2:179); cf. Heb. 9:14, 27.

re-presented, or made present, when the priest celebrates the Liturgy of the Eucharist.

This sacrificial reality of the Eucharist is not limited to Christ's sacrificial work but also includes the sacrifice of the Church as it participates in Christ's offering: "With him, she [the Church] herself is offered whole and entire. She unites herself to his intercession with the Father for all men. In the Eucharist the sacrifice of Christ becomes also the sacrifice of the members of his Body."[46] Indeed, with every Eucharistic celebration is associated the pope, the local bishop, the priest who presides in the bishop's place, the deacons, all the living faithful, as well as the Virgin Mary and all the saints who are in heaven. This point is powerfully portrayed during the celebration as the priest's hands offer the Eucharist "in the name of the whole Church in an unbloody and sacramental manner."[47] "The Eucharistic sacrifice is also offered for the faithful departed who 'have died with Christ but are not yet wholly purified,' so that they may be able to enter into the light and peace of Christ."[48]

In addition to thanksgiving and sacrifice, the third Eucharistic reality is "the presence of Christ by the power of his word and his Spirit."[49] Acknowledging that Christ "is present in many ways to his Church"—e.g., in the Word of God and when it prays—the *Catechism* emphasizes that "he is present . . . most especially in the Eucharistic species" of the consecrated bread and chalice.[50] This is so because the mode of Christ's presence in this sacrament is unique: "[T]he body and blood, together with the soul and divinity, of our Lord Jesus Christ and, therefore, the whole Christ is truly, really, and substantially contained."[51] The adverbs used in this affirmation are significant: "This presence is called 'real' . . . because it is presence in the fullest sense: that is to say, it is a *substantial* presence by which Christ, God and man, makes himself wholly and entirely present."[52]

This unique Eucharistic presence of Christ occurs by means of *transubstantiation*. From two Latin words—*trans* (change) and *substantia*

[46] CCC 1368.
[47] CCC 1369; citation is from Vatican Council II, *Presbyterorum ordinis* 2.4.
[48] CCC 1371; citation is from the *Canons and Decrees of the Council of Trent*, 22nd session (September 17, 1562), *Doctrine on the Sacrifice of the Mass* 2 (Schaff, 2:180).
[49] CCC 1358.
[50] CCC 1373; citation is from Vatican Council II, *Sacrosanctum concilium* 7.
[51] CCC 1374 (emphasis removed); citation is from the *Canons and Decrees of the Council of Trent*, 13th session (October 11, 1551), *Decree Concerning the Most Holy Sacrament of the Eucharist* 1 (Schaff, 2:126).
[52] CCC 1374; citation is from Pope Paul VI, *Mysterium fidei* (September 3, 1965), 39. Accessible at http://www.vatican.va/holy_father/paul_vi/encyclicals/documents/hf_p-vi_enc_03091965_mysterium_en.html.

(substance or nature; that which makes something what it is)—transubstantiation is the change of the substance of the consecrated bread into the body of Christ, and the change of the substance of the consecrated wine into the blood of Christ. "It is by the conversion of the bread and wine into Christ's body and blood that Christ becomes present in this sacrament."[53] The *Catechism* notes that both Tradition—e.g., John Chrysostom and Ambrose[54]—and Scripture affirm transubstantiation. Significantly, the Council of Trent, appealing to Christ's words of institution, "summarizes the Catholic faith by declaring,"

> Because Christ our Redeemer said that it was truly his body that he was offering under the species of bread, it has always been the conviction of the Church of God . . . that by the consecration of the bread and wine there takes place a change of the whole substance of the bread into the substance of the body of Christ our Lord and of the whole substance of the wine into the substance of his blood. This change the holy Catholic Church has fittingly and properly called transubstantiation.[55]

The *Catechism* makes three more important points regarding transubstantiation. The first concerns *the timing and nature of this change*: "The Eucharistic presence of Christ begins at the moment of the consecration and endures as long as the Eucharistic species subsist."[56] As explained earlier, this change is effected when the priest engages in the *epiclesis* and recites the narrative of Christ's institution of the sacrament, and the presence of Christ effected by this change is continuous rather than momentary.[57] Furthermore, "Christ is present whole and entire in each of the species and whole and entire in each of their parts, in such a way that the breaking of bread does not divide Christ."[58] In other words, Christ, the God-man, is present neither in his divine nature alone, nor in his human nature alone, but in the totality of both his divine and human natures. Additionally, in the totality of both his divine and human natures, Christ is present in the

---

[53] CCC 1375.
[54] CCC 1376. John Chrysostom, *De Prod. Jud.* 1:6; Ambrose, *On the Mysteries* 9.50, 52 (*NPNF*[2] 10:324).
[55] CCC 1376; citation is from the *Canons and Decrees of the Council of Trent*, 13th session (October, 11, 1551), *Decree Concerning the Most Holy Sacrament of the Eucharist* 4 (Schaff, 2:130).
[56] CCC 1377.
[57] "For in the sacrifice of the Mass our Lord is immolated [sacrificed] when 'he begins to be present sacramentally as the spiritual food of the faithful under the appearance of bread and wine'" (Pope Paul VI, *Eucharisticum Mysterium*, 3b [VC II-1, 102–103]); citation is from Pope Paul VI, *Mysterium fidei* 34.
[58] CCC 1377.

bread and in each of its grains and, in the totality of both his divine and human natures, he is present in the wine and in each of its drops. Accordingly, the faithful participating in the Eucharist do not receive more or less of Christ if they take Communion in "one kind"—that is, they receive the consecrated wafer only and not the wine—or if they take Communion in two kinds—that is, they receive both the consecrated wafer and the wine. By their participation in the Eucharistic celebration, they receive all of Christ. Finally, if some consecrated species remain after the sacrament has been distributed, Christ remains present.

This continuous presence of Christ in the remaining elements prompts *ongoing worship*, which is the *Catechism*'s second important point concerning transubstantiation: "The Catholic Church has always offered and still offers to the sacrament of the Eucharist the cult of adoration [worship], not only during the Mass, but also outside of it, reserving the consecrated hosts with the utmost care, exposing them to the solemn veneration of the faithful, and carrying them in procession."[59] In practice, then, any consecrated wafers remaining after the distribution of the sacrament during the mass are housed in the tabernacle—a sacred container consecrated for holding the Eucharistic elements and "located in an especially worthy place in the church"—and reserved for two purposes: distribution to the sick (*viaticum*) and silent adoration by the faithful who gather at the tabernacle.[60]

The third point regarding transubstantiation is its *comprehension*. With appeal to Thomas Aquinas, the *Catechism* affirms, "That in this sacrament are the true Body of Christ and his true Blood is something that 'cannot be apprehended by the senses,' says St. Thomas, 'but *only by faith*, which relies on divine authority.'"[61]

In summary, Catholic theology views the presence of Jesus Christ in the sacrament of the Eucharist in terms of transubstantiation, a doctrine denied by evangelical theology.

As for participants in the sacrament of the Eucharist, the *Catechism* affirms that all the faithful are invited to come—by Christ himself: "Truly, truly, I say to you, unless you eat the flesh of the Son of man and drink his blood, you have no life in you" (John 6:53). Those who respond to Christ's

---

[59] CCC 1378; citation is from Pope Paul VI, *Mysterium fidei* 56.
[60] CCC 1379. Eventually, these stored hosts will be consumed.
[61] CCC 1381; citation is from Thomas Aquinas, *Summa Theologica* pt. 3, q. 75, art. 1.

call must prepare themselves for the celebration, meaning that "[a]nyone conscious of a grave sin must receive the sacrament of Reconciliation before coming to communion."[62] By means of this sacrament (to be discussed later), the faithful who have committed mortal sin, and thus have lost divine grace, confess to a priest, who absolves them of their sin, enabling them once again to participate in the sacrament of the Eucharist. For all the faithful who are in a proper state of grace, participation in the Eucharist is urged each time they attend mass. Indeed, the *Catechism* speaks of obligation: "The Church obliges the faithful 'to take part in the Divine Liturgy on Sundays and feast days' and, prepared by the sacrament of Reconciliation, to receive the Eucharist at least once a year, if possible during the Easter season.'"[63] A daily rhythm of participating in the Eucharist is encouraged.[64]

Participation in this sacrament provides many benefits for the faithful. It *augments union with Christ*; specifically, such union "preserves, increases, and renews the life of grace received at Baptism. This growth in Christian life needs the nourishment of Eucharistic Communion."[65] The sacrament also *separates the faithful from sin*, with two specific values: it cleanses from past sins and preserves from future sins. With respect to the first value, "[t]he Eucharist is not ordered to the forgiveness of mortal sins [grave sins by which grace is lost]—that is proper to the sacrament of Reconciliation. The Eucharist is properly the sacrament of those who are in full communion with the Church."[66] As such, "the Eucharist strengthens our charity . . . and this living charity wipes away venial sins [less grievous sins by which grace is wounded but not lost]."[67] With respect to the second value, "[b]y the same charity that it kindles in us, the Eucharist preserves us from future mortal sins."[68] An additional benefit is that "the Eucharist *makes the Church*," because by it the faithful are more united to Christ and thus united in one body.[69] As a final benefit, the sacrament *commits the Church to the poor*, as it recognizes Christ in them.[70] Importantly, the

---

[62] CCC 1385. Biblical warrant is given as Paul's instructions to avoid eating the bread or drinking the cup "in an unworthy manner" (1 Cor. 11:27–29).
[63] CCC 1389; citation is from Vatican Council II, *Orientalium ecclesiarum* 15, and canon 920 of the Code of Canon Law.
[64] CCC 1389.
[65] CCC 1392.
[66] CCC 1395.
[67] CCC 1394 (emphasis removed).
[68] CCC 1395 (emphasis removed).
[69] CCC 1396.
[70] CCC 1397.

degree of fruitfulness of these benefits for the faithful depends on the life and attitude of those participating: "Like the passion of Christ itself, this sacrifice, though offered for all, 'has no effect except in those united to the passion of Christ by faith and charity. . . . To these things it brings a greater or lesser benefit in proportion to their devotion.'"[71]

The *Catechism* concludes its presentation of the sacrament of the Eucharist with a somber reflection on the present state of its celebration and an expression of hope for how it will be celebrated in the age to come. As for its reflection, the *Catechism* laments the present state of "the divisions in the Church which break the common participation in the table of the Lord."[72] This pain is expressed with regard to the Orthodox churches "that are not in full communion with the Catholic Church," yet which possess the true Eucharistic sacrament and celebrate it with love.[73] More grief is expressed over Protestant ecclesial communities; these "have not preserved the proper reality of the Eucharistic mystery in its fullness, especially because of the absence of the sacrament of Holy Orders," which is necessary for apostolic succession and the proper administration of the sacraments, including the Eucharist. Accordingly, "Eucharistic intercommunion with these communities is not possible for the Catholic Church."[74] This ruling means that Protestants/evangelicals are prohibited from taking the Eucharistic elements at a Catholic mass.[75]

As for its hope, the *Catechism* cherishes the Eucharist as "an anticipation of heavenly glory" in which the Church will participate when Christ returns and celebrates the sacrament in the Father's kingdom that he (Christ) will establish (Matt. 26:29; cf. Luke 22:18; Mark 14:25). Then, and only then, the Lord who "comes even now in his Eucharist," who is there in the Church's midst, will be present, no longer in a "veiled" manner but in his full glory, for the faithful to see face-to-face. In the meantime, the Church celebrates the Eucharist in hope, praying "Marana tha!" ("Come, Lord Jesus!") and nourishing the faithful on "the food that makes us live for ever in Jesus Christ."[76]

---

[71] Pope Paul VI, *Eucharisticum Mysterium* 12 (VC II-1, 111); citation is from Thomas Aquinas, *Summa Theologica* pt. 3, q. 79, art. 7.

[72] CCC 1398.

[73] CCC 1399.

[74] CCC 1400; citation is from Vatican Council II, *Unitatis redintegratio* 22.3.

[75] A provision for exception is made: In a situation of grave necessity—e.g., imminent danger or death—Catholic ministers are permitted to administer the sacraments of the Eucharist, Penance, and the Anointing of the Sick to Christians who are not in full communion with the Catholic Church, with several qualifications: These Christians must willingly request the sacraments, they must give evidence that they accept the Catholic theology of these sacraments, and they must be rightly disposed in life and attitude to receive them (CCC 1401).

[76] CCC 1402–1405.

Evangelical Assessment

The fact that the Catholic Church prohibits Protestants/evangelicals from participating in its sacrament of the Eucharist underscores the vast divide between Catholic and evangelical theology on this matter. Indeed, it may not be an overstatement to say that this sacrament is one of the top two or three divergences between the two theologies. Accordingly, even if some similarities exist between the Catholic sacrament of the Eucharist and the various types of evangelical celebration of this ordinance, such likenesses— e.g., the elements of bread and wine, the recitation of the institution narrative, the solemnity and regularity of observation, the giving of thanks when it is celebrated—are only external family resemblances at best.

Evangelical theology's critique of this sacrament focuses on the following matters: the sacramental interpretation of Jesus's "Bread of Life" discourse (John 6); the prefigurations of the Eucharist in both Old and New Testament Scripture; the dogma of transubstantiation; the notion of the re-presentation of the sacrifice of Christ by means of that event's sharing in the eternality or atemporality of God; the Church's participation in the offering of Christ; the infusion of grace through the sacrament; ongoing worship of Christ who is present in the unconsumed consecrated wafers stored in the tabernacle; and the relationship of this sacrament to that of Penance.

Sacramental Interpretation of the "Bread of Life" Discourse

The sacramental understanding of Jesus's "Bread of Life" discourse in John 6:22–58, an interpretation that is crucial for Catholic theology's doctrine of the actual presence of Christ in the sacrament of the Eucharist, is highly unlikely. In the first part of his address (vv. 22–48), Jesus emphasizes the necessity of faith in him in order to be saved:

- "This the work of God, that you *believe in him* [the Son] whom he [the Father] has sent" (v. 29);
- "For this is the will of my Father, that everyone who looks on the Son and *believes in him* should have eternal life, and I will raise him up on the last day" (v. 40);
- "Truly, truly, I say to you, whoever *believes* has eternal life" (v. 47).

In the second part of the discourse (6:49–58), Jesus switches to an extended metaphor about eating his flesh and drinking his blood:

- "This is *the bread* that comes down from heaven, so that one *may eat of it* and not die" (v. 50);
- "I am *the living bread* that came down from heaven. If anyone *eats of this bread*, he will live forever. And *the bread* that I will give for the life of the world is *my flesh*" (v. 51);
- "Truly, truly, I say to you, unless you *eat the flesh* of the Son of Man and *drink his blood*, you have no life in you" (v. 53);
- "Whoever *feeds on my flesh and drinks my blood* has eternal life, and I will raise him up on the last day" (v. 54);
- "Whoever *feeds on my flesh and drinks my blood* abides in me, and I in him" (v. 56);
- "As the living Father sent me, and I live because of the Father, so whoever *feeds on me*, he also will live because of me" (v. 57);
- "This is *the bread* that came down from heaven, not like the bread the fathers ate, and died. Whoever *feeds on this bread* will live forever" (v. 58); (all emphasis added).

A common evangelical understanding of Jesus's "Bread of Life" discourse goes something like the following: In the first part, Jesus underscores the necessity of faith in himself—the one sent by the Father, and the one who will sacrifice himself for the world—in order to have eternal life. In the second part, Jesus "provide[s] a striking metaphor that makes the teaching of the previous verses more vivid, but can hardly be taken to introduce fundamentally new (and 'sacramental') meaning."[77] There are several reasons for this: As he did in the first part of his discourse ("I am the bread of life"; vv. 35, 48), Jesus presents himself in the second part as "the living bread" (vv. 50–51). He further explains what he means by the metaphor of bread: "And the bread that I will give for the life of the world is my flesh" (v. 51). Whereas this expression may recall his words of institution ("This is my body"; Matt. 26:26), Jesus uses the word "flesh" (Gk. σαρξ; *sarx*), not the word "body" (Gk. σωμα; *sōma*) as is found in the institutional narrative.

A better association, therefore, is from the prologue of John's Gospel: "And the Word became *flesh* and dwelt among us" (John 1:14). The Word of God (John 1:1–2), the eternally existing Son, became incarnate, taking on human flesh (the whole of human nature, not just a body); as the incarnate

---

[77] D. A. Carson, *The Gospel according to John* (Leicester, England: Inter-Varsity Press; and Grand Rapids, MI: Eerdmans, 1991), 277.

God-man, "Jesus is able to give his 'flesh' for the life of the world."[78] This is Jesus's sacrifice: not his body present in the bread of the Eucharist, but his incarnate self on the cross. Yet, he does insist, negatively, that without eating this flesh, no one has eternal life (6:53), and, positively, that whoever does eat his flesh, has eternal life (v. 54). Moreover, Jesus adds the necessity of drinking his blood (vv. 53–54). Is this not sacrificial language referring to the bread and cup of the Eucharist?

Caution is urged for the following reasons: First, the parallelism between Jesus's affirmation, "Whoever feeds on my flesh and drinks my blood has eternal life, and I will raise him up on the last day" (v. 54), and his earlier affirmation, "everyone who looks on the Son and believes in him should have eternal life, and I will raise him up on the last day" (v. 40), underscores that the proper interpretative approach is to understand that "the former is the metaphorical way of referring to the latter."[79] Accordingly, in the first part of the discourse, Jesus speaks directly about believing in him for eternal life, leading to resurrection on the last day. In the second part, he metaphorically repeats the first idea, now with feeding on his flesh and drinking his blood for eternal life, leading to resurrection. To take this metaphorical expression as a reference to the bread and cup of the Eucharist makes the sacrament necessary for salvation, thus contradicting Jesus's emphasis on faith in the earlier part of his discourse. Second, Jesus's point that, on the last day, he will resurrect people who consume him, "proves he does not think that eating the flesh and drinking the blood themselves immediately confer resurrection/immortality."[80] But this is precisely what Catholic theology of the Eucharist maintains; indeed, one of the names for the Eucharist is the "medicine of immortality."[81] Third, Jesus's later comment on his discourse—"It is the Spirit who gives life; the flesh is no help at all. The words that I have spoken to you are spirit and life" (v. 63)—warns against a sacramental interpretation of the discourse. Clearly, "flesh" in this passage does not refer to Jesus's incarnation, which does indeed avail for everything regarding eternal life. Rather, "it is impossible not to see in 'flesh' a direct reference to the preceding discussion, and therefore a dismissal of

---

[78] Ibid., 295. Carson's citation is from Francis J. Moloney, *The Gospel of John* (Collegeville, MN: Liturgical Press, 1998), 115.
[79] Carson, *Gospel according to John*, 297.
[80] Ibid.
[81] CCC 1331.

all *primarily* sacramental interpretations. But if flesh does not give life, what does?"[82] Jesus points to the Holy Spirit as the giver of life. This move resonates with the Old Testament presentation of the Spirit and his work (e.g., Gen. 1:2), reflects Jesus's earlier explanation to Nicodemus that the Spirit is responsible for the new birth (John 3:1–15), and will be repeated later when Jesus invites the thirsty to be quenched by "rivers of living water," a reference to the Holy Spirit who would come as life giver after Jesus's death, resurrection, and ascension (7:37–39). Though this event was still future, Jesus now affirms that his words are "spirit"—"they are the product of the life-giving Spirit"—and "life"—"Jesus' words, rightly understood and absorbed, generate life."[83]

Accordingly, evangelical theology does not embrace Catholic theology's interpretation of Jesus's "Bread of Life" discourse as biblical support for the sacrament of the Eucharist.

Prefigurations of the Eucharist

As for the prefigurations of this sacrament in Scripture, the only Old Testament type that seems to offer some harbinger of the Eucharist is Melchizedek's offering to Abram (Gen. 14:18). This prefiguration alone has elements of both bread and wine; however, the fact that the New Testament does not make appeal to this action of Melchizedek as an anticipation of the Eucharist cautions us from freighting his offering of simple and common foodstuffs with too much importance. As for the other Old Testament prefigurations, the unleavened bread of the exodus is explicitly employed in Scripture to symbolize the people of Israel's need for a definitive break from sin (Ex. 12:14–20) as well as the need of the church for a similar decisive break (1 Cor. 5:6–8), but it has no connection with a sacrifice for sin (that was the Passover lamb; Ex. 12:1–13). Rather than a harbinger of something to come, the manna from heaven was provided for the people of Israel so that God might "test them, whether they will walk in my law or not" (Ex. 16:4). And when his audience brought up the manna in the wilderness, Jesus seemed to emphasize the *discontinuity* between it and the true bread that he will offer—that is, himself (John 6:31–35, 48–51). Finally, the cup of blessing at the Passover feast was not

---

[82] Carson, *Gospel according to John*, 301.
[83] Ibid., 301–302.

an Old Testament element of that celebration but a later development within Judaism.

As for New Testament prefigurations, Jesus's multiplication of the loaves of bread at the feeding of the five thousand (Matt. 14:19) and the four thousand (15:36) seem to be strangely linked to the sacrament, for both of these mighty acts involved bread and fish, not bread and wine. Indeed, the key elements of anticipation to which the *Catechism* draws attention are Jesus's giving of thanks and breaking of the loaves (14:19; 15:36). But the blessing he offered was surely part of his Jewish tradition before eating, and the breaking of the bread was necessary, not to symbolize his broken body (as the broken Eucharistic bread portrays), but to divide the few loaves that he had been given so that he could supply bread for the multitudes that needed to be fed. The typological significance of these actions seems quite stretched. Moreover, how Jesus's miracle of turning the water into wine at the marriage in Cana (John 2:11) was a harbinger of the Eucharistic is not clear.

In summary, it seems that Catholic theology's emphasis on these weak prefigurations of the Eucharistic celebration is a function of the Catholic interpretive approach of finding multiple hidden or mysterious meanings in biblical passages rather than strong scriptural support for this sacrament. For evangelical theology, the fact that Jesus instituted the Eucharist as one of the two rites of the new covenant between God and his people, the church, and the fact that Scripture presents this dominical institution (e.g., Matt. 26:26–29) and provides instructions for how to celebrate this ordinance (1 Cor. 10:14–22; 11:17–34), are sufficient biblical warrant.

The Dogma of Transubstantiation

Implicit in this criticism of Catholic theology's interpretation of Jesus's "Bread of Life" discourse and its reliance on weak prefigurations for its biblical support for the sacrament of the Eucharist is evangelical theology's critique of transubstantiation as an explanation of the presence of Jesus Christ when the Church celebrates this sacrament. In terms of evangelical theology's general criticism of transubstantiation, it harkens back to its earlier critique of the Christ-Church interconnection: the whole Christ—both the head and his body, the Catholic Church as the prolongation of the incarnation of Christ—is present here and now. For Catholic theology of the Eucharist, Christ, the God-man, is present neither in his divine nature alone nor in his human nature alone but in the totality of both his divine and human nature. It is able to affirm such a Eucharistic presence of Christ because the Catholic system is grounded on the axiom of the Christ-Church interconnection. To repeat earlier critiques of this concept, it has a defective view of the ascension (Christ, in his human nature, left the earth and went into heaven; Acts 1:9–11), his session (in terms of his human nature, he was seated and continues to be at the right hand of the Father; e.g., Rom. 8:34), his absence from earth (as to his human nature, Christ is not present here and now, but has sent the Holy Spirit to take his place; e.g., John 14:26; 16:7), and his future return (in what meaningful sense can it be said that Christ will return to earth if he is already present here with the entirety of his being, including his human nature?). Evangelical theology's criticism of the axiom of the Christ-Church interconnection as the ground of the Eucharistic presence of Christ—"the body and blood, together with the soul and divinity, of our Lord Jesus Christ and, therefore, the whole Christ is truly, really, and substantially contained"[84]—means that transubstantiation is critiqued as well.

Other specific reasons exist for evangelical theology's rejection of transubstantiation. To provide a bit of historical background (which the *Catechism* does not supply), transubstantiation was proclaimed as the authoritative position of the Catholic Church at the Fourth Lateran Council (1215), and Thomas Aquinas (1225–1274) later provided the philosophical underpinnings for this doctrine. Aquinas relied on the philosophy of Aristotle, specifically his distinction between *substance*—an essence or nature existing in itself (and not in something else)—and *accidents*—the characteristics or attributes not of its core and, thus, that can be lost without losing the thing itself. Some of these accidents can be perceived by the senses. In keeping with this distinction, Aquinas proposed the following: in the case of the Eucharistic bread and wine, though the *accidents* remain the same—the bread and wine still look like, smell like, feel like, and taste like bread and wine—the *substance* of the bread is changed into the body of Christ and the substance of the wine is changed into the blood of Christ. This change of substance is

---

[84] CCC 1374; citation is from the *Canons and Decrees of the Council of Trent*, 13th session (October, 11, 1551), *Decree Concerning the Most Holy Sacrament of the Eucharist* 1 (Schaff, 2:126).

called *transubstantiation*. Ultimately, Aquinas appealed to divine power to explain this miracle:

> God is infinite act; thus, his action extends to the whole nature of being. Therefore, he can work not only formal conversion [the change in the form of some substance], so that diverse forms succeed each other in the same subject; but also change the being [the substance] itself, so that the whole substance of one thing be changed into the whole substance of another. And this is done by divine power in this sacrament. For the whole substance of the bread is changed into the whole substance of Christ's body, and the whole substance of the wine into the whole substance of Christ's blood. Thus, this is not a formal, but a substantial conversion; nor is it a kind of natural movement. Rather, with a name of its own, it can be called *transubstantiation*.[85]

Aquinas was definitive in the historical development and explanation of this dogma.

Evangelical theology offers four criticisms of this development and explanation: First, the dogma of transubstantiation is of late origin; as Martin Luther complained, the Church had gotten along fine for about twelve hundred years without it, rendering transubstantiation suspect and unnecessary.[86] Second, because the doctrine is grounded philosophically rather than biblically, it cannot be binding on the conscience of the faithful. As Luther objected, "What is asserted without the Scriptures or proven revelation may be held as an opinion but need not be believed."[87] Third, and tied to the second criticism, the distinction between substance and accidents, and what happens to both realities during the Eucharist, does not seem to be supported by Aristotelian philosophy itself.[88] As for the fourth criticism, without clear and substantial biblical support for the alleged power of God to effect this miracle, evangelical theology refuses to embrace transubstantiation.

---

[85] Thomas Aquinas, *Summa Theologica* pt. 3, q. 75, art. 4.
[86] Martin Luther, *The Babylonian Captivity of the Church* (LW 36.31).
[87] Ibid., 36.29.
[88] Again, Luther criticized Aquinas because he built "an unfortunate superstructure [philosophical, rather than biblical, support for transubstantiation] upon an unfortunate foundation [a misunderstanding of Aristotle's philosophy]" (ibid.). Transubstantiation also raises the question of what happens to the substance of the bread and the substance of the wine at the moment of consecration: Are they annihilated, or are they dissolved into their original matter? Does the atmosphere become the substance of the accidents of the bread and wine? Aquinas himself dealt with some of these questions (Thomas Aquinas, *Summa Theologica* pt. 3, q. 75, art. 3, and pt. 3, q. 77, art. 1).

Still, while uniformly standing against the Catholic idea of the Eucharist, evangelical theology does not have one alternative view of it, but several.[89] Though Catholic theology is highly critical of the variety of evangelical views on this sacrament, the view of transubstantiation that it offers is not (for the reasons discussed above) a viable alternative. Like its Catholic counterpart, evangelical theology bemoans the division that exists with respect to the Lord's Supper and calls for further study and dialogue between the opposing positions. The reality is, however, that such disagreement will continue until Christ comes again, and evangelical theology does not look to Catholic theology for a biblically warranted solution to the division.

Re-presentation of Christ's Sacrifice

Catholic theology's doctrine of transubstantiation is closely associated with its idea of the *re-presentation* of the sacrifice of Jesus Christ when the sacrament of the Eucharist is celebrated. The whole Christ, both his divine and human natures, is present in the Eucharist, and the God-man's once-and-for-all atoning sacrifice on the cross of Calvary two thousand years ago is made present such that the sacrament is truly propitiatory, atoning for sin and consequently assuaging the wrath of God. Catholic theology's explanation of this phenomenon is that the cross work of Christ participates in the divine attribute of eternality (God always exists), or atemporality (God does not have time limitations). As a result of this participation, Christ's unique atoning sacrifice is not time-bound to that moment but is re-presented, or made present, when the Liturgy of the Eucharist is celebrated.

Evangelical theology objects to this explanation because it has no biblical warrant; indeed, it is based on a misinterpretation of Scripture,

---

[89] Lutheran evangelical theology, following Martin Luther, embraces consubstantiation (or sacramental union). While resoundingly rejecting transubstantiation (the idea that the bread and the cup *become* the body and blood of Christ), this view believes that the physical body and blood of Christ are present "in, with, and under" the Eucharistic elements. Following Huldrych Zwingli, evangelical theology as developed among the Anabaptists and Baptists (as well as many other denominations) holds to a memorial view of the Lord's Supper. With this theology, the emphasis is on remembering what Christ has done on behalf of sinful human beings. The signs of the bread and the cup serve as memorial tokens of the broken body and shed blood of Christ, prompting the church to remember his work on the cross. Reformed evangelical theology, following John Calvin, holds to a spiritual presence view of the Lord's Supper: While Jesus is not physically present in the bread and the cup (thus, it disagrees with both transubstantiation and consubstantiation), he is spiritually present when the church celebrates the Lord's Supper; thus, Reformed evangelical theology goes beyond the memorial view. It agrees that the bread and the cup are signs, but it maintains that they are not empty signs; rather, they render what they portray. Christ is spiritually present, such that the church, when it administers the Lord's Supper, shares in him and all of his salvific benefits: "The cup of blessing that we bless, is it not *a participation in the blood of Christ?* The bread that we break, is it not *a participation in the body of Christ?*" (1 Cor. 10:16, emphasis added). For further discussion of these evangelical views, see Allison, *SS*, 375–386; idem, *HT*, 635–658.

specifically Jesus's institution of his Supper with the words "This is my body. . . . This is my blood of the covenant" (Matt. 26:26, 28). Interpreting theses phrases literally, Catholic theology maintains that Jesus Christ as the sacrificial victim is really present, and his sacrifice on the cross is truly re-presented, when the Eucharistic sacrament is administered. But a literal interpretation of these phrases is wrong.

First to be noticed is the fact that it is not the bread itself that is at the forefront of Jesus's institution of the Supper, but the bread that he has broken; this action is a powerful symbol pointing beyond itself to the upcoming fracturing of Christ's body on the cross. Second, it is not the wine itself that is the focus of attention of Jesus's institution, but the cup of wine that is "poured out" ("This cup that is poured out for you"; Luke 22:20); this action is a powerful symbol pointing beyond itself to the upcoming shedding of Christ's blood on the cross for the forgiveness of sins (Matt. 26:28) and the establishment of the new covenant (Luke 22:20; 1 Cor. 11:25). Third, Jesus's giving of the bread and the cup to his disciples, with instructions that they should take and eat the bread and drink the wine from the cup, finds a response of eating and drinking on their part; these actions constitute a powerful symbol of Christ's upcoming gracious accomplishment of salvation and his followers' response of faith to appropriate his cross work. Fourth, these actions-as-symbols underscore that Jesus's words cannot be taken literally. The bread could not have been Jesus's physical body when he instituted his Supper; how could it have been, given that his body had not yet been broken on the cross? The wine could not have been Jesus's physical blood when he instituted his Supper; how could it have been, given that his blood had not yet been poured out on the cross? When Jesus gave the bread and the cup to his disciples with instructions when he instituted his Supper, the bread and the wine could not have been his body and his blood; how could they have been, given that he had not yet accomplished the forgiveness of sins on the cross and inaugurated the new covenant in his blood? When Jesus's disciples took and ate the bread and drank from the cup when he instituted his Supper, they could not have been his body and his blood; how could they have been, given that the disciples could not yet have appropriated Jesus's cross work? A literal interpretation of Jesus's words of institution is not plausible; therefore, invoking divine eternality or atemporality to explain the re-presentation of the cross work of Christ is not necessary. If such an explanation is not needed for the original celebration of the Eucharist, neither is it needed for the Eucharistic celebrations that have followed and that occur today.

Furthermore, evangelical theology does not consider Paul's discussion of the Lord's Supper to offer support for the transubstantiated presence of Jesus Christ and the re-presentation of his sacrifice in this sacrament.[90] Two Pauline passages are key. The first consists of two rhetorical questions that the apostle poses to the church of Corinth: "The cup of blessing that we bless, is it not a participation in the blood of Christ? The bread that we break, is it not a participation in the body of Christ?" (1 Cor. 10:16). The blessed cup is not the blood of Christ; the broken bread is not the body of Christ. Rather, *participation* in his blood and body is the apostle's point. There is no hint of transubstantiation or atemporal re-presentation; it is not sacrifice but participation that Paul underscores.

The second passage warns of abuse of the Lord's Supper by the church of Corinth. Immediately after recounting the tradition of the Lord's Supper as he had received it (1 Cor. 11:23–25), Paul explains, "For as often as you eat this bread and drink the cup, you proclaim the Lord's death until he comes. Whoever, therefore, eats the bread or drinks the cup of the Lord in an unworthy manner will be guilty concerning the body and blood of the Lord. Let a person examine himself, then, and so eat of the bread and drink of the cup. For anyone who eats and drinks without discerning the body eats and drinks judgment on himself. That is why many of you are weak and ill, and some have died" (1 Cor. 11:26–30). Several points deserve consideration. First, what Paul underscored about the Lord's Supper was *proclamation*: By celebrating it, the church proclaimed the death of Christ. Paul's reference is not to a verbal announcement of the gospel but to an enactment of it by means of the Lord's Supper. The powerful symbolism of its celebration—the broken bread portraying the fractured body of Christ; the cup of wine portraying the poured out blood of Christ; Christians eating and drinking the elements, portraying their participation in the body and blood of Christ—vividly depicted the gospel of Christ's death for sinful human beings. But proclamation is neither transubstantiation nor re-presentation. Second, the tragedy exposed and denounced by the apostle was the disrespect shown by the church's rich

---

[90] See Allison, *SS*, 395–398.

members toward its poor members. At the love feast, during which the Lord's Supper would be administered, the wealthy Christians would not wait for the poor Christians but ate all the food and drank all the wine, becoming gluttons and drunkards and humiliating the others (vv. 20–22, 33–34). The rich Christians failed to "[discern] the body" (v. 29); that is, they did not grasp the interdependence of the members of the church and their consequent responsibility to defer to and honor its poorer members. As a result of divine judgment, some of the Corinthians were sick and ill, and others had even prematurely died. Accordingly, the problem with the Corinthian church's celebration of the Lord's Supper was not a misunderstanding of the transubstantiated presence of Christ and/or the re-presentation of his sacrifice.

But the apostle does warn that whoever "eats the bread or drinks the cup of the Lord in an unworthy manner will be guilty concerning the body and blood of the Lord" (v. 27); such a warning does underscore the seriousness of observing the Lord's Supper and seems to point, along with 1 Corinthians 10:16, to the presence of Christ when it is celebrated. Some varieties of evangelical theology concur, with this understanding of the rite: Christ and all of his salvific benefits are indeed present when the Lord's Supper is administered. This idea is based on two theological truths: *divine omnipresence* (God is present with his whole being in every point of space) and *spiritual* or *moral presence* (God manifests his presence in different ways at different times). Applying these truths to the discussion of the Lord's Supper, these versions of evangelical theology affirm both the ontological presence of Christ and the particular manifestation of his covenantal presence either to (1) bless rightful celebrations of this new covenant ordinance, or (2) judge improper celebrations of it (as exemplified by the Corinthian church; 1 Cor. 11:29–31).[91] Historically, John Calvin embraced this view of the sacrament, known as the spiritual presence view,[92] and Reformed theology that flowed from him continues to affirm the actual presence of Christ in this rite. To be underscored, however, is the fact that this perspective is not transubstantiation, and it does not embrace the re-presentation of the sacrifice of Christ on the cross, for many of the same reasons offered above.

---

[91] For further discussion, see Allison, *SS*, 395ff.
[92] Calvin, *Institutes* 4.17 (LCC 21:1359–1428).

The Church's Participation in the Offering of Christ

Another criticism of Catholic theology concerns its idea that during the mass, the people—represented by the laity, not the clergy—bring the necessary sacrifices forward to the altar: "fruit of the earth and work of human hands" (the bread offered to God) and "fruit of the vine and work of human hands" (the wine offered to God).[93] These sacrifices are received by the priest, who later offers them to God as he leads the Liturgy of the Eucharist. He does so both on his own behalf and on behalf of the people, praying first to God, "may our sacrifice in your sight this day be pleasing to you, Lord God,"[94] then saying to the people, "Pray, brethren (brothers and sisters), that my sacrifice and yours may be acceptable to God, the almighty Father."[95]

Evangelical theology disagrees that the elements of this sacrament are offerings given to God. The critique of this idea focuses on the wrongness of the nature-grace interdependence: the idea that nature—in this case, bread and wine—possesses a capacity to convey grace, which must be tangibly communicated through nature. Accordingly, in this sacrament, the natural elements of bread and wine are capable of being offered to God so that they will be transubstantiated into an embodied grace, the body and blood of Jesus Christ himself. This axiom of the nature-grace interdependence has already been critiqued (ch. 2).

As for specific criticisms of the Catholic idea that the bread and wine of this sacrament are offerings presented to God, evangelical theology underscores the biblical discussion of sacrifice: The sacrifices called for in the new covenant are the once-and-for-all sacrifice of Jesus Christ (Heb. 9:26; 10:12); the offering by Christians of their entire being to God (Rom. 12:1–2); "praise to God, that is, the fruit of lips that acknowledge his name" (Heb. 13:15); doing good and sharing with others (Heb. 13:16); supporting the ministry of others (Phil. 4:18); and the offerings of spiritual sacrifices acceptable to God through Jesus Christ (1 Pet. 2:5), which are not detailed but which may be the proclamation of "the excellencies of him who called you out of darkness into his marvelous light" (v. 9). No biblical warrant is

---

[93] Roman Missal, Order of the Mass, 23, 25. Other offerings such as gifts for the poor may be brought as well. Moreover, during the celebration of the mass when the sacrament of Matrimony is administered, the man and the woman to be married unite the offering of their lives, which they are giving to each other, to the offering of Christ for his church in the Eucharist (CCC 1621).

[94] Ibid., 27.

[95] Ibid., 29.

found for the notion that the bread and the wine of the sacrament of the Eucharist are sacrifices offered by laypeople through their priest to God in the re-presentation of the sacrifice of Christ.

Infusion of Grace

Flowing from the evangelical critique of the nature-grace interdependence is its disagreement with Catholic theology's notion that grace is infused into the faithful through the Eucharist. According to this axiom, not only is nature capable of conveying grace, but grace must be made concrete; thus, grace operates through nature so as to elevate and perfect it. With regard to the Eucharist, the grace of the re-presented Christ in the sacrament effects a change in the (human) nature of the faithful who receive it/him. Because this axiom is wrong, the notion of infused grace based on the axiom is also wrong. The specific evangelical criticism of infused grace awaits the later discussion of justification and the imputed righteousness of Christ.

Ongoing Worship of Christ

The Catholic system's other axiom, the Christ-Church interconnection, supports the Catholic practice of the ongoing worship of Christ who is present in the unconsumed consecrated wafers stored in the tabernacle. The reasoning is tight: the Catholic Church is the continuation of the incarnation of the ascended Christ; through the Catholic Church's mediation the whole Christ is made present in the sacramental elements of the Eucharist; therefore, when some hosts/wafers remain from the celebration of the Liturgy of the Eucharist, the whole Christ continues to be present in those wafers and thus must be accorded worship. This reasoning makes sense within the Catholic system. Evangelical theology, finding fault with the Christ-Church interconnection, dismisses the ongoing worship of Christ in the unconsumed wafers as grounded on a wrong axiom that results in the downfall of the whole Catholic system.

Relationship of the Eucharist to Penance

A final aspect of this evangelical theological assessment of Catholicism's theology of the Eucharist focuses on this sacrament's relationship to another sacrament: the sacrament of Penance and Reconciliation. According to Catholic theology, participants are obligated to prepare themselves for the celebration of the Eucharist, meaning that "[a]nyone conscious of a grave sin must receive the sacrament of Reconciliation before coming to communion."[96] The fruit of this sacrament enables these participants to participate in the sacrament of the Eucharist.

An evangelical critique observes that this notion of preparation for grace flows from the axiom of the nature-grace interdependence: nature possesses the capacity to receive grace, but nature must be prepared or made worthy for grace. Evangelical theology notes the error of this axiom and thus offers a critique of its corollary that the faithful must be prepared to receive the grace offered in the Eucharist. As for more specific criticisms, evangelical theology suspects that this idea is based on a misunderstanding of Paul's warning about the proper recipients of the Lord's Supper. According to 1 Corinthians 11:27–30, the apostle does not forbid unworthy *participants* (for example, people who have committed mortal sin) in the sacrament; rather, he warns against unworthy *participation*—engaging in the celebration without the proper regard for and relationship with the other members of the church.[97] Appropriately, evangelical theology emphasizes the gospel: Christians are not, and can never be, worthy participants in the blessings of God. Try as they might, they can never become recipients of divine grace through readying themselves to receive it. Rather, because of the gospel—God's work through Christ—Christians are rendered fully righteous through the imputation of the righteousness of Jesus. And through Christ's work rendering them worthy participants, they are welcomed to participate in a worthy manner—with love and respect for their fellow communicants.

In summary, one of the most significant areas of divergence between Catholic and evangelical theology is the differences in their views on the sacrament of the Eucharist.

---

[96] CCC 1385. Biblical warrant is given as Paul's instructions to avoid eating the bread or drinking the cup "in an unworthy manner" (1 Cor. 11:27–29).
[97] For further explanation, see Allison, *SS*, 406–407.

10

The Celebration of the Christian Mystery
(Part 2, Section 2, Chapter 2, Articles 4–5)

The Sacraments of Healing: Penance and
Reconciliation; Anointing of the Sick

The Sacraments of Healing (Sec. 2, Ch. 2)

Having presented the three sacraments of Christian initiation by which
people are introduced into and nourished in the new life of Christ, the
Catechism turns next to a discussion of the two sacraments of healing. The
sacrament of Penance and Reconciliation and the sacrament of Anointing
of the Sick are celebrated whenever this new life is weakened or lost by sin,
or is threatened to end by illness and death. By these sacraments the Church
continues, by the power of the Spirit, Christ's "work of healing and salvation, even among her own members."[1]

The Sacrament of Penance and Reconciliation (Sec. 2, Ch. 2, Art. 4)

The first sacrament of healing is designed for the faithful who have committed sins against God after their Baptism, for it provides "pardon from
God's mercy" and reconciles the offenders "with the Church which they
have wounded by their sins and which, by charity, by example, and by prayer
labors for their conversion."[2] The sacrament goes by several names, each of
which reflects an element of the rite:

> It is called the *sacrament of conversion* because it makes sacramentally
> present Jesus' call to conversion, which is the first step in returning to
> the Father from whom one has strayed by sin. It is called the *sacrament*

---
[1] CCC 1421.
[2] CCC 1422; citation is from Vatican Council II, *Lumen Gentium* 11.2.

of Penance, since it consecrates the Christian sinner's personal and ecclesial steps of conversion, penance, and satisfaction. It is called the *sacrament of confession*, since the disclosure or confession of sins to a priest is an essential element of this sacrament. . . . It is called the *sacrament of forgiveness*, since by the priest's sacramental absolution God grants the penitent "pardon and peace." It is called the *sacrament of Reconciliation*, because it imparts to the sinner the love of God who reconciles: "Be reconciled to God" [2 Cor. 5:20].[3]

An important question that the *Catechism* raises and answers is why such a post-baptismal sacrament is necessary. Certainly, God's gracious work is bountiful and diverse—encompassing cleansing, sanctification, and justification (1 Cor. 6:11)—in the sacraments of Christian initiation, a generosity that underscores "the degree to which sin is excluded" for the faithful.[4] At the same time, the reality of their ongoing sin is undeniable (1 John 1:8). Furthermore, Jesus himself emphasized that the faithful's prayer—"Forgive us our trespasses" (Luke 11:4; Matt. 6:12)—is linked to their forgiveness of the sins of others. Accordingly, the new life received by conversion to Christ and the sacraments of initiation "has not abolished the frailty and weakness of human nature, nor the inclination to sin"—concupiscence.[5] Because of this present feeble and flawed reality, the toilsome Christian life, "the struggle of conversion," to which Christ calls the faithful is one for which he supplies his grace.[6]

Christ's call to conversion consists of two moments. The *first conversion* involves the Church's preaching the gospel to the unevangelized. Attached closely to this proclamation is the sacrament of Baptism, which provides for "the first and fundamental conversion" involving faith and repentance leading to "salvation, that is, the forgiveness of all sins and the gift of new life."[7] The *second conversion* is an ongoing response to Christ's call that "continues to resound in the lives of Christians." As such, it demands "an uninterrupted task for the whole Church" along "the path of penance and renewal," and it features a cooperative effort between human work and divine grace: "It is the movement of a 'contrite heart,' drawn

---

[3] CCC 1423–1424; citation is from *Ordo paenitentiae* (Vatican City: Vatican Polyglot Press, 1974), 46; formula of absolution.
[4] CCC 1425.
[5] CCC 1426.
[6] Ibid. (emphasis removed).
[7] CCC 1427.

and moved by grace to respond to the merciful love of God who loved us first."[8] This second conversion is exemplified by Peter's conversion after his threefold denial of Christ, who later restored the apostle (Luke 22:61; John 21:15–17).[9]

Conversion is first and foremost the fruit of divine grace prompting the human heart, which in turn is "shaken by the horror and weight of sin and begins to fear offending God by sin and being separated from him."[10] This awakening is "the *conversion of the heart, interior conversion*," which is the first aim of Christ's call.[11] Such conversion is "a radical reorientation of our whole life," including hatred of sins committed and "accompanied by a salutary pain and sadness."[12]

At the same time, "interior conversion urges expression in visible signs, gestures and works of penance."[13] These tangible manifestations are principally of three types: "*fasting, prayer, and almsgiving,* which express conversion in relation to oneself, to God, and to others."[14] Other expressions include reconciliation with others, tears of repentance, concern for the salvation of others, prayers of the saints, love, concern for the poor, social justice, accountability with others, living with suffering and persecution, and taking up one's cross daily and following Jesus.[15] Furthermore, ongoing conversion and penance are nourished by participation in the Eucharist, which is "a remedy to free us from our daily faults and to preserve us from mortal sins."[16] Other elements that foster ongoing conversion and penance include reading Scripture, praying, observing the seasons and days of penance (e.g., Lent; each Friday), and the like.[17]

As noted above, sin is two-sided: Before all else, it is an offense against God, but it also harms communion with the Church. "For this reason conversion entails both God's forgiveness and reconciliation with the Church, which are expressed and accomplished liturgically by the sacrament of

---

[8] CCC 1428; citation is from Vatican Council II, *Lumen Gentium* 8.3; the biblical reference is Ps. 51:17; cf. John 6:44; 12:32; 1 John 4:10.
[9] CCC 1429. The *Catechism* further refers to Ambrose's comment on the two conversions in the Church: "there are water and tears: the water of Baptism and the tears of repentance" (Ambrose, *Epistle* 41.12 [*NPNF²* 10:447]).
[10] CCC 1432.
[11] CCC 1430 (emphasis added).
[12] CCC 1431.
[13] CCC 1430.
[14] CCC 1434 (emphasis original).
[15] CCC 1434–1435.
[16] CCC 1436; citation is from the *Canons and Decrees of the Council of Trent*, 13th session (October 11, 1551), *Decree Concerning the Most Holy Sacrament of the Eucharist* 2 (Schaff, 2:128).
[17] CCC 1437.

Penance and Reconciliation."[18] As for the first reality, the *Catechism* underscores that God alone forgives sin (Mark 2:5, 10; Luke 7:48). But additionally, by his divine authority, Christ "gives this power to men to exercise in his name."[19] Specifically, "he entrusted the exercise of the power of absolution to the apostolic ministry which he charged with the 'ministry of reconciliation.' The apostle is sent out 'on behalf of Christ' with 'God making his appeal' through him and pleading: 'Be reconciled to God.'"[20] Regarding the second reality, the *Catechism* affirms, "[i]n imparting to his apostles his own power to forgive sins the Lord also gives them the authority to reconcile sinners with the Church."[21] This ecclesial reconciliation was exemplified by Jesus's reintegration of sinners into God's people from whom they had been alienated by sin, seen especially in his eating with sinners at his table (e.g., Luke 15; 19:9). This dimension of reconciliation with the Church is warranted biblically by Christ's promise to Peter: "I will give you the keys of the kingdom of heaven, and whatever you bind on earth shall be bound in heaven, and whatever you loose on earth shall be loosed in heaven."[22] The *Catechism* notes that "[t]he office of binding and loosing which was given to Peter was also assigned to the college of apostles united to its head."[23] As far as what Jesus was promising by *binding* and *loosing*, the *Catechism* explains: "[W]homever you exclude from your communion, will be excluded from communion with God; whomever you receive anew into your communion, God will welcome back into his. *Reconciliation with the Church is inseparable from reconciliation with God.*"[24]

The sacrament is designed "for all sinful members of his [Christ's] Church: above all for those who, since Baptism, have fallen into grave sin, and have thus lost their baptismal grace and wounded ecclesial communion."[25] As described by Tertullian, Penance is "the second plank [of salvation] after the shipwreck which is the loss of grace" because it offers ruined people "a new possibility to convert and to recover the grace of justification."[26] The

---

[18] CCC 1440.
[19] CCC 1441.
[20] CCC 1442; the biblical reference is 2 Cor. 5:18, 20.
[21] CCC 1444.
[22] Ibid.; the biblical reference is Matt. 16:19; cf. 18:18; 28:16–20.
[23] CCC 1444; citation is from Vatican Council II, *Lumen Gentium* 22.2.
[24] CCC 1445 (emphasis added).
[25] CCC 1446.
[26] Ibid.; citation is from Tertullian, *On Penance* 4, 7 (*ANF* 3:659–660, 662–663). The *Catechism* briefly treats the historical development of the sacrament, noting its public, lengthy, and non-repeatable structure in the early church, and its significantly changed configuration—private (i.e., in secret between a penitent and a priest),

sacrament consists of "two equally essential elements: on the one hand, the acts of the man who undergoes conversion; . . . on the other, God's action through the intervention of the Church."[27]

As for the acts of the penitent, three are required: contrition, confession of sins, and satisfaction. In first place is *contrition*, which is "sorrow of the soul and detestation for the sin committed, together with the resolution not to sin again."[28] Contrition is of two types: (1) *perfect contrition* (also called *contrition of charity*) "arises from a love by which God is loved above all else"; (2) *imperfect contrition* (also called *attrition* and *contrition of fear*) "is born of the consideration of sin's ugliness or the fear of eternal damnation."[29] The fruit of perfect contrition is the remission of venial sins as well as the "forgiveness of mortal sins if it includes the firm resolution to have recourse to sacramental confession as soon as possible."[30] The fruit of imperfect contrition is the disposition to initiate the process leading to absolution, but by itself such contrition "cannot obtain the forgiveness of grave sins."[31]

The second act of the penitent is the *confession of sins*, which entails acknowledgment of one's sins, taking responsibility for them, and opening oneself to God and to the Church. There is more. "Confession to a priest is an essential part of the sacrament of Penance: 'All mortal sins of which penitents after a diligent self-examination are conscious must be recounted by them in confession.'"[32] Such sins include both open and secret sins. The penitent says, "Forgive (or bless) me, father, for I have sinned. It has been ____ [the length of time; e.g., three months] since my last confession and these are my sins: _____" (they are confessed). After the priest has given counsel, the penitent makes an act of contrition; for example: "O, my God, I am heartily sorry for having offended you. I detest all my sins because of your just punishment, but most of all because they offend you, my God, who are all-good and deserving of all my love. I firmly resolve, with the help of your grace, to sin no more and

relatively brief, and repeatable—beginning with Irish monasticism in the seventh century and continuing along that trajectory to today (CCC 1447).

[27] CCC 1448.

[28] CCC 1451; citation is from *Canons and Decrees of the Council of Trent*, 14th session (November 25, 1551), *The Most Holy Sacraments of Penance and Extreme Unction* ch. 4 (Schaff, 2:144).

[29] CCC 1452–1453.

[30] CCC 1453. The distinction between venial and grave (or mortal) sins will be explained shortly.

[31] Ibid.

[32] CCC 1456; citation is from *Canons and Decrees of the Council of Trent*, 14th session (November 25, 1551), *The Most Holy Sacraments of Penance and Extreme Unction* ch. 5 (Schaff, 2:147).

to avoid the near occasion of sin."[33] Participation in the sacrament of Penance is required once a year as a minimum.[34] Access to the sacrament of the Eucharist is barred in the case of unconfessed mortal sin, even if the person "experiences deep contrition" but has not yet had the mortal sin absolved through the sacrament of Penance.[35] Children are to participate in this sacrament prior to their first Holy Communion. As for venial sins, daily confession is "strongly recommended by the Church" without it being "strictly necessary."[36]

Following contrition and confession, the third penitential act is *satisfaction*, which is the reparation of the harm caused to others by one's sin. Specific acts include restitution of stolen property, restoration of the reputation of others who have been slandered, and payment of compensation for injuries sustained by others. "Absolution takes away sin, but it does not remedy all the disorders sin has caused. Raised up from sin, the sinner must still recover his full spiritual health by doing something more to make amends for the sin: he must 'make satisfaction for' or 'expiate' his sins. This satisfaction is also called 'penance.'"[37] The priest who hears the confession (called a "confessor") imposes the appropriate satisfaction or penance, taking "into account the penitent's personal situation" and aiming for "his spiritual good. It must correspond as far as possible with the gravity and nature of the sins committed. It can consist of prayer, an offering, works of mercy, service of neighbor, voluntary self-denial, sacrifices, and above all the patient acceptance of the cross we must bear."[38] The *Catechism* offers the rationale for such acts of satisfaction: They "help configure us to Christ, who alone expiated our sins once for all. They allow us to become coheirs with the risen Christ, 'provided we suffer with him' [Rom. 8:17; Rom. 3:25; 1 John 2:1–2]."[39] Accordingly, satisfaction is rendered through, and finds its effectiveness in, Jesus Christ, who strengthens penitents to offer it.

In summary, the sacrament of Penance and Reconciliation consists of

---

[33] Taken from Catholic Online: http://www.catholic.org/prayers/prayer.php?p=421.
[34] As stipulated by canon 989 of the Code of Canon Law and *Canons and Decrees of the Council of Trent*, 14th session (November 25, 1551), *Canons concerning the Most Holy Sacraments of Penance and Extreme Unction*, canon 8 (Schaff, 2:166). This stipulation was first made by the Fourth Lateran Council (1215).
[35] CCC 1457.
[36] CCC 1458.
[37] CCC 1459. Cf. *Canons and Decrees of the Council of Trent*, 14th session (November 25, 1551), *The Most Holy Sacraments of Penance and Extreme Unction* ch. 8 (Schaff, 2:155–158).
[38] CCC 1460.
[39] Ibid.

three acts on the part of the penitent: contrition, the confession of sin, and satisfaction.

As for the acts of God through the intervention of the Church, the ministers of this sacrament are bishops and their assistants, the priests, upon whom has been conferred the power to forgive sins by virtue of the sacrament of Holy Orders. Penance is administered ordinarily in a confessional, to ensure privacy. The priest first greets and blesses the penitent, then reads a portion of Scripture "to illuminate the conscience and elicit contrition," and finally urges repentance.[40] The penitent verbalizes her sin or sins, for which the priest imposes a penance, which in turn is accepted by the penitent. The priest then absolves the penitent of her sin or sins, offers a prayer of thanksgiving and praise, and dismisses with a blessing. Strict confidentiality is to be observed in this sacrament; indeed, "the Church declares that every priest who hears confessions is bound under very severe penalties to keep absolute secrecy regarding the sins that his penitents have confessed to him. He can make no use of knowledge that confession gives him about penitents' lives. This secret, which admits of no exceptions, is called the 'sacramental seal,' because what the penitent has made known to the priest remains 'sealed' by the sacrament."[41] At the same time, "[c]ertain particularly grave sins incur excommunication," an ecclesial penalty that bars people from the sacraments of the Church and that cannot be absolved, "according to canon law, except by the Pope, the bishop of the place, or priests authorized by them."[42]

The effects of this sacrament are twofold: restoration to the grace of God, which reunites penitents with him in intimate friendship, and reconciliation with the Church, which revitalizes community life. Additionally, it usually results in "peace and serenity of conscience with strong spiritual consolation . . . [and] the dignity and blessings of the life of the children of God."[43] Moreover, in this sacrament, the faithful anticipate in a certain way the final judgment that will come at their death, choosing life so as to "not come into judgment' [John 5:24]."[44]

Closely associated with the sacrament of Penance and Reconciliation

---

[40] CCC 1480.
[41] CCC 1467.
[42] CCC 1463. The absolution of excommunication is treated in canons 1331 and 1354–1357 of the Code of Canon Law.
[43] CCC 1468.
[44] CCC 1470.

is the doctrine and practice of *indulgences*, of which the *Catechism* gives a brief treatment. "An indulgence is a remission before God of the temporal punishment due to sin whose guilt has already been forgiven, which the faithful Christian who is duly disposed gains under certain prescribed conditions through the action of the Church which, as the minister of redemption, dispenses and applies with authority the treasury of the satisfaction of Christ and the saints."[45] Indulgences are of two types: *plenary* indulgences, which remit all of the temporal punishment due to sin, and *partial* indulgences, which remit part of that punishment.

To help in understanding indulgences, the *Catechism* offers several explanations. The first explanation focuses on the *double consequence* of sin. *Grave* or *mortal* sin ruptures communion with God and leads to eternal punishment in hell. *Venial* sin, while not destroying such fellowship and not ending in condemnation, still leaves a taint or stain from which people must be purified either during their earthly life or, after death, in purgatory. "This purification frees one from what is called the 'temporal punishment' of sin."[46] Though the sacrament of Penance remits the eternal punishment of sin, the temporal punishment due to sin remains. Accordingly, penitents are forgiven of sin and restored to communion with God, but the taint of forgiven mortal sin and the stain of venial sin persist. In this earthly life, strides must be taken—e.g., through patiently bearing sufferings, doing works of mercy and charity, praying, engaging in the acts of penance—to break with the old life and walk in the new life of Christ. If the faithful are not fully obedient during their earthly pilgrimage, their souls go to purgatory for further purification.

The second explanation of indulgences focuses on the *communion of saints* as help for those in purgatory. As noted earlier, this communion mystically unites the saints in heaven, the souls expiating their sins in purgatory, and the faithful on earth. As part of this communion, there is an exchange of spiritual goods: "In this wonderful exchange, the holiness of one profits others. . . . Thus recourse to the communion of saints lets the contrite sinner be more promptly and efficaciously purified of the punishment for sin."[47]

---

[45] CCC 1471; citation is from Paul VI, apostolic constitution, *Indulgentiarum doctrina*, norm 1. Accessible at: http://www.vatican.va/holy_father/paul_vi/apost_constitutions/documents/hf_p-vi_apc_19670101_indulgentiarum-doctrina_en.html.
[46] CCC 1472.
[47] CCC 1475.

These communicable spiritual goods are the *treasury of the Church*, which consists of the infinitely valuable merits of Christ, "the prayers and good works of the Blessed Virgin Mary," and "the prayers and good works of all the saints."[48]

The third explanation treats *obtaining indulgences*: They are gained through the Church, which "intervenes in favor of individual Christians and opens for them the treasury of the merits of Christ and the saints to obtain from the Father of mercies the remission of the temporal punishments due for their sins."[49] Importantly, indulgences can be obtained for the souls in purgatory.

In summary, indulgences can help the faithful obtain the remission of temporal punishment due to sin both for themselves and for the souls in purgatory. Such help is possible because of the treasury of the Church and the sharing of the merits of Christ, the Virgin Mary, and the saints on behalf of the faithful on earth and those in purgatory.

Evangelical Assessment

Penance Is Not a Sacrament

Of the four Catholic sacraments presented so far, this sacrament, along with that of Confirmation, is not considered to be a sacrament by evangelical theology. As discussed earlier, the reason for this rejection is that Jesus did not ordain it as a rite to be administered by his church. Appeal to Jesus's words, "Do penance, for the kingdom of God is at hand" (Matt. 4:17), to argue that he did indeed institute Penance as a sacrament, fails because that citation, based on the Latin Vulgate, is a mistranslation of the command as expressed in the Greek New Testament. What he actually ordered was, "Repent, for the kingdom of God is at hand."[50] Jesus never commanded his people to engage in penitential acts of fasting, praying, almsgiving, and the like as prescribed by an ecclesial rite of penance, but to make an about-face, reorient their life, change their mind and heart. Moreover, Martin Luther

---

[48] CCC 1476–1477.

[49] CCC 1478. Specific examples of obtaining indulgences are certain activities associated with the Year of Faith (October 11, 2012 to November 24, 2013) and participation at the 28th Annual World Youth Day (Rio de Janeiro, July 22–29, 2013). For the Year of Faith, see http://www.vatican.va/roman_curia/tribunals/apost_penit/documents/rc_trib_appen_doc_20120914_annus-fidei_en.html. For the World Youth Day, see http://www.vatican.va/roman_curia/tribunals/apost_penit/documents/rc_trib_appen_doc_20130709_decreto-indulgenze-gmg_en.html.

[50] Whereas the Latin Vulgate, the Bible of the Catholic Church, presented Jesus urging "Pœnitentiam agite" ("Do [acts of] penance"), the Greek version narrated Jesus saying "Μετανοεῖτε" (*Metanoeite*; "Repent").

excluded penance as a sacrament, though at first he considered it to be one, because there is no tangible sign associated with it.[51] Evangelical theology, heir of this legacy, dismisses Penance as a sacrament.

Despite setting aside penance as a sacrament, evangelical theology agrees with its Catholic counterpart that confession of sin, repentance, and, in the case of damage done to others by sin, restitution or restoration are necessary. What it disagrees with is Catholic theology's structuring these ongoing actions as part of a sacrament, and it dissents from most of the elements of this rite. These disagreements will be the focus of the following assessment.

Pre- and Post-Baptismal Sins

One problematic area that evangelical theology finds is Catholic theology's division of sins into the two categories of pre- and post-baptismal, with the sacrament of Baptism dealing with pre-baptismal sins and the sacrament of Penance treating post-baptismal sins. Though this division developed in the early church, it has no biblical basis and hence is another case of unchastened Tradition. Furthermore, at the heart of this division is the nature-grace interdependence, an axiom of the Catholic system that has already been critiqued (ch. 2) and demonstrated to be in error. This axiom manifests itself in the Catholic concept of grace as a divine substance or power that is infused into people through the Church's sacraments, thereby elevating and potentially perfecting (human) nature. Accordingly, Baptism is the remedy for pre-baptismal sins, providing the infusion of grace to cancel original sin and to grant a new nature in the case of infants and, in the case of adults, to cancel original sin and the actual sins they have committed up to the point of their Baptism—and to give them a new nature. When baptismal or justifying grace is forfeited by the commission of mortal sin, plunging sinful people into a dreadful situation of the loss of salvation and

---

[51] As Luther expressed his conviction at the end of his 1520 work *On the Babylonian Captivity of the Church,* "It has seemed best, however, to consider as sacraments, properly so called, those promises which have signs annexed to them. The rest, as they are not attached to signs, are simple promises. It follows that, if we speak with perfect accuracy, there are only two sacraments in the Church of God, Baptism and the Bread; since it is in these alone that we see both a sign divinely instituted and a promise of remission of sins. The sacrament of penance, which I have reckoned along with these two, is without any visible and divinely appointed sign; and is nothing else, as I have said, than a way and means of return to baptism. Not even the schoolmen can say that penitence agrees with their definition; since they themselves ascribe to every sacrament a visible sign, which enables the senses to apprehend the form of that effect which the sacrament works invisibly. Now penitence or absolution has no such sign; and therefore they will be compelled by their own definition either to say that penitence is not one of the sacraments, and thus to diminish their number, or else to bring forward another definition of a sacrament" (*LW* 36:243–244).

impending divine condemnation in hell, another means for the infusion of grace is necessitated. The sacrament of Penance is this means, as the grace that it confers rectifies all post-baptismal sins, particularly mortal sins, and reinstitutes the process of elevating (human) nature, restoring penitents to friendship with God and fellowship with the Church. But if salvation does not depend on the progress of character transformation rendering the faithful more and more perfect in love, and if grace is not infused into them so as to foster this transformation, and if the division of sins into pre- and post-baptismal categories is without foundation, then the sacrament collapses. This is the assessment of evangelical theology.

Two Moments of Conversion

Another contrived distinction in this sacrament that presents a problem for evangelical theology comes as the result of assigning two moments to conversion. Evangelical theology clearly embraces what is called the "first conversion," involving the proclamation of the gospel to nonbelievers and the correlative call to repent and believe in Christ. That baptism is part of the appropriation of salvation is also embraced by much of evangelical theology, though without the Catholic accompaniments, as already discussed. As God operates powerfully to convict nonbelievers of their sin, calls them to embrace salvation, regenerates them, and the like, the human response is turning from sin, trusting in Christ, obeying the command to be baptized, and so on. This, indeed, is conversion, or the "first conversion."

It is with the other moment of conversion—the "second conversion"—that evangelical theology has difficulty. This ongoing response to Christ's call is not a foreign concept to, nor is it rejected by, evangelical theology. As Wayne Grudem discusses it, "although it is true that *initial* saving faith and *initial* repentance occur only once in our lives, and when they occur they constitute true conversion, nonetheless, the heart attitudes of repentance and faith only begin at conversion. These same attitudes should continue throughout the course of our Christian lives."[52] At the same time, biblically speaking, this ongoing process should more properly be called sanctification, not conversion. This precision helps avoid two problems with Catholic theology's presentation of ongoing conversion. First, Scripture presents

---

[52] Grudem, *ST*, 717 (emphasis original).

sanctification, not conversion, as featuring an ongoing, cooperative effort between divine grace and human work. God, in ways that are appropriate to his divine agency, supplies his grace to guide, discipline, empower, correct, and bless his people who, in ways that are appropriate to their human agency, read and memorize Scripture, pray, fast, fellowship with other Christians, avoid sin, and much more. Calling this second conversion "sanctification" brings a certain degree of precision and greater conformity to Scripture. It also avoids the difficulty of the weak biblical support for this "second conversion" as offered by Catholic theology. Peter's "conversion" after his three denials of Christ, who later restored him, seems more related to his restoration to ministry than a model for how the faithful are to convert in an ongoing manner. But the ongoing synergistic process of sanctification has much biblical support (e.g., Phil. 2:12–13; 1 Thess. 5:23; Heb. 13:20–21).

All stripes of evangelical theology applaud Catholic theology's emphasis on conversion being first and foremost the result of divine grace to bring awareness of sin, stir repentance, prompt faith, and so forth. In this regard, two theological persuasions attempt to discern the actual order of the events that occur in salvation. The debate is particularly focused on the relationship between regeneration and conversion. Arminian theology holds that, first, in response to prevenient grace, people who hear the gospel repent and express faith in Christ (conversion), then God gives them a new nature (regeneration). Reformed theology maintains that God first regenerates people, who then respond by converting through repentance and faith.[53] Attention should be called to the fact that both theologies emphasize the priority of divine grace for salvation. Though the doctrine of salvation will be discussed later, Catholic theology is similar to the Arminian position, which is also held by a large swath of evangelical theology. The other part of evangelical theology embraces the Reformed view and is opposed, therefore, to the Catholic order of salvation.

Acts of Penance

With the priority assigned to grace clearly affirmed, Catholic theology turns to a discussion of the human side of conversion, particularly its "expres-

---

[53] Without prejudicing this discussion toward either position, it seems that the clearest biblical passage that links regeneration and conversion places these two events in that order: "Everyone who believes that Jesus is the Christ has been born of God" (1 John 5:1). Belief in Christ (conversion) is grounded on, or is the fruit of, the new birth (regeneration).

sion in concrete signs, gestures and works of penance."[54] Again, evangelical theology is in full accord that genuine conversion will—indeed, must—bear fruit in terms of good deeds that are evident to others. As James underscored, "Faith apart from works is dead" (James 2:26). A question arises, however, as to why Catholic theology considers these acts of penance to be principally of three types: fasting, prayers, and almsgiving (which are expressions of conversion in relation to, respectively, oneself, God, and others). Certainly, Scripture associates fasting and prayer with repentance (e.g., Neh. 1:4); it is also frequently linked with weeping and lamenting, and dressing in sackcloth and ashes (e.g., Est. 4:3; Dan. 9:3; Jonah 3:6–10). Almsgiving—material aid given to assist the poor and needy—is also connected with conversion (e.g., Zaccheus; Luke 19:1–10). And almsgiving receives particular attention in some of the apocryphal writings. For example, Ecclesiasticus urges, "Store up almsgiving in your treasury, and it will rescue you from all affliction; more than a mighty shield and more than a heavy spear, it will fight on your behalf against your enemy" (Ecclus. 29:12–13). Tobit commands, "Give alms from your possessions to all who live uprightly, and do not let your eye begrudge the gift when you make it. Do not turn your face away from any poor man, and the face of God will not be turned away from you" (Tobit 4:7).

Importantly, however, Scripture does not seem to elevate these three acts above numerous other acts as being the principal fruits of turning to God. For example, John the Baptist clearly promoted almsgiving in his commands to the penitents who came to him for baptism: "Whoever has two tunics is to share with him who has none, and whoever has food is to do likewise" (Luke 3:11). But his instructions about acts of genuine repentance were also tailor-made, and thus varying, for the specific people who questioned him: "Tax collectors also came to be baptized and said to him, 'Teacher, what shall we do?' And he said to them, 'Collect no more than you are authorized to do.' Soldiers also asked him, 'And we, what shall we do?' And he said to them, 'Do not extort money from anyone by threats or by false accusation, and be content with your wages'" (Luke 3:12–14). Moreover, the apostle John presents four realities that flow from being born of God. One is a break with habitual sin, which is no longer able to dominate (1 John 3:9). Love for others is a second fruit (4:7). A third is resisting the enticements

---

[54] CCC 1430.

and temptations of the world and obeying God's commandments, which are not onerous duties, by an ongoing faith (5:3–4). This continuing faith is due to divine protection from Satan, a fourth concrete result (v. 18).

For evangelical theology, these biblical examples urge caution in accepting fasting, prayers, and almsgiving as the principal fruits of conversion. Not to be overlooked in this critique is Catholic theology's emphasis on other expressions of conversion, including some of the ones presented above. But its elevation of fasting, prayers, and almsgiving is resisted by evangelical theology because such selectivity lacks basis in Scripture, which presents the fruits of repentance and faith in an expansive way. Moreover, evangelical theology, as heir to the Protestant Reformation, also rejects Catholic theology's historical pattern of emphasizing "spiritual" good works over other types—collecting a fair amount of taxes, refusing to extort money, being content with one's paycheck, and the like (Luke 3:12–14).[55]

The Two-Sided Nature of Sin

Another duality that Catholic theology emphasizes in its discussion of conversion is the two-sided nature of sin and the implications of this complex reality for conversion. According to Catholic theology, sin both offends God and injures fellowship with the Church, necessitating both God's forgiveness and reconciliation with the Church. This double-sided nature of sin is addressed by this sacrament's two most common names: Penance (bringing divine forgiveness) and Reconciliation (fostering reparation with the Church).

With respect to the first reality, evangelical theology affirms Catholic theology's insistence that God alone forgives sin. This point is commonly misunderstood by evangelical theology because of the following additional affirmation by its Catholic counterpart: Christ entrusts the power of absolution to the apostolic ministry—the apostles and their successors, the bishops—of the Catholic Church, whereby its ordained clergy exercise the authority to forgive in the name of Christ. Biblical support is found in Paul's description of the apostolic ministry as being divinely commissioned, with God pleading through Paul as an apostle, urging people to be reconciled to God (2 Cor. 5:18–20), the first reality. This same authority to grant forgive-

---

[55] Martin Luther took a particularly strong stand against this Catholic tendency in his *Sermon on Good Works*.

ness is wielded by the clergy to reconcile sinful people with the Church, the second reality. The key biblical warrant is Jesus's granting of the keys to Peter and, through him, to the college of apostles, which in turn transferred this authority to its successor, the college of bishops. The power of the keys is that of binding and loosing: exclusion from communion with the Church because of entrenched sin and refusal to repent and be restored; or reception into fellowship by and with the Church because of availing oneself of the forgiveness its clergy offers.

Taking these two realities together, evangelical theology denies the delegation of the divine power to forgive sins to the clergy of the Catholic Church. An overarching critique of this position has already been offered when evangelical theology dismissed the Christ-Church interconnection upon which the Catholic system is constructed. Evangelical theology dissents from the axiom that the Catholic Church is the prolongation of the incarnation of Jesus Christ, making the Church—in this case, the clergy with its power to absolve the faithful of their sins—the mediator between grace and nature. In terms of specific criticisms, what Christ entrusted to the church was not a structure of apostolic succession whose members possess and employ delegated authority to grant absolution. Rather, he gave a commission to his apostles to make disciples of all people, the fulfillment of which they took to be the proclamation of the message of salvation accomplished by the death of Jesus Christ (see Acts). This fact is confirmed by the very passage invoked by Catholic theology in support of its position (2 Cor. 5:18–20). The apostle Paul did indeed receive the ministry of reconciliation. Yet, in the same breath, he describes its nature: "in Christ God was reconciling the world to himself, not counting their trespasses against them, and *entrusting to us the message* [Gk. λόγος (*logos*), literally, *the word*] *of reconciliation*" (v. 19, emphasis added). Through the message of the gospel, God effects restoration of our fellowship with him. As discussed earlier, the messengers whom God employs to proclaim this message are only stewards of it, servants through whom the gospel is announced and believed; they do not possess any delegated authority to make forgiveness take place.

Furthermore, Catholic theology's understanding of the keys of binding and loosing is critically inverted. Jesus did not promise to do what the *Catechism* explains: "whomever you exclude from your communion, *will be excluded* from communion with God; whomever you receive anew into your communion, *God will welcome* him back into his."[56] Rather, Jesus promised "whomever you exclude from your communion, *has already been excluded* from communion with God; whomever you receive anew into your communion, *God has already welcomed* him back into his."[57] The divine action is not subsequent to the church's action, thereby reflecting it or depending on it. On the contrary, the divine action is prior to the church's action, which in consequence reflects it and depends on it. This misunderstanding of the power of the keys is a specific reason for evangelical theology's rejection of Catholic theology's idea of God's delegation of the power to forgive sins to the Church's hierarchy. The messenger of the gospel proclaims, "For our sake he [God] made him [Christ] to be sin who knew no sin, so that in him we might become the righteousness of God" (2 Cor. 5:21). When this message is embraced, the messenger assures its recipients that they are no longer bound in their sins, but loosed from them to be in relationship with God. When the word is rebuffed, the messenger warns its detractors that they are still bound in their sins, and divine judgment and condemnation await them if they do not embrace Christ.

Mortal and Venial Sins

Turning to an assessment of who are required to avail themselves of the sacrament of Penance and Reconciliation, another duality is introduced: mortal sin and venial sin. Though this topic will be discussed more fully later on, it is sufficient to know that mortal sin is a deliberately chosen, grave wrongdoing committed with full awareness of violating the divine law. It results in the loss of baptismal or justifying grace; because grace is forfeited, one who commits mortal sin is destined to hell, apart from a new infusion of grace. Venial sin involves a less serious matter than does mortal sin: It is not a grave violation of the divine law, or, if it is, something less than full knowledge and/or deliberate consent is involved. It does not result in the loss of divine grace. This distinction has a great bearing on the sacrament of Penance: Penance is required in every case of mortal sin, but it is not needed in the case of venial sin. The sacrament provides new justifying grace for those who, through mortal sin, have lost it. Moreover, because

---

[56] CCC 1445 (emphasis added).
[57] Emphasis added. For a technical discussion of the Greek construction of future periphrastic perfects that give this sense, see D. A. Carson, "Matthew," in Frank E. Gaebelein, ed., *Expositor's Bible Commentary*, 12 vols. (Grand Rapids, MI: Zondervan, 1984), 8:370–372.

venial sin does not result in the loss of grace, the sacrament is not needed to restore that which was not lost.

Though a full assessment will be given later on, evangelical theology decries this distinction between mortal and venial sins. According to Scripture (e.g., James 2:10–11; Gal. 3:10), whether a sin is serious or minor, it results in guilt before God; thus, the one committing the sin stands in need of divine grace for forgiveness. Accordingly, if evangelical theology embraced a sacrament of Penance for post-baptismal sins, it would require participation in the sacrament for each and every sin, whether great or small. But, rejecting both the underlying distinction between mortal and venial sins as well as the sacrament itself, evangelical theology insists instead on confession of all sins, repentance from them, and restitution in all cases that require the restoration of honor, property, relationship, or the like.

Human and Divine Action

Catholic theology underscores yet another duality that is at the heart of the sacrament of Penance: the human action of conversion, and the divine action of forgiveness through the intervention of the Church. As for the human element, three acts are required of penitents: contrition, confession of sins, and satisfaction. The first of these, *contrition*, has some overlap with evangelical theology's concept of repentance, which involves acknowledgment that sin is wrong, sorrow for and hatred of sin, renunciation of it, and resolution to break with sin. Where evangelical theology disagrees is with the proposal that contrition is of two types, perfect and imperfect. Granted, Scripture makes a distinction between godly sorrow and worldly sorrow: "For godly grief produces a repentance that leads to salvation without regret, whereas worldly grief produces death" (2 Cor. 7:10). The godly sorrow about which Paul writes was the proper grief that his severe letter to the Corinthians prompted; it manifested itself in repentance, eagerness to do what was right, indignation over sin, and the like (vv. 9, 11). Though the apostle does not explain what he means by worldly grief, one could surmise that it consists of sorrow that one got caught in sin, that one is suffering because of sin being exposed, or the like. If this distinction between perfect and imperfect contrition is what Catholic theology means, then there is some common ground. But when Catholic theology goes on to attribute the remission of venial sins as well as the forgiveness of mortal sins (if the act includes the determination to avail oneself promptly of the sacrament) to perfect contrition, evangelical theology dissents.

The second penitential act is *the confession of sins*, and again there is some overlap with evangelical theology's notion of confession as involving acknowledgment of one's sins, agreeing with God that they are wrong, and admitting responsibility for them. Part and parcel of evangelical theology's view, however, is also trusting the divine promise that, "If we confess our sins, he [God] is faithful and just to forgive us our sins and to cleanse us from all unrighteousness" (1 John 1:9). Confession of sins, therefore, entails faith that those sins are forgiven and that the one confessing them is now cleansed from all filth. This is not a matter of autosuggestion or wishful thinking, nor is it something that is lightly regarded or done flippantly. On the contrary, it is an act of faith in God who through Christ has accomplished salvation from sin and who promises the forgiveness of sin to his people. Such confession does not involve going to a priest to seek absolution, which is an essential part of the Catholic sacrament. Such confession is demanded not only in the case of mortal sins; on the contrary, any sin that is brought to consciousness by the Word of God (e.g., Heb. 4:12) and the Spirit of God (e.g., John 16:8–11) must be confessed. The frequency of this confession is not ecclesially regulated to consist in a minimum of once a year. Indeed, given that all sin brings guilt before God, resulting in the impairment of one's relationship with him, sins should not be "stored up" for an ecclesial act of penance but should be promptly confessed to God; any accumulation of sins can only be disastrous for one's daily walk with him. If this continuous pattern of confession is what Catholic theology envisions in the case of venial sins, there is some formal overlap with evangelical theology at this point. Finally, the barring of the sacrament of the Eucharist to Catholics who have committed mortal sin and have not availed themselves of absolution through the sacrament of Penance has been addressed earlier (ch. 9).

The third penitential act is *satisfaction*, which focuses on repairing the harm wrought by sin to others' reputation, honor, property, character, well-being, family, and the like. With this notion of satisfaction, evangelical theology is in full agreement. Forgiveness or absolution deals with the sin itself, but when that sin has wreaked havoc in the lives of others, restitution or restoration is necessary. However, agreement stops here, for evangelical theology strongly dissents from the other aspects of Catholic theology's explanation of satisfaction.

The principal disagreement focuses on the idea that those who sin must "do penance," that is, make amends for or expiate their sins. This notion of satisfaction has its roots in the eleventh-century model of the atonement (what Christ's death on the cross accomplished) offered by Anselm.[58] This leading theologian-philosopher developed his theory amid the medieval culture of feudalism. In this system, feudal overlords protected serfs, who in turn worked for them by providing food and services. Importantly, restitution of honor through satisfaction was a key idea. If a serf dishonored his lord by stealing ten chickens, for example, the satisfaction that was demanded was not only the restitution of what had been stolen (ten chickens); rather, the serf had to render satisfaction by doing something more to restore his lord's honor—he owed, for example, fifteen chickens. For Anselm, what Christ accomplished on the cross was a response to human sin that had robbed God of his honor. What was required to restore God's honor was for sinful human beings to render satisfaction, but they could do nothing more than offer what they already owed to God—a humble heart, or obedience, for example. Moreover, sinful human beings could do nothing to help other sinful human beings. Accordingly, only Jesus Christ, the God-man, could save humanity, and he did so by offering himself to die in their place. This act of satisfaction went beyond what the sinless Savior owed to God, thus restoring God's honor. Rewarded by God for his obedience that went beyond the call of duty, Jesus Christ gives this reward to fallen human beings so as to provide satisfaction for their sins.

Though not Anselm's point, his atonement model was applied to the need of sinful human beings to make satisfaction for their sins, that is, to do something more to make amends for or expiate their sins through the sacrament of Penance. Evangelical theology, as heir of the Protestant Reformation, adheres to a different model of the atonement that, while similar in some ways to Anselm's satisfaction theory, has this major difference: Instead of grounding the atonement in the honor of God—that of which God has been robbed by the sin of humanity—the penal substitutionary theory grounds it in the justice of God. Because God is holy, he hates sin with wrathful anger; accordingly, sinful human beings have an eternal

---

[58] Anselm, *Why God Became Man.*

penalty to pay. Because they cannot atone for their own sins, Jesus Christ did: as the substitute for humanity, he died as a sacrifice to pay the penalty for sin, suffered the divine wrath against it, and removed its condemnation forever. With this penal substitutionary model of the atonement at its core, evangelical theology rejects the sacrament of Penance, because sinful human beings cannot do more than they are required to do, cannot make amends for or expiate their sin, and cannot render satisfaction to God—indeed, they not only *cannot* do these things; they *need not* do them, because Jesus Christ has provided full satisfaction to God through his death as a substitute for sinful humanity.

Flowing from this disavowal of the sacrament itself, evangelical theology also objects to Catholic theology's provision for a confessor-priest who imposes the appropriate satisfaction on the penitents. Whatever the penance might be—prayer (a common prescription is for the penitent to recite the "Hail Mary" five times and the "Our Father" five times), an offering, good deeds, and the like—none of them can nor need accomplish what Catholic theology envisions for it. Additionally, the penance cannot help "configure" (conform) the penitents to Christ or allow them to become his coheirs through suffering. Finally, Catholic theology's insistence that satisfaction is rendered through and finds its effectiveness in Christ cannot alter the fact that penance is not and cannot be needed, because of the supremely sufficient, satisfactory death of Jesus Christ by which he paid the penalty of sin as the substitute for sinful human beings.

Two Effects of Penance

As a final duality, Catholic theology considers the effects of the sacrament of Penance to be twofold: restoration to the grace of God and reconciliation with the Church. Confessed and absolved mortal sin is removed, and penitents are infused with new justifying grace so as to be restored to a relationship with God. Additionally, community with the faithful is revitalized. Evangelical theology concurs that the fruit of confession, repentance, and, when necessary, restitution of honor or property, or restoration of a broken Christian friendship, is indeed rich. Such fruit does not include justification, because that verdict of "not guilty" but "righteous instead" has already been pronounced and is therefore true of penitents. Nor does such fruit of penance entail a new infusion of divine grace. Rather, the effects are more on the order of the additional results of the sacrament detailed by Catholic theology: peace, a clear conscience, comfort, intimacy of relationship with God and others, and so forth. A bit more needs to be said about this aspect of confession.

I am fully aware of Catholic testimonies of how a priest's pronouncement of absolution of their sins as part of this sacrament overwhelmed those penitents with assurance and comfort of God's gracious work of forgiveness. The same is true for evangelical friends and disciples who have pulled me aside and confessed their sins, prompting me to rehearse 1 John 1:9 to them: "If we confess our sins, he is faithful and just to forgive us our sins and to cleanse us from all unrighteousness." Indeed, Scripture pictures the church as being the grace-filled place in which Christians regularly confess their sins to one another (James 5:16). But here is the point, according to evangelical theology: the human articulation of forgiveness, whether uttered by a priest or by a Christian friend, is a pronouncement of *what is true*, but it is not a declaration that *makes it true*. A clear example comes from Jesus himself when he explained the apostles' use of the keys of the kingdom: "whatever you bind on earth shall be bound in heaven, and whatever you loose on earth shall be loosed in heaven" (Matt. 16:19; 18:18). The apostolic pronouncement that an unrepentant person is still bound in her sins reflects a divine declaration that she is still bound in her sins, and the apostolic pronouncement that a repentant person is now loosed from her sins reflects a divine declaration that she has been loosed or forgiven of her sins. In both cases, the human pronouncement echoes a state of affairs—bound in sin; loosed from sin—that is *already true*; it *does not make it true*. Accordingly, when a priest or a Christian friend hears a confession and assures the penitent that her confessed sin is forgiven on the basis of the faithful and just God's forgiveness of it and his cleansing of her from all sins, the truth of forgiveness is spoken, not accomplished.

This evangelical theology of forgiveness encourages two things. One is for Christians during the regular course of their day to confess their sins promptly to God and, in accordance with the promise of Scripture, believe that their sins are indeed forgiven. Confession of sins and the appropriation of forgiveness becomes a matter of trust. Accordingly, whether Christians feel comfort and assurance that their confessed sins are forgiven is not the key issue. Rather, the promise of God in his Word, and the believers' trust that what God declares is true because he has made it true, is key. Failure to appropriate the forgiveness of sins through confession is not the result of lacking a human intermediary who pronounces the truth that God has forgiven them, but is due to a lack of faith in the promise of the Word of God. If the biblical promise of forgiveness is a divine speech-act,[59] then God's utterance of 1 John 1:9 is more than just a pronouncement of words; on the contrary, it is a declaration that *makes forgiveness the case.*

Second, this evangelical theology of forgiveness encourages Christians to confess their sins to one another. As noted above, something powerful transpires when corporate confession takes place. Sometimes it involves bringing into the light hidden sins that have heretofore isolated and burdened the one who now confesses them. Sometimes it entails reminding a forgetful, distracted, or depressed person of the divine promise of forgiveness. Though many churches—evangelical churches as well as the Catholic Church—encourage people to put on a facade of Christian piety and discourage transparency about the way things actually are, churches should be safe havens that take the lead in confession of sin and repentance among their members, grace-filled places that are not shocked by immorality, embezzlement, pride, laziness, broken relationships, anger, and other sins, but that move quickly to comfort, rebuke, correct, and forgive. This evangelical theology of the confession of sin does not depend on the sacrament of Penance for its reality or fruitfulness.

Indulgences

One final topic that is associated with the sacrament of Penance is the doctrine and practice of indulgences. It is related in this fashion: Through the sacrament, the eternal punishment of sin is remitted; however, Penance does not remove the taint of forgiven mortal sin, and the stain of venial sin persists. If the faithful are not fully obedient in this life, their souls go to purgatory to face further purification of remaining corruption.

Evangelical theology, following in the footsteps of Reformers such as Martin Luther and John Calvin, denounces this aspect of Catholic doctrine. Salient points of disagreement are the following: Designed to remit

---

[59] A "speech-act" is an utterance that does something. For example, when a pastor concludes a wedding ceremony by saying to the man and woman before him, "I now pronounce you husband and wife," his pronouncement effects the joining of those two people in marriage. Speech-act theory has become quite popular among evangelical theologians and philosophers.

the temporal punishment due to forgiven sins, indulgences are superfluous because Jesus Christ, through his supremely sufficient sacrifice on behalf of sinful human beings, has already remitted all punishment due to sin. He has fully paid the penalty; thus, no guilt remains and there is no temporal punishment for forgiven sinful people to face. Moreover, salvation is not dependent on the complete purification of human beings' sinful nature in this life; rather, it is a matter of justification, which is God's forensic declaration that repentant sinners are not guilty but righteous instead because the perfect righteousness of Christ is credited to their account. While justification is not the only mighty work of God in saving fallen human beings, it is the one upon which rest such promises as, "There is therefore now no condemnation for those who are in Christ Jesus" (Rom. 8:1). No condemnation means no guilt, and if there is no guilt, there is no temporal punishment to pay in purgatory, release from which is aided by indulgences.

Furthermore, the concept of the treasury of the saints, by which an exchange of spiritual goods applies the merits of Christ, together with the prayers and good works of Mary and the saints, to the souls of the faithful in purgatory, has no biblical basis and is illogical. If Christ's merits are indeed infinite, as Catholic theology maintains, then what possible benefit could be superadded to what is already infinite by the deeds and prayers of Mary and the saints? And what interest could be compounded to the treasury by full or partial remission of sin earned or purchased by the living faithful? At the heart of these questions lies evangelical theology's critique of the Christ-Church interconnection, which views the Catholic Church as the extension of the incarnation of Christ, thereby rendering the Church's mediation of forgiveness and other spiritual goods necessary. Evangelical theology balks at the doctrine and practice of indulgences.

In summary, the sacrament of Penance and Reconciliation, which provides for the forgiveness of mortal sins but does not remove the stain of those forgiven sins nor the taint of venial sins, is not considered a sacrament by evangelical theology. While applauding such aspects as the affirmation that God alone forgives sin, the call to Christians to confess their sins, the insistence that genuine conversion leads to concrete results, and a few other points, evangelical theology has many substantive areas of disagreement with this sacrament.

The Sacrament of the Anointing of the Sick (Sec. 2, Ch. 2, Art. 5)

The second sacrament of healing is the Anointing of the Sick, by which "the whole Church commends those who are ill to the suffering and glorified Lord, that he may raise them up and save them."[60] It is known also as *extreme unction*, in that it is the anointing of the faithful at the point of their death (the nearly exclusive use of this sacrament prior to Vatican Council II), and the *sacrament of those departing (sacramentum exeuntium)*.

The biblical basis for this sacrament begins with the common experience of human illness and suffering, which can provoke despair and even revolt against God, or which can prompt maturity and even a search for God. In the Old Testament, sickness is closely connected to sin and evil, together with the hope that God is the healer of all illness, if not during one's earthly lifetime, then certainly in a future time. As Jesus announced the inauguration of that time in his message that the kingdom of God is at hand (Mark 1:15), he followed up his proclamation with compassion for the sick and healings of many types (Mark 1:21–2:12). Often he asked the sick to believe (Mark 5:34, 36; 9:23), and he employed signs (e.g., spittle, Mark 7:32–37; mud and washing, John 9:6–7), along with the laying on of hands (Mark 8:22–25). Conversely, the sick tried to touch him, "for power came forth from him and healed them all" (Luke 6:19; cf. Mark 1:41; 3:10; 6:56). Matthew's Gospel presents Jesus's healing of the sick as a fulfillment of Isaiah's prophecy: "He took our infirmities and bore our diseases" (Matt. 8:17; Isa. 53:4). Yet Jesus did not heal everyone, for his healings were signs of the arrival of the kingdom pointing beyond themselves to "a more radical healing: the victory over sin and death."[61] Through his death on the cross, "Christ took upon himself the whole weight of evil and took away the 'sin of the world' [John 1:29; cf. Isa. 53:4–6], of which illness is only a consequence."[62] The sacrament of Anointing is a means by which Jesus continues to touch the faithful in order to heal them and unite them to his redemptive suffering.

Moreover, Christ invited his disciples to take up their cross and follow him (Matt. 10:38) and, as they became associated with his poverty and service, he commissioned them to heal: "[T]hey cast out many demons, and

---

[60] CCC 1499; citation is from Vatican Council II, *Lumen Gentium* 11.
[61] CCC 1505.
[62] Ibid.

anointed with oil many that were sick and healed them" (Mark 6:13). To some were granted a special gift of healing (Mark 16:17–18), yet recovery does not take place all the time; accordingly, the apostle Paul learned that divine grace is sufficient even when healing is not forthcoming (2 Cor. 12:9) and that suffering means that "in my flesh I complete what is lacking in Christ's afflictions for the sake of his Body, that is, the Church" (Col. 1:24).

Accordingly, this sacrament is needed because the Church has received the Lord's command: "Heal the sick!" (Matt. 10:8). Furthermore, James attests to the rite: "Is any among you sick? Let him call for the elders [*presbyters*] of the Church and let them pray over him, anointing him with oil in the name of the Lord; and the prayer of faith will save the sick man, and the Lord will raise him up; and if he has committed sins, he will be forgiven" (James 5:14–15).[63]

Until Vatican Council II, the administration of the sacrament of the Anointing of the Sick was almost exclusively for those about to die; following the Council, the new rite "is not a sacrament for those only who are at the point of death. Hence, as soon as anyone of the faithful begins to be in danger of death from sickness or old age, the fitting time for him to receive this sacrament has certainly already arrived."[64] Moreover, the sacrament is repeatable, both in the case of a grave illness for which the anointing was administered, followed by recovery and then another grave illness, and in the case of a deteriorating condition during the same grave illness. It is also proper to administer the sacrament before any serious operation and in the case of the increasing frailty of the elderly.

The proper ministers of the Anointing of the Sick are priests (or bishops), upon whom the faithful call in order to receive it. The priests do not administer the sacrament to one who is already dead. The rite is administered in the following way, whether it takes place in a home, a hospital, or a church building, and whether it is dispensed upon one person or a group of the faithful: Ideally, its administration is preceded by the sacrament of Penance and followed by the sacrament of the Eucharist, which "should always be the last sacrament of the earthly journey, the 'viaticum' for 'passing over' to eternal life."[65] Specifically, the celebration opens with an act of

---

[63] *CCC* 1509–1510.
[64] *CCC* 1514; citation is from Vatican Council II, *Sacrosanctum concilium* 73; cf. canons 1004.1; 1005; 1007 of the Code of Canon Law.
[65] *CCC* 1517. The Latin word *viaticum* refers to provisions for a journey.

repentance, followed by the Liturgy of the Word. The priests silently "lay hands on the sick; they pray over them in the faith of the Church—this is the epiclesis proper to this sacrament; they then anoint them with oil blessed, if possible, by the bishop."[66]

The particular grace conferred through this sacrament produces several effects: As a particular gift of the Holy Spirit, the effect is a renewal of trust in God that strengthens the resolve of the faithful not to fall into the temptations of Satan toward discouragement and anguish at their approaching death. This Spirit-empowerment works upon and heals their soul and, if God wills, also their body. Additionally, the sick experience union with the passion of Christ: "[I]n a certain way he [the sick person] is consecrated to bear fruit by configuration to the Savior's redemptive Passion. Suffering . . . acquires a new meaning; it becomes a participation in the saving work of Jesus."[67] Furthermore, the recipients of this sacrament "contribute to the good of the People of God" by adding their suffering to the suffering of the Church and its offering of itself to God.[68] Finally, the sacrament completes the faithful's conformity to the death and resurrection of Christ, "just as Baptism began it." That is, the whole Christian life is marked out by three "holy anointings": The first anointing is that of Baptism, the seal of new life; the second is that of Confirmation, the strength for the struggles of this life; and the last is the Anointing of the Sick, the fortification at the end of this life in anticipation of the life to come.[69] As noted earlier, this last Anointing is joined with the Eucharist as viaticum, "the sacrament of passing over from death to life, from this world to the Father."[70]

Evangelical Assessment

For the most part, evangelical theology concurs with what Catholic theology affirms about healing. Specific points of agreement include the connection between sin and sickness; the compassion that Jesus exhibited toward the sick; his healing of some but not all who were afflicted; his ministry of physical restoration as a sign of the arrival of the kingdom of God (which itself pointed to a more radical intervention to conquer sin and death); heal-

---

[66] CCC 1519.
[67] CCC 1521.
[68] CCC 1522; citation is from Vatican Council II, *Lumen Gentium* 11.2.
[69] CCC 1523.
[70] CCC 1524.

ing as an integral part of Jesus's commission of his disciples; and James's instructions for how the church is to engage in the ministry of healing prayer today. Because these latter instructions do not limit this ministry to prayer and anointing only in the case of Christians who are on the verge of death, evangelical theology agrees with the change introduced by Vatican Council II, opening this ministry to anyone who is in danger of death, in failing health because of sickness or old age, about to undergo a serious operation, and the like.

Anointing of the Sick Is Not a Sacrament

The central point of disagreement is Catholic theology's determination that this ministry of healing is a sacrament. For evangelical theology, the rite does meet one requirement for a sacrament or ordinance: anointing with oil is its tangible sign. What it lacks, however, is Christ's institution of it as a sacrament. Certainly, he healed the sick, and occasionally his act of restoration was accompanied by a physical sign—e.g., spittle, the laying on of hands, mud and washing. But the variety of these tangible symbols, which Jesus sometimes employed and sometimes did not, cautions against seeing this ministry as being ordained by Christ with a specific sign. It is also the case that Jesus commissioned his disciples to heal the sick, but as this healing ministry was only one aspect of a broader ministry that Christ gave to them (it also included exorcisms and preaching the gospel), it should not be isolated from those other aspects and then elevated to the status of sacrament. Catholic theology also points to the phrase "in the name of the Lord" as part of James's instruction about this rite (James 5:14), as support for Christ ordaining it as a sacrament. The phrase, however, does not indicate the *dominical origin* of this ministry but the *divine authority* with which it is carried out. An example that underscores the authoritative nature of the name of Jesus is a man lame from birth, whom Peter and John healed "in the name of Jesus Christ of Nazareth" (Acts 3:1–16, esp. vv. 6, 16). When later asked by the Sanhedrin, "By what power or by what name did you do this?" Peter explained, "if we are being examined today concerning a good deed done to a crippled man, by what means this man has been healed, let it be known to all of you and to all the people of Israel that by the name of Jesus Christ of Nazareth, whom you crucified, whom God raised from the dead—by him this man is standing before you well" (4:7–10).[71] Accordingly, as the elders of the church pray over sick people and anoint them with oil "in the name of the Lord," they exercise their ministry under the sovereign authority of Jesus Christ, without that phrase indicating that he ordained such a ministry to be a sacrament for his church.

Other Disagreements

Other points of disagreement are found in Catholic theology's ideal administration of this sacrament in conjunction with Penance (preceding it) and the Eucharist (following it). Having already treated the Eucharistic sacrament administered as viaticum and the sacrament of Penance as forgiving mortal sins, it only needs repeating that a final infusion of grace through these sacraments is not needed for departing this life and entering into salvation in the life to come. Moreover, evangelical theology questions Catholic theology's point that, through the conveyance of grace in this sacrament of Anointing the Sick, the Holy Spirit heals the souls of its recipients and, if God wills, also their bodies. At no point does Scripture indicate that inner healing is the intended result of prayer for physical healing; rather, the Bible's emphasis—in Jesus's ministry of healing, in his commissioning of his disciples to engage in healing, and in James's instructions about this ministry—is always on physical healing. In response, Catholic theology may point to the accompanying promise "and if he has committed sins, he will be healed" (James 5:15); from this phrase, it draws the conclusion that healing of the soul is an effect of the sacrament. However, this further effect is attached, not to the anointing with oil, but to the confession of those sins: "Therefore, confess your sins to one another and pray for one another, that you may be healed" (v. 16).

Furthermore, Catholic theology's proposal that the suffering of the faithful more closely unites them with the passion of Jesus Christ, so that their suffering means a participation in his saving work, is far removed from Scripture. The sufferings of *Jesus* are redemptive, not those of the faithful. That Christ promises suffering to his followers (Phil. 1:29), leaves them an example of how to suffer righteously (1 Pet. 2:21–25), calls them to endure

---

[71] Another example is the disciples' prayer that God would grant them boldness in evangelism while "you [God] stretch out your hand to heal, and signs and wonders are performed through the name of your holy servant Jesus" (Acts 4:30). Biblical parallels to healing in the name of Jesus are casting out demons in his name (e.g., Matt. 7:22; 8:16; 10:1; 12:27–28; Acts 16:18; 19:13), again with the emphasis on the authority with which these exorcisms are carried out.

(1 Pet: 1:6–9), and provides all the resources necessary for them to bear up in the midst of trials and heartache (2 Cor. 12:10) is certainly affirmed by Scripture. But it does not present the sufferings of the faithful as a joining with Christ in his saving work, nor do the recipients of this sacrament add their sufferings to the suffering of the Church. This view is grounded on the Christ-Church interconnection: The Catholic Church is the ongoing incarnation of the whole Christ, both the head and his body being joined together and present in the Church. Thus, the sufferings of the body—the faithful—are joined to the sufferings of the head—Jesus Christ. This axiom has already been demonstrated to be fundamentally flawed.

More specifically, this position seems to be based on a misunderstanding of Paul's affirmation that, "I rejoice in my sufferings for your sake, and in my flesh *I am filling up what is lacking in Christ's afflictions for the sake of his body, that is, the church*, of which I became a minister according to the stewardship from God that was given to me for you, to make the word of God fully known" (Col. 1:24–25, emphasis added). The apostle, through his suffering, is not compensating for any deficiency in the sacrifice of Jesus Christ. Rather, he fills up what the church of Colossae lacked by becoming its servant, "to make the word of God fully known," specifically through his pioneering ministry to the Gentiles, for which he struggles mightily through God's power (vv. 26–29). The New Testament narratives of the apostle's missionary journey note the fierce persecution that he encountered as he introduced the gospel of Christ into heretofore unevangelized areas. Accordingly, with reference to the Colossians, Paul explains

that he is stepping ahead of the church in uncharted territory to make an initial unveiling of the gospel. In so doing, he bears the brunt of the world's antagonism towards God and his word. As a servant of the church, he steps before her to take the first blow of the falling sword. Paul can say that such Christ-based suffering is "lacking" in regards to the church because it is the inevitable outworking of the church's gospel-based existence. Because the word will inevitably go forth, and the world hates that word, active persecution is also inevitable. Paul willingly and joyfully steps before the church to suffer a more public and extreme persecution.[72]

---

[72] Robert L. Plummer, *Paul's Understanding of the Church's Mission: Did the Apostle Paul Expect the Early Christian Communities to Evangelize?* Paternoster Biblical Monographs (Waynesboro, GA: Paternoster, 2006), 133–134.

Thus, the sufferings experienced by the apostle Paul were not the generic heartaches and pains of living life in this fallen world but were instead the persecutions he encountered as he proclaimed the gospel in hostile territories. To generalize Paul's experience so that the sufferings of the recipients of the sacrament of Anointing of the Sick participate in Christ's saving work and contribute to the merits in the treasury of the saints, is unwarranted.

In summary, evangelical theology appreciates aspects of Catholic theology's Anointing of the Sick but dissents from other aspects, specifically in considering such healing activity not to be a sacrament.

11

The Celebration of the Christian Mystery (Part 2, Section 2, Chapter 3, Articles 6–7)

The Sacraments at the Service of Communion:
Holy Orders; Matrimony

The Sacraments at the Service of Communion (Sec. 2, Ch. 3)

Having presented the three sacraments of Christian initiation—Baptism, Confirmation, and the Eucharist—and the two sacraments of healing—Penance and Reconciliation and the Anointing of the Sick—the *Catechism* concludes its discussion of the seven sacraments with two sacraments at the service of communion:[1] Holy Orders and Matrimony. These rites "are directed towards the salvation of others . . . [and] confer a particular mission in the Church and serve to build up the People of God."[2] Specifically, the sacrament of Holy Orders consecrates priests "to feed the Church by the word and grace of God," and the sacrament of Matrimony consecrates Christian spouses "for the duties and dignity of their state [marital relationship]."[3]

The Sacrament of Holy Orders (Sec. 2, Ch. 3, Art. 6)

Apostolic ministry—the ongoing mission entrusted by Christ to the apostles and passed down to their successors, the bishops of the Catholic Church—is dependent on the sacrament of Holy Orders. The name is derived from the Latin word *ordo*, which in Roman antiquity referred especially to a governing body. *Ordination* (Lat., *ordinatio*), therefore, means "incorporation

---

[1] "Communion" in the sense that the recipients of these sacraments receive grace to serve in relationship to others.
[2] CCC 1534.
[3] CCC 1535; citation is from Vatican Council II, *Lumen Gentium* 11.2.

into an *ordo*." In the Catholic Church, three degrees of Holy Orders are present: *ordo episcoporum* (the episcopate, for bishops), *ordo presbyterorum* (the presbyterate, for priests), and *ordo diaconorum* (the diaconate, for deacons). The sacramental act that integrates certain men into these three orders "goes beyond a simple election, designation, delegation, or institution by the community, for it confers a gift of the Holy Spirit that permits the exercise of a 'sacred power' (*sacra potestas*) which can come only from Christ himself through his Church."[4] Another name for the sacrament is *consecration* (Lat., *consecratio*), involving "a setting apart and an investiture by Christ himself for his Church."[5] The sign of this ordination or consecration is the laying on of hands by a bishop.

In terms of the biblical basis for this sacrament, the old covenant Levitical priesthood, which engaged in liturgical service for the people of Israel, is a prefiguration of the Church's new covenant priesthood. Consecrated by a specific rite, these Levites were "appointed to act on behalf of men in relation to God, to offer gifts and sacrifices for sins" (Heb. 5:1; cf. Ex. 29:1–30; Leviticus 8). Another prefiguration of the ordained ministry is the establishment of the seventy elders (Num. 11:24–25). The Church's Tradition also "considers Melchizedek, 'priest of God Most High,' as a prefiguration of the priesthood of Christ, the unique 'high priest after the order of Melchizedek'; 'holy, blameless, unstained,' 'by a single offering he has perfected for all time those who are sanctified,' that is, by the unique sacrifice of the cross."[6] As explained earlier, though this one sacrifice of Christ was accomplished once for all, it is made present in the sacrament of the Eucharist. "The same is true of the one priesthood of Christ; it is made present through the ministerial priesthood without diminishing the uniqueness of Christ's priesthood: 'Only Christ is the true priest, the others being only his ministers.'"[7]

More specifically, this one priesthood of Christ consists of two participations, because Christ has made of the Church "a kingdom, priests for his God and Father" (Rev. 1:6; cf. 5:9–10; 1 Pet. 2:5, 9); thus, the Church consists of the priesthood of all believers, in two senses. The first, the baptismal or common priesthood, is that in which all the faithful participate as

---

[4] CCC 1538 (emphasis removed).
[5] Ibid.
[6] CCC 1544; the biblical citations are from Heb. 5:10; 6:20; 7:26; 10:14; Gen. 14:18.
[7] CCC 1545; citation is from Thomas Aquinas, *Commentary on the Epistle to the Hebrews* 8:4.

they engage in Christ's mission. The second, the ministerial or hierarchical priesthood, is that in which bishops and priests participate. Though the two are closely related, they are essentially different in this way: "[T]he ministerial priesthood is at the service of the common priesthood."[8] This difference is why the hierarchical priesthood requires its own sacrament of Holy Orders. Indeed, by means of this sacrament, the priest "acts *in persona Christi Capitis*,"[9] that is, the ordained minister acts in the person of Christ the Head, such that Christ himself is present to his Church: "It is the same priest, Christ Jesus, whose sacred person his minister truly represents. Now the minister . . . is truly made like to the high priest and possesses the authority to act in the power and place of the person of Christ himself."[10]

Such sacramental consecration does not preserve the ordained ministers from weakness, error, and sin, but it does guarantee that their "sin cannot impede the fruit of grace" when they administer the sacraments.[11] Indeed, apart from their celebrations of the sacraments, the ministers leave "human traces that are not always signs of fidelity to the Gospel and consequently can harm the apostolic fruitfulness of the Church."[12] Accordingly, the *Catechism* underscores the fact that the "sacred power" conferred on priests by Holy Orders renders their priesthood *ministerial*, that is, in *service* to the Church. Furthermore, this ministerial priesthood is dually directional: representing Christ to the Church, and "acting in the name of the whole Church when presenting to God the prayer of the Church, and above all when offering the Eucharistic sacrifice."[13]

The three degrees of the sacrament are actually divided into two types: the two degrees of priestly participation—the episcopacy (the order of bishops) and the presbyterate (the order of priests); and the one degree of service—the diaconate (the order of deacons), which exists to help the bishops and priests. Yet all three degrees are conferred by the sacrament of Holy Orders.

The *Catechism* treats first the two degrees of priestly participation. The order of bishops, or the episcopacy, is conferred on men through episcopal

---

[8] CCC 1547.

[9] CCC 1548; citation is from Vatican Council II, *Lumen Gentium* 10; 28; cf. *Sacrosanctum concilium* 33; *Presbyterorum ordinis* 2; 6.

[10] Pope Pius XII, encyclical, *Mediator Dei* (November 20, 1947), 69. Accessible at http://www.vatican.va/holy_father/pius_xii/encyclicals/documents/hf_p-xii_enc_20111947_mediator-dei_en.html.

[11] CCC 1550.

[12] Ibid.

[13] CCC 1552. Cf. Vatican Council II, *Sacrosanctum concilium* 33; *Lumen Gentium* 10.

ordination, which is the fullness of the sacrament of Holy Orders. This office transmits the apostolic line, the unbroken succession of bishops that goes back to the apostle Peter at the beginning of the Church. Christ endowed his apostles with a special outpouring of the Holy Spirit, and they in turn transmitted to their successors, the bishops, the gift of the Spirit through the laying on of hands; the same practice has continued up to today through episcopal consecration. This conferring of the fullness of the sacrament "is called the high priesthood, the acme (*summa*) of the sacred ministry."[14] Specifically, episcopal ordination confers three offices or responsibilities—teaching, ruling, and sanctifying—such that bishops "take the place of Christ himself, teacher, shepherd, and priest, and act as his representative (*in Eius persona agant*)."[15] Such consecration, conferred by several bishops and by "a special intervention of the Bishop of Rome [the pope],"[16] gives the grace of the Holy Spirit, which is an indelible mark. The bishops so consecrated enjoy a hierarchical communion with one another and form an episcopal college. "As Christ's vicar, each bishop has the pastoral care of the particular Church entrusted to him, but at the same time he bears collegially with all his brothers in the episcopacy the solicitude [concern] for all the Churches."[17]

The order of priests, or the presbyterate, shares in the authority of Christ but not in a supreme degree as does the order of bishops. Specifically, "[t]he function of the bishops' ministry was handed over in a subordinate degree to priests so that they might be appointed in the order of the priesthood and be co-workers of the episcopal order for the proper fulfillment of the apostolic mission that had been entrusted to it by Christ."[18] The sacrament of Holy Orders confers on these men the priesthood of priests and, as it does in episcopal consecration, bestows the grace of the Holy Spirit, which is an indelible mark. Additionally, ordination configures them to Christ "in such a way that they are able to act in the person of Christ the head,"[19] and it delegates to them to a lesser degree the three responsibilities of teaching, ruling, and sanctifying. At the same time, priests share "in the universal dimensions of the mission that Christ entrusted to the

---

[14] CCC 1557; citation is from Vatican Council II, *Lumen Gentium* 21.2.
[15] CCC 1558; citation is from Vatican Council II, *Lumen Gentium* 21.
[16] CCC 1559.
[17] CCC 1560 (emphasis removed).
[18] CCC 1562 (emphasis removed); citation is from Vatican Council II, *Presbyterorum ordinis* 2.2.
[19] CCC 1563; citation is from Vatican Council II, *Presbyterorum ordinis* 2.

apostles."[20] This is especially seen in their celebration of the sacrament of the Eucharist, in which "they exercise in a supreme degree their sacred office" and from which "their whole priestly ministry draws its strength."[21] The priests, together with their bishop, constitute a sacerdotal, or priestly, college (*presbyterium*). United to their bishop, the priests "'represent, in a certain sense, the bishop, . . take upon themselves his duties' . . . [and] exercise their ministry only in dependence on the bishop and in communion with him."[22]

Having treated the two degrees of priestly participation in the sacrament of Holy Orders—the episcopacy (the order of bishops) and the presbyterate (the order of priests)—the *Catechism* turns next to discuss the one degree of service—the diaconate (the order of deacons). Deacons "receive the imposition of hands 'not unto the priesthood, but unto the ministry,'" and thus exist at "a lower level of the hierarchy."[23] As it does in both episcopal and priestly consecration, the sacrament confers on these men an indelible mark and "configures them to Christ, who made himself the 'deacon' or servant of all."[24] Specifically, deacons exist to help the bishop and priests, especially in the celebration of the sacraments (e.g., they distribute the Eucharistic elements and bless marriages), the communication of the gospel and preaching, the supervision of funerals, and the like. Though widespread in the early church, the diaconate fell out of use and was restored following Vatican Council II; its implementation is an ongoing task in the Church today. "This *permanent diaconate*, which can be conferred on married men, constitutes an important enrichment for the Church's mission."[25]

In summary, the sacrament of Holy Orders exists in three degrees: the two degrees of priestly participation (the episcopacy and the presbyterate) and the one degree of service (the diaconate).

The administration of this sacrament is a solemn celebration on a Sunday in the cathedral (the church in which the seat of the bishop is located) during the Eucharistic liturgy. The essential rite is the imposition of the bishop's hands on the head of the ordinand (i.e., the one to be ordained) and the bishop's prayer of consecration requesting the outpouring of the

---

[20] CCC 1565.
[21] CCC 1566; citation is from Vatican Council II, *Lumen Gentium* 28; cf. 1 Cor. 11:26.
[22] CCC 1567; citation is from Vatican Council II, *Lumen Gentium* 28.2.
[23] CCC 1569; citation is from Vatican Council II, *Lumen Gentium* 29.
[24] CCC 1570; the biblical allusion is to Jesus's words in Mark 10:45; Luke 22:27.
[25] CCC 1571.

Holy Spirit and his requisite gifts for the specific office to which the ordinand is being ordained. Other elements include "the initial rites—presentation and election of the ordinand, instruction by the bishop, examination of the candidate, and litany of the saints [a structured prayer invoking the Lord's mercy]."[26] Other rites for the consecration of a bishop are "an anointing with holy chrism . . . [and] giving the book of the Gospels, the ring, the miter [hat], and the crosier [staff]." The oil is "a sign of the special anointing of the Holy Spirit who makes their ministry fruitful," and the gifts are signs of the bishop's "apostolic mission to proclaim the Word of God, of his fidelity to the Church, the bride of Christ, and his office as shepherd to the Lord's flock." For the ordination of a priest, the other rites are the anointing with oil and the giving of the paten (the tray on which the Eucharistic wafers will be placed) and the chalice (the cup for the Eucharistic wine and water); these gifts are signs of "the offering of the holy people" that the priest "is called to present to God." For the ordination of a deacon, the anointing with oil is accompanied by the gift of the book of the Gospels, a sign of the deacon's "mission to proclaim the Gospel of Christ."[27]

The one who confers the three degrees of this sacrament is Christ himself through the bishops; as successors of the apostles, the bishops "hand on the 'gift of the Spirit,' the 'apostolic line.'"[28] The ordinand must be a baptized man, in keeping with Jesus's choosing of men to be his apostles, who in turn chose other men.[29] Because the Church is "bound by this choice made by the Lord himself . . . the ordination of women is not possible."[30] More specifically, in the case of bishops and priests, the ordinands must be "men of faith who live a celibate life and who intend to remain *celibate* 'for the sake of the kingdom of heaven' [Matt. 19:12]."[31] As "a sign of this new life to the service of which the Church's minister is consecrated," celibacy is to be "accepted with a joyous heart" and maintained.[32] Permanent deacons, conversely, may be married men.

The effects of the sacrament of Holy Orders are several: As already

---

[26] CCC 1574.
[27] Ibid.
[28] CCC 1576; citation is from Vatican Council II, *Lumen Gentium* 20.
[29] CCC 1577. Biblical support is Mark 3:14–15; Luke 6:12–16; 1 Tim. 3:1–13; 2 Tim. 1:6; Titus 1:5–9. Post–New Testament confirmation is Clement of Rome, *Letter to the Corinthians* 42, 44 (*ANF* 1:16, 17).
[30] CCC 1577. Cf. Pope John Paul II, *Mulieris dignitatem* (August 15, 1988), 26–27. See http://www.vatican.va/holy _father/john_paul_ii/apost_letters/documents/hf_jp-ii_apl_15081988_mulieris-dignitatem_en.html.
[31] CCC 1579.
[32] Ibid.

noted, one effect is configuration to Christ by the grace of the Holy Spirit for the purpose of participation in the mission of Christ and his Church. The consecrated man acts in the person of Christ in his threefold office of priest, prophet, and king. Another effect, as is true with Baptism and Confirmation, is the conferring of an indelible spiritual mark or character on its recipient, meaning that the sacrament is unrepeatable. Accordingly, though it is possible for a man consecrated by this sacrament to be removed from his office and stripped of his responsibilities, such disqualification does not render him a layman; he remains essentially marked out as a bishop/priest/deacon. Indeed, the *Catechism* recalls that, because "it is ultimately Christ who acts and effects salvation through the ordained minister, the unworthiness of the latter does not prevent Christ from acting."[33] Another effect of the sacrament is the gift of the grace of the Holy Spirit configuring its recipient to "Christ as Priest, Teacher, and Pastor, of whom the ordained is made a minister. For the bishop, this is first of all a grace of strength . . . to guide and defend his Church" by sanctifying, teaching, and governing it.[34] For the priest, this grace enables him to proclaim the gospel and preach, to offer the Eucharistic sacrifice and baptize, and the like. For the deacon, this grace promotes dedication to the faithful, in conjunction with the bishop and his priests, for the service of the liturgy, the gospel, and works of love.

Evangelical Assessment

As noted in the discussion and assessment of Catholic theology's doctrine of the church (ch. 5), one of the major points of divergence between it and evangelical theology is this particular doctrine. This deep divide is brought out once again in the sacrament of Holy Orders. For an overarching critique of this sacrament, evangelical theology once again turns to the two axioms on which the Catholic theological system is constructed, and demonstrates how these faulty pillars constitute the foundation for Holy Orders. First, the nature-grace interdependence makes a substantial contribution to the sacrament: human nature (in this case, the men consecrated by Holy Orders) possesses the capacity to mediate grace; accordingly, the ordained priests act in the person of Christ the Head, as particularly evident when they administer the sacraments that convey grace on the faithful. Immediately, the

---

[33] *CCC* 1584.
[34] *CCC* 1585–1586.

second axiom can be detected at work: the Christ-Church interconnection means that the Catholic Church is the continuation of the incarnation of Christ, who is present in his body the Church (in this case, its consecrated ministers, the priests) and acts through them to convey grace. The nature-grace interdependence also appears as the support for the Catholic Church's hierarchical structure: Because there is a hierarchy between nature (at the low end) and grace (at the high end), a similar hierarchy must be present in the Church. Accordingly, the essential difference between the laity (at the low end) and the clergy (at the high end) finds justification in this axiom. So also does the structure of the three degrees of Holy Orders: the degree of service, or the diaconate (at the low end), the second degree of priestly participation, or the presbyterate (in the middle), and the first degree of priestly participation, or the episcopate (at the high end). Finally, these three degrees are consecrated by Holy Orders as this sacrament "confers a gift of the Holy Spirit that permits the exercise of a 'sacred power' (*sacra potestas*) which can come only from Christ himself through his Church."[35] Transparently, the Christ-Church interconnection provides the foundation for the sacrament being viewed in this way. Critiques of these two axioms, having already been expressed (ch. 2), will not be repeated here, but this evangelical theological assessment underscores that the Catholic system on which Holy Orders is grounded is faulty.

Church Government/Offices

Other criticisms must also be voiced, and the first area of assessment regards church government or offices. In many of its variations, evangelical theology affirms that the New Testament presents three offices in the church: the apostolate, the eldership, and the diaconate. The apostolate, consisting of the Twelve apostles and a few more in the apostolic circle (Paul, Barnabas, and James),[36] was established by Jesus himself (Mark 3:13–18), required its members to have been with Jesus from the beginning of his ministry and to have witnessed one of his post-resurrection appearances (Acts 1:15–26),[37] and constituted the foundation of the church of Jesus Christ (Eph. 2:19–20; Rev. 21:14). Almost all stripes of evangelical theology agree that this office

---

[35] CCC 1538.
[36] Paul (Acts 26:12–18); Barnabas (Acts 14:14; 1 Cor. 9:6; Gal. 2:9); James (Gal. 1:19; 2:9).
[37] The apostle Paul noted the unusual circumstances of his office (1 Cor. 15:8).

was divinely designed to terminate with the death of the last apostle; consequently, it no longer functions today. The men who constitute the eldership, consisting of elders, bishops, or pastors (these are interchangeable terms),[38] engage in leading the church under the headship of Jesus Christ; preach and teach sound doctrine (1 Tim. 3:2; 5:17; Titus 1:5–9); pray, especially for the sick (James 5:13–16); and shepherd the flock through exemplary leadership (1 Pet. 5:1–5). In the New Testament, in every instance in which the composition of a church's government is known, the church has a plurality of elders.[39] The diaconate, consisting of deacons (many would add deaconesses), is the office of service or ministry (1 Tim. 3:8–13; cf. Rom. 16:1–2; Acts 6:1–7).[40]

In contradistinction to the cessation of the apostolate, these last two offices are ongoing; indeed, the early church had a twofold order of elders/bishops and deacons (Phil. 1:1; 1 Tim. 3:1–13). This structure continued in some churches in the first two centuries. For example, Clement of Rome cited Isaiah 60:17 (in the Septuagint) in support of the choosing of bishops and deacons as church leaders;[41] the *Didache* called for Christians to appoint for themselves bishops and deacons;[42] and Polycarp urged the church in Philippi to submit to its presbyters and deacons.[43] Accordingly, many evangelical churches are led by two groups with different responsibilities: pastors or elders (some churches call them priests, presbyters, or ministers) and deacons (some churches call them servants or trustees). This twofold leadership structure is commonly found in congregational churches. *Congregationalism* rests ultimate authority in the congregation, that is, the members of a local church, above which there is no person (e.g., a bishop) or graded authoritative court (e.g., a synod, a general assembly).

Other evangelical churches, while noting the New Testament presentation of the two offices of eldership and diaconate, detect as well other leadership structures in the early churches. For example, proponents of *episcopalianism* (the form of church government by *episcopos*, or bishop, in whom ultimate authority resides) consider James at the council of

---

[38] The case for the interchangeable nature of these terms makes appeal to Acts 20:17; Titus 1:5–7; and Eph. 4:11.
[39] E.g., the first churches started by Paul and Barnabas (Acts 14:23); the church of Jerusalem (15:1–29); the church of Ephesus (Acts 20:17; 1 Tim. 5:17); the churches of Crete (Titus 1:5).
[40] For further discussion, see Allison, *SS*, 206–247.
[41] Clement of Rome, *Letter of the Romans to the Corinthians* 42 (ANF 1:16).
[42] *Didache* 15 (ANF 7:381).
[43] Polycarp, *Letter to the Philippians* 5 (ANF 1:34).

Jerusalem to be the prototype of a bishop. Additionally, the establishment of a threefold leadership very early in the church's development (more below) is considered as pointing to the rightness of this form of government. For example, when the early churches were faced with dangerous heresies and confronted with potential divisions within them, Ignatius responded with a new form of church government. Distinguishing between the office of bishop and presbyter/elder, he called for one bishop, along with the presbytery and diaconate, to lead these churches in the following manner: "your bishop presides in the place of God, and your presbyters in the place of the assembly of the apostles, along with your deacons."[44] Episcopalianism, therefore, consists of a threefold hierarchical structure—bishop, elders/pastors/priests, and deacons.

Another variety found within evangelical theology is *presbyterianism*, the form of government with *presbuteroi*, or elders/presbyters, as representatives of the church who exercise their responsibilities not only in their local session or consistory but also in graded courts above their local church level—the geographical area of a presbytery or classis, the more expansive region of a synod, and the national level of a general assembly. Support for this polity includes evidence of a "church" structure above the local church level (e.g., Acts 9:31; 1 Cor. 12:28) and elements of presbyterianism at the council of Jerusalem (Acts 15:1–16:5).[45]

Despite this great variety of church polity under the umbrella of evangelical theology, there is complete agreement that Catholic theology's proposal of apostolic succession, and the Catholic Church's episcopalian form of government with the pope at its head, are wrong. Congregationalism and presbyterianism deny the propriety of episcopalianism. Not only do they find a lack of biblical warrant for that structure, but they dissent from the authority its proponents give to the early church tradition that fueled its development. They note as well that the tradition was not uniform. For example, as late as the end of the fourth century, Jerome emphasized that the apostle Paul considered that presbyters/elders are the same as bishops,[46] signifying that the earliest churches were led by a plurality of elders, without a separate office of the bishop. Moreover, Jerome underscored the pragmatic

---

[44] Ignatius, *Letter to the Magnesians* 6 (ANF 1:61); cf. idem, *Letter to the Smyrneans* 8 (ANF 1:89).
[45] For further discussion, see Allison, *SS*, 249–295.
[46] Jerome, *Letter 146, to Evangelus* 1–2 (NPNF² 6:289).

reasons for the early church's adoption of the threefold office of leadership with a bishop elevated above the other presbyters,[47] a development to which he did not take kindly.[48] Even evangelical episcopalianism, while maintaining the threefold office, denies apostolic succession[49] and the supremacy of the bishop of Rome, the pope, over the worldwide church.

Old Covenant Levitical Priesthood

Many versions of evangelical theology reject Catholic theology's sacrament of Holy Orders because of its appeal to the old covenant Levitical priesthood as a biblical precursor to the Church's new covenant priesthood. Certainly, the old covenant high priests were "appointed to act on behalf of men in relation to God, to offer gifts and sacrifices for sins" (Heb. 5:1). But the point of the Letter to the Hebrews is that the old covenant is "faulty" (8:7, 8), "obsolete," and "ready to vanish away" (v. 13). Additionally, its priests "serve a copy and shadow of the heavenly things" (v. 5), and its priesthood has yielded its place to the priesthood of Christ (7:23–28), whose "ministry . . . is . . . much more excellent than the old" (8:6). Indeed, the old covenant has been replaced by a new covenant that is "better, since it is enacted on better promises" (v. 6); it is "not like the [old] covenant" (v. 9). Underscoring the discontinuity between the old covenant and the new covenant, evangelical theology asks why, if the old covenant has been abrogated, Catholic theology seeks to pattern its new covenant priesthood after it. Correlatively, if the Levitical priesthood was not able to provide perfection for the old covenant people of God, who received the law under that priesthood, why would the Catholic priesthood—which must provide perfection for the new covenant people, who receive grace from that priesthood—be modeled after something that failed (7:11)?

A further implication of this discontinuity between the old and new covenants is the nature of the ministry of their priests. Under the old covenant, the priesthood was indeed dually directed, as Catholic theology affirms: the priests represented Yahweh to their people, especially by revealing his

---

[47] Ibid., 1 (*NPNF*[2] 6:288).

[48] Jerome, *Commentary on Titus* 1.6–7, in John Harrison, *Whose Are the Fathers?* (London: Longmans, Green, 1867), 488.

[49] The Anglican ministry, the leadership structure of the Anglican Communion, does hold to apostolic succession, but not in the same manner that Catholic theology does, and it does not acknowledge the pope as its supreme leader. Rather, the Archbishop of Canterbury is the first among equals in his relationship with the other Anglican bishops.

Word and calling the people to covenant faithfulness; and they represented the people to Yahweh, especially through the offering of sacrifices on the people's behalf. In the new covenant, however, priests/pastors/bishops represent Christ to the church, especially by proclaiming the gospel and calling the people to covenant faithfulness, but they do not represent the people to Christ in terms of offering sacrifices on their behalf, as Catholic theology maintains. This criticism is not due to a misunderstanding of the Eucharist (Catholic theology clearly explains that this sacrament is not a new or a different sacrifice than the one offered on the cross nearly two thousand years ago; rather, it is a re-presentation of that once-and-for-all sacrifice). Instead, it is a criticism of Catholic theology's idea that, during the mass, the people (represented by the laity, not the clergy) bring the necessary sacrifices forward to the altar: "fruit of the earth and work of human hands" (the bread offered to God) and "fruit of the vine and work of human hands" (the wine offered to God).[50] These sacrifices are received by the priest, who later offers them to God as he leads the Liturgy of the Eucharist. As rehearsed earlier (ch. 9), the idea that the bread and wine—elements of nature—possess the capacity to receive and communicate grace as the Church's offering to God is based on the nature-grace interdependence, a faulty axiom. Moreover, as also previously noted, Scripture presents numerous sacrifices that are to be offered by the people of the church, but no passage encourages the offering of bread and wine as sacrifices to God.

Two Aspects of the Priesthood

As Catholic theology gets more specific and explains that the one priesthood of Christ actually consists of two aspects—the baptismal or common priesthood, and the ministerial or hierarchical priesthood—evangelical theology senses with respect to the first aspect something approaching one of the key doctrines of the Protestant Reformation: the priesthood of all believers. All the members of Christ's church "like living stones are being built up as a spiritual house, to be a holy priesthood, to offer spiritual sacrifices acceptable to God through Jesus Christ" (1 Pet. 2:5). Indeed, Peter calls them "a chosen race, a royal priesthood, a holy nation, a people for his

---

[50] Roman Missal, Order of the Mass, 23, 25. Other offerings such as gifts for the poor may be brought as well. Moreover, during the celebration of the mass when the sacrament of Matrimony is administered, the man and the woman to be married unite the offering of their lives, which they are giving to each other, to the offering of Christ for his church in the Eucharist (CCC 1621).

own possession, that you may proclaim the excellencies of him who called you out of darkness into his marvelous light" (v. 9). As heir of the Protestant doctrine of the priesthood of all believers, evangelical theology encourages all Christians to engage in intercessory prayer for each other, hear others' confession of sin and assure those penitents of God's forgiveness, engage missionally together for the cause of Christ, teach and admonish one another with the Word of God (Col. 3:16), and much more. Catholic theology's emphasis on the baptismal or common priesthood is, therefore, a welcome development.

Agreement stops here, however, as evangelical theology dissents from Catholic theology's understanding of the ministerial or hierarchical priesthood. It disagrees specifically with the notion of an essential difference—a distinction in their very nature—between laity and clergy. Again, as heir of the Reformation, evangelical theology resonates with Martin Luther's emphatic denial of this difference:

> It is pure invention that pope, bishops, priests and monks are to be called the "spiritual estate"; princes, lords, artisans, and farmers the "temporal estate." That is indeed a fine bit of lying and hypocrisy. Yet no one should be frightened by it; and for this reason—viz., that all Christians are truly of the "spiritual estate," and there is among them no difference at all but that of office, as Paul says in I Corinthians 12:12, We are all one body, yet every member has its own work, where by it serves every other, all because we have one baptism, one gospel, one faith, and are all alike Christians; for baptism, Gospel and faith alone make us "spiritual" and a Christian people.[51]

Tearing down the essential difference between clergy and laity did not mean, for Luther, the destruction of all differences between them, as he continued to affirm the office of ministry that would lead the church. Expanding on what he mentioned above, Luther maintained that ordained men "are charged with the administration of the Word of God and the sacraments, which is their work and office,"[52] and he included this office of church leadership as one of the seven marks of the church.[53]

According to Catholic theology, this essential difference between laity

---

[51] Martin Luther, *To the Christian Nobility of the German Nation.*
[52] Ibid.
[53] Martin Luther, *On the Councils of the Church* (LW 41:154).

and clergy is bestowed on the latter group through the sacrament of Holy
Orders, which confers an indelible spiritual mark on clergymen. In consequence of this feature, even if a priest is deposed from his ministerial office,
such disqualification does not mean that he reverts to the nature of a layman. Evangelical theology searches in vain for any biblical warrant for the
existence of human beings whose nature is masculine laity, human beings
whose nature is feminine laity, and human beings whose nature is (masculine) priestly. On the contrary, when the apostle Paul lists the qualifications
for elders/bishops (1 Tim. 3:1–7; Titus 1:5–9), the only requirement for
men consecrated for that office that is different from the traits envisioned
and promoted for all Christians is "able to teach" (1 Tim. 3:2) or, more
expansively, "He must hold firm to the trustworthy word as taught, so that
he may be able to give instruction in sound doctrine and also to rebuke
those who contradict it" (Titus 1:9). To be noted is that this distinguishing qualification is not a matter of character but of ability.[54] Returning to
Luther's point, no difference of nature distinguishes laypeople from clergy;
rather, the distinction is one of office, with the latter being charged with
the responsibilities of preaching/teaching sound doctrine, leading and shepherding the church, and more.

Ministerial Effectiveness

According to evangelical theology, as these elders/pastors/bishops engage
in their various responsibilities, they are to maintain and advance the qualities that, present in their lives from the outset of their candidacy for office,
rendered them suitable for entering into the office. But the reason that such
personal development (requisite for all Christians) is needed by these leaders is not that their effectiveness in teaching, leading, shepherding, administering the sacraments, and other responsibilities depends on their individual
holiness. On the contrary, the fruitfulness of their ministry depends on the
Word of God that they proclaim being the divine power (Rom. 1:16–17) that
calls sinful human beings to salvation (2 Thess. 2:13–14), causes regenera-

---

[54] Someone may object that Paul holds out another qualification for elders/bishops that is not a requirement
for common Christians: "If anyone aspires to the office of overseer, he desires a noble task" (1 Tim. 3:1). In one
sense, this objection is on target: In order for men to be ordained to the eldership/episcopate, they must aspire
to that office. In another sense, however, this desire is neither a character trait to possess nor an ability to exercise;
evangelical theology often associates this aspiration with a divine call to this office. In any case, the desire to be
an elder/bishop is different from an indelible spiritual mark conferred by Holy Orders, for that desire certainly
must exist in those to be ordained before they receive the sacrament.

tion (1 Pet. 1:22–25), exposes disobedience (Heb. 4:12), teaches sound doctrine, and rebukes, corrects, and trains in righteousness (2 Tim. 3:16–17). Furthermore, the validity of their administration of baptism and the Lord's Supper similarly depends on those ordinances being enacted words of the gospel, as baptism vividly portrays identification with the death, burial, and resurrection of Jesus Christ (Rom. 6:3–5), and the Lord's Supper concretely depicts his broken body and shed blood (Matt. 26:26–29) while rendering its celebrants participants in his blood and body (1 Cor. 10:16).

As already explained, this gospel emphasis of evangelical theology differs from Catholic theology's doctrine of *ex opere operato*, that is, the sacraments are valid by the priests' administration of them. Because of Holy Orders, the indelible spiritual mark of consecration guarantees that the personal situation of the priests (e.g., being in sin) cannot obstruct the effects of the grace that is conferred through the sacraments. Evangelical theology agrees that the holiness or sinfulness of pastors cannot hamper the effectiveness of the sacraments, but it disagrees that such is the case because the sacraments are valid *ex opere operato*. Rather, it insists that baptism and the Lord's Supper are effective because they are ordinances of the gospel that they portray, sacraments of the Word of God that undergirds and empowers them.

Celebration and Recipients of the Sacrament

Concerning the administration of Holy Orders, evangelical theology is not in principle opposed to the Catholic celebration of the sacrament, including the laying on of hands, giving gifts that represent the ordinand's mission and faithfulness to Christ, and so forth. Most types of evangelical churches have some sort of ordination service that functions for the confirmation of the candidate's calling, character, theological and pastoral competencies, and the like, as well as for an act of public recognition of his installation as pastor/elder. For the varieties of evangelical theology that are not episcopalian, the requirement that bishops confer the sacrament is rejected; even those versions that do follow this polity deny that such episcopal consecration hands on the apostolic line in terms of Catholic apostolic succession.

In terms of who may be ordained, Catholic theology stipulates that it must be a baptized man; it prohibits Holy Orders from being conferred on women. Justification for this view is Jesus's choice of men only as his disciples. Though historically evangelical theology as a whole embraced this restriction, recent developments have led to a division within its ranks over women's roles in ministry. Those who restrict the office of pastor/elder to qualified men (the position is often called "complementarianism") do so on the basis of Paul's prohibition of women from teaching and exercising authority over a man (1 Tim. 2:11–15), biblical parallelism between male leadership in the home and male leadership in the church, biblical parallelism between authority and submission in the Trinity and authority and submission in the church (1 Cor. 11:3–16), and other arguments. Those who permit women to hold the office of pastor/elder (the position is often called "egalitarianism") appeal for biblical support to Paul's affirmation of the equality of men and women (Gal. 3:28), Christ's resurrection appearances to women (Matt. 28:1–10), the Holy Spirit's gifting and empowering of women (Joel 2:28–32; fulfilled in Acts 2:17), the important roles of women in the early church (e.g., Euodia and Syntyche, Phil. 4:2–3; Phoebe, Rom. 16:1–2), and other arguments.[55] Thus, some proponents of evangelical theology agree with Catholic theology's limitation of ordination to qualified men, while others disagree with it.

Despite this disagreement within its ranks, evangelical theology is of one accord in terms of its response to Catholic theology's limitation of this sacrament to "men of faith who live a celibate life and who intend to remain celibate," with appeal made to Matthew 19:12.[56] This demand for priestly celibacy comes into clear conflict with Scripture that certainly allows for, if it does not envision the common practice of, marriage for elders/bishops. The apostle Paul, in his list of qualifications for the office of elder, explains that "an overseer must be . . . the husband of one wife" (1 Tim. 3:2). Though the precise application of this requirement is debated—some see it as a prohibition against polygamy; others see it as enjoining marital faithfulness;[57] still others believe it to demand marriage—the point stands: this Pauline instruction is tailored to married men in this office. Reinforcement of this

---

[55] For a detailed discussion, see Allison, *SS*, 223–240.

[56] *CCC* 1579.

[57] An exception to this point would be Augustine's view that Paul's instruction prohibits the office to any man who has been married more than once (e.g., after the death of his first wife) (Augustine, *On the Good of Marriage* 21 [*NPNF*[1] 3:408]). Nothing in the context of Paul's discussion would warrant this restriction to men married only once, and Paul certainly could have used the Greek word ἅπαξ (*hapax* = once) if he had intended this meaning. Additionally, other Pauline comments about the propriety of widows remarrying (Rom. 7:1–3; 1 Cor. 7:39) would seem to contradict Augustine's interpretation.

understanding is found in a parallel passage in which the apostle details an elder as one who is "the husband of one wife, and his children are believers and not open to the charge of debauchery or insubordination" (Titus 1:6; cf. 1 Tim. 3:4–5). Given that these passages present apostolic teaching about the episcopal or priestly office, celibacy cannot be required of bishops and priests who are consecrated to the position. Catholic theology underscores the weightiness of these biblical passages, noting that clerical celibacy was not a requirement in the early church. Indeed, it admits that celibacy, "which at first was recommended to priests, was afterwards in the Latin [Roman] Church imposed by law on all who were to be promoted to holy Orders."[58] Evangelical theology decries this move that goes beyond the instructions of Scripture, thus calling into question its sufficiency.

This specific teaching about the marital status of church leaders fits well with general apostolic instruction about marriage elsewhere, particularly Paul's warning against people who "will depart from the faith by devoting themselves to deceitful spirits and teachings of demons, through the insincerity of liars whose consciences are seared, *who forbid marriage . . .*" (1 Tim. 4:1–3, emphasis added). The implied denunciation of clerical celibacy may be dodged by Catholic theology by pointing out that its ban of marriage is not universal for all the faithful, but is directed toward its clergy only. The point is well taken, but evangelical theology dissents from Catholic theology's taking heart with respect to its observance of this general apostolic instruction while failing in respect to the specific apostolic teaching about marriage for bishops/elders/pastors (1 Tim. 3:2; Titus 1:6).

Catholic theology's position on clerical celibacy is driven by Jesus's words about "eunuchs who have made themselves eunuchs for the sake of the kingdom of heaven" (Matt. 19:12). Is the application of Jesus's comments to celibate priests warranted? In context, Jesus's discussion centers on his endorsement of marriage as ordained by God from the very beginning of the human race (Matt. 19:3–6; reflecting Gen. 1:28 and 2:24) and on his allowance for divorce, which was never God's design, in only one case: adultery on the part of one of the marriage partners (Matt. 19:7–9). Jesus's teaching prompts his disciples to wonder if it is "better not to marry," to which he responds positively, with this qualification: refraining from marriage is only for those to whom the gift of celibacy "is given" (vv. 10–11).

[58] Vatican Council II, *Presbyterorum Ordinis* 16 (VC II-1, 893).

Jesus illustrates such gifted people with three types of eunuchs; the last of these three categories, kingdom-oriented eunuchs, becomes the justification for Catholic theology's restriction of the episcopate and presbyterate to celibate men.

Jesus's teaching is echoed by the apostle Paul's instruction about marriage and singleness in his First Letter to the Corinthians. A key point in this discussion is giftedness: "I wish that all were as I myself am. But each has his own gift from God, one of one kind and one of another. To the unmarried and the widows I say that it is good for them to remain single as I am. But if they cannot exercise self-control, they should marry. For it is better to marry than to burn with passion" (1 Cor. 7:7–9). To some, God gives the gift of celibacy; because these gifted people are able to master their sexual desires, they may forgo marriage and remain single. Many advantages accrue to them (vv. 32–35). To others, God gives the gift of marriage; because these gifted people are not able to control their sexual desires, they should marry. Though the marriage state brings many anxieties and results in divided attention (i.e., married Christians are devoted to their spouse as well as to the Lord; vv. 32–35), those who marry do well and certainly do not sin. And those with the gift of celibacy do even better by not marrying (vv. 36–38).

Accordingly, with respect to marriage and singleness/celibacy, both Jesus and Paul underscore the key point of giftedness. Evangelical theology raises this question: Is it realistic to expect that all the men who commit themselves to being celibate for the rest of their lives so that they may enter the priesthood, have the needed gift? If they do not, they will not succeed in controlling their sexual desires but will express them in God- and Church-dishonoring ways. The history of sexual immorality of both heterosexual and homosexual varieties among Catholic clergy testifies to tragic failure in this regard. It is not a testimony against those priests and bishops who have joyfully and constantly lived their gift of celibacy; indeed, they are to be applauded for their faithfulness to their pledge of celibacy. Rather, it bears witness against the requirement that all priests and bishops be celibate when some clergy have not been gifted with self-restraint so as to be unmarried.[59]

---

[59] Evangelical theology wonders, then, how Vatican Council II can state that it "feels confident in the Spirit that the gift of celibacy, so appropriate to the priesthood of the New Testament, is liberally granted by the Father,

Evangelical theology objects to Catholic theology's insistence on clerical celibacy also because it was not true of Jesus's apostles—for example, Peter was married (1 Cor. 9:5)—and it was not the practice of the early church; indeed, the requirement was not made and enforced until the turn of the first millennium. The Church acknowledges this point. Addressing the history of clerical celibacy, Vatican Council II admitted, "It is true that it [celibacy] is not demanded of the priesthood by its nature. This is clear from the practice of the primitive Church and the tradition of the Eastern Churches. . . ."[60] Furthermore, John Calvin expressed the sentiment of many people, including faithful Catholics who disagree with their Church's position: the demand for celibate priests has "deprived the church of good and fit pastors."[61] A perplexing point for evangelical theology is that its Catholic counterpart appeals to the *continuity* of the old and new covenant priesthoods in prohibiting sexual intercourse—the Levites were banned from engaging in it during their tenure of service in the temple (Lev. 22:4)—yet also underscores the *discontinuity* between the two when it comes to the old covenant priesthood being hereditary, transmitted by natural generation, and the new covenant priesthood being a gift conferred by a spiritual mark through Holy Orders. Finally, Catholic theology's desire for its priests to represent and portray Christ to his Church overlooks the clearest biblical image of this Christ-church relationship: marriage. A husband's leadership of his wife, and her respect for and submission to him, is a powerful picture of Christ's love and sacrifice for the church, and its honoring of and submission to Christ (Eph. 5:22–33). Evangelical theology's adherence to Scripture, as demonstrated by the fact that it permits, even encourages, clergy to be married, means that churches led by married pastors/elders offer their members close-up, though certainly imperfect, illustrations of the relationship between Christ and his church.[62] And this opportunity is not afforded by the Catholic Church with its sacrament of Holy Orders conferred only on celibate ministers.

In summary, the sacrament of Holy Orders, by which the Catholic

provided those who share Christ's priesthood through the sacrament of Order, and indeed the whole Church, ask for that gift humbly and earnestly" (Vatican Council II, *Presbyterorum Ordinis* 16 [*VC II-1*, 893]).

[60] Vatican Council II, *Presbyterorum Ordinis* 16 (*VC II-1*, 892).

[61] Calvin, *Institutes* 4.12.23 (LCC 21:1249).

[62] Where evangelical churches fall short in implementing sound evangelical theology on this topic is in their failure to readily accept single pastors/elders. This practice seems to discount Paul's instructions about the advantages of the single state, and is often driven by fear that unmarried ministers will use their position to engage in sexual immorality (as if that were not a potential problem for married pastors as well).

Church ordains certain men to the ministry, though bearing some resemblance to ordination as found in many varieties of evangelical theology, is actually quite removed from its evangelical counterpart. Holy Orders is grounded on both of the faulty axioms of the Catholic system; moreover, it is susceptible to several specific criticisms by evangelical theology.

The Sacrament of Matrimony (Sec. 2, Ch. 3, Art. 7)

The second sacrament at the service of communion is Matrimony, which is the initiation and sealing of a marital covenant between a husband and wife, a partnership that "is by its nature ordered toward the good of the spouses and the procreation and education of its offspring."[63] The biblical basis of this sacrament begins with the opening chapters of Genesis, which present God as "the author of marriage" who has endowed it with a specific meaning, origin, purpose, and "its own proper laws."[64] Indeed, God created human beings in his image and etched the vocation to marriage into their very nature; accordingly, it is a universal institution with certain common and permanent characteristics, and designed for both the well-being of individuals and the flourishing of human society. Moreover, creation in the divine image—the image of God who loves—means that human beings are called to love as a reflection of that divine love. This mirroring is accomplished in a particular manner through marital love, which is also fruitful in terms of procreation and is "realized in the common work of watching over creation" (Gen. 1:28).[65] Indeed, "Holy Scripture affirms that man and woman were created for one another: 'It is not good that the man should be alone' [Gen. 2:18]."[66] The woman, who was taken from the man's own body—"'flesh of his flesh' [Gen. 1:23], i.e., his counterpart, his equal, his nearest in all things"—"is given to him by God as a 'helpmate'; she thus represents God from whom comes our help."[67] The two become one flesh (Gen. 2:24), forming "an unbreakable union of their two lives," as emphasized by Christ himself (Matt. 19:6).[68]

Tragically, this idyllic portrait and design of human marriage is spoiled by the regime of sin, such that it is characterized universally by discord,

---

[63] CCC 1601; citation is from the Code of Canon Law 1055.
[64] CCC 1602–1603; citation is from Vatican Council II, *Gaudium et Spes* 48.1.
[65] CCC 1604.
[66] CCC 1605.
[67] CCC 1605. The discussion is from Gen. 2:18–25.
[68] Ibid.

domination, infidelity, jealousy, conflicts, hatred, separation, lust, and the like. This disorder is not natural to marriage—it is not proper and original to human nature, nor to the relationships between man and woman—but is due to sin; indeed, the originating sin of Adam and Eve "had for its first consequence the rupture of the original communion between man and woman" [Gen. 3:12].[69] Procreation now involves painful childbearing and vocation entails toilsome work (Gen. 3:16–19). "Nevertheless, the order of creation persists, though seriously disturbed" by sin,[70] and healing the wounds necessitates the grace of God that is provided by this sacrament. Moreover, following the fall into sin, "marriage helps to overcome self-absorption, egoism, pursuit of one's own pleasure, and to open oneself to the other, to mutual aid and to self-giving."[71]

The Old Testament sought to develop and regulate the institution of marriage. Its use of "the image of exclusive and faithful married love" to portray God's covenant relationship with Israel prepared the way for the new covenant featuring the Son of God uniting "to himself in a certain way all mankind saved by him, thus preparing for the 'wedding-feast of the Lamb' [Rev. 19:7, 9]."[72] For his first miraculous sign ("at his mother's request"[73]) Jesus turned water into wine at the wedding at Cana (John 2:1–11). The Church sees in this event "the confirmation of the goodness of marriage and the proclamation that thenceforth marriage will be an efficacious sign of Christ's presence."[74] Jesus also "unequivocally taught the original meaning" of marriage—it is indissoluble—as willed by God from its outset; specifically, Moses's concession of divorce was not the Creator's intent for marriage but was due to human callousness (Matt. 19:8).[75] Accordingly, Jesus came "to restore the original order of creation disturbed by sin" by giving "the strength and grace to live marriage in the new dimension of the Reign of God. . . . This grace of Christian marriage is a fruit of Christ's cross, the source of all Christian life,"[76] as affirmed by the apostle Paul (Eph. 5:25–26, 31–32). Characterized in its entirety by the marital love between Christ and his Church, the Christian life begins with a "nuptial

---

[69] CCC 1607.
[70] CCC 1608.
[71] CCC 1609.
[72] CCC 1611–1612.
[73] CCC 1613.
[74] Ibid.
[75] CCC 1614.
[76] CCC 1615.

mystery," Baptism, or the "nuptial bath which precedes the wedding feast, the Eucharist."[77] Similarly, because Christian marriage symbolizes and communicates grace, it is a new covenant sacrament.

Even as it elevates marriage, the Church also exalts virginity. This renunciation of the good of marriage means total commitment to Christ and his calling (Rev. 14:4; 1 Cor. 7:32; Matt. 25:6). Moreover, his invitation to become "eunuchs for the sake of the kingdom of heaven" (Matt. 19:12) is a way of life that he modeled. Such celibacy "is an unfolding of baptismal grace, a powerful sign of the supremacy of the bond with Christ and of the ardent expectation of his return, a sign which also recalls that marriage is a reality of this present age which is passing away."[78] Just as meaning and grace for marriage are conferred by Christ himself through the sacrament of Matrimony, so they are granted by him in virginity; accordingly, the Church associates and esteems highly both marriage and virginity.

The celebration of the sacrament of Matrimony takes place during the mass—the appropriate event because of its celebration of the new covenant "in which Christ has united himself for ever to the Church, his beloved bride for whom he gave himself up. It is therefore fitting that the spouses should seal their consent to give themselves to each other through the offering of their own lives by uniting it to the offering of Christ for his Church made present in the Eucharistic sacrifice, and by receiving the Eucharist so that, communicating [sharing in] the same Body and the same Blood of Christ, they may form but 'one body' in Christ."[79] The sacrament of Penance is preparatory for the sacrament of Matrimony so that it is proper.[80] By their expression of consent before the Church, "the spouses, as ministers of Christ's grace, mutually confer upon each other the sacrament of Matrimony by expressing their consent before the Church."[81]

Recipients of this sacrament are a baptized man and a baptized woman who are "free to contract marriage"; that is, they are not "under constraint": no one, including one or the other of them, is coercing or externally threatening them to marry, and they are "not impeded by any natural or ecclesial law," that is, they are not blood relatives (e.g., biological brother and sis-

---

[77] CCC 1617. For the idea of the nuptial bath, cf. Eph. 5:26–27.
[78] CCC 1619. For this idea, cf. Mark 12:25; 1 Cor. 7:31.
[79] CCC 1621.
[80] CCC 1622.
[81] CCC 1623.

ter) and neither one is currently married.[82] Because mutual consent is "the indispensable element that 'makes the marriage,'" if it is absent, "there is no marriage."[83] Such consent is voiced as vows—"I take you to be my wife/husband"—and consummated through sexual intercourse. If later on the marriage is judged to have lacked the consent of one or both of the parties, it can be annulled—that is, declared to have never existed. Before entering into the state of marriage through its sacrament, the two parties should go through marriage preparation.

The *Catechism* next deals with two special categories of marriage: mixed marriages and marriages with disparity of cult.[84] In the first case, the marriage that is covenanted is between a Catholic and a baptized non-Catholic (e.g., a Protestant Christian). This situation "does not constitute an insurmountable obstacle for marriage," but it certainly offers stiff challenges. Mixed marriages require "the *express permission* of ecclesiastical authority." In the second case, the marriage that is covenanted is between a Catholic and a non-baptized person (e.g., a Hindu). This situation demands even more careful consideration because the difficulties noted above are more easily aggravated. Marriages with disparity of cult require "an *express dispensation* from this impediment" by ecclesiastical authority. Additionally, both spouses must be open to "the essential ends and properties of marriage," and the Catholic spouse is obligated to ensure that the children of the marriage are baptized in the Catholic Church and educated in the Catholic faith.[85]

The effects of the sacrament of Matrimony are the creation of a permanent and exclusive bond between the spouses, and the conferring of a special grace on them. As for the first effect, God himself seals the covenant, rendering it indissoluble and guaranteed by his faithfulness. In terms of the second effect, the grace of this sacrament has Christ as its source and is "intended to perfect the couple's love and to strengthen their indissoluble unity."[86]

Furthermore, this conjugal love has certain requirements. First, "it demands *indissolubility* and *faithfulness* in definitive mutual giving."[87] Clearly,

---

[82] CCC 1625.
[83] CCC 1626. This point is according to canon 1057.1 of the Code of Canon Law.
[84] CCC 1633–1637.
[85] CCC 1635. This point is according to canon 1125 of the Code of Canon Law.
[86] CCC 1641.
[87] CCC 1643.

this obligation excludes polygamy and receives support from "the fidelity of God to his covenant"[88] and from the gospel of God's love as "a definitive and irrevocable love."[89] Practically speaking, this first demand precludes divorce, yet, in difficult situations, permits the separation of the couple; still, the best solution is reconciliation. The Church denounces Catholics who get divorced and remarry in civil unions, because this act creates the situation of adultery and contradicts Jesus's instructions (Mark 10:11–12). As long as this situation exists, they are barred from the sacrament of the Eucharist and are prohibited from exercising certain ecclesial responsibilities. It is only through the sacrament of Penance—including repentance for breaking their marital covenant and the promise to live in complete continence—that they can be reconciled.

The second requirement of conjugal love is *openness to fertility*. This duty is based on natural law: "By its very nature the institution of marriage and married love is ordered to the procreation and education of the offspring and it is in them that it finds its crowning glory."[90] Fruitfulness, then, consists of both physical procreation—conception, *in utero* development, childbirth, and physical development—and the moral, spiritual, and social education of those children. In the case of infertile couples, marital love can still be full of meaning and "radiate a fruitfulness of charity, of hospitality, and of sacrifice."[91] Affirming that "there can be no conflict between the divine laws governing the transmission of life and the fostering of authentic married love," the Church insists on the protection of life "with the utmost care from the moment of conception: abortion and infanticide are abominable crimes."[92] Furthermore, the Church has established certain objective criteria in the matter of birth control, permitting natural family planning—the serious practice of "married chastity"—and forbidding the use of contraception—"methods disapproved of by the teaching authority of the Church in its interpretation of the divine law."[93]

The *Catechism* concludes its discussion of the sacrament of Matrimony

---

[88] CCC 1647.

[89] CCC 1648

[90] CCC 1652; citation is from Vatican Council II, *Gaudium et Spes* 48.1; 50. Natural law is the rule, in accord with the eternal rule that God has prescribed for human conduct, which is found in human nature itself. Two parallels may help: just as nothing should inhibit the development of a tadpole into a frog, and just as nothing should inhibit the development of an acorn into an oak tree, so also should nothing—e.g., contraception, abortion—inhibit the fertilization and *in utero* development of a human fetus into a human being living outside of the womb.

[91] CCC 1654.

[92] Vatican Council II, *Gaudium et Spes* 51 (*VC II-1*, 955).

[93] Ibid.

with a brief treatment of the "domestic church" (*Ecclesia domestica*), which refers generally to the Church as "the family of God" and more specifically to the core of the Church as consisting of believers and their whole household (Acts 18:8; 16:31; cf. 11:14). By both their words and their examples, parents are "the first heralds of the faith with regard to their children" and bear the responsibility to foster their development in accord with "the vocation which is proper to each child," including "any religious vocation."[94] All the members of the domestic church "exercise the priesthood of the baptized in a privileged way 'by the reception of the sacraments, prayer and thanksgiving, the witness of a holy life, and self-denial and active charity.'"[95] Finally, the *Catechism* acknowledges the large number of single persons in the Church and affirms that they "are especially close to Jesus' heart and therefore deserve the special affection and active solicitude of the Church, especially of pastors." They are encouraged to find their home in the domestic church and to acquire their human family in "the great family which is the Church."[96]

Evangelical Assessment

Evangelical theology applauds many areas of Catholic theology's doctrine of marriage, to say nothing of its defense of this institution and its staunch support for a culture of life against an encroaching culture of death—typified by abortion, infanticide, physician-assisted suicide, geronticide, and the like—especially in the Western world. Areas of agreement include the following: Marriage is a covenant that entails two people, a man and a woman, making vows before God and other people for an exclusive commitment; by divine design, this marital state has meaning, purpose, origin, and laws that govern it. Two such requirements are indissolubility and faithfulness, thereby excluding immorality, polygamy, and divorce; whereas separation under difficult circumstances may be permitted, it is always enacted with the goal of reconciliation. The benefits of marriage are many, chief of which are the good of the husband and wife who were not designed to be alone, and procreation and the education—including spiritual, moral, social, civil, and vocational dimensions—of the children so generated. Personal benefits

---

[94] CCC 1656; citation is from Vatican Council II, *Lumen Gentium* 11.
[95] CCC 1657 (emphasis removed); citation is from Vatican Council II, *Lumen Gentium* 10.
[96] CCC 1658.

include help in overcoming sinful attitudes and actions like egoism and self-absorption; that is, marriage is a means of sanctification for the husband and the wife. Though the *Catechism* does not explicitly mention other benefits (which are particularly the good fruit of sexual intercourse expressed in marriage), evangelical theology would add the unity of the couple (they become "one flesh" through sexual intercourse; Gen. 2:24), comfort in the midst of tragedy (e.g., 2 Sam. 12:24), and a protection against sexual immorality (1 Cor. 7:5).

Further agreement consists in the excellent discussion of biblical support for marriage, beginning with reference to the opening chapters of Genesis. Following a divine deliberation ("let us make man in our image"; Gen. 1:26), "God created man in his own image, in the image of God he created him; male and female he created them" (v. 27). The dual genderedness within the human society reflects the plurality of persons in the divine society of the Trinity. Moreover, as the Father, the Son, and the Holy Spirit eternally love one another, men and women reflect this reality as they love one another, with the highest, though not exclusive, expression of this being marital love. The divine design for human beings to be gendered also provides for men and women alike to fulfill the so-called "cultural mandate" (v. 28), consisting of procreation ("be fruitful and multiply and fill the earth") and vocation, or civilization building ("and subdue it and exercise dominion"). Catholic theology rightly underscores that the call to marriage is etched into the very nature of the divine image-bearers, which is the reason why the vast majority of people are married, with most of those marriages producing children.

Another area of agreement centers on the brokenness of marriage as a tragic consequence of the fall. This disorder is not natural, not by God's design, but is unnatural, the result of sin. The disobedience of Adam and Eve resulted in pain in childbirth and toilsome work. Many proponents of evangelical theology would add that a disruption of the original, divinely designed hierarchical relationship—with the husband exercising gentle, affirming authority and the wife engaging in joyful, willing submission—was another disastrous result of their fall into sin. In some instances, the devastating impact of this fall leads to marital disaster. For example, when divorce for unbiblical reasons takes place and another marriage is contracted, a situation of adultery is created (Mark 10:11–12); the Catholic Church consequently bars those involved from the sacrament of the Eucharist and removes them from certain ecclesial ministries. Certain proponents of evangelical theology concur, exercising church discipline in such sinful cases. Because of the insidiousness of sin, a Christian husband and a Christian wife need the grace of God for the overcoming of their personal sins, the brokenness in their relationship, their missteps in parenting, and much more. Indeed, because marriage in itself is so wrought with difficulties, Catholic and evangelical theology agree that it is ideally contracted between two Christians (though each theology would define that reality differently, as will be seen).

Interspersed among this widespread agreement are particular points of disagreement. First and foremost, evangelical theology does not consider Matrimony to be a sacrament. The primary reason for this rejection is that marriage is a creation mandate; that is, God ordained marriage for his image-bearers from the first moment of the creation of human beings (Gen. 1:26–28; 2:18–25). Though Jesus Christ certainly affirmed marriage and clarified the grounds for its dissolution through divorce (Matt. 19:3–9), blessed a particular wedding with his first miracle (John 2:1–11), and strengthens marriages through his saving work in the lives of Christian men and Christian women, these actions of Jesus did not originate this relationship between husband and wife; marriage is not uniquely Christian but a universal human institution instead.

In terms of the biblical case for marriage presented by Catholic theology, some adherents to evangelical theology would make two points of clarification. First, when appeal is made to the divine assessment of Adam's condition—"it is not good that the man should be alone" (Gen. 2:18)—it should be specified that this pronouncement applies to people whom God has designed to be married, not to single people. In this latter case, God has gifted them to be unmarried, alone without a spouse; thus, their singleness is good. Second, the implication that Catholic theology draws from God's formation of Eve to be Adam's "helpmate"—"she thus represents God from whom comes our help"—needs qualification. Certainly, the Hebrew word 'ezer is used to describe God as helper, but it also describes human aid, angelic assistance, military support, and even the intervention of false gods; accordingly, caution needs to be exercised in transferring connotations of the divine to particular uses of the word. Indeed, as it was God who formed Adam of the dust of the ground, and as it was God who formed Eve out of

Adam's body, it is difficult to see how she represents God in this context. A more likely explanation of her helpmate role is actually supplied by the context (Gen. 1:28): Eve would help Adam as they together discharged the divinely designed cultural mandate to be fruitful (procreation) and exercise dominion (vocation).

Evangelical theology is also suspicious of its counterpart's appeal to the incarnate Son of God's uniting "to himself in a certain way *all mankind saved by him*, thus preparing for the 'wedding-feast of the Lamb' [Rev. 19:7, 9]."[97] Is this another assertion of inclusivism—taking the italicized phrase to mean that people are saved by the incarnate Son even if they have not heard of him through the gospel—or should it be understood in an exclusivist way, with the phrase meaning that only people who are saved by the incarnate Son have been united to him and will enjoy his wedding banquet? Another question is raised over the implication that Catholic theology draws from Jesus doing his first miracle at the wedding at Cana— "thenceforth marriage will be an efficacious sign of Christ's presence."[98] This allegorical approach seems to overlook the obvious point, supplied by the narrative itself, of Christ's presence at the wedding: "This, the first of his signs, Jesus did at Cana in Galilee, and manifested his glory. And his disciples believed in him" (John 2:11). This point fits very well with the overall purpose of this Gospel: "Now Jesus did many other signs in the presence of the disciples, which are not written in this book; but these are written so that you may believe that Jesus is the Christ, the Son of God, and that by believing you may have life in his name" (John 20:30–31). Out of all the miracles that the apostle could have included in this account of Jesus, John chose seven—the first of which is the turning of water into wine at a wedding—for the explicit purpose of provoking belief leading to eternal life. Prompting saving faith is John's intended purpose for narrating Jesus's presence and performance of a miracle at the wedding; it was not to establish marriage as a sacrament of Christ's presence and grace.

Further disagreement comes over Catholic theology's provision for annulment of marriage and its denial of divorce for any reason. Before these contentious matters can be discussed, a reminder of a few agreements is necessary. Evangelical theology concurs with its counterpart that this rite

---

[97] CCC 1612 (emphasis added).
[98] CCC 1613.

is properly administered to two Christians who consent to marriage (they are not under constraint) and who do so legally. Consent is voiced as vows, and the covenant is consummated by sexual intercourse. The announcement of the presiding church official—a declarative speech-act, commonly expressed as, "I now pronounce you husband and wife"—makes it so; the two are married, with consummation a foregone conclusion.[99] For evangelical theology, no subsequent annulment can declare undone what has already been declared as done. Catholic theology's clarification—the annulment does not signify that the marriage never took place, but only that the sacrament of Matrimony was not performed—means that annulments pertain to the Catholic Church and the marriage sacrament performed by its clergy only. Annulments are especially pursued in the case of Catholic marriages that end in divorce. Because the Church does not permit divorce, divorced Catholics who wish to be married in the Church must first obtain an annulment; otherwise, they will not be allowed to be married. Many proponents of evangelical theology disagree with Catholic theology's denial of permission to be divorced. The New Testament gives two biblical grounds for divorce: Jesus allows it in the case of adultery (Matt. 19:9), and Paul permits it when, in a mixed marriage, the unbelieving spouse seeks divorce (1 Cor. 7:12–16). Accordingly, evangelical and Catholic theology disagree over annulment and divorce.

The above statement that Catholic and evangelical theology agree that marriage should be between two Christians requires a bit of clarification, because that general statement masks some specific areas of disagreement. Evangelical theology, for the most part, insists on marriage between two Christians, defined as a man and a woman who have embraced the gospel, repented of their sins, and trusted in Christ for salvation. Given that evangelicalism encompasses a wide spectrum of Christians, an evangelical Presbyterian and an evangelical Baptist, or an evangelical Episcopalian and an evangelical Methodist, could readily unite in marriage. While recognizing that some difficulties may lie ahead because of denominational differences, these diverse evangelicals could be married. Catholic theology holds out the ideal of two Catholics being married to each other, but it also makes provision for two other categories of marriage. First, mixed marriages are those involving a Catholic and a baptized

---

[99] Sadly, in a high percentage of cases, the consummation has already occurred.

non-Catholic (e.g., a Protestant Christian); second, marriages with disparity of cult are those involving a Catholic and a non-baptized person (e.g., a Hindu). Both of these categories require some special ecclesial action in order to be permitted, and the Catholic spouse has obligations regarding the baptism and education of the children in the Catholic faith. In the case of a mixed marriage, in which both the Catholic and the non-Catholic are genuine Christians in the sense defined above, proponents of evangelical theology would disagree as to the advisability of the marriage: some would not allow it because they would doubt that the faith of the Catholic is genuine; some would not permit it because the difficulties would be insurmountable, especially the obligations of the Catholic spouse with respect to the children; others would allow it while strongly cautioning about the challenges that would inevitably arise. In the case of a marriage with disparity of cult, because this marriage involves a Christian and a non-Christian, and Scripture clearly calls for marriage between two Christians (1 Cor. 7:39), proponents of evangelical theology generally would not permit it.

Agreement regarding some of the requirements of marriage—specifically, indissolubility and faithfulness—has already been addressed. Another requirement of Catholic theology, openness to fertility, is a point of disagreement. This difference has a practical application in terms of Catholic theology's prohibition of the use of contraception and evangelical theology's permission of its use (as long as the contraceptive method does not cause an abortion). At the heart of this divide is evangelical theology's doctrine of the authority and sufficiency of Scripture, and Catholic theology's use of natural law and the Church's authoritative teachings to provide additional and binding guidance on this issue. For evangelical theology, the authoritative and sufficient instruction on procreation is the mandate to "be fruitful and multiply and fill the earth" (Gen. 1:28). This command does not stipulate how many children a married couple must have, nor that they must be open to having children with every act of sexual intercourse; moreover, Scripture does not prohibit the use of (non-abortifacient) contraceptive means. Evangelical theology, while not rejecting natural law outright, is cautious in using it and questions if one of its tenets is openness to fertility. More importantly, evangelical theology rejects any moral teachings outside of Scripture as being authoritative and binding; this includes additional moral instruction given by the Catholic Church.[100]

In summary, evangelical theology applauds much of Catholic theology's understanding of, support for, and defense of the sacredness of marriage, even while it dissents from certain aspects of this sacrament of Matrimony.

Conclusion

Part 2 of the *Catechism*, the Celebration of the Christian Mystery, comes to completion, having treated the sacramental economy of the Catholic Church, together with its seven sacraments. Working through this second part section by section, and cognizant of the Catholic system's two axioms, an evangelical assessment of this sacramental theology and practice in the light of Scripture and evangelical theology has been offered, resulting in areas of both intrigue and critique. Part 3, Life in Christ, with its focus on human vocation and human community, becomes the next topic of discussion.

---

[100] For Catholic theology, the duty to be open to fertility is based on natural law; because this is an aspect or reflection of divine law, it provides moral guidance in these matters. From that foundation, the teaching office of the Catholic Church has authoritatively established rules for birth control, allowing for natural family planning while prohibiting the use of any type of contraception. Condoms, IUDs, birth control pills, and all other artificial methods of preventing fertilization are ruled out.

III

Catholic Theology according to the
Catechism of the Catholic Church

Part 3: Life in Christ

12

Life in Christ
(Part 3, Section I, Chapters I–2)

Human Vocation: Life in the Spirit; the Human Community

Following its presentation of the doctrines of the Church under the heading "The Profession of the Faith" and its expanded discussion of the liturgy of the Church under the title "The Celebration of the Christian Mystery," the *Catechism* next turns to instruction about life in Christ. Reborn by the sacrament of Baptism, "Christians are called to lead henceforth a life 'worthy of the gospel of Christ' [Phil. 1:27]" and are enabled to do so "by the grace of Christ and the gifts of his Spirit, which they receive through the sacraments and through prayer."[1] This catechesis for the new life in Christ focuses on the Holy Spirit, grace, the beatitudes, sin and forgiveness, human virtues, Christian virtues (faith, hope, and charity), and the twofold commandment of charity (the Ten Commandments). Additionally, it is an ecclesial catechesis that is centered on Jesus Christ.

Human Vocation: Life in the Spirit (Sec. I)[2]

This first section treating life in Christ is dedicated to life in the Holy Spirit (Ch. 1), which is life consisting of divine love and human solidarity (Ch. 2) and graciously offered as salvation (Ch. 3). Our discussion and evangelical assessment will treat the themes of life in the Spirit and human solidarity together (ch. 12 of this book) and will address the doctrine of salvation by itself (ch. 13).

---

[1] CCC 1692.
[2] Though the actual title of this section in the *Catechism* is "*Man's* Vocation," the generic term "human" will substitute for the term "man" to ensure that the discussion is clearly oriented to both men and women, as is the intention of the *Catechism* itself.

The Dignity of the Human Person (Sec. I, Ch. I)

Life in Christ through the Holy Spirit is presented under eight articles ranging from the image of God to the overcoming of sin so that the faithful may arrive at the perfection of love.

Man: The Image of God (Sec. 1, Ch. 1, Art. 1)

"The dignity of the human person is rooted in his creation in the image and likeness of God."[3] This divine image is especially human intellect or reason, the capability "of understanding the order of things established by the Creator," and free will, the capability of directing oneself toward, and loving, one's true good, i.e., "what is true and good."[4] Tragically, the fall of Adam and Eve into sin involved an abuse of their freedom. Their reason, which urged them "to do what is good and avoid what is evil,"[5] succumbed to temptation and decided to do evil. As a result, human nature, while desiring the good, "bears the wound of original sin . . . [and] is now inclined to evil and subject to error."[6] Rescue from this internal division was accomplished by Christ and his grace, and it is applied by belief in Christ and following his example. Such relief signifies return to human dignity as divine image-bearers.

Our Vocation to Beatitude (Sec. 1, Ch. 1, Art. 2)

Such dignity is specifically fulfilled in the human vocation to divine beatitude, which is the subject of Jesus's Beatitudes (Matt. 5:3–12). "The Beatitudes are at the heart of Jesus' preaching . . . [and] depict the countenance of Jesus Christ and portray his charity. They express the vocation of the faithful . . . [and] shed light on the actions and attitudes characteristic of the Christian life."[7] Moreover, they "respond to the natural desire for happiness," a desire that has a "divine origin" because "God has placed it in the human heart in order to draw man to the One who can alone fulfill it."[8] Seeking happiness, human beings will find that only God can satisfy this divinely implanted desire. Finally, "[t]he Beatitudes reveal the goal of

---

[3] CCC 1700.
[4] CCC 1704; citation is from Vatican Council II, *Gaudium et Spes* 15.2.
[5] CCC 1706; citation is from Vatican Council II, *Gaudium et Spes* 16.
[6] CCC 1707.
[7] CCC 1716, 1717.
[8] CCC 1718.

human existence, the ultimate end of human acts: God calls us to his own beatitude."[9]

In Scripture, this divine invitation to beatitude is further described as the coming of the kingdom of God (Matt. 4:17), the beatific vision (seeing God; Matt. 5:8; cf. 1 John 1:2; 1 Cor. 13:12), entering into the joy of the Lord (Matt. 25:21–23), and entering into God's rest (Heb. 4:7–11). These descriptions underscore that beatitude is the divinely established goal of human existence: "God puts us in the world to know, to love, and to serve him, and so to come to paradise."[10] Entrance into beatitude is entirely dependent on God's grace and thus is supernatural; at the same time, the promised beatitude "confronts us with decisive moral choices" such as purifying our hearts, seeking God's love above everything else, and valuing rightly—not placing ultimate hope in—human wealth, health, notoriety, power, and achievement.[11]

Human Freedom (Sec. 1, Ch. 1, Art. 3)

Freedom to direct oneself toward this beatitude is the essence of human existence and dignity; accordingly, the *Catechism* returns to its discussion of the divine image, consisting of human rationality and free will. Being rational, human beings can initiate and control their own actions, direct themselves to seeking God, and "freely attain his full and blessed perfection by cleaving to him."[12] Specifically, freedom is defined as "the power, rooted in reason and will, to act or not to act, to do this or that, and so to perform deliberate actions on one's own responsibility."[13] When directed toward God, such freedom attains perfection; when it "has not bound itself definitively to its ultimate good which is God, there is the possibility of choosing between good and evil, and thus of growing in perfection or of falling and sinning."[14] Freedom of choice in the first case brings praise and merit; in the second case, the abuse of freedom results in blame and reproach. Habitual choosing of the good brings greater and greater freedom; habitual disobedience results in enslavement to sin (Rom. 6:17). Furthermore, freedom makes human beings responsible for their acts, assuming they are voluntary and not coerced

---

[9] CCC 1719.
[10] CCC 1721.
[11] CCC 1723.
[12] CCC 1730; citation is from Vatican Council II, *Gaudium et Spes* 17; cf. Sirach 15:14.
[13] CCC 1731.
[14] CCC 1731–1732 (emphasis removed).

acts. In the case of "ignorance, inadvertence (lack of attention), duress, fear, habit, inordinate attachments, and other psychological or social factors," personal responsibility "can be diminished or even nullified."[15] The importance of this point is underscored by the *Catechism*'s insistence that "[t]he right to the exercise of freedom, especially in moral and religious matters, is an inalienable requirement of the dignity of the human person."[16]

Placing this discussion of freedom in the context of the work of salvation, the *Catechism* notes several important themes.[17] The first theme, *freedom and sin*, underscores that human freedom, being limited and fallible, failed; Adam and Eve freely sinned, thereby becoming slaves to sin and plunging all humanity into a multitude of other sins. *Threats to freedom*, the second theme, notes that deviation from the moral law results in violation of freedom. For the third theme, *liberation and freedom*, attention is given to the work of Christ as achieving salvation and freedom from all that enslaves human beings (Gal. 5:1; John 8:32); the gift of the Holy Spirit also brings freedom (2 Cor. 3:17), which is the glory of the redeemed (Rom. 8:21). *Freedom and grace*, the fourth theme, emphasizes that the two are not rivals "when this freedom accords with the sense of the true and the good that God has put in the human heart."[18] Indeed, an increasing response to divine grace results in greater and greater freedom.

The Morality of Human Acts (Sec. 1, Ch. 1, Art. 4)

"Freedom makes man a moral subject. When he acts deliberately, man is, so to speak, the father of his acts." Such acts, being "freely chosen in consequence of a judgment of conscience, can be morally evaluated" as either good or evil.[19] The morality of human acts consists of three sources or constitutive elements: "the object chosen; the end in view or the intention; [and] the circumstances of the action."[20] First, the *object chosen* is the act itself, "a good toward which the will deliberately directs itself" as assessed by human reason "in conformity with the true good."[21] For illustrative purposes, a major example (which is positive) is tutoring a student who is strug-

---

[15] CCC 1735.
[16] CCC 1738 (emphasis removed).
[17] CCC 1739–1742.
[18] CCC 1742.
[19] CCC 1749 (emphasis removed).
[20] CCC 1750.
[21] CCC 1751.

gling in school. Objective norms of morality and the human conscience factor into this rational judgment. Consequently, some acts are intrinsically disordered (e.g., fornication [e.g., homosexual activity], blasphemy, perjury, murder, and adultery)[22] and can never count as good moral actions, no matter the intention—the second element—with which they are undertaken. For illustrative purposes, a minor example (which is negative) is exaggerating the abilities and accomplishments of a colleague at work.

The second element, the *end in view* or *intention*, resides in the human moral agent who acts, not in the act itself. This element is the goal of the intention, the purpose pursued in the action. "The intention is a movement of the will toward the end: it is concerned with the goal of the activity. It aims at the good anticipated from the action undertaken."[23] In the major example, the goal or intention of the tutoring is to help the student overcome his educational struggles and become proficient in the subject studied in order to move on to advanced studies, graduate from school, and secure employment in an occupation that uses the developed skill. Such aid is a good intention. As noted above, however, "a good intention . . . does not make behavior that is intrinsically disordered . . . good or just. The end does not justify the means."[24] In the minor example, exaggerating the abilities of a colleague at work (the act), in order that she may get a well-deserved promotion (the intention), does not render the act a good one, because lying is inherently evil.

As for the third element, the *circumstances of the action* include its consequences and "contribute to increasing or diminishing the moral goodness or evil of human acts . . . [and] the agent's responsibilities." However, these "[c]ircumstances of themselves cannot change the moral quality of the acts themselves."[25] In the main example, the tutoring of the student to help him prepare for a career succeeds; that is, the aim to equip the student through tutoring results in his making a significant contribution in his vocation. The moral goodness of the act itself, while not dependent on its consequences, nevertheless is magnified by its successful outcome. In the minor example, the lying to promote one's colleague does indeed result in her getting the promotion and, as a result, paves the way for a significant expansion of the

---

[22] CCC 1755–1756.
[23] CCC 1752.
[24] CCC 1753.
[25] CCC 1754.

company, benefiting all the employees. However, the positive consequences do not make the lying, which is evil in itself, good or right; moral culpability for the lie is not diminished in any way by the positive outcome. Changing the minor example slightly, if the lying is committed out of fear that the colleague will in some way retaliate if the deceit is not carried out, the culpability for the lying may be diminished to some degree.

Accordingly, a moral act consists of three sources or constitutive elements. Importantly, "a morally good act requires the goodness of the object, of the end, and of the circumstances together."[26] And a good intention cannot render as good an act that is inherently evil.

The Morality of the Passions (Sec. 1, Ch. 1, Art. 5)

Moving from acts to passions, the *Catechism* emphasizes that human passions or feelings can dispose moral agents to beatitude and contribute to it. By way of definition, "[f]eelings or passions are emotions or movements of the sensitive appetite that incline us to act or not to act in regard to something felt or imagined to be good or evil."[27] They are mediators between the life of the mind and the life of the senses, as shown here:

the life of the mind
(reason, will)

passions/feelings

the life of the senses
(body)

Accordingly, passions "form the passageway and ensure the connection between the life of the senses and the life of the mind."[28] As will be discussed shortly, moral perfection is the result of all human aspects functioning well together under the ordering of the reason and will.

Passions are numerous, but the most fundamental affection is love,

---

[26] CCC 1755 (emphasis removed).
[27] CCC 1763.
[28] CCC 1764.

aroused by the attraction of the good. "Love causes a desire for the absent good and the hope of obtaining it . . . [and] finds completion in the pleasure and joy of the good possessed."[29] Love is the source of all other feelings. Oppositely, "[t]he apprehension of evil causes hatred, aversion, and fear of the impending evil . . . [and] ends in sadness at some present evil, or in the anger that resists it."[30] Accordingly, passions "are evil if love is evil and good if it is good."[31]

This last statement means that passions are neither good nor evil in and of themselves, but become morally qualified when "they effectively engage reason and will" and are ruled by them.[32] When reason/will governs the affections or does not put obstacles in their way, the passions are voluntary. Ruled by reason/will so as to contribute to a good action, the passions are morally good; when not rightly governed and thus contributing to an evil action, the passions are morally evil. To put it another way, "[t]he upright will orders the movements of the senses it appropriates to the good and to beatitude; an evil will succumbs to disordered passions and exacerbates them."[33] In summary, passions "can be taken up into the virtues or perverted by the vices."[34]

The *Catechism* concludes its discussion by underscoring the importance of sanctification, through the Holy Spirit, of the entire human being. When reason and will, passions, and bodily appetites and senses are moved together toward the good, moral perfection results.

Moral Conscience (Sec. 1, Ch. 1, Art. 6)

Earlier, in its discussion of the sacrament of Matrimony, the *Catechism* made appeal to natural law in its support for the vocation to marriage.[35] Natural law is the rule, in accord with the eternal rule that God has prescribed for human conduct, which is found in human nature itself. Now, in its discussion of life in Christ, the *Catechism* revisits this idea and describes this law in terms of moral conscience: "Deep within his conscience man discovers a law which he has not laid upon himself but which he must obey.

---

[29] CCC 1765.
[30] Ibid.
[31] CCC 1766; citation is from Augustine, *The City of God* 14.7 (NPNF[1] 2:267).
[32] CCC 1767.
[33] CCC 1768.
[34] CCC 1768 (emphasis removed).
[35] CCC 1603.

Its voice, ever calling him to love and to do what is good and to avoid what is evil, sounds in his heart at the right moment."[36] The apostle Paul explains this phenomenon in Romans 2:14–16.

Specifically, this law of the heart or conscience is inscribed by God and is a judgment of human reason (not of passions or bodily appetites). An upright conscience functions in the following ways: It recognizes moral principles; perceives their application in given circumstances; makes a judgment about concrete actions, approving those that are good and denouncing those that are evil; promotes engagement in good and avoidance of evil; and acknowledges the truth about the moral good, so as to make it the object of actions. *Interiority* is necessary for the conscience to function properly; that is, a human being must "be sufficiently present to himself in order to hear and follow the voice of his conscience."[37] Human dignity "implies and requires uprightness of moral conscience"; indeed, because of conscience, human beings are able to assume responsibility for their actions.[38] When conscience is violated by doing evil, the judgment of conscience convicts of wrongdoing yet still witnesses to the truth of the good; additionally, conscience "calls to mind the forgiveness that must be asked, the good that must still be practiced, and the virtue that must be constantly cultivated with the grace of God."[39] Human dignity further means that human beings must be free to act according to conscience and not forced to act contrary to it.

Though implanted by God, conscience must be formed by a process of lifelong education; in this way, it becomes upright and truthful, formulating its judgments by reason in accordance with the good as willed by God. Such formation of conscience is indispensable in light of the negative influences and temptations to sin that seek to wreak havoc with human beings. Key to conscience formation are the Word of God, the gifts of the Holy Spirit, the counsel of others, and the authoritative teachings of the Church. Three principles of conscience always apply: "One may never do evil so that good may result from it; the Golden Rule: 'Whatever you wish that men would do to you, do so to them' [Matt. 7:12]; [and] charity always proceeds by way of respect for one's neighbor and his conscience [1 Cor. 8:12; Rom. 14:21]."[40]

---

[36] CCC 1776; citation is from Vatican Council II, *Gaudium et Spes* 16.
[37] CCC 1779.
[38] CCC 1780–1781.
[39] CCC 1781.
[40] CCC 1789.

It is possible for conscience to err. Ignorance and wrong judgment of conscience result from a blindness that develops through habitual sin, unawareness or rejection of Christ and the gospel, the bad example of others, enslavement to passions, assertions of autonomy of conscience, rejection of the Church's authoritative teachings, and an absence of conversion and love. To violate one's conscience, to act deliberately against it, results in self-condemnation and culpability for the evil committed.[41] Through formation of conscience, errors of conscience can be corrected.

The Virtues (Sec. 1, Ch. 1, Art. 7)

Taking its cue from Philippians 4:8,[42] the *Catechism* addresses the topic of human and theological virtues. By way of definition, "[a] virtue is an habitual and firm disposition to do the good."[43] Virtuous people holistically incline toward the good, giving the best of themselves to choose the good in concrete actions.

There are two types of virtues: human and theological. In terms of the first category, "[h]uman virtues are firm attitudes, stable dispositions, habitual perfections of intellect and will that govern our actions, order our passions, and guide our conduct to reason and faith."[44] These habits include four cardinal, or principal, virtues: prudence ("right reason in action"),[45] justice (giving God and others their due), fortitude (perseverance through difficulty and in pursuit of the good), and temperance (moderation in pleasures). These cardinal human virtues, and others that derive from them, are "purified and elevated by divine grace."[46] Virtuous living that is hard for sinful human beings to pursue and practice becomes aided by the grace of salvation.

Human virtues "are rooted in the theological virtues," the second category of virtues.[47] These dispositions or habits are oriented toward God, enable the faithful to live in relationship with him, and assist them in meriting eternal life. The three theological virtues are faith, hope, and charity (love).

---

[41] The *Catechism* allows for certain situations—e.g., "the ignorance [of conscience] is invincible [i.e., so absolutely and utterly complete that it cannot be rectified], or the moral subject is not responsible for his erroneous judgment"—that result in the evil committed not being imputed to the moral agent (CCC 1793).

[42] Paul sets forth truth, honor, justice, purity, beauty, grace, excellence, and praiseworthiness as the objects of human meditation.

[43] CCC 1803.

[44] CCC 1804 (emphasis removed).

[45] CCC 1806; citation is from Thomas Aquinas, *Summa Theologica* 2nd pt. of pt. 2, q. 47, art. 2.

[46] CCC 1810.

[47] CCC 1812.

"Faith is the theological virtue by which we believe in God and believe all that he has said and revealed to us, and that Holy Church proposes for our belief, because he is truth itself."[48] The righteous live by faith (Rom. 1:17), which in turn works through love (Gal. 5:6). Faith must be joined with hope and love, and faith must be professed. Indeed, "faith apart from works is dead" (James 2:26), meaning that by itself "faith does not fully unite the believer to Christ and does not make him a living member of his Body."[49] Moreover, according to Jesus's words about acknowledging or denying him before others (Matt. 10:32–33), "[s]ervice of and witness to the faith are necessary for salvation."[50]

"Hope is the theological virtue by which we desire the kingdom of heaven and eternal life as our happiness, placing our trust in Christ's promises and relying not on our own strength, but on the help of the grace of the Holy Spirit."[51] The tenacious hope of Abraham (Rom. 4:18) is a stellar example of this virtue. Jesus's beatitudes foster hope through trial and persecution, and prayer—especially the Lord's Prayer—both expresses and nourishes hope.

"Charity is the theological virtue by which we love God above all things for his own sake, and our neighbor as ourselves for the love of God."[52] Love is the new commandment that Jesus gives (John 13:34), and love between his disciples imitates Jesus's love for them (15:9, 12). As the fruit of the Spirit and the fullness of the divine law (Rom. 13:8), love obeys the divine commandments (John 15:9–10). As Jesus demonstrated his love for sinners by dying for them, his disciples are told to love sinners (Rom. 5:10; Matt. 5:44). Love is particularly depicted in Paul's hymn to charity (1 Cor. 13:1–7), placing it at the head of the other theological virtues. Accordingly, love animates, inspires, links, articulates, and orders faith and hope; it is "the form of the virtues," their source and goal.[53]

In addition to the human virtues and the theological virtues, the gifts of the Holy Spirit sustain the moral life of the faithful. These seven gifts—wisdom, understanding, counsel, fortitude, knowledge, piety, and fear of the Lord—render the faithful submissive to the Spirit's promptings and "complete and perfect the virtues of those who receive them."[54]

---

48 CCC 1814; citation is from Vatican Council II, *Dei Verbum* 5.
49 CCC 1815.
50 CCC 1816.
51 CCC 1817.
52 CCC 1822.
53 CCC 1827 (emphasis removed).
54 CCC 1831; the biblical reference is Isa. 11:2.

Sin (Sec. 1, Ch. 1, Art. 8)

As its discussion of the Dignity of the Human Person draws to a close, the *Catechism* focuses on the reality of sin, which is the backdrop for the need for divine mercy and Eucharistic grace leading to salvation. Citing Augustine, the *Catechism* affirms that "God created us without us; but he did not will to save us without us."[55] In other words, while creation was accomplished without human participation, redemption is another matter. Specifically, human participation in salvation includes confession of sin (1 John 1:8–9); indeed, divine grace, operating through the Word and Spirit of God, must "uncover sin"—cast "a living light on sin" or convict of sin—in order to accomplish its work, which is conversion and the bestowal of righteousness (Rom. 5:21).[56]

By way of definition, "[s]in is an offense against reason, truth, and right conscience; it is failure in genuine love for God and neighbor caused by a perverse attachment to certain goods."[57] It may also be defined as "an utterance, a deed, or a desire contrary to the eternal law."[58] Other elements included in sin are an offense against God and his love for human beings (Ps. 51:4); disobedience, or rebellion against the will of God so as to become autonomous (self-determining) creatures (exemplified in the first sin; Gen. 3:5); self-love, even to the point of contempt of God; and proud self-exaltation, as opposed to the obedience of Christ that accomplished human salvation. As for this last point, the passion of Christ reveals sin's "violence and its many forms: unbelief, murderous hatred, shunning and mockery by the leaders and the people, Pilate's cowardice and the cruelty of the soldiers, Judas's betrayal—so bitter to Jesus, Peter's denial and the disciples' flight."[59] Yet, from these sufferings due to many sins comes the forgiveness of sins.

From the various Pauline lists of sins[60] comes the notion of different kinds of sins and a categorization of them. After noting various classification systems, the *Catechism* proposes that "[s]ins are rightly evaluated

[55] CCC 1847; citation is from Augustine, Sermon 169, in *The Works of Saint Augustine: A Translation for the 21st Century*, Part 3: Sermons, vol. 5: *Sermons 148–183*, ed. John E. Rotelle, trans. Edmund Hill, *Sermons* (Hyde Park, NY: New City, 1992), 231.
[56] CCC 1848.
[57] CCC 1849.
[58] Ibid.; citation is from Augustine, *Reply to Faustus the Manichean* 22.27 (NPNF[1] 4:283); Thomas Aquinas, *Summa Theologica* 1st pt. of pt. 2, q. 71, art. 6.
[59] CCC 1851.
[60] Gal. 5:19–21; Rom. 1:28–32; 1 Cor. 6:9–10; Eph. 5:3–5; Col. 3:5–8; 1 Tim. 1:9–10; 2 Tim. 3:2–5.

according to their gravity";[61] hence, it makes a distinction between mortal and venial sin. "*Mortal sin* destroys charity in the heart of man by a grave violation of God's law; it turns man away from God, who is his ultimate end and his beatitude, by preferring an inferior good to him. *Venial sin* allows charity to subsist, even though it offends and wounds it."[62]

More specifically, the two categories can be discussed and distinguished by noting the sin itself, its immediate results, its eternal result, and the solution to overcome it. *Mortal sin* is a grave violation of the law of God, meeting three conditions. First, its object is a *grave matter*, as specified by the Ten Commandments; thus, it contradicts either love for God or love for neighbor, or both. Second, it is committed with *full knowledge* of "the sinful character of the act, of its opposition to God's law."[63] Third, mortal sin is committed with *complete consent*, involving a deliberate personal choice that is not diminished by—indeed, is increased by—"[f]eigned ignorance and hardness of heart."[64] As an example, "[s]in committed through malice, by deliberate choice of evil, is the gravest";[65] indeed, Jesus himself spoke of blasphemy against the Holy Spirit as an unpardonable, eternal sin (Mark 3:29; cf. Matt. 12:32; Luke 12:10). An *immediate result* of mortal sin is the destruction of love in the heart and a turning away from God through the preference of an inferior (i.e., created) good over the ultimate good, who is God. Another *immediate result* is the loss of sanctifying grace; one is no longer in a state of grace. In terms of its *eternal result*, if mortal sin is not redeemed, and should one die in this state, "it causes exclusion from Christ's kingdom and the eternal death of hell."[66] The *solution* for mortal sin is the sacrament of Penance and Reconciliation.

Venial sin involves a less serious matter than does mortal sin: the standard prescribed by the moral law is not observed, or the law is disobeyed "in a grave matter, but without full knowledge or without complete consent."[67] Two examples are "thoughtless chatter or immoderate laughter."[68] An *immediate result* of venial sin is an offense against and a wounding of love, but not its destruction, as in the case of mortal sin. Manifesting a disor-

---

[61] CCC 1854.
[62] CCC 1855.
[63] CCC 1859.
[64] Ibid. As for feigned ignorance and hardness of heart, the *Catechism* refers to Mark 3:5–6; Luke 16:19–31.
[65] CCC 1860.
[66] CCC 1861.
[67] CCC 1862.
[68] CCC 1856. The examples are from Thomas Aquinas, *Summa Theologica*, 1st pt. of pt. 2, q. 88, art. 2.

dered affection for an inferior (i.e., created) good, venial sin also impedes progress in exercising virtue and the practice of the moral good, a second *immediate result*. In terms of its *eternal result*, unlike mortal sin, venial sin does not result in the loss of sanctifying grace; covenantal friendship with God, love, and eternal happiness remain. However, venial sin does merit temporal punishment in purgatory. The *solution* for venial sin is not the sacrament of Penance and Reconciliation; rather, "[w]ith God's grace it is humanly reparable" through confession and repentance.[69] A warning is offered: "Deliberate and unrepented venial sin disposes us little by little to commit mortal sin."[70]

To conclude its discussion, the *Catechism* addresses the proliferation of sin: "Sin creates a proclivity to sin; it engenders vice by repetition of the same acts. This results in perverse inclinations which cloud conscience and corrupt the concrete judgment of good and evil."[71] Following early church tradition, the *Catechism* discusses vices not in terms of the virtues they oppose, but as they are linked to the seven capital sins (commonly known as the "deadly" sins; "'capital' because they engender other sins"): pride, avarice (greed), envy, wrath, lust, gluttony, and sloth (acedia).[72] It also mentions the traditional "sins that cry to heaven": Abel's blood; Sodomite homosexuality; the cry of God's people enslaved in Egypt; the outcry of the foreigner, the widow, and the orphan; and unjust business practices.[73] Additionally, sin goes beyond personal responsibility: "[W]e have a responsibility for the sins committed by others when we cooperate in them"[74] through our participation, our supervision or approval, our cover-up, and our protection of sins and those who commit them. Such sins are systemic, social, or structural sins; as such, they foster a reign of sin.

Evangelical Assessment

Much of this section on "Life in Christ" treats the topics of anthropology (the doctrine of humanity) and morality (ethics) from a philosophical

---

[69] CCC 1863.
[70] Ibid.
[71] CCC 1865.
[72] CCC 1866. These capital sins were discussed by John Cassian in *The Conference of Abbot Serapion* 5 (NPNF[2] 11:339–351), and by Gregory the Great, *Moralia in Job* 31.45.
[73] CCC 1867 (emphasis removed); the biblical references for these sins are: Abel's blood (Gen. 4:10); Sodomite sin (Gen. 18:20; 19:13); Israel's cry (Ex. 3:7–10); the cry of the downtrodden (Ex. 22:21–24); and unjust payment (Deut. 24:14–15; James 5:4).
[74] CCC 1868 (emphasis removed).

perspective; accordingly, an assessment of these topics must be measured and selective, focusing on those areas that Scripture and evangelical theology directly address. Generally speaking, because Catholic theology's teaching on these topics is neither explicitly biblical nor explicitly unbiblical, it may be welcomed as a possible contribution to anthropology and morality, yet without considering it definitive and binding. These areas include human freedom,[75] the morality of human passions,[76] moral conscience,[77] the human virtues,[78] the theological virtues, and the morality of human acts.

Taking this latter topic as an example, Catholic theology's teaching on the morality of human acts is a well-developed, coherent moral theory. Its emphasis on the three sources or constitutive elements of human moral acts—the object chosen, the end in view or intention, and the circumstances—reminds proponents of evangelical theology that good works and evil works do not just depend on the rightness or wrongness of the acts themselves. Were these deeds done to the glory of God (Rom. 15:7; 1 Cor. 10:31), from faith (Rom. 14:23), out of "love that issues from a pure heart and a good conscience and a sincere faith" (1 Tim. 1:5; 1 Pet. 1:22), in accordance with a proper and sincere attitude (1 Cor. 4:5; Col. 3:22)? Then they would qualify as good deeds; if not, they are deficient in some manner. Jesus warned about "false prophets, who come to you in sheep's clothing

---

[75] Evangelical theology embraces a number of views of human freedom, including libertarian freedom, dovetailing with indeterminism and with much overlap with Catholic theology's position, and compatibilistic freedom, dovetailing with (soft) determinism.

[76] For an evangelical exploration of the passions, see Kevin J. Vanhoozer, *Remythologizing Theology: Divine Action, Passion, and Authorship*, Cambridge Studies in Christian Doctrine (New York: Cambridge University Press, 2012).

[77] While evangelical theology agrees with its Catholic counterpart that the human conscience is inscribed by God on the hearts of all people and that it serves to accuse them when they do wrong and applaud them when they do right (Rom. 2:14–16), many versions of evangelical theology have a more pessimistic assessment of the role and importance of the conscience (because of its corruption due to sin) than does the Catholic perspective.

[78] For the most part, evangelical theology, if it is even familiar with Catholic theology's discussion of human virtues, will first of all question the grounds for them (Catholic theology appeals to the apocryphal writing Wisdom 8:7 in support) and then dismiss the *Catechism*'s proposal that "[t]he moral virtues are acquired by human effort . . . [and] dispose all the powers of the human being for communion with divine love" (CCC 1804). For evangelical theology, human virtues may be appreciated and even applauded as attitudes and dispositions that are virtuous on a human level, but they are not so before God, at least in terms of securing his favor and/or as preparations for his grace. That one's non-Christian neighbor is virtuous, exhibiting consistent patterns of prudence, justice, fortitude, and temperance, is cause for thanksgiving and fosters a good relationship with him. However, his human virtues do not merit favor before God and thus should not mitigate one's concern to call him to repentance and faith through the gospel. Even God-fearing Cornelius, from whom Peter learned the lesson "that God shows no partiality, but in every nation anyone who fears him and does what is right is acceptable to him" (Acts 10:34–35), needed to hear the apostle's message about Jesus Christ, repent, be baptized, and receive the Holy Spirit in order to be saved. Most importantly, evangelical theology underscores the nature-grace interdependence at the foundation of Catholic theology's position on the human virtues. According to this axiom, nature—in this case, the human virtues—possesses a capacity for grace, which operates so as to elevate and perfect those virtues. As the *Catechism* affirms, the cardinal virtues, and others that flow from them, "are purified and elevated by divine grace" (CCC 1810). The evangelical theological critique of this nature-grace interdependence has already been presented.

but inwardly are ravenous wolves," and he promised that his disciples "will recognize them by their fruits," which will be evil because they are evil people (Matt. 7:15–20). Jesus also explained that prophecies uttered, demons exorcised, and mighty works done, all in his name, do not guarantee entrance into the kingdom of God (Matt. 7:21–23). Good and evil do not just pertain to the rightness or wrongness of deeds themselves. This Catholic philosophy further underscores personal moral responsibility—"man is, so to speak, the father of his acts"[79]—and the intrinsically disordered nature of certain acts (e.g., homosexual activity, murder, adultery). This emphasis can be helpful to proponents of evangelical theology in the midst of a cultural shift away from taking personal responsibility for one's actions to a denial of accountability (e.g., "no fault" divorce; the victim syndrome), and from moral absolutes to ethical relativism (e.g., offering justification for one's evil with "God wants me to be happy" or "it was done for a good cause").

Two issues on which Catholic and evangelical theology part ways are the image of God and the distinction between mortal and venial sins. As for the first matter, and as discussed earlier, Catholic theology focuses its attention on the divine image as expressed in human reason or intellect and free will. In its support, it has a long tradition that was initiated by Irenaeus and developed by Thomas Aquinas.[80] Though some varieties of evangelical theology have followed this emphasis, other versions consider the identification of the image of God with human rationality and freedom to be problematic for several reasons. For one, it is needlessly reductionistic. Scripture itself does not make this limited identification; indeed, in the opening chapter of Genesis, the narrative flows from the divine deliberation to create man in the divine image (Gen. 1:26) to the actualization of that plan (v. 27), which is the creation of a man and a woman in their wholeness. Second, the past century of research into ancient Near Eastern literature has shifted attention to divine image-bearing as being primarily the function of exercising dominion over the created order.[81] Third, through the enormous influence of Karl Barth, the divine creation of both male and female image-bearers has been underscored, with the result that human relationality, reflecting the

---

[79] CCC 1749 (emphasis removed).
[80] Irenaeus, *Against Heresies* 4.4.3 (*ANF* 1:466); Thomas Aquinas, *Summa Theologica* pt. 1, q. 93.
[81] For example, Gerhard von Rad, *Genesis: A Commentary*, trans. John H. Marks (Philadelphia: Westminster, 1972), 60. For a summary of this development, see J. Richard Middleton, *The Liberating Image: The* Imago Dei *in Genesis 1* (Grand Rapids, MI: Brazos, 2005), 24–34.

relationality inherent in the triune God, has gained importance.[82] These developments toward embracing a more holistic approach to the divine image serve to critique and ward off the speculative view of Catholic theology that, even before the fall, for Adam and Eve, their reason/intellect was responsible for ruling over their passions and bodily appetites.

Turning to the second area of disagreement, evangelical theology rejects Catholic theology's distinction between mortal and venial sins, primarily because Scripture does not make a corresponding distinction. Certainly, Scripture explicitly distinguishes between unintentional sins and intentional, "high-handed" sins:

> If one person *sins unintentionally*, he shall offer a female goat a year old for a sin offering. And the priest shall make atonement before the LORD for the person who makes a mistake, when he *sins unintentionally*, to make atonement for him, and he shall be forgiven. You shall have one law for him who does anything *unintentionally*, for him who is native among the people of Israel and for the stranger who sojourns among them. But the person who *does anything with a high hand*, whether he is native or a sojourner, reviles the LORD, and that person shall be cut off from among his people. Because he has despised the word of the LORD and has broken his commandment, that person shall be utterly cut off; his iniquity shall be on him. (Num. 15:27–31, emphasis added)

Importantly, in the case of unintentional sin, an atoning sacrifice was still required, and in the case of intentional sin, no sacrifice could avail to forgive it. But this biblical distinction finds no parallel with Catholic theology's notion that venial sin does not require a new infusion of sanctifying grace to be forgiven, while mortal sin does require the sacrament of Penance so that it can be forgiven.

Furthermore, Scripture distinguishes between degrees of sin, at least in terms of the consequences that different sins produce: "Some sins are worse than others in that they have more harmful consequences in our lives and in the lives of others, and, in terms of our personal relationship to God as Father, they arouse his displeasure more and bring more serious disruption to our fellowship with him."[83] Biblical warrant for distinguishing between

---

[82] Karl Barth, *Church Dogmatics*, ed. G. W. Bromiley and T. F. Torrance, 13 vols. (Edinburgh: T & T Clark, 1936), 184–188.
[83] Grudem, *ST*, 502.

greater and lesser sins in terms of the greater or lesser seriousness of their consequences is found in Ezekiel's vision of "still greater abominations" (Ezek. 8:6, 13, 15) and the charge that because Judas delivered Jesus over to Pontius Pilate, that disciple "has the greater sin" (John 19:11). But this distinction focuses on the gravity of sin in terms of harmful consequences in people's lives and in terms of the loss of intimacy of people's relationship with God. It does not, however, address the issue of guilt before God. In the case of one's legal standing before God, each and every sin, no matter how serious or minor it may be, makes one guilty before God and thus incurs divine wrath. As James explains, "For whoever keeps the whole law but fails in one point has become accountable for all of it. For he who said, 'Do not commit adultery,' also said, 'Do not murder.' If you do not commit adultery but do murder, you have become a transgressor of the law" (James 2:10–11; cf. Gal. 3:10, citing Deut. 27:26). Accordingly, failure to keep the entire divine law, even a breakdown in just one point, renders one a violator of it, and that transgression spells divine judgment. Accordingly, whether the sin is a serious or minor sin, guilt before God is the result. Therefore, Catholic theology's distinction between mortal sin—entailing the loss of justifying grace, bringing guilt before God, incurring his wrath, and requiring the sacrament of Penance to be forgiven—and venial sin, by which grace is not lost, does not represent biblical teaching.

Two areas of serious disappointment that evangelical theology has with its counterpart's presentation of "Life in Christ" are the lack of attention given to Scripture as a critical component for Christian living and the nearly exclusive focus on human beatitude as the divinely established purpose for human existence. As for the dearth of consideration of Scripture, at the outset of its discussion of this topic, the *Catechism* attributes the faithful's ability to lead a life "worthy of the gospel of Christ" to "the grace of Christ and the gifts of his Spirit, which they receive through the sacraments and through prayer."[84] Other sanctifying elements enjoined explicitly on the faithful include conformity to the mind of Christ and following his example, the Holy Spirit, grace, sin and forgiveness, human virtues, and Christian virtues (faith, hope, and charity). As for Scripture's role in this life in Christ, three key sections of it—the Beatitudes, the Ten Commandments, and the Golden Rule (Matt. 7:12)—are the center of attention, and

---

[84] CCC 1692.

Scripture's importance in the formation of conscience is mentioned, but that is the extent of any explicit role of Scripture for Christian living. By this critique, evangelical theology is not denying that a good portion of this section of the *Catechism*'s discussion is grounded on Scripture; indeed, references to biblical support are common. Neither does this criticism overlook the fact that the *Catechism* as a whole dedicates a significant discussion to divine revelation—including a presentation on the inspiration, truthfulness, canon, interpretation, unity, and effectiveness of Scripture—in its opening pages. Rather, the criticism reflects what evangelical theology is known for—the Word of God and its authority, sufficiency, and necessity for life in Christ.

Key to this emphasis on the Word of God is what Scripture affirms for itself: "All Scripture is breathed out by God and profitable for teaching, for reproof, for correction, and for training in righteousness, that the man of God may be complete, equipped for every good work" (2 Tim. 3:16–17). As the last phrase underscores, there is no good work that God will call his faithful people to do that he will fail to equip them to do through his Word. The knowledge of the gospel and sound doctrine, exposure to what displeases God, conviction of sin, guidance on the right path, wisdom for knowing God's will, assurance during trial and persecution, the pursuit of purity—the Word of God supplies all this and much more for living the Christian life.

Evangelical theology offers a rich presentation of Scripture and how it mediates this saving work of Christ and fosters the faithful's progressive walk with him. For a first example, Scripture as the mighty speech-acts of God is more than just words, as its utterances effect what they communicate. To illustrate, the divine declarative known as justification is the legal pronouncement of God the Judge that sinful human beings are "Not guilty!" but are instead "Righteous!" because the declaration makes it so. To illustrate further, the divine commissive "Whoever has the Son has life" (1 John 5:12) commits God as its speaker to the truth of that promise, which is consequently true in the life of sinful human beings who embrace Christ. A second example appeals to an explicit biblical injunction: "Like newborn infants, long for the pure spiritual milk, that by it you may grow up into salvation—if indeed you have tasted that the Lord is good" (1 Pet. 2:2–3). Accordingly, Scripture is the spiritual milk for the nourishment of the faithful—all of whom are portrayed as newborn babies—in order to make progress in salvation. Evangelical theology laments the minimal attention given by Catholic theology to the Word of God as a crucial element in living the life in Christ, and it pleads for its counterpart to highlight the essential role of Scripture in Christian living.

A second area of serious disappointment that evangelical theology has with Catholic theology's presentation of "Life in Christ" is the latter's nearly exclusive focus on human beatitude as the divinely established purpose for human existence. This critique is not that the salvation and eternal blessing of people who embrace the gospel of Jesus Christ is not true or of minimal importance. On the contrary, the future eminence of the faithful is described richly in Scripture: full conformity to the image of Christ (Rom. 8:29; 1 Cor. 15:49; 1 John 3:1–3); resurrection bodies that are imperishable, glorious, strong, and dominated by the Spirit (1 Cor. 15:42–44); the experience of seeing God "face to face" (the "beatific vision") as he forever dwells with his people in the new heaven and new earth (1 Cor. 13:12; Revelation 21–22). Accordingly, the future eminence of the faithful is of signal importance in the biblical vision of the future beatitude that is in store for Christians. Rather, the criticism focuses on the missed opportunity to underscore that which is even more important than human beatitude: human beings were created, and thus are divinely designed, for glorifying God through their lives.

The Westminster Shorter Catechism, one of evangelical theology's popular expressions, puts the matter succinctly: "Question: What is the chief end of man? Answer: Man's chief end is to glorify God, and to enjoy him forever."[85] The highest end of human beings—not denying the other purposes for which they were created—does not terminate on them, but on God. As Paul rehearsed in a benediction of God, "For from him and through him and to him are all things. To him be glory forever. Amen" (Rom. 11:36).[86] Elsewhere, the apostle underscored that the eternal purpose of God was, in one sense, the future eminence of his people; yet beyond that exaltation of human beings would be something more: the preeminence of his Son. "For those whom he foreknew he also predestined to be conformed to the image of his Son, in order that he might be

---

[85] Westminster Shorter Catechism, question 1.
[86] Cf. Ps. 86; Isa. 60:21; 1 Cor. 6:20; 10:31; Rev. 4:11.

the firstborn among many brothers" (8:29). From all eternity, the divine plan (foreknowledge, predestination) is for human beings rescued by divine grace to be fully conformed one day to the image of the Son; yet, among the eminence of these redeemed brothers and sisters, the preeminence of the Son ("the firstborn," in terms of exalted status) will stand out. Accordingly, evangelical theology places the emphasis on the divine design for humanity, not on human beatitude, happiness, eminence, and the like, as important as that indeed is. Rather, foremost in its theological vision is the glory of God and the preeminence of Christ, with human beings existing for spreading the fame of their Creator and Savior. Consequently, evangelical theology laments the misplaced emphasis of Catholic theology on human beatitude.

The Human Community (Sec. I, Ch. 2)

Having treated life in Christ as life in the Holy Spirit (Sec. 1, Ch. 1), the *Catechism* next discusses the corporate dimensions of this life, that is, human community and human solidarity. As this chapter (Sec. 1, Ch. 2) focuses on the social and political theory of the Catholic Church, it will be presented very briefly.

The Person and Society (Sec. 1, Ch. 2, Art. 1)

Created in the image of the triune God who eternally exists in community as Father, Son, and Holy Spirit, human beings are called to reflect this divine community in human society. Indeed, because of this divine design for human nature, human beings need to live in society, specifically in the societies of the family and the state. Other voluntary associations and institutions—economic, social, cultural, recreational, athletic, professional, and political—foster human socialization, but they also present dangers. To ward off these potential threats, the Church proposes the principle of subsidiarity and a "just hierarchy of values, which 'subordinates physical and instinctual dimensions to interior and spiritual ones.'"[87] Because of human and systemic evil—for example, treating people as means to an end—"[i]t is necessary, then, to appeal to the spiritual and moral capacities of the human person and to the permanent need for his inner conversion, so as to obtain

---

[87] CCC 1886; citation is from Pope John Paul II, *Centesimus annus* (May 1, 1991), 36.2. Accessible at http://www.vatican.va/holy_father/john_paul_ii/encyclicals/documents/hf_jp-ii_enc_01051991_centesimus-annus_en.html.

social changes that will really serve him."[88] Indeed, the gospel is the only true solution to the social problem.

Participation in Social Life (Sec. 1, Ch. 2, Art. 2)

Human society requires authority that is oriented to, and demonstrates respect for, the common good. Authority is defined as "the quality by virtue of which persons or institutions make laws and give orders to men and expect obedience from them."[89] All human authority derives from God (Rom. 13:1–2; 1 Pet. 2:13–17). "By common good is to be understood 'the sum total of social conditions which allow people, either as groups or as individuals, to reach their fulfillment more fully and more easily.'"[90] This common good consists of three essential elements: respect for and promotion of human beings as such and their fundamental rights; prosperity, or the well-being and development of society; and peace, or the stability and security of society through the maintenance and development of a just order. Clearly, the presupposition that undergirds this discussion is the existence of a universal common good, the pursuit of which is required to secure and advance the dignity of human beings. Such responsibility to promote the common good is first personal, then institutional, especially involving the state and the family.

Social Justice (Sec. 1, Ch. 2, Art. 3)

Linked to both the exercise of authority and the pursuit of the common good is social justice, which society ensures "when it provides the conditions that allow associations or individuals to obtain what is their due, according to their nature and their vocation."[91] At the heart of social justice is respect for human beings and their transcendent dignity as image-bearers of God. Such respect is shown through the promotion of human rights, enacting the principle that "everyone should look upon his neighbor (without any exception) as 'another self,'"[92] and treating all human beings equally, despite their many divinely designed differences. Other differences—"sinful inequalities" that are opposed to the gospel—are to be countered and eliminated; one

---

[88] CCC 1888 (emphasis removed).
[89] CCC 1897.
[90] CCC 1906; citation is from Vatican Council II, *Gaudium et Spes* 26.1; cf. 74.1.
[91] CCC 1928.
[92] CCC 1931; citation is from Vatican Council II, *Gaudium et Spes* 27.1.

way is through reducing social and economic disparity between individuals and groups.[93] Key to this is the Christian virtue of human solidarity, which leads to the sharing of both material goods and the spiritual goods of the Christian faith.[94]

Evangelical Assessment

Generally speaking, because Catholic theology's treatment of these issues reflects social and political theory that is neither explicitly biblical nor explicitly unbiblical, it may be welcomed as a possible contribution to discussions on corporate dimensions of human existence, yet without considering it definitive and binding. Evangelical theology overlaps in areas such as the divine design for human beings to flourish in community, the two institutions of the family and government as ordained by God, the dangers inherent in voluntary associations and institutions because of systemic evil, the need for authority that is properly exercised, the promotion of biblically sanctioned human rights, the blessing of prosperity and peace (for which the church is to pray; 1 Tim. 2:1–2), the pursuit of a universal common good, the equality of all human beings because of their creation in the image of God, and the solidarity of the human race. Where disparity is to be found is in areas such as the principle of subsidiarity and the rather optimistic view that Catholic theology has of human community, government, and other institutions.

Before leaving this chapter, attention must be drawn to one area not yet assessed. In its discussion of life in Christ, especially as that existence is disrupted by the reality of sin, the *Catechism* quotes Augustine approvingly: "God created us without us; but he did not will to save us without us."[95] An evangelical assessment of this affirmation was not offered, because the next chapter concentrates on Catholic theology's doctrine of salvation in which this cooperative arrangement between God and human beings is discussed and defended at length. It is to that presentation, and its corresponding evangelical assessment, that we now turn.

[93] CCC 1938.
[94] CCC 1939–1942.
[95] CCC 1847; citation is from Augustine, Sermon 169, in Rotelle, *Works of Saint Augustine*, Part 3: Sermons, vol. 5: *Sermons 148–183*, 231.

13

Life in Christ
(Part 3, Section I, Chapter 3)

Salvation; Law; Grace and Justification; Merit;
the Church, Mother and Teacher

God's Salvation: Law and Grace (Sec. I, Ch. 3)

Having treated life in Christ as life in the Holy Spirit (Sec. 1, Ch. 1), and having discussed the corporate dimensions of human community and human solidarity (Sec. 1, Ch. 2), the *Catechism* turns next to a presentation of the salvation of human beings, who are "called to beatitude but wounded by sin" and thus in need of salvation (Sec. 1, Ch. 3).[1] Specifically, this redemptive help that God gives in Christ comes through the law that guides human beings and the grace that sustains them, as underscored in Philippians 2:12–13.

The Moral Law (Sec. 1, Ch. 3, Art. 1)

In his wisdom, God gave the moral law to human beings for their salvation. "It prescribes for man the ways, the rules of conduct that lead to the promised beatitude; it proscribes the ways of evil which turn him away from God and his love."[2] The law has four interrelated expressions: "eternal law—the source, in God, of all law; natural law; revealed law, comprising the Old Law and the New Law, or Law of the Gospel; finally, civil and ecclesiastical laws."[3]

As for the first type, the *Catechism* does not develop the idea of the

---

[1] CCC 1949.
[2] CCC 1950.
[3] CCC 1952.

414 Life in Christ

eternal law, but it seems to correspond to God's own eternal character of righteousness. Because he is perfectly righteous in himself, God is the source of natural law and revealed law, reflections of the eternal law.

In terms of the second type, "natural law expresses the original moral sense which enables man to discern by reason the good and the evil, the truth and the lie."[4] It is universal, engraved in the human conscience by God, expressed in the Ten Commandments, established by reason, supra-cultural (i.e., applicable to all people at all times in all places), immutable and permanent, foundational for the human construction of moral rules for building the human community, and the basis for civil law. Because of the present condition of human sinfulness, "[t]he precepts of natural law are not perceived by everyone clearly and immediately."[5] Rather, sinful humanity "needs grace and revelation so moral and religious truths may be known 'by everyone with facility, with firm certainty and with no admixture of error.'"[6] Importantly, then, natural law, as divinely designed and crafted, provides a foundation for revealed law and grace.

This third type of law, revealed law, consists of two stages: the Old and the New. The Old Law, or the law of Moses, was divinely revealed to the people of Israel and "expresses many truths naturally accessible to reason" but resituated in the context of God's work of salvation.[7] It is summed up in the Ten Commandments, or Decalogue, which "is a light offered to the conscience" of all human beings to make known to them the call and ways of God and to protect them from evil.[8] Though in and of itself the Old Law is "holy, spiritual, and good" (Rom. 7:12, 14, 16), it is imperfect. Specifically, though it functions as a tutor (Gal. 3:24) by showing "what must be done," it "does not of itself give the strength, the grace of the Spirit, to fulfill it."[9] Because it cannot remove human sin, "it remains a law of bondage."[10] Indeed, its special purpose is "to denounce and disclose sin, which constitutes 'a law of concupiscence' [Romans 7] in the human heart."[11] At the same time, "the Law remains the first stage on the way to the kingdom. It

---

[4] CCC 1954.
[5] CCC 1960.
[6] Ibid.; citation is from Pope Pius XII, *Humani generis* (August 12, 1950), 3. Accessible at http://www.vatican.va /holy_father/pius_xii/encyclicals/documents/hf_p-xii_enc_12081950_humani-generis_en.html.
[7] CCC 1961.
[8] CCC 1962.
[9] CCC 1963.
[10] Ibid.
[11] Ibid. (emphasis removed).

prepares and disposes the chosen people and each Christian for conversion and faith in the Savior God."[12] In other words, it is "a preparation for the Gospel," prophesying and foretelling Christ's work of salvation from sin.[13] Lastly, the Old Law is completed by the rest of the Old Testament, which consists of the Writings and the Prophets.

The second stage of the revealed law is called the New Law, or the Law of the Gospel. It is "the perfection here on earth of the divine law, natural and revealed"[14] and, as the work of Christ, it is expressed especially in his Sermon on the Mount. Prophesied in the Old Testament (e.g., Jer. 31:31–34; cited in Heb. 8:8–12), this New Covenant Law "becomes the interior law of charity" through the work of the Holy Spirit;[15] indeed, it is "the grace of the Holy Spirit given to the faithful."[16] Furthermore, "it uses the Sermon on the Mount to teach us what must be done and makes use of the sacraments to give us the grace to do it."[17] As noted by Jesus, his Sermon does not abolish or devalue the moral prescriptions of the Old Law. On the contrary, the New Law fulfills the Old Law's commandments (Matt. 5:17–19); specifically, it "releases their hidden potential and has new demands arise from them,"[18] demands that are not additional external precepts, but ones that reform the human heart for the accomplishment of good and the formation of faith, hope, and love. Moreover, the New Law "practices the acts of religion: almsgiving, prayer and fasting, directing them to the 'Father who sees in secret,' in contrast with the desire to 'be seen by men' [Matt. 6:1–6, 16–18]. Its prayer is the Our Father [Matt. 6:9–13; Luke 11:2–4]."[19] Furthermore, this Law demands a choice between "the two ways"—entrance by the narrow gate rather than by the wide gate; building one's house on the rock rather than on the sand (Matt. 7:13–14, 21–27)—and it requires obedience to its words as summarized by the Golden Rule (Matt. 7:12; cf. Luke 6:31). Additionally, this entire Law is summed up in Jesus's new commandment "to love one another as he has loved us" (John 15:12; 13:34).

Beyond the Sermon on the Mount is added "the moral catechesis of

---

[12] CCC 1963.
[13] CCC 1964 (emphasis removed).
[14] CCC 1965.
[15] Ibid.
[16] CCC 1966 (emphasis removed).
[17] Ibid. "This sermon contains . . . all the precepts needed to shape one's life" (CCC 1966, citing Augustine, *The Sermon on the Mount* 1.1 [*NPNF*[1] 6:2]).
[18] CCC 1968.
[19] CCC 1969 (emphasis removed).

the apostolic teachings, such as Romans 12–15, 1 Corinthians 12–13, Colossians 3–4, Ephesians 4–5, etc."[20] These additional elements of the New Law focus especially on "the virtues that flow from faith in Christ and are animated by charity, the principal gifts of the Holy Spirit."[21] They also appropriately form the conscience of the faithful in light of their relationship to Christ and to the Church. Also included in the New Law are the evangelical counsels: chastity, poverty, and obedience. These counsels relate to the precepts of the law with respect to charity: "The precepts are intended to remove whatever is incompatible with charity. The aim of the counsels is to remove whatever might hinder the development of charity, even if it is not contrary to it."[22] Specifically, the three counsels underscore "the more direct ways, the readier means" to love God and neighbor, and the faithful are to obey whichever counsels are appropriate for their vocation, station in life, opportunity, strength, and the like.[23]

Finally, this New Law goes by several other names. It is a *law of love*, because obedience to it comes not from fear but from the love of the Holy Spirit that is infused into the faithful. It is called a *law of grace*, because it confers grace for obedience, through faith and the sacraments. It is known as a *law of freedom*, because it releases the faithful from "the ritual and juridical observances of the Old Law," inclines them to act spontaneously through love, and, in place of a master-to-servant relationship, fosters a friend-to-friend relationship with Christ by elevating the faithful to the status of sons and daughters of God, and even fellow heirs with Christ.[24]

Finally, the fourth type of law includes civil and ecclesiastical laws, but this legal category is not further developed.

Grace and Justification; Merit (Sec. 1, Ch. 3, Art. 2)

In addition to the help provided by the law of God, the work of salvation that God provides for sinful human beings also involves grace and justification. Before defining these two terms, the *Catechism* affirms that the grace of the Holy Spirit powerfully works to justify people. This divine work is associated with cleansing from sins and communicating "'the righteousness

---

[20] CCC 1971 (emphasis removed).
[21] CCC 1971.
[22] CCC 1973.
[23] CCC 1974.
[24] CCC 1972. This section appeals for biblical support to John 15:15; James 1:25; 2:12; Gal. 4:1–7, 21–31; Rom. 8:15.

of God through faith in Jesus Christ' [Rom. 3:22] and through Baptism,"[25] as explained by the apostle Paul in Romans 6:1–11. Accordingly, the faithful participate in Christ's death—they die to sin—and his resurrection—they are born again to a new life; indeed, the faithful become members of Christ's body (1 Corinthians 12), branches grafted onto the vine (John 15:1–4), and partakers of the divine nature (2 Pet. 1:3–4). Conversion precedes justification: "The first work of the grace of the Holy Spirit is conversion, effecting justification";[26] biblical support is Jesus's proclamation "Repent, for the kingdom of heaven is at hand" (Matt. 4:17). "Moved by grace, man turns toward God and away from sin, thus accepting forgiveness and righteousness from on high."[27] With this presentation functioning as context, the *Catechism* repeats the definition of justification from the Council of Trent: "Justification is not only the remission of sins, but also the sanctification and renewal of the interior man."[28] The *Catechism* adds, "Justification is at the same time *the acceptance of God's righteousness* through faith in Jesus Christ," where righteousness is defined as "the rectitude of divine love."[29]

The *fruit of justification* includes the following: It "detaches man from sin . . . and purifies his heart of sin. . . . It reconciles man with God. It frees from the enslavement to sin, and it heals."[30] Moreover, faith, hope, and love are poured in the hearts of the faithful with justification, "and obedience to the divine will is granted" to them.[31] Additionally, justification "conforms us to the righteousness of God, who makes us inwardly just by the power of his mercy."[32] The *ground of justification* is the atoning sacrifice of Jesus Christ; he has merited justification for the faithful. The *appropriation of justification* is through faith and Baptism: "Justification is conferred in Baptism, the sacrament of faith."[33] The *purpose of justification* is twofold: the glory of God and the gift of eternal life (Rom. 3:21–26).

The *Catechism* explains that justification establishes a relationship of cooperation between grace and human freedom. As for the human ele-

[25] CCC 1987.
[26] CCC 1989 (emphasis removed). Cf. 1990: "Justification follows upon God's merciful initiative of offering forgiveness."
[27] CCC 1989.
[28] Ibid.; citation is from *Canons and Decrees of the Council of Trent*, 6th session (January 13, 1547), *Decree on Justification* 7 (Schaff, 2:94).
[29] CCC 1991 (emphasis added).
[30] CCC 1990 (emphasis removed).
[31] CCC 1991.
[32] CCC 1992.
[33] Ibid.

ment in the cooperation, "it is expressed by the assent of faith to the Word of God, which invites him to conversion, and in the cooperation of charity with the prompting of the Holy Spirit who precedes and preserves his assent."[34] This latter, initiating and sustaining work of the grace of the Spirit is the divine element in the cooperation. Citing the Council of Trent, the *Catechism* affirms, "When God touches man's heart through the illumination of the Holy Spirit, man himself is not inactive while receiving that inspiration, since he could reject it; and yet, without God's grace, he cannot by his own free will move himself toward justice in God's sight."[35] Clearly, this work of justification is marvelous, "the most excellent work of God's love."[36] Appealing once more to the apostle Paul (Rom. 6:19, 22), the *Catechism* again links justification, regeneration, and sanctification: "The Holy Spirit is the master of the interior life. By giving birth to the 'inner man,' justification entails the sanctification of his whole being."[37]

Having defined and discussed the work of justification, the *Catechism* next offers its presentation on grace, which is closely tied to justification; indeed, "justification comes from the grace of God."[38] Grace is defined as "favor, the free and undeserved help that God gives us to respond to his call to become children of God, partakers of the divine nature and of eternal life."[39] The fruit of grace is participation in the life of the triune God and the supernatural vocation to eternal life. Such grace is initiated by the sacrament of Baptism, but grace itself "is the gratuitous gift that God makes to us of his own life, infused by the Holy Spirit into our soul to heal it of sin and to sanctify it."[40]

Grace comes in various types: *Sanctifying grace* (also called *deifying grace*) is received in Baptism; it is "an habitual grace, a stable and supernatural disposition that perfects the soul itself to enable it to live with God, to act by his love."[41] Such *habitual grace*, "the permanent disposition to live and act in keeping with God's call,"[42] is to be distinguished by *actual graces*, specific

---

[34] CCC 1993.
[35] Ibid.; citation is from *Canons and Decrees of the Council of Trent*, 6th session (January 13, 1547), *Decree on Justification* 5 (Schaff, 92).
[36] CCC 1994 (emphasis removed).
[37] CCC 1995 (emphasis removed).
[38] CCC 1996.
[39] Ibid. (emphasis removed). This section appeals for biblical support to John 1:12–18; 17:3; Rom. 8:14–17; 2 Pet. 1:3–4.
[40] CCC 1999.
[41] CCC 2000.
[42] Ibid.

acts of God's intervention at the beginning or during the course of his work of sanctification. *Preparatory grace* (often called, in evangelical theology, *prevenient grace*) goes before sinful human beings and prepares them for the reception of divine grace.[43] Additionally, this divine initiative "demands man's free response" to know and love God; a person "only enters freely into the communion of love."[44] *Sacramental graces* are those "gifts proper to the different sacraments";[45] e.g., the grace of the sacrament of Penance absolves the penitent of her confessed mortal sin. *Special graces* (*charisms*) are gifts such as miracles and speaking in tongues that are "oriented toward sanctifying grace and are intended for the common good of the Church."[46] The *grace of final perseverance* is the divine work by which God holds and empowers the faithful to the very end, at which point he will recompense them "for the good works accomplished with his grace in communion with Jesus."[47]

The *Catechism* concludes its treatment of grace by underscoring two important points: Because of its supernatural character, "grace escapes our experience and cannot be known except by faith."[48] Accordingly, the faithful's feelings and good works are not to be relied upon in order to gain certainty of salvation. At the same time, in keeping with Christ's affirmation—"Thus you will know them by their fruits" (Matt. 7:20)—"reflection on God's blessings in our life and in the lives of the saints offers us a guarantee that grace is at work in us and spurs us on to an ever greater faith and an attitude of trustful poverty."[49]

Having treated the relationship between justification, grace, and human freedom, the *Catechism* concludes this section with a discussion of merit. It begins with a statement from the Roman Missal: "You [God] are glorified in the assembly of your Holy Ones, for in crowning their merits you are crowning your own gifts."[50] Merit is defined as "the recompense owed

---

[43] CCC 2001. The *Catechism* discusses this kind of grace as "[t]he preparation of man for the reception of grace" (emphasis removed). From the Latin *praevenire* ("to go before"), prevenient grace is biblically warranted, according to Augustine, because of Ps. 59:10 (Latin translation): "We read in Holy Scripture . . . that God's mercy 'shall meet me' [*praevenient*]. . . . It goes before the unwilling to make him willing" (Augustine, *Enchiridion on Faith, Hope, and Love* 32 [NPNF[1] 3:248]). For further discussion, see Augustine, *On Nature and Grace* 35[31] (NPNF[1] 5:133); *Treatise against Two Letters of the Pelagians* 2.21 (NPNF[1] 5:401).

[44] CCC 2002 (emphasis removed).

[45] CCC 2003.

[46] Ibid.

[47] CCC 2016.

[48] CCC 2005 (emphasis removed).

[49] CCC 2005.

[50] CCC 2006 (introduction); citation is from the Roman Missal, preface 1 *de Sanctis*, from Augustine's statement in *Exposition on the Psalms* 102.7; cf. *Letter* 194.

by a community or a society for the action of one of its members, experienced either as beneficial or harmful, deserving reward or punishment."[51] Through sanctifying grace, the faithful are enabled to earn merits and thus to gain eternal salvation. At the heart of the idea of merit is the fact that "God has freely chosen to associate man with the work of his grace."[52] Divine grace initiates, and a free human response follows; thus, there is divinely designed cooperation between God and human beings "so that the merit of good works is to be attributed in the first place to the grace of God, then to the faithful."[53] Such merit does not at all pertain to the beginning of salvation, for that grace belongs to the divine initiative alone: "[N]o one can merit the initial grace of forgiveness and justification, at the beginning of conversion."[54] But merit enters in when the faithful, prompted by the Holy Spirit and love, merit for themselves and for others "the graces needed for [their] sanctification, for the increase of grace and charity, and for the attainment of eternal life."[55]

Merits are of two types: *Condign merits* are real merits, or merits of worthiness, accomplished by the faithful through divine grace. God is morally obligated to reward the faithful who are righteous with condign merits. *Congruous merits*, or merits of fitness, are not strictly merits; rather, they are human works reckoned as merits because in doing them, the faithful do what is in them to do. Considered in and of themselves, good works do not achieve any real merit—condign merit—before God, because the faithful who engage in good works are in a state of sin and have received everything—especially grace—from God in the first place. But as long as the faithful do what is within their ability to accomplish, according to the way that God has designed them to use their free will to do good, they are rewarded with congruous merit. When God sees the faithful's good works that, in other circumstances, would be meritorious, he credits those works to their account as being meritorious.

The Church, Mother and Teacher (Sec. 1, Ch. 3, Art. 3)

God's work of salvation, brought about through the law that guides the faithful and the divine grace that sustains them, is always set in the context

---

[51] CCC 2006 (emphasis removed).
[52] CCC 2008 (emphasis removed).
[53] CCC 2008.
[54] CCC 2010 (emphasis removed).
[55] CCC 2010.

of the Church, which is both mother and teacher of the faithful. Specifically, the Church gives to her children and pupils the Word of God (especially the law of Christ and the Ten Commandments), the grace of the sacraments (especially the Eucharistic sacrifice), the outstanding examples of holiness in the Virgin Mary and the saints, saving truth, and moral principles (the "deposit" of Christian moral teaching) by which they are to live their lives.

Within the Church it is especially the Magisterium who is the authentic teacher of the faith that is to be believed and obeyed. This role of the Magisterium is ensured by the charism of infallibility, the gift of teaching without error. "This infallibility extends as far as does the deposit of divine Revelation"—including both written Scripture and Church Tradition—but goes beyond this deposit to include two other categories of teachings: First, it extends to "all those elements of doctrine, including morals, without which the saving truths of the faith cannot be preserved, explained, or observed."[56] Second, it extends to "the specific precepts of the natural law, because their observance, demanded by the Creator, is necessary for salvation."[57] The Church, through its Magisterium, is entrusted with this law of God and must teach it to the faithful, who have both the right to be instructed in it and the duty to obey it. While the conscience of the faithful must be free and cannot be coerced, it is not free to follow "individualistic considerations in its moral judgments of the person's own acts" and "should not be set in opposition to the moral law or the Magisterium of the Church."[58] As an example, a Catholic cannot take a pro-choice position on the issue of abortion; indeed, even the claim to be following one's conscience in favor of abortion demonstrates a malformed conscience and is to be rejected.

Beyond all these teachings, the Church also offers its precepts to its faithful. These instructions "are set in the context of a moral life bound to and nourished by liturgical life."[59] The five precepts are the following: (1) "you shall attend Mass on Sundays and holy days of obligation"; (2) "you shall confess your sins at least once a year"; (3) "you shall humbly receive your Creator in Holy Communion at least during the Easter season"; (4) "you shall keep holy the holy days of obligation"; and (5) "you shall observe the

---

[56] CCC 2035.
[57] CCC 2036 (emphasis removed).
[58] CCC 2039.
[59] CCC 2041.

prescribed days of fasting and abstinence." An additional precept is the faithful's duty to give financially to support the Church.[60]

When the faithful are obedient, they authenticate the message of salvation, foster the advancement of the Church's mission in the world, build up the Church, and hasten the coming of the kingdom of God.

Evangelical Assessment

In its preceding discussion of life in Christ, the *Catechism* quoted Augustine approvingly: "God created us without us; but he did not will to save us without us."[61] This synergistic effort of divine and human cooperation comes to the forefront in the *Catechism*'s discussion of the doctrine of salvation, and for this reason evangelical theology is strongly critical of Catholic theology on the following topics.

By way of introduction, *monergism*[62] is used in discussions of salvation to refer to a *sole source that works* redemption; that is, God is the single agent that operates the rescue of fallen human beings. By contrast, *synergism*[63] refers to two (or more) sources that *work together* in salvation; that is, God and fallen human beings together operate the rescue of the latter group. Evangelical theology, following key tenets of the Protestant Reformation, adheres to monergistic salvation, whereas Catholic theology holds to synergistic salvation. This comparison and implicit critique of synergism does not overlook or disagree with Catholic theology's insistence on salvation as a gracious work of God; the *Catechism* is replete with discussions of divine grace as the foundation of salvation. Rather, the criticism is raised with respect to the application of salvation and the idea that God has designed salvation to include the participation and empowerment of the faithful in meriting eternal life. At the heart of such synergism is the nature-grace interdependence: Nature—in this case, fallen human beings—possesses a capacity for grace, which operates in nature to elevate and perfect it; a cooperative engagement takes place. Critique of this axiom has already been offered (ch. 2). Accordingly, as this evangelical theological assessment of the Catholic view of salvation

---

[60] CCC 2042–2043.

[61] CCC 1847; citation is from Augustine, Sermon 169, in *The Works of Saint Augustine: A Translation for the 21st Century*, Part 3: Sermons, vol. 5: *Sermons 148–183*, ed. John E. Rotelle, trans. Edmund Hill (Hyde Park, NY: New City, 1992), 231.

[62] *Monergism* is derived from two Greek words: μόνος (*monos* = sole, only one) and ἔργον (*ergon* = work).

[63] *Synergism* is derived from two Greek words: σύν (*syn* = with, together) and ἔργον (*ergon* = work).

begins, it should be noted that the two sides on this doctrine are at polar opposites.

Law

Before further discussion of monergism and synergism, however, this assessment begins with Catholic theology's starting point, which is a presentation of the moral law as a God-ordained means by which he provides help for the redemption of fallen human beings. Without getting into the details of the four types of law that compose this moral law, it is the concept of law as a divinely given aid for salvation to which evangelical theology objects. Recognizing that evangelical theology encompasses a broad spectrum of views on the law, the following summary represents a fairly typical version (all of the following points relate especially to the old covenant law, or law of Moses, which Catholic theology also calls the Old Law).[64]

Coming from God himself, the law is holy, righteous, and good (Rom. 7:12). It reveals who God is, articulates what his people need in order to be righteous in his sight, and promises blessings for obedience and threatens curses for disobedience. Specifically, as it sets forth the divine requirements, it demands perfection, as Moses urges the people: "Be careful to *obey all these words* that I command you, that it may go well with you and with your children after you forever, when you do what is good and right in the sight of the LORD your God" (Deut.12:28, emphasis added). This demand for perfection is in keeping with the perfect holiness of the God who gave the law ("be holy, for I am holy"; Lev. 11:44; 1 Pet. 1:16) and is reflected in the all-encompassing sweep of the law, which regulated the whole of life for God's people. Importantly, the law "commands obedience and lacks the power to bring about that obedience, but it was never meant to be the source of obedience";[65] rather, "through the law comes knowledge of sin" (Rom. 3:20). Furthermore, "the law came in to increase the trespass" (5:20). Specifically, the impact of the law was to make the people of Israel *worse*; for example, immediately after receiving the Ten Commandments, they forged the golden calf and fell into heinous idolatry (Exodus 32). Because it exposes sin for what it is—thus, no one can feign ignorance—the law brings

---

[64] Much of the following reflects the discussion in Brian Vickers, *Justification by Grace through Faith: Finding Freedom from Legalism, Lawlessness, Pride, and Despair*, Explorations in Biblical Theology, series ed. Robert A. Peterson (Phillipsburg, NJ: P & R, 2013).

[65] Ibid., 99; cf. 133, 155, 175.

divine wrath (Rom. 4:15) and death (7:24), the very opposite of blessing and life. Accordingly, the law—and works associated with it—cannot bring justification, as Paul underscores:

> For by works of the law no human being will be justified in his [God's] sight, since through the law comes knowledge of sin. But now the righteousness of God has been manifested apart from the law, although the Law and the Prophets bear witness to it—the righteousness of God through faith in Jesus Christ to all who believe. (Rom. 3:20–22)

> Yet we know that a person is not justified by works of the law but through faith in Jesus Christ, so we also have believed in Christ Jesus, in order to be justified by faith in Christ and not by works of the law, because by works of the law no one will be justified. (Gal. 2:16)

Accordingly, "Paul does not condemn anyone for having a high regard for the law; he condemns people for trying to use the law to establish their own righteousness."[66]

Paul's discussion of the old covenant law and its inability to bring justification is part of a larger story that the apostle tells. First, "[t]he law distinguished Israel, setting it apart from every nation on earth by defining its identity and bringing attention to the greatness of its God."[67] In other words, the law of Moses was not a generic law given to the human race but was intended specifically for the people of Israel (e.g., Deut. 4:8). Second, "[t]he giving of the law is an act of grace to Israel because it is set in the context of redemption from Egypt, [and] functions as a response on Israel's part to its covenant relationship with God."[68] That is, the old covenant law did not create a relationship between God and his people; that covenant had already been established with Abraham and God's promises to him (e.g., Genesis 15). "The law, therefore, was never given as a way to find God but was given after God made a way for Israel to leave slavery in Egypt and become his people."[69]

Though narrowly focused on the people of Israel, the law of Moses—specifically, the failure on the part of those people to obey it—has startling

---

[66] Ibid., 99. It bears emphasizing that the apostle distinguishes between the Old Law, by which no one can be justified, and the Old Testament, to which the phrase "the Law and the Prophets" refers. The Old Testament bears witness to the manifestation of the righteousness of God apart from the works of the Old Law.
[67] Ibid., 100.
[68] Ibid., 100–101.
[69] Ibid., 106.

repercussions for the world at large: "What then? Are we Jews any better off? No, not at all. For we have already charged that all, both Jews and Greeks, are under sin, as it is written: 'None is righteous, no, not one; no one understands; no one seeks for God. All have turned aside; together they have become worthless; no one does good, not even one'" (Rom. 3:9–12). Paul argues from the specific to the general, calling "the law as Exhibit A to prove beyond a shadow of doubt that God's contention against [all] humanity is just. . . . [I]f those who live under the law show themselves unable and unwilling to keep the law, then what hope can there be for those outside the law?"[70] Under no circumstances can any single human being ever be justified by keeping the law, whether the law of Moses or any other code.

So, if it is impossible to establish righteousness on the basis of the law, on what basis can it be grounded? Scripture points to Jesus Christ the righteous, and faith in him, as the foundation for and means of appropriating the righteousness of God. In seed form, this focus begins with Abraham, who "believed the LORD, and he counted it to him as righteousness" (Gen. 15:6). Commenting on Abraham's faith, Paul explains,

> For the promise to Abraham and his offspring that he would be heir of the world *did not come through the law but through the righteousness of faith.* For if it is the adherents of the law who are to be the heirs, faith is null and the promise is void. For the law brings wrath, but where there is no law there is no transgression. That is why it depends on faith, in order that the promise may rest on grace and be guaranteed to all his offspring—not only to the adherent of the law but also to the one who shares the faith of Abraham, who is the father of us all. (Rom. 4:13–16, emphasis added)

Long before the law was given, Abraham believed God and his promise of a multitude of future offspring. If righteousness could come through the law—which it cannot, because the law brings wrath—then the beneficiaries of a relationship with God would be limited to the law-receiving people of Israel. But righteousness does not come in that way; rather, resting on the foundation of divine grace, it comes to all who, like Abraham, have faith.

This provision of grace was prophesied in the Old Testament (Rom.

---

[70] Ibid., 33. In a similar vein, Vickers employs the failure of Adam to address the fate of all other human beings, noting, "after all, if Adam did not obey in his innocence, what is going to happen to people living under his curse when they are given commands from God?" (ibid., 28–29).

3:21). Before the ink was dry on the end of the Pentateuch, Moses himself foresaw the people of Israel's abject failure to obey the law, and he offered this hope: "And the LORD your God will circumcise your heart and the heart of your offspring, so that you will love the LORD your God with all your heart and with all your soul, that you may live" (Deut. 30:6). With this prophecy, "Moses exposes the fact that this is not just a law problem but a heart problem. The law presents God's righteous standards and shows what it takes to attain righteousness, but the problem is that the law does not give the thing needed to keep it—a new heart."[71] This hope for transformation was echoed by Jeremiah's prophecy of a new covenant, in which the law would be written on the people's hearts and God would completely forgive their sins (Jer. 31:31–34), and by Ezekiel's prophecy of God's action to cleanse his people from their sins, give them a new heart, and put his Spirit within them (Ezek. 36:25–27).

The Old Testament hope pointed to Jesus Christ and his saving work as the ground of righteousness, which would be appropriated by faith. After his prophecy of the circumcision of the heart (Deut. 30:6), Moses returns to his presentation of the law, saying that it "is not too hard for you, neither is it far off. . . . But the word is very near you. It is in your mouth and in your heart, so that you can do it" (Deut. 30:11, 14). According to Paul, Moses's word is the gospel, "the word of faith" that is proclaimed and that provides, not "the righteousness that is based on the law," but "the righteousness based on faith, . . . because, if you confess with your mouth that Jesus is Lord and believe in your heart that God raised him from the dead, you will be saved" (Rom. 10:5–9). Thus, it can be said that the law pointed to Jesus Christ, and faith in him, for the obtaining of righteousness before God.

Tragically, the vast majority of the Jewish people missed this point, as Paul laments over them: "For, being ignorant of the righteousness of God, and seeking to establish their own, they did not submit to God's righteousness. For Christ is the end of the law for righteousness to everyone who believes" (Rom. 10:3–4). Gone, therefore, is the epoch of the law. As the old covenant has been rendered obsolete and replaced by the new covenant as the way that God now relates to his people, the church, so too has the old covenant law run its course. "The law is not of faith," explains Paul, but a curse is upon everyone who fails to keep every part of the law. But,

[71] Ibid., 114.

Paul continues, "Christ redeemed us from the curse of the law by becoming a curse for us—for it is written, 'Cursed is everyone who is hanged on a tree'" (Gal. 3:13). Through his death on the cross, Jesus rescues people from the demands of the law and the desperation of the failed old covenant. The former era is over; in its place is Christ: "Now before faith came, we were held captive under the law, imprisoned until the coming faith would be revealed. So then, the law was our guardian until Christ came, in order that we might be justified by faith. But now that faith has come, we are no longer under a guardian, for in Christ Jesus you are all sons of God, through faith" (vv. 23–26). Faith in Christ, and the righteousness of God that is appropriated by faith, was the goal of the law all along. Now that faith in Christ has come, the law that was like a guardian has played out its role. Faith is front and center for the church, which joyfully echoes Paul's affirmation: "For through the law I died to the law, so that I might live to God. I have been crucified with Christ. It is no longer I who live, but Christ who lives in me. And the life I now live in the flesh I live by faith in the Son of God, who loved me and gave himself for me" (2:19–20). It is the life of faith, not the life of law, that the church now lives.

With this framework of an evangelical theology of law, key points of disagreement with Catholic theology's focus on law in its presentation of salvation can be outlined. For one, the idea of law as divine help leading to the promised beatitude is certainly off target; nothing in the above discussion even hints at that notion. This is first of all true of natural law, whose development by Catholic theology goes far beyond the limited mention of it in Scripture. Even granting for the sake of argument this lofty idea of natural law, Catholic theology's point that human sinfulness creates a problem for the clear and immediate perception of the principles of natural law—with the corollary that sinful humanity stands in need of grace and revelation to overcome its nearsightedness—is far too limited. Sinful humanity's problem is not just an epistemological one—the failure to know natural law's precepts. Rather, its plight is moral—the culpable failure to obey those precepts—resulting in Paul's assessment that "all who have sinned without the law will also perish without the law" (Rom. 2:12). Those who do not have the law of Moses still have a law "written on their hearts"—natural law, or "conscience" (vv. 14–15)—but they fail to keep it and thus will perish. Accordingly, natural law does not provide a foundation for revealed law and grace; rather, sinful humanity's disobedience to the precepts of natural law creates the need for divine revelation and grace.

Second, the notion of the Old Law as divine help leading to the promised beatitude of all of humanity is wrong. This law was never intended for a general audience; on the contrary, it was given as a gift of divine grace to the people whom God had rescued from slavery in Egypt, and it was intended to distinguish Israel from the rest of the nations (Deut. 4:8). Moreover, its function as a tutor was not just due to its showing "what must be done,"[72] as if this were some positive role for it. Rather, as a guardian, the Old Law, which operated "before faith came," held people captive, "imprisoned until the coming faith would be revealed" in and through Jesus Christ, who would justify his people through faith (Gal. 3:23–26). With faith in place, the guardian is displaced; it is no longer operative for the church. To be fair, Catholic theology does underscore some good points about this law: it is good and holy in and of itself, yet imperfect; it does not in itself provide the resources necessary for its fulfillment; it does not take away human sin but exposes it instead. But when Catholic theology considers the law to be "the first step on the way to the kingdom" as a preparation for conversion and faith,[73] it finds no biblical support. Key points that Catholic theology overlooks are: the law demanded perfection, not merely doing what was in one's ability to do; it worsened the situation of the people of Israel rather than bettering it; because of human sinfulness, the law resulted in wrath and death, the very opposite of blessing and life; the law, and works associated with it, cannot make people righteous before God; and justification is grounded on the grace of God and is appropriated only by faith without any admixture of law-keeping or good works done in obedience to the law. These points will be resurrected in the next discussion, on justification.

Third, the idea of the New Law, the Law of the Gospel, as divine help leading to the promised beatitude is also incorrect. Taking its cue from the establishment of the Old Law as God's gracious gift to his people who were already rescued from enslavement and already in old covenant relationship with God, evangelical theology regards the establishment of the New Law, the law of Christ (Gal. 6:2), as the gracious gift for the benefit of Christians who are already justified not by law (of any kind) but by faith in Christ and

[72] CCC 1963.
[73] Ibid.

already in new covenant relationship with God. Thus, obedience to the New Law as an entry requirement into the new covenant people of God, the church, is to be rejected; rather, the New Law becomes the lifestyle of Christian disciples who have been saved by God's grace through faith.

Ringing in the ears of evangelical theology is Martin Luther's call to distinguish between law and gospel.[74] His distinction was not between the Old Testament (law) and the New Testament (gospel). Rather, law is anything in Scripture that expresses God's demands while emphasizing the inability of sinful human beings to live up to those standards (e.g., Jesus's command to be perfect as God himself is perfect; Matt. 5:48). Oppositely, gospel is anything in Scripture that expresses God's promises by emphasizing that Jesus has met all of his demands. Gospel, then, brings grace to rescue sinners awakened to their need by law. Evangelical theology, following Luther's trajectory, would profoundly disagree with Catholic theology's view of the New Law (and the Old Law, for that matter). There is no such thing as the Law of the Gospel, for those two are mutually exclusive. Law (of any kind) prepares the way by exposing and arousing sin, driving sinners to despair, and out of this hellish nightmare the only hope of escape is the gospel of Christ by which divine grace, which is embraced by faith, is made known and received.

While not disputing the attention that Catholic theology gives to Jesus's Sermon on the Mount, evangelical theology might approach the question of the content of the law of Christ differently. It would begin by focusing on what Jesus and the apostles do with Old Testament laws. Accordingly, the law of Christ would include those Old Testament laws that have come over intact into the new covenant (e.g., the Ten Commandments; Rom. 13:9; James 2:11)[75] and those Old Testament laws that have been modified for observance by new covenant members (e.g., the "fulfilled" commands regarding murder, adultery, and the like; Matt. 5:17–48).[76] The law of Christ would not include any of the laws that he and the apostles abrogated (e.g., the sacrificial laws and the dietary laws; Mark 7:19; 1 Tim. 4:3–4; Hebrews

[74] Though Luther made this distinction a key principle to observe when interpreting the Bible, its application can be broadened.
[75] The issue of the fourth commandment regarding the Sabbath raises the only significant question about whether it continues intact or whether it has been modified.
[76] "Fulfilled" in the sense that Jesus offers his definitive interpretation of these Old Testament laws. While some variations of evangelical theology would agree with Catholic theology that Jesus's language of contrast—"you have heard that it was said . . . but I say to you"—means that his new laws release the hidden potential of the old laws and have new internal demands that arise from them, many varieties would disagree.

8–10). Certainly, it would also include the laws revealed in the New Testament, which would include Jesus's Sermon on the Mount and the apostolic teachings. Because the evangelical counsels of chastity and poverty contradict Scripture (as discussed earlier), these are not included in the New Law. This principled approach to determining the content of the New Law, while not without its problems, achieves a balance between absolute continuity between the Old and New Testaments and absolute discontinuity between them.

Evangelical theology makes a final correction or, better, asks for greater emphasis with regard to the relationship of the Holy Spirit to law. Catholic theology does affirm that the New Law becomes the internal law of love through the work of the Spirit, who also gives faith and love, from which flow the virtues that are demanded by the New Law. But evangelical theology desires more emphasis on the Spirit's role in relation to law, both Old and New. The apostle Paul underscores this point: "There is therefore now no condemnation for those who are in Christ Jesus. For the law of the Spirit of life has set you free in Christ Jesus from the law of sin and death. For God has done what the law, weakened by the flesh, could not do. By sending his own Son in the likeness of sinful flesh and for sin, he condemned sin in the flesh, in order that the righteous requirement of the law might be fulfilled in us, who walk not according to the flesh but according to the Spirit" (Rom. 8:1–4). Paul exposes the failure of the law—the law of Moses given to people enfeebled by their sinful nature—to free them from sin and death. Such salvation, while impossible for the law, was what God accomplished through the death of his Son, and it leads to the verdict of no condemnation for all those united to Christ. Another important component of what Christ accomplished is the obedience of his followers to the law, a reality that is actualized by life in the Spirit. As the faithful walk in step with the Spirit, they fulfill the "righteous requirement of the law," which, in accordance with Scripture, is summed up by the two great commandments about loving God and loving others.[77] Importantly, obedience does not come from the law itself, nor from grace conferred by the law, but by walking in the Spirit.

This same idea is repeated elsewhere: "But I say, walk by the Spirit, and you will not gratify the desires of the flesh. For the desires of the flesh are

[77] Vickers, *Justification by Grace through Faith*, 159–160.

against the Spirit, and the desires of the Spirit are against the flesh, for these are opposed to each other, to keep you from doing the things you want to do. But if you are led by the Spirit, you are not under the law" (Gal. 5:16–18). The relationship between sinful human beings and the law is a deadly one, as explained above. When people living in accordance with their sinful nature connect with the law, it brings only conviction, wrath, guilt, enslavement, and condemnation; it stands against them. But the reverse is true for people living in accordance with the Spirit. They are not under the law's judgment and conviction; they do not feel its burden, but they bear fruit instead—"the fruit of the Spirit is love, joy, peace, patience, kindness, goodness, faithfulness, gentleness, self-control"—with this important conclusion: "against such things there is no law" (vv. 22–23). Accordingly, evangelical theology calls for a greater emphasis on the necessity of the Holy Spirit's filling and guiding those who belong to Christ so that they will "by (their new) nature" fulfill the law's demands as disciples.

Grace and Justification

If evangelical theology is largely disapproving of its counterpart's insistence on the law as a divinely given aid for the salvation of fallen human beings, it is even more critical of Catholic theology's discussion of grace and justification. Unlike the preceding critique, which focused on the inability of the law—even its lack of design—to help in redemption, this present critique will not deny the role—even the necessity—of grace and justification for salvation, but it will disagree with Catholic theology's understanding of these two matters. As the doctrine of justification through God's grace appropriated by faith was the material principle, the content at the heart, of the Reformation, this section treats one of the areas that most deeply divides evangelical and Catholic theology.[78]

Broadly speaking, an evangelical theology of justification and grace can be summarized as follows:[79] In terms of definition, justification is a forensic, or legal, act of God by which he declares sinful human beings not guilty but righteous instead. He does so by imputing, or crediting, the perfect

---

[78] As Martin Luther expressed it, "If the doctrine of justification is lost, the whole of Christian doctrine is lost" (Martin Luther, *Lectures on Galatians: Chapters 1–4* [LW 26:9]). John Calvin echoed Luther's conviction by calling justification "the main hinge on which religion turns" and urging the church "to devote the greatest attention and care to it" (Calvin, *Institutes* 3.11.1 [LCC 20:726]).

[79] Because of its novelty, not to mention the many strong challenges raised to it, the so-called "new perspective on Paul" will not enter into this discussion.

righteousness of Jesus Christ to their account, so that while they are not actually righteous, God views them as being so because of Christ's righteousness. Through his obedience in life and death, Christ fulfilled all of the requirements of the law, and through the mighty divine act of justification, sinful human beings are credited with his righteousness and stand before God as those "who [live] up to the entirety of God's will."[80]

Grace is often defined as unmerited favor; indeed, the *Catechism* defines it as "favor, the free and undeserved help that God gives us."[81] But as Vickers points out, this definition is not quite right, because "grace as it connects to salvation is not just *unmerited* but *de-merited* favor."[82] The biblical case for this definition includes Paul's point that those who "are justified by his grace as a gift" (Rom. 3:24) are not "morally neutral [people] who simply [have] done nothing to deserve God's favor";[83] rather, they are part of the group identified as "all have sinned and fall short of the glory of God" (v. 23). As a confirmation, Paul notes that those who "were once foolish, disobedient, led astray, slaves to various passions and pleasures, passing [their] days in malice and envy, hated by others and hating one another" are said to be "justified by his grace" (Titus 3:3, 7). The recipients of divine grace not only do not merit it, but because of their sin they are derelict in person and duty, deserving of the opposite of favor. Only justification through grace can rescue them.

The forensic nature of justification can be readily gleaned from Scripture. For one, the term is found in opposition to the term "condemnation" (e.g., Deut. 25:1; Prov. 17:15; Rom. 5:16, 18); indeed, as those justified by divine grace, Christians can be assured "there is therefore now no condemnation for those who are in Christ Jesus" (Rom. 8:1). Furthermore, Paul uses legal language when he offers a psalm of David in support of the contention that God "justifies the *ungodly*" (Rom. 4:5, emphasis added): "David also speaks of the blessing of the one to whom *God counts righteousness* apart from works: 'Blessed are those whose lawless deeds are forgiven, and whose sins are covered; blessed is the man against whom *the Lord will not count his sin*'" (Rom. 4:6–8, emphasis added). While this Old

[80] Vickers, *Justification by Grace through Faith*, 2; cf. 31. On page 48, Vickers cites John Piper: "[I]n Christ we are counted as having done all the righteousness God requires" (ibid., 48n30); citation is from John Piper, *The Future of Justification: A Response to N. T. Wright* (Wheaton, IL: Crossway, 2007), 171.
[81] CCC 1996 (emphasis removed).
[82] Vickers, *Justification by Grace through Faith*, 27.
[83] Ibid.

Testament quote (from Ps. 32:1–2) affirms God's counting, or imputation, of righteousness to people (a second aspect of justification, to be discussed shortly)—it also underscores God's non-counting, or non-imputation, of sin (the first aspect of justification), that is, the forgiveness of sins. God in Christ does not count or reckon people's sins against them, which is a legal notion through and through.

This biblical evidence for the legal nature of justification has served to introduce the two aspects of justification. The first is the forgiveness of sins, which is the result of Christ's substitutionary death on the cross (Rom. 3:25; 5:9) and is emphasized in God's declaration that sinful people are "Not guilty!" Jeremiah prophesied that forgiveness would be a key element in the new covenant: "I will forgive their iniquity, and I will remember their sin no more" (Jer. 31:34). Paul underscores this aspect in his description of God's work in Christ "reconciling the world to himself, not counting their trespasses against them. . . . For our sake he made him to be sin who knew no sin, so that in him we might become the righteousness of God" (2 Cor. 5:19–21). By making the sinless Son of God to be sin, and through Christ's death for sin, God now does not count sinful people's sins against them.

The second aspect is the imputation of the righteousness of Jesus Christ. Biblical support begins with Paul's statement that, "Therefore, as one trespass led to condemnation for all men, so one act of righteousness leads to justification and life for all men. For as by the one man's disobedience the many were made sinners, so by the one man's obedience the many will be made righteous" (Rom. 5:18–19). The parallel is clear:

Adam's trespass *condemnation for all*		Christ's act of righteousness *justification and life for all*
Adam's disobedience *all made sinners*		Christ's obedience *all will be made righteous*

On the one side of the parallel stands Adam and his trespass/disobedience, which plunged all human beings into condemnation as they are *made sinners*. On the other side of the parallel stands Christ and his act of righteousness/obedience, which brings justification and life for all who receive him (Rom. 5:17) as they *will be made righteous*. As Vickers explains, "When Paul speaks of being 'made' sinners and 'will be made' righteous, he is speaking legally. He is not emphasizing, at least here, either sinful or righteous actions. He is speaking of a status, a position that people occupy before God."[84] Why can Vickers affirm that Paul is using legal language here? "In the New Testament, the same word translated as 'made' in [Rom.] 5:19 is most commonly used to designate the place and/or status a thing or person holds or to which a thing or a person is appointed. Less commonly the word carries the sense of *become, cause to be*, or *make* and refers to some state of being."[85] A key reason for understanding "made sinners" or "will be made righteous" to mean "to be put into a position or appointed" is found in Romans 5:18, where Paul affirms that, "the legal status that one has before God is on the basis of *someone else's* actions. People are recognized in connection to Adam as those who sinned and in connection to Christ as those who fulfilled everything needed to be deemed righteous."[86] Again, this explanation does not mean that the word *righteous* is not often used to refer to "behavior and/or personal character."[87] "[B]ut when he [Paul] pairs it with *made*, which refers to being appointed or placed into a position, then *righteous* is not focused on behavior or character but on our position with God. We are made to hold the position of those whose acts and behavior are righteous on the basis of Christ's obedience."[88] Accordingly, God declares sinners "righteous" in a legal sense; "what is typically recognized through character traits and/or actions is declared *apart from* any actions done on the part of those made righteous. . . . God judges those connected (by faith) to Christ . . . as *having fully accomplished all manner of righteousness in his eyes*."[89]

---

[84] Ibid., 47.

[85] Ibid., 46–47. For "made" as a designation of status or position, he lists Matt. 25:21, 23; Luke 12:14; Acts 6:3; Titus 1:5; Heb. 5:1 (ibid., 47n28). For "made" as a designation of a state of being, he lists James 4:4; 2 Pet. 1:8 (ibid., 48n29). Elsewhere he illustrates this idea with Phinehas (Ps. 106:30–31), who was recognized as being righteous by his righteous action of killing an Israelite and the Moabite woman with him, an idolatrous relationship that had been strictly forbidden by Moses. According to the psalmist, Phinehas's action "was counted to him as righteousness" (ibid., 59).

[86] Ibid., 48.

[87] Vickers lists Joseph (Matt. 1:19), Simeon (Luke 2:25), Joseph of Arimathea (Luke 23:50), and Cornelius (Acts 10:22); he further notes Paul's use in this sense (Rom. 3:10; Col. 4:1; Titus 1:8; 2 Tim. 4:8) (ibid., 49).

[88] Ibid., 49.

[89] Ibid. (emphasis original).

Confirmation of the imputation of Christ's righteousness as the second aspect of justification is the case of Abraham. After Abraham complained that he was childless and had only Eliezer as his heir, God told Abraham that the patriarch's own son would instead be his heir, thus giving rise to the great nation that God had promised to Abraham (Gen. 12:1–3). "And he [God] brought him outside and said, 'Look toward heaven, and number the stars, if you are able to number them.' Then he said to him, 'So shall your offspring be.' And he believed the LORD, and he counted it to him as righteousness" (15:5–6). In the very moment that Abraham was going to take matters into his own hands and establish Eliezer as his heir, the patriarch instead trusts God to fulfill his promise, and God reckons Abraham's faith as righteousness. "The status or description typically reserved for actions is here counted to Abraham on the basis of faith. Abraham's faith is counted to him as something it inherently is not, righteousness. . . . [W]hen paired with *counted* and *faith*, righteousness here refers to a judgment and declaration about Abraham's position before God."[90] The technical theological term for this reckoning is *imputation*.

What is imputed to those who are justified is the righteousness of God. After rehearsing his illustrious pedigree that had qualified him for renown among his Jewish compatriots, Paul placed all of his accomplishments in the loss column, for, as he explained, they had only achieved "a righteousness of my own that comes from the law." Instead of this rubbish, the apostle desired the righteousness that "comes through faith in Christ, the righteousness from God that depends on faith" (Phil. 3:8–9). Martin Luther referred to this as "alien righteousness," that is, not the righteousness that is proper to oneself through human achievement but the righteousness of another, that which comes by faith from the outside and is imputed to one's account. "The righteousness that comes to us as a gift from God through faith that unites us to Christ remains Christ's righteousness. The righteousness in view is not our righteousness, as though God has transferred a certain amount of righteousness to us like a commodity or something that can be quantified in a point system. We have Christ himself and all his benefits of a perfect life and his death and resurrection on our behalf."[91]

As a gift to sinful human beings from God, his righteousness is, and can

---

[90] Ibid., 60.
[91] Ibid., 135–136.

only be, appropriated by faith. The case of Abraham, once again, supports this point:

> What then shall we say was gained by Abraham, our forefather accord-ing to the flesh? For if Abraham was justified by works, he has something to boast about, but not before God. For what does the Scripture say? "Abraham believed God, and it was counted to him as righteousness." Now to the one who works, his wages are not counted as a gift but as his due. And to the one who does not work but believes in him who justifies the ungodly, his faith is counted as righteousness. (Rom. 4:1–5)

Workers earn wages, the payment contracted and thus due for work per-formed. Assessing this system as a way of being right before God, Paul explains that if Abraham was justified by the good works he did, he could be proud and brag about his accomplishment as a godly man. But if the idea of boasting before God is ludicrous, then the idea of being justified before God by works is wrongheaded, and it certainly was not the way that Abraham followed. On the contrary, this idol worshiper from Ur did not work, but believed in God who does *not* justify *the godly*, but *the ungodly*. By faith Abraham was reckoned as righteous before God. As confirmation of his point, Paul underscores that Abraham's justification came before he was circumcised (Rom. 4:10–11) and apart from the law, which came much later (Rom. 4:13).

This language of the righteousness of God as a gift received by faith is re-peated: "But now *the righteousness of God* has been manifested apart from the law, although the Law and the Prophets bear witness to it—*the righ-teousness of God through faith in Jesus Christ for all who believe*. For there is no distinction: for all have sinned and fall short of the glory of God, and are *justified by his grace as a gift*, through the redemption that is in Christ Jesus, whom God put forward as a propitiation by his blood, *to be received by faith*" (Rom. 3:21–25, emphasis added). Achieved by Christ's perfect obe-dience, especially his death as an atoning sacrifice to assuage the furious wrath of God (propitiation and its effect), justification as the gracious gift of the righteousness of God is appropriated by faith in Jesus Christ.

To be especially noted is that the ground of justification leading to the gift of divine righteousness is the cross of Jesus Christ. Faith is not the ground of the gift, but is the means of receiving the gift, and it is placed in a proper object, who is Jesus Christ; indeed, "faith must not be thought of apart from its object. The righteousness in view is not made up of faith but is found in faith's object. Paul does not say that justification is *because* of faith but *by* faith. Faith is the means by which we are made righteous with God through Christ, the object of faith and the foundation of our righteousness."[92] Specifically, through union with Christ, and on the basis of the work of God in Christ, sinful human beings "stand before him without guilt and as having done all matters of obedience."[93] But such righteousness should not be considered as some kind of substance or commodity infused into people; rather, "[t]he righteousness in view is incarnate, and imputation is sharing in the Christ who is our righteousness."[94]

This conferring of the righteousness of God through his declarative act of justification, and its appropriation by faith, stands over against a false view exposed and denounced by Scripture: justification by works. As noted earlier, Abraham is the stellar example of one who did not work to earn God's righteousness but believed in the one who justifies the ungodly (Rom. 4:1–5). His was "the righteousness of faith" (v. 13) that was not based on circumcision nor on the law. As Paul summarizes this common point, "For we hold that one is justified by faith apart from works of the law" (3:28). The example of Abraham highlights that this scriptural denunciation of works is not reserved for those in association with the law of Moses. That old covenant law was not even in existence when the Patriarch believed God for righteousness. On the contrary, Scripture stands against works of any kind being done to achieve righteousness. This is because not only justification, but salvation in general, is not earned by good works: "For by grace you have been saved through faith. And this is not your own doing; it is the gift of God, not a result of works, so that no one may boast. For we are his workmanship, created in Christ Jesus for good works, which God prepared beforehand, that we should walk in them" (Eph. 2:8–10).

Evangelical theology is often charged at this point as siding with the apostle Paul and his emphasis on justification by faith over against the apostle James and his contention "that a person is justified by works and not by faith alone" (James 2:24). While much debate has occurred over this

---

[92] Ibid., 76 (emphasis original).
[93] Ibid., 74.
[94] Ibid.

issue, it is simply not the case that Paul and James are at odds as to the right way to appropriate justification, nor that evangelical theology pits faith against works.

As for the first point, Paul's emphasis is on the means of embracing the righteousness of God, which is his gift to sinful human beings: receiving this gift so as to be justified before God is by faith and not by anything else (e.g., circumcision, the works of the law, any good work). James's focus is not on saving faith but on bogus faith: such faith cannot save. His emphasis on the nature of faith is clear from his illustration of false faith: "You believe that God is one; you do well. Even the demons believe—and shudder!" (James 2:19). Demons have a type of faith, but it certainly is not saving faith! Moving out of the demonic realm, James illustrates this false faith among human beings: "If a brother or sister is poorly clothed and lacking in daily food, and one of you says to them, 'Go in peace, be warmed and filled,' without giving them the things needed for the body, what good is that?" (vv. 15–16). This faith is called "faith by itself . . . [that] does not have works," and James's evaluation is that such faith "is dead" (v. 17). Accordingly, the answer to James's questions—"What good is it, my brothers, if someone says he has faith but does not have works? Can that faith save him?" (v. 14)—is clearly, "No, of course not!" With this as his definition of faith, James emphasizes that justification before God is not, and cannot be, by *this* faith. False faith, or bogus faith, cannot save anyone.

Switching from this concept of faith, James describes the kind of faith that does bring justification: *saving* faith. What is this faith? He first illustrates it with the example of Abraham: "Was not Abraham our father justified by works when he offered up his son Isaac on the altar? You see that faith was active along with his works, and faith was completed by his works; and the Scripture was fulfilled that says, 'Abraham believed God, and it was counted to him as righteousness'—and he was called a friend of God" (vv. 21–23). Interestingly, James presents the nature of true faith first by noting Abraham's work of sacrificing his son (on Mount Moriah; Genesis 22), then by underscoring that this work fulfilled the Scripture affirming that Abraham was counted as righteous before God by faith (on Mount Hebron; Gen. 15:6). Abraham's justification before God was by faith, and as vividly demonstrated decades later through the patriarch's offering of his son, "that faith was active along with his works, and faith was completed by his works," which fulfilled the earlier Scripture. "The word *fulfilled* does not mean that Abraham's works made the Scripture true . . . but that Abraham's works brought the declaration in Hebron to its appointed end. The declaration was meant to be displayed so that God's word would be vindicated. God declared Abraham's faith as righteousness, and Abraham's actions, particularly his test with Isaac, affirmed the truth of Scripture."[95] Moreover, there was nothing wrong with Abraham's faith—by faith, Abraham had been counted righteous before God!—but such saving faith results in good works.

James's second illustration of saving faith is Rahab: "And in the same way was not also Rahab the prostitute justified by works when she received the messengers and sent them out by another way?" (James 2:25). How can one know that the faith of this prostitute was not just some last-ditch effort to save her own life, an example of the false faith that James is combatting in this passage? Bogus faith would not have resulted in such a courageous deed, but because she rescued the Israelite spies, her good work enables one to see her saving faith. As the Letter to the Hebrews, in its chapter on faith, highlights, "By faith Rahab the prostitute did not perish with those who were disobedient, because she had given a friendly welcome to the spies" (Heb. 11:31). The conclusion that James draws from this illustration is that "faith apart from works is dead" (James 2:26). Rahab's faith was not a bogus faith or dead faith; rather, it was a genuine faith—a saving faith—that showed itself to be such by her works.

Paul himself, rather than being at odds with James's discussion, completely agrees with it and even uses the same illustration of Abraham in support. As discussed above, the apostle quotes Genesis 15:6 in his letter to the Romans, underscoring the point that Abraham was not justified by works but by faith (Rom. 4:1–5). Interestingly, at the end of his discussion of justification by faith and not by works (at the end of Romans 4), Paul rehearses the Patriarch's life and again references Genesis 15:6. While being fully aware of Abraham's many actual failures, Paul describes him in this way:

> In hope he believed against hope, that he should become the father of many nations, as he had been told, "So shall your offspring be." He

---
[95] Ibid., 153.

440 Life in Christ

did not weaken in faith when he considered his own body, which was as good as dead (since he was about a hundred years old), or when he considered the barrenness of Sarah's womb. No unbelief made him waver concerning the promise of God, but he grew strong in his faith as he gave glory to God, fully convinced that God was able to do what he had promised. (Rom. 4:18–21)

Paul then quotes Genesis 15:6 for a second time—"That is why his faith was 'counted to him as righteousness'" (Rom. 4:22)—confirming two things: "(1) Abraham's life of faith was the evidence of his justification; and (2) what God in Scripture declared about Abraham was true."[96] These points correspond to those that James makes with his emphasis that justification is appropriated not by bogus faith, but by saving faith, and such saving faith always results in good works. Accordingly, it is simply not the case that Paul and James are at odds as to the right way to appropriate justification, so evangelical theology does not side with Paul against James in developing and defending its doctrine of justification.

But there is a second charge against evangelical theology, specifically, that it pits faith against works, or at least demonstrates a casual attitude toward good works as part and parcel of life in Christ. To repel such a charge, evangelical theology need only reach back to its Reformation heritage. Martin Luther made a distinction between "two kinds of Christian righteousness. . . . The first is alien righteousness, that is, the righteousness of another, instilled from the outside. This is the righteousness of Christ, by which he justifies through faith."[97] Here, Luther describes the imputation of Christ's righteousness that has been discussed. Regarding the other type, "The second kind of righteousness is our proper righteousness, not because we alone work it, but because we work with that first and alien righteousness. This is that manner of life spent profitably in good works."[98] Importantly for Luther, the first type "is primary; it is the basis, the cause, the source of all our actual righteousness."[99] Accordingly, those who have been justified by faith, thereby having the righteousness of Jesus Christ imputed to them, engage in actual works of righteousness. Luther clearly

---

[96] Ibid., 90.
[97] Martin Luther, *Two Kinds of Righteousness* (LW 31:297).
[98] Ibid. (LW 31:299).
[99] Ibid. (LW 31:298).

joined faith (in an alien righteousness) and works (one's proper righteous-ness that flows from the alien righteousness).

The relationship of these two kinds of righteousness is a paradoxical one, according to Luther, who set forth two propositions regarding the freedom and slavery of the human spirit: "A Christian is a perfectly free lord of all, subject to none. A Christian is a perfectly obedient servant of all, subject to all. These two theses seem to contradict each other."[100] As for his first thesis, Luther maintained that justification by grace through faith alone and not works completely frees Christians, especially from the divine law. Additionally, "If works are sought after as a means to righteousness . . . and are done under the false impression that through them one is justified, they are made necessary and freedom and faith are destroyed. And this addition to them makes them no longer good but truly damnable works."[101] As for his second thesis, Luther explained that justification establishes Christian service and the duty to engage in good works for the sake of all others: "This is a truly Christian life. Here, faith is truly active through love [Gal. 5:6], that is, it finds expression in works of the freest service, cheerfully and lovingly done, with which a man willingly serves another without hope of reward."[102] Luther concluded, "We do not reject good works; on the con-trary, we cherish and teach them as much as possible."[103] Noteworthy in this regard is Luther's denunciation of Catholic theology's restriction of good works to religious deeds such as praying, fasting, and almsgiving[104]—a criti-cism already echoed above.

Evangelical theology thus has a centuries-old legacy of embracing good works in relation to faith and justification. The charge that it pits faith against works, or at least demonstrates a casual attitude toward good works for the Christian life, is simply not true.

To avoid confusion or possible misunderstandings of evangelical theol-ogy's doctrine, a bit more needs to be said with regard to the relationship between justification, grace, faith, and good works. Justification of the un-godly through divine grace appropriated by faith is a declarative act of God—that sinful people are not guilty but righteous instead—and "God

---

[100] Luther, *The Freedom of a Christian* (LW 31:344).
[101] Ibid. (LW 31:349–350).
[102] Ibid. (LW 31:365).
[103] Ibid. (LW 31:363).
[104] Luther, *Treatise on Good Works* 3.

plans on keeping his word with a particular kind of people—those who follow him in obedience"[105] through engaging in good works. The declaration stands firm and is unconditional. Its reality does not depend on the good works of its recipients, but its reality is "concurrent, or parallel, with obedience."[106] Simply put, saving faith that justifies results in good works, but it is not contingent on those works. Accordingly, there is not "a double basis for justification, that of both faith and works. But faith, the single foundation for justification, works."[107] This means that the verdict of justification does not await evidence to support it but is declared before the evidence is given. To return to Abraham as an illustration, "Abraham's faith was counted as righteousness *before*, and not on the basis of, the evidence shown in his life."[108] The ground of justification is the work of Christ on behalf of sinful human beings, and the means of appropriation is faith, and only faith, but saving faith brings forth the evidence of justification, which is good works. Moreover, though the public verdict awaits a future moment, it has been rendered in the present for all who by faith rely on Christ for justification. Finally, as part of saving faith, assurance of salvation is the privilege of all Christ-followers.

With this framework of an evangelical theology of justification, grace, faith, and good works, key points of disagreement with Catholic theology's developments of these topics can be outlined. Most importantly, its definition of justification is incorrect. Justification is a forensic or legal act, the declaration of the forgiveness of sin and the imputation of righteousness. Catholic theology errs when it mixes justification with two other mighty acts of God, sanctification and regeneration: "Justification is not only the remission of sins, but also the sanctification and renewal of the interior man."[109] This critique does not mean that evangelical theology minimizes or denies these other two divine acts. On the contrary, while affirming that justification is linked with regeneration and sanctification, evangelical theology distinguishes these three, as does Scripture (e.g., 1 Cor. 6:11). Tragically, conflating justification, regeneration, and sanctification results in Catholic theology's false idea of justification.

---

[105] Vickers, *Justification by Grace through Faith*, 152.
[106] Ibid.
[107] Ibid., 153.
[108] Ibid., 90.
[109] CCC 1989; citation is from *Canons and Decrees of the Council of Trent*, 6th session (January 13, 1547), *Decree on Justification* 7 (Schaff, 2:94).

Equally important, Catholic theology's idea of righteousness as "the rectitude of divine love" that is infused into people, especially through the sacraments, is wrong.[110] This emphasis on infusion can be seen in Catholic theology's list of the fruit of justification, which underscores among other results the purification from sin; the pouring out of faith, hope, and love into the hearts of the faithful; and the conformity of the faithful "to the righteousness of God, who makes [them] inwardly just by the power of his mercy."[111] Evangelical theology's critique of the nature-grace interdependence, upon which Catholic theology's doctrine of infused grace depends, has already been presented. It is simply not true that nature—in this case, fallen human nature—possesses a capacity for grace, which is infused into the faithful through the sacraments so as to elevate and potentially perfect their nature. Rather than the *infusion* of grace that brings about inward conformity to the righteousness of God, evangelical theology embraces the *imputation* of Christ's perfect righteousness. An *infused* righteousness is capable of increase or decrease, depending on the faithful's participation in the means of grace (the sacraments) or their failure to participate. For evangelical theology, *imputed* righteousness through a divine declaration means that the ungodly now stand before God as those who have fully met the standard of the law and have rendered perfect obedience to him; there cannot be, nor is there, any need for an increase of righteousness. Neither can righteousness decrease, because justification is a declaration that makes it so. Moreover, Catholic theology's view of justifying grace being capable of being lost means there is no assurance of justification. But justification according to evangelical theology grants this security.

Furthermore, Catholic theology's linking of faith with the sacrament of Baptism as the means of appropriating justification is incorrect. Not only does it contradict the many passages in the Pauline writings that insist on faith as the sole instrument for receiving the divine gift of justification, but it seems incapable of explaining the discussion of salvation and its means of appropriation at the council of Jerusalem (Acts 15). At issue was the Judaizing Christians' insistence that the Gentile Christians must be saved by faith in Christ plus something else—namely, circumcision and obedience to the law of Moses (vv. 1, 5, 24). The Council's firm stance—"we believe

---

[110] CCC 1991.
[111] CCC 1992.

that we will be saved through the grace of the Lord Jesus, just as they will" (v. 11)—underscored that salvation for both Jews and Gentiles alike is by God's grace received by faith (vv. 7–11). "If there were ever a time for the early church to insist on the necessity of baptism for salvation, certainly this debate was the opportune moment. But no such proposal was made, discussed, or ratified at this council."[112] As explained earlier, this point about the non-necessity of baptism for salvation does not render baptism unimportant, but it does break Catholic theology's linkage of faith and the sacrament of Baptism for justification. Catholic theology makes the bond between faith and baptism because of the nature-grace interdependence, the axiom that grace must be concretely conveyed through tangible means—in this case, water. Another reason for this link is Catholic theology's interpretation of Jesus's statement that, "unless one is born of water and the Spirit, he cannot enter the kingdom of God" (John 3:5), but as discussed earlier, this is a misunderstanding of Jesus's words.

For a final critique of Catholic theology's doctrine of justification, an earlier discussion comes into play. Catholic theology affirms that justification establishes a relationship of cooperation between divine grace and human freedom. This formula is what was earlier referred to as *synergism*: Two agents, God and human beings, *work together* to operate the rescue of the latter group. On the part of God, the many types of grace work powerfully to bring about the justification of the faithful, whose part is to give "the assent of faith to the Word of God," respond with conversion, and obey "the prompting of the Holy Spirit who precedes and preserves [their] assent."[113] By contrast, evangelical theology's doctrine of justification is a clear example of *monergism*. One agent—God—*works alone* to justify the ungodly (Rom. 4:5), who do not—indeed, cannot—contribute anything to their justification. One agent—God—*works alone* to declare the unrighteous "Not guilty!" but "Righteous instead!" not making them actually righteous (and thereby cooperating agents), but counting them righteous through the gift of the perfect righteousness of Jesus Christ.

Once again, at the heart of Catholic theology's synergistic salvation is the nature-grace interdependence. Nature—in this case, fallen human beings—possesses a capacity to receive divine grace, and grace renders na-

---

[112] Allison, *SS*, 358.
[113] CCC 1993.

ture able to cooperate with the operation of grace conveyed through the sacraments. Because this axiom is faulty, salvation as a synergistic, cooperative venture between grace and nature, between God and human beings, is wrongly grounded. Moreover, if divine grace imputes righteousness as a gift, then the very idea of a gift dispels any notion that the one who receives it contributes anything to it or cooperates with the one who gives it. Furthermore, the appropriation of this gift is by faith, and this response of faith to the grace of God, while surely a human response, is wrongly seen as human cooperation. As Paul affirms, salvation by grace through faith—the whole of it—is itself a gift of God. For the apostle, this means salvation "is not your own doing" and "not a result of works," thereby precluding boasting or taking credit of any kind. Walking in good works, as the fitting response and fruit of being "created in Christ Jesus for good works, which God prepared beforehand," is the point of cooperation, but human beings contribute nothing to their justification (Eph. 2:8–9). Monergism, not synergism, is the proper framework for justification by grace through faith.

Merit

Accordingly, evangelical theology's framework of monergism critiques the next topic in the doctrine of salvation, namely, merit, the recompense that God owes to the faithful for both the good works that they do (reward) and the bad works that they do (penalty). At the heart of Catholic theology's idea of merit is its belief that "God has freely chosen to associate man with the work of his grace."[114] Divine grace initiates and is followed by human response (synergism), and God appropriately remunerates this human response. This response is person-specific: each of the faithful is expected "to do what is in him to do" (*facere quod in se est*). Importantly, Catholic theology denies that any merit is achieved at the start of salvation, for salvation's beginning depends solely on the grace of God; thus, "no one can merit the initial grace of forgiveness and justification."[115] But merit enters in when the faithful, prompted by the Holy Spirit and love, achieve for themselves and for others the grace for ongoing sanctification, the increase of grace and love, and the attainment of eternal life.

While respecting this differentiation between initial grace that cannot

---

[114] CCC 2008 (emphasis removed).
[115] CCC 2010 (emphasis removed).

be merited, and ongoing grace that can be merited, evangelical theology denies any possibility of earning grace of any kind—initial, ongoing, or final—and considers human effort toward the attainment of eternal life to be superfluous. Transparently, the idea of merit is grounded on the axiom of the nature-grace interdependence. Nature—in this case, fallen human nature—possesses the capacity to receive divine grace and, once it has obtained such grace through the sacraments, it is rendered free and thus capable of meriting eternal life. As the nature-grace interdependence has been demonstrated to be in error, the notion of merit that rests upon this axiom is wrong as well. Furthermore, evangelical theology's correct doctrine of justification underscores the wrongness of merit: Because fallen human beings are declared "Not guilty!" but "Righteous instead!" the obtaining of eternal life is based not on this gracious act of God plus human effort (even effort undergirded by divine grace), but on God's declaration alone received by faith alone. Considered fully righteous because of the righteousness of Christ imputed to their account by faith, Christians have nothing to add to this salvation. As if this full pardon and rescue from sin were not enough, they are also rewarded for their good works that come from their union with Christ, derive from the new nature given to them through regeneration by the Holy Spirit, and flow out of hearts that are full of gratitude for their salvation.

Evangelical theology underscores that such rewards, however, have nothing to do with Catholic theology's doctrine of merit. As John Calvin pointed out, the example of Abraham clarifies the difference between reward and merit. Before Isaac was born, Abraham received by faith the promise that his offspring would be as numerous as the stars in the heavens (Gen. 15:5); that is, he would become the father of many nations (Gen. 17:4–6). Years later the Patriarch stood obediently with a knife raised over the head of his son Isaac, proving that he feared God (22:12). Having acted in obedience, Abraham received this promise: "By myself I have sworn, declares the LORD, because you have done this and have not withheld your son, your only son, I will surely bless you, and I will surely multiply your offspring as the stars of heaven and as the sand that is on the seashore. And your offspring shall possess the gate of his enemies, and in your offspring shall all the nations of the earth be blessed, because you have obeyed my voice" (22:16–18).

As Calvin explained, "What is this that we hear? Did Abraham merit by his obedience the blessing whose promise he had received before the commandment [to kill his son] was given? Here, surely, we have shown without ambiguity that the Lord rewards the works of believers with the same benefits as he had given them before they contemplated any works, as he does not yet have any reason to benefit them except his own mercy."[116] Abraham did not, indeed could not, merit by his good works something that had already been promised to him and received by faith. God promised, Abraham believed by faith, his justification was declared, he obeyed, and Abraham was rewarded—but not so as to be saved through grace and merit. As noted previously, "God plans on keeping his word with a particular kind of people—those who follow him in obedience" by engaging in good works.[117] Their justification is firm and unconditional. Its reality is not dependent on their good works but is simultaneous or synchronized with them. Simply put, saving faith that justifies results in good works, but it is not contingent on the faithful cooperating with divine grace so as to merit eternal life by grace and works. That Christians are rewarded by God is certainly true, as underscored often in Scripture (e.g., Matt. 16:27; Luke 6:23; 1 Cor. 3:8, 15; 2 Cor. 5:10). That such engagement in good works merits eternal life for the faithful, and is required for obtaining that salvation, is wrong.

The Church, Mother and Teacher

The *Catechism* concludes its discussion of the doctrine of salvation by locating this divine work to rescue fallen human beings out of sin and to bring them to eternal beatitude in the context of its doctrine of the Church. Two themes already addressed are reprised: The Church is Mother and the Church is Teacher. Both topics are undergirded by the axiom of the Christ-Church interconnection: Because the Church is the extension of the incarnation of the whole Christ (both the head and the body), then it is the Catholic Church, and the Catholic Church alone, that is the mediator of salvation. As this axiom has received critique already, it suffices to point out that the foundation of Catholic theology's notion of the Church as Mother and Teacher is incorrect.

In terms of specific criticisms of the maternal metaphor for the church, evangelical theology underscores that while Scripture employs a vivid

116 Calvin, *Institutes* 3.18.2 (LCC 21:822–823).
117 Vickers, *Justification by Grace through Faith*, 152.

feminine image for the church—it is the bride of Christ (2 Cor. 11:1–4; Eph. 5:25–33; Rev. 19:7; 21:2, 9, 17)—it does not employ the metaphor of mother. Moreover, evangelical theology critiques Catholic theology's link between the Church as Mother and Mary as the Mother of the Church. At the same time, and understood in a different way, the church as the mother of Christians, serving as the Spirit-anointed minister of the grace of God through the preaching of the gospel and the celebration of the ordinances, is proper within an evangelical theological framework. As for specific criticisms of the church as teacher, one aspect of this idea, the doctrine of papal infallibility, is soundly rejected by evangelical theology, for the following reasons: it is based on a misunderstanding of Christ's promise that "the gates of hell shall not prevail against it [the Church]" (Matt. 16:18); it fails to reckon with the actual fallibility of popes; it was promulgated as official Catholic dogma very late (1870) and under questionable circumstances; and the setting forth of authoritative teachings under its operation are a violation of the sufficiency of Scripture.[118]

As for this last point, the *Catechism* explains that the Church's charism, or gift, of infallibility extends beyond *ex cathedra* pronouncements by the pope to include (1) other doctrines and moral principles "without which the saving truths of the faith cannot be preserved, explained, or observed";[119] (2) "the specific precepts of the natural law, because their observance, demanded by the Creator, is necessary for salvation";[120] (3) five ecclesial precepts regarding attendance at mass, confession of sin, participation in the Eucharist, keeping holy days of obligation, and observing designated days of fasting and abstinence;[121] and (4) an additional precept to give financially in support of the Church.[122] With exasperation, evangelical theology objects to the burdensome nature of these additional laws that the Catholic Church prescribes for and obligates the faithful to obey. It wonders, at what point do such additions to the requirements for salvation come to an end? Connecting this point to the first topic in this chapter, evangelical theology underscores and rejects the very heavy emphasis on law as an essential component of Catholic theology's doctrine of salvation. Not law, not good

---

[118] See the earlier critiques in chapter 3.
[119] CCC 2035.
[120] CCC 2036 (emphasis removed).
[121] CCC 2041–2042.
[122] CCC 2043.

works cooperating with grace, not grace in order to merit eternal life, but the gospel "is the power of God for salvation to everyone who believes, to the Jew first and also to the Greek. For in it the righteousness of God is revealed from faith for faith, as it is written, 'The righteous shall live by faith'" (Rom. 1:16–17).

Conclusion

"Life in Christ," Part 3 of the *Catechism*, has to this point treated the human vocation of life in the Spirit (Sec. 1), focusing on the dignity of the human person (Ch. 1) and the human community (Ch. 2), and God's salvation, focusing on law, justification and grace, merit, and the church as mother and teacher (Ch. 3). Though it contains another section covering the Ten Commandments (Sec. 2), an evangelical discussion and assessment of this topic will not be offered. There are three important reasons for this decision. First, Catholic theology's presentation of the Ten Commandments rests on its emphasis on law as an essential component of salvation. As Vatican Council II underscored, "all men may obtain salvation through faith, Baptism and the observance of the [Ten] Commandments."[123] As this evangelical assessment has already critiqued this emphasis on law, additional criticism directed at Catholic theology's detailed explanation of this law, as set forth in the Ten Commandments, seems superfluous. Second, the *Catechism*'s treatment of this section features a great deal of biblical interpretation of the Exodus 20:2–17 and Deuteronomy 5:6–21 passages. As this book is designed to be a *theological assessment* of Catholic doctrine and practice, an assessment of Catholicism's *biblical interpretation* would take this book far afield. Third, even when biblical interpretation of these passages flows into theological reflection and doctrinal discussion, the theological issues presented repeat the topics already covered in the preceding sections of the *Catechism*, rendering further comment redundant.

For similar reasons, Part 4, "Christian Prayer," will not be discussed. Section 1 treats prayer in the Christian life. Some of this discussion will and should resonate with evangelicals, while other parts will and should be critiqued, in the same way and for the same reasons that this evangelical

---

[123] CCC 2068; citation is from Vatican Council II, *Lumen Gentium* 24.

assessment has criticized Catholic theology and practice in the preceding sections of the *Catechism*. Section 2 is a detailed exposition of the seven petitions of the Lord's Prayer (Matt. 6:9–13). Again, because an assessment of this biblical interpretation would take this book far afield, it will not be rendered on this treatment.

Conclusion

14

Evangelical Ministry with Catholics

Roman Catholic Theology and Practice has been an evangelical assessment of Catholic theology and practice as articulated by the *Catechism of the Catholic Church*. It has been uniquely designed to express *intrigue* because of the many commonalities that are shared between Catholic and evangelical theology as well as to offer *critique* of the many divergences between these two counterparts. Another unique aspect has been the criticism's focus on both the Catholic system as a whole, grounded on the two axioms of the nature-grace interdependence and the Christ-church interconnection, and specific issues related to each Catholic doctrine and practice.

Throughout the writing of this book, my fascination with the theological agreements between Catholic and evangelical theology has grown, and this intrigue has been of great encouragement. Oppositely, the clear and pointed critique of the doctrines and practices on which Catholic theology disagrees with evangelical theology has not given me any joy. However, this criticism of such divergences, as burdensome as it has been, is necessary for several reasons. Evangelical readers of this book know many Catholics and want to understand what they believe and why. Additionally, Catholic readers of this book know many evangelicals and want to understand what they believe and why, and also what their assessment of Catholic theology is. Moreover, dialogue between Catholics and evangelicals will move ahead constructively only if both theological perspectives thoroughly understand each other, both their commonalities and divergences. Finally, Catholics who are journeying toward evangelicalism, and evangelicals who are journeying toward Catholicism, need to know what they are getting themselves into. I am not unaware of the reality that one of the most decisive factors in these journeys between faiths is the counsel of a spiritual guide or mentor from the faith toward which the person is traveling. A corollary of this fact is that the doctrinal and practical issues that are the focus of this book may not play the key role in the decision making process; indeed, they may exercise little influence on the move. This reality, however, does not make theological matters any less important, because when evangelicals become Catholic, for example, they must accept Catholic theology in its entirety. Accordingly, they must embrace the Catholic Church's Tradition and its Magisterium; the role of Mary as Advocate, Helper, Benefactress, and Mediatrix; justification as not only a declaration of acquittal before God and the imputation of Christ's righteousness, but also as their ongoing progress in holiness; the commission of mortal sin as resulting in the loss of salvation and leading to eternal punishment in hell; no possibility of the assurance of salvation; the reality of purgatory; the infallibility of the pope and the episcopal college; the sacramental economy; transubstantiation; participation in the sacraments of the Church so as to receive divine grace, with which they must cooperate in order to merit eternal life; requirements that go beyond Scripture and that are necessary for salvation; and much more. If this book succeeds in underscoring the vast divide on the above issues that separates Catholicism and evangelicalism, as difficult as the process of critique has been, at least it will make people aware of the theological distance between the two, even if such issues are not at the heart of journeys of faith.

My interest at the conclusion of this book is to address evangelicals who want to understand how to engage in ministry with Catholics. Assuming the contents of this book as a foundation to what will be next offered, I draw attention to the following points: First, in light of the nature-grace interdependence as one axiom of the Catholic system, evangelical ministry with Catholics needs to break the dependence of grace on nature. It does so by underscoring the depth and intractability of sin that renders nature incapable of receiving and transmitting grace, and it emphasizes the irremediable situation of nature and the desperate need not for revision or renewal but for re-creation. Additionally, evangelical ministry highlights the radical intervention of divine grace communicated through a gospel that comes from outside of human beings and that proclaims an alien righteousness imputed by justification—the declaration that sinful people are now righteous instead—rather than a righteousness that is infused, thus elevating human nature with the possibility of perfection.

Second, evangelical ministry with Catholics needs to unbind the strict interconnection between Christ and the church, but not by attacking the importance of the church or rendering it any less crucial. Evangelical ministry should underscore the sovereign rulership of the God-man who has ascended into heaven, operates through the Spirit of God and the Word of God, and has not transmitted his authoritative prerogatives to the Catholic Church and its hierarchy. Additionally, evangelical ministry should emphasize the *instrumental* nature of the church and its ministry that does not act in the person of Christ, possess infallibility, determine the canon of Scripture and its authoritative interpretation, or in general mediate between nature and grace. Again, this point is not intended to deprecate the church, its leaders, or its ministry, but it must distance a proper view of those realities from the axiom of the Christ-Church interconnection that considers the Catholic Church to be the prolongation of the incarnation of the ascended Jesus Christ.

In terms of practical counsel for evangelical ministry with Catholics, a number of suggestions focus on the gospel and flow from the doctrine of Scripture and its interpretation. One strategy, based on the general biblical illiteracy prevalent among Catholics, is to engage them in long-term exposure to the gospel through the reading and study of Scripture. A tool that we used when working with Catholics in Rome was to meet weekly in Reading Groups of the Gospel to study the Gospel reading (e.g., Luke 19:1–10) scheduled for the upcoming Sunday mass. Following a very simple Bible study method— reading the text, observation, interpretation, application, and prayer—such reading groups help Catholics become familiar with the person and work of Jesus Christ as he is revealed in Scripture. Believing that "faith comes from hearing, and hearing through the word of Christ" (Rom. 10:17), evangelical ministry can offer long-term exposure to the word of Christ, igniting faith in him, through such Reading Groups of the Gospel. A second suggestion is that evangelical ministry needs to constantly focus on biblical authority as conversations with Catholics occur. Familiarity with Scripture, love for the Word of God, affirmation of biblical truth, trust in scriptural promises, submission to biblical commands, and so forth not only underscores an evangelical doctrine of Scripture but, as importantly, communicates a deep and living commitment to the Word of God. To engage in debate in which evangelical opinion is pitted against Catholic teaching accomplishes little if anything, but if the constant reference point for discussion and dispute is Scripture, the proper authority is at the center of conversation.

Several other suggestions are designed to help clarify the gospel. The first counsel is specifically directed toward clarifying the application of God's saving work in Christ through repentance and faith. A critical question to be asked before inviting Catholics to embrace salvation is the following: "Have you ceased to rely on all of your own efforts to earn God's love and forgiveness?" The point of the question is to underscore that engagement in good works, attending mass, reliance upon one's Baptism and participation in the other sacraments, and so forth, still expresses dependence on one's self-righteousness and own works to render one ready for salvation. A negative response to the question—or a response indicating that the person grasps the importance of faith but is still committed to adding something *to* faith alone for salvation—signifies that the person is not yet ready to embrace Jesus Christ. A positive response indicates that the biblically prescribed means of appropriation of salvation by God's grace through faith has been understood, and encouragement to take that step of faith should be offered to the person. To express the conviction of evangelical ministry with regard to the proper appropriation of salvation, the simple formula "faith + _____" (fill in the blank: good works, obedience to the law, Baptism, sacramental grace, praying the rosary, etc.) cancels faith and renders divine salvation null and void. This issue needs to be clarified.

A second counsel with regard to the gospel is directed toward clarifying the impact that the gospel has on every area of life. Too often, evangelical ministry with Catholics limits its focus to the good news as the entry point into salvation, but it then abandons the importance of the gospel for ongoing transformation. Instead, evangelical ministry should insist on the good news of God's grace as prompting repentance from sin and igniting faith in Jesus Christ, mending broken relationships, overcoming addictions, replacing lying with truth-telling, calming insecurities and conquering fears, rescuing marriages, supplying love and compassion for the unlovable and marginalized, uniting disparate people, fostering courage to bear witness to Christ, and much more. Because the gospel impacts and transforms everything, evangelical ministry must make much of the gospel all of the time.

Several suggestions may be offered regarding the sufficiency of Christ and his work of salvation. Interestingly, one element of Catholicism that draws evangelicals toward the Catholic Church is the authority of its Magisterium and the certainty it provides concerning divine revelation, truth, grace, and the like. Importantly by way of contrast, Catholic theology denies that the faithful may possess the assurance of their salvation, so it seems that the most important point of certainty, that of one's own eternal destiny, is actually not to be found in the Catholic Church. But evangelical theology, at least those camps that embrace the perseverance of the saints, does indeed offer such assurance. By focusing on the fruit of the divine work of justification—the "not guilty" verdict, freeing us from condemnation; the imputation of Christ's righteousness, giving us an assured standing before God—such assurance is communicated. Additionally, by underscoring the intercessory work of Christ (Heb. 7:25), his pledge to hold Christians firmly to the end and so grant them eternal life (John 6:38–40; 10:27–29), the sealing of the Holy Spirit as the pledge of the Christian inheritance (Eph. 1:13–14), the promises of the Word of God (1 John 5:11–13), and the faithfulness and power of God to effect completed salvation (1 Cor. 1:7–9; Phil. 1:6; 1 Pet. 1:5), evangelical ministry offers the truth of perseverance in the faith and its accompanying assurance of salvation in contrast with Catholic theology's denial of that truth. An implication of this point is that purgatory does not exist, nor is such a state of complete purification for the taint of forgiven sin needed. It further highlights the fact that the mediatorial role of Mary and the intercessory work of the saints are unnecessary.

Another suggestion that flows from the sufficiency of Christ and his work of salvation is that evangelical ministry with Catholics should emphasize the daily application of the gospel because of their constant need for forgiveness. Christians dare not wait to deal properly with their ongoing problem of sin by accumulating sins over a long period of time (for example, for an entire year) before confessing them. Trust in the divine promise that God is faithful and just to forgive sins when they are confessed should be lived concretely whenever sin is exposed. Moreover, evangelical ministry should never present the Christian journey under the facade of a perfect life. Rather, modeling and championing ongoing confession and repentance should characterize evangelical ministry with Catholics.

Numerous reasons exist for the drifting of evangelicals toward the Catholic Church, including a desire to feel connected to the past and to be organically related to the church of ancient times, a longing for unity among Christians, a yearning for a sure authority, and the appeal of the mystery and majesty of the mass. These reasons highlight the central role that the reality of the Catholic Church plays in such journeys of faith. They also give rise to another practical counsel: evangelicals involved in ministry with Catholics need to be involved in robust churches that are characterized by being oriented to the glory of God, centered on the Word of God (intended as both the incarnate Word, Jesus Christ; and the inspired Word, Scripture), and Spirit-activated and empowered. These gospel-focused churches reject entertainment for the sake of attracting new people and adding to their numbers; nurture genuine community and do not just run programs; shun giving mere lip service to faithfulness and obedience but instead concretely live out joyful submission to authoritative Scripture; rely desperately on the presence and power of the Holy Spirit as expressed in prayer; disciple their members through preaching, teaching, pastoral care, community life, personal mentoring, and church discipline; administer the ordinances of baptism and the Lord's Supper with both seriousness of intention and celebration of what Christ's death has accomplished; and so forth. Many conversations with former evangelicals reveal that their evangelical church experience was lightweight and shallow. Evangelical ministry with Catholics needs to acknowledge that such superficial engagement in church will not hold evangelicals in their churches, and it will even encourage them to search for community, unity, authority, and mystery elsewhere—including the Catholic Church. Evangelical ministry needs to be rooted in robust evangelical churches.

Two final pieces of practical counsel: First, evangelical ministry, as heir to the Protestant doctrine of the priesthood of all believers, should encourage Christians to engage in intercessory prayer for one another, hear each other's confession of sin and give assurance of God's forgiveness, engage missionally together for the cause of Christ, and teach and admonish one another with the gospel. Living life and engaging in ministry together presents the evangelical faith as something different from its Catholic counterpart's reality (even if Catholic theology acknowledges the importance of the common or baptismal priesthood of all its members). Second, evangelical ministry should embrace a biblical vision for life with God and human flourishing and, supplied with God's grace, Christ's forgiveness, and the Holy Spirit's empowerment, strive with all it is and has to actualize that vision, keenly aware of how Scripture and evangelical theology engage in both intrigue and critique of Catholic theology and practice.

General Index

assurance of salvation, 41, 157, 212, 220, 454, 457

atemporality (of Christ's death), 232, 235, 306, 312, 319, 320

Athanasius, 93, 101–102

atomistic approach, to Catholic doctrine, 42, 43

atonement, 37, 144–146, 152, 214, 218, 265, 286–287, 345–346

Augsburg Confession, 92n51, 170

Augustine, 96n65, 149, 210n9, 397n31, 401, 412, 422
  on baptism, 261, 273–275
  on canon, 102–105
  on dichotomy and trichotomy, 124n29
  on marriage, 372n57
  on prevenient grace, 419n43
  on procession of Spirit, 122
  on sacraments, 160n7, 238
  on *totus Christus*, 58–60

Augustinian tradition, 46n28, 49

authority, 411

avarice (greed), 403

"Babylonian Captivity of the Church," 193–194

Baptism, sacrament of, 260–289
  cancels/effaces original sin, 122, 130, 207, 336
  and faith, 109–110, 115, 443–444
  and forgiveness of sins, 207–208
  as initiatory rite of Christian faith, 267–268
  mode of, 262–263
  as necessary for salvation, 265, 268–269, 285–289, 337, 444
  not to be repeated, 267
  as ordinance, 40
  and resurrection, 210
  with the Spirit, 40
  Trinitarian formula, 282
  triple immersion in, 263

baptismal priesthood, 239, 246, 381, 458

baptismal regeneration, 278, 281, 282, 284, 289

baptistery, 249, 256

Baptist Faith and Message, 244–245

Baptists, 158, 278

Barth, Karl, 405–406

Barth, Markus, 274

Baruch, 82, 100, 101, 103

Basilica of St. John Lateran, 196

beatific vision, 213, 409

beatitude, 72, 407, 409–410

beatitudes, 391, 392–393

Beckwith, Frank, 93n55, 99n67

believer's baptism, 33, 267, 279, 280, 281, 289

Benedict XII (Pope), 213n19

Benedict XVI (Pope), 71, 171n58

Bible. *See* Scripture

birth control, 380

bishop, office of, 167, 181–182, 183, 192, 358–360, 362, 364, 365–366

bishop of Rome, 101, 185, 193, 195, 195n130, 360, 367

blasphemy against the Holy Spirit, 152n123, 213, 219

blessed, Mary as, 132, 133, 135, 137, 138, 140, 142, 163, 190, 335

bodily assumption of Mary, 80, 190, 196, 204, 210

body, 119, 210–211

body of Christ, church as, 58–59, 60, 65, 153, 160, 161, 168, 273, 293

body of Christ, and blood of Christ, in Eucharist, 63, 305, 308, 309, 317, 321

Book of Wisdom, 103

born again, 269, 284

Bread of Life discourse, 301, 312–315

Breaking of Bread, 300

bride of Christ, church as, 161

Byzantine rites, 250, 257

Calvin, John, 170
  on allegorical interpretation, 107
  on angels, 123–124
  on Catholic Tradition, 84–85, 86
  on celibate priests, 375
  on church as mother, 115–116
  on indulgences, 348
  on infallibility of the church, 89

Catholic Church as post-ascension
mediator, 56, 64
circumcision of, 143
crucifixion of, 144–145, 147, 202, 203,
death of, 36, 37, 39, 85, 135, 144,
145–146, 147, 148, 151, 155, 161, 168,
177, 180, 190, 203, 204, 209, 211, 216,
227, 229, 230, 232, 245, 248, 260, 261,
272, 274, 282, 288, 293, 300, 301, 302,
306, 315, 321, 341, 345, 346, 350, 352,
371, 417, 427, 430, 432, 433, 435, 436,
458
deity of, 27, 35, 131, 134, 179
fulfilled the law, 143
as High Priest, 149, 174, 205, 228,
230, 231, 235, 302, 358
humanity of, 131, 134
intercession of, 114, 201–202, 302,
307, 457
and liturgy, 232–233
offices of, 62, 266, 363
as only Mediator, 66, 191, 204
passive obedience of, 134
person and work of, 35, 106, 130, 455
preeminence of, 409–410
presence in Eucharist/Lord's Supper,
65, 236, 307–309, 312, 319n89, 322
resurrection of, 37, 39, 61, 85, 87,
143, 146–149, 167, 168, 177, 180,
183, 190, 203, 216, 227, 229, 230,
232, 248, 261, 277, 282, 288, 293,
315, 371, 417, 435
ruling his church from heaven, 64, 194
second coming/return of, 36, 41, 64,
79, 84, 150–152, 160, 164, 166, 167,
173, 193, 204, 210, 214–216, 221–223,
236, 237, 240, 245, 251, 274, 296, 301,
304, 311, 317
session of, 149, 317
sufferings of, 64, 202, 354, 355
sufficiency of, 456–457
Jews, salvation of, 175, 179–180
John of Damascus, 208n6
John Paul II (Pope), 26, 71, 118n3,
138n69, 178n74, 179n76, 410n87
John the Baptist, 154, 295, 339

Jordan River, crossing of, 261, 271
Joseph (Saint), patron of a happy death,
211, 212
Judas Maccabeus, 218
Judith, 82, 100, 101, 103
justice, 399
justification, 39, 148, 216, 416–418, 424,
431–445, 457
Catholic doctrine of, 217, 266,
272–273, 328, 346, 420, 428
and faith. *See* faith, and justification
as forensic, 349, 408, 431, 432–433,
442, 447, 457
fruit of, 417
and good works, 441–442
and grace. *See* grace, and justification
ground of, 273, 417, 436–437, 442
and Holy Spirit. *See* Holy Spirit, and
grace
and law. *See* law, and justification/
righteousness
and purgatory, 201, 216, 219–220, 349
and regeneration. *See* regeneration,
conflated with justification
and sanctification. *See* sanctification,
conflated with justification
justification by faith alone, 45n23, 98,
172, 216, 428, 437, 446
Justin Martyr, 137, 255, 302

keys of the kingdom, 134, 143n93, 182,
185, 192, 208, 330, 341–342, 347
kingdom of God, 35, 134, 160, 193, 215,
222, 229, 242, 260, 261, 265, 266, 268,
269, 272, 284, 335, 350, 352, 393, 405,
422, 444
König, Cardinal Franz, 96n65
Kreeft, Peter, 93–94, 95n62, 104

laity of the church, 51, 57, 62, 184,
187–188, 194, 197, 237, 323, 364, 368,
369, 370
last judgment, 42, 150–152, 214–216,
219, 221–223
Last Supper, 144, 236, 242, 299, 300, 301,
303

Scripture Index

61:1–2	154
63:9	288n79

Jeremiah

1:5	135
31:31–34	83, 415, 426
31:34	433
32:17	139n74

Ezekiel

8:6, 13, 15	407
36:25–27	83, 105n83, 270, 274, 426
36:25–28	154
44:1–3	142n85

Daniel

9:3	339
10:13, 20	123
12:1	123
12:1–13	210n7
12:7	223

Joel

2:28–32	105n83, 154, 270, 372

Jonah

3:6–10	339

Micah

5:2–3	136

Zechariah

8:6	139n74
11:12	96n65

NEW TESTAMENT

Matthew

1:18–25	35, 132, 135
1:18, 25	141
1:19	434n87
1:22–23	136
1:24–25	141, 141n83
1:25	141
3:13	261
3:13–17	268
3:15	261
4:4	37
4:17	242, 335, 393, 417
4:19	182n82
5–7	35
5:3–12	392
5:8	393
5:13	182n82
5:14–16	182n82
5:17–19	83, 143, 415
5:17–48	429
5:22, 29	214
5:44	400
5:48	173, 429
6:1–6, 16–18	415
6:9–13	415, 450
6:12	173, 328
7:12	398, 407, 415
7:13–14, 21–27	415
7:15–20	404–405
7:20	419
7:21–23	112, 405
7:22	354n71
7:23	113
8:8	305n34
8:16	354n71
8:17	350
10	180, 193
10:1	354n71
10:1–4	36
10:6–42	182n82
10:8	351
10:19–20	154–155
10:28	214
10:32–33	400
10:38	350
10:40	166
11:25–27	36
11:29	131
12:27–28	354n71
12:31	152n123
12:32	151n122, 152n123, 213, 219, 402
12:46	142
13:3	77
13:11	229
13:24–30	162n20

12:15	123
13:9	293
14:8–18	34, 55n48, 75, 178
14:14	364n36
14:23	181, 365n39
15	193, 443
15:1, 5, 24	443
15:1–29	365n39
15:1–16:5	366
15:7–11	444
15:11	444
16:15	261, 279
16:15, 33	264
16:18	354n71
16:25–33	280
16:31	381
16:31–33	261
16:33	279
17:10–12	98
17:22–28	75
17:22–31	55n48, 178
17:22–34	34
17:30	39
17:30–31	42, 75
18:5	280
18:8	264, 279, 280, 381
18:27	39, 116
19:2–7	295
19:3–7	279
19:5–6	290n84
19:13	354n71
20:7	255
20:7, 11	300
20:17	365n38, 365n39
20:28	167n44
22:16	279, 282
26:12–18	364n36
26:18	281

Romans

1:3–4	147
1:4	37
1:5	108
1:16–17	370, 449
1:17	400
1:18–25	34, 55n48, 73, 75, 178
1:19	247, 253

1:20–23	75
1:21, 25	1651:28–32, 401n60
2:12	427
2:12–16	34
2:13–16	73, 75, 178
2:14–15	427
2:14–16	398, 404n77
3:9–12	425
3:10	434n87
3:19–22	39
3:20	423
3:20–22	424
3:21	425–426
3:21–25	436
3:21–26	417
3:21–31	114
3:22	417
3:23	34, 432
3:23–26	37
3:24	432
3:25	39, 332, 433
3:28	437
4	439
4:1–5	436, 437, 439
4:5	432, 444
4:6–8	432
4:10–11	436
4:13	436, 437
4:13–16	425
4:15	424
4:17	55
4:17–22	54
4:18	400
4:18–21	439–440
4:19	55
4:22	440
4:22–25	98
4:24–25	37
5:5	155
5:8	131
5:9	433
5:10	400
5:12–21	128, 137
5:16, 18	432
5:17	434
5:18	434